**FRANK KESSLER**

Missouri Western State College

# THE DILEMMAS OF PRESIDENTIAL LEADERSHIP

## Of Caretakers and Kings

PRENTICE-HALL, INC.

Englewood Cliffs, New Jersey 07632

*Library of Congress Cataloging in Publication Data*

Kessler, Frank P., (date)
    The dilemmas of Presidential leadership.

    Includes index.
    1. Presidents—United States.    I. Title.
JK516.K4        353'.03'1        81-10731
ISBN 0-13-214593-6        AACR2

Editorial production/supervision
    and interior design: *Edith Riker*
Cover design: Wanda Lubelska
Manufacturing buyer: *Edmund W. Leone*

Printed in the United States of America

10   9   8   7   6   5   4   3   2

ISBN 0-13-214593-6

Prentice-Hall International, Inc., *London*
Prentice-Hall of Australia Pty. Limited, *Sydney*
Prentice-Hall of Canada, Ltd., *Toronto*
Prentice-Hall of India Private Limited, *New Delhi*
Prentice-Hall of Japan, Inc., *Tokyo*
Prentice-Hall of Southeast Asia Pte. Ltd., *Singapore*
Whitehall Books Limited, *Wellington, New Zealand*

To my parents (Joseph and Margaret)
who always loved and believed

and

To Mary Meeks Kessler
(my most precious gift) who loves, shares, smiles, and cares

# CONTENTS

v

## PART 4
## CHOOSING AND DISPOSING OF PRESIDENTS

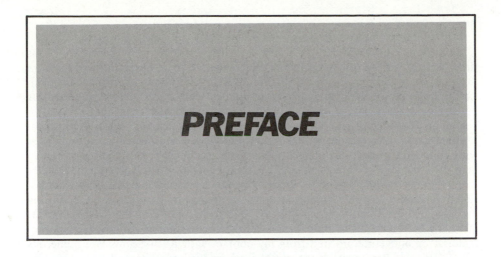

# PREFACE

At one time or another, every instructor imagines that there must be a single book that can cover the basics of the presidency, without need of numerous supplements. The ideal text would be clear and thorough, yet pithy, and have numerous anecdotes to maintain reader attention. Professor Fred Greenstein recently noted in a book review that a scholarly work asks more questions than it answers. Hopefully in this case scholarly and soporific need not be synonymous. It is hoped that this volume will approach those ideals in the limited space available.

While the themes of leadership and the complications that democracy presents for a president recur throughout this book, the material has not been altered to fit a predetermined set of notions. Although suggestions are sometimes provided for getting around some of the dilemmas being noted, the major thrust has been to ask many more questions than can be answered. Vignettes and anecdotes have been used extensively to give the reader food for thought and to provide attractive tidbits to stir group discussion.

This work is based on the belief that the presidency is not now, and never was, as powerful as many post-Vietnam and post-Watergate writers would lead us to believe. If anything, recent presidents have been modern-day Gullivers tied down by numerous political and legal restraints. Only in the foreign policy area has the White House been granted some flexibility.

Throughout we shall question whether Congress, the press, and other political institutions have overreacted to Watergate and have hampered the president's leadership capacity beyond justification. Democratic process and foreign leadership can coexist in the complex modern world of the final two decades of the twentieth century. Presidents who can encourage debate and shape a national consensus on crucial issues may find that cooperation and support of Congress, the press, the public, and interest groups are not beyond their grasp. Leadership from the White House need not imperil democratic institutions and the system of checks and balances that the Founding Fathers crafted two centuries ago.

In undertaking and completing a project of the magnitude of this book, a writer accumulates enormous debts of gratitude to a number of individuals. In this case some of them are the teachers who sparked my interest in the field: the late Paul G. Steinbicker (St. Louis University) introduced me to presidential studies; the late Paul Bartholomew (University of Notre Dame) nurtured that interest. Louis

Koenig (New York University), a noted presidency scholar, gave generously of his time, advice, and personal warmth to encourage me to set down my thoughts on the presidency and to refine them. Without a National Endowment for the Humanities grant to study the presidency in a summer seminar for college teachers, our paths would never have crossed, and this work would have been long delayed in beginning. This book began as a research project for that seminar. Words of appreciation are also due to persons whom I have interviewed and been in correspondence with about this project including the late Ambassador Robert Murphy who was so helpful in the area of foreign policy; Dr. Henry Kissinger who helped with some of the state department contacts; J. Brian Atwood who provided assistance in congressional relations; Joseph Califano who was a wellspring of ideas for the staffing discussion of the Johnson administration; and other guests at the Koenig seminar including Secretary of Commerce John T. Conner and General Andrew Goodpaster. Material on budgeting profited from my contact with Allen Schick and numerous OPM (Office of Personnel Management) teaching-the-budget materials provided by J. Edward Murphy.

Beginning a text from scratch would be next to impossible. This text began years ago as lecture notes for my classes in the American presidency and benefited from the enthusiasm and intellectual curiosity of students at Missouri Western like Tom McPherson, Tim Willis, Dan Radke, Denise Bartles, Bryant Hertel, Pat Conway, and Mark Hendrickson, who challenged me to challenge them. Cheerful research help from Doug Ernest, Elaine Jurries, Paula Spurlock, Elizabeth Castle, and Helen Wigersma made the going easier. Support and encouragement from my colleagues Jim Jordan, Tommie Ragland, Pat McLear, Roy Askins, Betty Phelan, Joe Ripple, David Steiniche, and Velva Hinderks made the burden lighter. If there is blame to be assessed for so many trees being made into paper for this work, part of it should be laid at the doorstep of Walter Kossmann, who had the audacity to suggest that I begin the project, and Stan Wakefield, Audrey Marshall, Edie Riker, and Sally Ann Clauss at Prentice-Hall, who tempered editorial justice with pleasant good humor, professional competence, and personal concern. To the anonymous professors who combed the early drafts, I might remind them that their reward will be great in heaven, and I appreciate their thoughtful and constructive suggestions. (No doubt I will regret having disagreed with some of their advice.)

A number of presidency studies people have given me helpful advice on the world of writing and publishing, and I acknowledge the following: Thomas Cronin, Stephen Wayne, Edward Kearny, Paul Scheele, William Lammars, Michael J. Francis and David R. Bradley, Jr. My greatest debt of gratitude goes to Caroline and E. Donnell Meeks for giving me the best proofreader, content analyst, and critic of "journalese," my wife Mary. Her expertise in both political science and teaching proved invaluable to me as she examined early drafts. She also developed great skill in explaining to Julie, Lori, Paul, and Tommy that they did have a daddy but that he had to work on his book, again. My name may appear on the cover of this work, but it was indeed a family effort. Lest the reader feel cheated, let me provide the appropriate disclaimer that, for any mistakes or inaccuracies that have crept into this manuscript, no one else need claim responsibility. "The buck stops here."

Frank Kessler

# PART

# 1

# EVOLUTION OF MODERN PRESIDENTIAL LEADERSHIP AND POWER

# Will the Real President Please Stand Up?

In 1976, Jimmy Carter, one-time naval officer, peanut farmer, and governor of Georgia, sought his party's nomination with the promise of integrity and "Leadership for a Change." His campaign slogan was a not-so-subtle questioning of Gerald Ford's ability to come to grips with the great problems confronting the nation and those that would arise in future decades. Didn't everyone know that Gerry Ford was a "nice guy" who, according to Lyndon Johnson, "couldn't walk and chew gum at the same time"? Nice evidently wasn't enough; presidents were expected to be competent leaders.

Within four years (by 1980) Carter was the target of similar salvos. Democrats and Republicans alike waxed eloquent about a "leadership crisis." Former Treasury Secretary John Connally, a Texas Republican, announced for the presidency because "Carter can't move anybody; he moves himself and he has difficulty doing that." Even fellow Democrat Senator Edward M. (Ted) Kennedy, in the unkindest cut of all, wondered aloud whether the president of his own party was permitting the nation to drift without decisive and knowledgeable leadership. Connally defined leadership as the ability to move others; Kennedy emphasized intelligence and decisiveness.

The election of Ronald Reagan in 1980 was testimony to the proposition that the image of being a more effective leader than one's opponent supersedes many other more negative images. Reagan's age, his reputation for being an "out of the mainstream" conservative, and his image as a hawkish Cold Warrior paled in comparison with Carter's perceived incompetence in holding down inflation and getting American hostages freed from the control of the Iranian militants. These perceptions helped to make 1980 an ABC (Anybody But Carter) year.

Conventional wisdom and a dollop of dreaming seems to indicate that the nation's economic woes, social ills, and international problems are solvable by the right leader. We need merely select another Washington, Lincoln, or FDR. But would we want another FDR or Lincoln in times other than war or economic crisis? Should the need for decisive leadership justify disregard for constitutionalism? Has the presidency become so powerful that it may endanger our democratic principles and individual rights?

The American presidency is an office of pomp and paradoxes. Since it is such a conspicuous office, impressions about its role, power potential, and accountability

3

differ widely. The breadth of decisions being made in the Oval Office today is even beyond the extravagant expectations of Alexander Hamilton. Still, it would be interesting to surmise whether Washington, in his day, had more control over the decision-making process than did his successors of the 1970s and 1980s. Is the president the ultimate problem solver or is he capable of solving anything? Does the president command the bureaucracies or is he their prisoner? Is the presidency so powerful and subject to abuse that it is a danger to our democratic institutions or has it become, in the post-Vietnam and Watergate era, dangerously impotent?

The answers to each of these questions lie in the nature of presidential power. In a system of checks and balances such as ours, questions about power become simply "powerful when compared with whom?" Bureaucratic foot dragging is capable of sabotaging seemingly simple directives from the White House. A case in point from a foreign policy perspective is President Kennedy's ordering the removal of the Jupiter missiles in Turkey in 1961. During the first days of his administration, JFK ordered the State Department to negotiate with Turkey to remove the missiles that were woefully obsolete. The Turkish government was not exactly enchanted with the idea so Secretary of State Dean Rusk pushed the matter to the back burner, hoping that JFK would not pursue the question. The president persisted and ordered the missiles prepared for transport out of Turkey. Attorney General Robert Kennedy reported in his memoirs of the missile crisis that his brother had "dismissed the matter from his mind." The president evidently felt that, since his wishes had been presented clearly "they would be followed and the missiles removed." Eighteen months later Soviet Premier Nikita Khrushchev sought to trade withdrawal of the missiles from Cuba for dismantling of U.S. missile sites in Turkey. A surprised Kennedy was reportedly livid that his earlier directives had evidently fallen on deaf ears.[1]

While the bureaucracies can bedevil presidents, Richard Nixon demonstrated how they could be used to a president's own political purposes. The shameful saga now known as Watergate was replete with examples of abuses of "the powers." Presidential campaign strategist Charles Colson drew up a short "enemies" list to make sure that those unfriendly to the president's reelection bid would not be invited to White House gatherings. Later, Counsel to the President John Dean, who was involved in campaign intelligence coordination, decided to expand the purpose of the list. In an August 1971 memo he wrote,[2]

> This memorandum addresses the matter of how we can maximize the fact of our incumbency in dealing with persons known to be active in opposition to our administration. Stated a bit more bluntly . . . HOW can we use the available federal machinery to screw our political enemies.

What had started out as an unassuming list of twenty or thirty on Colson's desk mushroomed into a veritable "Who's Who" of the liberal scene. The enemies could be subject to IRS audits and even FBI investigations. John Erlichman, for example, decided that getting Democratic National Committee Chairman Lawrence O'Brien was a necessity, and he felt that the IRS was the most capable of doing just that. When the investigation proved fruitless, IRS Commissioner Johnnie Walters reported later that Erlichman angrily dressed him down for "dragging his heels." Erlichman eventually testified before the Ervin (Senate Select Committee investigating Watergate abuses) committee, "I wanted to turn up something and send him to jail before the election; but, unfortunately, it didn't materialize." The FBI was called in to investigate, among others, CBS newsperson Daniel Schorr. He had the audacity to suggest on the air that a Nixon speech in New York promising aid to Catholic schools was made for "political" effect. The president was reportedly so incensed by the matter that, in response to his anger, aide Lawrence Higby took it upon himself to call J. Edgar Hoover to demand a complete background on Schorr.[3]

As these presidential abuses of power came to light, many of the most ardent disciples of strong presidential leadership during the Kennedy and Johnson years began expressing serious reservations about excessive presidential power.[4] The most vocal critics of the Nixon presidency decried his self-serving, imperious, and anti-democratic disrespect for American political institutions. The deeper reality of his administration was that it was not merely a temporary detour from the democratic straight and narrow. It was, instead, the culmination of what the presidency had become under his predecessors, especially Lyndon Johnson. Deceit, misinforma-tion, and excessive dependence upon secrecy had become a way of life.[5] Post-World War II presidents had placed little stock in the public and congressional "need to know." As the nation became hopelessly bogged down in Indochina quagmires and the Watergate abuses began to surface, the public and professional president watch-ers began to sense a need for reassessing not only Nixon but the powers of the office he occupied. Thomas Cronin asked menacingly, "Can the Presidency be made safe for democracy?"[6]

In light of Gerald Ford's need to govern by vetoing legislation and Jimmy Carter's early lackluster domestic record despite his advantage of having a "friendly" Democratic Congress, students of the presidency could wonder whether the frontal assaults on the office in the late 1960s and early 1970s might have done serious damage to presidential authority, prestige, and leadership. If the presidency was weakened, who should pick up the slack? Could it be argued that a constructive alternative to executive domination might be legislative supremacy? Would rule by public opinion polls or the media or interest groups be preferable? It would seem that in our complicated twentieth-century world, which finds domestic goals and international economic realities intertwining, more than ever, presidential leader-ship will be indispensible. Unfortunately, there are no simple answers to such questions as "How much leadership from the White House is enough, and how much is too much?"

In this chapter, our search for the real president will take us up the following avenues: (1) public perceptions of the office and its occupants, (2) the incumbents' attitudes toward the powers, and (3) analysts' views on the nature of the office and factors affecting the uses of presidential power in the modern world.


## THE MYTHICAL PRESIDENCY

The presidency is not just another executive office. It is surrounded by myths, symbols, and rituals, each of which serves to encourage misconceptions about the advantages the office gives to its occupants. Even presidents, when they first take office, may be unable to distinguish myth from reality. Richard Neustadt recounts that, in the early summer of 1952, President Truman appreciated the frustrations the office would present to General Eisenhower if he were elected. Command in the military hardly prepared Ike with the type of leadership skills he would need to function effectively in the White House. With his tongue firmly planted in his cheek, Truman lamented,[7]

> He'll sit here . . . and he'll say, "Do this! Do that!" And nothing will happen. Poor Ike . . . it won't be a bit like the Army. He'll find it very frustrating.

## SYMBOLISM

Every society has its temples to heroes and legendary figures as a part of its political culture, the mythical characters and the legends surrounding them serving to provide a nation with a perceptual set of rose-colored glasses that helps to make the reality appear attractive. The family, school, church, occupational association, and other social institutions reinforce these national sources of pride.[8]

America's mythical presidency has been evolving since the earliest days under the federal constitution. It has enveloped the occupants of the Oval Office in an aura that has tended to hide the limitations of the office. In response to the question "Shall we have a king?" the Founding Fathers replied with a qualified "no." They recognized the need for central leadership even though they were hardly monarchists. Their experience with the British, however, had not predisposed them to consider separating the ceremonial and administrative roles of their chief executive. The architects of the Constitution seemed to realize that a sense of national identity was lacking. The ritual surrounding a single national executive presented the stuff of which myths might be made. A president elected by the people represented the best of both worlds, the forms of democracy and the unifying symbolism of royalty.

Although the role and title of King of the United States offended George Washington's sensibilities, he still felt quite at ease with the trappings. He rode to his inauguration astride a white steed draped with leopard skin, and he traveled the country later in a fine coach drawn by six show horses. John Adams later sniped about Washington's penchant for pomp, "if he was not the greatest President, he was the best actor that we ever had."[9]

THE "ABOVE POLITICS" IMAGE. The pattern had been set, and even Andrew Jackson's raucous "people's" inaugural did not weaken the "above politics" image of the presidency. Even today, few Americans can avoid feelings of respect when they hear the strains of "Hail to the Chief" as a president enters a public function. When he travels overseas, the public feels a sort of pride from hearing the national anthem played for him. Jimmy Carter decided to forego much of the hoopla associated with the office only to find that just plain Jimmy in a cardigan sweater and carrying his own suitbag did not arouse the public support and respect he needed to compete with Congress and the interest groups for the power to sell his policies. The former Washington "outsider" came to realize that the symbolism surrounding the presidency was one of its most potent political assets. Before too long, the sweater was consigned to mothballs and replaced by a blue business suit, and the Marine band resurrected "ruffles and flourishes."[10]

Today's presidents are able to bask in the reflected glory of their predecessors. They sit in the chair once occupied by a host of legendary figures. They succeed to the shadow of Washington, who guided the nation through its turbulent years of infancy. They live in the home of Lincoln, savior of the Union and liberator of the slaves. They struggle to meet modern-day crises in the tradition of Franklin Roosevelt, who capitalized on public support through his fatherly fireside chats aimed at seeing the nation through the dark days of depression and world war. Present-day presidents may have a reservoir of public support built up by their predecessors, but they are somehow expected to emulate the best qualities of national heroes.

PERKS. The emoluments (perks) of the office may make it difficult for presidents to view themselves in proper democratic light. Dan Cordtz reported that during the Nixon years, for example, the president received a $200,000-per-year salary and a $50,000-per-year expense account and had a staff to care for the White House costing over $1.3 million and a discretionary fund of $1.5 million. In the White House and nearby buildings, the president also has almost any recreational facility he might desire (tennis, bowling, swimming, golf, viewing rooms for first-run movies, and ballrooms for galas involving nationally recognized entertainers).[11] Until Jimmy Carter sold it, the president had the use of the massive Presidential yacht, *Sequoia*. Should he find a need to get away from it all, the president could repair to the retreat at Camp David, Maryland, with its lavish appointments and facilities for recreation comparable to those at the White House. When he travels he flies in Air Force One, has a massive bullet-proof Lincoln limo waiting for him, and has his entourage accompanying him on one of the White House-assigned 707s or helicopters. The list goes on and on.

CONSTITUTION IN CRISIS. It should not be surprising, in light of the trappings surrounding the office, that some of our most revered presidents were capable of exhibiting less than democratic tendencies. Leadership abilities and charisma in candidates for the White House do not ensure their constitutional orthodoxy. Crisis situations pose the most perplexing dilemmas and potential dangers for constitutional democracies. Majority-rule political systems seek consensus whereas crisis situations leave precious little time for debate.

Two of our most notable presidents shed few tears over constitutional niceties when, in their judgments, emergencies called for suspension of its provisions. Among other things, Lincoln (1) spent funds not appropriated by Congress to carry on the war, (2) instituted a wartime draft when Congress had not declared war or authorized the draft, (3) imposed martial law on the border states even though in many cases fighting was not going on there, and (4) permitted military tribunals to replace civilian courts, thus ending *habeus corpus* rights in those states.[12] In a letter to his friend, A. G. Hodges, Lincoln defended his actions by drawing an analogy to the survival of the human body endangered by an unhealthy limb:[13]

> Was it possible to lose the nation and yet preserve the Constitution? . . . life and limb must be protected yet often, a limb must be amputated to save a life; but life is never wisely given to save a limb. I felt that measures otherwise unconstitutional might become lawful by becoming indispensable to the preservation of the nation.

Franklin Roosevelt, like Lincoln, saw extenuating circumstances as justification for suspension of civil liberties. Citing wartime considerations, Roosevelt ordered persons of Japanese-American descent to detention camps far inland from their homes on the Pacific Coast. For the sake of ensuring that these people would not consort with the Japanese at the expense of U.S. security, he deprived them of their rights as citizens to liberty, property, and due process of law ensured by both the Fifth and Fourteenth Amendments.[14]

The dangers lurking in these examples is that crisis and national security are not easily defined and are thus subject to individual interpretation. President Richard Nixon would find it possible to justify burglaries, illegal wiretaps, and other violations of civil liberties in the name of "national security." It was his highly debatable view that any action "if undertaken because of a Presidential determination that it was in the interest of National Security would be legal."[15]

## EGOTISM AND THE PALACE MENTALITY

Numerous presidents have enhanced their own sense of self-esteem with the aid of the trappings and perceived status that accompanies a job in the Oval Office. Presidents have jealously protected the integrity of the office from those who might hold it in less than proper awe. Presidents can begin to see themselves as royalty and permit the pomp surrounding the office to go to their heads. The careers of two recent presidents could be examined to show the dangers of the "l'état c'est moi" (I am the state, so said Louis XIV) mentality.

LYNDON'S COURT. George Reedy and other former aides of Lyndon Johnson characterized the climate in the administration with such phrases as "the life of the White House was the life of the court."[16] Clearly, LBJ had an exalted image of his role. Joseph Califano recounts a situation typical of Johnson's ego. The president was returning from a long trip in Air Force One and was preparing to take a helicopter back to the White House. A helpful Marine staff sergeant saw him heading to the wrong copter so he explained, "Your helicopter is the next one, Mr. President." Johnson reportedly replied, "They're all mine, son."[17] His strong sense of importance may well have contributed to his worsening press relations. He was not adverse to berating reporters for wasting his valuable time. He once barked at an unsuspecting reporter during a press gathering for delaying him with a mundane question, "Why do you come and ask me, the leader of the Western world, a chicken s- - - question like that?"[18]

Presidents holding majestic views of the office can discourage questioning even when opposition would have been in the national interest. Although it is true that effective leaders cannot brook insubordination for very long, it is likewise correct to assume that they need constructive criticism. During the Johnson years, especially in the area of foreign affairs, any criticism was considered to be destructive. The president habitually taunted his in-house critics, especially George Ball and Bill Moyers, on Vietnam. Irving Janis indicated that during the LBJ years, whenever members of the "in group" began to express doubts, they were treated in a rather standard way that "domesticated them through social pressures." The dissenters were made to feel at home provided that they lived up to two restrictions: first, they did not publicly display their doubts, thus aiding the opponents, and, second, they did not challenge the fundamental assumptions of the group on wartime commitments. George Ball arrived at war-related meetings as the "in-house devil's advocate on Vietnam," whereas Moyers would be greeted by the president with "Well, here comes Mr. Stop the Bombing." If aides overstepped accepted grounds, they placed themselves in danger of having their "effectiveness" questioned. Anyone who became too negative about existing policy might hear a colleague say none too discreetly, "I am afraid he's losing his effectiveness." This generally meant to tone down opposition or face removal from the inner circle.[19] This type of peer pressure ensured consensus but stifled necessary opposing views mainly because LBJ was so ultrasensitive to criticism.

KING RICHARD.  In numerous ways, Richard Nixon was cut from the same cloth as Johnson. Like his predecessor, he was taken by the grandeur of the office. Not only did he expect elegant surroundings in the White House, but he sought to create similar atmospheres in his vacation White Houses at San Clemente, California and Key Biscayne, Florida. The General Services Administration proved to be highly capable decorators for the Nixons, and the list of items paid for by the public was long indeed. It included, according to a report to the Joint Committee on Internal Revenue,[20]

> A forced-air heating system ($18,494), four picture windows ($1,600), a flagpole ($2,329), another flagpole for Key Biscayne, a shuffleboard court ($2,000), a gazebo ($4,981.50), and sewer construction ($3,800) in addition to the cost of security on these estates of approximately $500,000 per year.

Nixon was also addicted to suspense as a part of the regal drama of decision making. Whenever important decisions had to be made, he reveled in leaving Washington with appropriate news coverage, to spend a weekend at the Camp David retreat in the Catoctin Mountains of Maryland. His critics theorized that he either envisioned himself as Moses seeking wisdom on Sinai before the burning bush or as a mythological god returning from Mount Olympus to convey his verdict to the mortals.

Early in 1970, not long after Nixon had returned from a trip to several European capitals, he decided to improve the surroundings at the White House by regaling the in-house police force in military-styled uniforms featuring, among other things, white tunics, patent leather holsters, dress formal shoes, and pointed Prussian helmets.[21] One press account saw the outfits as comic opera costumes; Hugh Auchincloss judged them to be appropriate to any self-respecting banana republic.[22] Within a month the administration scrapped the outfits only to replace them with a set of revolutionary war uniforms.

The Prussian helmet incident could be considered laughable were it not symptomatic of a lack of judgment and respect for democratic appearances. The history of Britain and France demonstrate what can happen when the pomp of the court hides the intrigues. Many a king lost his head because the court created to do him homage erected a wall around him, thus isolating him from the realities of revolution brewing outside of the castle walls. Presidential staffers, likewise, in feeding the president's ego can create false impressions that can be devastating to his political awareness and hence his very political survival.[23]

Not every president has succumbed to the temptation to be a "king." Jefferson walked to his inauguration and back. Others such as Jackson, Harrison, and Lincoln were revered for their frontier heritage. More recently, Jimmy Carter sought to project that type of image by staying in voters' homes during the campaign and instituting "town meetings" and telephone call-in shows as president. But, as we noted earlier, there was not much political capital to be made with such "down-home" tactics. Ronald Reagan's star-studded pre-inaugural gala in 1981 and his desire that members of Congress wear tuxedos to the inauguration ceremonies signaled his recognition of the value in pomp and ceremony.

# PUBLIC SUPPORT

Usually, presidents have a decided advantage over political opponents in gaining and maintaining public support. At the beginning of the Nixon hearings on impeachment in the House, for example, even those who had never supported him were uncomfortable about the prospect of removing the president from office no matter how overwhelming the evidence.[24] Fears that impeachment might destabilize the government must have been on the minds of many. This instinctive reaction, however, could easily have been a manifestation of a learned respect for the institution of the presidency nurtured in homes and schoolrooms across the nation. Saccharine biographies of Washington and his immediate successors convinced generations of Americans that presidents were scrupulously honest, benevolent, and effective leaders.

## *THE TEXTBOOK PRESIDENCY*

Thomas Cronin coined the phrase "textbook presidency" to categorize the nature of discussions of the office in American government texts. As a whole, writings have tended to reinforce the myths about the nature of the office and the goodwill of its occupants. American youth, he asserts, grow up expecting their presidents to be powerful enough to win wars or to end them and to cure the nation's social and economic woes. Research related to the attitudes of children regarding politics has found youthful impressions of the president as powerful, wise, and benevolent. As the child matures and moves up the educational ladder, a certain skepticism about government and the political figures who run it emerges.[25] Media exposure no doubt plays a part in this, but "introductory high school and college-level textbooks and intermediate treatments may reinforce rather than measurably refine youthful expectations about presidential leadership."[26]

HIDING BEHIND THE PRESIDENTIAL SEAL. The recurrent assertions in textbooks that the president is a symbol of national unity may present some serious complications for our democracy. Textbook and school norms suggest that a person should question *candidates* thoroughly, but, after the election, citizens should rally around the new *president.* By implication, opposition to a particular president's policies would be, at the very least, unpatriotic, especially if newly elected and in need of presenting an image of national solidarity for the benefit of dealing with the world community.[27] This pressure to unite behind the new president, even among those who did not vote for him, tends to discourage separation of the president as symbol of the nation from the president as chief executive and policy maker. This type of thinking can be twisted into such pernicious slogans as "America, love it or leave it." Differing opinions would be stifled as presidents espousing unpopular policies could wrap their policies and themselves in the American flag to ward off all criticism, constructive or otherwise.

During the weeks and months prior to Richard Nixon's resignation, he hid behind the presidential seal arguing against impeachment by suggesting that it would damage the presidency. Even his ardent supporters doubtlessly recognized that these scare tactics were aimed at salvaging his administration. Since the public views the presidency as the pivotal part of our political system, weakening the institution would be seen as endangering the effective functioning of the federal government as a whole.

Although the citizenry might not understand the intricacies of the White House, the role of a single executive is far easier to comprehend than are those of 535 members of the House and Senate, numerous federal and state judges, and the maze of 80,000-plus local governments dotting the American political landscape. The information explosion through the print and telecommunications media has helped to encourage president-centered thinking. His every movement is news. Analysis of *The New York Times* from 1958 to 1974 comparing column inches given over to presidential news as compared with congressional news and joint presidential-congressional news shows presidential news receiving a lion's share of the coverage. In fact, between 1970 and 1974, presidential news as a proportion of total government news was 73.1 percent, whereas congressional news in the same period was 17.8 percent. In 1958, the figures were 61.9 percent presidential and 33 percent congressional.[28] It would be interesting to see if any relationship exists between the passivity of the Eisenhower administration and the larger coverage given to Congress versus increasing presidential coverage since then.

In Chapter 9 we shall examine the tendency of the press to assign more coverage to personal qualities of presidential candidates than to the issue positions they take. In campaigns, it is the image that the candidate projects that shows whether he will measure up to public expectations.[29]

Since so much press time is taken up with presidentially related subject matter, one would expect the public to be at least conversant with the incumbent. Fred Greenstein, in assessing the awareness of political leaders among various age groups, found that the president, not surprisingly, was the most visible federal official. Ninety-four percent of the thirteen-year-olds he surveyed could name the president, but only 16 percent could name one senator from their respective home states. Among the adults, the figures climbed slightly to 98 percent recognition of the president and a more healthy increase to 57 percent for those who could name a home-state senator. While it is not too difficult to imagine that a substantial percentage of the electorate would be unfamiliar with its home state's senators, it almost defies comprehension that even 2 percent of the adult population in 1969-1970 missed out on the news that Richard Nixon had won in 1968.[30]

Since presidents are so visible and their roles are easier for the public to understand than are those of other officials, it is logical for the voters to view them as symbols of stability and security. They are viewed as the hub of the governmental wheel. Public responses to the death of President Kennedy point out the importance that voters attach to the Oval Office. The National Opinion Research Center found psychosomatic (mentally-induced) problems in a large percentage of the sample they questioned immediately after JFK's death. Among the maladies reported, 68 percent of the sample experienced nervousness and tension, 48 percent loss of appetite, 26 percent rapid heartbeats, and 25 percent persistent headaches. These responses crossed party lines and were not in reaction so much to the death of John Kennedy as to the death of the president. Numerous psychologists found similar public reactions to the deaths of presidents Lincoln, Roosevelt, McKinley, Garfield, and, even in spite of the Tea Pot Dome Scandal, Harding.[31]

If the public identifies so positively with the president and has such an emotional attachment to the office, why is it that, within fifteen months or so of assuming the position, modern-day occupants of the White House have seen their popularity plummet? One might attempt to explain the embarrassingly low ratings for both Gerald Ford and Jimmy Carter (see Table 1.1) as a backlash of disillusionment with the presidency in light of Watergate abuses. While Watergate was no doubt a factor, presidents long before Richard Nixon had to deal with declining popularity after their first years in the White House.

## TABLE 1.1
## PRESIDENTIAL POPULARITY AFTER FIFTEEN MONTHS IN OFFICE

| PRESIDENT | APPROVE | DISAPPROVE | NO OPINION |
|---|---|---|---|
| J. Carter | 40% | 44% | 16% |
| G. Ford | 41 | 46 | 13 |
| R. Nixon | 56 | 31 | 13 |
| L. Johnson | 68 | 18 | 14 |
| J. Kennedy | 77 | 13 | 10 |
| D. Eisenhower | 68 | 21 | 11 |

Source: *Gallup Opinion Index,* no. 156, July 1978, p. 2.

THE PASSAGE-OF-TIME EFFECT. Numerous possible explanations could be given for this decline. Some would argue that loss of presidential popularity is inevitable with the passage of time.[32] The public holds a naïve admiration for the new president because he has won, because of his campaign promises, and because of relatively uncritical media reporting about him during the honeymoon period immediately after his election. The euphoria inevitably gives way to disillusionment when the president proves incapable of conjuring up instant magic for making long-standing problems disappear. Presidents who misread public thinking on a matter or decide to buck public opinion early in their administrations are courting disaster. Gerald Ford, for example, mistakenly thought that he could pardon Nixon rather than put the nation through a destabilizing trauma that indictment of Nixon would have been. While he had the power to do so, his standing in the public opinion polls plummeted. No matter what accomplishments the new president can log, the public asks "what have you done for us lately." Given unrealistic voter expectations of the presidents and the increasing complexity of American economic problems, downturns in presidential fortunes in the opinion polls seem unavoidable.

COALITION OF MINORITIES. Loss of ratings has also been attributed to the "coalition of minorities effect."[33] This interpretation suggests that, even if a president does what the majority wants, he stands to fall into disfavor with more intensely interested minorities whom he has angered by his decision. Single-issue politics is becoming common enough that presidents can presuppose that any decision they make will bring praise from one interest group and the wrath of another through their respective political action committees.[34]

A classic example of this sort of dilemma may be found in Jimmy Carter's speech to farmers in Columbia, Missouri in 1978. He shared with them the difficulties of being responsible for the problems of an economy in which "everyone wants theirs." The president scolded the medical community for the soaring rate of inflation in the health care industry and launched into attacks on several other sectors of the economy. Still, he made no mention of farm price supports and their potential effects on food prices for urban consumers. He pledged to reverse prior policy that had permitted imported beef to be shipped in large quantities to the United States to lower meat prices.[35] That decision, when its effects hit the supermarkets, will make the president who proposed it a number of enemies.

Even as universally lauded a program as a "tax cut" can make both enemies and friends depending on whose ox is being gored. Appreciative middle- and upper-class tax law beneficiaries must be balanced against enemies made in the minority community and in the ranks of organized labor who will be enraged by cuts in or deletion of federal programs for full employment and public assistance coinciding with shrinking revenues. President Carter, for example, took a tongue lashing from Representative Parent Mitchell of the congressional black caucus in a meeting at the White House on the Humphrey-Hawkins full employment legislation. Carter had campaigned on his support for the 4 percent unemployment target and willingness to spend the funds necessary to create federal jobs to reach that goal. As the recession began to turn around, it became clear to the administration that a public jobs program would be inflationary and Carter's economic brain trust, including aide Stuart Eisenstadt and Secretary of Treasury Blumenthal, were pointing to inflation as the more pressing problem. Eventually, however, due to the attendant political fallout in the black community, Carter realized that he desperately needed the support of the black vote if he intended to be reelected, so he signed a scaled-down version of the Humphrey-Hawkins bill.

## REASONS FOR POPULARITY

Presidents need not despair after their first year in office. Impoving their images is not impossible. Swings upward in the pollster's figures usually accompany two situations: (1) U. S. involvement in an overseas crisis and (2) public perception that the economy has improved. In a now classic article entitled "The Two Presidencies," Professor Aaron Wildavsky envisioned the office duties as divisible into domestic and foreign affairs responsibilities. He contended that the public permits the White House much more latitude and support in the latter area than it does in the former.[36]

THIRD LEVEL FOREIGN AFFAIRS AND CRISES. Public deference to presidential judgments reaches its zenith in times of real or perceived world crises. John Mueller, in *War, Presidents, and Public Opinion*, recognized that Americans, when the need arises, will "rally round the flag."[37] Respect for the White House role in crises may well be based on more than mere patriotism, however. Fear of war may also be a determining factor. For our purposes, crisis will be defined as John Spanier has in *Games Nations Play*, that is, as a situation "in which one state demands a change in the status quo and the other resists, creating a heightened perception of the possibility of war."[38]

A careful examination of the *Gallup Opinion Index* on foreign affairs questions over the past thirty years shows that a majority of the public tends to support presidential action at least in the early stages of the policy. One explanation for this support might be that the public approves of presidential action, regardless of its nature, if there is not enough information available to challenge his interpretation of the situation. Approval might also be based on the fact that the president is the focal point of national attention in times of crises or major international events. When international situations become prolonged and public attention is focused on them for a protracted period, popular support that appeared like a meteor will flicker and then fade (see Table 1.2).

Table 1.2 provides several interesting insights into public response to presidential action in crisis worth noting at this juncture. In only one case, Laos in 1971, did the public respond negatively to the use of troops in crisis. In two-thirds of the cases cited, the support did not extend even half a year. Evidently, a strong argument can be made to defend the proposition that increased information on the crisis will erode public support for the president. Today's instant media communications capability should make more information available more quickly.

In addition to crises and military involvements, public reaction to other presidential activities in the area of foreign affairs has enhanced presidential prestige (see Table 1.3).

Probably the ultimate in visible presidential foreign affairs activity is summit diplomacy. It can mean a veritable bonanza for the president in public support. Summitry can include U.S. presidents going abroad or foreign dignitaries of major nations visiting Washington. Due to complications in travel, summit diplomacy in person is a fairly recent phenomenon. President Wilson was the first to visit foreign

### TABLE 1.2
### WAR AND MILITARY CRISES AND POPULARITY, 1945-1975

| DATE | PRESIDENT | WAR OR CRISIS | % POPULARITY | | DURATION |
| | | | PRE | POST | (months) |
|---|---|---|---|---|---|
| 4/48 | Truman | Berlin blockade | 36% | 39% | 1 |
| 6/50 | Truman | North Korea invades South Korea | 37 | 46 | 5 |
| 7/58 | Ike | Troops to Lebanon | 52 | 58 | 3 |
| 7/61 | JFK | Berlin crisis | 71 | 79 | 12 |
| 10/62 | JFK | Cuban missile crisis | 61 | 73 | 8 |
| 2/65 | LBJ | Bombing North Vietnam | 68 | 69 | 1 |
| 4/65 | LBJ | Troops to Dominican | 64 | 70 | 3 |
| 6/66 | LBJ | Extends bombing of Hanoi, North Vietnam | 48 | 56 | 2 |
| 6/67 | LBJ | Mideast war | 44 | 52 | 1 |
| 4/70 | Nixon | Troops to Cambodia | 56 | 59 | 2 |
| 1/71 | Nixon | Expand war to Laos | 56 | 49 | 14 |
| 5/75 | Ford | *Mayaguez* incident | 40 | 51 | 8 |

Source: Adapted from Jong R. Lee, "Rally Around the Flag: Foreign Policy Events and Presidential Popularity," *Presidential Studies Quarterly*, (Fall 1977), 254. Lee uses the Gallup poll for his data.

## TABLE 1.3
### AVERAGE % POPULARITY CHANGE AND DURATION, 1938-1975

| SITUATION | APPROVAL | DISAPPROVAL | DURATION (months) |
|---|---|---|---|
| War and military crises | 6.38% | −5.38% | 5.08 |
| Peace efforts | 5.50 | −5.13 | 2.00 |
| Summits | 3.73 | −3.55 | 1.82 |
| New policy initiatives | 7.40 | −6.20 | 4.40 |
| International setback in presidential plans | −2.36 | 3.20 | 2.36 |

Source: Adapted from Jong R. Lee, "Rally Around the Flag," *Presidential Studies Quarterly,* (Summer 1977), p. 255.

capitals officially and to participate personally in an international conference outside the United States. During World War II, Franklin D. Roosevelt met numerous times with Allied leaders (Casablanca, Quebec, Cairo, Teheran, and Yalta). Harry Truman took part in the Potsdam conference. Eisenhower attended an East-West conference in Geneva in 1955 and went to Paris in 1960 for the ill-fated meeting with Khrushchev after a U.S. U-2 spy plane had been shot down over the Soviet Union. John Kennedy's meeting with Khrushchev at Vienna in 1961 proved inconclusive as did Johnson's meeting with Soviet President Kosygin at Glassboro, New Jersey in 1965. Richard Nixon's trips to China and the Soviet Union in 1972, while not that productive internationally, measurably enhanced his already excellent chances for reelection and immediately improved his standing in the public opinion polls.[39] Gerald Ford also cemented his image as a capable U. S. spokesperson in foreign affairs at the Vladivostok summit on strategic arms limitations.[40] Summitry has become a major building block in the development of a president's prestige.

Blessed also are the peacemakers. Presidents involved in mediation and conciliation efforts have received national and international acclaim for their efforts. Theodore Roosevelt not only enhanced his standing at home through his successful mediation of the conflicts between Russia and Japan at the time of the Russo-Japanese war in 1905, but he also lent credence to the "world power" status of the United States. Jimmy Carter's public opinion stock jumped twelve points in one month in 1978 by bringing the Israelis and Egyptians to Camp David and cajoling them into a settlement at a time when momentum for peace had seemed hopelessly stalled. In light of his gargantuan efforts, Carter was being promoted as a possible recipient of the Nobel Peace Prize, which was eventually to be shared by Egypt's President Sadat and Israel's Prime Minister Begin.[41] In retrospect, however, it becomes clear that public adulation heaped on presidents for their parts in summits and peace initiatives tends to be more short-lived than the approval that is given to presidents in times of full-blown crisis.

As international issues become increasingly centered on energy matters and balance-of-payments questions, presidential popularity based on foreign policy decisions could become a thing of the past. Economic issues such as these will tend to have a more individual effect on the average consumer and on particular interest groups than did past policies that affected the future of unknown masses of populations overseas. The electorate's instincts will be shaped by their perceptions of the chances that their life-styles or livelihoods will be adversely affected by changes.

POPULARITY AND THE ECONOMY. An old bromide in politics makes the distinction between a recession (when your neighbor is out of work) and a depression (when you are out of work). In peacetime, "butter issues" (those related to domestic economic health) are most important. The president is expected to keep the economy productive, prosperous, and inflation free. On the other hand, American folkways value both free market economics and a full employment economy. Free market economics would oppose government-created jobs whereas a full employment economy would require some jobs along the lines of the Depression-era PWA, WPA, and CCC programs. Conflicting public values leave the president on the horns of some nasty dilemmas.

Unfortunately, the president has neither the public support nor the tools under the Constitution to control economic policy in the same way that he can handle foreign and military affairs. The typical voter, while perhaps not feeling the tension of an overseas crisis, can relate to the pinch of inflation at the supermarket and the despair that accompanies recession-related layoffs. When government policies exacerbate these problems, presidents, because they are so visible, are bound to take the blame. John Mueller has argued that "public perception of a particular situation is almost as important as the reality."[42]

High rates of unemployment have traditionally been considered the fault of the president. If the voters were given a choice between high joblessness or high inflation, the impact of joblessness would be less immediately threatening to the average voter.[43] Democratic presidents will find their popularity waning if they do not recognize and try to act upon labor and minority goals of full employment for all employables.

As inflation has been growing at a faster pace over the last ten years, its impact on the prestige of presidents has increased proportionately. Overall increases in food and other consumer-related prices can correlate with declining presidential popularity. "As an indicator of economic conditions that could affect popularity," Henry Kenski contends that "inflation appears to be considerably more sensitive than unemployment."[44]

When presidents act to deal with international crises, public response is almost immediately favorable, but reaction to domestic economic decisions are longer ranged. Congress might wish to stall the president's proposals. It may take months for the bureaucracies to implement the programs and longer still for their impact to be seen in commerce and labor statistics.

Long delays may well make the programs inadvisable as the situations that encouraged them may have changed before Congress gets around to them. Back in the early 1960s President Kennedy commented that both he and Prime Minister Macmillan of Great Britain were seeking a tax cut. Macmillan's made its way through Parliament in six weeks. Kennedy's plan was still pending in Congress when he died. Jimmy Carter's early proposals to enact both a tax cut and tax reform were sufficiently slowed down in Congress that the original purpose of the cuts—to spur the economy to create jobs—had to be scrapped because of inflationary pressures that had not been evident when he made the original proposals. Even the full employment goals of the Humphrey-Hawkins jobs bill proved to be inflationary, and the public seems to fear inflation more than recessionary joblessness.

Even if the president is successful in implementing his program, there will be at least a six-month lag in the public opinion poll reaction to it.[45]

CREDIBILITY AND POPULARITY. During the last two decades, there has been a steady decline in public trust in the integrity of the leaders of government, and the presidency has not escaped this skepticism.[46] Executive credibility had clearly sunk to an unprecedented low when President Nixon found it necessary to inform the public that he was not a crook. Upon reading many of the news accounts of Watergate, one would get the impression that deception was something new in American politics but numerous past presidents have engaged in bouts of plausible lying.

In 1846, President Polk asked Congress to declare war on Mexico for crossing U. S. boundaries and shedding American blood. A careful check into the location of first contact between the forces of the two countries shows that the conflict took place in disputed territory between the Rio Grande and the Nueces rivers. Polk had created a customs port there hoping to goad the Mexicans into action. He clearly lied to Congress to get that body to declare war.[47] Woodrow Wilson, Franklin Roosevelt, and Lyndon Johnson campaigned on the slogan that they would keep our troops out of wars overseas. In each case, early in their respective new terms the nation was deep into World Wars I and II and the Vietnam conflict, respectively. If one prefers not to view these situations as involving lies to the public, it is clear nevertheless that both Roosevelt and Johnson knew that the nation was already deeply committed and that further involvement was a most likely option.

During the 1950s presidents and high administration officials had been caught in several lies about the extent of U.S. involvement in coups against the governments of Indonesia and Guatemala. Three of the obvious examples in the 1960s were (1) the U.S. reaction to the downing of a U-2 spy plane over Russia, (2) the U.S. version of the Tonkin Gulf incident, and (3) the reports of atrocities in the Dominican Republic in 1965, which encouraged U.S. intervention there. In the first case, President Dwight Eisenhower denied that the U-2 was on a spy mission even though he had authorized these overflights. Four days later he had to retract his denial since the Soviets had captured both the plane and its pilot, Francis Gary Powers. Several years afterward, Ike was to comment,[48]

> The lie we told about the U-2, I didn't realize how high a price we were going to have to pay for that lie. And, if I had it to do all over again, we would have kept our mouths shut.

In August 1964, an attack by North Vietnamese PT boats against two U.S. ships, the *Maddox* and the *Turner Joy,* off the Tonkin Gulf was reported. President Johnson had approved CIA programs of covert warfare in February 1964, including aiding South Vietnamese navy raids on North Vietnam. Defense Secretary Robert McNamara told the Senate Foreign Relations Committee that the navy played no part in and was not associated with any South Vietnamese actions if there were any. He added that the *Maddox* "was not aware of" any South Vietnamese raids. Four years later, in the *Pentagon Papers* leaked by Daniel Ellsberg, these and other statements used to gain congressional support for the U.S. military action in the area were proved inaccurate if not purposely false.[49]

President Johnson's decision in 1965 to interpose U.S. marines between warring factions in the Dominican Republic was reportedly based on the need to protect American lives and property in the face of atrocities taking place during the conflict. Johnson reported at a press conference that[50]

> some 1,500 innocent people were murdered and shot, and their heads cut off. . . . As we talked to our ambassador to confirm the horror and the tragedy and the unbelievable fact that they were firing on an American and the American embassy, he was talking to us from under a desk while bullets were going through his windows.

Subsequent investigations proved both the 1,500 bodies comments and the story about Ambassador W. Tapley Bennett squeezing his 6 foot 2 inch frame under his desk were, at best, gross exaggerations.[51]

Lyndon Johnson was so much in the habit of lying that he hardly recognized he was doing it. It could be said that he raised presidential lying to an art form. Throughout his White House years he was being caught in lies about his family roots, his schedule, his health, and his friends like Bobby Baker as well as in attempts from 1967 onward to convince the public that he was winding down the war.

Lying had become a sufficiently institutionalized way of doing things that many would defend Richard Nixon during Watergate because he was doing nothing that his predecessors had not done, but they had not been caught. So much has been penned about the burglary, wiretaps, cover-up, and the eighteen-minute gap in one of the tapes that it would be useless to burden the reader with yet another account. Suffice it to say that there was so much press coverage of these events that the public was bound to become less than respectful of the White House and its occupant. Not only did trust in Nixon evaporate, but trust in the office was severely undermined. By the time Governor Jimmy Carter took to the campaign trail in 1976, he was able to strike a responsive chord with the public by promising to "never tell a lie." Credibility had hit a new low.

During the Nixon years, the president's lack of candor contributed to precipitous declines in his popularity in the Gallup polls. In less than six months, his rating declined from about 67 percent approval in 1973 at the time of the Vietnam settlement to about 30 percent by midyear. The polls also dipped when the *Pentagon Papers* were released. (See Chart 1.1.) It must have been public disenchantment with the institution that caused this decline as Nixon had not been involved in the situations reported in those papers.

Gerald Ford's reputation for candor took a severe pounding and his approval rating plummeted from a 65 percent approval rating in September 1974 to about 50 percent a mere one month later.[52] In the interim, he had announced his decision to pardon Richard Nixon. Although there was no evidence of collusion between Ford and the man who appointed him, his timing of the decision was at best unfortunate so soon after Nixon's unceremonious exit from the White House.

Even an outsider such as Jimmy Carter found his white-knight image muddied by reports of past financial improprieties of his long-time friend and nominee for OMB director, Bert Lance. Carter, like Truman, stuck by his friends and paid the price of his loyalty in the opinion polls. His low point came in 1977 after he decided to fire Republican David Marston who was hot on the trail of two Democratic representatives, Josuah Eilberg and Daniel Flood, for conflicts of interest and kickbacks from federal contracts. (See Chart 1.2.) Representative Eilberg

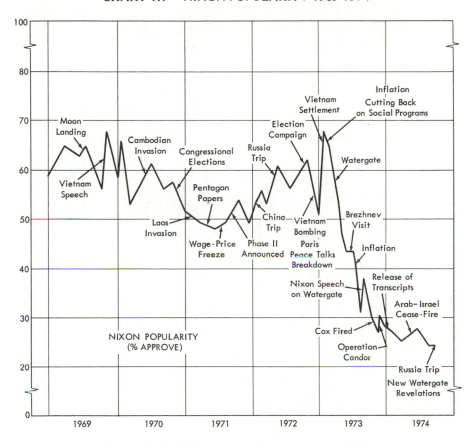

**CHART 1.1   NIXON POPULARITY 1969-1974**

Source: *Gallup Opinion Index,* September 1974, p. 12.

reportedly received funds for his efforts in getting a $14.5-million federal grant to construct a new wing for Hanneman Hospital in Philadelphia. Flood was accused, among other things, of receiving over $100,000 in exchange for favors related to a $60-million defense contract and a $10-million livestock program. Even though Carter was evidently unaware of these problems when Eilberg approached him with the request to dispose of Marston, the president paid for his decision to fire U.S. Attorney Marston.[53]

Credibility, like foreign affairs performance and the state of the economy, has been a major factor in recent public attitudes toward the White House. Public perceptions of poor performance in these areas spells political difficulties for any president.

The presidents of recent decades tarnished the office's image. It was somehow accepted that the gift of public trust would enhance the ability and character of the

# CHART 1.2 PRESIDENT CARTER'S JOB RATING

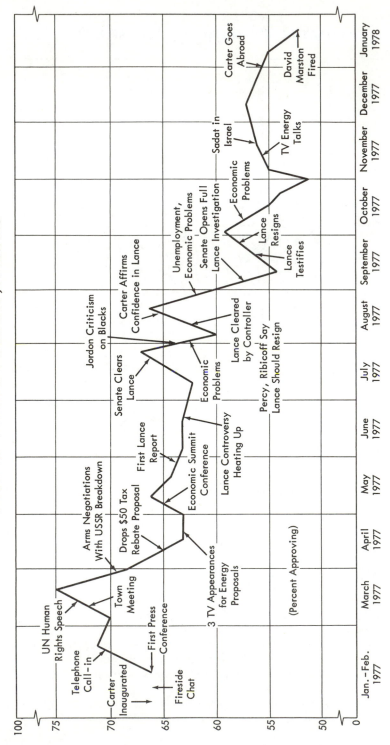

Source: *Gallup Opinion Index*, January 1978, p. 17.

20

man the voters selected. Theodore White, in *Breach of Faith,* contends that the public felt that "His [the president's] duties would, by their very weight, make him a superior man, fit to sustain the burden of the law, wise . . . enough to resist the clash of selfish interest."[54] Richard Nixon's transgressions exploded the publicly accepted myth that the office could somehow make the man. Optimists viewing Watergate could note, however, that those incidents may have awakened a healthy skepticism in the minds of the American voter.

## PRESIDENTIAL VIEWS:
## LITERALISTS AND ACTIVISTS

The powers of the office of president have come to be not what the Constitution says but what might be implied from what it says. Like the Bible and Thomas Jefferson, the U.S. Constitution may be interpreted in any creative way the fertile imagination of a public official might deem appropriate. Some presidents have taken a highly legalistic view of their roles, contending that they were empowered to do only what the Constitution or statute law specifically authorized. The presidents who espoused these views have come to be known as *literalist* or *weak* presidents.

The very words are negative value judgments. Marcus Cunliffe suggests that the term "weak" might be misleading. Some presidents were truly weak in that they were "inept, timorous, and petty." Others, like Taft and Eisenhower, were "weak" out of conviction, not inability to do the job.[55] They had a passion for checks and balances and did not think it was right for the president to muscle in on congressional territory.

Critical value judgments aside, there are dangers inherent in the literalist mentality in times of crisis. The pre-Civil War administration of James Buchanan could serve as a case in point. Although Buchanan denounced secessionist thought as "nothing short of revolution," he refused to act with sufficient determination to quell the impending conflagration. Instead, he contended that[56]

> apart from the execution of the laws . . . the Executive has no authority to decide what shall be the relations between the federal government and South Carolina. He has been invested with no such discretion. . . . It is therefore my duty to submit the whole question to Congress.

The Congress in which he was placing his faith was hopelessly divided on both slavery and the state of the Union. While it debated, the Union continued to dissolve.

Literalist thinking among the Republican presidents of the 1920s led them to expect the free market system to eventually halt the growing recession. As a group, Harding, Coolidge, and, until late in his administration, Hoover viewed presidential intervention in the economy as not only unnecessary but as potentially harmful. In 1930, for example, there was a severe drought in the Southwest and the secretary of agriculture recommended a relief fund of $25-million. In reaction to that suggestion Congress opted for a $60-million fund. President Hoover, however, reacted by saying "prosperity cannot be restored by raids on the public treasury . . . playing politics with misery." The president's alternative was a plan to provide loans for farmers for seeds, fertilizer, and cattle feed. There was to be no direct relief. Hoover fully expected private charities to provide relief. In 1931 he said that, if the time came that voluntary agencies were unable to find resources to prevent hunger and suffering, then he would use every resource of the federal government to meet the needs.[57]

As the Hoover example points out, executive branch leadership seems to be anathema to literalists. Historians and political scientists have tended to assign little more than an asterisk to them in texts on the office since few literalists left many personal marks on the institution. It has been common in academic writings on the presidency to complain about the shortcomings of literalists and to applaud activists.

The creed of the activist is a testament to personal leadership. Theodore Roosevelt is often cited for his "stewardship" approach to presidential leadership. He viewed the presidency as the voters' political fortune that had been given to the president as the steward or trustee. He felt required to invest that authority to make it grow for future presidents. "The executive," he contended, "is limited only by specific restrictions and prohibitions appearing in the Constitution or imposed by Congress under its Constitutional powers."[58] Theodore Roosevelt felt few restrictions from Congress and was in the habit of making important foreign policy decisions without even informing it.[59]

Teddy Roosevelt's cousin Franklin, in a message to Congress on wartime stabilization, put it this way: "In the event Congress should fail to act and act adequately, I shall accept the responsibility and I will act."[60] Vigorous leadership from the White House is not merely expected but, according to John Kennedy, demanded by the American voters.

> They demand a man capable of acting as commander-in-chief of a grand alliance, not merely a book keeper who feels that his work is done when the balance sheet comes out even. They demand a man who will formulate and fight for legislation.[61]

Unfortunately, excessive emphasis on leadership can breed arrogance, which might discourage compromise when a situation demands.

## THE GREATS AND
## THOSE WHO ALSO SERVED

Ultimately, which presidents are destined for a prominent place in history and which are doomed to obscurity? Fate may answer the question in part. Clinton Rossiter contends that "a man cannot possibly be judged a great president unless he holds office in great times." Washington, Lincoln, Wilson, and FDR rate high because they presided over a nation in crisis. Buchanan and Hoover were fated to lead the nation in extraordinary times too, but they were mere also-rans in the greatness sweepstakes. Great presidents are expected to meet problems head on even if it means violent clashes with Congress, dilatory tactics from the bureaucracy, and grumbling among the voters. Personal political consequences are not expected to lessen their resolve. Deference has rarely been judged as the stuff of which greatness is molded. Rossiter, after analyzing over one hundred presidential biographies, suggested the following criteria for greatness:[62]

1. Great presidents must serve in great times.
2. Each must be imaginative and brave and make decisions later perceived to be right ones.
3. He must be a Theodore Roosevelt stewardship type.
4. He must be a recognized organizer and administrator.
5. He must be capable of putting together a good system of advisors.
6. He must have the traits of character that make him loved, quoted, and remembered.
7. He must leave his mark on the office and on the social history of the nation.

Few of Rossiter's criteria seem to consider the massiveness of the federal government or the visual media that affect the functioning of today's presidents. Modern presidents have numerous expectations that did not encumber their predecessors. There are over 2.8 million federal employees and more than 1,900 federal agencies over which a president supposedly presides. Television coverage of the president and his appointees requires that he carefully select capable administrators who are personally above reproach. Eisenhower felt the aftershock of his assistant Sherman Adams's indiscretion of accepting a vicuna coat from financier Bernard Goldfine. LBJ aide Bobby Baker embarrassed his boss and ultimately went to jail due to business manipulations that had helped to parlay his modest government salary into a $2-million nest egg in ten short years. Johnson tried to disavow close ties to his former Senate aide Baker, but the scandal still hurt the White House.[63] Chief White House aide Walter Jenkins was arrested on a morals charge and eventually hospitalized. Johnson reacted by saying that the Eisenhower administration had had the same type of problem. Making things worse, Johnson crony Abe Fortas was forced to resign because of his consultant ties to the Wolfson foundation while he was on the bench. Whether or not Nixon was involved in the original order to wiretap at the Watergate, the transgressions of Haldeman, Erlichman, Mitchell, Magruder, et al. chipped away at the foundation of the administration. Gerald Ford had his administrative dirty linen aired via the controversial resignation, over the Nixon pardon, of his press secretary Jerald ter Horst. In the spirit of Harry Truman, Jimmy Carter stood up for his friends who were hurting his own public image. Attorney General-designate Griffin Bell's civil rights record was questioned, OMB director Bert Lance was suspect for irregular banking practices, and U.N. Ambassador Andrew Young developed political anthrax (foot-in-mouth disease) making controversial statements that reflected unfavorably on the man who chose him to a sensitive international position.

In addition to being careful about the company they keep, the media age requires presidents to exhibit leadership qualities, a sense of mission, and the oratorical ability to convey that zeal to the public. Presidents will be required to be able to inspire confidence in times of crisis and elicit sacrifice when necessity requires. Franklin Roosevelt could serve as a guide in these areas. He was able to use radio to encourage public confidence during the Depression and to request public sacrifice during World War II. John Kennedy used his energy and personal mystique to great advantage with the media. Even though his New Frontier legislation lay dormant and his foreign policy, with the exception of the Cuban missile crisis, was handled in a pedestrian manner, he had excellent ties with the press and the public which helped to enhance his political image. Only recently have revisionist analysts such as Henry Fairlie pointed up Kennedy's shortcomings both as a goal formulator and a legislative manipulator.[64]

It is noteworthy that, up to this point, the measures of greatness discussed have not touched on the attitudes of presidents toward democracy and the constitutional process. Those presidents most severely criticized were, interestingly, those who showed the greatest respect for the checks-and-balances system. Was this simply an oversight on the part of presidency analysts or does the absence of democracy in such discussions stem from a consensus that the leadership necessary in this modern age supersedes considerations about the democratic process?

## PERSONALITY AND PRESIDENTIAL TYPES

Do some personality types produce effective leaders? Are others more attuned to the democratic process? Without placing presidential hopefuls on a Freudian couch, is there any method for determining how they will react under stress in the office? In a step toward prediction rather than mere description, James David Barber's now classic study, *Presidential Character,*[65] diverted the attention of analysts away from strict adherence to history and public law as the explanatory media for discussing presidential power. Barber pointed presidential scholars toward the psyche and personality of the candidates as important concerns. He contended that a president's personality (character, style, and worldview) determine the way in which he will handle the office.

Others have approached the presidency from similar perspectives. Erwin C. Hargrove plowed similar ground in his *Presidential Leadership: Personality and Political Style.*[66] Both were following in the footsteps of Alexander and Juliette George[67] in their study of *Woodrow Wilson and Colonel House: A Personality Study* who tried to explain Wilson's stubborn and intractable approach to the handling of the League of Nations issue before the Senate as part of the character traits already evident in his upbringing. Ironically, Alexander George would later be one of the most vocal of the critics of Barber's personality categories.

Barber's studies suggested that four types of personalities have been noticeable among American presidents: (1) active-positive, (2) active-negative, (3) passive-positive, and (4) passive-negative. The actives wore the "white hats" because they were envisioned as social-minded problem solvers. Passives, on the other hand, seemed capable of fabricating mountains of excuses for deferring or totally avoiding action. These classifications bear a close resemblance to the activist and literalist categories that had been circulating in the field for some time. Barber's greatest contribution was his attempt to explain how a president's enjoyment of his job affected his use and understanding of presidential powers. Positives are painted as persons who enjoy the flush and challenge of the job. Negatives are portrayed as persons who consider their years in the White House as a painful national duty. Putting the characteristics together would produce the following definitions:[68]

1. Active-positive: constant activity, enthusiasm for the job, and self-confidence.

2. Active-negative:    constant activity, lack of real direction in some cases, hostility envisioned from others.
3. Passive-positive:   moderate work at the job but enjoys it nonetheless.
4. Passive-negative:  low activity and frustration with the duties of the office.

The perspective that a president has of his own competence is an important factor in deciding how he will handle the office. Does he see himself as possessing extensive skills, or is he haunted by self-doubts that force him to prove himself? Does he seek the respect and love he never had as a child, or is success for him the esteem to be bestowed in the history books? Every story of presidential decision making is really two stories: an outer one in which a rational man calculates and an inner one in which emotional man feels.

Another part of "character" according to Barber is "style." It could be defined as the president's way of dealing with people singly or in groups and his ways of handling problems that come to his desk. Some presidents may be most effective in one-to-one persuasion types of contacts. Lyndon Johnson was notorious for his dazzling interpersonal approach cynically dubbed "the treatment." He often used his physical size to advantage by standing on his tip toes and staring down into the eyes of his unwitting victims. He habitually wagged his finger in this type of encounter while maintaining a solid hold on the lapels of the intimidated person. He would threaten then beg, heap scorn then ply with flattery. LBJ was mercilessly unpredictable even with his own staff.[69] As a case in point, then Senate Majority Leader Johnson dressed down his long-time Senate aide George Reedy with expletives worthy of deletion from the Watergate tapes. Within a few minutes of the encounter, the senator gave Reedy a new station wagon for Christmas. Johnson felt that "you never want to give a man a present when he's feeling good. You want to do it when he's down."[70] His style in dealing with his staff did not alter radically when he assumed a new role as president.

A person's interpersonal relationships are shaped by his perceptions of human beings and the context within which he must deal with them. Barber refers to this as a person's *worldview*.[71] Various analysts of Richard Nixon's political career have identified his tendencies to view life as a series of crises and friendships as fleeting. In his book *Six Crises,* he commented about the 1960 campaign.[72]

> I have seen many men become bitter after an election defeat when they saw friendships melt away. . . . And what really hurt the worst was that those for whom they had done the most were often the first to desert. I was not unprepared for this reaction because I had already gained that experience during my mercurial career.

Nixon viewed most people as lazy and lacking in drive, daring, and courage. The key, to him, was willpower, personal mobilization, effort, and struggle. It should come as no surprise that a man with a philosophy such as that could seek to ferret out communist conspirators as he did in the Alger Hiss case. Further, as Barber so insightfully pointed out in his book written before Watergate, Nixon's obsessions with fate and his siege mentality were to be his undoing.

Even though the Barber typologies have been criticized in some academic circles, his work has been recognized so broadly that members of the press sought Barber's reflections on the type of character that each of the presidential hopefuls in 1976 might display. Candidate Jimmy Carter was sufficiently influenced by Barber's writings that he is reported to have said in a *Washington Post* interview that he planned to be a leader and that he thought that he would enjoy the job.[73] This self-assessment placed him in the active-positive category, which Barber considered optimum for modern-day America.

Other researchers into the psychological aspects of the presidency, in contrast to Barber, emphasized not individual character traits but interaction between the president and groups that either assisted or hampered him in reaching his goals. Robert Sickels, for example, pictured the role of the president as a mass of inter-actions (transactions) between interested groups and the chief executive. Sickels theorized that the president and other political activists interact only if each sees a chance to profit from discussion and/or cooperation.[74] He contended that the president, thinking like an economist, applies a sort of cost-benefit analysis to his decisions to maximize the advantages that might accrue from his efforts. Instead of pointing out the ways in which the man shapes his White House environment, as Barber did, Sickels illustrates the ways in which the environment hones the ultimate decisions.

Following a similar line of thinking, Irving Janis has suggested that a sort of mob psychology develops especially within the "in" crisis decision-making group. Presidential advisors will tend to adopt positions that they think coincide with the president's own views. In analyses of the Korean decision-making process, the Cuban missile crisis, and the Vietnam conflict, Janis attempts to explain how major policy options can be virtually ignored by "experts" both inside of government and from the outside who provide advice to presidents during crises. Numerous "Watergate" works have criticized the "team player" mentality so characteristic of the Nixon administration;[75] and Jimmy Carter has been criticized for depending too much on his "Southern-fried Mafia" of Georgia "good ole boys" with limited or nonexistent federal government expertise.

## CONCLUSIONS

The "real" presidency is not as powerful as perceived by the public. In the later decades of the twentieth century domestic economic problems may become increasingly traceable to international realities that are beyond White House control. Since our presidents are surrounded by the trappings of royalty, they might begin to believe it is their due. Frustration with the checks and balances system which stymies their initiative might encourage presidents to side-step the Constitution or laws in order to conjure up miracles that the public seems to demand of the successors of Washington, Lincoln, and Franklin Roosevelt.

## NOTES

[1] Robert Kennedy, *Thirteen Days: A Memoir of the Cuban Missile Crisis* (New York: W. W. Norton, 1968), pp. 94-95.

[2] Theodore White, *Breach of Faith* (New York: Atheneum, 1975), p. 152.

[3] *Ibid.,* p. 157.

[4] A case in point would be Theodore Sorensen who was enamored with the strong presidency in the mid-1960s and wrote two works extolling its virtues. See Sorensen, *Decision Making in the White House* (New York: Columbia U. P., 1963) and Sorensen, *Kennedy* (New York: Harper & Row, 1965).

His tone changed markedly to one of decrying the abuses of presidential power and the need for accountability in Sorensen, *Watchmen in the Night: Presidential Accountability after Watergate* (Cambridge, Mass.: MIT Press, 1976).

[5] Deceit in American politics from the U-2 to Watergate is handled in an excellent manner in David Wise, *The Politics of Lying: Government Deception, Secrecy and Power* (New York: Vintage Books, 1973). See also Townsend Hoopes, *Limits of Intervention* (New York: David McKay, 1970), esp. pp. 105-116.

[6] Thomas E. Cronin, "Making the Presidency Safe for Democracy," from Center Magazine, September-October 1973 as reprinted in *Readings in American Government, 1978/79,* Bruce Steinbrickner, ed. (Guilford, Conn.: Dushkin, 1978), pp. 109-116.

[7] Richard Neustadt, *Presidential Power: The Politics of Leadership* (New York: New American Library, 1976), p. 9.

[8] Harold M. Barger, "The Prominence of the Chief of State Role in the American Presidency," *Presidential Studies Quarterly,* (Spring 1978), pp. 127-139.

[9] Mary Klein, ed., *Viewpoints the Presidency: The Power and the Glory* (Minneapolis: Winston Press, 1974) pp. 18-19.

[10] *Gallup Opinion Index,* no. 156 (July 1978), 5, reports that Carter's high was March 1977 with 75 percent but that it had dropped by thirty-five points by July.

[11] See Dan Cordtz "The Imperial Lifestyle of U.S. Presidents," *Fortune,* October 1973, pp. 143-147, 220-224. See also *The New York Times,* January 1, 1974. A long and entertaining list of the "elevating" perks of the White House can be found also in William Mullen, *Presidential Power and Politics* (New York: St. Martin's Press, 1976), pp. 156-216.

[12] For a discussion of these and other constitutional violations, see Rowland Egger, *The President of the United States,* 2nd ed. (New York: McGraw-Hill, 1972), pp. 22-24.

[13] Robert S. Hirschfield, ed., *The Power of the Presidency: Concepts and Controversy,* 2nd ed. (Chicago: Aldine, 1973), pp. 79-80.

[14] Court reaction to this line of thinking can be found in *Hirabayshi* v. *U.S.,* 320 U.S. 81 (1943), pp. 217-18, and also in *Korematsu* v. *U.S.,* 323 U.S. 214 (1944), p. 218.

[15] Nixon took this position in an interview with David Frost. See *The New York Times,* March 14, 1976.

[16] George Reedy, *The Twilight of the Presidency* © 1970 by George E. Reedy. Reprinted by arrangement with New American Library, Inc.

[17] Joseph A. Califano, *A Presidential Nation* (New York: W. W. Norton, 1975), p. 227.

[18] James David Barber, *The Presidential Character: Predicting Performance in the White House* (Englewood Cliffs, N.J.: Prentice-Hall, 1972), p. 84.

[19] David Halberstam, *The Best and the Brightest* (New York: Random House, 1972), pp. 522-532, gives excellent insights into the total loyalty Johnson demanded.

On the LBJ pressures to conform, see also Irving Janis, *Victims of Groupthink* (Boston: Houghton Mifflin, 1972), pp. 119-126.

[20] *The New York Times,* January 1, 1974.

[21] *The New York Times,* January 29, 1970.

[22] *The New York Times,* February 3, 1970.

[23] Charles Peters and James Fallows, eds., *Inside the System,* 3rd ed. (New York: Praeger, 1976), p. 3.

[24] Erwin C. Hargrove, *The Power of the Modern Presidency* (New York: Knopf, 1974), p. 15.

[25] On youth, political socialization, and the presidency, see Fred Greenstein, "The Benevolent Leader: Childrens' Images of Presidential Authority," *American Political Science Review,* (December 1973), 1383ff. See also Christopher Atherton, "Watergate, Children's Attitudes Towards Political Authority Revisited," *Political Science Quarterly,* (Fall 1975), 488ff. Also Fred Greenstein, "Popular Images of the President," in *Perspectives on the Presidency,* eds. Stanley Bach and George Sulzner (Lexington, Mass.: D. C. Heath, 1974), pp. 136-137.

[26] Thomas Cronin, "The Textbook Presidency," in *Inside the System,* eds. Charles Peters and John Rothschild (New York: Praeger, 1973), pp. 6-19.

[27] Samuel Kernell, Peter Sperlich, and Aaron Wildavsky, "Public Support for Presidents," in *Perspectives on the Presidency,* ed. Aaron Wildavsky (Boston: Little Brown, 1975), pp. 152-153.

[28] Alan P. Balutis, "The Presidency and the Press: The Expanding Presidential Image," *Presidential Studies Quarterly* (Fall 1977), p. 248.

[29] See Chapter 10 of this text.

[30] Fred Greenstein, "What the President Means to Americans," in *Choosing the President,* ed. James D. Barber (Englewood Cliffs, N.J.: Prentice-Hall, 1974), p. 125.

[31] *Ibid.,* pp. 122-123.

[32] See John Mueller, "Presidential Popularity Truman to Johnson," *American Political Science Review* (March 1970), pp. 18-34. See also Samuel Kernell, "Explaining Presidential Popularity," *American Political Science Review* (June 1978), p. 506.

[33] James A. Stimson, "Public Support for the American Presidency: A Cyclical Model," Mimeo, 1974, as cited in Kernell, "Explaining Presidential Popularity," p. 507.

[34] On the role of interest groups and their action committees, see Carol Greenwald, *Group Power: Lobbying and Public Policy* (New York: Praeger, 1977), pp. 210-266.

[35] President Carter's address to the MFA Convention in Kansas City, Missouri.

[36] Aaron Wildavsky, "The Two Presidencies," in Wildavsky, ed., *The Presidency* (Boston: Little Brown, 1969), pp. 230-248. By permission of *Transaction,* 4:2 © 1966 by Transaction, Inc.

[37] John Mueller, *War, Presidents, and Public Opinion* (New York: John Wiley, 1973), pp. 53, 58-59.

[38] John Spanier, *Games Nations Play* (New York: Praeger, 1978), p. 194.

[39] *Gallup Opinion Index,* No. 111, (September 1974), 12.

[40] *The New York Times,* November 25, 1974.

[41] *The Wall Street Journal,* September 8, 1978. Carter's Gallup rating as of August was 39 percent but, by September 18, it had increased to 51 percent. See also *Congressional Quarterly Weekly Reports,* September 23, 1978, p. 2548.

[42] John Mueller, *War, Presidents, and Public Opinion.* See also Henry C. Kenski, "The Impact of Economic Conditions on Presidential Popularity," *Journal of Politics* (August 1977), pp. 764-773.

[43] Kenski, *op. cit.,* pp. 764-773.

[44] *Ibid.,* p. 767.

[45] Samuel Kernell, "Explaining Presidential Popularity," *American Political Science Review* (June 1978), p. 506.

[46] *Gallup Opinion Index,* no. 150 (January 1978), pp. 19, 22-24, 27, discuss public distaste for government officials.

[47] Rowland Egger, *The President of the United States,* 2nd ed. (New York: McGraw-Hill, 1972), p. 76.

[48] Wise, *op. cit.,* p. 44.

[49] *Ibid.,* p. 62.

[50] *Ibid.,* p. 60.

[51] *Ibid.,* p. 61.

[52] On Ford's popularity, see *Gallup Opinion Index,* no. 113 (November 1974), pp. 18-19.

[53] For more on the Marston problem and the investigations of Flood and Eilberg, see *Congressional Quarterly Weekly Reports,* 1978 volumes at pp. 89, 139, 176, 383, 1078.

[54] White, *op. cit.,* p. 324.

[55] Marcus Cunliffe, *American Presidents and the Presidency.* © 1968 American Heritage Publishing Co., Inc.

[56] James Buchanan, "Fourth Annual Message to Congress," excerpted in Robert S. Hirschfield, *The Power of the President*, p. 68.

[57] Barber, *op. cit.*, pp. 28-29.

[58] Hirschfield, *op. cit.*, p. 82.

[59] Theodore Roosevelt, "An Autobiography" in *The Works of Theodore Roosevelt*, ed. Herman Hagedorn (New York: Scribner's, 1926), vol. 220, pp. 535-540.

[60] Franklin Roosevelt, "War Time Stabilization Message to Congress," September 7, 1942 as excerpted in Hirschfield, *The Power of the President*, p. 107.

[61] *Ibid.*, p. 129.

[62] The list is a synopsis from Clinton Rossiter, *The American Presidency* (New York: Harcourt Brace, 1960), pp. 179-181.

[63] Rowland Evans and Robert Novak, *Lyndon Johnson: The Exercise of Power* (New York: New American Library, 1966), pp. 436-437.

[64] Henry Fairlie, *The Kennedy Promise: The Politics of Expectations* (Garden City, N.Y.: Doubleday, 1973).

[65] Barber, *op. cit.*, pp. 3-14.

[66] Erwin C. Hargrove, *Presidential Personality and Political Style* (New York: Macmillan, 1966).

[67] Alexander L. and Juliette L. George, *Woodrow Wilson and Colonel House* (New York: John Day, 1956).

[68] Barber, *op. cit.*, pp. 12-14.

[69] Erwin C. Hargrove, *The Power of the Modern Presidency*, p. 36.

[70] Patrick Anderson, *The President's Men* (Garden City, N.Y.: Doubleday, 1968), p. 364.

[71] Barber, *op. cit.*, pp. 441-442.

[72] Richard M. Nixon, *Six Crises* (New York: Pyramid, 1968), p. 425.

[73] Walt Anderson, "Looking for Mr. Active-Positive," as reprinted in Bruce Steinbrickner, *Readings in American Government 1978-79* (Guilford, Conn.: Dushkin, 1978), p. 97.

[74] Robert J. Sickels, *Presidential Transactions* (Englewood Cliffs, N.J.: Prentice-Hall, 1974), p. 1.

[75] Typical of the Watergate works that excoriate the "team player mentality" is Dan Rather and Gary Gates, *The Palace Guard* (New York: Harper & Rowe Publishers, Inc., 1974).

# The Evolving Presidency: Whatever Happened to James Buchanan?

Who gets angry at the thought of President James Buchanan? If he is remembered at all, it is for being Lincoln's predecessor and for what he didn't do. Was the Civil War his fault? Didn't he want to see the issues of slavery and sectionalism addressed? He kept begging Congress for guidance and legislation to enable him to deal with those problems. Voters today would demand leadership from the president in crisis even if Congress were left on the sidelines. If the president waited for congressional directions, he would become unpopular. The electorate has come to expect something other than a wait-and-see attitude from the White House.

The summer of 1974 saw the unthinkable happen, however. A president of the United States was forced to resign due to evidence that he had obstructed justice. Richard Nixon covered for his associates who had botched a "third-rate" burglary of the Democratic National Committee headquarters at the Watergate complex in Washington, D.C. Could a president be involved in raw politics like that? Wasn't he supposed to be above such things? What had become of the heroic seat of social change that produced the New Deal, the New Frontier, and the Great Society? What tragic flaws in the institution permitted this vehicle of social betterment to become the epitome of the worst connotations of the word politics? Possibly, the expectations of the office were unrealistic. Surely, considering the fact that the presidency is a human institution, shouldn't human frailties be expected? What other institution could record only one resignation under fire of well over thirty chief executives?

Public disenchantment in the aftermath of Watergate and Vietnam might encourage changes in executive power through constitutional amendment. The idea of a national convention to amend the Constitution is not as outlandish as it might sound at first. In recent years, twenty-six states have petitioned Congress for a new constitutional convention to write an amendment to the Constitution requiring that the federal budget be balanced every fiscal year. Nineteen other state legislatures have asked Congress to call for a convention to outlaw abortions except when the mother's life is endangered. The Constitution simply requires petitions from two-thirds of the state legislatures (thirty-four states) to set a new convention into motion.

At present, it is unclear whether these national conventions, if called, would be limited to the single topic addressed in the petitions from the states. What if the convention strayed into the executive branch? Would delegates of the 1980s opt for just one president, or, given the burdens of the office, would they suggest several? Would a single executive have one six-year term, two four-year terms, or indefinite reeligibility? Would the selection process remain the same including the continuation of the Electoral College system? Would a new executive be given more powers than today's president or less? Would removing a president be made easier than the impeachment procedures under our present Constitution? Experiences of the past few decades would no doubt weigh heavily on the minds of delegates at any future national convention. Could a new convention change the leadership role the presidency has assumed in the American political process?

## ATTITUDES TOWARD EXECUTIVE POWER: THE PROBLEMS WITH THE ARTICLES

The position of chief executive created by the first convention at Philadelphia in 1787 was established partially in response to discontent with the weakness of American government under the Articles of Confederation. Were the delegates from that convention to return to examine the system of government they pieced together in the blistering summer meetings, those "demigods" as Thomas Jefferson so impetuously called them, would be awed at the power that has gravitated toward the executive they created. They might well wonder if they had overresponded to the frustrations of the helter-skelter administrative processes that had plagued the government under the Articles of Confederation. Under that system, the Union amounted to a mere marriage of convenience among sovereign states against the specter of anarchy that haunted the fledgling nation. Congress had been the only branch of government, and, by present-day standards, its powers were meager indeed.

This feeble organization was able to function relatively effectively in dealing with the British in wartime because life under the rule of England had become intolerable to her free-spirited colonists. They recognized that unity was the key to their survival or, as Benjamin Franklin put it at the signing of the *Declaration of Independence,* "We had best hang together or, assuredly, the British will hang us separately."

As the war began to wind down, internecine feuding erupted among the thirteen sister states that had entered into a "firm league of friendship."[1] Whatever that meant exactly, it did not leave the impression of a strong national government. Issues such as trade policies, tariff restrictions among the states, and slavery encouraged much of the bickering; but also at issue was the very makeup and power of the government itself. The basic flaw of the increasingly threadbare system was the inability of the Articles of Confederation to "faithfully execute" national laws especially in the areas of trade and taxation. The questions before the delegates to the Philadelphia convention boiled down to, as Gouverneur Morris of Pennsylvania put it, "Should there be a national government or general anarchy?"[2] We might add another overriding question too: Who should be responsible for seeing that a *national* government could work? Who should lead the nation?

In this chapter, as we explore the new chief executive and his powers, we shall investigate (1) the views of the public and Philadelphia convention delegates, (2) the state governors as presidential models, (3) the conflicts at the convention over powers and the very nature of the executive, and (4) some of the factors that encouraged the growth of presidential leadership and powers. In Chapter 11 we shall examine the relationship between leadership and accountability in the context of impeachment, resignation, and vacancies in the Oval Office in general.

The distaste for executive tyranny among the delegates at Philadelphia and the public at large had grown out of the Stamp Act, the "Townsend Acts," the results of the Boston Tea Party, and other experiences with the British king and his royal governors.[3] Legislatures, on the other hand, were commonly viewed as the guardians of the rights of every person. This attitude was reflected in the various state constitutions that tended to severely curtail the prerogatives and powers of state governors. The first national constitution, the Articles of Confederation, likewise relegated the enforcement and administration of laws to a hodgepodge of congressional committees rather than to a single strong executive.

The writers of the new Constitution faced a perplexing dilemma that haunts our nation even to the present. They feared a strong executive, yet they realized that one would be needed to ensure an effective national government. Many, like Alexander Hamilton, who was a monarchist at heart, would argue that "Energy in the executive is the leading characteristic in the definition of good government."[4] Others, including James Madison whose *Journal* provides today's closest thing to a firsthand account of the convention, recognized that legislatures could also usurp powers in much the way that an executive could. As a result, he cautioned against rigid opposition to a strong executive.[5] Legislatures, due to their ties to the people, might be pressured more easily by the whims of the masses. Even George Washington was uncomfortable with the practical application of the theory of popular sovereignty. Shortly after Shay's rebellion, he lamented in a letter that those events,[6]

> exhibit a melancholy verification of what our transatlantic foes have predicted; and of another thing perhaps still more to be regretted, That mankind left to themselves are unfit for their own government.

Such sentiments were hardly for public consumption. Still, the problem for the Founding Fathers became one of incorporating the concepts of a strong executive into the Constitution and still being able to sell the document to a skeptical public.

Contrary to some glorified impressions of the Philadelphia convention delegates, they were less philosophers than pragmatists, less visionaries than political realists. They hoped to fashion the best document that they could sell. In pursuit of that goal, they proved quite capable of citing the writings of political theorists whose views and prestige could be used to defend the new Constitution. Advocates of a strong executive could look to John Locke's defense of broad discretionary power for the executive.[7] They could also find support in the writings of Montesquieu who envisioned each branch of government as being strong enough to intrude into the bailiwicks of the others. A weak executive would be unable to check the excesses of a popularly elected legislature.[8]

## STATE GOVERNOR MODELS:
## ERRAND BOYS OR EMPERORS?

Since it was generally agreed that a different method for executing the laws was called for, the delegates had thirteen models from which to choose. In the early state constitutions, governors tended to be "pledges" in the governmental fraternities as they were little more than errand boys of the legislature. It was an accepted principle that, for the safety of the rights of the masses, the executive should be subordinated to the legislatures. James Wilson, destined to be an architect of the presidency at Philadelphia, contended that the people exhibited excessive partiality toward the legislatures at the expense of *effective* law enforcement.[9] State constitutions were laced with provisions for reducing the executive to virtual obscurity. Governors were restricted to short terms of one, two, or three years. They were not eligible for reelection except in Massachusetts. Commonly, they were elected not by the people but by state legislatures, which showed them none of the deference a prime minister could expect from the Parliament that selected him. Prime ministers were given the courtesy of selecting their own cabinets; but state constitutions usually saddled the governor with a privy council chosen by the legislature. That council then shared the executive powers with the governor. As a result of the workings of these councils, Edmund Randolph, as governor of Virginia, referred to himself as a "member of the executive."[10]

Many delegates believed that a stronger, more national executive would be necessary to protect the peoples' liberties, and John Adams championed the position[11] forcefully even before the convention. The best available working model was that of the governor of New York. That state's constitution provided numerous insights to the Philadelphia delegates. First, it was not written until 1777, after the other states had penned theirs. As a result, the mistakes of the other states in creating their executives were known to the New York convention delegates. Contrary to the constitutions of most of its sister states, the New York charter did not assert the dominance of the legislative branch. The New York governor was given a longer term, three years versus one or two in other states. He could be reelected, and he was selected by the voters rather than by the legislature so that he retained an independent political base. He was not strapped with a council to limit his authority and was granted numerous powers eventually granted to the president of the United States.[12] He was commander-in-chief of the militia, could call the state legislature into special session and grant reprieves and pardons, and possessed qualified appointments and veto powers.[13]

The New York system proved to be effective under fire from the battlefields of the war with England and the cauldron of internal civil disorders including the Doctor's riot and the cleanup operation against the remnants of Shay's rebellion.[14] But would it prove acceptable when adapted to providing a single executive for the entire nation?

## DEBATES AT PHILADELPHIA

From the opening gavel of the Convention, the delegates found themselves in a quandary. While a strong executive seemed necessary to effectively enforce the laws passed by Congress, widespread popular resentment toward monarchy limited the shape of the options available. The issues raised about the executive could be lumped into two broad categories: (1) How should he be selected? and (2) How broad a leadership role should be given?[15]

SINGLE VERSUS MULTIPLE EXECUTIVES. Instituting a line of kings could have saved hours of debate over a selection process and the term of office for any new chief executive. Prior to the constitutional convention, John Jay, in a letter to George Washington, asked, evidently in all seriousness, "Should we have a king?"[16] Rumors circulated that the Bishop of Osnaburg, Germany, second son of George III, had been suggested as the first in a line of U.S. kings.[17]

No one at the Convention, not even Hamilton, seemed bent on creating an ancient-styled Asiatic or European court to hold forth in the United States. Abraham Baldwin of Georgia wrote in his diary that[18]

> it appeared to be the opinion of the Convention that he [the executive] should be a character respected by the Nations as well as the federal Empire. To this end . . . as much power should be given to him as could be . . . guarding against all possibility of his ascending in a tract of years or Ages to Despotism and absolute monarchy.

Hamilton tried to convince convention members that they might have misread public attitudes and that a limited monarchy could be both effective administrative machinery under the Constitution and a salable political commodity. The people, he argued, were becoming "tired of an excess of democracy."[19]

The four often-cited major plans for constructing the new government suggested at Philadelphia (Virginia, New York, New Jersey, and South Carolina) all recognized the need for a separate executive, but their advocates parted company over a number of issues. They had different answers to such questions as: Should there be more than one executive? Should his term be short or long? Should he be selected by the state legislatures, the Congress, or the public at large?

Among the first issues to come before the Committee of the Whole at Philadelphia was the question of a single executive.[20] Edmund Randolph, characterizing a single executive as the "foetus of monarchy," proposed an executive council composed of three men from different regions of the nation. He reasoned that this triumvirate would more adequately represent all regions of the country and gain their support. One man, he felt, could be co-opted by a single powerful region. James Wilson and Charles Pinckney spoke for the single executive. In answer to Randolph's previous assertions that a monarchy might develop, Wilson reminded the delegates that all thirteen states had single executives. In fact, he viewed them as the "best safeguard against tyranny." Wilson would later push these views from his position as chairman of the Committee on Detail and would be bolstered by the convictions of his fellow Pennsylvanian, Gouverneur Morris who chaired the Committee on Style.[21] The drafts and final copies of the presidential article bore the indelible stamp of these advocates of a strong executive.

ADVISING THE EXECUTIVE: CABINET OR COUNCIL. Disenchantment with a strong single executive did not evaporate merely because a few influential delegates were eloquent in their support of it. Opponents envisioned some type of privy (advisory) council as a mechanism for limiting the chances of executive tyranny. One suggestion would have created a council of state consisting of six members (two each from East, South, and Middle states) appointed by Congress. Franklin lent his support to this approach because he reasoned that a council "would not only be a check on a bad President, but a relief to a good one."[22] In the ensuing debate, Morris worried aloud that the president might pressure his council to approve an ill-conceived idea and then cloak himself in their support when the inevitable critics materialized.

Eventually, support coalesced around something akin to today's cabinet. The Constitution, however, does not use the term cabinet, and its provisions for advice to the president are nebulous. Throughout the Convention, there was a consensus that, as Franklin put it, "the first man put at the helm will be a good one."[23] The fact that Washington was odds on choice to be the first president encouraged wavering delegates to leave the question of an advisory council up to him. The Constitution simply provided that a president[24]

> may require the opinion, in writing, of the principal officer in each of the Executive departments, upon any subject relating to the duties of their respective offices.

In opting for this approach to a system of presidential consultation, they retained the separation of powers intact by resisting the temptation to include members of the Supreme Court and Congress in a constitutionally mandated advisory system.

SELECTION AND TENURE. How simple and short the Convention would have been had the number of executives and the nature of consultation been the only bones of contention. Instead other questions concerning the selection process and the length of term for the executive also aroused passions. During early deliberations over these matters, proposals for election of a new president by Congress were almost adopted.[25] To lessen the chances that the president might knuckle under to congressional pressures, these plans called for long terms for the president with no reeligibility (seven years). He would not have to return to Congress for reelection, and so he would remain independent of the legislature that chose him.[26] Advocates of long terms also reasoned that only a long term would attract the "best" candidates and, once elected, these types of persons would be unafraid to take firm stands on issues while in office. Given the reality, today, that presidents, in their first terms are running constantly for their second four years, although they are required to "make their mark" to get reelected, they are often afraid to make waves. Some would argue that, if the president doesn't have to explain some damage done during his administration, he might be reelected rather than requiring a change of horses in midstream. Given these realities, longer terms and no re-eligibility look even more attractive. In recent years, former President Lyndon Johnson and former Attorney General Griffin Bell have been among the more vocal advocates of one six-year term.[27]

Some delegates argued that the people, not Congress, should select the national executive. Direct popular election for governor had worked in New York, they noted; why not try it nationally? These radically democratic suggestions did not sit well with most of the delegates, and objections leveled at involving the masses in the process were numerous. Skeptics considered the public incompetent to be making such momentous decisions. No doubt, they argued, the masses would be ignorant of the issues and would vote for the candidate from their state or region regardless of his qualifications. Finally, direct democracy of this type would give an undue advantage to candidates from large-population states.[28] The Founding

Fathers, then, when confronted with the dilemma of selecting a president capable of dynamic leadership or one chosen for his popularity with the masses, opted for leadership and settled for "indirect" democracy as the safest, most politically acceptable, way.

A variation on the popular election theme was offered by James Wilson.[29] He suggested that the president be chosen by electors chosen by the people. This novel idea was resurrected and retooled on July 17 as discussions returned to electoral procedures. Calls for selection of electors by state legislatures fell on deaf ears. The question was shifted to the Committee on Detail to construct something salable, and the Electoral College system of today was the handiwork of that committee.[30] In Chapter 10, we shall discuss the anachronistic Electoral College in more detail.

## BROAD POWERS FOR THE PRESIDENT

When questions arose about the powers to be given to the new president, the belief that Washington would use them wisely and set proper precedents encouraged the Founding Fathers to resolve differences in favor of the chief executive. The first phrase of Article II instructed that "The executive power shall be vested in the President of the U.S." There is not a broader grant of authority anywhere in the Constitution.

To correct the chaotic administration of government by Committees of Congress under the Articles of Confederation, the new Constitution created a unified executive system. The president was mandated *broad appointive powers*.[31] He was to nominate "ambassadors, other public ministers and consuls, the judges of the Supreme Court and all other officers of the United States whose appointments were not otherwise provided for by the Constitution." These nominations were made subject to majority Senate approval.

Fears about legislative supremacy encouraged supporters of checks and balances to advocate a *veto power*[32] for the president. Memories of the arbitrary rule of the king and of royal governors made some delegates nervous about bestowing a veto on another potential tyrant simply because he would be holding court in New York or Philadelphia instead of in London. A Council of Revision was considered as a middle-of-the-road solution to differences of opinion over a presidential veto. It would have shared the veto power by including representatives of all three branches of the "veto" council. The Committee of the Whole at the convention eventually removed the judiciary from consideration on veto matters and awarded the president a "qualified" veto with a two-thirds vote in both houses needed to override it.

The "royal prerogatives" in foreign affairs created substantial controversy too. Should the president have the powers of the king in his dealings with other nations? Logic dictated that a single executive rather than a more diverse legislature should speak for the nation as a whole. To that end, the president was empowered to send and receive ambassadors, to negotiate treaties subject to a two-thirds consent in the Senate, and to serve as commander-in-chief of the army and navy.

Ironically, many of the same worries expressed by members of Congress in the 1960s over U.S. involvement in Indochina had bothered the delegates at the Philadelphia convention almost two centuries earlier. While some considered a broad war-making power[33] a necessity for the president, others were clearly uncomfortable with such generosity to a single executive. The convention opted for keeping declarations of war close to the people by giving Congress the power to "declare war," even though some, like Charles Pinckney, felt that the Senate alone would be capable of the speed necessary to handle crisis decisions. The term "declare" was a compromise fashioned by Gerry and Madison who preferred it to "make" war. By giving Congress the power to declare war, the Constitution did not foreclose on the president's options as commander-in-chief to "make" war in order to repel invasions. In Chapter 6 on the president, Congress, and foreign affairs, we shall examine these issues in greater detail.

PRESIDENTIAL POWERS ABUSED: PUNISHMENT UNDER THE CONSTITUTION. Removing a king would call for revolution and removing a prime minister would require a "no-confidence" vote by the legislature. But how does a nation remove a president? Max Farrand, respected analyst of the convention, contends that "the clearest indication of the intention to make the office an important one is that the executive was rendered subject to impeachment."[34] Even noted advocates of a strong executive like James Wilson agreed with George Mason that some method of impeachment would be in the national interest. "Shall any man," Mason cautioned his colleagues, "be over Justice?" He also reminded them that "The community requires protection against incapacity, negligence, or perfidy of the Chief Executive."[35]

Impeachment proceedings necessitated accusation and trial. The delegates had to determine who should impeach (accuse) and who should convict. Some felt that impeachment and conviction should be handled by judges from each state constituting a temporary tribunal. Others leaned toward some role for Congress while a third group envisioned the Supreme Court as the ultimate arbiter in matters of accusation and conviction. Determining how the state judges would work together proved a problem. Even the politically naïve had cause to wonder how the Supreme Court, many of whose members might have been appointed by the accused president, could handle impeachment and conviction proceedings objectively. Eventually, the delegates agreed to having the House draw up the letters of impeachment (the accusation or indictment) and the Senate sit as trial jury under the watchful eye of the chief justice who would preside over any eventual trial.

## THE CONVENTION IN SUM

The friends of a strong single executive had every reason to leave the Convention crowing proudly about their accomplishments. They succeeded in turning the tide in their direction during the last two weeks of the deliberations. Had the Convention disbanded only two weeks sooner, the Senate would have been given the power to appoint ambassadors and judges and to make treaties with foreign powers. The new president, ultimately, was more magnificently empowered than any of the delegates could have imagined when the Convention began. The framers had painted the presidency in bold, broad strokes leaving the details to Washington and his successors. Choice of a single rather than a multiple executive and the military and diplomatic powers given to him enhanced the potentials of the office. Despite the checks and balances incorporated into the document, the president initiated most of the important national decisions and Congress was relegated to a position of responding to national initiatives.

# CUSTOM AND USAGE
# SHAPE THE PRESIDENCY

When George Washington became President, he realized how little guidance the Constitution gave him and how important his early decisions would be. Washington wrote,[36]

> Few who are not philosophical spectators can realize the difficult and delicate part which a man in my situation has to act. . . . I walk on untrodden ground. There is scarcely any part of my conduct which may not hereafter be drawn into precedent.

From the earliest days of government under the new document to the present, growth in presidential leadership and power is attributable less to the Constitution and laws of Congress than to evolving customs and day-to-day usage. *Custom* refers to practices not based in statutes or the Constitution that become acceptable modes of behavior over long periods of time. *Usage* refers to interpretation of powers and privileges already granted to a public official under the Constitution or a statute.

## WASHINGTON PRECEDENTS

The first president found the Constitution less than specific in a number of areas, and it became necessary for him to plow quite a bit of virgin territory. As a consequence, he established a number of precedents creating leadership roles for his successors.

**ADMINISTRATIVE LEADERSHIP.** In one case, for example, the Constitution had provided that all governmental machinery not otherwise provided for under the document would be created by Congress. In the first session of the new legislature, the House and Senate established three departments (State, War, and Treasury) and instituted the post of attorney general. During the debates some senators argued that the fact that they were to approve appointments included a right to veto dismissals as well. This interpretation was clearly at odds with Washington's reading of the intent of the Constitution. Fortunately for the new president and his successors, Madison persuaded House members to vote against giving this implied power to the Senate. Vice President Adams broke a Senate tie over the issue in support of the president's view of his appointments power under the Constitution.[37] A less popular figure than Washington as president might have lost that vote, and a precedent could have been set forcing future presidents to work with department heads, generals, and so on whose performance was substandard or whose loyalty was suspect. In appointing Jefferson, Knox, Hamilton, and Randolph, Washington was acting on the presupposition that Senate consent meant after the fact of nomination, not consultation in advance.

In Washington's view, the president was to be an involved administrator. He took literally the constitutional provision that he could require the departments to provide him with reports about their duties; and he used these reports to intervene in their operations and give them direction. In doing so he opened the door to the use of executive orders to shape the day-to-day operation of departments, even though the Constitution had not provided for executive orders. Louis Koenig has summarized Washington's involvement in the departments to include reading all departmental communications, approving all loans and debt transactions, and approving the use of the U.S. seal. The president even jealously guarded patronage. "No lighthousekeeper, customs collector, or captain of a cutter could be appointed without his approval."[38] No bureaucrat wondered who was boss.

LEGISLATIVE DIRECTION. Given the time that must have been involved in such careful scrutiny of the bureaucracy, it is hard to imagine that Washington had time to do much else. Nevertheless, he worked diligently behind the scenes to blaze a legislative path for Congress. Treasury Secretary Alexander Hamilton served as a legislative aide for Washington and was intimately involved in drafting legislation and building coalitions and congressional majorities behind the bills as well as providing the president a sense of what would be salable in the House and Senate. In public, Washington always maintained an above-the-battle posture in his dealings with Congress, and he was careful to accord the members of the House and Senate the courtesy to which their station entitled them. To him, the separation of powers did not preclude presidential leadership in the legislative process.

Washington was jealously protective of the prerogatives given to the presidency, and he made every effort to deflect any attempts at legislative encroachment. While he avoided open conflict with Congress over policy questions, he was not afraid to stand his constitutional ground, considering the veto as his ultimate defense. (He used it only twice.)[39]

Foreign affairs problems caused some of his most serious battles with Congress. On one occasion the president decided to go the extra mile and answer Senate questions on a treaty that the administration had negotiated with the Creek Indians. The Constitution had not required consultation with the Senate on treaties. It merely required Senate ratification by a two-thirds vote. When the president finished answering the senators' inquiries to their satisfaction, Washington was asked to leave the chamber so that the committee members could deliberate in private. That request so angered Washington that he reportedly stormed from the chamber murmuring that he would be "damned if he ever went there again."[40] From that day until Gerald Ford went to Capitol Hill to explain his pardon of Richard Nixon before a congressional committee, no other president testified on Capitol Hill.

On another occasion Washington clashed with the House over papers related to the Jay treaty. The president brusquely swept aside their request to view the instructions he gave to John Jay. Washington wanted no part in Republican attempts to get ammunition to impeach Jay because of the highly unpopular treaty he had negotiated.[41] The president offered two explanations for his decision. First, he lectured the House on its lack of constitutional standing in the treaty process, and then he argued that secrecy and dispatch in negotiation of treaties required that the president be free to confer with his subordinates without undue fear of public scrutiny. In essence, he was invoking what would now be called "executive privilege." Noted constitutional scholar Raoul Berger has recently referred to executive privilege as a constitutional myth.[42] But the fact that it was not in the Constitution did not seem to bother Washington in the least. We shall examine secrecy, national security, and executive privilege in more detail in Chapter 5.

Another donnybrook between branches arose over Washington's Neutrality Proclamation of 1795 and the Genêt incident. In declaring the United States neutral in the ongoing conflict between Britain and France, the president was acting in a manner not provided for under the Constitution. Likewise the Constitution left the president broad discretion in dealing with ambassadors assigned to the United States. When Washington informed the French government that he wanted Genêt recalled for causing problems between the president and Congress over neutrality, he reasoned that, if he could receive ambassadors, he could also request their ouster from the United States. In both cases he claimed that powers existed by implication from responsibilities imposed under the Constitution.

ADVISORY SYSTEM. As his administration evolved, the president began meeting more and more frequently with four major department heads.[43] Debate became common in these meetings as Jefferson and Hamilton were invariably on opposite sides of most issues. The Constitution made no provision for a cabinet to advise the president, and Washington never used the word, but he did set a precedent that a president would meet regularly with the "heads of the great departments" and seek their counsel on a broad range of issues. Custom had created for the future what the Founding Fathers had been unwilling to impose on the presidency.

TWO TERMS. Washington could not even retire without setting a precedent. In his Farewell Address he suggested that two terms[44] should be enough for any man and that practice evolved into a custom that stood for 144 years until Franklin Roosevelt, referring to the need for continuity in dealing with the troubled national economy and the war in Europe, was elected for a third term in 1940. The first president left a heritage of prestige,[45] authority, and respect for the Constitution and a sense of dignity on which his successors could build. He received the adulation of a king, yet he demonstrated measured respect for the role of Congress. Above all, he set high standards of integrity and he jealously guarded the prerogatives that the Constitution had granted to the presidency.

## JEFFERSON TO LINCOLN

While Washington shaped administrative, legislative, and foreign policy roles for the president, Thomas Jefferson introduced political parties into the presidential leadership equation. The sprouts of his grass-roots presidential campaign matured into the Democratic-Republican Party. Taking advantage of his party leadership role, Jefferson united the party caucus (all the members of his party in Congress) behind his legislative agenda. Federalist John Marshall had prophesied that Jefferson would weaken the office of president while enhancing his own power as party leader, and E. S. Corwin concluded from studying Jefferson's administration that he was primarily a party leader and only secondarily the chief executive.[46] Nevertheless, his contribution to the presidency was a new leadership dimension through political parties that served presidents like Woodrow Wilson, Franklin Roosevelt, and later Lyndon Johnson, as they pressed the New Freedoms, the New Deal, and the Great Society programs through the legislature.

No one waiting in the wings to replace Jefferson could approach his charismatic style or his party leadership abilities.[47] As a result, presidential leadership fell upon hard times as the White House came under the sway of the party caucus of the Democrats. (The same party caucus nominated Presidents Madison and Monroe.) When the Electoral College proved unable to choose a president in 1828, Congress once again chose the president (John Quincy Adams). Even though the Founding

Fathers decided against letting Congress select the president, in fact this is what happened in each election from Jefferson to Jackson.[48]

The presidency quickly emerged from its limbo of checks and balances with the coronation of "King Andrew I" Jackson. While historians remember his administrations for such terms as the "spoils system" and "kitchen cabinet," his greatest contribution to presidential power and leadership was not his interpretation of patronage jobs or advisory systems. Rather, he staked out an independent position for the presidency, free from the congressional restraints that had cast the presidency into a position of subservience to the leadership on Capitol Hill.

Although his opponents berated him for his independent thinking, rough demeanor, and "despotic" ways, Jackson envisioned himself as the single federal official capable of claiming special ties to the mass of voters in the nation as a whole. His election by "universal suffrage" encouraged him to consider himself the champion of the causes of the "humble members of society." Even Jefferson, who is usually viewed as the voice of the freeholder, had not attempted to develop such close ties to the common man. In a battle with Congress over the Second Bank of the United States, Jackson vetoed the recharter, and his philosophy of presidential leadership and independence were evident throughout his veto message, a part of which said[49]

> The Congress, the Executive, and the Court must each for itself be guided by its own opinion of the Constitution. Each public officer who takes an oath to support the Constitution swears that he will support it as he understands it, and not as it is understood by others. . . . The opinion of the judges has no more authority over Congress than the opinion of Congress has over the judges, and on that point, the President is independent of both.

Neither the Congress nor the courts, then, in his view, had any right to instruct him in policy matters or in the way in which he should handle the office that the voters had entrusted to him.

Abraham Lincoln made the last major contribution to presidential leadership before recent decades by expanding the concept of inherent powers (powers implied from the nature of the office even though not specifically stated in the Constitution or statute) beyond previously recognized bounds. In interpreting the "commander-in-chief" and "take care that the laws be faithfully executed" phrasing in the Constitution, Lincoln acted to save the strife-torn Union oblivious to court criticism and congressional foot dragging. Dutifully, and more out of a sense of protocol than of need for approval, Lincoln took the list of decisions he had implemented to Capitol Hill for an after-the-fact seal of approval. Congress had not been in session during his first eleven weeks as president. He justified his actions on the grounds that the moves were made in response to "popular demand and public necessity."[50] The crisis model of the presidency Lincoln constructed required broad prerogative power for the president with the expectation that Congress would follow his leadership and approve his actions.

Congress, to Lincoln, was a more or less necessary nuisance and his cabinet a usually unnecessary one.[51] His courtesies toward Congress bore fruit as the House and Senate eventually approved the *faits accomplis* from his early days in office. His decisions to unilaterally free the slaves had no constitutional precedent, and his "with malice toward none" views on Reconstruction hardly endeared him to the

Radical Republicans in Congress. Even though these issues were of a "peacetime" nature and were not precipitated by crisis, Lincoln stood his ground, arguing that, as president, he had extraordinary legal resources that Congress lacked.[52] A century later Richard Nixon would contend that inherent powers permitted the president to send troops into Cambodia in an affront to congressional intentions because, as commander-in-chief, he had to protect the lives of American soldiers.

## PRESIDENTIAL LEADERSHIP: MODERN EXPECTATIONS

Presidents Jefferson and Jackson began the process of moving the presidency closer to the public, and public expectations that the president could deal with their problems grew. As property qualifications for voting began to disappear from state statutes, the president's political base broadened even further. The flood of immigration in the middle to late decades of the nineteenth century and the trek of people westward served as further catalysts to the development of a "people's" presidency. With public support, however, came increasingly high public expectations for White House leadership.

DOMESTIC ARCHITECT AND ECONOMIC MANAGER. With the dawn of the twentieth century, the role of government began to detour from the traditional narrow "law and order" road. Gradually, a more "positivist" state philosophy emerged geared toward federal involvement in the quest of solutions to long-festering economic and social maladies. The often thankless task of steering new programs through a less than enthusiastic Congress fell to the only individual who represented the public at large, that is, the president.

He was to chart the national course with new initiatives and to generate a sense of national purpose and mission in the minds of the public so that his initiatives would have a good chance of success. Theodore Roosevelt viewed the presidency as a "bully pulpit" for preaching change to the electorate. His cousin Franklin recognized the unassailable leadership posture that a president could assume if he knew how to utilize popular support. Leadership became a standard by which presidents would be judged as they sought reelection. The president who senses the popular mood and spots the tides before they start to flow, who is deft in acting as spokesperson for the nation, who realizes the position he has for initiating and controlling discussion of national problems, and who can effectively call upon Christian morality and tradition can be heard over any other voice in the nation. The most powerful leaders in the White House are those who possess a sixth sense for public opinion and the personal attributes to use it to their advantage.

From the 1890s onward, the public viewed presidential involvement in the affairs of business and labor as necessary to protect the "little man" from abuse by corporate giants. "Trustbuster" Theodore Roosevelt and his corpulent successor, William Howard Taft, brought monopoly practice in the American business community under careful public and government scrutiny. Government had already intervened in labor disputes through Grover Cleveland's decision to dispatch troops to Chicago at the time of the Pullman strike in 1894. The White House soon gained further credibility in resolving labor disputes, and both the Sherman and Clayton acts involved the executive branch in dealing with the rights and dignity of labor and with the excesses of big business. Woodrow Wilson, in fact, is said to have personally drafted the clause in the Clayton Act that declares that "the labor of human beings is not a commodity or article of commerce."[53] Developments in later decades involved the president in protecting labor's rights to organize and bargain collectively under the Wagner Act (National Labor Relations Act of 1935) and the Taft-Hartley Act which called for "cooling-off periods" in labor disputes.

The broad range of federal services to individuals would be impossible without the income derived from the income tax. The federal income tax became the economic birthright of the federal government, and what had initially amounted to a "soak the rich scheme" (1 percent of net incomes of up to $20,000 and a surtax on larger incomes) provided the eventual mothers' milk for the ever-expanding list of social programs begun during the New Deal years. Each new bureaucracy owed its existence and allegiance to the president who fashioned it. Each assisted him in formulating solutions to social problems for which he would take the credit. In Chapter 8 we shall explore the extent to which presidential control of swollen bureaucracies might well become more an illusion than a reality.

BUDGET DIRECTION. "Politics," according to Harold Laswell, noted British political scientist, boils down to "who gets what, when and how." With a federal budget of one-half trillion dollars plus, control of the budget process permits the president to set the priorities for allocation of resources and receive the gratitude of those who receive the benefits of his decisions. Even though Congress initiated its own budget process in 1975, the president still sets initial priorities for the distribution of inflation-shrunken dollars. He strongly suggests through his budget messages and State of the Union address whether national defense should take spending priority over domestic social programs in any given year.

Still, some budget categories are virtually *uncontrollable* by the president or by Congress. The federal government must pay the interest on the national debt and pay back banks that lent money used to build public housing. It also must pay on construction contracts signed in previous years for weapons systems, highways, and so forth. Unless Congress changes previous laws that created entitlement programs (Social Security, retirement pensions from the government, and so on), these programs guarantee large sums to major segments of the population. Inflation in certain sectors of the economy also forces up the percentage of the budget that entitlements can consume. In recent years, the burgeoning costs of health care has diverted increasing amounts of federal funds into the Medicare and Medicaid coffers. In 1967, the Office of Management and the Budget classified 59 percent of all federal outlays as beyond the reach of the appropriations process. By 1975, that figure had reached almost 75 percent.[54] It would be politically difficult for a president to propose cuts in these entitlement programs, although he might be in a position to stunt their growth a bit. He might suggest, as Jimmy Carter did in 1979, elimination of certain benefits. Carter asked Congress to cut out burial money for families of Social Security recipients. We shall examine the budget process in much greater depth in Chapter 8, on the president and the economy.

INFORMATION MANAGEMENT AND ADMINISTRATIVE LEADERSHIP. In a complex modern society as in twentieth-century America, information is power. The White House machinery for gathering and disseminating data puts the president at a distinct advantage vis-à-vis Congress. Franklin Roosevelt is often cited as the father of the modern presidential staffing system. FDR's predecessors had managed the White House with skeletal staffs. Lincoln is reported to have answered most of his own mail; Cleveland personally manned the White House phones; Calvin Coolidge read all incoming mail and dictated replies; and Woodrow Wilson typed a number of his own speeches. Since FDR, the presidential bureaucracy has proliferated until it has reached some 600 individuals on the White House staff and over 5,000 serving the executive office of the president. Staff personnel have not only freed the president of many of his daily chores, but they have served him as filters of information being sent through the cabinet bureaucracies and provided him independent sources of information and analysis. Chapter 3 analyzes the ways in which different presidents have used and organized their staffs.

As presidential sources of information were ballooning, Congress was scarcely showing any interest in keeping up. Its data resources were meager indeed.[55] In the aftermath of Vietnam, Congress began to beef up the Congressional Research Service, created the Office of Technological Assessments, expanded the use of the General Accounting Office's analytical services, and created a Congressional Budget Office. Each of these helped to improve the information acquisition, storage, and retrieval capacities of the House and Senate. Still, in the areas of foreign policy and national security, Congress must depend on the White House or executive branch agencies for their information.

CONTROLLING BUREAUCRATS. Voters expect presidents to tame run-amok bureaucrats. The cabinet departments, though created by laws of Congress, owe their allegiance to the president who appoints their secretaries. In some cases, as in the case of the Department of the Treasury, however, the legislation creating it put it in the position of being forced to serve two masters. The Treasury secretary's duties were minutely spelled out to include supervision of the collection of revenues, prescribing accounting forms, issuing warrants for the expenditure of public funds, selling of public lands, and so forth. The question went from the theoretical to the practical in 1833 in the controversy between President Andrew Jackson and Congress over the Second Bank of the United States.

Jackson, an implacable foe of the bank because of its bias toward the financially well-to-do and its tight money policy toward Westerners like himself who sought loans, prepared to close the doors on the bank by removing federal funds. When Congress passed legislation in 1832 to renew the bank charter, Jackson vetoed the bill. The bank continued in existence because its prior charter had not yet expired. To break the bank's hold on credit and its favoritism toward Establishment friends, Jackson needed the cooperation of Treasury Secretary William Duane. Shortly after Duane took office in 1833, he informed the president that he felt that Congress should be called in on any decisions to remove funds from the National Bank.[56] Duane agreed to investigate the propriety of transferring the funds to state banks, but, when he reached the conclusion that he could not do so and proved unwilling to resign, Jackson relieved him of his duties by appointing Attorney General Roger Taney. Soon thereafter the funds were transferred.

The matter was far from settled, however, since Henry Clay submitted a resolution of censure of the president for assuming authorities not given under the Constitution. Jackson, in his defense, sent the following message to the Senate:[57]

> Thus was it settled by the Constitution, the laws and the whole practice of the Government that the entire executive power is vested in the President of

the United States; that as incident to that power the right of appointing and removing those officers who are to aid him in the execution of the laws, with such restrictions as only the Constitution prescribes, is vested in the President; that the Secretary of the Treasury is one of those officers; that the custody of the public property and money is an Executive function which, in relation to the money, has always been exercised through the Secretary of the Treasury and his subordinates; that in the performance of these duties he is subject to the supervision and control of the President, and in all important measures having relation to them consults the Chief Magistrate and obtains his approval and sanctions; that the law establishing the bank did not, as it could not change the relation between the President and the Secretary—did not release the former from his obligation to see the law faithfully executed nor the latter from the President's supervision and control.

Even though the Senate refused to consider the president's comments, the Senate finally retracted its previous censure of the president. The arguments he made stand as a testimonial that history has recognized a broad latitude for the White House in administration of the departments.[58]

The dilemma faced by Treasury Secretary William Duane is somewhat analogous to the problem encountered by Attorney General Elliot Richardson when Richard Nixon ordered him to fire special Watergate prosecutor Archibald Cox even after the secretary had promised the Senate that Cox would have a free hand. Richardson resigned rather than violate his word, leaving the President to find others who would follow his directions. Normally, a president can command loyalty from department heads, and, if he does not receive it, he can fire them.

NATIONAL SECURITY: PRESIDENTIAL LEADERSHIP AND POWER. While the President finds riding herd on bureaucracies and Congress a problem in domestic affairs, foreign affairs has traditionally been an executive preserve. As the Cold War of the 1950s, 1960s, and 1970s with the Soviets extended American interests and commitments against both real and imagined Soviet aggression, "pact-itis" became a chronic American diplomatic disease. Presidents spearheaded the competition for allies in a world confused by the death of European colonial empires and the emergence of developing nations in Asia, Africa, and Latin America. The president's constitutional role as chief diplomat (send and receive ambassadors) and his commander-in-chief responsibilities permitted him to commit American prestige, honor, and power through an ever-expanding number of defense treaties and base agreements.

More often than not, Congress was asked to cooperate with the president on the basis of information that he or some other executive agent provided. Legislators, on the other hand, were incapable of questioning and verifying. Not only did tradition encourage them to rally around the president in foreign affairs, but their lack of independent sources of information rendered them powerless to criticize or suggest alternatives when situations demanded.

Although the issue of an "information gap" will be examined in greater detail in Chapter 5, at this juncture a look at the sale of Airborne Warning and Control System aircraft (AWACS) to Iran can demonstrate the advantage that information sources give the president and executive agencies as they interact with Congress.[59]

During the year prior to the decision, several senators, prominent among them being John Culver (D., Iowa) and Thomas Eagleton (D., Missouri), were expressing misgivings about the vast quantities of sophisticated U.S. weaponry being ticketed for Iran. After a November 1976 fact-finding tour of the Middle East, the two senators called for independent U.S. judgments on future requests. In May 1977, Culver and Eagleton approached the congressional investigative and analysis arm of the General Accounting Office (GAO) seeking an independent interpretation of the AWACS deal. Fearing that Russian intelligence agents might be in a position to get information on the system from defectors, they sought some assurance that U.S. intelligence assessments on the dangers to the security of the technological gear had been made and were supportive of the sale.

The GAO report concluded that the Carter administration had not given Congress adequate justification for the sale.[60] The Pentagon immediately took exception to the report citing twenty-three errors. Director of Pentagon Arms Sales Eric von Marbod termed the report "a very inaccurate and misleading document." Defense Department criticisms infuriated GAO Comptroller General Elmer Statts who complained to the responsible congressional committees that the Pentagon had provided GAO with one set of data and then changed it without even informing GAO.[61] In this case, and in numerous others, Congress received what the executive wanted to give, period.

Even as domestically successful a president as Lyndon Johnson saw his achievements in social welfare and civil rights eclipsed by the shadow of Vietnam. With few exceptions, recent presidents have rarely left marks on the history books because of their domestic decisions. Modern-day presidents, especially those since the advent of the Cold War, are remembered for their pursuits on the international scene. Harry Truman is remembered more for his A-bomb decisions, the Truman Doctrine, and the Marshall Plan than for his efforts in civil rights and his Fair Deal. Reminiscences of Eisenhower conjure up images of the Cold War and its crises: Quemoy and Matsu, Lebanon, Berlin, and the U-2 spy plane flights over the Soviet Union. It is all but overlooked that the general-turned-president attempted to balance the federal budget before it became popular to do so. Memories of John Kennedy conjure up images of his tragic assassination, but aside from that the Cuban missile crisis comes to mind more quickly than his lackluster efforts to reach a New Frontier of social policy and civil rights. Johnson and Nixon tend to be known as the Vietnam presidents, and the Great Society legislation that LBJ so effectively shepherded through Congress fades by comparison with the troubles in Southeast Asia. Had it not been for Watergate, Nixon would have been remembered for his trips to China and the Soviet Union and not for any outstanding domestic record. Even Jimmy Carter, whose only previous high governmental experience had been in social policy and fiscal management as governor of Georgia, carved out a sizable niche for himself in foreign policy via his conclusion of the Panama Canal treaty and Egyptian-Israeli accords, which had involved such migraines for his three predecessors. Clearly controversial and noteworthy were Carter's efforts in negotiating the SALT arms agreements with the Soviets and recognition of the People's Republic of China.

Ironically, voter-related rewards for foreign policy efforts are fleeting at best, yet expectations are still high. It is often domestic economic considerations that spell life or death for the political aspirations of any incumbent, however.

The direction that the presidency of the 1980s may take has been predetermined to a degree by the ebbs and flows of executive-legislative relations in recent decades.

Hamilton's "heroic" presidential leadership model has superseded the "party government" model of Jefferson and the checks-and-balances approach espoused by Madison.[62] Almost two centuries later, the president has assumed virtually unquestioned leadership in the areas of domestic social policy, economic management, budgeting and administration, diplomacy, and national security. With greatly enhanced information sources at his disposal and increasing centralization of policy making in the Oval Office, it should have been no surprise that the excesses of the Nixon administration and the "imperial" thinking they represented would eventually arise.

More recent complaints about "drift" in domestic policy, foreign affairs, and economic management in the Carter White House might indicate that, in the aftermath of Watergate, the pendulum of power had swung too far from the president in the direction of Congress and the special interest groups it increasingly represents. Some critics suggest that it was merely Carter's personal deficiencies in leadership style that were the cause of his problems. Still, viewing the presidential role and the breadth of its powers, the question should not be whether certain leadership types can abuse the office but, rather, whether any person would be permitted by the system to enhance the position and prerogatives at the expense of the public trust. In the final chapter we shall discuss how presidents can be held accountable for violating their sacred oaths.

## NOTES

[1] Articles of Confederation, Articles II and III as reproduced in Clinton Rossiter, *1787: The Grand Convention* (New York: Macmillan, 1966), pp. 351-360. All subsequent references to the Articles will refer to this citation.

[2] Carl Van Doren, *The Great Rehearsal* (New York: Viking Press, 1948), p. 171.

[3] C. Herman Pritchett, "The President's Constitutional Position," in *The Presidency Reappraised (2nd ed.)*, eds. Rexford Tugwell and Thomas Cronin (New York: Praeger, 1977), p. 3.

[4] Alexander Hamilton, *Federalist Paper 70*, as cited in Charles Thach, *The Creation of the Presidency* (Baltimore, Md.: Johns Hopkins U.P., 1923; 1969 paper) p. v.

[5] James Madison, *Federalist Paper 48*, in *The Federalist*, ed. Edward Meade Earle (New York: Modern Library, 1937), pp. 321-326.

[6] Thach, *op. cit.*, p. 21.

[7] Pritchett, *op. cit.*, p. 4.

[8] This is discussed in Louis Fisher, *The Constitution Between Friends* (New York: St. Martin's Press, 1978), p. 8.

[9] Thach, *op. cit.*, p. 27.

[10] Randolph's letter to George Washington, November 24, 1776 as cited in Thach, *op. cit.*, pp. 28-29.

[11] Louis Fisher, *The President and Congress* (New York: Free Press, 1972), p. 20.

[12] Thach, *op. cit.*, pp. 35-43.

[13] Louis Koenig, *The Chief Executive*, 3rd ed. (New York: Harcourt Brace, 1975), p. 19.

[14] Max Farrand, *The Framing of the Constitution of the United States* (New Haven, Conn.: Yale U.P., 1976), p. 129.

[15] Edward Stanwood, *A History of the Presidency*, vol. 1 (Boston: Houghton Mifflin, 1912), p. 9.

[16] Thach, *op. cit.*, p. 22.

[17] *Ibid.*, p. 80.

[18] Farrand, *op. cit.,* p. 162.

[19] Farrand, *op. cit.,* p. 89. Gerry felt that many delegates, not including himself, would have viewed a constitutional monarchy as ideal. For more on this, see Charles Warren, *The Making of the Constitution* (New York: Barnes & Noble, 1967), pp. 17-20.

[20] The Committee of the Whole report called for a single executive to have a seven-year term, no reeligibility, and be chosen by the legislature. Votes on these issues were 8-3 in the first form and 7-3 in the second.

[21] These two committees did much to shape the presidency due to their roles of providing proper form and wording for the positions taken by the committees or the whole convention.

[22] Pritchett, *op. cit.,* p. 5.

[23] Rossiter, *op. cit.,* p. 222.

[24] Article II.

[25] Warren, *op. cit.,* p. 325.

[26] See Pritchett, *op. cit.,* p. 5.

[27] Johnson's support of the six-year term is in Lyndon B. Johnson, *Vantage Point,* (New York: Holt, Rinehart & Winston, 1971), p. 344.

[28] Stanwood, *op. cit.,* p. 3.

[29] *Ibid.,* p. 4.

[30] Pritchett, *op. cit.,* p. 6.

[31] Thach, *op. cit.,* p. 128.

[32] Gerry proposed an absolute veto; see Warren, *op. cit.,* p. 185.

[33] Pritchett, *op. cit.,* p. 6; more on war powers appears in Chapter 7.

[34] Farrand, *op. cit.,* p. 79.

[35] Warren, *op. cit.,* p. 660.

[36] James Flexner, *Washington: The Indispensable Man* (Boston: Little, Brown, 1974), p. 220.

[37] *Ibid.,* p. 221.

[38] Koenig, *op. cit.,* p. 30.

[39] On presidential vetoes, see Jong R. Lee, "Presidential Vetoes from Washington to Nixon," *Journal of Politics* (May 1975), pp. 522-524.

[40] Marcus Cunliffe, © 1968 American Heritage Publishing Co., Inc. Reprinted by permission from *American Presidents and the Presidency.*

[41] Stanwood, *op. cit.,* p. 43.

[42] Raoul Berger, *Executive Privilege: A Constitutional Myth* (Cambridge, Mass.: Harvard U.P., 1974).

[43] The four were Hamilton, Jefferson, Knox, and Randolph.

[44] Flexner, *op. cit.,* pp. 260-262.

[45] *Ibid.,* pp. 349-350.

[46] Edward S. Corwin, *The President: Office and Powers* (New York: New York U.P., 1957), p. 19.

[47] Jefferson model in James McGregor Burns, *Presidential Government* (Boston: Houghton Mifflin, 1965), pp. 27-29.

[48] Corwin, *op. cit.,* p. 19.

[49] *Ibid.,* p. 21.

[50] J. G. Randall, *Constitutional Problems under Lincoln* (Glouster, Mass.: Peter Smith Press, 1963), p. 58.

[51] Corwin, *op. cit.,* p. 23.

[52] Randall, *op. cit.,* p. 514.

[53] Koenig, *op. cit.,* p. 172.

[54] Joel Havermann, "Budget Report/Ford, Congress Seek Handle on Uncontrollable Spending," *National Journal,* November 29, 1975, p. 1620.

[55] Thomas Cronin, *The State of the Presidency* (Boston: Little, Brown, 1975), p. 153.

[56] Rowland Egger, *The President of the United States,* 2nd ed. (New York: McGraw-Hill, 1972), p. 32.

[57] *Ibid.,* p. 35.

[58] *Ibid.,* p. 36.

[59] *Current American Government,* "Case Study: Carter and Congress on AWACS," *Congressional Quarterly* (Spring 1978), p. 43.

[60] *Ibid.,* p. 43.

[61] *Ibid.,* p. 44.

[62] Burns, *op. cit.,* pp. 28-31.

# PART 2

# PRESIDENTIAL ADVISORY SYSTEM

# Buddies, Brains, Bootlickers, and Some Yahoos: The Personal Staff

All the rhetoric about leadership and promises to work miracles with the economy that are made along the campaign trail might tempt a new president to imagine himself as a modern-day St. George capable of single handedly slaying the nation's dragons. The job seems much more manageable from the outside than from the inside. Jimmy Carter, for example, came into the White House swearing that he would make the decisions and would never have a chief of staff like Nixon did. He feared that Watergate-like abuses would creep in with such tight staffing practices. Three years later, though, he promoted Hamilton Jordan from assistant to the president to chief of staff. That summer, Carter also reshuffled his cabinet. At the same time, more power was diverted to the highly centralized staff. Why did he make this radical departure from his campaign promises? Were his sentiments out on the hustings mere salesmanship or outright flimflam? Carter's experiences in the Oval Office changed his thinking. The "outsider" from Plains, Georgia had learned that a president couldn't keep up with energy policy, SALT II, and the Panama Canal treaties and still handle staff disputes over who could use the White House tennis courts. He came to realize that there weren't enough hours in the day to listen to departmental gripes, see everyone who wanted to converse with him, and read every report ground out by prolific bureaucrats. Each president, sooner or later, realizes that he must meld the demands of the presidency with his own personal philosophies about staffing and accessibility.

## EVOLUTION OF WHITE HOUSE ADVISORS

Presidential staffers have not always been key figures in the advisory system. The cabinet evolved first as the vehicle for assisting a president in decision making. The Founding Fathers resisted the urge to impose some body of advisors on the president. George Washington began the custom of seeking collective advice from his attorney general and secretaries of state, war, and treasury.[1] Early cabinet meetings were hardly models of decorum and subservience to Washington's whims. A hotheaded Secretary Hamilton (Treasury) and an equally strong-willed Secretary

Jefferson (State) clashed constantly. Those fiery weekly meetings have evolved into today's rather lackluster and infrequent get-togethers of more numerous (thirteen)[2] and less prestigious cabinet secretaries. Theoretically, the cabinet was to have been a forum for high-level debate on national issues to aid the president in making policy. Department secretaries[3] were to dissect present policy and suggest innovative alternatives. Theory was one thing, but the pressures of the job dictated changes in practice.

In the late 1930s, the White House staff was added to the information network to aid the president with increasingly complicated domestic economic problems. Franklin Roosevelt enlarged the existing token staff, and it has been growing, almost unabated, ever since. Since the Kennedy years, it has eclipsed the cabinet in prestige and public recognition.[4] Although many of the trappings still remain, only the secretaries of state and defense retain the aura of power that once accompanied cabinet positions. Eventually, according to a Lyndon Johnson aide, "The cabinet became a joke; it was never used for anything near what could be called Presidential listening and consultation."[5]

Increasing staff specialization for the president (domestic, foreign policy, economic, press relations, and so on) has made simple flow charts with tidy boxes for department and agency heads under the president and a tiny White House staff of generalists a relic of a bygone era.[6] In this chapter we shall examine (1) who tends to be chosen to the president's inner circle, (2) what their personal goals are, (3) how recent presidents have tended to use them, (4) who are the close friends and selected outsiders, and (5) how these people can affect presidential leadership and the president's ability to respond to crises and public discontent.

## STAFF PERSONNEL: GENERALISTS

The select few who occupy the West Wing of the White House near the president's office are bestowed grand titles such as counselor to the president, chief of staff, and special assistant to the president. Their power stems from their proximity to the Oval Office. Being near the president as he is making momentous decisions is the epitome of "clout." A vignette from the Carter White House illustrates this point. A young aide of an out-of-town politician was in Washington for the gala ceremony accompanying the signing of the twin Panama Canal treaties in 1978. At one point, the aide found himself shoulder to shoulder with Chief of Staff Hamilton Jordan. When President Carter completed his comments, Jordan was assailed by a steady stream of persons eager to talk with him, touch him, or in some way be able to brag that they had been in contact with him. An official of the AFL-CIO slipped him a calling card and whispered, "Have him [the President] sign it, will you?"[7]

Originally, the White House staff was a mere skeleton crew of anonymous personal assistants. Reportedly, George Washington dug into his own pocket to hire his nephew and another aide and that was the extent of his staff.[8] By the time Gerald Ford took leave of the White House, the staff numbered 510 and had exceeded 600 under Lyndon Johnson. The numbers don't tell the whole story, either. Presidents since Franklin Roosevelt have habitually borrowed staffers from other federal agencies and departments. These individuals were not counted against the White House budget.[9]

Former Eisenhower aide Emmet John Hughes suggests that today's staffers are really liaisons (ambassadors) for the president with Congress, the executive departments, and the mass media. They are expected to provide a broad range of personal services for the president including gathering data, verifying rumors, drafting speeches, screening visitors, answering mail, preparing messages, scheduling trips, prodding departments, coaxing Congress, courting journalists, recommending appointments, summarizing news, smothering scandals, baffling opponents, and cheering followers while keeping the president and the world beyond the White House on speaking terms.

The modern White House staff was born with Franklin Roosevelt's Executive Order 8248 issued in 1939. On the advice of management specialists whom Roosevelt had appointed to study administrative practices (the Brownlow commission),[10] the president was given a small retinue of executive assistants who were to help him in dealing with the agencies and departments. They included a secretary to the president, two additional secretaries, and six administrative assistants. Roosevelt used them to help him maintain some control over the sprawling New Deal programs[11] and the bureaucracies that were growing up around them.

Only Plato could have expected more from potential applicants for the White House staff than the Brownlow commission did. Future staffers were to be of such high character and stamina that they would "shun personal power, be highly competent, possess great physical vigor and have a passion for anonymity."[12] Hamilton Jordan's antics in Washington and New York discos, Dr. Peter Bourne's (special assistant on Drug Abuse Control) bogus drug prescriptions and alleged cocaine sniffing, and the myriad "Watergate" abuses of the Nixon staff illustrate something less than staff disinterest in personal power and passion for anonymity. In fact, a number of analysts contend that all recent White House staffers have shared uncommon ambition, a thirst for power, a willingness to sacrifice family and personal health, and an ability to suffer personal humiliation to satisfy their own blind ambitions.[13] They want to get ahead, so they are encouraged to keep their bosses happy by telling them what they want to hear rather than telling it "like it is." It is the jester, after all, who survives at court. The emperor doesn't want to be told that he has no clothes, and nay sayers are banished from the kingdom. Banishment may be a gradual process. Midge Costanza, public liaison assistant for President Carter, made the mistake of telling him and the press that it was time for controversial OMB director to resign for the good of the administration because of his questionable banking practices as officer in several Georgia banks. For that and other unappreciated outbursts, she found herself moved to the basement in a cubbyhole of an office. She eventually resigned.

Staffers are expected to keep the president on top of problems even before they arise. They are not supposed to be policy makers in their own right.[14] In recent administrations, however, people such as Joseph Califano, special assistant to Lyndon Johnson, and Stuart Eisenstadt in the Carter White House were the major architects of most of those administrations' domestic initiatives. Although personal staffers are expected to perform any services the president might ask, they have three broad roles: (1) to capsulize data, (2) to provide options for their boss, and (3) to do his bidding outside the White House.

Closest White House aides must also be capable of understanding not only what a president says but what he doesn't say. Califano recounts a situation in which he found himself as he was forced to interpret Johnson's wishes when the president gave him orders in the midst of a temper fit. Prior to LBJ's decision to abandon the race for president in 1968, he was often angered by press reports that various cabinet and subcabinet officers were announcing their support for Robert Kennedy and Hubert Humphrey. An article about the Agriculture Department aides' choosing up sides raised Johnson to the boiling point one night. He not only called in and dressed down the hapless assistant secretary named in the article but he demanded his resignation by the next morning. When Johnson left the office, Califano called the aide and told him to forget about sending in the resignation. The assistant secretary protested, saying that he had direct presidential orders. Califano convinced him to let the dust settle. In retrospect, he said, Johnson didn't want that resignation:[15]

> After three years serving on his White House staff, he would have expected me to have some sense of how to measure his true meaning when he spoke in anger. I am sure he would have felt ill-served by me had I accepted the resignation on his behalf.

## STAFFER TALENT POOL

Theodore Sorensen, close friend and special counsel to Presidents Kennedy and Johnson, suggests that the role of the White House staffer can be a valuable yardstick of a president's effectiveness. "A good White House staff can give a President that crucial margin of time analysis and judgment that makes an unmanageable problem more manageable."[16] Nevertheless, presidents tend to choose generalists for top staff duties. Since White House aides are often facilitators, mediators, and personal service personnel for the president,[17] they must speak his language and he must be at home with them. For this reason, it is common to see top staffers being selected from the President's preelection aides and cronies. Frederic Malek, former deputy OMB director and personnel talent scout for the Nixon administration, calls the traditional means of recruiting in American politics the BUGAT (Bunch uh guys around the table) system. Intimates sit around combing through "old buddy" lists to find names to fill slots. "You don't get the best people," Malek laments, "You get people you know."[18]

Usually, faithful servants from along the campaign trail find prominent places in the White House even though they lack preparation for their new responsibilities. Key Nixon staffers like Ron Ziegler, Bob Haldeman, and John Erlichman were campaign workers as were Hamilton Jordan and Jody Powell during the Carter administration. Ziegler's job experience as a tour guide at Disneyland and Jody Powell's duties as chauffeur to candidate-for-governor Jimmy Carter were hardly the advanced preparation one would expect for the responsibilities they took on.

Franklin Roosevelt tapped a broad range of sources as he sought out aides. Among his advisors were old friends from his early days in Washington during the Wilson years, people who had served him while he was governor of New York, stalwarts from the 1932 campaign, and persons recommended on the Harvard "ole boy" network.[19] Kennedy drew names from among his Harvard classmates, promoted his "Irish Mafia" (campaign aides, O'Brien, O'Donnell, Powers, and so on), and chose others recommended highly by his former Harvard professors. Six of Lyndon Johnson's aides were from Texas, and virtually all the Nixon higher-ups hailed from New York or California. Gerald Ford depleted the leadership pool in Grand Rapids, and the Carter White House was largely populated with long-time campaign aides and various "good ole boys" from Georgia. In each of these cases, the president chose people with whom he felt comfortable. Rarely was a staffer chosen as a political favor to someone else as was often the case with cabinet selections.[20]

## LOYALISTS AND BOOTLICKERS

In recent years, most of the White House office staffers have been young men "on the make," in marked contrast to the cabinet political appointees and career bureaucrats with whom they must often deal. Since these climbers invariably have plans for the future in well-paying private jobs, they are acutely aware of the need to be team players.[21] Today, few of the close White House aides are selected on the basis of their previous government service. In many cases, they are on leaves of absence from positions in the business world. Since a job in the White House can be a stepping stone, aides are not eager to make waves.[22]

Serving the president well should mean being willing to be honest with him when he needs advice. These aides are friends and close comrades from past political wars; if they can't give a president bad news and criticism, who can? Even intimate friends find that the mystique of the presidency creates artificial barriers. Dwight Eisenhower felt this when his long-time military compatriot General Omar Bradley insisted on calling him Mr. President rather than Ike. Likewise, Theodore Sorensen saw his relationship with "Jack" Kennedy change when he entered the White House too:[23]

> He was the same human being with the same faults and virtues with whom I had worked, joked, argued and traveled almost night and day for eight years. Yet my attitude was instantly characterized by a greater degree of not only deference but awe. Addressing him at all times, at play as well as at work, as Mr. President . . . was but a symbol of change.

As we noted in an earlier chapter, the regal life-style provided for a president adds even more to the deferential treatment accorded him by his staff.

In some administrations, bootlicking became almost a part of the job description even for the closest of White House advisors. Wilson's unofficial aide Colonel Edward House fed the president's vanity even though he simultaneously filled his diary with criticism of the administration. He once told Wilson in a letter, "I do not put it too strongly when I say, you are the one hope left in this torn and distracted world."[24] Such fawning over the boss was not limited to the Wilson years. Lyndon Johnson demanded unflagging devotion from his staffers. Circumstances surrounding his rise to the White House left his early administration haunted with the ghost and personnel of the New Frontier. Eric Goldman remembered that the Johnson White House was like Noah's Ark: "there were two of everybody."[25] The new president was sensitive to the fact that few of the Kennedy staffers promised to be able to make the transition easily, and within six months the faint-hearted and disenchanted had jumped ship. Vacancies were almost invariably filled by young Texans like Bill Moyers, George Christian, and so on.[26]

Presidents could be crude and insulting to their close advisors when the spirit moved them. David Halberstam recounts an incident that illustrates this tendency in Lyndon Johnson. As the president was examining the credentials of an applicant for a White House job in 1965, he asked a staffer, "How loyal is this man?" When the staffer replied, "he seems loyal, Mr. President," Johnson fired back, "I don't want loyalty, I want *loyalty.* I want a man to kiss my ass in Macy's window at high noon and tell me it smells like roses."[27] Another Johnson aide, Jack Valenti, was notorious for pumping the president's ego to the point of making a laughing stock of himself. "If Johnson would drop the H-bomb," so the story went around Washington, "Valenti would call it an urban renewal project." These situations seem laughable; but beneath the salty language and sycophancy is an undercurrent of presidential weakness, which the advisory system fails to correct. Too often, as Watergate demonstrates, young staffers leave their ethical antennas at home when they move to Washington. It is so easy for them to believe that the orders they receive must be acceptable because they come in the president's name. When a president has a poorly defined sense of what is just and ethical, he can't expect his aides to correct that flaw. Jeb Magruder recounts a battle of conscience he had when he was ordered to help use the powers of the Oval Office to discredit Nixon opponents. He convincéd himself that he had to do what he was told to keep his job. "Although I was aware that they were illegal, and I am sure others knew—we had become somewhat inured to using some activities that would help us in accomplishing what we thought was a legitimate cause."[28]

Why do presidents demand deep loyalty? Answers may vary from personality to personality with each president; but each needs people to whom he can divulge confidences. Criticism accompanies almost everything a president does in the unsheltered world outside the Oval Office. Not surprisingly, then, a president develops a sensitivity to criticism and seeks out people who can think as he does and will not compete with him for the powers of the office.

Some presidents demand loyalty because they equate it with a staffer's personal integrity. Truman defended his aide Harry Vaughn from accusations of wrongdoing in office because Truman knew that he was a decent man who stuck by the president. Eisenhower couldn't fathom the possibility that Sherman Adams would take a vicuna coat as a gift from Bernard Goldfine because it would embarrass the president, and Adams was too loyal to hurt Ike. When Johnson and his aide and friend Bill Moyers came to a parting of the ways over Vietnam, Johnson could not imagine that an honest disagreement was possible from a loyal staffer. The president concluded that Moyers must have been trying to make a name for himself. Throughout his service in the White House, Moyers had received better press than his boss. Johnson felt Moyers was enhancing his name at the president's expense and he reasoned that "that boy lacks integrity."[29]

## STAFFING PHILOSOPHIES
## AND INFORMATION FLOWS

Since staffers are so close to the president, the way in which he uses them can affect the nature and flow of information and advice that gets to the Oval Office.[30] Essentially there are two ways that recent presidents have structured their staffs:

the pyramid style or the hub-of-the-wheel style.[31] In the first, the president is perched on a tightly organized system with a chief of staff immediately below who controls the flow of people and information. Presidents Franklin Roosevelt, Truman, Kennedy, Johnson, and to a degree Ford and Carter were hub-of-the-wheel types, although both Ford and Carter moved toward more structured operations after a while in the White House. Presidents Eisenhower and Nixon and Reagan erected pyramids, since they were most comfortable with order and disliked one-on-one contact with others. By contrast, the hub system permits large numbers of staffers, cabinet secretaries, members of Congress and others to have relatively easy access to the president. There is also no chief of staff to filter out "less important" information or restrict access.

## HUB-OF-THE-WHEEL PRESIDENTS

FRANKLIN ROOSEVELT'S STAFF: FOMENTING UNREST. As the Depression struck in 1929, it became clear that the existing bureaucracies had been incapable of handling the economic crisis. Roosevelt opted to create new agencies in 1932 that could be used to circumvent the Harding-Coolidge-Hoover Republicans entrenched in the federal bureaucracy. The White House staff was to be one of Roosevelt's most potent weapons in dealing with the departments and agencies. Until 1939, no large White House staff even existed, but FDR borrowed various assistant secretaries whom he had appointed to the departments. Although they were technically on the payroll of the departments of state, justice, war, and so on, people like Raymond Moley, Rexford Tugwell, Adolph Berle, and others made up a "braintrust" for the White House.

As assistant secretary of the navy, young Franklin Roosevelt developed a strong aversion to going through channels. Accordingly, he was to reject the idea of a tightly structured staff system for his administration.[32] Instead, he opted for a wide-open, free-wheeling, conflict-riddled system. Management and public administration specialists would have given him low grades for his scatter-shot approach. Still, there was never the slightest doubt as to who was in charge at the White House; below the president, however, the line of authority was left purposely unclear.

Encouraging and cultivating chaos in his staff seemed to delight Roosevelt. Often he would assign two of his aides to research the same problem without informing either that someone else had the same project. In a variation of this theme, the president once pitted Secretary of State Cordell Hull against staffer Raymond Moley at the International Monetary and Economic Conference held in London in 1933. Both were outspoken about protective tariffs, which proved to be a major bone of contention at the conference. Hull considered protective tariffs a horrible mistake, whereas Moley was convinced that they would be crucial to industrial recovery at home under the New Deal. When the conference stalled, Roosevelt sent Moley as his liaison even though Hull was there chairing the U.S. delegation. Was Moley's authority to supersede Hull's? Who knew? Which view was closer to Roosevelt's? No one could say until FDR finally sided with Hull. Moley was so incensed by the whole affair that he resigned as assistant secretary of state and left the inner circle as well. The Hull-Moley conflict demonstrates Roosevelt's capacity to build up a man one minute and destroy him the next. The psychological roller coaster could be devastating to staff morale.[33] Nevertheless, he was determined to make it clear to the great minds around him that he expected them to do their homework well, to do his bidding faithfully, and to "avoid going into business for themselves." He was to get the headlines, not they. By contrast, Ronald Reagan placed a sign on his desk in the Oval Office that reminded him "A man can do great things if he doesn't care who gets the credit."

Roosevelt had no intention of letting himself be sealed into a cocoon spun by his aides. Lines of communications were kept open to a broad range of people outside the White House to avoid isolation.[34] One hundred or so persons could get to him directly by telephone without being diverted by a secretary. He employed no chief of staff and permitted few of his staffers to become subject matter specialists. Except for Harry Hopkins, to whom he turned almost exclusively for foreign policy assignments, staffers were assigned problems in a variety of areas. He wanted to be sure that no staffer would become so steeped in an issue area that he would be forced to lean on that person for advice.[35] Everyone but FDR had to be expendable.

Professor Richard Neustadt recognized that no president in this century, with the possible exception of Lyndon Johnson, had "a keener sense of power, what it is and how to get it."[36] Roosevelt's "competitive" system and his insistence on being accessible assured him that he would remain on the top of things better than any flow chart that might have said so on paper.

HARRY TRUMAN: A STREAK OF ORTHODOXY. Historians and political scientists have debated for decades as to whether the presidency makes the man or the man makes the presidency. Harry Truman, unlike Roosevelt, had no burning desire for power. He would have been happy to have lived out his days as senior senator from Missouri. When FDR strongly suggested that Truman be his running mate in 1944, the salty senator responded, "Tell him to go to hell, I'm for Jimmie Byrnes." FDR eventually maneuvered him onto the ticket, but his ninety days as vice president left him ill-prepared to make the quantum leap from constitutional oblivion to the Oval Office.[37] It was at his first cabinet meeting, for example, that he learned from War Secretary Stimson about the Manhattan Project and the atomic bomb.[38]

Since he entered the White House virtually blind to the problems and policy options that lay before him, he was quick to ask the Roosevelt cabinet to stay on, and he met with them regularly. Gradually, he built his White House staff operations and assigned specific roles to each aide. There was no chief of staff, and Truman valued contacts with a broad range of people, so his was also a hub-of-the-wheel system. Still, several aides were influential. Assistant to the President John Steelman, a conservative, was entrusted with responsibility for handling labor disputes and coordination of federal agency programs. Problems of this sort were to be brought to the president through him. Another assistant, Clark Clifford, a liberal by reputation, served as a high-level jack-of-all-trades giving domestic policy advice, writing speeches, drafting legislation, wording executive orders, and handling the delicate task of White House liaison with State and Defense departments. Three lower-ranking aides were detailed to congressional liaison (Charles Murphy), overseer of personnel and patronage matters (Donald Dawson), and liaison with minorities (FDR holdover David Niles).

Key staffers like Clifford carried greater weight with Truman than did all but a few of the cabinet members. The president, for example, vetoed a weak price control bill and the Taft-Hartley Labor Act at Clifford's urging even though the entire cabinet opposed those vetoes.[39]

Remaining members of the Truman staff, derisively tagged "the Missouri gang," gave the White House a bad name. Many of them were old cronies whose ties to Truman often stretched back to his Jackson County, Missouri days. Others, like Harry Vaughn, were Truman's military friends and comrades. These hangers-on left the administration burdened with scandals over petty graft including accepting mink coats, deep freezers, free hotel rooms, and so on. Several were convicted of tax evasion and influence peddling. Vaughn, the center of quite a bit of the controversy, proved to be honest but hopelessly naïve. Former Atomic Energy Commission Chairman David Lillienthal wrote in his journal that the president in 1951 "had close around him since Clark Clifford left two years ago, as sorry a bunch of third-raters as I have seen in many a moon."[40]

During his administration two new units were added to the executive office of the president. One was to synthesize information in foreign affairs (National Security Council) and the other provided expertise in economic policy planning (Council of Economic Advisors). Truman also expanded the one-person congressional liaison office under FDR into a staff with the same responsibilities but more horses.

Theoretically, Truman was as much committed as Eisenhower proved to have been to straight lines and tidy boxes on organizational charts. In practice, however, his was not a pyramid system because he had more feel for personalities than for formal jurisdictions. His instinct was to improvise arrangements around a problem rather than to work it through rigid procedures. Still, during the Truman years, the White House staff grew from sixty to two hundred, and the presidential bureaucracy became a part of the study of the presidency.[41] The larger the White House staff became, the greater the tendency among observers to judge a president's leadership in terms of his ability to choose and use the staff mandated for his service.

JOHN KENNEDY: THE THUMB IN EVERY PIE OPERATION. Skepticism of entrenched bureaucrats seemed inbred in President Kennedy, even before he entered the Oval Office. Like Roosevelt,[42] he was convinced that a president, if he is not careful, can become a prisoner of his own information network. As his first order of business, Kennedy dismantled the apparatus from the elaborately organized Eisenhower White House. In its place he erected a much more loosely knit operation. He had no chief of staff, although Special Assistant Theodore Sorensen was especially close to him. He blamed much of Eisenhower's lack of progress on civil rights and other social issues on his rigid staffing system and sacred channels that were rarely bypassed. These restrictions on communication and access inhibited innovative ideas from getting to the upper echelons, in Kennedy's estimation. As a result, he was determined to know what was going on throughout the executive branch. Protocol, proper channels, and the sensitivities of bureaucrats were not permitted to stand in his way. To that end, he appointed trusted advisors to number two and three positions in cabinet-level departments so he could have personal listening posts for new ideas and could keep ahead of any foot dragging that might be planned to shanghai White House policies. He intended to be in charge in fact, not merely in name. At the State Department, for example, he appointed Secretary of State Dean Rusk only after he had tapped George Ball as an assistant secretary,

Joseph Sisco as undersecretary, and Adlai Stevenson as U.N. ambassador.[43] To keep the bureaucracies off balance, Kennedy was known to personally call departments on the phone seeking immediate information. His ultimate harassment was to visit department meetings unannounced and uninvited.

The idealistic and eager New Frontiersmen resorted to guerilla warfare in an attempt to deal with permanent government. Kennedy directed his staffers to prod, double-check, and even circumvent the bureaucracy when situations demanded.[44] Like Roosevelt, he was convinced that the White House could coordinate and direct the efforts of each of the federal departments and agencies it cared about. Since there were well over a thousand at the time, such thinking was as pretentious as it was unsophisticated and inaccurate.

To further enhance White House sway over the bureaucracies, Kennedy replaced the maze of interdepartmental committees common in the Eisenhower administration with special-issue presidential task forces. As new problems arose, task forces were gathered together at the president's request and membership included personnel from relevant departments and several White House staffers. By naming "presidential" task forces, Kennedy added immeasurably to their prestige. When members sought information in the bureaucracies, they were acting at the president's request.

Although Kennedy followed Truman's lead in assigning specific roles to staffers, he nevertheless built a close staff of generalists. He rotated persons into and out of roles rather frequently. At various times, and often simultaneously, Sorensen[45] wrote speeches for the president, formulated legislative packages, briefed him before press conferences, helped draft the budget, and participated in crisis policy making. Obviously he could not have been an expert in each of these areas, but Kennedy's philosophy was that brilliant generalists could do anything if they had the raw talent. Richard Goodwin was chosen to serve as a pinch-hitter staffer or a staffer without portfolio. At various times he wrote speeches, studied urban issues, and even went to meet with Cuban leaders in a Brazilian hotel to see if some accommodation with Castro might be possible in 1962. As special assistant for national security, the president tapped a former Harvard dean, McGeorge Bundy. While Bundy had had a distinguished record in those hallowed halls, it hardly provided him with the practical experience in international relations that his duties seemed to call for. Some of the staffers could have been considered specialists of sorts. Lawrence O'Brien seemed ideally suited to handle his congressional liaison duties due to prior campaign and administrative experience for Representative and later Senator Kennedy. Campaign operative Kenneth O'Donnell just switched offices to the White House where he handled appointments, arranged travel, and juggled relations with national, state, and local party machinery.

To Kennedy's credit, when he decided to dismantle Eisenhower's staff system, he did not discard everything on principle. Instead he selected the congressional liaison operation and the national security assistant for special attention. He beefed up the congressional affairs office with trusted aide Lawrence O'Brien and permitted him regular access. Bundy served as something of a latter-day John Foster Dulles (key Eisenhower advisor in foreign affairs). The national security assistant cleared incoming cables from the departments of state and defense and the CIA. Kennedy joked about Bundy's expansive role, "I will continue to have some residual functions."[46]

In the Truman and Roosevelt tradition, Kennedy remained accessible, especially to his staff, the press, and some members of the bureaucracy. Like his two immediate Democratic predecessors, the president was a voracious reader. No one summarized newspapers for him; he read a number of them daily. Department reports on foreign affairs received his undivided attention from cover to cover. To him, time was spent more profitably reading the views of cabinet-level department heads and agency directors than talking with them. A senior Kennedy staffer once recalled the president's preferences in this regard as they surfaced when a cabinet member sought an appointment with the president.[47]

> He kept calling and calling to get an appointment with the President. Finally, about the forty-third time after I had told him again and again that this wasn't the type of problem the President wanted to discuss with Cabinet members . . . I finally relented and scheduled an appointment.

Immediately after the secretary left, Kennedy stormed into the staffer's office and chewed him out for letting the secretary in.

In sum, Kennedy was determined to inject himself or his staff into every executive branch operation. Aides were to be an extension of him, gathering information, serving as trusted advisors, and tiptoeing around in the bureaucracies to keep them apprehensive. One of the major weaknesses of this system was that the volume of information potentially available to the president was more than any one mere human could hope to assimilate and use. It also left Kennedy bogged down in bureaucratic politics, leaving less time after hassling with details for strategic planning.

**LYNDON JOHNSON: THE BRANDED STAFF.** Johnson's massive ego rivaled his Texas-sized build. He tried to put his brand on everyone who served him. Dean Rusk became "my" secretary of state, Robert McNamara was "my" defense secretary, McGeorge Bundy was "my" national security assistant, and so on. Reminiscent of Kennedy and Roosevelt, he wanted to be involved in everything and often became obsessed with details.

Effective leadership to Johnson involved manipulating others, so he eagerly combed records and files for proof of other people's weaknesses and vulnerabilities. When he served on Capitol Hill, he was a two-legged encyclopedia on the fallibilities of his colleagues. During the Dominican Republic crisis in 1965, he devoted hours to scouring the backgrounds of the various leaders on the right and left in the strife-torn Caribbean nation.[48] Johnson manipulated his staff as he did everyone else. Life in the Texan court was not always pleasant as the president sought to keep his staff in line.[49]

> The President could berate his aides in lashing language. Sometimes he did it collectively . . . as when he exploded . . . "How can you be so goddamn stupid! Why can't I get men with the brains of the Kennedy bunch?"

As a true student of Franklin Roosevelt, his political mentor, Johnson drove staffers to the brink with punishing fits of anger only to follow them up with fatherly concern. Eric Goldman, Johnson's resident intellectual at the White House, put the psychological warfare this way:[50]

> He would heap praise on a particular aide for a period, much to the discomfort of the others, then, suddenly shift his attitude giving the man no assignments, rejecting his suggestions in toto, scarcely speaking to him. Just

as suddenly, the assistant would be lifted from hell and transformed into an angel once again.

From the beginning, the Johnson staff was a loosely knit operation, although Walter Jenkins, a Johnson aide since the late 1930s was given responsibilities a cut above those of his younger peers. George Reedy, whose ties to the president stretched back to the 1950s, also held a somewhat higher position than did his colleagues. Eventually, when Kennedy holdover Pierre Salinger stepped down as press secretary to run for the Senate from California (1964), Johnson turned those duties over to his friend Reedy.

Generalists abounded in the Johnson White House. Staffers might be asked to do anything, including washing windows. Press Secretary Reedy, for example, also served as speechwriter, domestic policy advisor, architect of the 1964 campaign, liaison with various bureaucracies, and roving ambassador on foreign affairs. Johnson never felt that he was overloading his staffers because he had worked so hard himself. His was a two-shift day (7 A.M. to 2 P.M. and then 4 P.M. to 9 P.M.). Although he allowed himself a two-hour break, his younger staffers were expected to be able to work through the full time. He selected young men for his staff in the belief that they would be able to keep up with his withering pace. His philosophy of staffing and advice was simple, "I get my action from younger men, and my advice from older men."[51] Most of the spaces in his circle of foreign policy advisors were reserved for the more seasoned hands (usually with some prior government service) like Bundy and secretaries Rusk and McNamara. Each of them carried more weight in the Johnson years than they had under the Kennedy scheme of things.

No demand on a staffer's time was too great in Johnson's estimation. They could be asked at any time to take on "just one more" job. Four days before Johnson announced his decision to withdraw as a presidential candidate in 1968, he propositioned Joseph Califano, his domestic special assistant, to take over the Peace Corps since Sargent Shriver was retiring. The shocked special assistant recalled:[52]

> Typically he asked me to take it on as an additional duty . . . and seeing the horror on the face of a White House aide who was already working 15 hour days, he said, "I will only ask you to do it if I run again."

Meetings with top advisors and verbal reports to the president were more in Johnson's style than reading the voluminous reports that consumed so many of John Kennedy's waking hours. Probably as an outgrowth of Johnson's brokering experiences as Senate majority leader, he habitually sought consensus among his advisors before announcing his own position. One of his favorite ploys was to paraphrase the book of Job from the Bible in its suggestion, "come let us reason together." Of course, reasonable men tried to read Johnson's mind and reason *his* way. Least-common-denominator decisions are likely to come out of consensus and compromise decision making.[53] Although these procedures may lessen friction among decision makers and contribute to *esprit de corps* in the group, a sameness of mind on issues can develop and this "group think,"[54] as Irving Janis has called it, can have a negative effect on decision making. Poor decisions can receive the seal of approval merely because they are acceptable. Although Johnson, in his memoirs *Vantage Point*,[55] says that he sought a broad range of advice on Vietnam, few who valued their lofty positions near the president's right hand dared to incur his wrath by openly breaking ranks with him. One who did question was Undersecretary of State George Ball. He played the unenviable role of in-house devil's advocate on Vietnam. Johnson wanted to make it clear that he heard all sides. But as George Reedy remembers, no one changed his thinking because of Ball's criticisms. Instead, his comments helped to increase support for the president's position. Reedy reported that[56]

> During the Johnson administration, I watched George Ball play the role . . . there would be an overwhelming report from Robert McNamara [secretary of defense] . . . another from Dean Rusk [secretary of state] another . . . from McGeorge Bundy [national security assistant]. Then five minutes would be set aside for Ball to deliver his dissent. The others . . . because they expected him to dissent . . . automatically discounted whatever he said. . . . [they] could quite honestly say, "We heard both sides of this issue discussed. . . ." They heard it with wax in their ears.

In his book, *The Lost Crusade,* NSC aide Chester Cooper reminisced about the president's habit of counting votes on issues among those advisors attending meetings. Few gave their uncensored opinions even when the president seemingly asked for it.[57]

> I would frequently fall into a Walter Mitty-like fantasy: When my turn came, I would rise to my feet slowly, look around the room and then directly at the President, and say very quietly and emphatically, "Mr. President, gentlemen, I most definitely do not agree." But I was removed from my trance when I heard the President's voice saying, "Mr. Cooper, do you agree?" and out would come a "Yes, Mr. President, I agree."

Dissenters from Johnson's Vietnam policy, although allowed to speak their piece, were subjected to severe group pressure to conform. Gradually, Bill Moyers became "Mr. Stop the Bombing," and his opposition to the war became the major reason for his decision to leave the Johnson White House.

As Vietnam began to consume the bulk of Johnson's time, appointments secretary Marvin Watson began screening out more and more people seeking individual meetings with the president. Johnson, who had been accessible to members of Congress, interest groups, and department and agency heads began to withdraw almost totally from domestic affairs.

Although Vietnam drove Johnson from the White House, it could not completely overshadow the legislative successes of the Great Society. Processes for developing ideas and writing legislation and implementing it helped to speed congressional responses to White House initiatives in the areas of housing, health care, and civil rights. Johnson placed Special Assistant Joseph Califano at the head of a number of task forces created to deal with issues listed in an "ideas book" drawn up through the efforts of Califano's staff and outside specialists. Next, task force members were chosen from the appropriate departments, his own staff, and the Bureau of the Budget. Task forces met in secret and developed reports on actions that should be taken on their assigned subject. Those reports were forwarded to appropriate departments for comments. Finally the Budget Bureau and the president decided whether legislation should be introduced. Task forces have been credited with the establishment of the Department of Housing and Urban Development and the bulk of the health, education, and antipoverty legislation of the Great Society. These task forces also involved the energy and ideas of approximately three hundred business people, labor leaders, and educators. Two of the most innovative pieces of domestic legislation in those years, model cities and head start for preschoolers, sought to concentrate federal funds in a way not previously acceptable to Congress or the bureaucracies. Keeping the task force meetings secret permitted the White House to get things done without tipping its hands to the bureaucracy in advance. Presidential Task Forces during the Johnson years were not always mere window dressing as they tended to be in most other administrations.

The many "yes men" around Johnson and his fixation on Vietnam combined to do him in. While it is true that he had no chief of staff filtering out information and reality, his immense ego demanded that he not be the first president to lose a war. It convinced him that the public was with him. He became a prisoner of his own delusions that the only opposition to his policies in Vietnam were members of the "Eastern Establishment" press and a few assorted radical students.

GERALD FORD: THE JERRY-BUILT SYSTEM. Instant President Gerald Ford was deprived of the luxury of being able to choose his own staff before he was catapulted into the Oval Office. Restoring the luster to the presidency after the tarnish of Watergate also complicated Ford's two-year interim presidency. For public consumption, at least, the Ford operation was hub of the wheel, but privately, White House officials acknowledged that a truly *open* operation was impractical because someone must act as traffic cop.

Early in his administration Ford declared that no one person would speak for him or would be considered senior to the others. Still, Donald Rumsfeld, a congressional colleague, did emerge as a first among equals as Ford unveiled a reorganization of the Nixon White House. The new flow charts included nine senior aides placed horizontally below the president. Rumsfeld handled White House operations, staff coordination, and recruiting for Ford. Both Rumsfeld and his successor, Richard Cheney, determined who could enter the Oval Office, but the president directed that the door be kept open to as many congressional party and interest group persons as possible.[58] It was this openness and accessibility that the president considered one of his greatest assets and he suggested that his staff emulate it.[59] Like other access-oriented presidents, much of Ford's time for long-range planning was eaten up by endless streams of visitors.

Initially, the Ford staff was a curious mix of Nixon carry-overs, cronies from Michigan, and enlistees from the House of Representatives. Henry Kissinger remained as national security assistant and the National Security Council subcommittee system was left intact. When Michigander Jerald ter Horst resigned in a huff over being "misled" about the president's decision to pardon his predecessor, Ron Nessen left NBC-TV news to take over the press operations. As counselors to the president, Ford intimates Robert Hartmann and Philip Buchen handled political matters and Hartmann doubled as a speechwriter. Nixon's Transportation Secretary James T. Lynn directed the budget operation (OMB after 1970) and former Rockefeller aide James Cannon presided over the remnants of the once vaunted Domestic Council.[60] If these aides had anything in common beyond their ties to Ford, it would have been that they were older than average for their jobs and that they were conservatives and Republicans.

His short tenure permitted Ford little chance to innovate in domestic or foreign affairs management. Even after the president put together "my own team" in December 1974, Henry Kissinger (Nixon's national security assistant) still retained a prominent place in foreign policy decision-making circles and the NSC system continued in place for Vietnam. When the Cambodian government seized an American merchant ship, *Mayaguez,* in 1975 the NSC was activated so that the president could direct member agencies about their roles in his plans to send marines to free the thirty-member crew of civilians being held on Tang Island off the Cambodian coast.

The December 1974 reorganization included (1) replacing Kissinger as national security assistant with his trusted aide, General Brent Scowcroft and (2) moving Donald Rumsfeld to secretary of defense. James Schlesinger was replaced because he made the tactical blunder of criticizing administration policy on arms control negotiations with the Soviets. George Bush, former Republican national chairman and U.S. ambassador to the United Nations, was tapped to pick up the pieces at the CIA in the aftermath of Watergate.

In response to public outcry over CIA aid to the Watergate burglars and the "Plumbers" who raided Daniel Ellsberg's (a Defense Department official who leaked information on the evolution of our Vietnam policy) psychiatrist's office to get files to discredit him, Ford created a Foreign Intelligence Board, quickly renamed Foreign Intelligence Advisory Board, because of the acronym the original title would have created (FIB). This three-member board of civilians with previous government service also had private job commitments so they could not devote full time to their new duties. Former Ambassador Robert D. Murphy who chaired the operation was acting simultaneously as president of Corning Glass International in New York. The FIAB was replaced by an Intelligence Oversight Board,[61] which was to review agency budgets and make recommendations for administrative reform directly to the president.

Even though Ford promised a more open atmosphere in the administration, he did not radically reorganize the Nixon-Kissinger system in foreign affairs. Things would most likely have been organized more tightly permitting less access in a second Ford administration, but it didn't materialize.

JIMMY CARTER: FROM HUB TO HIERARCHY. When "outsider" Jimmy Carter entered the Oval Office, he brought a clique of Georgia staffers with him who, like their boss, had virtually no Washington experience. One disenchanted aide quipped that the Carter White House was "like a movie set for a Marx brothers' picture only instead of four brothers, there were about a dozen."[62]

Early in his administration, Carter professed a great respect for the cabinet as an institution. "I believe in Cabinet administration," he declared. "There will never be an instance while I am President where members of the White House staff dominate or act in a superior position to the Cabinet."[63] This disclaimer about unbridled staff power had a familiar ring to it. Nixon and Ford and later Ronald Reagan said essentially the same thing. Two and one-half years in office taught Carter a certain skepticism about the motives of cabinet members, however. Health, Education, and Welfare Secretary Joseph Califano became expendable (his resignation was accepted) partly because he was often at loggerheads with presidential assistant Hamilton Jordan. The fact that he had been close to the Kennedys didn't help either.[64] Treasury Secretary Michael Blumenthal's tendencies to criticize administration spending on domestic problems and his alleged bickering with presidential domestic policy insider Stuart Eisenstadt did little for his longevity in the Carter cabinet. As the administration progressed, the role of the staff overshadowed that of most of the cabinet secretaries.

Cabinet administration would have provided the perfect excuse for cutting the White House staff. That had been one of the promises that candidate Carter had made in 1976. Frugality was to be a trademark of the Georgian White House. The "superstaff" was due to be cut down a few pegs. Hugh (Cousin Cheap) Carter was ordered to cut the frills and applied his trusty axe to such "perks" as door-to-door limo service for staffers, multiple magazine subscriptions, use of White House facilities, and so on. On paper, at least, the personal staff for the president was cut by about a third.[65] Through a bit of administrative *legerdemain,* those duties didn't disappear. Instead, many of the jobs such as the White House Office postal crew, payroll handling, and housekeeping were merely shifted to a new Office of Administration housed not in the WHO personal staff but in the Executive Office of the President along with other bureaucracies that serve him.

Throughout his administration, Georgians and former campaign aides held down key positions. In fact, of the original nine top-ranking aides, six came from Carter's home state:[66]

> Jody Powell [press secretary], Frank Moore [congressional relations], Jack Watson [intergovernmental affairs and cabinet secretary], Stuart Eisenstadt [director of the domestic policy staff], and Hamilton Jordan [political and patronage duties and later chief of staff].

The three carpetbaggers were Public Liaison Margaret "Midge" Costanza, National Security Assistant Zbigniew Brzezinski, and Energy Coordinator James Schlesinger.

Initially, the White House staff organization was developed along functional lines rather than on a strict line of command. There were three administrative levels: Carter at the top, nine key aides on the next plateau, and all the rest somewhere below. Theoretically, there was no pecking order, but Jordan and Powell, who had been long-time campaign aides, became two of Carter's closest advisors. In a highly publicized July 1979 shake-up of the staff and cabinet, Jordan moved from a first among equals to a de facto position as chief of staff.

As we suggested earlier, presidents use their staffing operations to fit White House needs as they perceive them. The stricter hierarchy should have freed President Carter from minutiae, but his passion for details didn't lessen measurably after reorganization. Often he overlooked the big picture because he was bogged down in particulars. Memos that crossed his desk in the Oval Office were often returned to the sender with Carter's comments penciled in the margin. He went so far as to correct his young staffer's grammar. One Carter aide noted that even after four months in office the President was[67]

> still preoccupied with details, as far as I can tell . . . as [the aide] took a memo out of his desk drawer and pointed to the handwritten notes in the margin. "I'm glad this went to the President since it is something I've been working on, but frankly, I'm surprised it ever reached that level."

Critics have suggested that Carter's passion for details stemmed from his need to persuade with facts and strong arguments because he lacked the style of a Kennedy or Roosevelt and was adverse to arm twisting in the style of the Johnson "treatment." Gradually, the president and staff became more political. When Jordan was advanced to chief of staff, Tim Kraft took over political and personnel matters. An early April 1978 staff meeting had concluded that the White House should begin to tamper with the departments by examining the performance and policy positions of subcabinet appointees who had been critical of the White House behind the scenes. As one assistant secretary noted, "There is a belief that some assistant secretaries are in business for themselves. Officially . . . they say the right things in respect to the President's budget and legislative programs. On the other hand, privately, they tell committee staffers on the Hill, I don't really think that."[68] Personnel people in the departments were told that the White House wanted to be consulted on all appointments whether they were to presidential staffs, to regional councils or advisory boards and commissions, or to high government service (GS-rated) positions.[69] Those directives were a far cry from the original practice of permitting cabinet secretaries to choose their top aides without White House interference. In the words of one Carter aide,[70]

> We need to let the Cabinet Secretaries know we are aware of what is going on. . . . If people are working against the President, we'll move on them. . . . Before, nobody in the White House acted on complaints or applied pressure on people kicking the President around. . . . It doesn't matter whether it's a regional appointee in Denver or San Francisco: if he's pounding the hell out of the President, we're going to find out about it and not let it happen again.

One of the major innovations of the Carter staffing patterns was in dealing with domestic policy issues. Nixon's domestic council, which had long since begun to atrophy, was permitted to die when the funds dried up in September 1977. On the remnants of Nixon's folly, the president built a domestic policy staff that bore some resemblance to the task force operations so common in the Kennedy and Johnson years. Loyalist Stuart Eisenstadt was tapped to direct the operation, which became something of an in-house think tank. The domestic policy staff reviewed domestic issues, defined problems, set up agency and department committees with policy staffers included, and then took recommendations to the president in memo form called presidential review memoranda (PRMs). Eisenstadt aides often drafted ideas for presidential speeches and met with members of Congress to explain administration policy. They also tried to resolve interagency differences over issues. Departments and agencies were known to complain about the arrangement because Eisenstadt's aides were handling virtually every major issue facing the White House. Eisenstadt's staff had expertise and responsibilities in areas such as agriculture, transportation, housing and urban affairs, justice, civil rights, government reforms, and consumer affairs.

Carter improved his advice on economic policy by creating a forum known as the Economic Policy Group, which brought together his major economic advisors for a weekly Thursday morning meeting with the president. Members included Charles Schultze (chairman of the Council of Economic Advisors), James McIntyre (second director of OMB), Vice President Walter Mondale, Treasury Secretary Michael Blumenthal, and inflation fighter Alfred E. Kahn, chairman of the Council on Wage and Price Stability. Eisenstadt also sat with the "core," as it was called, to lend his political advice on what would sell and what was administratively feasible to the advice of the president's key economists. Reminiscent of the competition in the Truman White House between conservative Steelman and liberal Clifford, Treasury Secretary Blumenthal's conservative political and fiscal philosophies clashed with Eisenstadt's moderate liberalism. In the July 1979 reorganizations, those conflicts and Blumenthal's tendencies to complain about administration spending on domestic problems hastened his departure from the cabinet.

Gradually, Carter the outsider and unorthodox, became Carter the insider who learned from early naïve mistakes. The much publicized reassessments in April 1978 and July 1979 did not radically change the Carter system but, rather, ratified the natural hierarchy that had begun to evolve over the previous two years or so. The courage to jettison the "cabinet-oriented" approach in favor of tighter White House control was partly in response to the success of bargaining for Senate consent to the twin Panama Canal treaties in 1978.

In Chapter 8, we shall examine the administration's efforts to reform the civil service system. For now, however, we can say that Carter and his aides learned that it was impossible to govern without politics. Tampering with the bureaucracies is not without its risks for a president's program.

## THE PYRAMID PRESIDENTS

DWIGHT DAVID EISENHOWER: THE GENERAL'S STAFF. When Dwight Eisenhower swapped his military jeeps for the White House limos, to no one's surprise his staffing system bore the stamp of a military mind. He delegated as much responsibility to his staff as possible. A clear pyramid developed with former New Hampshire Governor and Congressman Sherman Adams at the top immediately below the president. Former New Deal "brain truster" Rexford Tugwell claimed that Eisenhower was more skilled in using staff and more willing to delegate than any of his predecessors.[71] In his memoirs, Eisenhower commented on his expectations as he entered the Oval Office. "It was inconceivable" he said, "that the work of the White House could not be better systematized."[72]

Of the original thirty-two members of the staff, twenty-two had worked in the presidential campaign, five had served under the general in the army, and two had been with him in his years as president of Columbia University. These choices reflect his philosophy that staffers are personal assistants. Eisenhower preferred staffers with "professional experience" in jobs related to planned White House assignments.[73] For example, his press secretary, James Hagerty, was not appointed as a friend or because he was a reporter but because he had been a press secretary. General Jerry Persons who first served as chief of Eisenhower's congressional relations office had experience as a lobbyist. Eisenhower also added a personal economist, an actor-producer to help him with television, and experts in science and foreign economic policy.

The linchpin of the Eisenhower system was Chief of Staff Sherman Adams. None of the hub-of-the-wheel presidents had a person with a comparable role. Adams acted almost as a deputy president. Eisenhower informed his chief that he had certain expectations of that role:[74]

> [Eisenhower] simply expected me [Adams] to man a staff that would boil down, simplify and expedite the urgent business that had to be brought to his attention and keep as much work of secondary importance off of his desk.

Ike placed so much confidence in the "governor" as he was known at the White House that he would not read memos or reports coming across his desk unless the appropriate "OK SA" was at the bottom to indicate that it was cleared through the chief of staff. Paperwork was reduced to a single page (typewritten) in keeping with Eisenhower's view that anything worth saying could be summed up in one page.

Adams was also responsible for scheduling appointments, and he reportedly sometimes sat in on meetings uninvited. With the exception of Secretary of State John Foster Dulles, who met with Eisenhower twenty-five to thirty times per week and on weekends, other cabinet secretaries were required to reach the president only through "Governor" Adams.

While Eisenhower was criticized for being isolated because of the Adams operation, he also took considerable flak for his deference to Dulles in foreign affairs.[75] He openly disagreed with his secretary of state only twice—on the Atoms for Peace and Open Skies proposals at the United Nations, which he supported and Dulles opposed. Both disagreements came late in his administration.

Although the president was all too familiar with the bureaucratic process from his days as a general, he had no real feel for or love of the politics involved in dealing with individuals. Adams's operation freed him of the burden of day-to-day personality clashes, permitting him to spend more time formulating longer-range planning. More recently Fred Greenstein has suggested that Eisenhower was not as adverse to politics as many have suggested.[76]

Expanding on Truman's congressional relations system by adding a number of assistants, he arranged for General Persons to report to Adams. Further institutionalizing the staff, he appointed Robert Cutler to a newly created post of special assistant for national security. Still, like Truman who sought most foreign policy advice from Secretary of State Dean Acheson, Eisenhower leaned on Dulles and not his national security assistant.

The entire Eisenhower system isolated aides from the president. Fortunately for him, his aides were, as a group, honest and self-effacing. To compensate for the possibility that necessary information might not get through Adams and Dulles, Eisenhower made extensive use of the NSC and interdepartmental committees, and he had regular, highly structured cabinet meetings. Critics enjoyed poking fun at the White House saying that there were "three presidents": president for foreign affairs, Dulles; president for domestic affairs, Adams; and president for protocol and golf, Eisenhower. In fact, however, Eisenhower realized the importance of being able to delegate to trustworthy subordinates, and he made every effort to cooperate with the Democratic leadership on Capitol Hill and make himself accessible to them. As his administration progressed, he, like an activist, took on more and more of the decisions and battles himself.

RICHARD NIXON: THE TEAM PLAYERS. Staffing philosophies learned at Eisenhower's knee as vice president had a profound effect on the Nixon operation. Like the former general he served, Nixon constructed a highly stratified system and as chief of staff he employed a latter-day Sherman Adams in the person of H. R. (Bob) Haldeman. Psychologically, Nixon resembled Eisenhower in that he shied away from personal confrontation with individuals, and he hated to muddy his hands with such distasteful chores as firing subordinates. Every president needs a few scrupulously loyal staffers who, as Joseph Califano so neatly phrased it, "bleed when he gets cut." Haldeman was that type of aide. He took on the unpleasant tasks for Nixon and he indelicately described his role with the comment that, "Every President needs a son-of-a-bitch and I'm Nixon's."[77]

Nixon's aides did not have the professional polish for their assignments that Eisenhower had tried to find for his staff. Nixon's team was made up of generalists more in the Kennedy mold, although there was no Ivy League intellectual flavor as the Massachusetts-bred president had brought to the White House. Nixon's aides had little or no Washington experience and, as a result, they were not schooled in the limits of acceptable behavior within the federal government. Political enemies even in the bureaucracies were envisioned as enemies, every bit as dangerous to the administration as the Soviets were to the nation as a whole.

The pin-striped public relations flavor of the Nixon White House earned it the label J. Walter Thompson East. Haldeman had been Los Angeles branch manager for that public relations firm before becoming a Nixon campaign aide and later chief of staff. Most of the aides had close ties to Haldeman:[78]

> John Erlichman [chief domestic advisor] was a Seattle lawyer and old Halde-man classmate. Dwight Chapin [appointments secretary] had worked for Haldeman at Thompson; Ron Ziegler [press secretary] had been employed at Disneyland and later at Thompson. Others once tied to Haldeman were Thompson employees, Bruce Kehrli [secretary], Haldeman's chief deputy Larry Higby, and Kenneth Cole [head of the domestic council]. Egil Krogh [on Erlichman's staff] had been a legal colleague of Erlichman's.

With such close personal ties, it should have been no surprise that a strong "team player" mentality evolved.

Since Nixon did not personally know many members of the White House staff as close friends, and because he had an aversion to face-to-face communication, he preferred to make decisions on the basis of option papers rather than "skull sessions." Not only did Nixon have a strong preference for the written page, but he liked to get away from the Oval Office to think through problems without interruption. He made many important decisions only after communing with nature at Camp David. In explaining these practices to inquisitive journalists, Nixon said[79]

> I find that up here on top of a mountain, it is easier for me to get on top of the job, to think in a generally relaxed way at times—although the work has been very intensive in these past few weeks, as it was before the other great decisions that have been made here—but also in a way in which one, if not interrupted either physically or personally or in any other way, can think objectively with perception about the problems one has to make a decision on.

Initially papers got through to Nixon much more easily than people. Haldeman who became known as the "Berlin Wall" jealously guarded the entrances to the Oval Office. Few, other than Henry Kissinger, could get around him to the president. Once, Federal Reserve Board Chairman Arthur Burns met Nixon for his allotted ten minutes but, on his way out, he remembered something else he wanted to tell the president. Haldeman reportedly thrust his arm across the doorway telling Burns to make another appointment.

Although Nixon was willing to read staff papers, he wasn't disposed to read newspapers as Roosevelt and Kennedy enjoyed doing. His negative reputation with the press as a crusading anti-communist senator, feisty vice president, and unsuccessful 1962 candidate for governor of California were hard for him to shake. Early in the administration, he tried to improve relations with the press with little success. So, instead of wading through newspapers, magazines, or using LBJ's favorite press tickers, Nixon asked White House aide Pat Buchanan and his staff to prepare morning news summaries for him. They included[80]

> four or five sections totaling around thirty-five pages. One section contained an edited UPI and AP wire service report, another dealt with what had been said about the administration on radio and T.V. news and talk shows, the third contained a news summary from several East Coast morning newspapers, and the fourth was a digest of analyses and editorials from around fifty papers from around the country. The final part of the summary was a report on how thirty to thirty-five magazines and newspapers were covering particular issues.

The Buchanan operation was light-years from the Johnson administration's interest in televised news. Johnson had a three-screen console in his office, and he watched the national network news on the majors simultaneously. Reportedly, TV viewing for Nixon was limited to a mystery series, "Kojak," and the Washington Redskins football games.[81]

Henry Kissinger, former foreign affairs advisor to New York Governor Nelson Rockefeller, was tapped to serve as national security assistant. He quickly built up a personal apparatus that rivaled the analysis capabilities of the departments of state and defense as well as that of the intelligence community. We shall examine that system in more detail in Chapter 4. Suffice it to say that Kissinger's operation became a potent voice of foreign policy counsel to the president. Unlike Defense Secretary Melvin Laird and Secretary of State Rogers, Kissinger did not have to approach the "Berlin Wall"; he had access on a regular basis to the Oval Office.

Executive office changes in the Nixon administration centered on reorganization of the old Budget Bureau into Office of Management and the Budget and creation of a new Domestic Council. A new responsibility for giving management advice to the departments was added to the former budget duties of the old BOB. The shakedown cruise of the Domestic Council in 1970 demonstrated that trying to coordinate the activities of all cabinet-level departments dealing with domestic programs was no easy proposition. In theory, it is laudable to try to correct overlap and duplication in services and personnel. Still, which programs should be eliminated and which departments will lose personnel?

The problems with these reorganizations pointed out to Nixon and his aides that, if they wanted to accomplish any of their domestic goals, they would have to develop some method of bringing the Democrats in the bureaucracy to heel at the order of the White House. He learned that cabinet members, no matter how politically strong in their own right, could not be depended on to ride herd over the bureaucracies. Richard Nathan in his book, *The Plot That Failed,* noticed that Nixon began creating a counterbureaucracy centralized under Haldeman. All reports got to the president only through the "Berlin Wall." In 1973, Nixon tried to salt loyalists into subcabinet positions to help the administration keep tabs on the bureaucracy, much in the way Kennedy had in the early 1960s.[82] Watergate destroyed any chance for success of Nixon's plans.

Haldeman's operation helped to free the president's time to think out broader-ranging policy initiatives. Working days for Nixon were often left virtually free of formal meetings while most days had at least one three-hour stretch without interruption. As a result, Nixon was able to spend large blocks of time in study and contemplation of foreign policy, which he considered his major set of responsibilities.[83] On almost every issue of international significance—Vietnam, Sino-American relations, arms limitations with the Soviets (SALT), and troop reductions between NATO and the Warsaw Pact (MBFR)—Kissinger was the president's primary advisor, negotiator, and contact with the bureaucracy, the public, and the press. Kissinger and his staff cleared cable reports and dispatches for the president. They also provided summaries of information relating to national security, and Dr. Kissinger supervised the covert operations of the intelligence community from his post as chairman of the Forty Committee, which was a subcommittee of the National Security Council. In many respects, Kissinger was the John Foster Dulles of his day.

For a system like Nixon's to work effectively, the president must permit criticism to filter through to him. Woodward and Bernstein pointed out in their book, *Final Days*,[84] that Nixon's staff was his undoing. Top aides like Haldeman, Erlichman, and Colson withheld the campaign problems from him. He demanded they get him elected in all fifty states and he didn't care how they did it.[85] Excesses were justified as loyalty to the president. Nixon withdrew farther and farther, delegating most of his duties to top aides. The pyramid remained intact, but it helped to topple the Pharoah.

## LEADERSHIP AND THE LESSONS OF STAFFING

It has been said that the hand that rocks the cradle rules the world. People with experience in government soon come to realize likewise that the power to "define" options is the power to choose some and eliminate others. That is often the power in the hands of the White House staff. Presidents must be careful, in creating a staffing system, to allow the operation to permit a certain amount of latitude without getting a totally free rein. For the most part, staffers need the direction of a seasoned political figure who can add a sense of reality to the fairyland atmosphere of the White House. Most staffers are generalists, are substantially younger than their boss, and tend to be subject to pressures to be a good team player. Too often, staffers believe that, because they have access to the president, they are intelligent enough to define options for him. As the president's extended person in hostile environs outside the antiseptic atmosphere of the White House, they must be attuned to gathering the information they know he will want, presenting it in the form he can use, and understanding both the letter and the spirit of the orders he gives them.

Rapid growth and specialization in the White House staff, especially during the Johnson and Nixon years, has made it difficult for a president to keep a handle on staffers and what they are saying in his name. Requests prefaced by "the President says," can be the best of bludgeons in the hands of an eager White House staffer. Watergate put presidents on notice that they may well be held accountable for crimes committed in their name. Still, presidents set the tone for their administrations. If they are disrespectful of democratic processes, can better be expected of their staffs?

Would-be presidents, the press corps, and others can point out the public relations liabilities of a staffer to help to discredit the boss, the president. Most aides are unfamiliar with the White House scene. The fishbowl existence of Washington and their own unquenchable ambitions can combine to make them develop an exalted sense of their own importance. They may, as a result, do things that reflect disfavor upon their bosses. Republicans questioned Truman's decision to stand behind his Missouri gang, and Eisenhower's reputation was hurt by the vicuna coat that financier-industrialist Bernard Goldfine left as a token of his esteem to Sherman Adams. When the sex life of old-friend and close Johnson aide Walter Jenkins broke in the press, the President showed less loyalty than he demanded and acted as if he hardly knew Jenkins. Hamilton Jordan, Dr. Peter Bourne, and OMB director Bert Lance at various times became political liabilities for Jimmy Carter due to their personal habits and alleged violations of the law.

Finally, most presidents come into office promising an open administration with an accessible Oval Office only to learn that leadership requires that the president be able to plan ahead. Time taken up being available is time that cannot be spent on policy planning and crisis management. So, the hub-of-the-wheel style, which is so congenial to democracy and generates many opinions, tends to overburden a president and becomes an unacceptable thief of his time. Open administration also finds that the bureaucracies can mount guerrilla actions against presidential initiatives when they are informed ahead of time.

## THE RASPUTIN SCHOOL
## OF INFLUENCE AND INFORMATION

Close friends who exert influence on the president without holding public office may be a relic of the pre-White House staff past. Nevertheless, Rasputin theories have abounded with respect to presidential friends who might be casting their spells on policy making from offices outside the government orbit. It becomes a sort of journalistic game to assess the influence of these "outsiders." Did Charles B. "Bebe" Rebozo influence Nixon's views on anti-Castro U.S. policies toward Cuba? What roles did Averell Harriman play in the Truman years, and Clark Clifford and Abe Fortas in the Johnson years? Did Bert Lance have policy input even after he resigned as OMB director in the Carter administration, and did Charles Kirbo need a White House job to be influential?

Lyndon Johnson probably made the greatest use of these types of individuals among the post-World War II presidents. One of them described his role this way:[86]

> I don't think he really expects answers from his friends most of the time. He uses his friends as sounding boards, letting his thoughts come out and bounce off of them. . . . The chief function of his friends, then, was to let him talk.

Clark Clifford's role in Johnson policy making on Vietnam demonstrates the value of these outsiders. He had been brought in in 1968, according to Irving Janis, as a "dependable hawk" who could function well in the cliquish company of the Tuesday lunch group. It was Clifford, however, free of bureaucratic constraints, job considerations for the future, and "group think" pressures who was capable of asking the necessary questions about the goals of the policy that provided a badly needed alternative perspective.

The epitome of inside "outsiders" have been the wives of some of the presidents.

These "first ladies," or in the case of Betty Ford who was given the CB handle "first mama," can exert influence over their husbands, especially in the areas of women's issues. Both Betty Ford and Rosalyn Carter were major influences in their husbands' support for the Equal Rights Amendment. They helped to keep the issue on the front burners at the White House even when energy policy, inflation, and foreign policy seemed destined to put White House efforts to place ERA on the shelf. Like Eleanor Roosevelt, Rosalyn Carter seemed to have been interested in being one of the White House staff, if not on the flow charts at least in access. She had a standing appointment for a business lunch with the president and was very active in her efforts to improve mental health services across the nation. Her personal visit to Cambodia in 1979 seemed to act as a spur to increase American relief efforts to head off the destruction of that nation through starvation.

A steady stream of outsiders was always willing to provide its wisdom to the White House so there was never a shortage of interest group representatives providing counsel. Late AFL-CIO President George Meany provided his guidance to a number of Democratic presidents, and Lyndon Johnson was in the habit of calling in congressional leaders to help him get a sense of what he could sell in domestic legislation at critical times during the legislative sessions.

"Think tankers" have also served as advisors to various administrations, especially in the areas of economic and defense policy. Academic consultants from the Brookings Institution (sometimes called the shadow government for out-of-office Democrats), the Rand Corporation (Research Associates for National Defense), and the Hoover Institute at Stanford University[87] have long been prominent sources of information and advice for the White House. Since 1975 the American Enterprises Institute (AEI) has been evolving into a moderate to conservative version of the Brookings Institution. In 1975 AEI hired former Defense Secretary Melvin Laird to chair its national energy project, former White House aide Bryce Harlow to handle its program priorities committee, and former Council of Economic Advisors (CEA) Chairman Paul McCracken to chair its academic advisory board. Brookings has served as a halfway house for former CEA chairmen like Arthur Okun and other Democratic cabinet members and White House staffers. It has become a regular ritual for Democratic presidents to call in people like Okun and Kennedy's CEA chairman Walter Heller for economic advice.

## SPECIAL TASK FORCES
## AND BLUE-RIBBON COMMISSIONS

Outsiders might take on the collective trappings of special task forces, commissions, or committees to deal with sensitive problems. Too often, however, the presidential purpose for gathering these outsiders together may be more political than informational or advisory. If things are flaring up in Latin American affairs, the solution is to create a Rockefeller commission[88] to investigate. A Kerner commission can respond to the civil disorders in places like Detroit and Watts (Los Angeles, 1968) that left sections of those cities charred monuments to racial unrest. When the public was fearful of the excesses of the intelligence community, President Ford called Rockefeller to the rescue again.[89] Pornography and pot smoking were examined during the Nixon years by special presidential commissions, but, when the president disagreed with their findings, the voluminous reports were filed in the wastebasket.

Elizabeth Drew, with her tongue firmly planted in her cheek, listed some of the reasons that presidents might use commissions.[90]

> To obtain the blessings of distinguished men for something you want to do anyway. . . . To postpone action yet to be justified insisting that you are at work on the problem . . . to act as a lightning rod to draw political heat away from the White House. . . . To conduct an extensive study of something you need to know more about before you act . . . to investigate and lay to rest rumors . . . to get [commission members] aboard on something you want to do . . . because you can't think of anything else to do. . . . To change the hearts and minds of men.

Even commission members can be suspect of presidential intentions in creating them. Robert D. Murphy, who chaired the Commission on the Organization of Government for the Conduct of Foreign Policy, suggested in an interview that Congress could be especially wary of these meetings. The ambassador pointed out that congressional members soured on his commission since they came to perceive it as an attempt by President Ford to make sure that the suggestions of the Rockefeller Commission on Intelligence would be buttressed by another commission that included members of Congress. Senator Mike Mansfield, Senate majority leader, had permitted his office to be used for the Murphy commission meetings until Rockefeller was added to the commission to replace Anne Armstrong.[91] Mansfield took this move as a White House ploy and later vehemently attacked the findings of the commission he had served on. Senator Edward Kennedy, in comments before a Senate subcommittee dealing with "presidential commissions," commented with obvious disenchantment that[92]

> It seems as though most Presidential Commissions are merely so many Jiminy Crickets chirping in the ears of deaf presidents, deaf officials, and perhaps a deaf public. They could be the nation's conscience spurring us on to do what ought to be done, showing us the way . . . but, all too often, we reject them, ignore them, or forget them.

Presidential commissions, committees, conferences, and the like demonstrate to the world that the president is not blind to the existence of a problem. Furthermore, they seem to bring together the sum total of conventional wisdom on a particularly sticky question. Thomas Wolanin, in an exhaustively researched and documented study of presidential commissions, is hardly encouraging about their impacts on presidential decisions.[93] Henry Kissinger probably described them best when he snipped, "committees are consumers and sometimes sterilizers of ideas, but rarely creators of them."[94]

## THE REAGAN WHITE HOUSE: A NINE-TO-FIVE PRESIDENT?

Soon after his swearing in on January 20, 1981, Ronald Reagan embarked upon an ambitious plan to restructure the system for managing the White House and the entire Executive branch. During the campaign he had raised the cliché call for

# CHART 3.1 WHO'S WHO IN REAGAN'S WHITE HOUSE

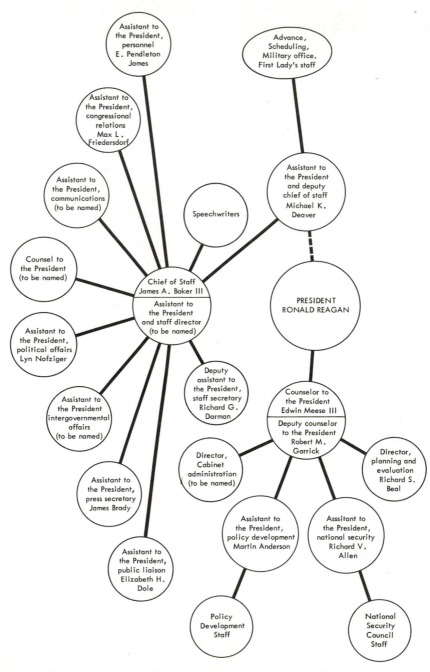

Assistant to the President, personnel E. Pendleton James

Advance, Scheduling, Military office, First Lady's staff

Assistant to the President, congressional relations Max L. Friedersdorf

Assistant to the President, communications (to be named)

Speechwriters

Assistant to the President and deputy chief of staff Michael K. Deaver

Counsel to the President (to be named)

Chief of Staff James A. Baker III
Assistant to the President and staff director (to be named)

PRESIDENT RONALD REAGAN

Assistant to the President, political affairs Lyn Nofziger

Assistant to the President intergovernmental affairs (to be named)

Deputy assistant to the President, staff secretary Richard G. Darman

Counselor to the President Edwin Meese III
Deputy counselor to the President Robert M. Garrick

Director, planning and evaluation Richard S. Beal

Assistant to the President, press secretary James Brady

Director, Cabinet administration (to be named)

Assistant to the President, policy development Martin Anderson

Asssitant to the President, national security Richard V. Allen

Assistant to the President, public liaison Elizabeth H. Dole

Policy Development Staff

National Security Council Staff

Source: "Transition Office," *National Journal*, January 1981, p. 89.

"cabinet government" as a solution to dictatorship by the White House staff. Former aide to Gerald Ford and campaign manager (in the primaries) for George Bush, James Baker was chosen as chief of staff in the new White House and he adamantly opposed both "cabinet government" or a super-cabinet of key staffers along the lines Richard Nixon had once suggested. His White House experiences lent credibility to his philosophies of staffing and gradually Reagan jettisoned the concept.

Instead, the White House deemphasized an advisory role for the cabinet or an executive committee of key cabinet members in favor of an innovative advisory system based on a novel structuring of the staff.

The traditional functions of a chief of staff in a pyramid system were divided between James Baker and Edwin Meese, III, who served as chief of staff for former Governor Reagan. As Chart 3.1 illustrates, Meese assumed policy formulation chores while Baker was bequeathed the unenviable task of handling the politics and selling programs to skeptics in the press, on Capitol Hill, and among interest groups and various constituencies. Another key part of the administrative inner circle was Michael K. Deaver, who coordinated the efforts of scheduling, appointments, and travel personnel. Erstwhile insiders in some administrations, like the press secretary and the National Security Assistant, were downgraded in position on the Reagan flow chart. Evidently he wanted no one to question that his chief spokesman in foreign policy would be Secretary of State Haig and not another Kissinger or Brzezinski in the person of National Security Assistant Richard V. Allen.[95]

Since leopards rarely change their spots, Reagan's nine to five style as Governor of California is likely to prevail throughout his four years as President. In this respect he resembles the pyramid presidents who were normally long on delegation and short on details.[96] For this reason channels of access and the insights to be gleaned from flow charts should be valuable in determining how policy is made in the Reagan administration.

## CONCLUSIONS

Presidents can use staffers, close friends, and professionals not merely as advisors but as psychological support. Staffers can permit a president to keep the bureaucracies off balance and responsive to his wishes. Professionals and think tankers can provide him with the vocabulary of expertise to defend his programs. None of them, it seems, can provide him with advice unless he really wants to receive it. Permitting access to the Oval Office for members of the cabinet, interest group representatives and members of Congress can leave the image of *multiple advocacy* decisions. Alexander George used the term to refer to the need for decision makers to reach conclusions on the basis of a broad range of information and advice. How much of the president's efforts to be accessible are mere window dressing rather than a sincerely motivated desire for different points of view can be difficult to determine while a particular administration still holds the Oval Office.

The Reagan administration's organization will position him atop a pyramid. As Governor of California he acted more as chairman of the board, leaving the details to subordinates much as Eisenhower and Nixon had done. Unlike Carter, Reagan is notorious for avoiding the "nuts and bolts" of government.[97] He must remain vigilant so that his sources of information do not become so closed that multiple advocacy becomes impossible. Whether his counselor, Ed Meese, or his Chief of Staff, Jim Baker, takes the top spot below the president remains to be seen. It is almost unimaginable that both men can indefinitely share the top spot and the authority for controlling the flow of information into the Oval Office.

# NOTES

[1] Emmet John Hughes, *The Living Presidency* (New York: Coward, McCann & Geoghegun, Inc., 1973), p. 146.

[2] Today's cabinet includes thirteen secretaries: Agriculture, Commerce, Defense, Education, Energy, Housing and Urban Development, Health and Human Resources, Interior, Justice, Labor, State, Transportation, Treasury. The U.N. ambassador is often considered a cabinet-level post, which would bring the number to fourteen. More on the cabinet in Chapter 7.

[3] Richard Pious, *The American Presidency* (New York: Basic Books, 1979), p. 240.

[4] Richard Neustadt, *Presidential Power: The Politics of Leadership* (New York: John Wiley, 1976), p. 14.

[5] Thomas Cronin, *The State of the Presidency* (Boston: Little, Brown, 1975), p. 120.

[6] *Ibid.*, p. 120.

[7] Nicholas Lehmann, "Jordan, Georgia and the Establishment," *Washington Monthly* (April 1978), p. 37.

[8] E. S. Corwin, *The Presidency, Office and Powers* (New York: New York U.P., 1957), p. 301.

[9] Stephen Hess, *Organizing the Presidency* (Washington, D.C.: Brookings Institution, 1976), p. 9.

[10] President's Commission on Administrative Management, *Report* (Washington, D.C.: G.P.O., 1937), p. 5.

[11] Marian Irish and Elke Frank, *U.S. Foreign Policy* (New York: Harcourt Brace, 1976), p. 200.

[12] President's Commission on Administrative Management, *op. cit.*, p. 5.

[13] Patrick Anderson, *The President's Men* (Garden City, N.Y.: Doubleday, 1968), p. 3. See also John Dean, *Blind Ambition* (New York: Simon & Schuster, 1976).

[14] Arthur Schlesinger, Jr., *The Imperial Presidency* (New York: Houghton Mifflin, 1973), p. 217.

[15] Joseph A. Califano, *A Presidential Nation* (New York: W. W. Norton, 1976), p. 145.

[16] Theodore Sorensen, *Decision Making in the White House* (New York: Columbia U.P., 1963), p. 7.

[17] Hess, *op. cit.*, p. 49.

[18] Frederic Malek, *Washington's Hidden Tragedy* (uncorrected proofs) (New York: Free Press, 1978), p. 64.

[19] Hess, *op. cit.*, p. 28.

[20] Congressional Quarterly, *President Carter*, Special Report (Washington, D.C.: Congressional Quarterly Service, 1978), pp. 15-18.

[21] Patricia Florestano, "The Characteristics of White House Staff Appointees from Truman to Nixon," *Presidential Studies Quarterly* (Fall 1977), pp. 184-190.

[22] *Ibid.*, p. 190.

[23] Theodore Sorensen, *Watchmen in the Night* (Cambridge, Mass.: M.I.T. Press, 1976), p. 140.

[24] Hughes, *op. cit.*, p. 144.

[25] Eric Goldman, *The Tragedy of Lyndon Johnson* (New York: Knopf, 1969), p. 22.

[26] George Reedy, *Twilight of the Presidency*. Copyright 1970 by George E. Reedy. Reprinted by arrangement with New American Library, Inc.

[27] As cited in John Stoessinger, *Crusaders and Pragmatists* (New York: W. W. Norton, 1979), p. 185.

[28] Jeb Stuart Magruder, *An American Life* (New York: Atheneum, 1974), pp. 56, 81 as cited in Pious, *op. cit.*, p. 245.

[29] Califano, *op. cit.*, pp. 189-190.

[30] Hughes, *op. cit.*, p. 140.

[31] Hess, *op. cit.*, p. 3. The two patterns are a slight variation from the models Hess suggests.

[32] James David Barber, *Presidential Character*, 2nd ed. (Englewood Cliffs, N.J.: Prentice-Hall, 1977), p. 237.

[33] *Ibid.*, p. 238.

[34] Erwin C. Hargrove, *The Power of the Modern Presidency* (New York: Knopf, 1974), p. 82. See also Richard Neustadt, "Approaches to Staffing the Presidency: Notes on FDR and JFK," *American Political Science Review*, (December 1963), 855. Also see Arthur Schlesinger, Jr., *The Coming of the New Deal* (Cambridge, Mass.: Riverside Press, 1959), pp. 527-528.

[35] William Mullen, *Presidential Power and Politics* (New York: St. Martin's Press, 1976), p. 196.

[36] Richard Neustadt, *Presidential Power*, p. 238. The exception of Lyndon Johnson was added as mine and was not in the original Neustadt.

[37] Barber, *op. cit.*, p. 248.

[38] See Chapter 11 for more on this from Truman's memoirs.

[39] Hess, *op. cit.*, p. 49.

[40] Anderson, *op. cit.*, p. 103.

[41] Hargrove, *op. cit.*, p. 86.

[42] Professor Neustadt advised Kennedy to follow FDR's lead as cited in Hess, *op. cit.*, p. 79.

[43] Technically, the U.N. ambassador is independent, but he works most often under the direction of the secretary of state.

[44] Anderson, *op. cit.*, p. 195.

[45] See comments by Lee White at the Montauk Symposium on the Presidency in the 1970s in R. Gordon Hoxie, ed., *The White House Organization and Operations* (New York: Center for the Study of the Presidency, 1971), pp. 67-68.

[46] Hargrove, *op. cit.*, p. 87.

[47] Cronin, *op. cit.*, p. 185.

[48] Barber, *op. cit.*, p. 86.

[49] Goldman, *op. cit.*, p. 120.

[50] *Ibid.*, p. 121. Joseph Califano spoke of his own period in President Johnson's dog house when Johnson would only speak to him through their secretaries. This lasted for almost three weeks because of some comments Califano gave to a friend about the defense budget that ended up in the *Washington Post*. Johnson was furious.

Talk with Califano was as a part of an NEH Summer Seminar on the presidency held at New York University under the direction of Louis Koenig, June 1976.

[51] Hess, *op. cit.*, p. 95.

[52] Califano, *op. cit.*, p. 210.

[53] See Louis Koenig, *The Chief Executive* (New York: Harcourt Brace, 1975), p. 201.

[54] Irving Janis, *The Victims of Groupthink* (Boston: Houghton Mifflin, 1972), p. 119.

[55] Lyndon B. Johnson, *Vantage Point* (New York: Holt, Rinehart and Winston, 1971), p. 410.

[56] As cited in Hughes, *op. cit.*, p. 153.

[57] Cooper is cited in Stoessinger, *op. cit.*, p. 185.

[58] Dom Bonafede, "Ford Leaves Office Structure Intact," *National Journal*, June 28, 1975, p. 974.

[59] Dom Bonafede, "White House Staffing in the Nixon-Ford Era," in *The Presidency Reappraised*, eds. Thomas Cronin and Rexford Tugwell (New York: Praeger, 1977), p. 65.

[60] Dom Bonafede, "Ford's Lobbyists Expect Democrats to Revise Tactics," *National Journal*, June 21, 1975, p. 926.

[61] Henry T. Nash, *American Foreign Policy* (Homewood, Ill.: Dorsey Press, 1978), p. 224.

[62] *National Journal,* November 10, 1979, p. 1894.

[63] *Congressional Quarterly Weekly Reports,* July 21, 1979, p. 1432. Hereafter *CQWR.*

[64] Califano had other problems, especially his antismoking crusade, that flew in the face of the president's promise of tobacco subsidies to North Carolina farmers.

[65] Pious, *op. cit.,* p. 248.

[66] Carter hired a management specialist, Alfonso McDonald, to aid Jordan. See *CQWR,* July 21, 1979, p. 1495.

[67] Dom Bonafede, "The Fallout from Camp David—Only Minor White House Changes," *National Journal,* November 10, 1979, p. 1897. See also, for more on Carter's administrative practices, James Sundquist, "Jimmy Carter as Public Administrator: An Appraisal at Mid-Term," *Public Administration Review* (January-February 1979), pp. 5-11.

[68] *Ibid.,* p. 1897.

[69] Dom Bonafede, "Carter Sounds Retreat from Cabinet Government," *National Journal,* November 18, 1978, p. 1854.

[70] *Ibid.,* p. 1854.

[71] As cited in Hess, *op. cit.,* p. 67.

[72] Dwight Eisenhower, *Mandates for Change* (Garden City, N.Y.: Doubleday, 1963), p. 67.

[73] Hess, *op. cit.,* pp. 67-68.

[74] Koenig, *op. cit.,* p. 193.

[75] Hughes, *op. cit.,* p. 155.

[76] Hargrove, *op. cit.,* p. 86. See also: Fred Greenstein, "Eisenhower as an Activist President: A Look at New Evidence," *Political Science Quarterly,* Winter 1979-80, pp. 575-96.

[77] Califano, *op. cit.,* p. 192.

[78] Mullen, *op. cit.,* pp. 210-211.

[79] John Kessel, *The Domestic Presidency* (North Scituate, Mass.: Duxbury, 1975), p. 89.

[80] Mullen, *op. cit.,* pp. 210-211.

[81] William Safire, *Before the Fall* (Garden City, N.Y.: Doubleday, 1975), p. 342. He takes the position that Nixon did feel a need to keep the press happy, however.

[82] Richard Nathan, *The Plot that Failed: Nixon and the Administrative Presidency* (New York: John Wiley, 1975), pp. 59-95 gives details on how the system worked and why it failed.

[83] Malek, *op. cit.,* p. 22.

[84] Bob Woodward and Carl Bernstein, *The Final Days* (New York: Simon & Schuster, 1976).

[85] Theodore White, *Breach of Faith* (New York: Atheneum, 1975).

[86] From Ben H. Bagdikian, "The Inner-Inner Circle Around Johnson," *The New York Times Magazine,* February 28, 1965, as cited in Nelson Polsby, *The Modern Presidency* (New York: Random House, 1973), p. 184.

[87] Professors or those holding Ph.Ds have been common. The list from the Nixon and Ford and Carter years is indeed impressive. The Nixon-Ford group includes Secretary of State Kissinger, U.N. Ambassador Daniel P. Moynihan, Attorney General Edward Levy, Secretary of Agriculture Earl Butz, Secretary of the Treasury George Schultz, Secretary of Defense James Schlesinger, Federal Reserve Board Chairman Arthur Burns, Labor Secretary John Dunlop, HEW Secretary David Matthews, and Chairman of the Council of Economic Advisors Herbert Stein. The Carter White House listed the following: Brzezinski, Brown, Schlesinger, Kreps, Marshall, Blumenthal, Schultze, and Campbell. See also Henry J. Aaron, *Politics and Professors* (Washington, D.C.: Brookings Institution, 1978).

[88] Nelson A. Rockefeller, *Quality of Life in the Americas* (Washington, D.C.: Agency for International Development, 1969).

[89] See Commission on the CIA Activities within the U.S., *Report to the President,* June 1975 (Washington, D.C.: G.P.O., 1975). A summary can be found in *The New York Times,* June 11, 1975.

[90] Elizabeth Drew, "On Giving Oneself a Hotfoot: Government by Commission," *Atlantic*, (May 1968), 44-45. © 1968 by Atlantic Monthly Company, Boston, Mass. Reprinted with permission.

[91] Frank Kessler, "Presidential Congressional Battles: Toward a Truce on the Foreign Policy Front," *Presidential Studies Quarterly*, (Spring 1978), p. 126. See note 60 on an interview with Ambassador Murphy.

[92] U.S. Senate, Committee on the Judiciary, Subcommittee on Administrative procedures, *Hearings On Presidential Commissions*, 92nd Cong., 1st sess., June 1971, p. 3.

[93] Thomas Wolanin, *Presidential Advisory Commissions: Truman to Nixon* (Madison: Univ. Wisconsin Press, 1975). See especially pp. 130-156 and appendices 2 and 3.

[94] Thomas Cronin and Sanford Greenburg, eds., *The Presidential Advisory System* (New York: Harper & Row, 1969), p. 160.

[95] William J. Lanouette, "Reagan Plays Chairman of the Board to Carter's Corporate Comptroller," *National Journal*, July 19, 1980, p. 1177.

[96] Dick Kirschten, "Reagan's Federal Machine—If It Doesn't Work, Then Fix It," *National Journal*, January 17, 1981, pp. 88-93.

[97] For a revisionist view of Eisenhower which emphasized his working familiarity with politics see both of the following: Fred I. Greenstein, "Eisenhower as an Activist President: A Look at New Evidence," *Political Science Quarterly*, Winter, 1980, pp. 575-596, and R. Gordon Hoxie, "The Not So Imperial Presidency," *Presidential Studies Quarterly*, Spring, 1980, p. 199. For a look into the future on possible directions in staffing see: Hugh Heclo, *A Presidency for the 1980s*, A Report by a Panel of the National Academy of Public Administration, Washington, D.C., 1980. See also Bradley D. Nash, "Staffing the Presidency: a 1980 View," in Bradley D. Nash with Milton S. Eisenhower, R. Gordon Hoxie and William C. Spraegens, *Organizing and Staffing the Presidency*, New York, Center for the Study of the Presidency, 1980, pp. 150-173.

# The President's Experts: Bureaucratic Advisors

At times it is difficult to fathom why anyone would want to take on the superhuman burden of being president. It could well be that the office is simply too complex for any one mortal to handle. Still, barring a constitutional amendment breaking the job down to more manageable proportions, the persons chosen in the quadrennial November election are expected to do the impossible. As they enter the Oval Office, new presidents are likely to have only a passing familiarity with the complicated problems facing them. Who could expect them to personally comprehend all the subtleties of history and culture of each of the 150-plus nations they will have to deal with? They are unlikely to have been privy to in-depth information on the U.S. conventional and nuclear arsenals they will command. As we noted earlier, Harry Truman did not even know that the atomic bomb existed until after his inauguration. Few things have befuddled presidents more than the intricacies of domestic and international economic policy. While professional economists have both advised and chastised presidents, none has ever sat behind the desk in the Oval Office. Even these common deficiencies among presidents have done little to lessen public expectations that they should each exercise bold, aggressive, and enlightened leadership in these complicated areas. Presidents need experts to educate them. Generalists on the White House staff rarely have the training to provide in-depth analyses comparable to those available through careerists in the departments and the executive office of the president.

In this chapter we will examine some of the major components of the system of specialists at the president's disposal including the cabinet, the National Security Council, the Office of Management and the Budget, the Council of Economic Advisors, the Treasury Department, and the Federal Reserve Board. Finally, since Vice President Walter Mondale held an unusually central role as an advisor to President Jimmy Carter, we shall also look into the potentials of the vice presidency to see if Arthur Schlesinger, Jr.'s suggestion that it be done away with by constitutional amendment might be a bit too hasty.[1]

# THE CABINET:
## SERVANTS OF MANY MASTERS

"A man," the Bible reminds the faithful, "cannot serve two masters. He will love one and hate the other." Imagine the frustration of cabinet secretaries who must demonstrate loyalty to the president who appointed them even though they also owe allegiance to such demanding masters as the department staff and bureaucrats, congressional committees that draw up their budgets, interest groups affected by the department, and personal career goals that might well include a stay in the White House for themselves sometime in the future. Presidents may be able to expect their staffers to be good and faithful servants, but they soon learn to question the motives of cabinet-level appointees as their advice makes its way to the Oval Office.

Neither the Constitution nor statute law provided for a cabinet. George Washington initiated the practice of meeting with his four major department heads (justice, state, treasury, and war) to seek their collective advice on a broad range of issues both foreign and domestic. The experiment did not pan out as Washington had hoped. By the summer of 1793 Jefferson had resigned to build his own political party. Treasury Secretary Hamilton took his leave not long after that. To replace these outspoken secretaries, Washington settled on cooler heads with more pedestrian skills. Because the new secretaries were men of lesser stature, Washington did not consult with them as he had with Hamilton, Jefferson, Knox, and Randolph. Instead, he considered the replacements merely as administrators and relegated them to strictly departmental chores.[2] In most every administration since, presidents have wrestled with the roles they wanted the cabinet to play.

Today's cabinet consists of thirteen department secretaries and presidents may invite others such as the U.N. ambassador to huddle with them as a collective advisory system. If status is to be measured, as it often is in the business world by the trappings of one's office, the cabinet meeting room near the White House rose garden and close to the Oval Office would seem to indicate that cabinet members are among the principal advisors to the president. Traditionally, they have been viewed this way. But appearances can be deceiving.

Tradition has labeled the cabinet as the major collective advisors to the president, so each administration seems to feel honor bound to profess its allegiance to a "strong" cabinet. It could well be that presidents fully intend to reinvigorate the cabinet but find that these moves, while theoretically attractive, are practically unworkable. Prior to his election in 1968, Richard Nixon called for a powerful cabinet capable of standing its ground in the face of pressure from the White House staff:[3]

> I don't want a government of yes-men. . . . [I want] a cabinet made up of the ablest men in America, leaders in their own right and not merely by virtue of appointment . . . men who will command the public's respect and the President's attention by the power of their intellect and the force of their ideas.
>
> Such men are not attracted to an Administration in which all credit is gathered to the White House, and the blame parcelled out to scapegoats or in which high officials are asked to dance like puppets on a presidential string.

Like his predecessors, however, Nixon learned that the political factors involved in selecting cabinet secretaries often rendered their advice suspect and self-serving.

## BUILDING A CABINET: FACTORS IN THE SELECTION

Since the daily duty of cabinet secretaries is to administer massive federal programs with multibillion-dollar budgets, logic would seem to dictate that nominees be chosen on the basis of their demonstrated budgeting and management skills. Administrative skills,[4] quite to the contrary, are often a secondary factor in appointments. A theoretical want-ad announcing a cabinet opening would seek a person of experience in the problems the department has to handle. The candidate should also be well respected by the public and hopefully members of Congress with whom he or she will be bartering. Samuel Huntington would demand even more than that:[5]

> [he should be] a man of dedication, acting and thinking purely in terms of the needs of the office. . . . the Secretary must be a man of policy. His greatest needs are breadth, wisdom, insight, and above all, judgment. He is neither operator, administrator nor commander. But he is a policy maker.

In the tight budget years of the 1980s, domestic programs from the Department of Health and Human Services (HHS, formerly HEW), Housing and Urban Development (HUD), the Department of Transportation (DOT), and the Department of Education will require careful shepherding through Congress. Secretaries will have to be salespersons, but they must also be accomplished practitioners of the give and take that is politics.

REPAYING SUPPORTERS. Given the complexities of the duties, presidents must exercise great care in finding people who are up to the tasks. Too often, however, appointments are made with past or future elections in mind. Appointments to the cabinet have been a long-standing reward for deserving campaign aides. The job of postmaster general, before postal reorganization removed it from the cabinet, traditionally went to the campaign manager of the successful presidential candidate. Later, though Winton Bount was named postmaster under Nixon, key campaign aides John Mitchell and Maurice Stans were rewarded with positions as attorney general and secretary of commerce. No doubt Jimmy Carter's decision to appoint Joseph Califano HEW secretary was due not merely to his key role as architect of the Great Society domestic program under Johnson, but was also Carter's way of repaying Califano for serving as a bridge between the Kennedy and Johnson segments of the party around the time of the Democratic national convention in 1976.[6]

Powerful interest groups use their organizations' finances and clout to assure the election of "their" candidates. In turn, a president must pay homage to the groups that were instrumental in his election by setting aside "their seats" in the cabinet. At the very least, major interest groups, whether they strongly supported a candidate or not, expect the right to veto unacceptable appointees. For this reason, labor secretaries are commonly union leaders themselves or persons that "big labor" will accept. The Nixon administration, for example, wanted to tap Daniel Patrick Moynihan to preside over the Labor Department, but the White House backed down when AFL-CIO chief George Meany complained publicly about Moynihan's "lack of experience."[7] When another vacancy developed at the Labor Department later in the Nixon years, the president's talent scouts recommended the president of the New York Building Trades (labor) Council Peter Brennan to be the next secretary of labor. As with most of the things Nixon proposed to do, Meany was singularly unimpressed. He was unwilling to fight Brennan's nomination in the Senate mainly because he wanted nothing to do with a squabble over confirmation of any labor "honcho."[8]

There are numerous other examples of occupational groupings and geographic regions commonly having "their" secretary. Department chiefs in the commerce and treasury departments are invariably tied to business and banking circles. Interior secretaries like Stewart Udall of Arizona (Kennedy administration), Walter Hickel of Alaska (Nixon administration), Cecil Andrus of Idaho during the Carter years, and Reagan appointee James Watt came from Western states with extensive open land. Regionally chosen candidates for the cabinet normally have a political following of their own in that locale so they have become accustomed to independence and freedom of action. They are likely to resent efforts by the White House to tinker with the operations of their department or limit their access to the president. Meddling presidential aides and hermetically sealed doors to the Oval Office have encouraged many a proud cabinet secretary to pack his bags and return to personal campaign politics, business, or private life.

CIVIL RIGHTS FACTORS. Since the early 1960s, a potential cabinet member's attitudes or record on civil rights issues can be a factor in his selection. When President John Kennedy was considering Arkansas Senator J. William Fulbright of the Foreign Relations Committee for the position of secretary of state, his voting record on civil rights legislation[9] and his attitudes toward the conflicts between Israel and her Arab neighbors made him totally unacceptable to both Black and Jewish leaders in the Democratic Party. Later, when Jimmy Carter prepared to appoint his old friend Judge Griffin Bell as attorney general, groups like the NAACP, the Urban League, and the Southern Christian Leadership Conference demanded that they be given assurances in public that the Georgia federal judge would be active in the area of civil rights in the tradition of previous Democratic attorneys general.[10] While the complaints about Bell could not be based on his previous record, they were understandable since the attorney general is in such a sensitive position with respect to civil rights. The Fulbright case, though, demonstrates that a negative civil rights record could be used to disqualify a person for *any* cabinet position. Ronald Reagan's nominee for attorney general made it a point to say that his participation in an all-male club should not bar his confirmation and the Senate agreed.

The majorities that elect Democratic presidents are created by piecing together numerous minority Americans. "Hyphenated" Americans (Irish-Americans, Polish-Americans, Spanish-speaking-Americans, etc.) and activist women have constituted a mother lode of votes for the party at least since the 1960s and as far back as the 1930s in some cases. As a result, Democratic presidents have a special incentive to include these types of people in their cabinets. The recent Carter cabinet included three women: Patricia Roberts Harris (first of HUD, then HHS), Juanita Kreps (Department of Commerce), and Shirley Hufstedler (Department of Education). Mrs. Harris and U.N. ambassadors Andrew Young and later Donald McHenry were blacks. Each of them owed both allegiances to the president and their own natural constituencies. Mrs. Harris could serve as a good case in point. She was openly critical of the president's fiscal 1980 budget for slighting HUD programs because it would "risk the disaffection" of blacks and others politically important to the administration. Her job, as she envisioned it, was to "speak for people who are unable to provide for their own needs and who have been disadvantaged by this society."[11]

Since both Presidents Nixon and Ford sought to forge a new Republican majority,[12] they were also sensitive to ethnic factors, and they shamelessly courted the Catholic ethnics of Eastern European descent in particular. Nixon talent scout Frederic Malek admitted that faulty staff work led to the selection of Transportation Secretary Claude Brinegar, who turned out to be a German Protestant rather than the Irish Catholic Malek's detectives thought they had unearthed.[13] Gerald Ford's cabinet, likewise, was a microcosm of Oscar Handlin's melting pot. Included in top positions in the Ford administration were Jewish Attorney General Edward Levi, black Secretary of Transportation William Coleman, woman Secretary of Housing Carla Hills, and Southern academician David Matthews at Health, Education, and Welfare.[14] In each of the cases, no doubt the administration had one eye on their vitaes and the other on the groups they represented. In contrast, Ronald Reagan drew fire for having only one woman (U.N. ambassador) and only one black (HUD Secretary) selected for his cabinet-level appointments.

MENDING FENCES. To mend fences after a tough nomination battle, a new president may decide to appoint either his opponent or someone representing his wing of the party to the cabinet. With this idea in mind, Richard Nixon chose George Romney to serve as HUD secretary so that he could speak for liberals and the needs of the cities because the administration had few ties to either group. Romney had been a major opponent to Nixon in 1968. By placing him in a responsible government position, Nixon, no doubt, hoped to mute any criticism that the former Michigan governor might be inclined to make. In hopes of reestablishing rapport with farmers, a normally Republican group angered by the "big farm" policies under Ezra Taft Benson in the Eisenhower years, Nixon chose Clifford Hardin as his agriculture secretary, calling him "a man who can speak eloquently for farmers, for rural America and agriculture to the President."[15]

Future presidents may follow Jimmy Carter's recent philosophy and go up to Capitol Hill to find potential cabinet members. It makes good sense for post-Watergate presidents to nod respectfully toward Congress in this way. "Outsider" Carter's transition team suggested Washington State Representative Brock Adams to head the Department of Transportation and encouraged him to select Minnesota farmer and Representative Bob Bergland to run the Department of Agriculture.[16] Likewise, Ronald Reagan tapped a three term Representative, David Stockman, to run OMB which is usually considered a cabinet-level position even though, like the U.N. ambassador's job, it has few administrative duties. Since presidential credibility has become chronicly suspect, it helps a president to have former members of Congress marching up to the Hill to defend White House initiatives and to beg for the budgets the administration seeks.

Finally, presidents seek out cabinet members who promise to be compatible with the White House staff, other members of the cabinet, and, of course, the president himself. Potential personality clashes must be taken into account in making cabinet choices. In 1972, for example, Richard Nixon felt that John Connally,[17] whom he had considered as his likely successor in the White House after 1976, should replace Secretary of State William Rogers. The idea was eventually scrapped, though, because the president found it impossible to imagine National Security Assistant Dr. Henry Kissinger working well with Connally given the strong personalities involved. The highly visible secretary of state job could have been an ideal public platform from which to launch a campaign for the White House. Nevertheless, effective foreign policy required that the president's two key foreign policy advisors be able to live together in peace.

LEADERSHIP IMPLICATIONS. It has become harder and harder for recent presidents to find capable managers and political types to serve in the cabinet. Proven managers must sacrifice comfortable salaries and the life-style they bring for the comparative penury of government service. Likewise, political figures, accustomed to personal clout, soon tire of being outsiders at the White House, so, even if they do accept a position, they resign all too quickly.[18] Respected president watchers Nelson Polsby and Stephen Hess, as they read the political tea leaves for the 1980s, suggested that presidents would be less beholden to others in the future selection of their cabinets.[19] Polsby surmised that voters no longer listen to political parties or interest groups as they once did in deciding how to cast their votes for president. Instead, he argues, it is the mass media that market candidates and that marketing sells the voter; the President need not worry about the parties and interest groups as much in choosing department heads. Should their crystal ball gazing prove correct, presidents would stand a much better chance of exercising leadership over the bureaucracies via the secretaries they appoint. Whether Polsby and Hess are correct or not, it is clear that their sentiments did not invade the Ford or Carter cabinet selection process. Carter's appointments were, in fact, a model of traditional considerations. Ronald Reagan's appointments, on the other hand, would tend to support Hess and Polsby's assertions.

## RECENT CABINET ROLES: ADVISORS?

Almost as if required by ritual, recent presidents have entered the Oval Office promising to cut staff and reinvigorate the advisory role of the cabinet. In 1968, the Nixon transition team vowed that the White House staff would be reduced in both size and stature. They were determined not to erect another Sherman Adams-type operation or even a successor to the procedures under Johnson's domestic affairs leader Joseph Califano. Nixon learned about Califano's reported tendencies to ride herd over distinguished cabinet members many years his senior. "There will be no repetition of this," Nixon warned, "where power would flow back to the Cabinet level departments from the White House staff."[20] However, cabinet members who had been ushered in with great fanfare soon found it virtually impossible to get their views to the president.

Historically, presidents have often had second thoughts about taking advice from the cabinet members they appointed. Andrew Jackson resorted to meetings with outsiders (the kitchen cabinet) rather than depending on the collective wisdom of his highest-level appointees. Woodrow Wilson's cabinet meetings quickly degenerated into gum flapping over the inconsequential. One of Wilson's cabinet members recalled, "nothing talked of at Cabinet meetings would interest a nation, a family, or a child."[21] By the time Franklin Roosevelt took the oath of office, the collective advisory role of the cabinet had all but disappeared from the modern presidency. Leadership and administrative control over the departments under FDR became part of the White House turf.

Cabinet meetings in the Roosevelt years were, according to Interior Secretary Harold Ickes's recollections, "pleasant affairs; but we skim only the surface of routine matters."[22] Henry Stimson, secretary of war, noted that the *real* value of cabinet meetings was the access that members had after the meetings ended. It was then that they could meet with the president individually and discuss their views and problems candidly with him.

For a short time, it seemed as if Roosevelt's successor, Harry Truman, would reinvigorate the cabinet. After all, he needed advice from the Roosevelt holdovers since he felt ill prepared to handle problems he had only learned about upon entering the Oval Office as president. Initially, Truman hired a secretary to take minutes and distribute agendas prior to meetings to aid members of the cabinet in preparing for discussions. But soon, cabinet meetings returned to limbo as Truman's preference for individual contacts, born of his Senate days, reemerged.

When General Eisenhower became president, he attempted to impose the order of the military on what had become chaotic cabinet politics. In place of the informal secretary arrangement Truman had used, Ike created a formal new position of cabinet "secretary." This aide went even farther than his predecessor from the Truman administration. Not only did he take notes and circulate meeting agendas, but he was responsible for preparing "cabinet papers" that presented proposals for discussion and presidential action. Eisenhower envisioned his cabinet members as field generals responsible for their own theaters of war or departments. Tactics, then, were essentially their business, but, as a group, they provided strategic advice. The president did not assume that cabinet secretaries were automatically carrying out his directives so, after each cabinet meeting, the special cabinet "secretary" met with a group of departmental assistant secretaries to check on compliance. Just to make sure, every couple of months a cabinet meeting was set aside strictly for "action reports," in which department heads demonstrated the extent to which they were following directives announced in cabinet meetings.[23] Ike was determined to lead, not to follow, the bureaucracies. In this respect he was an activist.

The New Frontiersmen had little use for the cabinet advisory system. President Kennedy appointed assistant secretaries in some departments before he appointed the secretaries. He selected the department heads almost as an afterthought or because every other president had them. Close Kennedy aide Theodore Sorensen said that the administration only held cabinet meetings because they were traditional and the public expected them.[24] The president saw little sense in the secretary of commerce and the postmaster discussing relations with the Soviets. Likewise it seemed ludicrous to him to have the secretaries of state and defense wrestling with domestic unemployment. When he interviewed the original cabinet members, he said that he planned to meet with them, but when he did call cabinet meetings they were fruitless exercises. The more deeply engrossed he became in foreign affairs, the greater the distance he kept from his domestic cabinet secretaries. His attitude toward the collective advice role of the cabinet was plain to his staffers; as one aide remembers shortly after the inauguration in 1961, Kennedy asked, "Just what the hell good does the Cabinet do anyway?"[25]

Lyndon Johnson found himself in a situation similar to Harry Truman's and responded to his sudden role as president by leaning heavily on cabinet holdovers from the late president's administration. Initially, at least, Johnson seemed to see more value in the cabinet than Kennedy. Secretaries, as individuals, became more important than they had ever been under the man who appointed them. In the Truman and Eisenhower tradition, he called regular cabinet meetings with predetermined agendas. Evidently, only Johnson saw much value in them, though. As one White House aide quipped, "Cabinet meetings were akin to sitting with the preacher in the front parlor on Sunday." To everyone but the president, they were a painful experience.[26] As Vietnam and campaign politics enveloped Johnson's waking hours and the Great Society momentum began to stall on Capitol Hill, domestic concerns became less important to him. Cabinet meetings became occasions for Secretary of State Dean Rusk to give foreign affairs briefings and for the president to give his department heads new political campaign marching orders. Johnson did set aside Saturday mornings for domestic cabinet members to make appointments with him, but few of them took advantage of the opportunity. Although it may be surprising that secretaries passed up the chance for one-to-one discussions with the president, one cabinet member explained, "Johnson had the uncanny way of asking favors of you or giving you a number of political chores to do that you knew you didn't want and often couldn't carry out."[27] As a result, politically astute cabinet secretaries kept their distance because by 1968 it was becoming evident that Vietnam was making Johnson unelectable.

With experience in the Eisenhower administration to draw upon, Richard Nixon entered the White House advocating a return to a strong cabinet. To make his point, he paraded his appointees before national TV cameras to brag about their credentials and promised to consult with them. Within six months he had retreated behind a wall erected by Haldeman and the White House staff. He became so disenchanted with the tendency of the cabinet members to speak for their bureaucracies rather than for the White House that he proposed a governmental reorganization that would have reduced the number of cabinet-level departments from twelve to eight. Shrewdly, he left the traditionally powerful departments like defense, treasury, justice, and state untouched, but he suggested that all the rest be merged into four superdepartments: human resources, community development, natural resources, and economic development. This 1971 thrust was blunted by guerrilla warfare in Congress. Congressional committees were not about to permit the president to adjust their jurisdictions by merging departments. Interest groups that had developed contacts at the highest levels in each of the vulnerable departments allied with their friends in Congress to "deep six" the Nixon plans. Richard Nathan noted that the president got what he wanted anyway by simply placing two hats on the heads of four cabinet members. Each maintained the departmental duties, but each also became a White House counselor to oversee the other related departments in the areas of human resources, community development, and so on.[28] Although Congress and the interest groups fumed, there was little they could do about the White House dodge.

Former Representative and interim President Gerald R. Ford had little time in office to become disenchanted with cabinet meetings. Like Truman, Eisenhower, and Johnson, he used a cabinet secretary (James Cannon) who drew up formal agendas. Ford's experiences as House minority leader shaped his consensus style of leadership in the White House. To him, cabinet meetings became a mechanism for gauging the views of the department heads on a broad range of issues. Department heads also learned of initiatives the president was planning or innovations he had already implemented at the cabinet meetings.[29]

Jimmy Carter's fanfare about reinvigorating the role of the cabinet proved to be little more than rhetoric. No doubt his intentions were to develop a mechanism for using the cabinet more. Aide Jack Watson became cabinet secretary, and the formal trappings of elaborate meetings were adopted. In an attempt to demonstrate the openness of the new administration, Carter ordered some of the early cabinet meetings televised. Obviously, little could be accomplished in this format since no department head would be willing to air his dirty linen in public or criticize his colleagues from other departments. Gradually the status of the cabinet began to tumble. In July 1979, the president requested that all cabinet secretaries tender their resignations.[30] Loyalty was a major factor in determining whether a secretary would be retained; cabinet survivors and future appointees could hardly be expected to be even the slightest bit critical of administration policy in cabinet meetings or anywhere else for that matter.

Most presidents eventually come to the conclusion that they can live without cabinet meetings. When they are called, they are simply being used for public relations or to give the departments their marching orders. Leadership-oriented presidents quickly become disenchanted with the cabinet. They want advice when they ask for it, but they also want the freedom to disregard it if they prefer.

Still, seasoned political veterans in the cabinet can provide a president one thing that the most dedicated and informed White House staffer often cannot, and that is a sense of perspective gained from years of experience and political savvy. Certain cabinet members by virtue of the department they head are more likely to have easy access to the president and be called upon for advice. The original department heads that Washington brought together as the first cabinet (war, treasury, state, and justice) now constitute what Thomas Cronin has called the president's *inner cabinet*.[31] Strategic information and crisis management advice from them gets careful hearing in the Oval Office. Since the president is normally very careful in making appointments to head these four departments, it is likely that the views of these secretaries will mirror his. Also, members of the inner cabinet are likely to be Washington veterans like Cyrus Vance, Edmund Muskie, and John Foster Dulles, secretaries of state for Jimmy Carter and Dwight Eisenhower. By contrast, the "outer cabinet" often has less experienced newcomers for whom a position in the cabinet is a step up from a metropolitan city hall or from the governor's chair in some statehouse.[32]

## CABINET MEMBERS AS ADVOCATES

It would be reasonable to assume that, since the president appoints the department heads, they would basically see eye to eye with their mentor at the White House. In fact, however, relationships between a president and the cabinet secretaries often break down in a matter of months. Friction can normally be traced to one of several bureaucratic and political realities. First, the cabinet member begins to adopt the views of his bureaucracy whether or not they agree with the president's philosophies. On the other hand, as leaders in their own right, secretaries possess both self-confidence and self-esteem, which limits their willingness to bend when they come into conflict with the president.

Members of the White House staff have a tendency to look down on cabinet secretaries. Once, for example, when Nixon White House aide John Erlichman was participating in a 1972 picture-taking session at the White House, he bragged, "The President and the staff rarely see the Cabinet," except on special occasions. "We only see them at the annual Christmas party; then they go off and marry the natives."[33] Those "natives" who staff the bureaucracies provide the expertise cabinet members must draw upon to run their departments. They learn the ropes in their new jobs from their staffs, and quickly realize that they cannot run their departments without unflagging staff support. Often, then, the secretary becomes the mouthpiece for the sentiments of the department in contacts with the president and the White House staff. As Richard Nathan so neatly phrased it, every secretary undergoes "the ritualistic courting and mating process with the bureaucracy."[34] Hugh Heclo suggests in his book, *A Government of Strangers,* that it is in the best interest of the secretary to battle for his bureaucrats:[35]

> Fighting your counterparts in other departments creates confidence and support beneath you. . . . Less politically effective executives may be person- ally admired by civil servants but have little to offer in return for bureaucratic support. [A secretary was described by one of his bureau chiefs] "He had charisma . . . a lot of the civil servants around here liked him. But he never got a grip on the department. He didn't really fight for what was needed and if he made a decision it was because he got maneuvered into it by his staff.

Department secretaries with their own prior political power base or support of their department personnel can frustrate the president who appointed them. Frank- lin Roosevelt complained about the difficulties that a president can have in trying to bring the major bureaucracies into line:[36]

> The Treasury is so large and far-flung and ingrained in its practices that I find it almost impossible to get the action and results I want even with Henry [Morgenthau] there. But, Treasury is nothing compared with the State Department. You should go through the experience of trying to get any changes in thinking policy and action of the career diplomats and then you'd know what a real problem was. But the Treasury and State Department put together are nothing compared with the Na-a-vy. The admirals are really something to cope with and I should know. To change anything in the Na-a-vy is like punching a feather-bed. You punch it with your right hand and you punch it with your left until you are finally exhausted, and then you find the damn bed just as it was before you started punching.

Careerists in the departments can change the views of their new bosses on the issues that come within their jurisdiction. When this happens, the secretary may get into the nasty habit of publicly breaking with the president's policy line. Ironically, they are supposed to be the president's voice over the bureaucracy, but independ- ent secretaries can become headaches for the White House. A perfect case in point would be Nixon's Interior Secretary Walter Hickel. He was not the president's first choice, but Nixon caved in to pressures from Western Republicans to appoint him instead of Rodgers Morton from Maryland. The appointment also produced an- guished howls from environmentalists who feared that the former Alaskan governor (Hickel) would swing the weight of his new department behind the proposed Alaskan oil pipeline planned to stretch across some Northern wilderness lands.[37] Actually, Hickel swung the other way much to the dismay of the White House and the friends of big oil in Congress. Hickel's views on the pipeline were problem enough, but he compounded his transgressions by passionately expressing himself whenever the spirit moved him. In the Nixon administration, leaving the impression of being anything but a "team" player was tantamount to political suicide. Unfortunately for both Hickel and the administration, the interior secretary was to die a slow death. In April 1969 he delivered a polemic against the Federal Reserve and its tight money policies in a cabinet meeting. "The fiscal policy is wrong," he reportedly thundered. Obviously he was speaking out of his element as he should have said "monetary" policy. From the day of that performance on, he was labeled a troublemaker. Hickel personally hammered the final nail in his own political coffin when he wrote a May 6, 1970 letter to the president asking him to muzzle Vice President Agnew after his Kent State University speech rebuking the nation's youth. The letter also contained criticism of administration policy in Cambodia and complaints about the fact that cabinet members could not get through Chief of Staff Haldeman to see the president. The whole series of complaints might have blown over but for the fact that one of Hickel's aides, without his superior's approval, leaked the letter to the press.[38] From that moment it was clear that Hickel would have to go; the only unresolved question was when. Disposing of the former Alaskan governor proved to be a ticklish proposition.

## SELF-ESTEEM, RESHUFFLING, AND RESIGNATIONS

Since many cabinet members are important figures in their own right, they are accustomed to giving rather than receiving orders. While presidents often seek seasoned political veterans for key cabinet positions, they can run into serious difficulties when they choose men with political constituencies of their own. Abraham Lincoln, for example, made the tactical error of choosing his opponent for the Republican presidential nomination in 1860, William Seward, to be his secretary of state. Seward complained both publicly and in private that the new administration had no foreign policy. In response Lincoln, reminding Seward who was to lead in foreign affairs, said simply, "If a policy is needed, I will write it."

FORCED RESIGNATIONS. Although cabinet members may become the bane of a president's existence, he rarely fires them. Normally, asking for their resignation is sufficient. Requests of this sort reach the cabinet members through White House channels. As was noted earlier, disposing of Walter Hickel became a thorny problem for the Nixon administration. As a political favor to Alaska's Senator Ted Stevens, the axe was permitted to fall on Hickel only after the November 1970 senatorial elections. Stevens feared that if Hickel were discharged too soon, he might decide to run against his fellow Alaska Republican in the party primary.[39] Still, the administration kept Hickel on the hot seat. When the election was over Hickel began complaining again. He told Attorney General Mitchell that all the speculation from the White House that he was soon to get his walking papers was disrupting his department.[40]

> I can take anything . . . but the White House says Hickel's going to get fired or Ziegler says, "we're thinking about this." Now look, you either cut this

horse - - - - out or fire me. I can take it, but it is disrupting my department. The only man who could ask me to quit would be the President.

To further make his point that he would leave only at the request of the president, Hickel told a CBS-TV interviewer about his meeting with Mitchell. "I am going," he said, "with an arrow in my heart, not a bullet in my back."[41] The following day Hickel had only his fourth appointment with the president, but it was to be his last. The president personally asked for and received his resignation. Shortly thereafter, Frederic Malek presided over housecleaning in Hickel's department and six heads rolled from among Hickel's staff.[42]

SECRETARY CHOOSES TO RESIGN. When cabinet secretaries decide to resign of their own accord, they can be making a politically damaging decision for the White House.[43] The October 1973 decision of Attorney General Elliot Richardson to resign rather than obey President Nixon's directive to dismiss Watergate Special Prosecutor Archibald Cox created quite a bit of political fallout for the administration at a time when it could least afford it. Richardson, with his own career and credibility at stake, chose to step down rather than to do the president's bidding. During his own confirmation hearings Richardson had promised members of the Senate Judiciary Committee that Cox would be given a free hand.[44] He had no intention of reneging on his promise even though Chief of Staff Alexander Haig reminded him, "This is an order from your commander-in-chief."[45] By the time the dust had settled Assistant Attorney General William Ruckelshaus was fired for refusing to remove Cox and eventually Solicitor General (number three in the Justice Department) Robert Bork axed Cox. The entire incident, later dubbed the "Saturday Night Massacre," along with press suggestions that Cox became vulnerable because he had evidence implicating the president, did even more to damage what was left of Nixon's credibility.

Respected secretaries with impeccable credentials may become so disenchanted with a White House policy that they take leave of the administration and publicly criticize those "misguided" positions. Carter's low-profile but highly respected Secretary of State Cyrus Vance gradually became worried about the increasingly "Cold War" directions that U.S. foreign policy was taking in the late 1970s. While he expressed these views internally, being ever the loyal trooper, he made no public complaint to that effect. Within three weeks of his resignation as secretary of state, however, he voiced these serious misgivings about the drift of the Carter foreign policy in a commencement speech at Harvard University. Vance, who was the most respected member of the Carter foreign policy team, both in the United States and Europe, added his voice to a growing chorus of criticism of the administration policy. It certainly reflected poorly on the Carter White House, which was gearing up for the 1980 general election, that the secretary of state found he could not serve out the full four years as he had planned.[46]

Presidents still tend to seek advice from their "inner-cabinet" secretaries individually, but it is likely that meaningful cabinet meetings have outlived their usefulness. A fear lurks in the minds of presidents that secretaries might be tempted to become competitors for leadership in their policy areas with the person who hired them. As long as presidents feel political pressures dictating the selection of many of their cabinet members, they are likely to be suspicious of those secretaries and their bureaucracies.

# FOREIGN AFFAIRS ADVISORY SYSTEM

A president's suspicion of bureaucrats could be justified in foreign affairs since in few areas of his job is the president more dependent on bureaucratic professionals and advice. Since World War II and the breakup of the European empires into numerous developing nations, handling international affairs has become an almost hopelessly complex and time-consuming problem for the occupants of the Oval Office. Foreign policy, defense, and intelligence communities keep the president abreast of the information and analysis that becomes involved in making day-to-day and crisis decisions. How can a president maintain control and exercise his decision-making responsibilities when the data he receives comes from bureaucratic competitors? Each has its own set of bureaucratic blinders and sees decisions in terms of its specialties. A president needs competing views; but the advice that each group gives normally promotes the positions prevalent within its bureacracy.

Graham Allison has offered three useful models[47] for understanding the thinking involved when presidents and their foreign affairs advisors interact to produce national security decisions. His *Rational Actor* model is based on the presupposition commonly held by historians that decision makers rationally calculate the advantages of options based on a set of generally accepted national goals and judgments about the way in which civilized nations should act. As an alternative Allison suggests the existence of an *Organizational Process* model. This view holds that each bureaucracy offers options in terms of its standard operating procedures (SOP). When, for example, the decision is made to bomb particular targets, the air force has "how-to-do-it" manuals that would encompass situations similar to the one at hand. Likewise, the State Department has standard procedures for handling diplomatic negotiations. The "manual" can often be a bureaucratic "sacred cow." When President Kennedy attempted to implement a naval blockade of Cuba to stop Russian ships from landing missile cargoes, he had almost as much problem with the navy foot dragging as he had with the Russians.[48] On October 21, the day the NSC placed its stamp of approval on a blockade, Kennedy asked Admiral George Anderson, chief of naval operations, to describe normal procedures for such operations. The request produced the following exchange between the president and the admiral:[49]

> Each approaching ship would be signaled to stop for boarding and inspection. If the ship fails to respond, a shot would be fired across the bow. If there was still no satisfactory response, a shot would be fired into the rudder to cripple but not to sink it. "You are certain that can be done," the President inquired. "Yes sir," the admiral responded.

Even though Kennedy had followed the proper amenities in discussing the matter with the admiral, the navy was still disturbed with the White House because the president, before deciding on a blockade, was personally directing the movement of each American ship likely to cross the path of the Russian vessels. This was, as Graham Allison pointed out, an unprecedented breach of SOP. Not only were civilians giving tactical directions to field naval officers but they were also bypassing the normal chain of command. Further complicating matters, the president had ordered a delay in implementing the operations to give Soviet Premier Khrushchev time to respond without forcing him to react to his vessels coming under fire.

In an attempt to make sure that the less than enthusiastic naval officers were following the White House directives, Defense Secretary McNamara was dispatched to check with Admiral Anderson. Elie Abel, in his book on the missile crisis, recounts the sharp encounter between the two. At first McNamara asked a number of questions including "Who would make the first intercept?" "Were there Russian-speaking officers on board to intercept ships?" "How would subs be handled?" "What would he do if a Soviet captain refused to answer questions about his cargo?" Undoubtedly angered and frustrated by this barrage, Admiral Anderson raised the *Manual of Naval Regulations* and waved it under McNamara's nose yelling, "It's all in there." The Secretary shot back, "I don't give a damn what John Paul Jones would have done; I want to know what you are going to do now." The confrontation between the president's emissary and the naval commander ended with Anderson's caustic jab, "Now, Mr. Secretary, if you and your deputy will go back to your office, the Navy will run the blockade."[50] No one could have stated a president's problems in getting things done his way any better. Presidents may give orders; but bureaucracies have *their* ways of carrying them out.

BUREAUCRATIC COMPETITION. Even though bureaucracies can frustrate a president with their SOPs as the organizational process model suggests, Allison contends that, when a president seeks advice from bureaucratic experts, members of each department and agency will compete for the chance to shape the policy. Allison labels this conflict among advisors to enhance the status of their particular department the *Bureaucratic Politics* model. Diplomats will favor negotiations as the first-line solution to international problems. There is a tendency among military minds to envision some sort of force. The air force will suggest bombing, while the navy would be partial to blockades. Their advice is colored, unwittingly or not, by their expertise and training. As each offers advice, it seeks to have its bureaucracy at the forefront of both the policy making and the implementation. It is not uncommon to see them clashing openly when called in to larger forums by the president as he seeks solutions to perplexing international problems. Once again, the missile crisis provides a good example of how bureaucratic politics can complicate a president's life and policies.

The Air Force and the CIA clashed over which should handle the reconnaisance overflights of Cuba to see if the reported missiles were actually being installed. Information had been filtering into the State Department and elsewhere from the Cuban exile community that large Soviet ships were riding high in the waters of the Caribbean (a sign of space-consuming rather than heavy cargo) on their way to Cuba. Overflights were required to document the evidence. Still, there was a ten-day delay between the decision that overflights were needed and the commencement of the flights themselves. Even though the very survival of the nation could have been at stake, bureaucratic politics intervened. At the October 4 meeting of the Committee on Overhead Reconnaissance, the decision was made to begin the flights over western Cuba. State Department representatives were quick to remind all others present about the U-2 aircraft shot down in similar flights over Russia in 1959. The Pentagon argued to have uniformed officers handle the flights rather than a civilian like Francis Gary Powers who had been shot down in 1959. The CIA argued that "intelligence gathering" operations of this sort were under its jurisdiction. The director also argued that CIA U-2s could better avoid Soviet surface-to-air missiles than could the air force version of the spy aircraft. In the interim, the State Department continued to push for a somewhat less risky method of gathering the needed intelligence data. The battle between the CIA and the Air Force was finally resolved by having Air Force pilots trained to fly CIA U-2s. It was October 16, a full twelve days after the decision had been made to use aircraft for photo reconnaissance, before the president received the first fruits of that decision.

Too many presidents seem to learn the hard way that intelligence assessments are often overly optimistic. President Kennedy only became skeptical of his institutional advisors after being escorted up the garden path by the CIA at the time of the ill-fated Bay of Pigs invasion. The administration produced a hopelessly flawed plan partly due to its dependence on severe miscalculations being provided as analysis by the CIA. Among the major miscalculations, Irving Janis noted the following:[51]

(a) that the invasion couldn't be traced back to the U.S. so there would be little diplomatic fallout,

(b) that the Cuban Air Force could be knocked out of action before the landing began,

(c) that the 1,400 exile Cubans in the Invasion force would fight vigorously even if no American forces were involved,

(d) that Castro's army was so weak that the invaders could quickly establish a beachhead,

(e) that the invasion would ignite the Cuban underground which could then easily topple Castro, and

(f) that if the forces did not succeed immediately they could simply retreat into the Escambray Mountains to reinforce guerrilla units holding out against Castro.

Each of these assumptions was fraught with half-truths, total misconceptions, and a large share of unwarranted optimism. First, was it reasonable to assume that a 1,400-man operation that was CIA trained in Nicaragua and supplied through Guatemala could have been kept a secret from the entire world? Was it likely that aged B-26 bombers based in Nicaragua could do more than merely cripple the Cuban Air Force since they were slated to return in one round trip to their home base? In fact, half of them were shot down and their camouflaged markings didn't cover up their origins. The exiled Cubans were not as eager to fight alone as the president had been misled into believing.[52] The "freedom fighters" had been told that they were merely the vanguard of a much larger invasion force, which, of course, never materialized. The presuppositions that Castro's army could not handle the invasion and that the anti-Castro underground could topple the bearded revolutionary leader proved grossly inaccurate and misleading. CIA Director Allen Dulles later admitted that the underground distrusted the agency and that CIA analysts did not expect underground cooperation. Finally, and most ludicrous of all, the CIA assured Kennedy and his advisors that, should the invaders get into difficulties, they could fade back into the Escambray Mountains. They neglected to tell the president, and no one even took a map out to check, that the second site they selected, the Bay of Pigs, was eighty miles from the original, which was a short distance from the Escambrays. From the Bay of Pigs, the invaders had two choices, fall back into the ocean or try to negotiate their way eighty miles through swamps and jungle to reach the mountains.

These missile crisis and Bay of Pigs examples tend to point up several serious difficulties a president has in working with information and advice coming from the foreign affairs bureaucracies. Kennedy was initially overawed by the CIA, so he and his advisors neglected to probe deeply enough. Janis suggests that Secretary of State Rusk asked few penetrating questions during the planning stages of the Bay of Pigs invasion.[53] Similarly, he complains that not a single Cuban affairs desk officer at the State Department[54] was privy to the plans or even asked to assess the potentials of plans of that sort. Even though Arthur Schlesinger, Jr., a respected historian and White House aide, questioned the value of an invasion, Kennedy opted for the advice of the military specialists over the misgivings of a social scientist. Kennedy explained his decision saying simply, "you always assume that the military and intelligence people have some secret skills not available to mortals."[55] Because of his confidence in the expertise of the military and intelligence establishments, Kennedy stifled criticism, even if unintentionally, by neither circulating Schlesinger's memo against the invasion nor seeking reaction to Senator J. William Fulbright's vote in opposition to the plan. During that last straw vote on the plan when Fulbright expressed his misgivings, no one chimed in and the president asked for no response. Since both the majority present and the president himself seemed committed to the plan, not one other member of the group saw fit to criticize it.[56]

## LESSONS

His experience with the Bay of Pigs fiasco taught Kennedy a number of valuable lessons that he later applied in handling the missile crisis. Instead of depending on the unassailable wisdom of the military and the intelligence community, he created a fifteen-member executive committee to encourage questioning and the cross-fertilization of ideas. Unlike the formal meetings on the Bay of Pigs invasion, protocol was cast to the winds. According to Theodore Sorensen,[57]

> Protocol mattered little when the nation's life was at stake. . . . We were fifteen individuals on our own, representing the President and not different departments. Assistant Secretaries differed vigorously with their Secretaries. I participated much more freely than I ever had in an NSC meeting; and the absence of the president encouraged everybody to speak his mind.

In retrospect, Monday morning quarterbacks might have faulted the decisions that Kennedy made during the missile crisis, but few could argue that all the proper questions had not been asked. Only a few years earlier, Kennedy could have been blamed because he did not sufficiently examine the alternatives to the exile invasion of Cuba.

## NATIONAL SECURITY ADVISORY SYSTEM

Although Kennedy resorted to the temporary executive committee during the missile crisis, most presidents tend to institutionalize their foreign policy advisory system under the leadership of either their secretaries of state or national security assistants. Among recent administrations, the prototype of the secretary of state-centered advisory system would be John Foster Dulles during the Eisenhower years. He saw himself as key foreign policy advisor, not merely overseer of the striped-pants bureaucrats at Foggy Bottom. During the transition from the Truman administration to its Republican replacement, Dean Acheson, the outgoing secretary, prepared a set of transition books detailing departmental policies, programs, and procedures. Dulles was unimpressed and admitted that he was not concerned with administrative management, personnel problems, or current operations. Ironically, Dulles, more than any recent secretary of state, was forced to become enmeshed in departmental business because Senator Joseph McCarthy kept claiming that there were communists behind the doors, in the closets, and beneath the rugs at the State Department.

The prototype of the White House-centered advisory system headed by an influential national security assistant would be the one presided over by Dr. Henry Kissinger during the Nixon administration. Later in this chapter we shall examine these White House-centered operations. Suffice it to say here that, as presidents become disillusioned with the State Department (Kennedy called it a "bowl of jelly") the chances are great that they will turn to White House apparatus that better serves their needs. It is safe to assume that White House-centered advisory systems will predominate well into the 1980s.

THE SECRETARY OF STATE: CAN HE WEAR TWO HATS? It remains to be seen whether Ronald Reagan's appointment of Alexander Haig as Secretary of State and Richard V. Allen's (National Security Assistant) comments that he will not use his position to make policy, will help to invigorate the role of the State Department. Historically, any discussion about the major foreign policy advisors to various presidents includes the secretary of state as an integral part of the group. This may or may not be accurate depending on the particular president's confidence in his secretary. As ranking U.S. diplomat and administration spokesperson before congressional committees and in public forums, the secretary's time for discussing policy in the Oval Office is severely limited. His diverse duties and his position atop the most venerable foreign policy establishment, the Department of State, gives him a unique set of perspectives from which he can draw either to aid the president or to get in his way. Secretaries chosen for mainly "political reasons" are not always courteous enough to show their appreciation for getting the nod. Lincoln's experience with awarding the job to "Mr. Republican" William Seward makes this point. Woodrow Wilson also suffered political complications from his decision to name former Democratic presidential candidate and antiwar pacifist William Jennings Bryan as his secretary of state. Harry Truman settled on James Byrnes whom many had considered FDR's other choice for the 1944 vice-presidential spot on the ticket. Because he remained highly visible as secretary, both Byrnes and Truman found themselves caught in the cross-fire between Commerce Secretary Wallace, who thought Byrnes was too tough on the Russians, and Senator Arthur Vandenberg, who viewed the secretary as too soft on communism.[58] When a president chooses a secretary of state who has self-confidence born of past campaign experiences, he runs the risk that the secretary will speak his mind whether the president agrees or not.

Still, the president needs a forceful leader to ride herd on the State Department and to negotiate in the name of the United States. Someone must do the president's bidding in the corridors of state, or careerists might be left free to handle foreign policy merely as they see fit, without paying attention to guidelines being set by the White House. President Truman once felt it necessary to demonstrate who was in charge by saying, "I want to make it plain that the President of the United

States and not the second and third echelon in the State Department is responsible for foreign policy."[59]

Since the witch hunts of the McCarthy era in the 1950s, career foreign service personnel are subject to departmentwide paranoia. One need only read departmental reports to Congress to see that the name Foggy Bottom is often appropriate. In the 1950s, reports grew nebulous to avoid offending either the political left or the communist hunters on the right. Like any bureaucrats, State Department personnel seek to protect their jobs. To careerists, even appearing innovative can be frightening. Franklin Roosevelt once quipped that a foreign service officer (FSO) could hope to become an ambassador only if he were loyal to the service, acting so as to offend no one, and not seen intoxicated at public functions.[60] From the 1950s on, incoming FSOs were reminded to play it safe with the warning, "There are old FSOs and there are bold FSOs; but there are no old, bold FSOs."[61]

While the likelihood that the department would act on its own without White House direction may not be as great as it once was, presidents can be frustrated to see some crafty bureaucrats adjusting or evading White House policies. If the president has settled on a less forceful new secretary of state, the appointee may quickly become mired in departmental quicksand. Each department has its normal ways of doing things, its standard operating procedures. These may differ from the way in which the president wants things done. SOP invariably slows down reactions to crisis and the flow of information, analysis, and current data to the White House. Dean Rusk, one of those less assertive types, felt obligated to operate through departmental channels. In testimony before a Senate subcommittee on national security, Rusk said that he had often read in morning telegrams coming into the department specific questions he felt prepared to answer immediately. He understood that normally each telegram was to go through channels to the regional bureaus, down to the appropriate individual country desk at the State Department in Washington. "If it doesn't go down there," Rusk testified, "somebody feels he is being deprived of his participation in a matter of his responsibility." Eventually, the answer would come back to him through channels about ten days later. How valuable can a secretary be as an advisor to the president if he is unwilling to cut through departmental red tape to get things done quickly?[62]

It should come as no surprise then that presidents are increasingly tempted to depend less on the State Department and the secretary and more on close friends, outside advisors, special groups brought together to handle crisis situations, and their national security assistants. McGeorge Bundy as national security assistant carried more weight with John Kennedy than Dean Rusk could muster. Although Rusk's status improved under Lyndon Johnson, his successors at the helm of the State Department have often tended to take a back seat to their White House office competitors, the national security assistants.

STATE AND WHITE HOUSE STAFF COMPETITION. Early in the Nixon years, journalists indulged in the game of trying to determine whether Secretary of State Rogers or National Security Assistant Henry Kissinger was the power behind the throne in foreign affairs. In presidential politics, access is power. Kissinger attended deliberations on foreign policy in the Oval Office while Rogers was often excluded. Kissinger briefed the president each morning on overnight international developments while meetings between the secretary of state and his old friend Mr. Nixon became rare enough to become newsworthy.[63] A similar set of parlor games was popular during the Carter administration. Even though the president went to great pains to be pictured in thoughtful conversation with his secretary of state Cyrus Vance, and despite the fact that he often referred to Vance as his major foreign policy advisor, it was National Security Assistant Zbigniew Brzezinski who seemed to come out on top when the two disagreed over policy. His neo-Cold War approach to the Soviets gradually emerged as the administration's position partly because of Soviet adventurism in Africa, the Middle East, and especially Afghanistan in 1979-1980. Brzezinski's contacts with the president were more regular than were those of Secretary Vance, who spent his time in jet plane diplomacy in the Middle East, Africa, and elsewhere.[64] In both these cases of conflict between the secretary of state and the national security assistant, the one who emerged victorious was both the most vocal and controversial and who had the most regular contact with the president.

THE NATIONAL SECURITY COUNCIL AND THE INTELLIGENCE COMMUNITY. If competition among personalities and bureaucracies for the president's ear is not to become counterproductive to presidential leadership, some efforts are needed to bring the competing views together so that he can use them in making decisions. Immediately after World War II, the foreign affairs and military advisory process was reorganized in an attempt to adjust to U.S.-Soviet tensions, the growing role of air power in national security, the age of nuclear weapons, and the flood of intelligence information being produced. The first step in the changes was the National Security Act, which created the Department of Defense (with a civilian secretary), the Department of the Air Force, the Central Intelligence Agency, and the National Security Council. While Congress created each of them ostensibly to aid the president, they were also intended as legislative responses to Franklin Roosevelt's tendency toward "lone ranger" negotiating with the Soviets. Members of both houses were especially critical of the Teheran and Yalta agreements, which shaped the map of postwar Europe by permitting expansion of the Soviet sphere of influence that would later be called the Iron Curtain countries. Though President Truman had not sought the legislation that created the NSC, he appreciated the idea of "integration of domestic, foreign, and military policies relating to National Security." He was reportedly quite frustrated by the overlap and duplications in intelligence gathering that often found the army and navy spying on each other as each spied on the enemy.

Under the original legislation,[65] the council included the president, the vice president, and secretaries of state and defense. Later Congress added the chairman of the Joint Chiefs of Staff (heads of the three armed services), the CIA director (DCI), and, in 1961, the director of the Arms Control and Disarmament Agency (ACDA). As the issues have warranted, presidents have also invited others, most often the secretary of the treasury (on tariff policies and balance of payments), the budget director (to see if a plan is affordable), and the attorney general (on domestic and foreign legal ramifications).[66] In general, the role of the NSC was to coordinate and synthesize material produced through the intelligence and military communities to usable format for the president. The meetings were designed to provide one place in which major advisors on national security could come together to "cuss and discuss" their differing views on what national security policy ought to be. Given the size and varying roles of the intelligence community alone, the job of coordinating and analyzing national security information can be monumental. Table 4.1 is intended to give some insight into the enormity of the task.

## TABLE 4.1
## MAJOR FOREIGN POLICY
## INFORMATION SOURCES FOR THE PRESIDENT

| AGENCY | SECRET AGENCY PERSONNEL (EST.) | MAJOR ROLES |
|---|---|---|
| Defense Intelligence Agency | 5,000 | Coordinates military intelligence from individual armed services. Prepares daily and weekly intelligence digests. |
| Intelligence and Research (State Department) | 350 | Develops policy position papers based on in-house analysis and reports of foreign service officers in the field. Contracts with academicians for policy papers. |
| National Security Agency | 24,000 | Responsible for cryptological analysis, radar analysis, communications intelligence, photointelligence. |
| Army Intelligence Navy Intelligence | 35,000 } 15,000 } | Handles intelligence support for tactical operations. |
| Air Force Intelligence  National Reconnaissance Office | } 56,000* | Develops reconnaissance satellites and rockets to orbit them. Operates satellite programs for the entire intelligence community. |
| Federal Bureau of Investigation | 19,312 | Handle internal security and counterespionage. |
| Energy Department (formerly AEC) | 20,147 | Provides information about nuclear developments in foreign nations. Detects and analyzes nuclear explosions. |
| Treasury Department | 120,025 | Responsible for drug abuse control, tariff policy, balance of payments. |
| Central Intelligence Agency | 18,000 | Advises NSC on intelligence activities of government departments and agencies related to national security. Coordinates and evaluates intelligence related to NSC and disseminates it within the government. Develops programs to collect information relative to politics, economics, military, science, technology, sociology, and geography to be provided to the president and the NSC. |

TABLE 4.1 (continued)

| AGENCY | SECRET AGENCY PERSONNEL (EST.) | MAJOR ROLES |
|---|---|---|
| Central Intelligence Agency (continued) | | Studies international terrorist activities and narcotics traffic. Conducts foreign counterintelligence and coordinates its findings with the FBI and works with approval of the attorney general. Provides services for intelligence community: monitors foreign radio broadcasts, TV, and other press foreign magazine translation and distribution photo interpretation. Contracts for or develops technological systems and devices for its uses. Protects security of installations including checks on personnel. Other functions as NSC shall request (including covert activities). |

*Air Force and National Reconnaissance Office combined.

Sources: Compiled from Philip Agee, *Inside the Company: CIA Diary* (New York: Bantam Books, 1976); David Wise, *The Politics of Lying* (New York: Vintage, 1973); L. Fletcher Prouty, *The Secret Team* (New York: Ballantine Books, 1973); *U.S. Government Organization Manual 1978-79* (Washington, D.C.: G.P.O., 1978); John Clements, *Taylor's Encyclopedia of Government Officials 1979-1980* (Dallas: Political Research, Inc., 1979); U.S. Department of Justice Law Enforcement Assistance Administration, *Sourcebook of Criminal Justice Statistics, 1979* (Washington, D.C.: G.P.O., 1980).

## PATTERNS BY ADMINISTRATIONS

Understandably, new presidents can be awed by the sheer size and brain power at the disposal of the White House. Whether a president decides to use the NSC to help him ride herd over this bureaucracy or as his major source of advice in foreign policy crises depends on his individual personality and administrative preferences. As an advisory institution, the NSC probably reached its heyday during the Eisenhower years with a temporary resurgence of prestige reflected from National Security Assistant Kissinger in the Nixon administration.

TRUMAN. The first president to have a council, Harry Truman, became almost as skeptical of it as he was of the "striped-pants" bureaucrats at the State Department. He was evidently afraid that the NSC system would compete with him for authority in policy making. In his memoirs he said, "There were times in the early days of the NSC when one or two of its members tried to change it into an operating Super-Cabinet on the British model." He had no intention of being a prime minister subjected to a vote of confidence of the NSC. To be sure that they would not try to make policy for him, Truman stopped attending NSC meetings. Before the outbreak of war in Korea, he attended only twelve of the fifty-one meetings. The decision to involve the United States in Korea was made through consultation with a small group of advisors rather than in the formal framework of the NSC.

EISENHOWER. Eisenhower's penchant for lines of command and tidy boxes on organization charts encouraged him to create an elaborate committee system for the NSC. His national security assistant, Robert Cutler, presided over a planning board made up of departmental assistant secretaries. They were to develop position papers as a group to submit to the NSC for their bosses to evaluate in charting future foreign policy courses. Eisenhower saw the system as a way to keep the president up to date or, as he put it to Patrick Anderson,[67]

> You walk into the Presidency and you've got problems all over the world. You have to examine each one from every viewpoint . . . military, economic, and political. How the hell can you do this for 100 sovereign countries? We tried to use the NSC to keep our policies up to date. . . . The NSC papers analyzed our position relative to each country. Regularly, you take the damn things out and you revise them.

To show his confidence in the system, Eisenhower not only met regularly with the NSC but he chaired the meetings. With no intent to exaggerate, he told his successor John Kennedy in 1960, "the NSC meetings have become the most important weekly meetings in government."[68] He later lamented the fact that his successors either discarded or ignored the NSC. "I think no greater mistake has been made," he said, "I suppose Kennedy thought one man could know all the answers heaven sent and did not need the analysis the NSC could give him."[69] One of the major difficulties with the Eisenhower system was that, to get a broad spectrum of advice, Eisenhower inadvertently politicized his system. Suggestions and reports became mere compromises among the various competing bureaucracies. These watered-down statements provided few innovative answers for the really difficult problems. He was not totally naïve about politics and bureaucracies, so he created an operations coordinating board for the NSC to monitor bureaucratic compliance with White House and NSC foreign policy decisions. Only the outsider believes a presidential order is consistently followed. As Dr. Henry Kissinger, Nixon's national security assistant, said, "I have to spend considerable time seeing that it is carried out and in the spirit the President intended."[70]

KENNEDY. John Kennedy deemphasized the role of the NSC. At the same time, the star of the National Security Assistant McGeorge Bundy rose higher and faster than had that of either of his predecessors, Sidney Soeurs and Robert Cutler. Under the umbrella of the National Security Council, Bundy developed a strong White House-centered foreign policy staff. Kennedy rarely assembled the formal NSC especially after the Bay of Pigs fiasco.[71] Instead he preferred calling on his close staffers and senior-level executives from previous administrations. These outsiders also acted as roving ambassadors. He used Averell Harriman from the Truman years, for example, as a special envoy to handle efforts to neutralize Laos in 1961 and to work out a nuclear test ban treaty with the Soviets in 1963.[72] Along with the suggestions and efforts of these outsiders, the Bundy operation developed policy options for approaching problems with Berlin, Laos, and, later, Vietnam.

Gradually, Kennedy developed a preference for using task forces to study problems. Often, the president assigned his brother Robert to chair them. Each would produce both majority and minority reports on ways of dealing with a particular problem. The "first brother" developed a reputation by 1963 as the best man in government to whom to bring an unconventional idea. It was his doubts about the civilian losses in Vietnam that led him to ask skeptics like Harriman, defense assistant Roger Hilsman,[73] and others, "Do you think those people really want us there? Maybe we're trying to do the wrong thing."[74]

Temporary arrangements like these, while attractive at first glance, are not without their flaws. When Kennedy created the executive committee[75] to deal with the Cuban missile crisis, he ordered members to put all their other duties aside. To protect the meetings from being shaped by member expectations of what Kennedy might want to do in the crisis, the president purposely stayed away from many of these deliberations of the "wise men." As long as no other business was pressing, the system could work; but imagine in 1980 if a system like that had to juggle the crises in Iran, Afghanistan, and Poland at the same time or if future crises dragged on for months rather than days.

Presidential task forces and White House staff-created options provided a certain creative chaos to the Kennedy system for gathering foreign policy ideas. The arrangements proved useful in moving from crisis to crisis but left much to be desired in heading off crises before they reached the flash point. Long-range policy making suffered, since the president had learned the hard way from the Bay of Pigs that the bureaucracies were hardly infallible.

JOHNSON. When Lyndon Johnson took over upon the death of his predecessor, he retained the Kennedy NSC operation under Bundy, initially at least. However, as the president's interest in Vietnam heightened, he tended to use the NSC less and less. He resorted instead to an ongoing informal group of advisors who lunched with him each Tuesday to discuss policy options (the Tuesday lunch bunch).[76] As Walt Rostow, Bundy's successor, realized, there was an inherent weakness in this closed advisory system centered around informal meetings. "The only men present," Rostow noted, "were those whose advice the President wanted most to hear."[77]

Under Rostow, the NSC became more institutionalized in the Eisenhower tradition. Rostow was determined to take full advantage of the available knowledge and skills in the foreign affairs bureaucracies, so he developed an elaborate system to include senior departmental officials (a senior interdepartmental group, SIG) and assistant secretaries (interdepartmental regional groups, IRGs). Formalities aside, these groups had little effect on Vietnam, so experts who might have been tempted to counsel a change in course had little access to the Oval Office.[78] Unfortunately for the nation, dissent and disloyalty were synonymous to Johnson, so this complicated system still produced the stock rather than the creative answer.

It was only when outsider Clark Clifford was added to the Tuesday lunch bunch that the basic assumptions on Vietnam came into question. In February and March 1968 Clifford fought ferociously to turn the tide of the war, to limit the number of troops, and to reduce the bombing. Instead of the hawk Johnson thought he appointed, Clifford proved to be an insufferable dove. David Halberstam recounts LBJ's response to this prestigious dissent within his inner circle:[79]

> Their relationship, once so warm and easy, turned cool and distant . . . he [Clifford] was cut off from important cable traffic . . . but he posed a special

> problem. . . . when McNamara [defense secretary] went soft on the war, that could be ascribed to his idealism, distaste for blood and his friendship for the Kennedys. None of this could be said of Clifford . . . he was no Kennedy enthusiast, no kook, there was nothing soft about him.

Gradually Clifford forced Johnson to a more realistic, albeit painful, assessment of the direction of the war. Johnson's policy-making machinery proved hopelessly flawed since it depended on outsiders to get both sides of a policy issue. His system provided not advice and expertise but adulation for the president.

NIXON. The Nixon NSC operation could be more accurately labeled the Kissinger apparatus. Dr. Kissinger, as national security assistant, chaired a maze of NSC subcommittees that he created to supplement the SIGs and IRGs from the Bundy-Rostow machinery. In times of crisis, formal NSC meetings were called mainly to ratify decisions made by the subcommittees. Each subcommittee had a specific area of responsibility including the Vietnam Special Studies Group, the Verification Panel (arms control and Soviet compliance), the Forty Committee (covert operations), the Washington Special Action Group (WASAG, crisis management), the Net Assessments Group (intelligence estimates), the Defense Policy Review Committee (DPRC, defense budget analysis), and the Undersecretaries Committee (aid in implementation along the lines of Eisenhower's Operations Coordinating Board).[80]

This network of subcommittees was intended to specialize foreign policy analysis capabilities and to synthesize information that would be available for the president's use. Still the IRGs (renamed IGs) produced reams of reports and position papers that former professor Kissinger seemed to relish correcting like term papers. Kissinger kept the bureaucracy productive and off balance by the manner in which he responded to reports submitted for his clearance. The following vignette circulated around Washington with a sufficient number of variations to demonstrate the Kissinger style, which permitted him to ride herd on the bureaucracy in the president's name.[81]

> When a person brought a paper to him, he would take it, wait a few days and call the author in and ask, "Is this the best you can do?" Usually the staffer would respond, "I guess I can do better." The same question and answer were likely a second time. If Kissinger balked a third time the aide might complain about the time he spent on the report and say, "This is the best I can do." At this point Kissinger would respond, "Good, now I will read it."

While the Nixon NSC resembled the Eisenhower operation, Dr. Kissinger played a central role unparalleled in any previous administration. It was Kissinger and his personal staff of a hundred with a budget of $2 million (two and a half times the size of Bundy's and three times Rostow's) and not the formal senior review group that was the center of foreign policy innovation, analysis,[82] and advice to the president. Kissinger was in daily contact with Nixon, and the number of formal NSC meetings dropped from thirty-seven to ten between 1969 and 1971. Unlike any of his predecessors, Kissinger was also the president's major negotiator with foreign governments and served as administration spokesperson with the press corps. It seemed as if Nixon's solution to difficulties he perceived at the State Department were being handled, in his first administration, by just creating a separate White House-centered foreign affairs operation.

FORD AND CARTER. President Ford made occasional use of the NSC, especially in "crisis" situations like the May 1975 Cambodian seizure of the merchant vessel *Mayaguez*.[83] Still, he followed the Nixon pattern in which policy options generated by the NSC system and the staff of the national security assistant came to the president through Kissinger. When Ford decided to assemble his own team, Kissinger remained as secretary of state, but his aide, Brent Scowcroft, took over as national security assistant.[84] Dr. Kissinger's involvements in "national security" wiretaps tarnished his shining image. Still, via Scowcroft, he remained intimately involved in informing the president on national security issues.

Under Jimmy Carter, the NSC system resembled the operation during the Kennedy and Johnson years. His National Security Assistant Zbigniew Brzezinski was to be a high staff aide. In describing his own job, Brzezinski said[85]

> I don't envisage my job as a policy making job. I see my job essentially as heading the operational staff of the President, helping him to facilitate the process of decision making in which he will consult closely with his principal Cabinet members.

President Carter seemed intent on adopting a middle-of-the-road approach between a Kissinger system and a Dulles operation. Initially, Brzezinski was not nearly as influential as Kissinger had been. Still, the fact that he had regular access helped him. He prepared the agenda for NSC meetings and informed the appropriate agencies of that list of issues. He also met daily with the president providing an intelligence briefing on international developments within the last twenty-four hours and then discussing pressing foreign policy questions including peace proposals for the Middle East, the problems in Iran and Afghanistan, the Cuban "freedom flotilla" of refugees headed for Miami in 1980, and so on. He was also responsible, as Kissinger had been, for monitoring departmental compliance with White House foreign policy directives.

Hedrick Smith of *The New York Times* suggested that Carter's attempts to create a balance between the NSC and the State Department were doomed to failure. It was clear that Carter had no desire to have another Henry Kissinger in his administration. He cut back on what remained of the security assistants staff from fifty to thirty.[86] In addition, he dismantled the maze of subcommittees so that the national security assistant would be unable to keep the cabinet-level departments and agencies from providing information he might need. Even the NSC-issued study reports titles were changed from National Security Study Memoranda to Presidential Decision Memoranda to demonstrate Carter's determination to stay on top in foreign policy decision making.[87] Carter, not Brzezinski or Vance, negotiated the Camp David agreements between Egypt and Israel in 1978. In addition, he permitted U.N. Ambassador Andrew Young to build bridges to Third World nations by visiting them and speaking his mind. The only problem with this system was that it gave other nations mixed signals about the U.S. policies. Vacillation on policy position led to charges that Carter lacked the ability to lead in foreign policy and that he merely followed one advisor one minute and another the next. It was only a matter of time before the system led either to resignations or to chaos.

Several international events encouraged President Carter to withdraw his support for a charter limiting the role of the CIA by legislation. First, when the CIA assessments of the ability of the Shah of Iran to ride out the storm of revolution in his nation proved falsely optimistic, the White House began to become skeptical. The Christmastime 1979-1980 Russian invasion of Afghanistan took place unannounced by the CIA, and the United States was in a poor position to respond even to the point of being able to covertly train the Mujahiden (Moslem freedom fighters) who sought to drive the Soviets from their soil. The pressures for untying the hands of the CIA in light of Soviet expansionism in the vital, oil-rich Persian Gulf area encouraged a reexamination of the restrictions on CIA covert operations that had been imposed in response to Vietnam and Watergate. A superspy agency of this type with little congressional restrictions can be a potent tool in the president's hands in directing foreign policy. It remains to be seen whether reinvigorating the CIA will produce more accurate intelligence data.

As the Plumbers operation during the Nixon years and the incident at the Watergate complex both demonstrated, though the CIA was intended to enhance the president's ability to exercise leadership in foreign affairs, an unbridled CIA can present serious implications for the democratic process both here and abroad. If a president finds it easier to defend secrecy and covert activities, the intelligence community might be able to conceal poor judgments from the public and the press. They might also get into the habit of concealing them from the president himself. Were this to happen, the bureaucracies created to serve the president could come to dominate him through their decisions to either supply or withhold information.

CONCLUSIONS ON NSC SYSTEM. Presidents tailor the NSC to fit their personal philosophies of staffing and their information demands. One can measure the importance of the NSC to any particular president by noting (1) the frequency with which it meets, (2) its role in crises, and (3) the size of the staff provided for the national security assistant who is responsible for NSC operations.[88] While the principal role of the council and the national security assistant is to define options for the president, it would seem that they make few decisions. In fact the power to define options in government is the power to choose some and eliminate others, and that is definitely a significant shaper of policy outcomes.

An institutionalized NSC system under a strong national security assistant permits presidents to centralize control over foreign policy in the White House. The Nixon-Kissinger operation demonstrated that the national security assistant can filter and shape the information that a president sees. These advisors are not subjected to Senate approval as are the secretaries of state, acting instead as extensions of the president who may invoke executive privilege or national security to cover a multitude of decisions from congressional and public scrutiny.

When Dr. Kissinger wore both hats as national security assistant and as secretary of state, he became increasingly vulnerable to second-guessers in Congress and the press. His presence on the seventh floor at the State Department enhanced the prestige of the department in Washington political circles. There was some speculation that Kissinger would serve as a bridge between the State Department and the White House so that the administration could take advantage of the expertise there to enhance the president's capacity to lead in foreign policy. Nixon's hopes to bridge the White House and the departmental gap were never realized. Kissinger, who had previously had difficulty in disguising his contempt for the department of "sorry administrators of the least common denominator," as he viewed it, tended to stay aloof from department business. Furthermore, the secretary's personal diplomacy style encouraged him to play his cards close to his vest, thus leaving the department in the dark about secret negotiations or White House discussions. His philosophy was simply, "the only way secrecy can be kept is to exclude from the making of decisions all those charged with carrying them out."[89]

THE ROLE OF THE CIA. Since information is power, anyone who can use secrecy to control information can force others to follow his or her lead. Presidents have used their ties to the intelligence community to monopolize national security information. The 1960s and 1970s produced a spate of exposés about the "company" (Central Intelligence Agency, CIA). The agency went to court to stop publication of books by Phillip Agee, Frank Snepp, Victor Marchetti, and John Marks,[90] and the courts were generally sympathetic to CIA fears. Although the CIA is not the nation's largest intelligence body, it has become the most controversial, and its director has been a major foreign policy advisor to the president since 1949.

When it was created by Congress in 1947, it was intended to be little more than an intelligence clearinghouse that collected and analyzed information gathered by others. But revision of the legislation creating the agency in 1949 directed it to perform "other functions as the President shall decide." In addition, the 1949 law permitted the agency to cloak itself in secrecy by exempting it from the normal agency reporting requirements before Congress.[91] As a result of the 1949 legislation, only estimates are available about the size of the CIA; and the functions it performs are likewise shrouded in secrecy. Its cost to the American taxpayer is hidden in the budgets of other agencies, especially those of the armed services. Four congressional committees have had some oversight responsibility over the activities of the CIA and until the mid-1970s permitted it a free rein. Typically, when the House and Senate "watchdog" committees responsible for oversight met, they not only did not get answers but they had difficulty in formulating questions. The philosophy of Congress in dealing with the CIA in those years could be summed up best in a quote from the Senate "watchdog" committee chairman John Stennis: "You have to make up your mind that you are going to have an intelligence agency and protect it as such and shut your eyes and take what is coming."[92]

Glaring reports of CIA wrongdoing finally pried open the eyes of Congress. Should the CIA be permitted, they had to ask themselves, to train and equip burglars who gather political information for the White House and the committee to reelect the president? Are CIA activities overseas since 1954 in the best traditions of a democracy? Press reports of CIA activities since the 1950s that became common fare in the newspapers and magazines of the 1970s painted a picture of an agency gone wild. The CIA was involved in armed interventions, disruptions of labor unions, propaganda operations, kidnappings, sabotage, spying, and like activities throughout the Third World. It could field its own army, navy, and spy planes. It was even referred to as a state within a state. If the CIA's involvement in the overthrow of elected governments in Iran (1953), Guatemala (1954), and Chile (1970) seems contrary to American democratic principles, one cannot overlook the fact that the presidents cleared these operations. It is also noteworthy that Congress, which had given a legislative blank check to both the CIA and the president in 1949, did little to limit CIA adventures.

In 1974 the worm began to turn, at least temporarily. Congress enacted legislation providing that the CIA could not spend money for operations in foreign countries for other than necessary intelligence unless the president considered other spending necessary to "national security." The president reports the description and breadth of the operation to the congressional "watchdogs" in a "timely fashion." That may or may not be after the action has taken place. President Ford commissioned Vice President Rockefeller[93] to study the workings of the intelligence communities[94] and by executive order in 1976 forbade the CIA to become involved in further assassination plots.

Jimmy Carter appointed his old Annapolis classmate Stansfield Turner to preside over housecleaning at the CIA. Turner was ordered to get the clandestine operations under control. In the process he reasoned that fewer clandestine officers could yield less temptation to launch those operations so his broom swept 500 senior officers out, and he cut the number in the covert operations division from 8,500 to 4,500.[95] The Reagan administration, on the other hand, seems intent upon cutting employees elsewhere and hiring more for the CIA.

## THE ECONOMIC ADVISORS

As complicated as foreign policy and national security issues can be, they pose no fewer headaches for the president than developing a national economic policy in an interdependent, shortage-plagued world. In fact, few things have bored recent presidents more than involved discussions of fiscal or monetary policy. John F. Kennedy supposedly had so much trouble remembering the difference between fiscal and monetary policy that he had to rely on the fact that the word monetary and the name of the Federal Reserve chairman (W. McChesney Martin) both began with the letter "m".[96] Richard Nixon's eyes tended to glaze over at the very mention of an economic topic. When he was involved in a meeting and the topic came up, he tried to speed up the discussion. William Safire recounted a meeting at the Oval Office involving the President, Haldeman, Arthur Burns, and Edward Morgan on a welfare-related matter. It demonstrated Nixon's impatience with the dismal science (economics):[97]

> Burns made a long, slow presentation of a conservative point of view: "As I said in my July 8 memorandum, Mr. President. . . ." The President interrupted to speed things along: "Yes Arthur, I read that." . . . "But you couldn't have Mr. President, I didn't send it yet, I have it here."

Since presidents have neither the expertise nor all-consuming interest in economics, they depend on the views of their major economic advisors. They also receive unsolicited advice from every department head or agency director about his department's needs. Four individuals tend to provide the lion's share of economic advice for the president. The secretary of the treasury, the chairman of the Federal Reserve Board, the director of the Office of Management and the Budget (OMB), and the chairman of the Council of Economic Advisors (CEA) form the "Quadrad"[98] as some have called it. With the exception of the chairman of the Federal Reserve (Fed), these advisors have views that mirror the president's at any given time. Since each is a professional economist, business executive, or banker and each heads a specialized economic bureaucracy, a president cannot expect unanimity among them, although consensus is possible.

Normally, presidents feel more comfortable with the OMB director and the CEA chairman than with the treasury secretary and the head of the Fed. There are a couple of reasons for this. First, OMB and CEA are parts of the executive office of the president, and the director of OMB and the CEA chairman are less likely to have their opinions shaped by their subordinates. Second, although the president appoints the secretary of the treasury and the chairman of the Fed, these two serve several masters and as a result can become suspect in White House circles. To understand the potential advisory impact of the Quadrad and the limits that they impose on presidential leadership in economic policy, we must examine the duties of each of them and their relationships with those serving in their departments.

## THE TREASURY SECRETARY

The first treasury secretary, Alexander Hamilton, skillfully used the position to interfere in Congress, tinker with the budget (which was handled by the treasury until 1921), and to act almost as a prime minister leaving Washington detached from Congress, as almost a national chairman of the board. More recently, presidents have become skeptical of the Treasury Department because of its size, complexity, and ability to stymie White House economic policies. The department can be awesome in its exercise of a broad range of responsibilities and thus can act as a counterweight to presidential leadership if a weak person in the White House cannot keep it in line. Treasury's responsibilities encompass income and corporate tax administration, currency controls, public borrowing (bonds), and counseling the president on such issues as the price of gold, the balance of payments, the federal debt, international trade policies, drug traffic, and currency exchange matters. The list is impressive and to those not immersed in business and financial analysis, a bit overpowering. Because the treasury department is involved with international trade and currency matters, the secretary is often brought into the foreign affairs inner circle. Obviously the department's expertise in public borrowing and the balance of payments can make the secretary's views valuable in dealing with such thorny issues as national energy policies, the sale of weapons to developing nations, the amount of defense spending, the balance of payments, and payments on the national debt.

An effective Treasury secretary must be a recognized expert in the field with the type of personality that is both informative and persuasive. With the creation of OMB and CEA, Treasury has competitors for the president's ear on economic policy. The secretary's access to the president may be limited by departmental duties and the time he must spend working with Congress, especially in the areas of taxes and public borrowing. Contacts with Congress help treasury secretaries in their advice to the president because they develop a healthy sense of what is salable on the Hill. Of the presidential advisors on economic policy, the treasury secretary and the OMB director are the ones most likely to notice the political implications of economic policy decisions. Henry Fowler, treasury secretary under Lyndon Johnson, pointed out that "a set of policy prescriptions is not good if they can't be implemented, and in deciding on the mix of tax policies, debt management policies, and expenditures in the budget . . . I want to be sure they can be implemented and that they work."[99] Treasury secretaries are judged effective then, not on the basis of how they run their departments, but whether the president takes their advice and whether it works. Carter's Treasury Secretary W. Michael Blumenthal put it this way:[100]

> You're perceived to be a good secretary in terms of whether the policies for which you are responsible are adjudged successful or not: what happens to the economy, to the budget, to inflation, and to the dollar, how well you run debt financing and international economic relations, and what the bankers and the financial community think of you.

It is the pressure to be respected internationally and by the members of the banking and financial community from which the treasury secretary comes that can cause friction between those secretaries and White House aides responsible for domestic policy innovations. What makes sound economic policy can be lousy politics and worse social policy. It should come as no surprise, then, that White House Domestic Counselor Stuart Eisenstadt and Treasury Secretary and former Bendix executive Blumenthal did not see eye to eye during Blumenthal's tenure in the Carter administration. Former Textron Corporation President G. William Miller, who moved from the Fed to Treasury to replace Blumenthal, came into office partial to much of the old-time religion of limiting government spending to fight inflation. If treasury secretaries can be adroit enough to avoid running afoul of close presidential aides they can be among the most influential members of the president's cabinet and help to shape fiscal (spending) policy in the administration.

## THE BUDGET DIRECTOR

Today's Office of Management and the Budget is the modern-day bearer of the budget pen and budget axe.[101] It is the successor to the old Budget Bureau that had been a part of the Treasury Department and then became part of the White House orbit in a massive executive reorganization in 1939. The Budget Bureau had come under close White House direction even before that, however. In 1921, the Budget and Accounting Act permitted the departments to draw up their budgets much as they had done since the days of Treasury Secretary Alexander Hamilton; but after 1921 the president was required to submit an annual budget to Congress. In 1970 President Nixon created the present OMB to replace the Bureau of the Budget with four major roles in mind for it: (1) to continue the budget-writing functions of the BOB, (2) to serve as a clearinghouse for new legislation and proposals for legislation, (3) to keep track of the status of the president's legislative program on the Hill, and (4) to provide management advice to the numerous departments and agencies in the executive branch.[102]

Nixon hoped to use the reorganized Budget Bureau as a sort of bludgeon over the heads of the federal bureaucracies. As the word "management" in the OMB title implies, the office was to provide "advice to departments" on ways to improve their administrative efficiency so that they could run with fewer budget dollars. Only a fool would totally disregard advice from an agency that could axe its budget proposals. Still, OMB did not prove to be the tool of presidential leadership in the agencies that Nixon had hoped for. Stephen Wayne insightfully suggests why the idea that seemed so sterling in theory tarnished in practice.[103] While OMB did provide management services, it did not threaten the bureaucracies with budget cuts as Nixon had hoped. The operatives in OMB have too many friends in the agencies and departments and on congressional committees that oversee the departments to participate in such unsportsmanlike conduct.

The Republican president imagined OMB as one of the first lines of attack against New Frontier and Great Society programs he disliked. What better machinery could be available to dispose of swollen bureaucracies overburdened with Democratic appointees? His budget cutting cries, vocalized by OMB Director Roy Ash, were nonpolitical, at least on the surface. Ash, for example, says that Nixon intended OMB to advise him on identifying and eliminating, wherever possible, "marginal and ineffective programs." [104] The president expected the OMB director to use his experience from his years at Litton Industries to keep the departments responsive to White House direction. Ash and his deputy, Frederic Malek, introduced a governmentwide management-by-objectives program [105] with the stated purposes to

1. Improve management throughout the federal government to deliver more effective services to the American people.
2. Assure that what the president wants accomplished is accomplished.
3. Provide a program that is so relevant, so important, and so simple that departmental heads will play the principal role in program input and operation.
4. Establish a method of setting priorities to focus personnel and fiscal resources of the president's staff including OMB.
5. Open lines of communication between top OMB officials and heads of departments and agencies problems.
6. Assure accountability for performance on the part of department heads.

To accomplish the last three tasks, OMB focused on departmental structures, research, and evaluation capacities, paperwork, and procedures and personnel management. [106] Then OMB could suggest changes to the president and the departments. Because the departments feared that OMB would encourage the president to authorize cuts in their budgets if they did not reach their departmental goals, agency executives began producing nebulous statements of goals so that no one could argue that they had not been reached. Since OMB, at the president's direction, found itself digging deeply into departmental dirty linens, the budget people found themselves mired in petty bureaucratic infighting. [107]

Nixon's insistence on advice on ways of trimming, merging, and otherwise streamlining the executive branch made headaches for OMB as it was intimately involved in resolving battles over who would get what programs after reorganization (jurisdictional fights) and how the dollars should be divided up. Those who administer and believe in the programs condemned to the chopping block will resist attempts to alter or abolish them. [108]

Even OMB, Nixon learned, could not be trusted to provide "objective" budget examiners who tow the president's line. Just as diplomats who stay in a foreign country may tend to become advocates for that nation or region in foreign policy circles, budget examiners may become advocates of the departments they examine in the budget review process. During the Ford years, for example, career examiners at OMB became suspicious of the Ash-Malek "management" division because many of the new "management associates" (hired since 1970) were fresh out of business school or business careers, and some of them had worked with Malek (he simply was not trusted by OMB careerists). [109]

In addition to the management analysts and budget examiners, OMB has legislative staff members. When departments have new program proposals, they clear them with OMB. Proposals for programs usually come to OMB after the interested agencies have negotiated among themselves for a piece of the action. As any proposal reaches OMB, the legislative staff notes whether it is in accord with the White House policy or not. Obviously, those lacking the seal of approval go no farther. Much of this clearance role is mechanical. Routinely, OMB processes thousands of bills each year that arise from the bureaucracy. Most of them are minor or technical adjustments of existing law and of little interest to the president and his chief policy advisors.[110]

Even though budget directors (OMB directors) might be coopted by legislative specialists, management analysts, or budget examiners who make up the five hundred or so employees at OMB, in most cases, they are clearly the president's people.[111] Hugh Heclo in an article on OMB and the presidency noted that "three Nixon budget directors, George Schultz, Casper Weinberger, and Roy Ash, each showed a strong tendency to position themselves as personal advisors to the president using their new offices in the West Wing of the White House as a symbol of that fact." According to Heclo, "the result was to identify OMB more as a member of the President's own family and less as a broker merely supplying an independent analytical service to the President."[112]

There have been times, though, when the ties between the budget director and the president have become cold, indifferent, and even hostile. In fact, Nixon's first OMB director, Robert Mayo, could serve as a case in point of this problem. Many of Mayo's proposed slashes in departmental budgets and staff met with disfavor at the White House. By the end of 1969, in fact, he no longer met directly with the president. Instead, he depended on John Erlichman for his marching orders. At the other extreme, one could use the relationship between Jimmy Carter and his budget advisor, Bert Lance, to demonstrate how close the two could be. Lance, a long-time friend of the president's from Georgia and a banking executive by experience, enjoyed the president's total confidence. This relationship was more personal than institutional, but it did not change even when allegations against Lance's banking practices threatened Carter's "clean as a hound's tooth" image via association with a person under investigation for illegal banking practices. At OMB, the professionals tolerated rather than respected Lance, and, when he resigned, his replacement James McIntyre was the darling of the bureaucratic experts. Still, he was infinitely more distant from presidential circles than Lance had been.[113] All things considered, OMB directors, like other potential presidential advisors, have clout in the Oval Office commensurate with the prestige of their agency and their personal relationship with the president. In fiscal and budgetary matters, OMB can help a president either justify expansion or dismemberment of existing programs, policies, and even departments and agencies.

## THE CEA CHAIRMAN

While OMB's major responsibility is to advise the president on budgets and provide management advice and suggestions on budget revisions, the president depends for longer-range forecasting and advice on the Council of Economic Advisors. One time Council Chairman Walter Heller who served under John Kennedy was asked what his major duty was. Speaking like an unrepentant professor (University of Minnesota), he replied that his main job was to teach the president some economics. As we noted, his boss (Kennedy) had difficulty distinguishing between fiscal and monetary policy. Dr. Heller had had experiences teaching government executives crash courses in economics dating back to his days as chief economic advisor to former Minnesota Governor Orville Freeman.[114]

While Congress did not include lectures for the president as a part of the job description given to applicants for council positions when the Employment Act of 1946 created it, the implication was there that he sorely needed help in those areas. The council was to assist the president in giving a report to the nation on the state of the economy and employment. No doubt some members of Congress noted Harry Truman's lackluster performance as a proprietor of a haberdashery shop in Independence, Missouri before he found his permanent niche in politics.

Although it was created by Congress, the Council of Economic Advisors responds to the wishes of the White House.[115] Commonly, the chairman is a professional economist, most often from the same academic background that produced Walter Heller. Truman, the first president to have a council, was often frustrated in dealing with Edwin Nourse, chairman. Nourse's professional style got on Truman's nerves, and the chairman rarely took a stand on issues. The president, so the story goes, despaired of ever hearing anything from them but "on the one hand, Mr. President, you might do this, but on the other hand you might do that." Truman reportedly quipped, "What I wouldn't give for a one-armed economist." In fairness to economists, it is important to note that Gardner Ackley, Lyndon Johnson's CEA chairman, contended that, if an economic advisor refrained from giving advice on gut issues of policy, the president should get another one.[116]

In carrying out its duties under law, the council serves as a three-member in-house group of analysts of the state of the economy always at the president's disposal. They can keep him abreast of present economic facts of life, project where the economy might be headed, and suggest ways in which to maintain an adequate rate of growth in the GNP while maintaining economic stability. They may also help him to monitor new economic policies and their effectiveness. The council chairman can serve as a spokesman for administration policies. In the process, they may float a trial balloon about a possible new policy to see how it is received. In showcasing innovative ideas, they can call on their status as experts to try to convert labor skeptics, business nonbelievers, or uncooperative mossbacks on Capitol Hill. If the idea becomes popular, then a chairman can step aside and give all the credit to the White House.

Few council chairmen have exercised a broader role than Arthur Burns did under President Eisenhower. Burns represented the council at cabinet meetings and also made reports on current and anticipated or proposed policies. The president assigned him to chair several cabinet committees. In light of Eisenhower's great respect for the advisory role of the cabinet, Burns was at the center of Eisenhower's economic policy operation. It was his expertise that provided him with the clout that he exercised.[117]

## ECONOMIC PLANNING BODIES: FORD AND CARTER INNOVATIONS

In an attempt to head off bureaucratic battles over economic policy, President Ford developed a new economic planning board. Like Nixon's domestic council, it was supposed to coordinate the ideas of interested departments into one super-advisory body. Members included all cabinet secretaries but defense and justice. Others involved were the CEA chairman, OMB director, and a representative of the Council for International Economic Policy.[118] Others could be invited as a particular issue warranted. As Richard Pious noted, the system proved less than a howling success because the planning board staff was too small and thus it had to depend on the cooperation of the departments and OMB.[119] Any idea that depends on cooperation among the departments and agencies to make it work has the same flaw as groups like the NSC and the Domestic Council have demonstrated. Who could expect a department to permit encroachment on its turf for the sake of co-ordinated economic policy? There is a plus side to the ledger on the economic planning board. It should help to limit the president's understandable tendency to lean on one aide or department for the bulk of his economic policy advice. In the Ford administration there was no economic czar with a role comparable to the one Kissinger had enjoyed in foreign affairs during the Nixon years. Still, cabinet members with access to Ford had no qualms about bypassing the system and taking their views to the Oval Office in person.

Carter's White House was not nearly as taken with "superpolicy" bodies like the Domestic Council, the Kissinger NSC system, or Ford's Economic Planning Board. As they tried to do away with many of the institutions they found on entering the White House, the Carter people opted for continued cooperation but streamlined the systems substantially. The retooled planning board was labeled the Economic Policy Group. Treasury Secretary Blumenthal presided over the operation, which included among its list of members for the weekly meetings the CEA chairman, OMB director, national security assistant, and secretaries of energy, commerce, labor, HUD, and the undersecretary of state for economic affairs. Still, even in this slimmed-down format, department secretaries ran the system, taking their economic advice to the president through White House aides.

The planning group fell into disarray as Treasury Secretary Blumenthal lapsed into disfavor with those in power at the White House. Some of his public statements condemned him to gradual obscurity. His influence and that of the planning group were damaged by statements that he was "sick and tired of seeing the President and the administration, two, three and four months behind on everything . . . this was ruining his [Carter's] Presidency by making him look foolish."[120] Under Blumenthal's successor, G. William Miller, neither the treasury nor the planning board returned to its once lofty perch. Questions about Miller's complicity in, or ineptitude in not knowing about, bribes paid to foreign governments while he was president at the Textron Corporation quickly eroded his effectiveness. In light of these types of complications and given the nature of problems of any superpolicy organ that might trample on the "sacred" turf of a number of bureaucracies, it remains to be seen whether innovations of this type can become a permanent part of the White House advisory system.

## THE FEDERAL RESERVE BOARD AND ITS CHAIRMAN

Unlike CEA and OMB, the Federal Reserve provides advice to the president but does not always follow his lead. Since presidents appoint the chairman of the Federal Reserve's Board of Governors, one might assume that he is responsive to White House concerns. In fact, the reality is often quite the opposite. Of all of the key economic advisors, the president has least control over the chairman of the Fed. Although presidents appoint them to four-year terms, the terms don't coincide with the president's. Jimmy Carter, for example, replaced Arthur Burns two years into his new administration after Burns had served out a full term. To understand the nature of the advisory role in which the Fed chairman is involved, we must examine: (1) the duties of the Fed,[121] (2) the number of reasons it acts independently of the president, and (3) the ways a president cooperates with it or tries to counteract it.

While the other members of the Quadrad are mostly involved in advising the president on spending and tax policies (fiscal policy), the Federal Reserve can influence the national economy through its control over the money supply (monetary policy). This is important, because the amount of money in circulation can have an effect on interest rates at which others can borrow to expand their output and thus the total output of the nation. When we think of money, most of us think of coins, paper currency, and checking accounts (demand deposits). Taken together, economists view these as $M_1$ but economists also look at time deposits in banks and savings and loan institutions $M_2$.[122]

In 1913, Congress created the Federal Reserve to create and implement monetary (money supply) policy. The Fed acts much like an independent regulatory commission in that the president appoints members to the seven-member board for a term of fourteen years. Since their terms are fixed and staggered, one president rarely appoints more than one or two of them and needs Senate consent on his choice. In addition, board members can only be removed for violations of the law or incompetence (malfeasance or misfeasance, cause). Since the Fed can create and implement money supply policies, its decisions can determine whether the supply of money will be sufficient to meet the demands of economic expansion or be squeezed to make less money available in hopes of controlling inflation.

When the Fed chairman advises the president, he speaks as a person capable of affecting the money supply through his involvement in selling or buying government bonds, raising or lowering the "discount rate," and adjusting reserve requirements for participating banks (federal and state member banks account for three-fourths of all bank deposits in the United States).[123] Each of these decisions can ultimately have an effect on the amount of money that will be available for the president's fiscal (spending and tax and tariff) plans.

BUYING AND SELLING GOVERNMENT BONDS. When the Fed sells government bonds to brokers, banks, and large corporations, each writes a check on its demand deposits in its own bank, thus limiting the amount of money that those banks will have available to lend to others in the private sector. The money supply, as a result, tightens up. If the Fed buys rather than sells bonds, that puts dollars in the bank accounts of the brokers, bankers, and the corporations who sold them to the Fed. In effect, the money supply available for lenders to distribute increases. Increases in money supply by this method are paper transactions between, let us say, the Chase Manhattan Bank and the Fed.[124] This paper shift has the side effect of making more money available for loans in New York City and its surrounding area.

DISCOUNT RATES. The Fed can also expand or contract the money supply by adjusting the "discount rate." That rate is simply the interest that the Fed charges member banks seeking loans to add to the amount of money they have available to loan to other customers. As collateral for the loans they seek from the Fed, banks can use either government bonds that they hold or signed loan agreements that they have received from their customers. Borrowing on these is called re-discounting.[125]

By raising or lowering the interest it charges the banks to borrow (discount rate) the Fed affects the whole structure of interest rates for borrowers seeking money for business expansion, home loans, and so on. The Fed uses the discount rate as a warning to member banks who are supposed to see that the Fed wants "tighter" money (to make fewer dollars available for loans) to cool inflationary pressures.[126] These decisions affect the survival of small businesses, farms, and the housing industry to name a few. The economy is bound to slow down and, of course, the voter blames the president for inflation and recession even though it is the Fed that ultimately decides if "tight" money and a cooled-down economy are preferable to full employment and high inflation. The Fed makes economic decisions that can have disastrous political consequences for the man in the White House.

RESERVE REQUIREMENTS. The third approach to controlling the money supply is often referred to by economists as the "meat axe" approach because the Federal Reserve cuts the amount of money available for loan in all banks at once by changing the reserve requirements. The Fed sets the percentage of a bank's outstanding loans that it must have in order to cover customer deposits. By adjusting reserves it can create extra money for borrowing or create money shortages across the board. Since this method hits all banks at once on an indiscriminate basis, it is rarely used by the Fed, but it is another weapon available in the arsenal of the Fed.[127]

To the noneconomist politician, the business of bonds, discount rates, and reserve requirements can be bewildering. It should come as no surprise, then, that political figures on Capitol Hill and even at the White House have difficulty arguing with the views of the Fed. The congressional experts on the Joint Economic Committee proved no match for Fed Chairman Arthur Burns in 1972 hearings. Committee Chairman Senator William Proxmire reacted to Burns's testimony as a virtuoso performance by commenting, "I can describe your performance only like Stokowski playing us as if we were an orchestra; and I feel like someone in the back playing the cymbals."[128]

Normally, chairmen of the Fed have business and/or banking experience and are much more likely to view economic problems from a monetarist perspective than from a Keynesian viewpoint. In other words, they are more likely to think that controlling inflation is possible mainly through controlling the money supply. Politicians, especially since the New Deal, are likely to lean toward solving economic problems and the social dislocations they present by priming the pump to expand the economy and bring it out of the doldrums with federal spending. When presidents disagree openly with the Fed, they run the risk of weakening business confidence in the economic good sense of the administration. The administration is likely to be berated in the business and banking communities for "playing politics with the economy."

NIXON AND THE FED CHAIRMAN: A CASE STUDY. Fed Chairmen can and often do act as a counterweight to a president's leadership of the economy. Richard Nixon's love-hate relationship with Arthur Burns, the Fed chairman during his administration, provides an interesting case study in peaks and valleys in interactions between the White House and the Fed. Nixon's fiscal 1971 budget (written in 1970) was a barebones package due to the president's stated hope that it could help stop inflation. More likely, however, it was skimpy due to pressures from the incoming Fed Chairman Burns.

In late December 1969, Budget Director Robert Mayo warned the president that under no circumstances could the fiscal 1971 budget allocations be cut enough to balance the budget, since the treasury's income was dropping sharply due to recessionary pressures throughout the economy. All the administration's economic advisors saw a balanced budget as the perfect "old-fashioned tonic" for the ills of the economy. However, all of them agreed with University of Chicago economist Dr. Milton Friedman that the Fed's tight money policies (high interest rates and high reserve requirements) were about to strangle the economy. Dr. Burns, due to replace William McChesney Martin at the Fed on January 31, made it clear that eased monetary policy would come only when the Fed could see that the president had placed his fiscal house in order by balancing the federal budget. Treasury Secretary David Kennedy hoped to bail out administration programs by proposing a $4.5-billion tax package, which included gifts and estate tax increases and higher excises on liquor, tobacco, and gasoline.[129]

Although Nixon had appointed him, Burns refused to stand still for this band-aid approach to balancing the budget. To him, the medicine of monetary restraint and the blood-letting from departmental budgets was the classic and only cure. Burns got his way and the 1971 Nixon budget carried with it an unrealistic $1.3-billion surplus. However, the recession-triggered loss in tax revenues dunked the federal government into a pool of red ink as deep as the worst deficits accumulated under Lyndon Johnson.

Ironically, the same Arthur Burns who had painted Nixon into a corner in 1970 was later to be accused of using the Fed to assist in Nixon's reelection effort in 1971-1972. The complaints were based on a Fed decision to accelerate the growth of the money supply in a manner similar to a suggestion prior to the 1960 election made by the CEA chairman, Arthur Burns. Richard Nixon reported on this discussion with Burns on this subject in his book, *Six Crises*:[130]

> Burns' conclusion was that unless some decisive governmental action were taken and taken soon, we were headed for another economic dip which would hit its low point in October, just before the elections. He urged strongly that everything possible be done to avert this development. He urgently recommended that two steps be taken immediately: by loosening up on credit and, where justifiable, by increasing spending on national security.

What the Fed eventually did in 1971-1972 bore a haunting similarity to what Burns had suggested, and his detractors began debates in *Fortune* magazine[131] about Burns's supposed sellout. Nixon White House aide William Safire suggests that Burns's decision in 1971-1972 might well have been due to pressure from the Oval Office.

When Burns publicly criticized the Nixon game plan, some White House aides began a game of "political hardball." Burns was calling for a more "stringent" incomes policy (i.e., economist's euphemism for controls), and the administration zealots struck back. There had been talk around the White House about bringing the Fed monetary power under closer presidential control and the time seemed right to float a trial balloon for Dr. Burns to see on this score.

In a blatant attempt to intimidate Burns, a White House staffer leaked a suggestion to UPI that the White House was considering trying to expand the Fed (in a manner akin to FDR's court-packing plan). To further belittle the Fed and Burns, the staffer said that Nixon would reject a request by Burns for a $20,000 salary increase. Burns was painted as little more than a greedy viper who called for tightening the federal belt on people programs and at the same time was going to the well himself for a salary increase. Nixon later publicly exonerated Burns at a news conference by saying that he had never asked for a raise and had specifically said he didn't think anyone in high office should take one. The president apologized for the fact that Burns had taken an unfair shot. Burns commented in response to Nixon's public apology that "This just proves what a warm decent man the President is. We will have to work more closely now." The date was August 5, 1971, and a shift in Fed monetary policy came soon after that.[132] This whole incident demonstrates the extent to which a president might be tempted to go to develop leadership over monetary policy. Since the Fed is immune from White House threats of firing, presidents who want to dominate it must go to great lengths to do so. While the president may exercise a leadership role in fiscal policy, monetary policy can shape an administration's program options.

Even after Nixon retired to San Clemente, Presidents Ford and Carter had to deal with Burns at the Fed. When election 1976 rolled around, Ford found Burns staying at arms length from the administration. After having been shanghaied by Charles Colson (Nixon's staffer), he had no intention of being rebuked in economic circles for helping to reelect Ford. Eventually, Carter crossed swords with Burns when the Fed raised interest rates late in 1977. The president chose not to reappoint him, opting instead for William Miller who later moved to the treasury secretary's position. Miller "struck a deal" to coordinate monetary and fiscal policy. The administration's part of the agreement was to cut the fiscal 1979 budget deficit from $25 billion to less than $15 billion.[133] In return the Fed agreed that, as the size of deficits decreased, the Fed would lower interest rates.

Evidently, Paul Volcker, Miller's replacement, followed the same game plan. It is noteworthy that no recent president has been able to force the Fed to do anything. In White House councils and deliberations of the Quadrad, it speaks with an independent voice. Neither Congress nor the president can use purse-string pressure and threats of budget cuts to bring the Fed to heel as they might try to do with other federal bodies. The Fed is funded independently from the interest in the bank and not by appropriations passed by the Congress and signed by the president. On the brighter side for the president, if Fed monetary policy helps to dampen economic growth and increase joblessness or even appears to do so, the president can shift the blame for it from the White House, since he has so little control over the Fed.

## THE VICE PRESIDENT:
## "HIS SUPERFLUOUS MAJESTY?"

While the economic advisors and foreign affairs professionals have specialized knowledge that gains them access to the president, his running mate, the vice president has tended to be an elected outsider far removed from White House inner circles and advisory councils..

The vice presidency has been variously described as an anachronism, a joke, and the consolation prize of American politics. The Founding Fathers provided that the person who got the most votes in the Electoral College would be president and the one with the next largest number would be vice president. Unfortunately for the runner-up, they didn't waste much time or effort designing meaningful things for vice presidents to do. John Adams, who once called his new job "the most insignificant office that ever the invention of man contrived or his imagination conceived,"[134] also said, "I am Vice President—in this I am nothing but I may be everything."[135] A vice president's importance stems not from who he is but from the fact that he might become president. One political wag commented that the vice president has two roles: to preside over the Senate and to check the president's health each morning.[136] History shows, though, that the office has served as a stepping stone to the Oval Office. Of the first forty presidents, thirteen were former vice presidents and eight moved into the Oval Office on the death of their predecessor.[137] One, Gerald Ford, even became president on the resignation of his predecessor. Of the twentieth-century vice presidents, Theodore Roosevelt, Coolidge, Truman, Johnson, and Nixon went on to be elected for terms of their own. The specter of presidential assassination also points up the fact that the vice president is a mere heartbeat away.

The earliest vice presidents (those prior to 1800) were often of much higher caliber than most of those of more recent vintage. John Adams, Thomas Jefferson, and Aaron Burr could just as easily have been elected presidents themselves. After the passage of the Twelfth Amendment to end the possibility of confusion between votes for president and vice president, the lesser office deteriorated and the vice presidential candidate rarely again had a substantial political following of his own. When Daniel Webster was approached to run for the vice presidency, his response to the request demonstrated the low estate to which the office had descended. The renowned orator reportedly quipped, "I do not propose to be buried until I am dead and in my coffin."[138]

Gradually, the office became a political appointment that a party's candidate for president could use to enhance his chances of winning in November. Just as Gouverneur Morris had warned after the ratification of the Twelfth Amendment, the separate vote for the vice president in the Electoral College converted the office into "a bait to catch state grudgeons." Presidential candidates used the job to soothe the dissident wings of their parties or to add a person of a different religious, social, or geographic background to gain votes from voters with similar backgrounds. This attitude toward the vice presidency resulted in the selection of running mates not on their ability to be president or to offer useful advice but to raise the stock of unknowns. In a nod to the border states, Woodrow Wilson chose Thomas Marshall of Indiana to run with him. Governor Spiro Agnew was Nixon's choice for vice president in keeping with the candidate's "Southern strategy," which he stretched to include the "law and order" governor of Maryland. Although rules in each of the parties indicate that the vice-presidential nominee will be chosen by the convention, he ends up being hand picked by the presidential candidate. In recent years, only Adlai Stevenson (1956 Democratic nominee) left the choice up to the convention.

## AS AN ADVISOR

Given the reasoning involved in selecting vice-presidential candidates, it would seem unlikely that the president would take them into White House inner circles. The degree to which a president makes use of the vice president depends on the depth of their personal relationship. Most vice presidents were forced to handle the things that bored their bosses the most. Richard Nixon complained that, as vice president under Eisenhower, he was merely, "Secretary of Catch-all Affairs."[139] Still, when he became president, Nixon treated Agnew the same way. Even though he spoke of Agnew's "important" role in intergovernmental affairs, it amounted to handling domestic issues that Nixon had no interest in.[140] Agnew seemed to realize his new state in life, however. On the day after the inauguration in 1969, he described the "principal part" of his role as that of serving the president: "Whatever the President wants is what I want. I envision that as the principal role of the Vice Presidency . . . to implement the policies of the Chief Executive."[141]

Loyalty is expected of any vice president even if he hurts his own reputation in the process. Hubert Humphrey linked his political fortunes with Lyndon Johnson's and in the process cast his reputation, at that time at least, to the four winds. In a televised interview Humphrey described his role this way:[142]

> I did not become Vice President with President Johnson to cause him trouble. I feel a deep sense of loyalty and fidelity. I believe that if you can't have that, you have no right to accept the office. Because, today it is so important that a President and Vice President be on the same wave length. . . . You can't have two leaders of the executive branch at a time.

This loyalty badly tarnished his political image. In the early months of 1965 when Humphrey got wind of George Ball's opposition to the war in Vietnam in the White House discussions, the vice president tried to meet with Ball since he agreed that opposition was in order. Ball's aides didn't want him to associate himself with Humphrey since "he had become a cripple and everyone knew it." Later Humphrey admitted with regret that "The only time I saw Johnson was when he ran out of people to chew on and raised hell with me."[143]

## JOB DESCRIPTION

No matter who the president, the job description for a post-World War II vice president will have certain common responsibilities. The constitution makes him presiding officer over the Senate, but according to Dom Bonafede, he "invariably feels like a political emigré seeking shelter in the legislative and executive branches and not being particularly welcome in either."

Since 1947 the vice president is on the National Security Council and commonly stands in for the president at various ceremonial occasions. In recent years presidents have sent their running mates on overseas "fact-finding" missions. Richard Nixon debated capitalism in Moscow with Nikita Khrushchev, the Soviet premier; he also dodged rocks and hecklers during a motorcade in Caracas, Venezuela in 1958. Vice Presidents Johnson, Humphrey, and Agnew all went on investigative trips to Vietnam to report on the status of the conflict. Even Walter Mondale, whom many considered to have a special status as vice president under Jimmy Carter, found himself following funeral corteges and congratulating newly inaugurated heads of state across the globe.

ADVANCE MEN AND LIGHTNING RODS. Normally, presidents expect their vice presidents to act as political surrogates for them when something controversial needs saying. Unfortunately for the vice presidents, they also have to take the heat, thus insulating the president from criticism. Nixon reveled in calling Spiro T. Agnew his "cutting edge." When he wished to speak out on an issue, he left it up to "Ted." In 1970, for example, Nixon dispatched him to campaign for Republican congressional candidates and instructed him to be tough on the opponents of the war in Vietnam.[144]

> Be prepared to blast hell out of the Scranton report (on campus violence). They are at least four months out of tune . . . 78% of the people think that college administrators are too soft. Hit the faculties, never the students. Force the Democrats to defend the Scranton report, be uncompromising and tough because we are right . . . we've resisted the overly tough stuff. . . . Anybody who bombs or burns a Federally assisted institution faces Federal prosecution.

In blasting the antiwar movement, Agnew was given to rhetorical overkill. Administration opponents became "nattering nabobs of negativism." Press opponents became an "effete corps of impudent snobs." George McGovern dubbed Agnew's alliterations "foaming fusillades." The vice president's oratorical outbursts brought the wrath of the press corps down upon him while Nixon hid behind his controversial partner. One editorial cartoonist pictured Agnew as a rod atop the White House taking bolts of lightning as he spoke while a sheepish-looking Nixon peeked out of the windows of the Oval Office. The arrangement worked so well for Nixon that he used Agnew's replacement, Gerald Ford, to deflect criticism during Watergate and to say what the president couldn't say. The president stayed above the fray, considering himself too busy with foreign affairs to soil his hands with petty partisan politics. When Ford decided to run for president, he chose Kansas Senator Bob Dole, "the sharpest-tongued hatchet man in the West," to be his running mate.[145]

LEGISLATIVE ROLE. In addition to his partisan political duties, the constitutional role as presiding officer might give a vice president a chance to advise a president on what will sell on Capitol Hill. It would seem at first glance that he could also help pedal the White House programs in the Senate. Still, translating contacts in the Senate from the past into clout later, as vice president, proved difficult for former Senate Majority Leader Lyndon Johnson. The presiding function is not as power laden in the Senate as it is in the House. Senator Mike Mansfield made that point once when he said that "here, presiding officers are to be seen and not heard, unlike the House where the Speaker's gavel is like a thunderclap."[146] In the Senate chambers, the vice president is viewed as little more than a stalking horse for the president, and Senators resent any semblance of interference or advice in their deliberations and voting. In July 1969, for example, Spiro Agnew who had no Capitol Hill experience, defied Senate etiquette by leaving the rostrum attempting to cajole Senate Republicans to support a tax surcharge the president wanted. Senator Len Jordan (R., Idaho) took offense telling Agnew to get back to the platform and be about his own business. An angry Jordan brought the incident up in a weekly meeting of Republican senators. The discussion produced what has come to be known as Jordan's rule:[147]

> Whenever the Vice President lobbies a Senator about anything on the floor, he should vote the opposite way, whether or not it violates his principles or convictions.

Not one Republican senator dissented from the suggestion. After the meeting Senator Gordon Allot of Colorado informed Agnew that no vice president had ever been allowed the liberty of lobbying on the floor. Agnew's effectiveness in the Senate had totally dissolved.

Before long, vice presidents also learn that they are expected to overlook the fact that Senate rules permit them to select those who may speak during floor debate. Some of them had to learn the hard way. When, for example, Vice President Nelson Rockefeller presided over debate on a proposed consumer protection agency, he followed the written rules and used his personal judgment in refusing to recognize Senator Jimmy Allen (D., Alabama). The senator sought the floor to begin a filibuster against the bill. Rockefeller saw no sense in the delay. At the end of the day, Jimmy Allen was fuming and Rockefeller defended himself by citing Senate rules. The Alabama senator later groused to the press that Rockefeller's acts may have been in accord with written rules as the press suggested, but Allen said, "what about the unwritten rules?" Senators are supposed to get the floor to speak whenever they want. Vice presidents who try to lead the Senate soon find that they have an angry tiger by the tail. They can make more friends for a president and get more accurate barometer readings of what is acceptable on the Hill to instruct the president if they keep a very low profile.

WALTER MONDALE: A BORN AGAIN VICE PRESIDENCY? Walter Mondale and Jimmy Carter plowed virgin territory in the broad advisory role they carved out for the office that had been considered the ultimate cliché in American politics. When Mondale's predecessors arrived in Washington amidst the euphoria of the election, they were usually promoted as key administration figures. Before long, however, they found themselves ensconced in offices across the street from the White House, far from the Oval Office. Access to the president is the stuff of power, and Mondale was given an office in the West Wing of the White House (the first ever for a vice president), only a few feet from the president's office. Such proximity gave Mondale clout wherever he went because legislators, interest group leaders, and other Washington power brokers knew that he had the president's ear. It is noteworthy that Ronald Reagan assigned the same office to George Bush, his vice president.

Carter had a novel view of the vice presidency long before he tapped Mondale to fill the number two spot on his ticket. During the campaign candidate Carter said,[148]

> I am certainly determined to make the Vice Presidency a substantive position. . . . I hope to have the kind of Vice President, if I am elected, who would share with me all the purposes of the administration in an easy unrestrained way. . . . I think the country loses when a competent Vice President is deprived of any opportunity to serve in a forceful way.

At first glance, the selection of Mondale might have been viewed as a traditional attempt to ticket balance. A moderate Southerner chose a liberal Northerner. That is where the similarity to past vice-presidential selections ended. Rarely since the 1800s has a person been chosen who was better prepared to take over the reins in an emergency. While Mondale still performed many of the ceremonial duties such as going to state funerals, Carter did not press him to spend all his time traveling. The president habitually sent his family (mother, wife, and son) to speak for him in roles once relegated to the vice president to give him something to do.

Mondale's main role was that of respected advisor who had both the experience and political stature to handle almost anything for the president. The vice president and his staff were permitted to see virtually every paper that went through the Oval Office. Mondale had several regularly scheduled meetings with the president including (1) Monday lunches; (2) weekly congressional leadership sessions; (3) twice-weekly intelligence briefings with Chief of Staff Jordan, National Security Assistant Brzezinski, and CIA Director Turner; and (4) Friday foreign policy breakfasts with Carter, Brzezinski, Jordan, and the secretary of state (Vance/Muskie).

Unlike his recent predecessors, he was not involved with special commissions or committees and councils. Mondale wasn't interested in any operational roles since he felt that "in the past, Vice Presidents often took on minor functions in order to make it appear that their role was significant, when if they were President, they wouldn't touch them at all." He preferred to be an available advisor and prized the fact that "I'm automatically included in things, invited to things. That was not the case in the beginning, but now we have the institutional experience so that the next Vice President is going to say, 'Well, I should be in the White House. I think I can help you and we've got precedent for it.'"[149]

Few could doubt the personal rapport that developed between Carter and Mondale, and it was that personal relationship that helped to enhance Mondale's role as vice president. Should a president's confidence wane, it is likely that the pedestal could collapse accordingly. A number of respected presidency watchers and analysts were skeptical about the potentials of this enhanced vice presidency. They seemed to think that it would not survive the two who created it. One Brookings Institution senior fellow contends that[150]

> The odds are it won't have long-lasting effect. There is no infra-structure; the whole thing rises or falls on two people. Their relationship depends on irreplaceable things that can't be reproduced in a test tube. Carter had the campaign sewed up and had time to find Mondale, . . . Mondale is young enough to wait patiently and Carter is young too. Also, Mondale was useful in the campaign and during the transition . . . Carter needed Mondale more than most Presidents need their Vice Presidents. . . . Another factor is Mondale's tranquil personality. He is less of a threat than most vice presidents.

In light of the special relationship that developed between Mondale and Carter and noting that no special office of the vice president has been created to institutionalize the advisory role of the vice president, it seems unlikely that subsequent presidents will emulate the pattern, even though the model will be available for them to use.

## CONCLUSIONS

Most of the institutional advisors discussed in this chapter present a dilemma for the president as he tries to be the captain of his own ship. Each provides a measure of specialization that the president needs as he attempts to make decisions. However, each also tends to be an accomplished and recognized expert in a substantive field or someone with a recognizable political following of his own. If a president is careful about whom he selects to cabinet, White House office, and similar key department head positions, he can hope that they won't be too easily compromised by their bureaucracies or see their positions as merely stepping stones to their own political aspirations. Vice presidents, on the other hand, with the exception of the Mondale experiment, have rarely graced White House inner circles and posed no serious threat to presidential leadership.

As presidents take the reins of government into their hands, they learn that the beasts can be hard to control. Bureaucracies and the people who lead them, though they are normally presidential appointees, prove to be both sources of information for and obstructions to their nominal boss in the White House. In Chapter 8 we shall examine how presidents try to use economic and administrative techniques to make bureaucracies more responsive to presidential leadership.

## NOTES

[1] Arthur Schlesinger, Jr., "On Presidential Succession," *Political Science Quarterly,* (Fall 1974), pp. 472-505; Also see Arthur Schlesinger, Jr., *The Imperial Presidency* (New York: Houghton Mifflin, 1973), pp. 480-482.

[2] James T. Flexner, *George Washington: Anguish and Farewell* (Boston: Little, Brown, 1974), p. 220.

[3] As stated in a radio address dated September 19, 1968 excerpted in Robert Hirschfield, ed., *Power of the Modern Presidency,* 2nd ed. (Chicago: Aldine, 1973), pp. 165-166. This book of documents is the best of its kind for statements by presidents, analysts, and members of the Supreme Court on the executive branch.

[4] A more administratively oriented view can be found in a classic on the cabinet, Richard Fenno, *The President's Cabinet* (Cambridge, Mass.: Harvard U.P., 1959), p. 224ff.

[5] Samuel Huntington, *The Soldier and the State* (Cambridge, Mass.: Harvard U.P., 1957), pp. 453-455, as cited in Stephen Hess, *Organizing the Presidency* (Washington, D.C.: Brookings Institution, 1976), p. 190.

[6] This was the impression this author gained in talking with Califano in a group discussion as part of a seminar sponsored by the National Endowment for the Humanities for college professors and organized and run by Professor Louis Koenig of New York University in June 1976. The meeting with Califano took place June 20, 1976 in the University library.

[7] Theodore White, *Breach of Faith* (New York: Atheneum, 1975), pp. 103-104.

[8] Hess, *op. cit.,* pp. 136, 201.

[9] Marian Irish and Elke Frank, *U.S. Foreign Policy* (New York: Harcourt Brace, 1975), p. 189.

[10] On the appointment of Griffin Bell and accompanying problems with it, see "A Completed Cabinet-Carter's Criticized Choices," *National Journal,* January 1, 1977, pp. 16-17.

[11] The statement by Mrs. Harris is cited in Robert J. Sickels, *The Presidency* (Englewood Cliffs, N.J.: Prentice-Hall, 1980), p. 158.

[12] A number of books have been written about the silent majority and the new Republican majority including Kevin Phillips, *The Emerging Republican Majority* (New Rochelle, N.Y.: Arlington House, 1969). See also: William Rusher, *The Making of a New Majority Party* (Ottowa, Ill.: Caroline House, 1975).

[13] Frederic Malek, *Washington's Hidden Tragedy* (New York: Free Press, 1978), p. 74.

[14] *Ibid.,* p. 67.

[15] Richard P. Nathan, *The Plot That Failed* (New York: John Wiley, 1975), p. 39.

[16] On the transition team, see "Carter's White House Staff is Heavy on Functions, Light on Frills," *National Journal,* February 12, 1977, p. 233.

[17] On Connally's stature, see William Safire, *Before the Fall* (Garden City, N.Y.: Doubleday, 1975), p. 498.

[18] William Lammars, *Presidential Politics* (New York: Harper & Row, 1976), p. 99.

[19] Nelson W. Polsby, "Presidential Cabinet Making," *Political Science Quarterly,* (July 1977), pp. 20-23; see also Hess, *op. cit.,* p. 189.

[20] Rowland Evans and Robert Novak, *Nixon in the White House* (New York: Vintage Books, 1972), p. 12.

[21] Emmet John Hughes, *The Living Presidency* (New York: Coward, McCann & Geoghegan, Inc., 1973), p. 148.

[22] Erwin C. Hargrove, *The Power of the Modern Presidency* (New York: Knopf, 1974), p. 49.

[23] Louis W. Koenig, *The Chief Executive*, 3rd ed. (New York: Harcourt Brace, 1975), p. 194.

[24] Theodore Sorensen, "Advising the President," *The Bureaucrat* (April 1974), p. 33, as cited in Thomas Cronin, *The State of the Presidency* (Boston: Little, Brown, 1975), p. 186.

[25] Hughes, *op. cit.*, p. 149.

[26] Hess, *op. cit.*, p. 107.

[27] Cronin, *op. cit.*, p. 187.

[28] Nathan, *op. cit.*, p. 130.

[29] "Ritual Governs Cabinet Meetings," *National Journal*, May 3, 1975, p. 653.

[30] Dom Bonafede, "Carter Turns on the Drama: But Can He Lead?" *National Journal*, July 28, 1979, pp. 1236-1240.

[31] Cronin, *op. cit.*, pp. 191-192.

[32] Examples in the Carter administration in 1979 were HUD Secretary Moon Landrieu, former mayor of New Orleans, and Cecil Andrus, secretary of interior and former governor of Idaho.

[33] Nathan, *op. cit.*, p. 40.

[34] *Ibid.*, p. 39.

[35] Hugh Heclo, *A Government of Strangers* (Washington, D.C.: Brookings Institution, 1977), p. 196.

[36] Richard Neustadt, *Presidential Power* (New York: John Wiley, 1980), p. 33.

[37] Safire, *op. cit.*, p. 192.

[38] Evans and Novak, *op. cit.*, p. 280.

[39] Safire, *op. cit.*, p. 193; see also Hess, *op. cit.*, p. 106.

[40] Evans and Novak, *op. cit.*, p. 355.

[41] *Ibid.*, p. 256.

[42] Firing of Hickel staffers noted in Safire, *op. cit.*, p. 288. Malek contends that he was not as brutal as the press portrayed him in the firings; in Malek, *op. cit.*, pp. 40-41.

[43] Louis Fisher, *Constitution Between Friends* (New York: St. Martin's Press, 1978), pp. 76-77.

[44] Theodore Sorensen, *Watchmen in the Night* (Cambridge, Mass.: M.I.T. Press, 1975), p. 94.

[45] William Mullen, *Presidential Power and Politics* (New York: St. Martin's Press, 1976), p. 190.

[46] Note the complications in Vance's resignation in *Christian Science Monitor*, April 28, 1980.

[47] A good summation of Allison's models is in Morton Halperin and Arnold Kanter, *Readings in American Foreign Policy* (Boston: Little, Brown, 1973), pp. 45-84.

[48] Graham Allison, *The Essence of Decision* (Boston: Little, Brown, 1971), p. 127.

[49] Theodore Sorensen, *Kennedy* (New York: Harper & Row, 1965), p. 710 as cited in Allison, *op. cit.*, p. 128.

[50] See Elie Abel, *The Missile Crisis* (New York: Bantam Books, 1966), pp. 156ff.

[51] Irving Janis, *Victims of Groupthink* (Boston: Houghton Mifflin, 1972), pp. 19-26.

[52] *Ibid.*, pp. 25-26.

[53] *Ibid.*, p. 39.

[54] *Ibid.*, p. 25.

[55] Arthur Schlesinger, Jr., *A Thousand Days* (Boston: Houghton Mifflin, 1965), p. 258.

[56] Others were critical but not in the meetings; see *Ibid.*, pp. 258-259. See also Sorensen, *Kennedy* (New York: Harper & Row, 1965), p. 679.

[57] Marian Irish and Elke Frank, *U.S. Foreign Policy* (New York: Harcourt Brace, 1975), p. 228.

[58] For the controversy, see Lawrence S. Kaplan, *Recent American Foreign Policy* (Homewood, Ill.: Dorsey Press, 1972), pp. 33-35.

[59] Richard Pious, *The Presidency* (New York: Basic Books, 1979), p. 359.

[60] Hargrove, *op. cit.,* p. 245.

[61] James Nathan and James Oliver, *United States Foreign Policy and World Order* (Boston: Little, Brown, 1976), p. 456.

[62] U.S. Congress, Senate, Subcommittee on National Policy Machinery of the Committee on Government Operations, Hearings, *Organizing for National Security,* 86th Cong., 2nd sess., 1960. See also Henry M. Jackson, ed., *The National Security Council* (New York: Praeger, 1966), pp. 255-257.

[63] For an interesting discussion of Kissinger's contempt for Rodgers, see Bob Woodward and Carl Bernstein, *The Final Days* (New York: Simon & Schuster, 1976), p. 198-199.

[64] On the differences in philosophy between Vance and Brzezinski that led to Vance's eventual resignation, see *Christian Science Monitor,* April 29, 1980.

[65] National Security Act 1947, Title 1, Sec. 101.

[66] Henry T. Nash, *American Foreign Policy* (Homewood, Ill.: Dorsey Press, 1973), p. 121. See also on this Nathan and Oliver, *op. cit.,* p. 449, and Hess, *op. cit.,* p. 56.

[67] Patrick Anderson, *The President's Men* (Garden City, N.Y.: Doubleday, 1969), p. 207.

[68] Dwight D. Eisenhower, *Waging Peace: The White House Years 1956-61,* Memoirs vol. II (Garden City, N.Y.: Doubleday, 1965), p. 712.

[69] Anderson, *op. cit.,* p. 207.

[70] Morton Halperin, *Bureaucratic Politics and Foreign Policy* (Washington, D.C.: Brookings Institution, 1974), p. 219.

[71] Pious, *op. cit.,* p. 365.

[72] David Halberstam, *The Best and the Brightest* (New York: Random House, 1972), pp. 114-358.

[73] A good discussion of this skepticism can be found in Roger Hilsmann, *To Move a Nation* (Garden City, N.Y.: Doubleday, 1967).

[74] As cited in Halberstam, *op. cit.,* p. 336.

[75] On this see John Esterline and Robert B. Black, *Inside Foreign Policy* (Palo Alto, Calif.: Mayfield Press, 1975), p. 242. Members of the executive committee were the president, Dean Rusk (state), Robert McNamara (defense), C. Douglas Dillon (treasury), Special Foreign Affairs Assistant McGeorge Bundy, Robert Kennedy (attorney general), General Maxwell Taylor (chairman, Joint Chiefs), Vice President Johnson, White House aide Theodore Sorensen, John McCone (CIA director), and "outsiders" Paul Nitze, George Ball, and Llewellyn Thompson.

[76] For a thorough handling of the dynamics of the Tuesday lunch group, see Henry Graff, *The Tuesday Cabinet* (Englewood Cliffs, N.J.: Prentice-Hall, 1970). See also Townsend Hoopes, *The Limits of Intervention* (New York: David McKay, 1969).

[77] Walt W. Rostow, *The Diffusion of Power* (New York: Macmillan, 1972), p. 360.

[78] The best comparison of the Kennedy and Johnson administrations is in I. M. Destler, *Presidents, Bureaucrats and Foreign Policy* (Princeton, N.J.: Princeton U.P., 1972).

[79] Halberstam, *op. cit.,* p. 793.

[80] Good coverage of the differences in the Kissinger operation when compared with Rostow's is in Esterline and Black, *op cit.,* p. 19. Also see Ernest S. Griffith, *The American Presidency* (New York: New York U.P., 1976), p. 70.

[81] Comments were made by a FSO on the Cuban desk at the U.S. Department of State, Washington, D.C., March 27, 1974 in conversation with this author who was a participant in a Scholar-Diplomat Seminar, March 25-29, 1974.

[82] On the reams of reports produced by the Kissinger system, see R. Gordon Hoxie, *Command, Decision and the Presidency: A Study of National Security Policy and Organization* (uncorrected proofs) (Pleasantville, N.Y.: Reader's Digest Press, 1977), p. 332.

[83] Henry T. Nash, *American Foreign Policy,* rev. ed., (Homewood, Ill.: Dorsey Press, 1980), p. 193. Comments to this effect were also made by a "high State Department source," in a "for background only" briefing attended by this author at the Muehlbach Hotel, Kansas City, Missouri on May 13, 1975.

[84] Hoxie, *op. cit.,* p. 333.

[85] Nash, p. 193, cites *The New York Times,* December 17, 1976.

[86] *The New York Times,* June 25, 1978.

[87] Pious, *op. cit.,* p. 368.

[88] Sickels, *op. cit.,* p. 145.

[89] Nathan and Oliver, *op. cit.,* p. 471.

[90] Two of the most controversial books on the CIA were Philip Agee, *Inside the Company* (New York: Bantam Books, 1976) and Victor Marchetti and John Marks, *The CIA and the Cult of Intelligence* (New York: Dell, 1974).

[91] For a thorough discussion of this see Harvey Howe Ransom, *Can Democracy Survive the Cold War* (Garden City, N.Y.: Doubleday, 1964), pp. 178ff.

[92] Nathan and Oliver, *op. cit.,* p. 509.

[93] *Report to the President by the Commission on CIA Activities Within the U.S.,* June 1975 (Washington, D.C.: G.P.O., 1975). This commission was chaired by Vice President Nelson A. Rockefeller. See also summary of the report in *The New York Times,* June 11, 1975.

[94] On the operation of the intelligence community in general, see *Commission on the Organization of Government for the Conduct of Foreign Policy* (Murphy commission) (Washington, D.C.: G.P.O., 1975) (several volumes and appendices) Also insightful on this subject is William Colby, Walter F. Mondale, P. Szanton and G. Allison, "Reorganizing the CIA: Who and How," *Foreign Policy,* Summer 1976, pp. 55-63. See also Renze Hoeksema, "The President's Role in Insuring Efficient Economical Intelligence Services," *Presidential Studies Quarterly,* Spring 1978, pp. 187-196.

[95] Robert Sherrill, *Why They Call It Politics,* 3rd ed. (New York: Harcourt Brace, 1979), p. 235.

[96] James Q. Wilson, *American Government: Policy and Institutions* (Lexington, Mass.: D.C. Heath, 1980), p. 456.

[97] Safire, *op. cit.,* p. 491.

[98] Lammars, *op. cit.,* p. 165.

[99] Cronin, *The State of the Presidency,* p. 195.

[100] Cronin, *The State of the Presidency,* 2nd ed., p. 280.

[101] On the importance of the budget director, see Lance LeLoup, "Fiscal Chief: Presidents and Their Budgets," in *The Presidency: Studies in Policy Making,* eds. Stephen A. Shull and Lance T. LeLoup (Brunswick, Ohio: King's Court, 1979), pp. 207-209.

[102] See Pious, *op. cit.,* p. 465.

[103] Stephen Wayne, *The Legislative Presidency* (New York: Harper & Row, 1978).

[104] Malek, *op. cit.,* p. 152.

[105] *Ibid.,* p. 153.

[106] Pious, *op. cit.,* p. 250.

[107] Joseph A. Califano, *Presidential Nation* (New York: W. W. Norton, 1975), p. 33.

[108] Elizabeth Drew, "Reports and Comments: Washington," *Atlantic Monthly,* February 1973, p. 8, as cited in Mullen, *op. cit.,* p. 236.

[109] Joel Havermann, "OMB's New Faces," *National Journal,* July 26, 1975, p. 1074.

[110] Mullen, *op. cit.,* p. 57.

[111] Hugh Heclo, "OMB and the Presidency: The Problem of Neutral Competence," *The Public Interest* (Winter 1975), pp. 86-87.

[112] *Ibid.,* p. 88.

[113] LeLoup, *op. cit.,* p. 208.

[114] Lammars, *op. cit.,* p. 118.

[115] Hargrove, *op. cit.,* p. 85; see also some of the following: Walter Heller, *New Dimensions of Political Economy* (Cambridge, Mass.: Harvard U.P., 1966) and also Arthur Okun, *The Political Economy of Prosperity* (New York: W. W. Norton, 1970). Both Heller and Okun have chaired the Council of Economic Advisors.

[116] Pious, *op. cit.*, p. 308.

[117] On Burns and tax cuts, see Eisenhower, *op. cit.*, pp. 310-311, *Waging Peace: The White House Years 1956-61.*

[118] John Edward Murphy, "Managing the Federal Budget," Civil Service Commission, Washington, D.C., 1977. Unpublished manual for teaching the federal budget to executive branch personnel. Murphy has done a masterful job of explaining the highly complicated budget process. This work will be used extensively in the "Economy" chapter of this book.

[119] Pious, *op. cit.*, p. 309.

[120] George C. Edwards, *Presidential Influences in Congress* (San Francisco: Freeman, 1980), p. 173, one of the most engagingly written books in the field.

[121] Good summaries of this subject are available in Richard B. McKenzie and Gordon Tullock, *Modern Political Economy* (New York: McGraw-Hill, 1978), p. 449, and Robert L. Heilbroner, *The Economic Problem*, 6th ed. (Englewood Cliffs, N.J.: Prentice-Hall, 1981).

[122] A lucid answer to the question "what is money?" can be found in Fred. R. Harris, *America's Democracy* (Glenview, Ill.: Scott, Foresman, 1980), pp. 570-571. See Heilbroner, *op. cit.*, p. 308.

[123] Harris, *op. cit.*, p. 571.

[124] Sherrill, *op. cit.*, p. 308.

[125] Heilbroner, *op. cit.*

[126] *Ibid.*, p. 323.

[127] *Ibid.*, p. 322.

[128] Sherrill, *op. cit.*, p. 311.

[129] Evans and Novak, *op. cit.*, p. 202.

[130] Richard M. Nixon, *Six Crises* (New York: Pyramid Books, 1968), pp. 309-310.

[131] See Sanford Rose, "The Agony of the Federal Reserve," *Fortune*, July 1974, pp. 90-93.

[132] Safire, *op. cit.*, pp. 492-495.

[133] Pious, *op. cit.*, p. 314.

[134] Adams is quoted in Louis Koenig, *The Chief Executive*, 3rd ed. (New York: Harcourt Brace, 1975), p. 187.

[135] Herman Finer, *The Presidency: Crisis and Regeneration* (Chicago: Univ. of Chicago Press, 1960), p. 272.

[136] Sorensen, *Watchmen in the Night*, pp. 153-154.

[137] Finer, *op. cit.*, p. 272.

[138] Cited in Stephen Wayne, *The Road to the White House* (New York: St. Martin's Press, 1980), p. 122.

[139] Hess, *op. cit.*, p. 169.

[140] Evans and Novak, *op. cit.*, p. 312.

[141] *Ibid.*, p. 310.

[142] Cronin (1980), p. 221.

[143] Cronin, *op. cit.*, p. 225.

[144] Safire, *op. cit.*, p. 324.

[145] Sickels, *op. cit.*, p. 273.

[146] Dom Bonafede, "Vice President Mondale, Carter's Partner without Portfolio," *National Journal*, March 11, 1978, p. 377.

[147] Evans and Novak, *op. cit.*, p. 311.

[148] Neal R. Pierce, "The Carter Presidency: Plans and Priorities," in *The Presidency Reappraised*, eds. Rexford Tugwell and Thomas Cronin, 2nd ed. (New York: Praeger, 1976), p. 51.

[149] Mondale, in *National Journal*, March 11, 1978, p. 377.

[150] *Ibid.*, p. 377.

# PART 3

# COMPETITORS
# FOR
# LEADERSHIP

# Presidents and Congress: Leadership and Followership

The upheavals of the 1970s, especially those of Vietnam and Watergate, have contributed to the growing power of Congress in its dealings with the White House. Still, the public, the Washington media, and the president's colleagues on the Hill tend to measure his performance as president, in part, according to his effectiveness as a legislative leader. Presidents willing to make an effort in that direction find the sledding tough. They can be bedeviled by the very size of Congress, its local allegiances, its lack of party line cohesiveness, and the Byzantine procedures that are a way of life on Capitol Hill. An assertive Congress can scuttle a president's attempts to make good on his campaign promises.

Today, the White House initiates most of the major legislation that Congress handles in a given session. The House and Senate, in response, seem to deliberate and drag their collective heels. Delay and deliberation need not always be considered vices. Sluggish congressional responses could help to sidetrack ill-considered programs concocted by a jittery White House staff acting in response to public clamoring for action.

It was fashionable in media and academic circles in the late 1960s and throughout the 1970s to sound the alarm that an "imperial presidency" had gradually reduced Congress to fawning subservience to the whims of the White House. Those concerns were probably being voiced as much out of disenchantment with the events in Southeast Asia, the "meat axe" Nixon methods for disposing of social programs, and the Watergate abuses as out of fear for the future of the constitutional system of checks and balances. In times of crisis, worry about democracy recedes, and demands for leadership grow. President Franklin Roosevelt, in a speech at Ogelthorpe University in 1932 put it this way: "The country needs, and unless I am mistaken about its temper, the country demands bold, persistent experimentation . . . above all, try something."[1]

When does presidential leadership in legislative matters become domination of Congress? Can congressional reassertiveness reach the bounds of constitutional propriety and endanger the efficiency necessary for effective government? Must combat rather than cooperation be a way of life in the give and take between members of Congress and occupants of the Oval Office? Effective presidential leadership in the legislative process will require an ability on the part of the president to work respectfully and harmoniously with Congress.

135

The normally tense, often strained, relationship between the White House and Capitol Hill worsened considerably during the Nixon-Ford years. The two Republican presidents jousted constantly with uncooperative Democratic majorities in both houses of Congress. The election of Democrat Jimmy Carter should have mellowed things considerably, but, as one Carter aide noted ruefully, "it's become a habit with Congress to oppose the Administration from the top down."[2] Even the staffers who served the Democrats in Congress were accustomed to bucking the president. A White House lobbyist noted that there were some 20,000 congressional staff aides, most of whom had never served under a Democratic president.[3] The adversary role had become, like smoking, a difficult habit to break.

Knee-jerk conflict between the two branches is highly counterproductive. The White House is in the best position to lessen these tensions, since it speaks with a single voice rather than 535 that represent local constituencies in Congress. Cooperation won't automatically endanger the delicate system of congressional checks on mushrooming presidential power. On the other hand, presidents need not necessarily lower their policy sights. They should, however, lower their voices and deal more respectfully with Congress. In the near future, it is unlikely that presidents will have congressional lambs to deal with; and they should not expect to be able to run roughshod over the prerogatives that Congress has been reasserting in the past decades.

Former Representative Gerald Ford, shortly after assuming the presidency, informed Congress that he was not looking forward to the traditional honeymoon that Congress usually grants a new president. Instead, he sought "a good marriage." Good marriages must be based on mutual respect and trust. These sentiments are too often lacking in the "shotgun marriage" that the Constitution imposes on the executive and legislative branches. To understand why these strange bedfellows are often seemingly one step from the divorce courts, we must examine the causes for their almost ceaseless bickering.

## FACTORS CAUSING CONFLICTS

Hostilities between the two branches housed seventeen blocks apart on Pennsylvania Avenue in Washington are as perennial as the cherry blossoms along the Potomac and as deeply rooted as the trees from which they sprout. Former White House fellow Thomas Cronin once suggested, "everyone believes in democracy until he gets to the White House." Likewise, it could be said that every senator or representative believes in shared powers until he occupies the Oval Office. There seems to be more than a small grain of truth in the old bromide, "where you stand on an issue depends on where you sit." Backbench Whig Representative Abraham Lincoln once lashed out at President James Polk's decision to involve the United States and Mexico in a war that the Illinois legislator castigated as "unconstitutionally and unnecessarily begun by the President."[4] Later Lincoln, this time sporting a Republican label and serving as president himself, did not feel restricted by the Constitution as he carried on the Civil War. He did what he considered necessary to save the Union and in doing so ignored one law and constitutional provision after another. He expanded the army and navy beyond congressionally authorized levels, called out volunteers for three-year stints in the service, spent funds without appropriations, suspended *habeus corpus* rights, and committed an act of war by blockading the Confederacy.

Presidents Harry Truman and Gerald Ford, who had relished their years on Capitol Hill, quickly found themselves at loggerheads with their old cronies. Truman won reelection in 1948 campaigning against the "do-nothing" Eightieth Congress, and Gerald Ford vetoed his way through two years of constant quarreling with both houses. The perspectives of the two branches are vastly different. Whereas the president must create speedy solutions to long-standing national problems, Congress is expected to find and plug holes in those programs. Lyndon Johnson, from experiences on the Hill and in the White House, put the differences this way: "While the President must live with crises and deadlines, a congressman can cultivate the art of delay and refrain from commitment."[5]

## THE SEPARATION OF POWERS: A CONSTITUTIONAL STRAIGHT JACKET?

Article II of the Constitution is tantalizingly vague and, as a result, encourages conflict between the two branches. Powers granted to the president are so broadly stated that he is left to interpret his prerogatives to a much greater extent than is Congress under Article I. What, for example, does the phrase, "the executive power . . . shall be vested in the President of the United States"[6] mean? The Constitution also refers to the president as "commander-in-chief of the Army and Navy."[7] It remains unclear whether that provision makes him lead the forces in battle, determine what weapons they need, or possibly even determine where U.S. forces should be engaged. To further confuse matters, the Constitution grants Congress the power to declare war. This vagueness and ambiguity permitted Richard Nixon sufficient latitude to justify extension of the Vietnam conflict into Laos and Cambodia under the pretext of protecting the lives of the military personnel under his command. Caches of arms were reportedly stored in North Vietnamese sanctuaries along Cambodia's border with South Vietnam. Nixon ordered the push into Cambodia even though Congress was on record as being opposed to any further expansion of the war.

As the separation of powers system has evolved, the lines of demarcation between the branches have grown fuzzier and less discernible, making presidential leadership infinitely more difficult. Theoretically, the Constitution created three co-equal branches with rights and responsibilities for each. Today, the simplest case studies of policy making demonstrate graphically that there are at least five branches: (1) executive, (2) legislative, (3) judicial, (4) the print and electronic media, and (5) interest groups. James Madison[8] recognized the roles that organized interests might play in the policy process, but the Constitution is silent on the subject.

The five branches regularly interact, especially when controversial issues surface.[9] When, for example, the Carter administration announced its plan to decontrol oil prices and slap a sizable windfall profits tax on oil company profits, the decision unleashed a chorus of howls. Petroleum producers cried that the windfall profits scheme was an unjustified encroachment on free enterprise. Consumer advocates were disenchanted with oil company profits so they resisted any further fattening of oil industry coffers that did not provide for the return of a sizable chunk to the government for redistribution to inflation-ravaged consumers. Both groups pressed their cases before congressional committee hearings that the media beamed into living rooms across the country. Whatever the outcome of national energy policy, those feeling aggrieved by the eventual plans will lobby Congress to support or undermine a president's program that hurts them. Simultaneously, they will be prepared to fight a holding action in the federal courts.

The case just cited should demonstrate that presidential leadership in legislative programs is subject to a number of moderating influences. Evidently the Founding Fathers expected that the president would be called upon to provide some regularized direction for government. To this end, they required that he present a "State of the Union" address in which he could convey his shopping list of programs to Congress. They also empowered him to select the upper ranks of the federal government. This permitted him to direct the day-to-day operations of the departments as he saw fit. Nevertheless, Congress was given the last say. The Senate could reject presidential appointments and treaties. Either house, by manipulating the purse strings, could curtail presidential spending plans. Congress could create new agencies and destroy others. Wary presidents might be forgiven for a tendency to look back over their shoulders before making a decision. An angry Andrew Jackson reportedly approved a site for the new Treasury Department building precisely because it obstructed his view of the Capitol. Richard Nixon once warned, "the moment a President is looking over his shoulder down to Capitol Hill before he makes a decision, he will be a weak President."[10]

It has become increasingly evident that Congress resents playing second fiddle to the president. When presidents encroach on congressional turf, they can expect frustrations and reprisals. In an unguarded moment, Theodore Roosevelt voiced his dismay at having to ransom his "progressive" programs to the whims of "conservative" fellow Republicans like Speaker Joe Cannon and Senators Aldrich, Platt, and Spooner who resented too much presidential leadership in legislation and sought to make him pay for his impudence. "If only I could be President and Congress too," Roosevelt fantasized, "for only ten minutes."

When institutional jealousies limit congressional receptivity to White House ideas, a certain creative atrophy may settle in among the president's men. James Fallows, a former White House speechwriter and "idea man" during the Carter years tendered his resignation due to his disillusionment with the gnawing frustrations of presidential-congressional relations. "It's time to go," he complained, "when your imagination is limited to ideas that are possible to get through Congress."[11] Fallows resented the need to pander to congressional prejudices:[12]

> Your imagination dies. You see yourself as foolish or arrogant for suggesting ideas, say, tax reform, that you can't get past the Ways and Means Committee. So you stop thinking those thoughts. You wonder what part of your brain has died during the night.

His myopic view recognized no middle ground. The options are not merely get things "past" Congress or resign. He neglected to explore the avenue of cooperation. That route, however, is littered with massive roadblocks.

## CONSTITUENCY DEMANDS:
## SERVING DIFFERENT MASTERS

Lyndon Johnson reveled in referring to himself as the president of "all" of the people. Congress, by implication, then merely serves limited special segments of society. This description is politically attractive for presidents; but, given the demographics of presidential elections, it is not wholly accurate. Johnson was not elected by "all the people." His pluralities came from urban areas and especially from the core cities dominated by labor unions and minority politics. Until the later 1960s, Congress represented a more conservative constituency that was based in rural areas. The Supreme Court's "one-man, one-vote" decisions changed the complexion of Congress to better reflect the attitudes of an "urban" nation.

Ironically, just as the central cities stood to gain political clout in Congress to go along with their preferred position in White House circles, their populations declined and the "urban" nation became an increasingly suburban and conservative one. The refugees from the city fled to escape its crime, decay, and oppressive tax burdens. They resented liberal social policies aimed at curing urban ills because they were paying for them. Richard Nixon capitalized on this discontent by demanding "law and order" and by criticizing big government and massive federal programs whose tax burdens were being foisted off on the middle class. These rallying cries galvanized the "Silent Majority" into a potent political force.[13] The presidency that had been the vehicle of social change shifted directions. Conservative messages so impossible for Barry Goldwater to sell in 1964 became much more acceptable when Ronald Reagan showcased them in 1980.

SUN BELT AND SUBURBANITES: NEW CONSERVATIVES. The cries of budget balancers and advocates of tax rollbacks could sound the death knell for welfare reform legislation and programs designed to revitalize cities that have been the common fare of liberal presidents. The population has been flowing steadily into the Sun Belt (Southeast and Southwest), an area that has had a long-standing conservative tradition. The once "solid" Democratic Southeast has also become a hotly contested area in races for the White House, and a liberal Democratic president will most likely consider it enemy territory. These shifts will make moderately conservative presidents[14] better able to work with Congress than more urban-oriented liberals, especially after congressional districts are redrawn to reflect migration to the suburbs and the Sun Belt.

Congress represents not only the various localities but the organized segments of the population in those areas.[15] Members of the House and Senate must be responsive to the needs of the dominant economic groupings in their state or district. Voters expect legislators from Kansas, Nebraska, or Iowa to be concerned first with the problems of farmers and only second with the ills of the nation as a whole. Representatives seek out committee assignments that provide them with a springboard to the constituency they service. The makeup of the 1979-1980 House Interior and Insular Affairs Committee (which deals with oil, coal, water, and wilderness areas, among other things) illustrates the point graphically. Of its nineteen most senior Democrats, eleven were from oil, coal, or Western states; of its fourteen Republicans, ten fit that description.[16] Obviously their views on water projects, strip mining of coal, deregulation of oil prices, and so on will mirror the needs of their constituents even when that means deserting a president from their own party and putting national interests on the back burner.

Predictably, Senate Finance Committee Chair Russell Long of Louisiana was critical of President Carter's hefty windfall profits tax on oil companies that was to be plowed back into social programs to aid the poor. The Carter program was neither pro oil nor politically conservative enough for Long's taste. He promised the president that his committee would "report out" a profits tax that the president could live with.[17]

House members face reelection every two years, so they must be even more sensitive to constituent sentiments than their colleagues in the upper chamber. Even senators, with the luxury of a six-year term, must eventually align themselves with the desires and prejudices of their electorates. They can be somewhat more nationally oriented in the first four years, but they must eventually hit the cardboard chicken circuit and press the flesh like a down-home politician during the last two years. J. William Fulbright, chairman of the prestigious Senate Foreign Relations Committee, lost a primary fight for his political life partly because his opponent questioned not just Fulbright's liberal voting record and criticisms of the war in Vietnam but also his value in helping the people of Arkansas with their economic problems. His opponent, Governor Dale Bumpers, asked, "How many jobs has the Foreign Relations Committee provided for Arkansas?" When members of Congress depend for their survival on this sort of local orientation, the difficulties for presidents in constructing majorities to support their legislative programs are multiplied by 535 or more.

## A RUDDERLESS CONGRESS

Too often, the lion's share of the blame for Congress's bended-knee, hat-in-hand posture toward the president is laid at the doorstep of the White House. Honest legislators should admit, as comic strip character Pogo once trenchantly observed, that "We have met the enemy and it is us." Presidential disdain for Congress is, unfortunately, often richly deserved. On one of the Watergate tapes, Richard Nixon described Congress as "irrelevant . . . irresponsible . . . and so enormously frustrated that they are exhausted."[18]

It should come as no surprise that senators and representatives are exhausted and that it is not just due to frustration as Nixon seemed to believe. Capitol Hill workdays are torturous, and the grueling schedules leave legislators little time to ponder presidential usurpations of congressional power. James Boyd, a former Senate staffer, gave this description of the early morning hours of a legislator's day.[19]

> He arrives at 9:30 . . . goes through a private door so visitors won't see him . . . has his usual committee meetings scheduled at 10:00. . . . His waiting room is crowded with people he can't ignore. One helped his campaign in the distant past. . . . Then there is a delegation of union leaders who aided his campaign last time.

The rest of the day is taken up with constituent requests for help with VA benefits, Social Security checks, research information for budding high school scholars, more committee and subcommittee meetings, floor votes, and preparations to fly back to the home district on the weekend for social functions, speeches, talk shows, town meetings, and on and on. Time is indeed a precious commodity for members of Congress. As she prepared to resign from Congress, Representative Barbara Jordan bemoaned the diversity of topics with which House members are expected to be familiar and the lack of time to learn much about most of the issues pending before Congress.[20]

> There is not enough think time for a member to bring a well-thought-out and considered decision to a question. There are simply too many different areas defying the expertise of the ordinary person. You have to vote on a neutron bomb, international microwave systems, or funding for the Export-Import Bank.

The frustrations that Representative Jordan expressed become even more acute when presidents withhold information that Congress needs to legislate effectively, especially in the troublesome area of international affairs, which we shall examine closely in the next chapter.

## CONGRESS DECENTRALIZED: TOO MANY CHIEFS

Since the average senator and representative becomes mired in daily routines, they should be able to expect that the institutional and party leadership will act to protect congressional prerogatives from presidential encroachments. However, Congress today is in a state of flux. Moves to democratize the upper ranks of both houses have produced the unfortunate side effect of weakening the leadership. Henry Kissinger, former secretary of state, complained that there was no leadership with whom to discuss foreign affairs on Capitol Hill.[21] Neither House Speaker Thomas P. O'Neill, Jr., or Senate Majority Leader Robert Byrd ruled with the iron hand that "Uncle Joe" Cannon, "Czar" Thomas Reed, "Mr. Sam" Rayburn, or Senate Majority Leader Lyndon Johnson wielded in their days.

It may well be that followership, not leadership, is the problem with Congress today. Distaste, distrust, and disrespect for authority are common within our society. Representatives and senators are, after all, a product of the society they serve. If our religious, social, and political institutions are under fire, it should not be surprising that members of Congress are unwilling to accept the direction of either the president or the party leaders on Capitol Hill. In the last decade or so, the ancient mores of Congress have been buffeted severely. Since 1975, freshman representatives and senators are demanding and receiving "a piece of the action." By 1979, over half the membership had served only *since* Watergate[22] and the "young Turks" spearheaded efforts to reshape Democratic Party congressional leadership to make it more responsive to the judgments and demands of the rank and file members.

Due to major changes in the seniority system implemented in the 1970s, the average legislator now votes in the party's caucus to select the chairperson for the standing committees that prepare legislation for floor action (i.e., debate and vote). The Democrats made election by one's peers the ultimate criterion for selection. A legislator's proximity to his or her eternal reward is no longer the greatest political asset. Individual clout has been enhanced at the expense of the committee barons who once lorded it over the legislators laboring in their fiefdoms.

These reforms have complicated the lives of presidents, however, as they attempt to work with Congress. A number of committee chairpersons who were respected and even feared by the White House have been swept out in the recent congressional housecleanings. Such committee fixtures as Wilbur Mills (House Ways and Means), W. R. Pogue (House Agriculture), Wright Patmann (House Banking), and Wayne Hayes (House Administration) have fallen victim to the changes. Reforms also included provisions that the top subcommittee positions must be spread among the members, not doled out as favors by committee chairpersons. Decentralization with an evident lack of effective leadership has plagued, in both houses, and, as a result, the president may no longer depend on merely gaining the support of a few key chairpersons and the speaker or majority leader to guarantee his administration's programs safe passage through the legislative process.

Unfortunately for the White House, congressional Democratic caucuses have reinvigorated the practice of debating and adopting policy statements independent of the president and often at odds with his wishes. In 1972, for example, the House Democratic caucus, after debating the issues of U.S. combat presence in Vietnam, issued instructions to Democrats on the House Foreign Affairs Committee to seek legislative restrictions on U.S. combat involvement. Later on, the House caucus set a party line on Watergate, proposed a new budget system, and supported the War Powers Act. In 1979, House Democrats in caucus rejected Jimmy Carter's oil deregulation plans by a better than 2-1 margin.[23] This habit of independence infected individuals too. Two senators, both possibly motivated by personal presidential aspirations, took strong public exception to the strategic arms limitations treaties with the Soviets and proposed an alternative to Carter's "piecemeal" approach to national health insurance.[24]

## THE PRESIDENT
## AND PARTY LEADERSHIP

Being loyal to the president, the party, or even Congress itself seemed to be the last thing on the minds of many Democratic legislators during the Carter years. Although a Democrat sat in the White House and the party held commanding majorities in the House, voting along party lines was at its lowest level in years. Given this independence-oriented mentality, presidents must gather allies where they may. Cooperation with the speaker of the House and Senate majority leader becomes even more important because their institutional and party prerogatives permit them to manipulate certain facets of the legislative process (see Table 5.1). In light

## TABLE 5.1
### INSTITUTIONAL AND PARTY POWERS OF HOUSE AND SENATE DEMOCRATIC LEADERS AND THEIR IMPACT ON THE PRESIDENT, 1980

| OFFICER | POWERS | IMPACT ON PRESIDENTIAL PROGRAMS |
|---------|--------|----------------------------------|
| Speaker | 1. Assigns bills to standing committees (institutional). | Bills can be speeded up or pigeonholed depending on the attitudes of the chairperson to whom he gives the bill. |
| | 2. Assigns members to select committees (institutional/party). | These committees get members favorable national exposure so speaker gets IOUs that can be used on later controversial legislation for votes. |
| | 3. Assigns members to Rules Committee (institutional/party). | Can get favorable treatment for a bill to speed it to the floor and limit debate and amendment on the proposal. |
| | 4. Chairs steering and policy committees (party). | May get IOUs for assigning members to attractive standing committees since Steering and Policy does this for Democrats. |
| | 5. Assigns House members to the conference committees (institutional). | Can assign members favorable to a piece of legislation. Conference puts bills passed under different forms in each into a compromise form likely to reach the president without major changes. |
| Senate Majority Leader | 1. Assigns bills to standing committees (institutional). | . . . . . . . . . . . . . . . . . . . . . . . . . . . . . . . . |
| | 2. Assigns members to select committees (institutional/party). | Select committees can investigate things the president might prefer to leave uninspected. One example: Senate Select (Ervin) Committee on Presidential Campaign Finances (Watergate). |
| | 3. Helps in controlling the flow of bills from committees to floor (party). | Can speed up or slow down a bill and can help get priority bills up for quick action. |
| | 4. Is a conduit of treaty and appointments information from the White House to the Senate (party). | Prestige used for a treaty or appointment will help; opposition could doom the president's plans. |
| | 5. Is major figure on Steering Committee. (party). | See speaker, impact 4. |
| | 6. Assigns to conference committees (institutional/party). | See speaker, impact 5. |

of the powers listed in Table 5.1, any president who expects to push his program through Congress without at least the tacit consent of the majority party leadership is merely fooling himself.

Presidents are not always fortunate enough to face cooperative majorities in Congress. Randall Ripley, in fact, found three distinct patterns of presidential-majority leader relations:[25]

1. The Presidential Majority—His party is in the majority. He tries to use Congress as a vehicle to pass his program. Party leaders are *expected* to line up behind him.
2. The Congressional Majority—The President and Congress are of the same party. Presidents give freedom to the leaders in Congress.
3. Truncated Majorities—At least one house differs in party allegiance from that of the President.

In recent years, presidential-congressional relations have become regularized and institutionalized, especially since the Kennedy and Johnson administrations. Long-time Kennedy intimate Lawrence O'Brien had liaison[26] chores for the White House during both administrations. The operation emphasized party loyalties during the Kennedy years; but Johnson's majorities were so monumental that he was able to seek moderate Republican support on his more liberal programs such as the twin civil rights acts in 1964 and 1965. That minority support enabled LBJ to offset the holding action that Southern conservatives launched. Johnson generously and sensibly recognized the contributions that those Republicans had made to his legislative successes. "Most of the key measures," he admitted candidly, "have received some support from progressive and moderate Republicans, and all Republicans in some instances."[27]

All good things do indeed come to an end. Even such presidents as Franklin Roosevelt and Lyndon Johnson who amassed legendary records of legislative success early in their administration suffered setbacks eventually. FDR, who steamrolled the bulk of the New Deal through the "me too" Seventy-third Congress, soon suffered delay and defeat on other critical legislation involving labor disputes, the administration of oil resources, unemployment insurance, and old age pensions.[28] Johnson sensed the urgency of selling his Great Society legislation as early as possible. His experiences on Capitol Hill had taught him that a president has precious little time to enact his programs before carping and sniping from Congress slow his momentum to a standstill. Presidential majority situations demand that the president call quickly and forcefully for party loyalty and make the most of a good thing while it lasts.

CONGRESSIONAL MAJORITIES. Some presidents blessed with majorities in both Houses have demonstrated no affinity for imposing their own imprints on the party's legislative activity. Warren Harding, Calvin Coolidge, and Dwight Eisenhower fit comfortably into this mold. Eisenhower imagined any White House tampering with the decisions of House and Senate Republicans would be unjustified seizure of congressional prerogatives. The president adopted a "hands-off" posture toward the Senate Republican selection of a Senate majority leader to replace Robert Taft, whose sudden death had left the position vacant. "This administration," Eisenhower declared, "has absolutely no personal choice for majority leader. *We* are not going to get into *their* [Congress's] business." Eisenhower's reward for his restraint was a new majority leader who proved to be a continuing thorn in the president's side. Conservative California Senator William Knowland seemed to spend more time worrying about Red China than trying to get along with Ike. Emmett John Hughes, a close Eisenhower aide, contends that this aloof demeanor and unwillingness to soil his hands with partisan politics in Congress helped to contribute to his lackluster legislative batting average. Hughes claims that the White House fashioned only two or three major victories during the entire administration.[29] In congressional majority situations, majorities in and of themselves do not ensure success for the president's legislative package. Presidents who disregard partisan politics in Congress are in no position to count partisan votes before they are cast.

TRUNCATED MAJORITIES: COOPERATION WITH THE "OUT" PARTY. Some presidents are destined to deal with a Congress in which at least one house marches to the beat of a drummer different from that of the president. Often members of Congress are willing to set politics aside when international issues are involved; the armistice breaks down when domestic questions arise, however. The president's program might have smooth sailing through one house and run aground in the other. When both houses belong to the opposition, the president's alternatives are severely limited. He may cooperate with them as much as possible through their party leaders; he may attempt to ram his programs down their throats; or he may content himself with obstructing congressional initiatives.

President Eisenhower, who was a dispassionate observer and ineffective practitioner of party politics, excelled in bipartisan politics. He found it easier to work with Democrats Lyndon Johnson and Sam Rayburn than with his fellow Republicans Senator Knowland and Representative Joseph Martin. Candidate Eisenhower had campaigned on the promise to restore Congress to its rightful place after the usurpations of legislative prerogatives by Presidents Roosevelt and Truman. The general-turned-president lacked both the interest and the skills to propose a "New Deal"-style package of domestic initiatives. To his credit, though, he made no attempt to dismantle the domestic programs that his predecessors and congressional majorities had constructed. He sought to neither build up nor tear down. By nature, Eisenhower was a unifier,[30] and as president he appealed to Congress for support in the national interest. This leadership approach won admiration and even affection for him from the Democratic majorities in Congress, but it produced few legislative victories.

Unlike Ike, other presidents facing hostile majorities battled them tooth and nail. Harry Truman, the belligerent bantam rooster from Missouri, certainly did not set the kind of example Eisenhower wanted to emulate. Truman crowed at and on occasion thundered publicly against congressional Republicans, saddling them with responsibility for the standstill in health care, civil rights, and the rest of his domestic package. They, in return, pushed through the Taft-Hartley Act, which restricted labor's rights to use union shops over the vehement opposition of the White House. Later, in 1951, Republican Senator Robert Taft sponsored a resolution against Truman's use of troops in Korea and his commitment of forces to NATO.[31]

Richard Nixon, who faced truncated majorities throughout his years as president, was as combative as Truman but remained low keyed about it. Instead of fusillades of rhetoric, which did not fit his style, Nixon claimed executive privilege to withhold information from Congress, indulged in budgetary sleights of hand, and regularly impounded funds. All these practices were aimed at circumventing Congress and the intent of the legislation it had passed. In his penchant for excessive use of impoundments (refusing to spend funds that Congress has already appropriated for a particular purpose), Nixon broke with two centuries of fiscal tradition. In the nineteenth and twentieth centuries, presidents used impoundments sparingly, and recent presidents from Roosevelt to Johnson resorted to them mainly to curtail wasteful spending on unperfected or unnecessary weapons systems or expansion of troop deployments in peacetime.[32] The bulk of Lyndon Johnson's impoundments were defense related, but he also withheld $5.3 billion from a wide variety of domestic programs in the interest of dulling their impact on an already overheated and inflation-prone wartime economy. Nixon, on the other hand, used impoundments as a tool of legislative leadership by making whopping cuts in a broad spectrum of social programs. As fiscal 1971 drew to a close, the White House's own estimates placed the figure for impounded funds at over $12.2 billion.[33] The president found it necessary in 1972 and 1973 to slash funds from agriculture, housing, and environmental programs. Waste and water treatment funds were cut in half, and housing and community development programs were put on an eighteen-month moratorium.[34]

The battle lines drawn between the Democratic Congress and Republican White House continued to plague Gerald Ford when he entered the Oval Office in the wake of the Nixon resignation. Ford resorted to the veto as his most potent tool for fighting a holding action against Democratic initiatives constantly brewing on Capitol Hill. Congress, by legislation, had foreclosed on the unrestricted use of impoundments as an alternative. When truncated majorities exist, it seems that the temptation to use presidential prerogatives to obstruct Congress is almost irresistable. Presidents who have opted for animosity and conflict in their dealings with Capitol Hill have usually lost more than they have gained.

JIMMY CARTER'S CONGRESSIONAL MAJORITY.  From the earliest days of American history, it was assumed that governors would make excellent presidents because they would have developed administrative and legislative skills on the job. Jimmy Carter's experiences with the "part-time" Georgia legislature predisposed him to underestimate the critical role that the U.S. Congress could play in his presidency. Less than one week after national political novice Carter took the oath of office, Senate Majority Leader Robert Byrd was complaining that the White House had breached political etiquette by failing to consult with the party leadership. Consultation would have helped Carter in appointing his first CIA director. Not since 1959 had Congress rejected a nominee for such a high-level cabinet-type position. Prior consultation with Senate Democrats would have demonstrated to the administration that the nomination of Theodore Sorensen would be in trouble due to Sorensen's distaste for CIA involvement in covert activities against foreign governments.[35]

Neither Carter nor his majordomo for congressional relations, Frank Moore, recognized that the House and Senate could not be dealt with in the same "hamfisted" manner that had sufficed for the Georgia legislature. Byrd was quick to inform both the president and Mr. Moore that snubbing the leadership might bring about a "slowdown" in the administration's legislation.[36]

Byrd was not the only member of the congressional leadership who developed a jaundiced view of the new president. House Speaker Thomas P. (Tip) O'Neill, Jr., was reportedly livid over two amateurish administration humiliations of the man who was considered the power in the House. The new president's first two appointments in the Speaker's home state of Massachusetts were, of all things, Republicans. Elliot Richardson was sent to lead the U.S. delegation to the Law of the Sea conference and Evan S. Dobelle was tapped to serve as protocol chief for the State Department. O'Neill's Irish-Democrat blood boiled not only because Republicans were appointed but also because he was not consulted in advance. Hamilton Jordan was responsible for the *faux pas*.[37] On another occasion during the summer of 1978 the speaker was so furious at the White House because the president dismissed an O'Neill crony from the scandal-plagued General Services Administration (GSA) that he barred Frank Moore from his office. In the summer of 1979, though, when the president was reshuffling his cabinet. Representative Thomas P. O'Neill, III's name surfaced as a front-runner for the job of secretary of transportation. The event obviously did not go unnoticed by his father, the speaker.

Fortunately for Carter, despite the less than genteel treatment O'Neill received, he was a staunch party loyalist. When other Democrats were prepared to desert the president and restore funds to the controversial B-1 bomber that the president had ordered scrapped, O'Neill stood shoulder to shoulder with the president and used his position to hold House Democrats in line with the president. The speaker was instrumental in guiding the Carter energy program through an often reluctant House of Representatives.[38] Even their rhetoric on the energy package overlapped. The president expressed "shock and embarrassment" over the House's initial repudiation of his request for standby authority to ration gasoline. The speaker repudiated his colleagues for "lack of guts."[39] Still O'Neill harbored resentment against the arrogance of the Georgians in the White House inner circle for underestimating the clout of the party leadership. In a fit of temper O'Neill caustically referred to the president's chief of staff as "Hannibal Jerkin." The "good ole boys" were unschooled in the intricacies and psychology of legislative leadership in Congress. As one Capitol Hill aide noted, "You have to deal with a lot of egos up here. . . . You've got to know where the power is and how to use it."[40]

## LEGISLATIVE LEADERSHIP: TOOLS OF THE TRADE

The Carter case study illustrates how naïve some presidents can be in their dealings with Congress. "Above politics" postures may work well in some election years for presidential hopefuls, but legislative leadership requires that the president get involved and give Congress a sense of direction.

LEGISLATIVE CLEARANCE. Since the 1920s the White House has actively interjected itself (to varying degrees) in setting the legislative agenda for Congress. Approximately 80 percent of the public bills that Congress handles are written up under White House auspices. In 1921, the Bureau of the Budget (BOB) assumed responsibility, under orders from President Coolidge, for central clearance of departmental budget requests. BOB approval was required before a department could submit its ledgers to the appropriate committees on Capitol Hill. Previously, each department carried its own budget figures to Congress without direct White House interference. Coolidge's innovation permitted the president, through BOB, to scrutinize departmental budgets and evaluate them in light of his own spending priorities. Franklin Roosevelt advanced the procedures a quantum leap by requiring that *all* legislation originating in the departments, not merely budget matters, needed a nod of approval from BOB prior to submission to Congress.

Gradually Congress came to accept the president's role as initiator of legislation and learned to expect the president to provide programs for congressional reaction. A Republican committee chairperson lectured the fledgling Eisenhower administration on its role in the legislative process by remarking "Don't expect us to start from scratch on what you people want . . . that's not the way we do things here. You draft the bills and we work them over."[41]

In the reexamination of roles that accompanied the fallout from Watergate and Vietnam, Congress, as it had sporadically in the past, took up the initiative in many areas of legislation. Nixon and Johnson had shown Congress the harvest that it would reap from excessive dependence on presidential leadership. Congressional reassertiveness evolved on an issue-by-issue basis. It did not supplant the system of legislative clearance but rather enhanced Congress's ability to address national issues from a non-White House perspective. Examples of legislative initiatives in the late 1960s are numerous. It was Representative Henry Reuss of Wisconsin, not the president who proposed revenue sharing; yet the program became the centerpiece of the Nixon administration's domestic proposals. The handling of radioactive wastes by the army was a subject unearthed by members of the House.[42] More recently, President Carter's decision to launch a Manhattan-type project (as was used to develop the atomic bomb quickly during World War II) to produce new synthetic fuels and spend billions doing it had been proposed in both the Senate and House before the president saw the wisdom of the suggestion.

Even with the increasing congressional tendency to raise issues and specify solutions, the practice of legislative clearance through the White House is very much alive. It remains a potent leadership tool in the hands of a president willing to use it. Members of Congress realize too that the legislation that they create themselves has a greatly enhanced chance of passage if it can be placed in the stack of bills considered as the "president's legislative package."[43]

EXECUTIVE ORDERS, RULES, AND REGULATIONS. If a president finds himself lacking in statute or constitutional authority to do something he considers in the national interest, he may use executive orders to implement his wishes. Executive orders are simply directives issued to departments and agencies by the president or others under his authority giving the bureaucracies instructions on applying a law, treaty, or court decision, or on discharging a constitutional duty. In 1955, Associate Justice of the U.S. Supreme Court Hugo Black expressed reservations about the constitutionality of executive orders. "They look," Black contended, "more like legislation to me than properly authorized regulations to carry out a clear and explicit command of Congress."[44] No similar misgivings seemed to encumber presidents, however.

In 1907, the State Department began to number executive orders. By January 1978, the number was 12,034. But that figure is most likely a gross understatement as the numbering system includes fractions (106½) and letters (108A). Congressional research Service analyst Louis Fisher estimated the number might be upwards of 50,000 or more.[45] Due to the broad and often nebulous language in the Constitution, laws of Congress, and court decisions, executive orders are justifiable. After all, the president is responsible to see that the laws be executed faithfully. When the laws are unclear, someone must interpret them. Executive orders permit the president the discretion to manipulate the day-to-day operating procedures for any agency should he wish to do so.

The White House can also issue executive orders to "end run" Congress if delay or resistance on the Hill seems likely. Franklin Roosevelt, for example, in June 1941, seized the strike-bound North American Aviation plant in California by executive order, which he justified doing as commander-in-chief. A short time later, he commandeered several other defense-related businesses in the national interest. It took Congress two years to authorize similar seizures by legislation that granted him the power under the War Labor Disputes Act of 1943.[46]

Executive orders have also proved invaluable to presidents committed to civil rights who find themselves facing a less than enthusiastic Congress. Harry Truman desegregated the armed services by executive order at a time when even his own party was deeply divided over equality for black Americans. His executive order (9981) established a committee on equal treatment and opportunity in the armed services and declared it a national policy that "equality of treatment and opportunity in the Armed Services without regard to race, color, creed or national origin" be observed immediately.[47] Since that time, Truman's successors have used executive orders to force compliance with the equal employment opportunities provisions in federal contracts. In Chapter 8 we shall discuss in more detail the manner in which presidents have used federal contracts to bring businesses into compliance with White House directives.

At times, presidents have used executive orders like a credit card, permitting the White House to buy now and pay later. While Congress was out of session, for example, Lincoln borrowed money and instituted a draft with no prior legislative authority. More recently, John Kennedy began the Peace Corps by executive order before seeking congressional financing for it.[48]

In sum, executive orders enhance presidential prerogatives while often chipping away at the importance of Congress's role in passing legislation. Congress, as we shall note shortly, has revised legislation and has become enamored with legislative vetoes to stunt the executive powers and the tendency of presidents to use executive orders to advance initiatives that might be defeated if presented as separate bills on Capitol Hill.

LIAISONS AND LOBBYING: HOW PRESIDENTS CONVERSE WITH CONGRESS. Given the broad range of presidential obligations and the size of Congress, personal contacts between the president and individual members of Congress on a regular basis are impossible. To bridge the gap that results, presidents have used go-betweens or liaisons to do their bidding for them on Capitol Hill. Since the Eisenhower years, a unified liaison operation has become a part of the White House staff. Prior to that time, responsibility was parceled out among a number of individual staffers. Some pushed for legislation, treaties, and consent on presidential appointments; others carried patronage requests (jobs) from the Hill to the Oval Office; still others arranged personal meetings between the president and members of Congress.[49] Eisenhower and later Kennedy preferred that the same people handle all these functions simultaneously as a part of their shared responsibilities. Kennedy and Johnson centralized operations further by ordering that departments and agencies that had been using their own liaison officers for a long time to coordinate their efforts with the White House liaison operation be directed by battle-hardened Kennedy campaign veteran Lawrence O'Brien.[50] The Eisenhower operation did not make much of an effort to pamper members of Congress with promises of pork barrel projects and political appointments; but it did provide information about his programs to members of Congress and sought to line up the votes necessary to sustain the president's positions on crucial issues. Lawrence O'Brien, like George Washington Plunkitt of Tammany Hall, recognized that jobs and boodle were the lifeblood of political coalitions, and so his liaison operation was used both to garner votes for the New Frontier and Great Society legislation.

Liaison officers can be helpful indeed to presidents who value a working relationship with Congress. They can serve as conduits taking information from the White House to the Hill and taking requests and complaints from the Hill to the Oval Office. These operations tend to work well if the president is willing to invest experienced personnel and his own personal time to assure a smoothly operating system. Still, the finest personnel are of little value if they cannot command the necessary attention on Capitol Hill. In Washington, regular access to the president is, in part, the stuff of which power and respect are fashioned. Kennedy and Johnson valued their liaison operations and permitted regular access to the Oval Office for O'Brien and members of his staff. Both JFK and LBJ had great respect for O'Brien's judgment and viewed congressional relations as crucial to the success of their administrations. Richard Nixon, on the other hand, had an experienced operation headed by former Eisenhower liaison Bryce Harlow;[51] but he held the legislative branch in such low esteem that, after the first year in office, both Nixon and Harlow became disenchanted with having to pamper Congress. Even though Nixon expanded the system to include an assistant to the president for congressional relations and deputy liaisons for House and Senate affairs, it deteriorated quickly after Harlow's departure and did little to improve Nixon's chronic difficulties with Congress.[52]

Former House Minority Leader Gerald Ford upgraded the operations that had atrophied in the later Nixon years. Ford met daily with his liaison chief, Max Friedersdorf, and other top assistants including counselor John Marsh to hammer out priorities for that day on Capitol Hill. When Ford decided to govern by issuing vetoes, Friedersdorf had the thankless task of lining up the votes to sustain.[53]

The job of assistant for congressional relations in the Carter administration went to Frank Moore, who had performed a similar role for the former Georgia governor several years earlier. The early months of the Moore operation have been variously described as a "comedy of errors," a "fiasco," and an "unmitigated disaster." It took Moore a while to realize that the U.S. Congress couldn't be handled like the Georgia legislature. Certain amenities were expected, and Moore bruised a number of egos in Congress by overlooking those niceties. He reportedly failed to return phone calls, overlooked requests, missed appointments with members of Congress, and neglected to consult with the congressional Democratic leadership.[54]

After what could be most charitably described as a shaky start and several mid-course corrections, the liaison operation perked up. Late in 1977, Vice President Mondale, a Senate veteran, scrutinized Moore's operation. Once again, the operation was under study in April 1978[55] as Carter and his senior staff aides went to Camp David to iron out a range of problems. After this second confab, the liaison office was increased from four to seven members. The administration also lowered its sights with respect to the number of bills it considered "priority." The number shrunk from an unrealistic sixty to a more manageable thirty.

The White House adopted a most effective innovation to deal with crucial legislation. The new "task force"[56] approach paid handsome dividends for Carter in his efforts to scuttle the B-1 bomber and sell the unpopular twin Panama Canal treaties to a wary Senate. The operation called for a senior White House aide to coordinate the effort to see that no presidential tool of persuasion was left unused. Lobbyists were responsible for identifying the undecided members who were brought in to talk with chief White House and State and Defense department leaders or even the president himself. The system was used to the advantage of the White House too on Carter's veto of an extensive public works bill and to engineer the president's much ballyhooed reform of the civil service promotion system. Liaison operations have worked relatively well for the presidents who were committed to making them work.

### PAMPERING CONGRESS: TECHNIQUES OF PERSUASION

The White House can be a mother lode of political riches for representatives and senators seeking favors. Dispensing this largess can yield stacks of IOUs for leadership-oriented presidents. One of the sweetest of these political plums has always been the patronage appointment. The various civil service acts have trimmed back on the "spoils" system for dispensing federal positions, but the White House still has a number of rewards it can distribute to the faithful on the Hill. The president and his department secretaries control about 6,700 positions including 3,500 top executive department jobs, 140 White House employees, 523 federal judges, 93 U.S. attorneys, 94 U.S. marshalls, and 2,100 positions on boards and commissions.[57] In local areas presidents may appoint U.S. marshalls, members of the Selective Service boards, and regional white-collar employees. Politics has been described as "who gets what, when, and how." Deciding who gets what federal job can be burdensome and even loathsome for some presidents. Dwight Eisenhower complained that he had little time to do anything but take requests from Republicans who wanted to cash in on their campaign efforts after twenty years of being members of the "out party" unemployed. Woodrow Wilson initially refused to let political considerations enter into his appointments. Wilson told his postmaster general, "On appointments, I am not going to advise with reactionary or standpat Senators or Representatives." The postmaster counseled the president,[58]

> the defeat of the measures of reform that you have next to your heart [will result]. The little offices don't amount to anything. . . . It doesn't amount to a damn who is postmaster at Paducah, Kentucky. But these little offices mean a great deal to the Senators and Representatives in Congress. . . . If they are turned down, they will hate you and will not vote for anything you want. It is human nature . . .

The president eventually came to see the wisdom of the postmaster's counsel.

Another president, Jimmy Carter, committed himself to making judicial appointments on a nonpolitical basis. By 1979, however, at least one candidate, Archibald Cox, found himself being passed over probably because of his long-standing friendship with Senator Edward Kennedy, then a potential Carter rival in 1980. A commission appointed by the president to suggest nominees for the federal court positions had placed Cox at the top of its list for a circuit court appointment.

White House liaisons to Capitol Hill during the Carter years have complained that the stocks of patronage jobs are shrinking. Eric Davis, in an interview with a few of these liaisons,[59] found them frustrated with the lack of jobs to use as bargaining chips:

> With patronage, there have been a lot of problems. First of all, there's simply a lot less patronage to go around. . . . The plum book . . . put out for John Kennedy in 1961 was a couple of inches thick. The plum book we had was maybe 1/5 the size. . . . What they [the Ford administration] did was take a political job, abolish it, and create a new civil service job. The job description had all the proper civil service code words in it, and it said nothing about being involved in political work. What happened, though, is that the guy who lost the political job got the new civil service job. So in . . . HEW, there's 135,000 employees, but the President and Califano together make only 115 appointments.

Even though the list of patronage jobs has shrunk, patronage can still be a valuable instrument in the hands of a president who wants to garner support on Capitol Hill.

Since senators are in the enviable position of approving presidential appointments and treaties, presidents are eager to practice senatorial courtesy (the White House consults with its own party's senators in each state in which federal appointments are to be made). In making other appointments, presidents must demonstrate appropriate deference to the resident committee barons. President Kennedy, for example, ran into problems in the Senate over his plan to nominate NAACP counsel and later Supreme Court Justice Thurgood Marshall to a federal judgeship on the Second U.S. Court of Appeals. James O. Eastland, the venerable chairman of the Senate Judiciary Committee who hailed from Mississippi, kept holding up the nomination from committee action. Later, Eastland met Attorney General Robert Kennedy in the Senate hallway and reportedly suggested, "Tell your brother that if he will give me Harold Cox, I will give him his nigger (a disparaging reference to Marshall who is black)."[60] Cox, a classmate from Eastland's college days, was appointed to a federal judgeship of his own. Kennedy had seen the handwriting on the wall. Any patronage appointment involves some political trade-offs. There are liabilities. As Lincoln reportedly said, "Filling a patronage job creates nine enemies and one ingrate."

PORK BARREL. Legislators with clout like Senator Eastland can also expect the White House to generously ladle out federal money for water projects, post offices, new courthouses, jail facilities, and the like in their states and districts. It should come as no surprise that large defense installations were being placed in the Southeast when the seniority system raised Southern senators and representatives to top committee positions in Congress. Could it be that the White House decision to place the manned space craft center in Houston had anything to do with the fact that the House Appropriations Committee chairperson then was George Mahon of Texas, the House Ways and Means was chaired by Wilbur Mills of neighboring Arkansas, and the House Banking and Currency Committee in the House was the fiefdom of Wright Patman, also from Texas? It is also a curious coincidence that the architect of the 1958 Space Act[61] was Senate Majority Leader Lyndon Johnson and his interest in space affairs was shared by Speaker Sam Rayburn, who like Johnson was a Texan.

For every decision on the placement of a defense contract, the building, transfer of forces, or closing of a military base and project approval for dams, recreational facilities, and the like, interested presidents who are willing to soil their hands with political promises can enhance their chances of congressional support on major programs that are dear to their hearts.

FAVORS, AMENITIES, AND PRESTIGE: SHARING THE GLITTER OF THE PRESIDENTIAL SEAL. In addition to jobs and pork barrel, the president can share his national spotlight with cooperative colleagues on Capitol Hill. Like Santa Claus at a shopping center, he can have his picture taken with eager, smiling members of Congress. He might invite them to special White House functions or give parties for them. Lyndon Johnson's barbeques, especially those at the Texas ranch, were legendary. Along with the food and festivity came very effective personal arm twisting. Harry Truman used to visit his old friends up on Capitol Hill for lunch. John Kennedy treated members of Congress to fine wines and sumptuous meals and serenaded them by trotting out the Marine Band's chamber ensemble for these occasions. Especially helpful members of Congress might be privileged to stand around before national television cameras for the signing ceremony accompanying the passage of an important piece of legislation.

These dollops of flattery are unlikely to change a member's vote on a particular issue. They can, however, help the president to build a reservoir of goodwill that can be tapped at a later date. Unlike patronage and pork barrel, presidents don't consider these courtesies as requiring anything specific in return. In some cases these courtesies can be rebuffed. President Kennedy, for example, tried to cultivate support with Senator Harry Byrd of Virginia even to the point of helicoptering to Byrd's Virginia ranch to wish him a happy birthday. Nevertheless, Kennedy had almost continual problems with powerful Southern conservatives like Byrd and Senator Richard Russell of Georgia.[62]

Presidents have even taken to the campaign trail for their friends in Congress. If the president's coattails are long and strong, his presence with the accompanying ruffles and flourishes can enhance the image of Senator Throttlebottom as he battles for reelection. If the president is not popular in a state, however, his visit can be the kiss of death to the often unsuspecting congressional candidates. At a Colorado stop, President Carter, in 1978, referred to Democratic Senator Floyd Haskell as a national treasure. On election night, Colorado voters who were not particularly enchanted with Carter and were disturbed with Haskell's liberal voting record and support of the Panama Canal treaties, buried the "national treasure" under an electoral landslide.

GOING OVER THE HEAD OF CONGRESS. Lyndon Johnson said in his memoirs that "there are times when a president must be willing to bypass Congress and take an issue to the people."[63] Unfortunately for Woodrow Wilson, there were no television airwaves on which to take his message in support of the League of Nations across the nation so he had to do so by train. The trip almost killed him. Today's presidents have mass media, especially television, to carry their messages into the homes of Middle America from the grandeur of the Oval Office. As we shall note in Chapter 9, however, the electronic media can be a mixed blessing.

By appealing to the public, a president might stir up the electorate on an issue and get the adrenaline flowing on Capitol Hill as a result of public outcry. In times of war appeals of this type can be highly effective as Franklin Roosevelt's fireside chats show. Still, on domestic issues of particular importance, a president might invoke a sense of national purpose to arouse public cooperation and congressional support. The last few decades provide several examples of this phenomenon. President Eisenhower pushed federal aid to education arguing that the first space satellite, "Sputnik," proved that our science education in the United States was inferior to that of the Soviets. Lyndon Johnson declared a "War on Poverty" and made impassioned appeals to the fairness of the American people as he sought support for the Civil Rights Act of 1964 and the Voting Rights Act of 1965. To dramatize the energy bind in which the nation found itself, Jimmy Carter, frustrated by congressional stalling on his energy program, termed the crisis the "moral equivalent of war" in hopes of convincing a skeptical public that a real, not a contrived, shortage did exist.

In taking an issue to the public, the president is in an excellent position to get prime-time media coverage (especially television) of his addresses. As we discussed in Chapter 1, it takes a special type of personality to use the media effectively. In Chapter 9, we shall analyze presidential addresses, press conferences, and media operations as tools of leadership. Suffice it to say here that presidential speeches over television garner better Nielsen ratings than do "equal-time" speeches that the networks grant to those with opposing views. Richard Pious reported that President Ford's State of the Union address reached 75 million TV viewers. Three broadcasts in reply on different evenings attracted a *total* audience of 47 million.[64]

THE PARADE OF EXPERTS: OTHERS SPEAK FOR THE PRESIDENT'S PROGRAM. The next best thing to a visit from the president himself is a visit from his advisors. Pressing White House business or the president's own ineffectiveness on the stump may discourage him from personally taking to the road to sell his programs to the people. In these cases, he may resort to staging some "road shows" manned by a cast of superstars who praise his policies from coast to coast. In an attempt to rescue the floundering strategic arms treaty with the Soviets (SALT II), President Carter dispatched former Arms Control Director and SALT negotiator Paul Warnke flanked by supportive experts from the State and Defense departments into the hinterlands. They presided over local seminars at which invited business executives, the press, and academic types were briefed on SALT and urged to let their senators know that they supported the final draft as negotiated.[65] This approach was not a Carter innovation, though. John Kennedy had sent administration officials to thirty-one cities in an attempt to sell Medicare in the countryside and to goad Congress into being more cooperative with the Kennedy health care package.[66]

Some presidents have adopted a variation on this theme by bringing former government leaders out of retirement to support the administration position before the House or Senate. When the Panama Canal treaties were having tough sledding in the Senate, President Carter paraded out former President Ford and his Secretary of State Henry Kissinger to add their support to the cause. This maneuver put the Senate on notice that the president's position had the support of the leadership of both parties.

## THREATS, COERCION, AND VETOES

If gentle persuasion and indirect advice to Congress prove fruitless, presidents may unleash their most potent weapons to intimidate their opponents. Lyndon Johnson used his role as commander-in-chief of the Defense Department like a master to line up votes for the 1964 Civil Rights Act. Defiant senators and representatives were informed that certain army, navy, and air force installations and the VA hospitals in their states or districts were obsolete and scheduled for closing. When those legislators recanted and lent their support to the civil rights legislation, almost miraculously, the shutdowns, after "reexamination," were rescinded.

Threats can be made to one member of Congress in the privacy of the Oval Office and then leaked to the press to produce maximum effect on other potential straying sheep. Lyndon Johnson was a master of this ploy. There was once a press report in *The New York Times* that Johnson called Senator Frank Church to the White House and dressed him down for writing an article for Walter Lippmann detailing his own opposition to the war in Vietnam. Reportedly, Church apologized to the president, "I didn't go any further than Walter Lippmann." Johnson, so the story goes, replied caustically, "Well Frank, the next time you need a dam for your state, you better go to Walter Lippmann." Senator Church later claimed that the conversation never took place and that the White House circulated the apocryphal story "trying to threaten the dissenters . . . to suggest the kind of punishment that could be taken against us." The press report also seemed calculated to portray Church as a bootlicker who trembled at the prospect of raising the wrath of the president.[67]

Typically, Nixon took the game of political hardball one step farther. When he realized that his nomination of Judge Clement Haynesworth to the Supreme Court was in jeopardy, he sensed an assault not just on the appointment but on his very capacity to lead the nation. In response, his administration tightened the thumbscrews on the undecided and unfaithful senators. Those who wavered were warned that access to the White House would be forfeited if they broke ranks with the president. Others were intimidated by threats that the Internal Revenue Service would carefully scrutinize the tax returns of senators who defied the president on the Haynesworth nomination. Nixon's abuses of power increased public revulsion over Watergate and should put future presidents on warning that, when they resort to such blatantly coercive methods to keep Congress at bay, they will be treading on the thinnest of ice.

CONSTITUTIONAL COERCION: THE VALUE OF THE VETO. Shortly after a bill has survived the obstacle course in Congress and makes its way to the Oval Office, as Table 5.2 shows, the president has four options that he must weigh.

Presidents who opt for signing or leaving a bill unsigned during the session are choosing a positive or at least relatively neutral posture with respect to Congress. Signing a bill is an admission on the president's part either that he is not opposed or that he recognizes that the bill is the best he can get on a particular issue. Letting a bill become law represents a cooperative nod toward Congress but leaves the president's options open. Vetoes are, by their very nature, negative and friction producing. They may weaken a president's standing in Congress enough to jeopardize the rest of his programs. Vetoes, like explosives, may get rid of a particular problem, but they must be handled with care lest the aftershocks be more dangerous than the original problem.

THE VETO: LEADERSHIP OF LAST RESORT. Although such presidents as Franklin Roosevelt, Grover Cleveland, and Gerald Ford wielded the veto regularly, it is normally a weapon of last resort especially when major legislation is involved. The chances of Congress's overriding the president with a two-thirds vote of those present in both houses are slim indeed. This is especially true when a president has

**TABLE 5.2**
## PRESIDENT'S OPTIONS WITH A FINISHED BILL

| OPTION | PROCEDURE | REASONS/VALUE | RESULTS |
|---|---|---|---|
| Signing | Affix signature within ten days of receiving bill. | Generally approves. | Bill is law. |
| Not signing during the session | Let bill remain on the desk for more than ten days. | Wants no blame for the bill's passage. | Bill becomes law without his signature. |
| | | Lets Congress have its way. | |
| | | Leaves door open to issue executive orders to negate the intent of the bill.* | |
| Simple veto | Refuse to sign bill and send message to Congress with explanation. | Law is unconstitutional.+ | Bill is returned to Congress for vote on override. |
| | | Can force Congress to correct the bill to the president's liking if a two-thirds vote for override is unattainable. | |
| | | Can argue that funds are not available for the program . . . the proposal is irresponsible and the president is responsible. | |
| | | To jettison pesky riders.‡ | |
| Pocket veto | Hold bill submitted with fewer than ten days left in the session. | No need to anger any person or group since no explanation is required. | Bill dies with the end of the session. Must be resubmitted and again go through each step in the legislative process. |

*President may also do this with bill he vetoes and is overridden by Congress.

+May also be used as a reason for not signing; invites court test.

‡No longer likely to have many riders due to the Legislative Reorganization Act of 1970 that can require a two-thirds vote in the Senate to add these amendments to bills.

cultivated a working coalition in Congress. Richard Nixon, for example, used a coalition of conservative Southern Democrats and Republicans to sustain all but six of his forty-three vetoes. Gerald Ford had comparable success taking advantage of the same coalition. Not all presidents were prone to resorting to the veto, but those who did had a high success rate.

Some presidents prefer to use the veto almost as a calling card to remind potential House and Senate mavericks that they are alive, well, and unafraid to confront a defiant Congress. Franklin Roosevelt has often been quoted as having directed his aides to find him bills that he could veto.

Contrary to conventional wisdom, which suggests that vetoes are used to interfere with major legislation, vetoes are more likely to be used on private rather than on public bills.[68] Private bills apply to individuals or small groups, whereas public bills encompass the nation as a whole. These private bills might involve such things as pension claims, special immigration exemptions, or money for relief to a citizen whose house has been damaged by debris from a plummeting U.S. satellite. Former White House fellow Thomas Cronin has estimated that 90 percent of the vetoed bills are not related to a major policy, and vetoes of these are usually sustained by Congress.

Major legislation accounts for a small percentage of the vetoes. Usually, presidents have used their liaison officers and party leaders to get tax, appropriations, and authorization legislation shaped into formats that the White House can at least live with. "The President rarely vetoes a tax bill," according to Brookings economist and tax expert Joseph Pechman, "even though very few of them satisfy him in every detail. In the past thirty years only two important bills [evidently referring to tax bills] have been vetoed and Congress passed both over the President's veto."[69]

Presidents who face hostile majorities in Congress are more likely to resort to using the veto on major bills than are those blessed with a more friendly cast of characters on Capitol Hill.[70] President Andrew Johnson, whose twenty-nine vetoes were more than double the number of any predecessor, found it necessary to use the veto to head off Radical Republican aims in Reconstruction legislation and the Tenure of Office Act. Congress overrode the hapless president on Reconstruction and later tried to use the tenure of office legislation as an excuse to impeach him. Harry Truman found it necessary to use vetoes to deal with a coalition of Republicans (majority party) and conservative Southern Democrats who had enacted the Taft-Hartley Act. He also used it to shanghai Joseph McCarthy-era internal security legislation like the McCarren Act.

USE AND ABUSE OF VETOES: THE NIXON-FORD YEARS. Presidents Kennedy and Johnson used the veto sparingly, and neither had one overridden. Their successors, Nixon and Ford, who had to interact with antagonistic Democratic majorities, found it a convenient way of squelching Democratic Party programs orchestrated from Capitol Hill. Both Nixon and Ford stretched tradition to the breaking point by using pocket vetoes during midsession adjournments (within the session for holidays and so forth) to kill health care, vocational rehabilitation, farm labor, and wildlife preservation legislation. No veto messages were required, and the bills died within ten days because Congress was not in session. Up to that point, pocket vetoes on major bills had been used to kill bills on the president's desk at the end of the session. To circumvent this cynical maneuvering from the White House, Congress began adjourning temporarily subject to recall by the party leadership. Later in a suit filed by Massachusetts Democratic Senator Edward Kennedy against the practice of midsession pocket vetoes, federal district court and appeals court judges ruled that the Nixon actions were unconstitutional. Nevertheless, the Ford administration continued the practice,[71] possibly waiting for a definitive statement on the practice from the U.S. Supreme Court. Despite the controversy surrounding the veto methods and frequency of use during these two administrations, both were quite successful in having the vetoes sustained by effective conservative coalition building.

THE VETO AS A PERSUADER: A QUESTIONABLE FUTURE. In his first three years as president, Jimmy Carter found it necessary to use the veto only three times in dealing with his Democratic colleagues in Congress. In each case, his position was sustained. The threat of veto has proved potent enough to force adjustments in a controversial piece of legislation especially when the president faces a Congress with substantial majorities from his own party. Mustering a two-thirds vote to override becomes highly difficult to virtually impossible in these situations.

In the future, presidents will continue to find vetoes useful for hatcheting private bills that amount to pork barrel for individuals or groups at the expense of the taxpayers as a whole. These types of vetoes can be highly effective "political statements." [72] to budget-conscious voters. The pocket veto may go the way of the great white whale since Congress, today, is in virtually continuous session and the courts have looked with a jaundiced eye at midsession pocket vetoes. Either type of veto (simple or pocket) will continue to be a two-edged sword. They can destroy poorly formulated or unduly expensive legislation, but they can also sabotage the working relationship between the White House and Capitol Hill.

Implicit in the continued use of the veto by a particular president is an attitude of contempt for Congress. Richard Nixon learned, when his political life was at stake before the House Judiciary Committee and the Senate Select Committee investigating Watergate, that haughty presidents can pay an awful price for their arrogant dealings with Congress.

DANGER OF PREROGATIVE GOVERNMENT. Representatives and senators are a proud and sometimes vindictive breed. When they feel themselves collectively abused, they eventually strike back with a vengence. Lincoln ran roughshod over Congress during the Civil War and Andrew Johnson paid the price for it. More recently, Lyndon Johnson and Richard Nixon bypassed, hoodwinked, and defied Congress on the Indochina war, and presidents since then have been strapped with legislation limiting use of troops and funds for certain geographic areas and now have a War Powers Act to contend with. These foreign affairs problems will be aired in more detail in Chapter 6, but they illustrate that the sins of one president are usually visited upon his successors. The ultimate in congressional restriction on a president is to hold him liable to letters of impeachment. Short of that worst case scenario, legislators can use statutes to hold him accountable and constrain any penchant he might have for leading the nation in flagrant violation of the principles embodied in the constitutional system of checks and balances.

# CONGRESSIONAL REASSERTIVENESS

The battles between the Democratic Congress in the Nixon-Ford years left in their wake an abundance of enactments restricting more recent presidents that did not burden most of their predecessors. Congress still avails itself of the traditional methods of checking the president via tight-fisted control of the purse strings (appropriations and revenues), Senate consent on appointments and treaties, and so forth. In the 1970s, however, the House and Senate augmented these with a number of innovative strategies to refill their time-honored bag of checks-and-balances tricks.

POWER THROUGH PROCEDURES. "If there is one word which describes the essence of Congress, that word is," according to Representative Les Aspin, "*proce-

*dures.*"[73] Legislators revel in open rules, closed rules, motions to table, consent calendars, and the like. It is not merely the fact that so many members of Congress are lawyers that predisposes them so favorably to legislative procedures and circumlocution. Sometimes they can permit legislators to conceal their votes from constituents. Imagine interested voters trying to figure out how their representatives voted on the first House attempt to end the war in Vietnam. The vote came on a motion to table a motion to instruct House and Senate conferees to insist on the House version of the Defense Reorganization Act in light of the legislative Reorganization Act of 1970. Confusing? To a layperson yes, but this maze provides a safe haven for timid members of Congress.

Procedures also enable Congress to defy the president without ever having to discuss the merits of the particular issue involved. In 1972, for example, Defense Secretary Melvin Laird presented recommendations to the House and Senate Armed Services Committee asking that a new weapons system be added to the Pentagon budget. The House Armed Services Committee obliged him by passing the new Hard Target Re-Entry Vehicle (HTRV) bill, but strong opposition surfaced in the Senate. Without dallying on the merits of the weapon, the Senate Armed Services Committee bailed out on the sticky issue by declaring that the request to include the HTRV in the Pentagon shopping list got to them too late. Thus, the Senate had not been permitted to examine the bill before it reached conference. (Note: A joint House-Senate committee that irons out differences between bills passed on the same subject but in different forms in each house.) Thus, Congress was able to reject the controversial addition on the transparent pretext that only one house had considered the matter.[74] The new missile the president wanted had been shot down on a technicality. Chalk up another one for procedures.

CONGRESSIONAL OVERSIGHT AND LEGISLATIVE VETOES. Congress is constantly attempting to increase its share of control over the activities of the agencies and departments of the federal government. Still, legislation usually delegates leadership to the president and the department heads, and a certain flexibility in application of the broadly stated provisions of any particular law. The Legislative Reorganization Act of 1946 instructed congressional committees to "exercise continuous watchfulness of the execution by administrative agencies concerned with any laws . . . within their jurisdiction." As the number of federal programs has grown, state and local governments affected have pressed Congress to make sure that loans, grants, and the like are distributed equitably. The practice of closely scrutinizing the enforcement of law by the executive branch agencies is usually referred to as Congress's *oversight* function.

Oversight is no simple proposition given the chronic problems Congress has had with information gathering and management. To improve its capacity to monitor the activities of the departments, Congress has beefed up its investigative and analysis arms, the General Accounting Office and the Congressional Research Service. Two more offices, the Office of Technological Assessments and the Congressional Budget Office were added to enhance the ability of the House and Senate to independently assess technological and budget questions on the basis of information gathered independently of the executive branch. Oversight has been especially difficult for Congress in the foreign policy and national security areas as we shall examine in more detail in Chapter 6.

For oversight to work effectively, senators and representatives need time, expertise, and information to examine the agencies carefully. Their personal workloads and pressures from their old friends and colleagues who represent the agencies or interest groups are obstacles to careful scrutiny of agency operations. Comptroller General Elmer Statts commented a few years ago that[75]

> We have trouble getting people on the Hill to read GAO reports despite the summaries and précis of our findings. . . . You would think they would want to ask their staff what's available.

As a result of these complicating factors, oversight tends to be sporadic at best. Morris Ogul suggests that oversight will be most likely in cases[76]

a) involving the concerns of their constituents,
b) involving narrow issues which do not cross committee lines of jurisdiction,
c) in which a crucial committee member is personally interested,
d) in which an agency official angers a Congressman or Senator, and
e) which might damage the President when he is a member of a different party from the Congressional majorities.

LEGISLATIVE VETOES.  One of the most significant, if not most often discussed, changes in the relationship between the branches has been the increasing use of "legislative vetoes." The House and Senate have begun to depend on them to keep departments and agencies and even the president, himself, accountable to Congress. The term *legislative veto* refers to any of a number of provisions that one house, both houses, or a committee in either house might enact to forestall or halt executive actions taken under discretion granted to them by Congress in a piece of legislation.

The whole concept of legislative vetoes can be confusing because we normally imagine presidents' vetoing laws passed by Congress not Congress's vetoing presidential decisions. Legislative vetoes reverse the customary roles of the two branches. The practice is not a new one, but it has been infinitely more popular since 1970 than in any previous decade. Congress has used concurrent (passed by both houses) and simple (passed by one house) resolutions to accomplish a variety of things:[77]

1. It has reserved power to terminate a statute or program by concurrent resolution.
2. It has asserted power to enable or require executive action by concurrent resolution.
3. It has made administrative exercises of delegated power contingent upon congressional approval or disapproval by concurrent or simple resolution.

Major policy conflicts between the White House and Capitol Hill have often resulted in concurrent or simple resolutions aimed at tying the hands of the president or agency heads with spending ceilings and thresholds (money spent beyond a certain figure must be reported to Congress), cut-off dates, prohibitions (e.g., no troops could be used in Angola in 1975 by legislative veto), and reporting provisions (Congress must be informed or veto), and "report and wait" provisions (Congress must be informed or consulted with under stated circumstances within a given period of time). These vetoes have been placed both in resolutions and in other types of legislation and have forced the president and the departments to (1) spend funds that were withheld, (2) end the sale of "peaceful" nuclear technology to certain nations, (3) suspend the sale of weapons to certain allies for violation of agreements on the use of the weapons (Turkey after its invasion of Cyprus), (4) limit special trade concessions to nations that Congress viewed as violators of the human rights of their citizens, and (5) report to Congress on troop movements, impoundments, executive agreements, and declarations of national emergency.

In addition to concurrent and simple resolution vetoes, another variation, *the committee veto*, has come into vogue in recent years. These obligate an executive agency to submit its programs, before implementing them, to a designated congressional committee or chairperson who may forbid the action that he or the committee judges violates the letter or spirit of applicable legislation. The first committee veto, dating back to 1867, illustrates the way in which they work. Appropriations for the White House building and grounds were restricted to $35,000 during the Andrew Johnson administration, and no further payments could be made unless submitted to and approved by a joint committee of Congress.[78] Committee vetoes usually include "coming to agreement" provisions that require department heads to make sure that their programs jibe with the judgments of the congressional committees that oversee their department. Provisions of this type cause agency heads dilemmas when the views of the oversight committee and the president's executive orders conflict.

Legislative vetoes have become so common that a committee of the American Bar Association found thirty-nine examples in the Health, Education, and Welfare (now HHS) appropriations alone. The controversial HEW regulations on sex equality in public education including sports were subject to legislative provisions and could not be effected until Congress had been given the opportunity to block them by concurrent resolution.[79] Evidently, even the most specific of regulations have not been beyond the gaze of congressional committee watchdogs.

LEGISLATIVE VETOES: PRESIDENTS RESPOND. Every president from Truman through Carter has voiced his displeasure with legislative vetoes. Lyndon Johnson and Gerald Ford even used their presidential veto power on bills because they included unacceptable legislative vetoes. Sometimes, however, a president may find it in his best interest to sign a bill despite its legislative veto provisions. Franklin Roosevelt signed Lend Lease and other wartime measures because of the powers they gave him and despite the restrictions imposed on the president. Likewise, Richard Nixon approved the 1974 Impoundment Control Act because he wanted the authority to defer spending funds already appropriated by Congress. He was willing to overlook the fact that deferrals were made subject to one-house vetoes. Presidents have come to realize that legislative vetoes are likely to be tacked onto any legislation that delegates congressional authority to the White House or a department. As a result, the president may be forced to sign legislation he is not totally happy with. In the words of an old song about love and marriage, "You can't have one without the other."

Jimmy Carter, typifying the attitudes of most of his predecessors said,[80]

> Legislative vetoes authorize Congressional action that has the effect of legislation while denying the president the opportunity to exercise his own veto.

The president realized that Congress might be hard pressed to enforce these veto provisions against a president so he said that he would view them as "report and wait provisions" but that he would not consider them legally binding.

# PRESIDENT AS LEGISLATIVE
# LEADER: ASSESSED

Convincing Congress to follow the president's lead in legislation is no easy proposition. He must demonstrate to members of the House and Senate that he has public support for his programs. Can he sell his domestic programs to deal with specific social and economic ills if there is no consensus that the problems are worth attacking? One of Jimmy Carter's greatest frustrations in pedaling his energy package on Capitol Hill was the fact that a large segment of the public refused to believe that a crisis really existed. If voters recognized no reason for alarm, is it reasonable to suppose that Congress would take steps to implement a set of policies that would raise oil and gasoline prices, ensure large profits to oil companies, and further limit available fuel supplies? The president's decision to require that thermostats in public buildings be raised to 78° fahrenheit in summer and lowered to 65° fahrenheit in the winter was much more valuable in raising public consciousness that a problem actually existed than it was in saving large quantities of oil.

Today, the president has become the keystone of the legislative process. There are a number of reasons why this is the case.[81] First, he has the information necessary to formulate defensible policies. In addition, he, more than any other political figure, has the prestige necessary to rally public support to formulate and implement "national" policy that might work hardships on some regions or groups in the interest of the nation as a whole. No other public figure is capable of using his prestige to reconcile feuding factions and lead them boldly and consistently in a particular policy direction. The most effective legislative leaders to sit in the White House were those who could intuitively sense and imaginatively articulate the needs and moods of the nation and construct policy accordingly.

Reformers often suggest that development of more party responsibility and party line voting in Congress would infinitely enhance the president's chances of acting as an effective legislative leader. In theory, the point is well taken, but practice in the 1960s and 1970s seems to relegate such thinking to the category of pipedreaming. A president's ability to lead Congress hinges more on what he does than on any changes in Congress that he might wish for.

To be an effective legislative leader a president must

1.   Respect the importance of his party and its leadership in Congress in guiding his programs through the House and the Senate.
2.   Recognize the dangers of overburdening Congress with a number of programs without setting priorities and being realistic in his expectations about what he can sell.
3.   Be willing to admit that patronage, pork barrel, and prestige are tools of the trade and use them to the utmost.
4.   Use Congress as a barometer of interest group and regional attitudes as he attempts to construct a domestic program that will deserve nationwide support.
5.   Consider consultation not as a sign of presidential weakness in his dealings with Congress but as a way to develop consensus and as a method to improve the quality of legislation.

While these suggestions are not a recipe for presidential domination of the legislative process, they do represent techniques for dealing with Congress that will enhance a president's chances of making policies that will endure because they have been fashioned with consensus in mind.

## NOTES

[1] *Christian Science Monitor,* July 2, 1979.

[2] Dom Bonafede, "Carter's Relationship with Congress—Making a Mountain out of a 'Moore-hill'," *National Journal,* March 26, 1977, p. 460.

[3] *Ibid.,* p. 460.

[4] Paul Angle, ed., *The Lincoln Reader* (New York: Pocket Books, 1954), p. 146.

[5] Lyndon Johnson, *Vantage Point* (New York: Holt, Rinehart and Winston, 1971), pp. 441-442.

[6] U.S. Constitution, Article II.

[7] *Ibid.*

[8] James Madison, *Federalist 10,* in *The Federalist,* ed. Edward Mead Earle (New York: Modern Library, 1937), pp. 53-62.

[9] Nelson W. Polsby, *Congress and the Presidency* (Englewood Cliffs, N.J.: Prentice-Hall, 1971), p. 3.

[10] Theodore Sorensen, *Watchmen in the Night* (Cambridge, Mass.: M.I.T. Press, 1975), p. 89.

[11] Robert Sherrill, *Why They Call It Politics* (New York: Harcourt Brace, 1979), p. 119.

[12] *Ibid.,* p. 119.

[13] See Kevin Phillips, *The Emerging Republican Majority* (New Rochelle, N.Y.: Arlington House, 1969) and, more recently, William Rusher, *The Making of the New Majority Party* (Ottowa, Ill.: Green Hill, 1975).

[14] Erwin C. Hargrove, *The Power of the Modern Presidency* (New York: Knopf, 1974), p. 206.

[15] *Ibid.,* p. 206.

[16] Sherrill, *op. cit.,* p. 124.

[17] *The New York Times,* July 25, 1979.

[18] Sorensen, *op. cit.,* p. 89.

[19] Charles Peters and Nicolas Lemann, *Inside the System* (New York: Praeger, 1979), p. 102.

[20] Sherrill, *op. cit.,* p. 119.

[21] Brief personal interview after a "For background only briefing" with Secretary Kissinger, May 13, 1975, in the Muehlbach Hotel, Kansas City, Missouri.

[22] This comment is based on evaluation of data in Congressional Quarterly Service, *Electing Congress* (Washington, D.C.: G.P.O., 1978), pp. 68-71.

[23] For a discussion of the reasons behind Carter's problems with Congress, see *National Journal,* May 19, 1979, p. 830.

[24] Senator Henry Jackson spoke out against SALT, and Senator Edward M. Kennedy had his own ideas about national health insurance.

[25] Randall Ripley, *Congress: Process and Policy* (New York: W. W. Norton, 1978), pp. 308-316. This section is based on the Ripley models on the cited pages.

[26] Liaisons will be discussed in more depth later in this chapter.

[27] *The New York Times,* March 23, 1966 as cited in Louis Koenig, *The Chief Executive* (New York: Harcourt Brace, 1975), p. 175.

[28] Ripley, *op. cit.,* pp. 322-323.

[29] Emmett John Hughes, *The Living Presidency* (New York: Coward, McCann, & Geoghegan, Inc., 1973), p. 63.

[30] Hargrove, *op. cit.,* pp. 60-61.

[31] Marion Irish and Elke Frank, *U.S. Foreign Policy* (New York: Harcourt Brace, 1975), p. 32.

[32] More on impoundment in Chapter 7.

[33] Mark J. Green, James M. Fallows, and David R. Zwick, *Who Runs Congress* (New York: Bantam Books, 1974), pp. 114-117, has a list of Nixon impoundments.

[34] John C. Hoy and Melvin H. Bernstein, eds., *The Effective President* (Pacific Palisades, Calif.: Palisades Press, 1976), p. 42.

[35] *National Journal*, March 26, 1977, p. 460.

[36] *Ibid.*, p. 460.

[37] *Ibid.*, p. 461.

[38] *Congressional Quarterly Weekly Reports* (hereafter CQWR) February 3, 1979, p. 195.

[39] *Christian Science Monitor*, May 17, 1979.

[40] *National Journal*, March 26, 1977, p. 460.

[41] Richard E. Neustadt, "Presidency and Legislation: Planning the President's Program," *American Political Science Review*, (December 1955) 981. See also John Johannes, *Policy Innovation in Congress (Morristown, N.J.: General Learning Press, 1972), p. 3.*

[42] William Lammars, *Presidential Politics* (New York: Harper & Row, 1976), p. 216.

[43] Thomas Cronin, *The State of the Presidency* (Boston: Little, Brown, 1975), p. 90.

[44] Ruth Morgan, *The President and Civil Rights* (New York: St. Martin's Press, 1970), p. 4.

[45] Louis Fisher, *The Constitution Between Friends* (New York: St. Martin's Press, 1979), p. 128.

[46] *Ibid.*, p. 128.

[47] Morgan, *op. cit.*, p. 11.

[48] Fisher, *op. cit.*, p. 130.

[49] A most thorough discussion of liaisons is to be found in Abraham Holtzmann, *Legislative Liaison* (Chicago: Rand McNally, 1970). More on this in the area of national security is in Chapter 6.

[50] To realize how battle-hardened O'Brien was, one need only read his own book: Lawrence O'Brien, *No Final Victories* (New York: Doubleday, 1974).

[51] On Harlow's techniques, see Rowland Evans and Robert Novak, *Nixon in the White House* (New York: Random House, 1972), p. 109.

[52] Ripley, *op. cit.*, pp. 202-203.

[53] *CQWR*, February 3, 1979, p. 195.

[54] *National Journal*, March 26, 1977, p. 456.

[55] *CQWR*, February 3, 1979, p. 195.

[56] *Ibid.*, p. 195.

[57] Ripley, *op. cit.*, p. 300.

[58] William Safire, *The New Language of Politics* (New York: Random House, 1972), p. 484.

[59] Eric Davis, "Carter's Legislative Liaison," *Political Science Quarterly*, (Summer 1979), 293.

[60] Sherrill, *op. cit.*, p. 38.

[61] Joseph Califano, *Presidential Nation* (New York: W. W. Norton, 1975), pp. 59-60.

[62] Patrick Anderson, *The President's Men* (Garden City, N.Y.: Doubleday, 1968), p. 309.

[63] Johnson, *op. cit.*, p. 450.

[64] Richard Pious, *The American Presidency* (New York: Basic Books, 1979), p. 197.

[65] One of these meetings was scheduled through the International Relations Council of Kansas City and another was scheduled 50 miles north in St. Joseph, Missouri, by the St. Joseph Chamber of Commerce. Both received State and Defense department organizational assistance. In the case of the Kansas City meetings, Secretary of State Vance sent out letters of invitation.

[66] Randall Ripley, *Kennedy and Congress* (Morristown, N.J.: General Learning Press, 1972), p. 15.

[67] Sherrill, *op. cit.*, p. 40.

[68] Cronin, *op. cit.,* p. 77.

[69] Pechman is quoted in Cronin, *op. cit.,* p. 77.

[70] Good recent articles on vetoes include Stephen J. Wayne, Richard L. Cole, and James F. C. Hyde, Jr., "Advising the President on Enrolled Legislation: Patterns of Executive Influence," *Political Science Quarterly,* (Summer 1979), 303-317. Also see Jong R. Lee, "Presidential Vetoes from Washington to Nixon," *Journal of Politics,* (May 1975), 522-546.

[71] William Mullen, *Presidential Power and Politics* (New York: St. Martin's Press, 1976), pp. 73-74.

[72] Cronin, *op. cit.,* p. 79.

[73] Les Aspin, "The Power of Procedure," in *Congress and Arms Control,* eds. Alan Platt and Lawrence D. Weiler (Boulder, Colo.: Westview Special Studies in International Relations and U.S. Foreign Policy, 1978), p. 47.

[74] *Ibid.,* pp. 49-50.

[75] Morris S. Ogul, *Congress Oversees the Bureaucracy: Studies in Legislative Supervision* (Pittsburgh: University of Pittsburgh Press, 1976), pp. 178-179.

[76] "The President versus Congress: The Score Since Watergate," *National Journal,* May 29, 1976, p. 739.

[77] See also Harvey G. Zeidenstein, "The Reassertion of Congressional Power: New Curbs on the President," *Political Science Quarterly,* (Fall 1978), 393-409.

[78] Fisher, *op. cit.,* p. 104. See also Fischer, *The President and Congress* (New York: Free Press, 1972), pp. 81-82.

[79] Robert G. Dixon, Jr., "Congress, Shared Administration and Executive Privilege," in *Congress against the President,* ed. Harvey C. Mansfield, Sr. (New York: Academy of Political Science, 1975), p. 127.

[80] Pious, *op. cit.,* p. 226.

[81] James McGregor Burns, "The Politics of the Presidency," in *Congress and the President,* ed. Ronald C. Moe (Pacific Palisades, Calif.: Goodyear, 1971), pp. 292-293.

# The Royal Prerogative: The President, Congress, and Foreign Policy

Presidents and Congress have not always seen eye to eye on matters of foreign affairs; but tradition has it that the White House draws up the plans and implements them with only sporadic opposition from Capitol Hill. Few presidents have put White House attitudes about leadership in foreign policy better than Lyndon Johnson who commented in 1966 that "There are many, many who can recommend advice and sometimes a few of them consent. But there is only one that has been chosen by the people to decide."[1] This frame of mind has encouraged presidents to make agreements with foreign nations, dispatch the army and navy, launch covert operations, and commit the United States to foreign powers without prior consultation with Congress. The more presidents sought to expand America's commitments in the name of our national security, the more docile, impotent, and isolated from the decision-making process Congress became.

During the later years of the Vietnam engagement, the worm began to turn. Congress began a measured assault on the prerogatives of the "imperial" presidency. The newly found legislative assertiveness, however, left allies and enemies alike scratching their heads as they pondered who was in charge of making U.S. foreign policy. Imagine the amazement of Soviet Party Leader Leonid Brezhnev on learning that Senate Majority Leader Robert Byrd planned to visit the Kremlin to discuss Senate misgivings about SALT II (Strategic Arms Limitations Treaty 1979) that the president had already signed in Vienna. Likewise, the Chinese communists, whose overtures to the West had begun a whirlwind courtship, were treated to a lesson in American Democracy when conservative forces led by Senator Barry Goldwater convinced a federal judge to rule that a president could not unilaterally sever a defense treaty with Taiwan without Senate consent.[2] In another case, after fourteen years of negotiations by four presidents, the House almost scuttled the Panama Canal treaty, which had been negotiated, consented to by the Senate, and ratified by the president. Members of Congress threatened to reject the legislation needed to turn the Canal Zone properties over to the Republic of Panama.

In light of these confusing signals from the United States, foreign nations could hardly be faulted for considering long-range commitments by the United States as risky indeed. Critics of American foreign policy during the Carter years faulted the White House for failing to provide sufficient, consistent leadership.

How could foreign nations be sure that the White House commitments assured

166

one day might not be undermined by congressional restrictions and reservations the next? A case in point would be the fact that, during the negotiations to end the war in Vietnam, Secretary of State Henry Kissinger promised $3 billion in reconstruction aid to Le Duc Toh and the North Vietnamese to make them more cooperative at the Paris peace talks. Congress, as it turned out, refused to appropriate the money to make good on the promise.

This chapter will examine why conflicts between the White House and Capitol Hill have been growing with respect to foreign policy. In doing so, it will sketch the evidence of congressional submissiveness in the face of mushrooming presidential prerogatives in foreign policy such as executive agreements, executive privilege, the budget, and control of information crucial to our national security. Throughout, we must ask two questions: (1) Can competition between the branches be lessened without permitting a president to disregard democratic concerns? and (2) Is it possible for a president to deal more openly with Congress without losing the image of leadership necessary for dealing effectively with foreign governments?

## THE ROLE OF CONGRESS

Some analysts such as Robert Novak complain that continued congressional encroachment in sensitive areas of executive responsibility weakens the capacity of the American system to survive in an increasingly hostile world.[3] Possibly Alexis de Tocqueville, an astute observer of the early American Republic under our present Constitution, was correct in his fears about the way in which foreign policy was to be made. He worried that the qualities needed for an efficient foreign policy (such as secrecy and speedy responses) are the very qualities that any democracy lacks.

If Congress is to avoid being doomed to rubber-stamping itself into foreign affairs oblivion, it will have to become more intimately involved in the foreign policy process. Does Congress have either the time or the interest given its vast array of duties?

While the voter, the professional politician, and the political scientist might differ about which congressional role is most important, the list of responsibilities would include at least the following: (1) lawmaking, (2) gathering information necessary for effective legislation, (3) informing the voters on issues, (4) acting as a "watchdog" over agencies, and (5) serving as a liaison between constituents and the bureaucrats buried in the bewildering layers of the numerous federal departments and agencies.[4] Today's better informed electorate makes more and more demands for assistance from its representatives, thus diverting precious staff time to parochial (local) considerations. Legislators attuned to political realities understand that, of all of their expected chores, direct constituent service provides them with the votes required for reelection. Is it any wonder, then, that the primary allocation of their resources and time are to be found applied in this area?[5]

Until very recently, the average member of Congress saw little beyond personal prestige as an incentive to become interested in foreign affairs. With the increasing evidence of domestic impact from foreign policy decisions such as wheat sales overseas and the purchase of crude oil from the nations of the Middle East, we can expect growing congressional interest and awareness in these matters. At the very least, the legislative branch should be able to scrutinize the activities of the executive branch to be able to blow the whistle on flagrant mismanagement and on executive decisions that are out of step with the political and economic realities at home and abroad. As the 1970s began, Congress was virtually incapable of gathering sufficient information to exercise effective oversight (review) functions in foreign affairs because it had surrendered the initiative over these processes almost totally to the president.

In contrast to the Congress, presidents and their subordinates have been better prepared to initiate, implement, and investigate the impact of foreign policy decisions. While the executive apparatus had been tightly centralized and hierarchical, Congress remained scarcely more than a hodgepodge of tiny kingdoms since the overthrow of congressional autocrats like "Czars" Cannon and Reed who were speakers of the House at the turn of the twentieth century. While the president was making increasing numbers of decisions on the basis of his own national view of international affairs, Congress has tended to adopt a basically regional view. While the executive branch skillfully crafted information gathering, storage, and retrieval networks,[6] Congress plodded along with patronage staffs handling constituency problems. While electronic communications enhanced executive speed in making and carrying out decisions and protecting national security information, Congress lived up to such derogatory labels as "a most deliberative body" and "a swamp."[7]

Possibly, reforms discussed in the previous chapter might be an indication of things to come. The increased role of the speaker, the growing importance of the party caucuses, and the modification of the seniority system could augur effective congressional involvement in foreign policy. Leroy Rieselbach suggests that there are three qualities of a legislature that can help in assessing its effectiveness. The first is *responsibility*, or the speed, efficiency, and success of the policy product. Next is *responsiveness* focusing on the ability of Congress to listen to and take account of the ideas and sentiments of those who will be most affected by its actions. The third is *accountability* to the voters. The deliberative nature of the legislative process encourages responsiveness, and reelection every two years for the House cannot help but to encourage accountability.[8] However, in any measures of responsibility, Congress comes up short.

## PROBLEMS AND CONGRESSIONAL REFORM

Whenever reforms are suggested that might increase the responsibility of Congress, the fact that Congress is made up of 535 individually elected persons makes it difficult to develop reforms that can satisfy some members without frightening others. Some members profess frustration over their inability to evaluate the depth and accuracy of executive-supplied information and to assimilate the data received into coherent and effective legislation. Others have developed a keen political sixth sense that triggers alarms and institutes avoidance mechanisms lest they be informed on "security" matters. Former Secretary of State Dean Rusk told the Senate Judiciary Committee investigating executive privilege claims that some members of Congress were sorry to have received sensitive information from him.[9] Being privy to secrets can be, as Congressman Lucian Nedzi, chairman, and Michael Harrington, member of the old House CIA watchdog committee, found out, politically fatal. Both were chastised by their colleagues. Nedzi's mistake was not blowing the whistle on CIA assassination plots on which he had been briefed. Harrington, on the other hand, leaked classified information about CIA covert activities in Chile. Eventually, the entire committee was reconstituted under a new chairman, Otis Pike, and without either Harrington or Nedzi as members.[10]

## CONGRESS TO BLAME

Too often, critics of the diminished congressional role in foreign affairs blame presidential excesses without recognizing that Capitol Hill, itself, shares much of the blame. The Bolling Select Committee on Committees researching legislative reorganization found stubborn resistance to most of its proposals to reform legislative committee "business as usual." In general, Congress has been less aggressive in protecting and defending its just constitutional interests than it has been in fighting reorganizations that have threatened committee jurisdictions.[11] Joseph A. Califano, former assistant to President Johnson and former HEW secretary, pointed out that the two branches had become separate but unequal. He contended that the reasons for congressional acquiescence into second-class citizenship have been both informational and institutional.[12] Reformers must remember Congressman Chet Hollifield's reminder about reorganizations:[13]

> If you affect . . . the powers of the various committees of Congress, you may as well forget it. The only way to get one or more of these proposals [for executive branch reorganization that will affect committee jurisdictions] is to allow the committees which now have these programs within their jurisdictions to continue to follow that program.

Members of Congress when surveyed in 1975 told the Murphy commission several things about their perceptions of their foreign policy roles. First, they were dissatisfied with the role they perceived that they were playing. Next, they thought that Congress should have a greater responsibility in foreign affairs and that the congressional role is limited by that of the executive whose role should be *broader* than theirs. Finally, members were predictably unimaginative in suggesting concrete remedies to deal with the lessened congressional role in foreign affairs.

Should role adjustment be viewed as a zero sum game (if one side increases the power it has, the other must lose a commensurate amount)? "Just because Congress can't take over foreign policy," Leslie Gelb and Anthony Lake remind observers, "doesn't mean it should abdicate its proper role."[14] Can adjustments be accomplished without weakening the initiative and secrecy that may be necessary for the president to exercise in certain foreign policy situations and area? There are no simple answers to such questions as How much secrecy is too much? and How much initiatives should Congress be able to exercise and How much should belong solely with the White House?

## PRESIDENTIAL PREROGATIVES

Traditionally, presidents have assumed leadership responsibility in foreign affairs while Congress has taken a back seat in these areas. In a televised interview with David Frost, former President Richard Nixon contended that, in matters of national security, the president possesses royal prerogatives. Although his successor, Gerald

Ford, was quick to disassociate himself from such inflammatory and antidemocratic rhetoric, in practice he too demonstrated a belief common among presidents that they command rather than consult in crisis. The king, of course, or in this case the president, defines what constitutes a crisis.

The Constitution's system of intersecting jurisdictions seems to make the struggle between the White House and Capitol Hill inevitable. Unfortunately, the document does not use the term "foreign policy" and is nebulous about the distinctions between the right to *make war* and the ability to get the men and money required to *carry it out*. Advocates of stronger roles for either the president or Congress have often resorted to dredging up time-worn arguments based on the "intent of the founding fathers."[15] The participants at the Philadelphia convention in 1787 had serious qualms about excessive concentrations of power so roles were often intertwined. The president was empowered to negotiate treaties, but the Senate was to consent to them. Congress was instructed to raise and support the armed forces while the president was assigned to command them. He could wield the weapons of war as commander, but only Congress was permitted to declare war. Ambassadors, special negotiators, and other U.S. representatives to foreign governments were presidential appointees, but they were subject to confirmation by Congress. Gradually, as the U.S. role in the world grew and international issues became both more complicated and delicate, the powers of the president expanded accordingly.

Crisis psychology accompanied the two world wars, and anxiety over aggressive intentions of the "world communist conspiracy" in the 1950s and 1960s reinforced congressional acceptance of White House leadership in the international arena.[16] Enormous advances in weapons technology ultimately made the presidents responsible for dispatching sophisticated military hardware capable of unleashing nuclear holocaust on any foreign adversary. Through radio and TV fireside chats and press conferences, presidents became father figures, fonts of wisdom, and professors capable of educating the public in the foibles and subtleties of international relations. No matter who is responsible in checks-and-balances theory, the public perceives the president as the practical lord in foreign policy.

In keeping with these images, presidents have tended to view foreign policy as their personal preserve while Congress has spent its energies on more mundane domestic pursuits. Former White House advisors have estimated that a third to half of a president's time is consumed by foreign policy and national security matters.[17] In fact, Richard Nixon once commented, "I've always thought that this country could run itself domestically without a President; all you need is a competent cabinet to run the country at home. You need a President for foreign policy."[18]

The complexity of international problems in recent decades has also enhanced the prerogatives of the president as he attempts to deal with well over 150 nations. Keeping up with the volume of information and necessary analysis requires large stables of experts, voluminous information, and strict secrecy to protect national secrets from foes and to maintain the confidentiality of discussions among our friends. Even determining who is our enemy became increasingly difficult. In the early days of active U.S. involvement in Vietnam during the mid-1960s, analysts had to determine whether the enemy to be defeated was simply the North Vietnamese, the Vietcong, or the Russians who helped to bankroll the operations bent on the capitulation of the South Vietnamese government.[19] Likewise, in the battles between Ethiopia and Somalia over the Ogaden Desert in Northern Africa, the American government had to be swift afoot to be able to switch sides from Ethiopia to Somalia when Marxist military leaders overthrew the remnants of the government of long-time U.S. ally Emperor Haile Selassie. Somalian President Mohamed Said Barré went from enemy to ally around the same time when he expelled Russian advisors as Anwar Sadat had done earlier in Egypt. The existence of international terrorism and kidnappings by networks of anarchists and Marxist-oriented groups like the Bader-Meinhoff gang of Germany, the PLO, the IRA, and so on have required delicate handling that Congress has left up to the White House. In the crisis in Iran (1979) involving the taking of American hostages, Congress as a body remained dutifully silent as the Carter administration wrestled with the problem of making appropriate and calculated responses. It became increasingly evident that merely pleasing the revolutionary leader of Iran, Ayatollah Khomeini, did not assure the safe release of the hostages because the "students" included Iranians tied to the Fadayeen Marxists and the Popular Front for the Liberation of Palestine. Congress demonstrated neither the expertise necessary to deal quickly with such crises nor the organizational leadership to be able to take united stands on such issues and respect the confidentiality of information[20] involved in learning about such conflicts.

## PRESIDENTIAL DECEPTIVENESS

The Cold War mentalities of the 1950s and 1960s accentuated the natural presidential tendencies to conceal information from Congress.[21] Open democratic societies and secrecy systems can often clash. The executive must safeguard the sensitive information that, if leaked, could endanger the national security; but who should have access to such data? The White House, its staff, and the executive departments have generated the lion's share. Capitol Hill, on the other hand, has no full-time equivalents to the analysts at the State and Defense departments and the National Security Council, on the White House staff, in the various agencies of the intelligence community, or on blue-ribbon task forces or commissions. If Congress has become a useless appendage in foreign policy, it is partly because Congress has abdicated its "need to know" by not demanding to know.

The conflict between secrecy for security and Congress's need to know presents a classic dilemma. How can Congress do an effective job of appropriating funds for weapons systems, defense installations, or assistance to foreign governments without adequate information and the ability to analyze what it receives? How can Congress oversee the agencies and blow the whistle on errors in judgment if it is kept in the dark on crucial executive agreements (nontreaty arrangements) with foreign heads of state, "stonewalled" by claims of executive privilege, bamboozled by budgetary sleights of hand by the White House, and misled or lied to by executive agents testifying before Congress? Ironically, Richard Nixon, before being elected to sit in the Oval Office himself, criticized the Kennedy administration for abusing the claim of national security. "The plea of security," he warned, "could become a cloak for errors, misjudgments, and other failings of government."[22]

A president must recognize that representatives and senators could be helpful consensus builders if they are provided appropriate and thorough information from a White House that is acting in good faith with Capitol Hill. How can legislators be expected to wholeheartedly support a policy to their constituents if they must fear that information will surface later to show that they have been mislead by the president? White House credibility with Congress was stretched to the breaking point during the Nixon and Johnson years as they used various subterfuges to weedle congressional support for their efforts in Vietnam.

TONKIN GULF RESOLUTION: A CASE STUDY IN DECEPTION. In August 1964, President Lyndon Johnson requested a congressional resolution of support for his decision to respond forcefully to "unprovoked attacks" on American fighting men in "international waters" off the coast of Vietnam in the Gulf of Tonkin. No dissenters to the request surfaced in the House, and only Senators Wayne Morse and Ernest Gruening stood their ground before a Senate stampede to support the president. The resolution applauded the president's decision to "take all necessary measures to repel any armed attack against the force of the U.S. and prevent further aggression."

Recent reevaluations demonstrate that the White House and the Pentagon purposely attempted to deceive Congress and the public to gain endorsements for strong action against the North Vietnamese. President Johnson was so sensitive to the possibility of criticism from congressional doves that he realized congressional blessings would be necessary for any engagement in a protracted conflict in Indochina.[23] *New York Times* columnist Tom Wicker reported that Johnson carried a copy of a text of a resolution in his pocket long before the Tonkin incident provided him with an excuse to use it.[24]

The *Pentagon Papers* (Defense Department study of decision making on Vietnam) and later Senate hearings about the Tonkin Gulf incident[25] point out early planned United States involvement in Vietnam. Even as President Johnson addressed the nation to explain his planned response to "aggressive" North Vietnamese acts, cables were being dispatched between Washington and Admiral U. S. Grant Sharp of the Pacific Command seeking to verify whether attacks had in fact taken place against the *Maddox* and the *Turner Joy* (two U.S. vessels operating in the Gulf of Tonkin). David Wise, in his provocative book, *Politics of Lying,* says that neither the president nor the secretary of defense were even sure that any engagement had actually taken place.[26] The commander of the task force on the scene cabled that it was doubtful that an attack had really taken place. He suggested, instead, that "freak weather effects and an overeager sonarman may have accounted for many reports."[27] During the hearings four years later, the Senate Foreign Relations Committee found a number of flaws in the president's accounts to Congress. Investigators unearthed evidence to show that (1) the *Maddox* was not on a *routine* patrol in *international* waters but on an intelligence mission close to North Vietnam, well within the twelve-mile limit and (2) American carriers and other ships were acting in support of a South Vietnamese operation against the North and were reinforcing the *Maddox* prior to the alleged attacks. In light of these discoveries, the attacks, if they even took place as reported, could hardly have been considered unprovoked.[28]

Congress took the bait and provided the president with a broad mandate to commit U.S. troops to combat with a declaration of war. Truman, at least, had the defense that he was carrying out his duties under the U.N. charter when he dispatched U.S. troops to combat as a part of the U.N. police force in Korea. The Tonkin Gulf situation presented no immediate threat to our national security as the Cuban missile crisis had, and no American property or civilian lives were at stake as was to be used as a justification in the Dominican Republic landing of the marines in 1965 and the reaction to the Cambodian seizure of the merchant ship *Mayaguez* in 1975. The Johnson administration envisioned the Tonkin resolution as what it had been seeking, namely, "the functional equivalent of an act of war,"[29] and it expanded the American role dramatically over the next few years. Although some in Congress may have intended to give a blank check to the president to use troops, the chairman of the House Foreign Affairs Committee, Representative Thomas Morgan, contended that[30]

> The resolution is definitely not an advanced declaration of war. The Committee has been assured by the Secretary of State that the Constitutional powers of Congress, in this respect, will continue to be scrupulously observed.

In the Senate, Kentucky Republican John Sherman Cooper asked the resolution's floor manager, Foreign Relations Committee Chairman J. William Fulbright, "If the President decided that it was necessary to use such force as could lead to war, will we give that authority by this resolution?" Fulbright responded, "That is the way I would interpret it." However he added optimistically, "I have no doubt that the President will consult with Congress in case a major change in policy becomes necessary."[31] That optimistic assessment turned out to be unjustified.

## COLD WAR CONSENSUS TO CONFLICT

As the Tonkin Gulf incident and congressional action illustrate, the president normally expects Congress to follow his lead in dealings with communist aggression anywhere in the world. Cold War presidents tended to view Congress as merely a "troublesome nuisance to be disposed of." From 1945 to 1965 executive-legislative relations in foreign affairs were relatively uncomplicated. The president simply made policy and Congress nodded its approval as if doing otherwise would have been, in the mood of the Joseph McCarthy era, downright un-American. There seemed to be fundamental bipartisan agreement about the gravity of the communist threat emanating from the Soviet Union. All international crises were suspected of being Soviet inspired, therefore requiring forceful American responses. Interbranch conflicts over foreign policy were the exception rather than the rule in the first twenty post-World War II years. From the mid-1960s to the present, conflict replaced consensus as the dominant theme. The bungled U-2 spy plane incident in which President Eisenhower first denied that the spy flights had taken place over the Soviet Union and later had to admit them[32] after the capture of pilot Francis Gary Powers was followed by the fiasco at the Bay of Pigs where U.S.-supported anti-Castro forces were mopped up by the Cuban government after an almost comic opera invasion. *Faux pas* like these and the growing public frustration that accompanied the U.S. role in Southeast Asia taught disenchanted voters and a wary Congress that the president and his advisors might not be infallible after all. It was no longer unpatriotic to question the veracity of White House pronouncements or the wisdom of a president's foreign policy designs.

Early in the Vietnam era, however, Congress had itself to blame, almost as much as the White House, for presidential tendencies to disregard the views on Capitol Hill. Under Presidents Kennedy and Johnson, Democratic Congresses permitted a massive growth in the executive office, approved presidential appointments without question, and presented Johnson the blank check of a Tonkin Gulf Resolution. The Senate awakened from its swoon in the later 1960s and early 1970s as it mirrored public discontent over Vietnam by drawing up a number of antiwar amendments aimed at extricating the United States from the Indochina quagmire. Most of these (such as Cooper-Church and McGovern-Hatfield) sought to bar U.S. funds for widening the conflict, to limit funds to troop withdrawal uses only, or to set dates for ending hostilities involving American forces. It took until 1972 to garner Senate majorities for these, and the House reacted to all of them by supporting the president. The *Congressional Quarterly* reported that, from 1966 through July 1973, Congress used 113 recorded votes (roll calls and tellers) in attempts to limit the Southeast Asian hostilities or to end the U.S. combat role altogether.[33] The Nixon administration was especially effective in defeating these pieces of antiwar legislation because it availed itself of a coalition of Democratic "hawks" and the Republican faithful. Although the efforts to wind down the war were of little value in doing that, they did encourage Congress to examine executive practices that helped to entangle the nation in these no-win conflicts. They also came to realize that the executive had a number of tools at its disposal that it could use to isolate Congress from foreign affairs realities.

## EXECUTIVE AGREEMENTS AND TREATIES

One of the tools that presidents have used extensively since World War II to enter into commitments with foreign nations without informing Congress has been the executive agreement. The Constitution provides for the president to act as negotiator in the treaty process, but it is conveniently silent on executive agreements.[34] Since the 1940s presidents have increasingly depended on these instruments as alternatives to treaties since the two-thirds vote needed for Senate consent to treaties is often difficult to amass. From 1940 to 1970, in fact, 95 percent of all formal U.S. agreements with foreign powers were executive agreements.[35] Although they were not in the Constitution, custom has placed them on equal footing with treaties in international intercourse.[36]

Essentially, there are two types of executive agreements: (1) congressional-executive agreements made by the president to carry out a law of Congress or existing treaty obligations and (2) "true," "sole," or "pure" agreements made under the president's constitutional authorities as commander-in-chief, chief diplomat, or chief executive.[37] The fact that the Constitution was silent about these instruments did not seem to bother George Washington who entered into a series of agreements (congressional-executive type) to aid in the handling of foreign mail under the Postal Act of 1792. Commonly, postal, trade, and nonmilitary aid congressional-executive agreements don't ruffle feathers on Capitol Hill. It is the other type—the "sole" agreements—that tend to spark tempers and raise blood pressure because major departures in foreign policy may be initiated with Congress left in the dark until dollars are needed to continue the policy at some later date. When, for example, Franklin Roosevelt sensed some isolationist balking on the Hill over his desire to provide weapons to the beleaguered British in the summer of 1940, he simply concluded a destroyers-for-bases deal with the British prime minister. Under the arrangement, the United States would receive lease rights to British bases in the Caribbean in return for transferring sixty vintage World War I destroyers to the Royal Navy.[38] Who would argue that the commander-in-chief had no authority to dispose of "surplus" goods? At the same time, FDR was providing other war materials to Britain, but it took until March 1941 before Congress agreed to fund an expanded operation under the Lend Lease Act. As the war was winding down, both Presidents Roosevelt and Truman were involved in negotiating a series of controversial executive agreements with Stalin's Russia through conferences at Teheran, Potsdam, and Yalta. Neither president sought congressional approval on these pacts, and both became targets of vitriolic criticism that lasted well into the 1950s.

Negative responses to Teheran, Potsdam, and Yalta, which charted the course of postwar Europe, and congressional discomfort over U.S. involvement in Korea spawned the "Bricker" amendment, which would have empowered Congress "to regulate all executive and other agreements with any foreign power or international organization." After heated debate in the Senate, the amendment went down to a remarkably close defeat.[39] The razor-thin margin placed later presidents on notice that executive agreements had merely survived an early test and that more salvos were in the offing.

Immediately after the Korean conflict, Congress refrained from challenging presidential leadership via executive agreements. Fear of communist expansionism encouraged congressional support for a spate of resolutions that gave the blessings of Capitol Hill to presidential use of armed forces when he judged that the national security was at stake. Congress relegated the issues of executive agreements to the back burner to present a show of national unity in the face of the communist threat. In a number of cases it passed resolutions of support. See Table 6.1.

As the Cold War consensus began to break down, the issue of executive agreements surfaced once again. Public disenchantment with the U.S. role in Indochina mounted, and Congress began to examine the wisdom of presidential commitments being made around the world via executive agreements. Second thoughts about the Tonkin Gulf Resolution also arose on Capitol Hill, especially in the Senate, as early

## TABLE 6.1
## COLD WAR RESOLUTIONS

| TITLE OF RESOLUTION | PURPOSE | YEAR |
|---|---|---|
| Formosa | To protect it and the islands of Quemoy and Matsu from Communist Chinese attack. | 1955 |
| Mideast | To protect these nations against aggression by communist-controlled nations. | 1957 |
| Cuba | To protect hemisphere nations from Castro-sponsored aggression or subversion. | 1962 |
| Berlin | To protect West Berlin from attack from East Germany or the Soviet Union and to assure Western access to city. | 1962 |
| Tonkin | To permit the president to use force to protect U.S. forces under fire in Southeast Asia. | 1964 |

Source: Compiled from Congressional Quarterly Weekly Reports.

as 1966. The Foreign Relations Committee called for a "National Commitments Resolution" in 1967 declaring that commitments could only result from the "Affirmative action of the executive and legislative branches by means of treaties, statutes, or concurrent resolutions." As any resolution, it was not legally binding on the president; but a similar resolution in 1969[40] further illustrated to the White House and the public that the bipartisan blank checks of the Cold War years were destined for the shredding machines.

The Senate sought explanations for presidential decisions to send treaties up to the Hill on such trivial matters as artifacts, student and cultural exchanges, copyrights, and the like while more monumental decisions were being handled by executive agreement. Foresaking the treaty process in the late 1960s and early 1970s, the White House concluded air and naval base arrangements with such widely spread nations as Ethiopia, Laos, Thailand, South Korea, and Portugal via executive agreements. Some of these arrangements even included the placement of nuclear weapons.[41] U.S. involvement in Vietnam, ostensibly undertaken because of U.S. commitments to the Southeast Asia Treaty Organization was, to a much greater degree, the product of a number of "sole" executive agreements with South Vietnam that dated to the Kennedy administration.

As late as 1973, Richard Nixon was still promising, in a private letter that later leaked to the press, that the United States would respond forcefully to any North Vietnamese violations of the 1973 peace accords. The Ford administration sidestepped that pledge. Evidently, Congress was not prepared to countenance any attempt to live up to Mr. Nixon's word to South Vietnamese President General Nugyen Van Thieu.[42] Nixon had also promised, through Henry Kissinger, to get most favored nations trade concessions for the Soviets to encourage further cooperation in a wide range of areas including arms control. The Senate response was simply to pass the Jackson-Vanik amendment to the Trade Act of 1974, which scuttled the White House plans by tying most favored nation status in the legislation to Soviet demonstrations that Jews could freely emigrate from the Soviet Union.[43]

CONGRESS REGULATES EXECUTIVE AGREEMENTS. Congress reacted to White House "abuse" of executive agreements by legislating limits on them. Since 1972, the secretary of state has been required to submit the final text of executive agreements to Congress within sixty days of their completion. There is one exception. Those having "national security" implications (as defined by the president) are to be submitted on a classified basis to the House International Relations Committee and the Senate Foreign Relations Committee. Senator Clifford Case, architect of this legislation, assured those fearful that it would render the president powerless in crisis and that "the executive branch does not have its hands entirely tied in dealing responsibly with foreign nations."[44] While Congress has demanded the right to examine these agreements, it has shown little stomach for the battle involved in limiting the president's ability to conclude them.

Even with the Case Act, Congress gets wind of executive agreements only after they have been concluded. Presidents can lead the nation into extended commitments that the Senate might well have rejected if submitted in treaty form. Too often, what begins as a few dollars' worth of weapons and a small group of "advisors" to another nation can snowball into prohibitive price tags in American lives and capital. Congress then has a difficult decision to make. Legislators must acknowledge the president's right to speak for the nation, but they must also try to limit his ability to commit American prestige and treasure to conflicts that can extend indefinitely.

Congress seemed prepared to bite the bullet and attack these problems in 1975 and 1976. One bill introduced in the House in 1975 sought to limit national commitments involving the introduction, basing, and deployment of U.S. forces on foreign soil and military training and equipment or financial resources sent to a foreign nation. These were to be subject to a sixty-day waiting period during which time Congress could disapprove by concurrent resolution. In 1976, the Senate held hearings on legislation to require that agreements that involve "siginficant political, military, or economic commitments" to a foreign nation must be submitted in treaty form to the Senate for its consent. On the critical issue of what is "significant," the Senate proposal remained tactically silent. Neither of these bills made it to the president's desk, though.[45]

A SUGGESTION. For Congress to assess effectively the implications of executive agreements that are submitted by the White House, it will require supportive data in the form of "impact statements" that could spell out personnel needs and provide projected cash outlay data. Had the Case Act and the impact statement provisions been operable throughout the 1950s and 1960s, Congress would have been in a position to recognize that U.S. involvement in Vietnam was escalating not by design but in a series of incremental moves aimed at striking the final blow to end the "nasty little war" that kept getting bigger and bigger. Impact statements would also have the spin-off effect of forcing policy makers in the executive branch to cost-benefit analyze situations more thoroughly. One of the most damaging criticisms leveled at the decision-making process on Vietnam during the Kennedy and Johnson years was that such basic questions as "How many lives lost are too many?" or "How many dollars are too many?" went unasked until Clark Clifford addressed them in the LBJ Tuesday lunches during 1968.

The election of Democrat Jimmy Carter dulled the sense of urgency for congressional action to restrict executive agreements. The issue is far from being resolved and could rise again when Congress represents one party and the White House marches to the beat of a different drummer. Ronald Reagan, for example, has a Democratic-controlled House and marginal Senate majorities complicating administration initiatives in foreign policy.

## TREATY POWER

The Constitutionally standard way in which presidents negotiate with foreign governments has been via treaties rather than less complicated executive agreements. John Hay, secretary of state under Presidents McKinley and Theodore Roosevelt, once suggested that a "treaty entering the Senate is like a bull going into the arena: no one can say just how or when the final blow will fall, but one thing is certain, it will never leave the arena alive." Hay lamented that the Senate "veto" on treaties was the "original mistake of the Constitution."[46] No doubt other negotiators and presidents wished that the Founding Fathers, in their wisdom, had not provided a mere one-third of the senators an axe to dismember the most meticulously negotiated treaties.

Garnering Senate consent for treaties has not always been as difficult as Hay suggested. In fact, from 1789 to 1965, nearly three fourths of the treaties submitted by the president gained Senate consent without any modification.[47] Even those creating the United Nations, making peace with a number of World War II enemies, and the later Nuclear Test Ban Treaty had reasonably smooth sailing through the Senate.[48] When presidents could convince senators that there were no hidden commitments, they have rarely been sent back to renegotiate a treaty.[49]

Controversy may arise at any number of stages in the treaty process. The Senate may question White House leadership as it decides on (1) appointments of ambassadors and negotiators, (2) requiring consultation between president and Congress, (3) the need for reservations or rejections of an already completed treaty, and (4) the value of continuation or termination of an existing treaty prior to the negotiations for a new one.

NEGOTIATIONS: WHO SPEAKS FOR THE UNITED STATES. British scholar Harold Laski once quipped, "Diplomatic negotiations are like a proposal of marriage, they must be made in private even if the engagement is later discussed in public." Members of Congress rarely questioned the leadership of the president in recognizing nations (whom we will deal with and whom we will not) or in negotiating treaties. Rather than directly undermining those prerogatives, however, senators and representatives have often used confirmation hearings as a forum for leveling broadsides at White House initiatives. The Nixon administration decision to move toward normalization of relations with Peking aroused some impassioned Senate dissent during hearings called to confirm David Bruce and George Bush as liaisons to Peking and later Leonard Woodcock as the first U.S. ambassador to the People's Republic of China.

Although the White House and its spokespersons have been the prime voices of the United States to foreign nations, private citizens and members of Congress may often contact and complicate matters with foreign governments as "unofficial diplomats."[50] During the war in Vietnam, for example, a number of "end the war" activists made pilgrimages to Hanoi in an attempt to gain a speedy resolution to the hostilities. Prominent among them were representatives of the American Friends Committee (Quakers) who met with North Vietnamese officials and Viet Cong representatives in both Paris and Hanoi. Critics of these liaisons argued that these Americans were, by their contacts, encouraging the North Vietnamese to think that the United States was hopelessly fragmented over the war. Congress likewise, in speaking critically of administration policy, was chastised by some for giving aid and comfort to the enemy. The actions of private citizens were, at least, a violation of the Logan Act (1799) aimed at persons who assumed executive authority by corresponding with foreign governments.

When Richard Nixon embarked on his 1976 journey to China as a retired elder statesman, Senator Barry Goldwater suggested that he would do the nation a favor to stay there. The trip, according to the senator, had violated the Logan Act as well. Goldwater reminded Nixon that, as the law put it, "unauthorized actions of private individuals have a potential of interfering with and disturbing the ability of the executive to make and carry out foreign policy."[51] More recently, in November 1979, it was disclosed that former Attorney General Ramsey Clark, a vocal critic of the repressive tactics of the Shah of Iran, had written to the Revolutionary Foreign Minister Ibrahim Yazdi with suggestions about ways to extradite the Shah from exile to stand trial. In this case, rather than criticizing Clark or prosecuting him under the rarely enforced Logan Act, the Carter administration found his ties to Iran useful enough to send Clark to speak for the U.S. government to the revolutionary leader, Ayatollah Ruhollah Khomeini. Still later, Clark participated in a "crimes of America" tribunal in Teheran, much to the anger of the Carter White House. It would not be difficult to imagine citizens' delegations complicating matters as some suggested was the case when several professors from the University of Kansas went to Teheran to seek the release of the Americans held hostage in the U.S. embassy there.

It has not been uncommon for individual members of Congress or delegations of them to set off for investigations overseas only to become involved in discussions with foreign governments. Representative Elizabeth Holtzman of New York headed a women's caucus group from Capitol Hill to meet with the Vietnamese-sponsored Heng Samrin government of Cambodia in 1979 to seek some basis for getting food to the victims of communist-inspired fratricide and the threatened extinction of the Cambodians as a people. Although the puppet Phnom Penh government was open to shipments of food through its eastern ports and government-controlled airports, the congressional delegations had no authority to promise equipment and personnel to transport the foodstuffs. Shortly thereafter, Representative George Hansen, without clearance from the White House or the State Department, showed up in Teheran, Iran in a personal attempt to negotiate the freedom of U.S. hostages being held by Iranian "students." This self-proclaimed ambassador without portfolio was the target of State Department criticism for diverting public and Iranian attention away from the hostage issue by suggesting that Congress would hold investigations into Iranian allegations about the Shah if the students would consider freeing the hostages. Hansen had no authorization from the congressional leadership to be making these statements, and his grandstanding did little more than convince the Iranian students that American public opinion was divided, making negotiating even more difficult for the White House. Hansen's trip was, at best, an embarrassment to the administration, but there was precious little that they were able to do to an elected representative.

CONSULTATION: ADVICE BEFORE CONSENT. When preliminary jockeying of unofficial diplomats and congressional fact finders ends, and discussions between nations reach the stage of negotiating treaties, logic would seem to dictate that presidents bring senators into the early stages of the process to help determine what elements could be sold to two thirds of the Senate. Prior consultation was not required under the Constitution, but George Washington kept the Senate up to date and sought its reactions to treaties even as they were being negotiated. Once, he personally appeared before the Senate to discuss a treaty. As we noted earlier, he left the Senate chambers in a huff, but he still preconsulted by letter with legislators whom he realized could make or break his efforts.

Gradually, presidents mothballed preconsultation with the Senate. They expected senators to rubber stamp treaties because the White House had committed the nation's honor in negotiating the provisions of these instruments. Congressional Scholar Woodrow Wilson, lacking the insights that occupancy in the Oval Office could provide, instructed presidents not to consult with the Senate or treat it as an equal partner in foreign affairs.[52] His reverence for presidential leadership was abundantly evident, but his understanding of Senate sensitivities left something to be desired. In rawest political terms, Wilson reasoned that a president could, by unilaterally negotiating a treaty,[53] force the Senate to consent because the country would be

> so pledged, in the view of the world, to a certain course of action, that the Senate would hesitate to bring about the appearance of dishonor which would follow its refusal to ratify the rash promises or to support the indiscreet threats of the State Department.

Wilson adopted this philosophy with disastrous consequences for his dream of U.S. leadership in a League of Nations. With isolationist sentiments swelling throughout the nation at the end of the war, senators who had no part in the negotiations saw little political capital in supporting the president. Opponents of the League such as Senator Henry Cabot Lodge were able to use the president's snub of the Senate as additional ammunition for torpedoing U.S. involvement in the international organization.

Wilson's tactical blunders left their marks on later administrations. President Truman, for example, astutely courted Senators Tom Connally, Arthur Vandenberg, and Walter George and openly consulted with them on the formation of the North Atlantic Treaty Organization (NATO, in 1948). The Senate, with drafting aid from the State Department, issued a resolution supportive of collective self-defense arrangements such as NATO. Later, Secretary of State Dean Acheson informed the Senate Judiciary Committee that three senators were with him during the NATO negotiations and that Senator George even authored one of the treaty provisions.[54] A congressional delegation participated in the Punta Del Este Conference of the Organization of American States (OAS) in 1962 that eventually expelled Castro's Cuba from the OAS and laid the groundwork for the much publicized $3-billion development aid package later dubbed the Alliance for Progress.[55]

RESERVATIONS AND RATIFICATION. The Constitution does not restrict the Senate to all-or-nothing options when treaties come to the Hill for a vote. Senators may condition their consent on amendments or reservations to the instrument. These reservations may take the form of interpretation of the meaning of particularly nebulous treaty terms. In other cases it might mean additions or deletions from the treaty that the other signatory nations might or might not accept. Reservations almost invariably send negotiators back to the conference table, but they usually leave the president one of three options: (1) renegotiate the pact, (2) ratify as amended (the Senate consents but the president ratifies) if the other signatories agree, or (3) refuse to ratify the treaty with Senate reservations.

From 1945 through 1974 the Senate left its marks on two score treaties, adding reservations to the OAS charter, the Japanese peace treaty, and treaties dealing with taxation, telecommunications, and sundry other matters.[56] These reservations were not crippling amendments, and so the treaties were eventually ratified in some form. If a president finds the Senate bent on crippling amendments, he can take a page out of Jimmy Carter's statements about Senate foot dragging on SALT II. The president let it be known that he would consider living up to the provisions in SALT II even if intensified unfriendly fire in the Senate made consent for the treaty impossible. The difficulty with SALT II as senators like John Glenn saw it was that, with the fall of the Shah of Iran, sensitive listening posts necessary to monitor Soviet compliance with the treaty were lost. In his judgment, the pact was unverifiable. Senators Jake Garn, Jesse Helms, and others worried about the massive fire power of the Soviet land-based system of SS 17, 18, and 19 missiles. Participation of some key senators in the early negotiations on SALT might have headed some of these differences off before they became national political issues in which liberals closed ranks behind the president and conservatives allied against him with moderates caught in the inevitable squeeze.

Often, treaties are vaguely worded so that each nation may claim a victory, at least for the sake of public relations. This purposeful lack of clarity can make the president's job of selling them on Capitol Hill difficult indeed.

The twin Panama Canal treaties provide an excellent case in point. Article I of the neutrality treaty provided for the return of the canal to Panama after the year 2000, with both nations agreeing to "maintain the regime of neutrality established in the treaty." The question of how this was to be accomplished was left unaddressed. Who was to determine when neutrality had been abridged? Did the United States maintain the right to intervene unilaterally to defend the canal or keep it open? The administration claimed those rights even though the treaty itself was silent on such specifics. To no one's real surprise, Secretary of State Cyrus Vance of the United States and Panama's chief negotiator, Dr. Romulo Escobar, presented different interpretations to their respective legislatures. In response to the flap in the Senate, Panamanian strongman General Torrijos issued a "Statement of Understanding" along with Mr. Carter supporting the U.S. view of the meaning of the treaties. A number of senators remained unconvinced of the value of Torrijo's unsigned *verbal* assurances. Senators Dennis DeConcini and Sam Nunn pressed for reservations to the treaties. The DeConcini reservation, later added to the treaty, permitted the United States to reopen the canal if necessary to ensure its operation. Nunn, on the other hand, called for a statement permitting the United States to enter into negotiations for stationing American troops even after the year 2000. The treaties, as amended, squeaked through with the barest of margins (68-32), a single vote over the required two-thirds.[57]

Only monumental and frantic last-minute White House lobbying salvaged the treaties. The administration had to neutralize extensive lobbying and media campaigns heavily financed by conservative treaty opponents. Carter decided to roll out the administration's most potent guns including his secretaries of State and Defense. He also dipped back into history a bit to add support from former Secretaries of State Rogers and Kissinger and former President Gerald Ford to blitz the nation in a roadshow designed to push the treaty at the grass roots, thus giving a gentle shove to senators soon to stand for reelection.[58] As was the case with SALT II, inclusion of senators in the delegation negotiating treaties might have helped to clear up problems without reservations or at least made the treaties more palatable on Capitol Hill. Had the president addressed these uncertainties about the twin treaties before his gaudy treaty signing flanked by seventeen Latin American leaders, he could have protected his credibility. He had given his pledge to Torrijos before he was sure that the Senate would abide by it. His leadership had been challenged but not undermined.

TERMINATING TREATIES. If presidents are not careful, Congress may begin questioning the value of already ratified treaties. In our quick-paced, ever-changing world, treaties may outlive their usefulness or at least become dated. Customarily they can be terminated in several ways: (1) by provisions within the treaty itself, (2) by giving notice of plans to terminate to other treaty partners, (3) in response to any breach of the treaty by other signatories, and (4) by claiming *rebus sic stantibus* (things have changed since the treaty was negotiated).[59] Who is supposed to determine when a treaty should be permitted to lapse or be abrogated? While the Constitution spells out the roles of president and Congress in negotiating, consenting to, and ratifying treaties, it avoids the thorny problems of deciding who has the right to take the lead in terminating them.

In principle, one could argue that, if the framers of the Constitution required the president to gain Senate consent to make treaties, consent should also be necessary to unilaterally terminate them. Senator Barry Goldwater took this tack to lambaste the Carter administration's decision to terminate long-standing defense treaty commitments with the Chinese Nationalists on Taiwan. Although a federal district court judge agreed with Goldwater's assertions, a federal court of appeals voted 6-1 to uphold the president's action, and the Supreme Court refused to consider the matter when Goldwater and his colleagues sought a final determination from the highest court in the land.[60]

Carter was not the first president to claim the authority to terminate a treaty. Franklin Roosevelt, for example, acting as chief diplomat, denounced an extradition treaty with Greece in 1933 because the Greek government did not extradite a notorious financier, Samuel Insull, who had been accused of mail fraud and extortion. Later on, in 1939, he terminated a treaty of commerce and friendship with Japan two years before the Japanese attack on Pearl Harbor.[61]

Even though the court decision in the Goldwater case might have changed things somewhat, it is likely that presidential leadership will prevail in determining when situations have changed and new directions in foreign policy are called for.[62] The Senate may continue to pass resolutions denouncing or seeking termination of particular treaties, but presidents are likely to view these statements as advice and nothing more. Ultimately, if Congress is unhappy with a treaty obligation, it can refuse to approve any implementing legislation that might be required to make the treaty operative. One such effort was launched in the House to undercut the Panama Canal treaties in 1979. Majority support for efforts of that sort could tie the president's hands and have the effect of voiding the treaty. Congress has always had the power of the purse as the weapon of last resort, but, as we shall note in our discussion of the War Powers Act later in this chapter, having the power and being willing to use it are two radically different things.

## EXECUTIVE PRIVILEGE

Not only has Congress complicated the president's leadership in choosing policy direction by treaties, but it has often tried to investigate the way in which White House decisions were reached. George Washington once argued that secrecy and dispatch in the negotiation of treaties required that the president be free to confer with his subordinates without fear of undue public scrutiny. His successors have often withheld information by claiming executive privilege such as the right of executive officials to refuse to appear before Congress and to withhold information from a legislative committee or a court. Present-day claims of "privileged" communication can be defended on the basis of precedents in the Adams, Jefferson, Jackson, and Buchanan administrations.[63]

The actual term and its modern-day applications are traceable to the Eisenhower

White House. The former general defended his decisions to withhold information from Congress by contending that "for efficient administration, executives must be completely candid in advising each other." He seemed to imply that his advisors might become more tight-lipped if they thought that their comments would eventually be examined by others.[64]

His attorney general, Herbert Brownell, argued that privilege extended to the cabinet members and other heads of executive departments also.[65] Among the items these confidants could retain as privileged included interdepartmental memoranda, advisory opinions, recommendations of subordinates, informal working papers, and materials in personnel files. Eisenhower did not view executive privilege as some abstract and rarely applicable right of the president. In fact, from June 1955 to June 1960, he invoked it at least forty-four times, which, as Arthur Schlesinger, Jr., pointed out, was more times than in the entire first century of U.S. history. These broad assertions of executive privilege denied Congress the information and analysis that could have helped in producing more realistic legislation.

Neither of Ike's immediate successors, Kennedy and Johnson, felt the need to invoke the privilege very extensively. Richard Nixon, on the other hand, found the urge irresistible. He used it to stymie a House Armed Services Committee investigation of bombing raids over North Vietnam that reportedly violated presidential directives. In August 1971 he instructed Secretary of State William Rogers to refuse to comply with a Senate Foreign Relations Committee demand for the five-year projections on plans for foreign military assistance.[66] Typical of the administration's disdain for Congress was a statement by Attorney General Richard Kleindienst in which he glibly insulted a bewildered Congress by declaring that none of the 2.5 million executive employees need appear before its committees. According to the arrogant head of the Justice Department, the only alternatives Congress had for getting the information it sought would be (1) to slice appropriations or (2) to impeach the president.[67] His pomposity shocked the Senate and further damaged the already tattered fabric of interbranch relations.

COURT HOLDINGS. In the aftermath of Watergate, the federal courts became enmeshed in the debates over the issue, since Nixon had claimed executive privilege to withhold the celebrated tapes of his Oval Office conversations with key aides from congressional and federal court scrutiny. After the president's landslide victory in 1972, the tangled web of intrigues in the Committee to Reelect the President began to unravel. House and Senate committees investigating the Nixon White House ties to the Reelection Committee and a special prosecutor (Archibald Cox) assigned to the Justice Department each considered court action to gain access to the tapes. The issue was finally resolved in U.S. v. Nixon, in which the Supreme Court upheld the right of privilege but denied the Nixon contention that it was "absolute." By an 8-0 vote, the justices upheld executive privilege but as a "qualified" right.[68]

The implications for presidential leadership in foreign affairs arose from the dictum of the case (an incidental opinion of a judge on a point not argued in the case but somehow related) written by Chief Justice Warren Burger. In his majority opinion the chief justice supported the right of a president to use executive privilege when his claim is advanced on the basis of a "need to protect military, diplomatic, or other sensitive national security secrets." The Burger dictum seemed to imply that only the president could determine what materials were sensitive enough to be withheld from congressional examination.[69] Presidents had finally received some court recognition for a long-standing practice of withholding foreign affairs information from Congress.

"INTERMESTIC" AFFAIRS: AN INCENTIVE TO CONSULT. It is becoming harder for the president to keep crucial foreign policy decisions secret. As the United States finds itself in the unenviable position of fighting inflation with one eye on our money supply and the other on OPEC oil prices, it becomes clear that foreign policy leadership from the White House has far-reaching domestic implications. Thus Congress will seek greater involvement in these decisions. The effect of oil prices on the domestic economy is but one example of the phenomenon that Bayless Manning has called "intermestic affairs" (international issues having domestic impact). Proposals to embargo wheat sales to the Soviets, OPEC members, hostage holders such as the Iranians, or the like can place a severe burden on the U.S. farmers who have come to depend on foreign sales to dispose of their bumper harvests in corn, wheat, and soy beans. Any move to cut those sales further complicates the farmers' efforts to stay ahead of the skyrocketing costs of raising cash crops with expensive equipment, costly fertilizers, high interest rates and high-priced land. Likewise, complaints that the Soviets were using sophisticated computers sold to them by U.S. corporations to improve their missile telemetry and guidance systems through miniaturization led to talk of embargoing those sales to the Soviet Union, much to the vocal dismay of major American electronic firms.

The other side of the coin applies too. Decisions intended for domestic consumption can have severe international repercussions. Greek-American lobbies labored tirelessly to get Congress to maintain an embargo on the sale of weapons to our NATO allies in Turkey in retaliation for Turkish use of U.S. weapons in the 1975 takeover of the Cypriot government from Greek-leading Archbishop Makarios. Some wags have suggested that two presidents have had trouble getting the ban lifted because there was no Turkish lobby to offset the potent Greek lobby. While it is true that Turkish actions violated U.S. legislative restrictions on offensive use of American-supplied weapons, representatives such as Paul Sarbanes and Nick Galifanikas had reason to nod to the views of Greek-American voters. Clearly, presidents cannot expect to sell their programs on Capitol Hill with calls to the national welfare. Heaven's first law in politics, after all, is, get yourself reelected.

## FINANCIAL SHELL GAMES
## AND FOREIGN POLICY

Although it is harder for the president to shield his plans than in the past, presidents have proved creative, if not devious, in recent years in hiding their foreign policy objectives from the financial axes that might be wielded by congressional committees. A huckster on the midway of a typical county fair can bewilder a gullible crowd with one green pea and three shells to cover it. Presidents have used numerous lids to shelter billions of dollars from a perplexed and often inattentive Congress. This tendency toward trickery has been manifested in such ploys as (1) confidential funds, (2) covert financing, (3) sales of excess stocks, (4) use of transfer authority, and (5) reprogramming among others.

CONFIDENTIAL AND DISCRETIONARY FUNDS. As early as 1790 Congress realized that unforeseen events might require speedy presidential response, so they granted President Washington the substantial sum of $40,000 and permitted him to decide whether the spending should be reported to the public.[70] During World War II, the concept was broadened considerably. The Manhattan Project to produce the atomic bomb was funded with secret monies. Congress authorized other discretionary funds to NASA (National Aeronautics and Space Administration), the Bureau of Narcotics, the secret service, and a number of others including the White House itself. These stashes of "mad money" were quite convenient for several recent presidents. Kennedy used them to fund the Peace Corps for its first year before congressional appropriations were voted for the program. Presidents Johnson and Nixon unearthed spending authorities originally granted during the Civil War to feed and forage the cavalry on the frontier for the purpose of funding troop movements in Vietnam and Cambodia even though Congress had prohibited new spending.[71] It is ironic that the original Feed and Forage Act was merely a stopgap measure intended to fill the needs of U.S. fighting forces at times when emergency dollars would be needed while Congress was on recess.[72] In hopes of providing greater control over these funds, Congress has recently considered, but did not pass, legislation to require specific authorization of all unvouchered spending. A companion proposal would have made the amount and nature of confidential funds visible in appropriations bills and provided for annual reports including limited General Accounting Office audits to ensure that funds are actually spent for the purposes intended in the law.

HIDE AND SEEK FINANCING. Using national security as their justification, post-World War II presidents have shielded agency expenditures from scrutiny by hiding them deep in the maze of Defense Department budget ledgers. Exposés on the intelligence community are consumed with efforts to solve the baffling mysteries that surround the way in which those agencies get their dollars to operate.[73] The federal budget is filled with "secret" accounts including funds for the FBI, the Atomic Energy Commission (now in ERDA), several White House stashes, the CIA, and others in the intelligence establishment whose accounts have been immune to audit by Congress. When the CIA director issues certificates to authorize the expenditure of funds, no public or congressional audit is ever made. The Central Intelligence Act of 1949 exempted the CIA from normal legal provisions relating to spending of government funds. The law also permits the White House to approve the transfer of funds from other agencies through the cooperation of the president's Office of Management and the Budget to the CIA. Most of these funds have been diverted for covert operations such as orchestrating the overthrow of the left-leaning government of Jacobo Arbenz Guzmán in Guatemala in 1954, the return of the Shah of Iran to the Peacock throne by the overthrow of the elected Mossadegh government in 1953, and the numerous bungled attempts to unseat Castro in Cuba since 1959.[74]

After public disclosures of CIA complicity in the overthrow of the elected government of Marxist President Salvador Allende Gossens of Chile in September 1974, Congress prohibited the agency from spending funds for covert operations, limiting it to spending for activities solely involving obtaining necessary intelligence.[75] These restrictions were not intended to short-circuit presidential leadership in crises, however. He was required to report to Congress on the size and scope of these operations, but only *after* they were completed. Ultimate decision on the need for covert operations rested with the president.

Both the White House and Congress have made efforts to make the CIA more accountable. Carter reorganized the "company" and his classmate Admiral Stansfield Turner, upon assuming the duties as director, did extensive housecleaning.[76] The House and the Senate created committees on intelligence and empowered them to demand information from the intelligence establishment through the director of the CIA. These committees were even permitted to review the budgets and subpoena information and require testimony. The urgent need for congressional oversight of intelligence became even more obvious when it became clear that the Watergate burglars had used CIA voiceboxes and burglar tools and disguises. The Nixon administration had even tried to use the CIA to undermine an FBI investigation of the Nixon campaign organization.

A Senate study committee on intelligence (the Church Committee after Senator Frank Church who chaired it) suggested in its final report that one of the major problems with secret funding was that the public was deceived as to the amount that other departments were spending because CIA and other intelligence dollars hidden in other department budgets tended to make those other departments look bloated.[77] By 1978, both President Carter and his CIA director agreed that national security would not be endangered by a disclosure of the total amount spent on all intelligence activities without any breakdown as to agency or function.[78]

SALE OF EXCESS STOCKS. If covering intelligence funds in the budget is analogous to a game of hide and seek, sale of excess stocks and reprogramming could be labeled musical chairs. The Defense Department became accustomed to declaring various weapons and munitions as "surplus" for the purposes of transferring them to other agencies within their departments or selling them to foreign nations for a nominal charge. If the president wants to provide weapons to a nation that had been budgeted a miniscule sum in military assistance, he could, as commander-in-chief, merely transfer "excess stocks," even though Congress might not have been willing to supply an equivalent amount of money for that nation's military assistance allotment. The pre-World War II destroyers for bases deal with the British (discussed earlier) is an example of action in this category.

When these weapons are transferred between agencies, a simple accounting procedure sale of, say, $1.00 permits the materials to move into places that Congress did not authorize it to go. L. Fletcher Prouty, a retired air force colonel who had served as a focal point for contacts between the CIA and the Pentagon on military support of special operations, has pointed out that these transfers to foreign governments for a pittance were invariably hidden from Congress. In fact, between 1966 and 1971, the increase in distribution of surplus stocks grew in direct proportion to congressional cuts in military assistance programs.

REPROGRAMMING. The president may also encourage an agency or department to *reprogram* funds. Reprogramming involves shifting funds within an appropriations account from one stated use to another without receiving specific congressional authorization. Timothy Ingram, in a *Washington Monthly* article,[79] cites an example of the navy's diverting funds earmarked for a tanker and three tugs to spending for a nuclear-powered aircraft carrier at a time when Congress was not enamored with the massive outlays that could be required for nuclear carriers. The navy would not have been permitted to divert the funds from the shipbuilding account to aircraft production as funds can only be shifted within one account category. Agencies would reprogram if a proposal they submitted were either unfunded or were underfunded and Congress could not be convinced to reconsider. Until 1974, Congress had fifteen days in which to figure out if diversions of this type had taken place, and, unless they disapproved, it was assumed that Congress had no complaints. Since then, Congress requires semiannual notification or prior clearance with appropriate congressional comittees.[80]

SURPLUS OR PIPELINE FUNDS. Given the inevitability of budget padding, executive departments have the potential for having unspent or surplus funds. The Defense Department and other agencies may be given congressional permission to carry funds over for use in the next fiscal year. The funds are often referred to as pipeline funds to indicate that they have already been pumped from the public trough but have not been spent yet. Pipeline funds can complicate presidential-congressional relations. In 1973, for example, Secretary of Defense Elliot Richardson candidly replied to congressional questions on what his department would do if funds for bombing Cambodia were not forthcoming. He indicated that the Defense Department would simply use funds in the pipeline or dig into its stockpiles of weapons and munitions that it could replenish later through future requests for appropriations or through later pipeline or carry-over funds.

TRANSFER AUTHORITIES. Another tool in the hands of a president seeking to circumvent congressional spending prohibitions is congressional authorization for department heads to transfer funds from one account within their budgets to another. President Nixon abused these authorities to expand the U.S. role in Cambodia even though Congress had soured on the idea of extended involvement there. He bankrolled the incursion into Cambodia with $90 million diverted from military aid money earmarked for Greece, Turkey, South Vietnam, and the Nationalist Chinese government on Taiwan. Nixon skillfully defended his decisions in these cases by referring to the Foreign Assistance Act, which allowed him to make transfers of up to 10 percent of the funds from one program to another. Congress, in the act, also gave the president the authority to spend funds if he found it "important" to the security of the United States. The Senate attached a $341-million total ceiling on Cambodian spending as a rider to the Foreign Assistance Act 1970, which the president found it necessary to sign, albeit with "great reluctance."[81] As a result of this legislation, if the president found that he needed more funds for Cambodia, he would have to return to Congress for additional authorization. Still, during 1972 and 1973, funds were being transferred in the defense budget to fund the bombing. The issue of the bombing, which had been kept secret from Congress, was, in fact, the subject of one of the proposed articles of impleachment against President Nixon. Although the House Judiciary Committee did not find the bombing an impeachable offense, it is clear that Nixon abused the transfer authority granted by Congress.

The example of the Cambodian incursion points out the problems with presidential adoption of any of these budgetary maneuvers. While it is true that Nixon was able to do what he wanted in that particular situation, he encouraged Congress to legislate limits on his budget authorities in foreign affairs. Use of these devices had so soured relations between the White House and the Hill that Congress has become accustomed to using legislative vetoes to foreclose on similar White House options in the future. We shall discuss some of these later in the chapter in a section on other congressional responses to presidential leadership in foreign affairs.

Hiding money can be difficult, but, to maintain secrecy and control in foreign policy, presidents have taken advantage of security classifications to hide information. Bill Moyers, press secretary for President Johnson, once observed that there are two major sources of foreign policy power: "One is information and the other is access to the President."[82] Even more valuable would seem to be access to the information available to the president. Critics of the "religion of secrecy" contend that presidents often classify documents to keep them from domestic opponents, not just from foreign enemies. Presidents have resorted to classification on a number of domestic fronts in efforts to embargo information from groups such as professors seeking research information, political opponents or investigative reporters seeking muck to rake, the courts seeking information pertaining to civil or criminal cases, and members of Congress and committees involved in legislative investigations.

Few would quarrel with a president's right to shield information about troop deployments in crisis, intelligence codes, strategic weapons and planning, or the like. Data of this type if leaked to a foreign power could severely undermine the national security. Sensitive negotiations with foreign powers could be scuttled if information were indiscriminately disseminated in the world press. Obviously, negotiations cannot be carried out in public because positions can change, bargains must be hammered out, and compromises are a way of life. President Wilson's promises of "open agreements" openly reached proved difficult to live up to at the time of the negotiations to end World War I and create the League of Nations. The public may be predisposed to view the give and take of diplomacy as a sacrifice of principle to gain concessions. For public consumption President Nixon took the posture of negotiating with the North Vietnamese to end the war in Vietnam on the principle of "peace with honor."[83] Secretary Kissinger's promise to Le Duc Tho to provide reconstruction aid to North Vietnam had to be soft pedaled. Likewise, as President Carter spoke of safety for the American hostages held in Iran and our national honor virtually in the same breath, negotiators at the United Nations including Ambassador McHenry let it be known that some concessions to Iran's desire for some investigation of the purported crimes of the deposed Shah were possible by letting the U.N. secretary general call for a U.N. Security Council session on the hostage issue to which representatives of the Revolutionary Council and Ayatollah Khomeini would not be invited.

**EVOLUTION OF THE SECURITY CLASSIFICATION SYSTEMS.** Since World War II, presidents have taken advantage of documents classification statutes and other devices to shield executive branch decisions and errors in judgment from press and legislative probers. The present system can be traced to 1917 when a general order of the American Expeditionary Forces set up *confidential, secret,* and *for official circulation only* categories. Army regulations broadened these in 1921 and 1935 and President Franklin Roosevelt issued Executive Order 8381 to cover maps, photos, drawings, and similar national security information. President Truman updated the order in 1951 extending the system to include "nonmilitary" agencies. By 1957, a congressional committee viewing the bloated system found 1.5 million persons authorized to brandish classification stamps. Mercifully, however, the number of stamp wielders has been cut since early 1970.[84]

Still, a familiar trinity of classifications has been used to sanctify stacks of government documents as "confidential," "secret," and "top secret." Excerpts from a Defense Department study on decision making about Vietnam (the *Pentagon Papers*) demonstrate the depth of U.S. involvement in Cambodia, Laos, and Vietnam that might never have come to the attention of Congress had the papers not been leaked by Daniel Ellsberg.[85] Imagine the chagrin among the members of the prestigious Senate Foreign Relations Committee to learn, during the Johnson years, that there were twenty categories above top secret with even the names classified as inaccessible to members of the Senate. A befuddled Senator Albert Gore asked Defense Secretary Robert McNamara at the time, "would you please clear up the identity of this clearance status that is something superior to top secret? I thought that top secret was *top secret*."[86] The names of these restricted categories, though taboo for circulation on Capitol Hill, were nevertheless available to several members of the cabinet and even some low-level military personnel.

Ironically, the Nixon administration, notorious for its passion for secrecy, instituted major reforms in the basic documents classification system. By a 1972 executive order the president reduced the number of agencies permitted to use the "top secret" stamp from thirty-four to thirteen. In addition, he cut the number of agencies permitted to use any documents classification back to thirty-five. At first glance, this may not seem like much of an improvement, yet it was a world of difference from the Truman administration. During those years there were no restrictions limiting the number of agencies that could classify documents. Security information management became a gargantuan problem. A retired air force security officer testified before Congress that in 1971 the Pentagon had amassed at least 20 million classified documents. To illustrate the problem further, another witness estimated that those documents constituted about 1 million cubic feet of paper. Former U.N. Ambassador Arthur Goldberg commented that "Seventy-five percent of these documents should never have been classified in the first place; another 15% quickly outlived the need for secrecy; and only about 10% genuinely required restricted access." Under the applicable executive order from the Eisenhower years, 55,000 government officials were authorized to classify documents as confidential, secret, or top secret. Mountains of paper were inevitable. It has been suggested, only partly in jest, that lower-level bureaucrats got into the habit of classifying documents and reports to make sure that their superiors would read them. Most of these classified materials were available to at least some members of Congress, however.[87]

WHITE HOUSE AND INTERNAL AGENCY SECRECY SYSTEMS. Increasingly media-conscious presidents have tended to worry that information supplied to Congress might leak to the press. As a result, they have developed internal White House classifications other than the normal categories. Lyndon Johnson warned his successor Richard Nixon that the success of his future policies could well depend on preventing leaks from the bureaucracies.[88] So, when Daniel Ellsberg leaked the *Pentagon Papers* to Senator Mike Gravel of Alaska who read excerpts in public, the administration worried that such practices might get out of hand. To avert disasters in the future, the administration sought court action to forbid the publication of the papers on the grounds of national security.

The potential for leaks grew as the pool of presidential advisors expanded. The National Security Council, created in 1947 to provide information and advice to presidents, became unwieldy and porous. How could meetings be kept secret? Statutory members (president, vice president, and secretaries of the state and defense departments) joined legions of others commonly invited including members of the joint chiefs of staff, CIA and OMB directors, the secretary of the treasury, and aides for each. During the Cuban missile crisis the greenest cub reporter could have sniffed out an NSC meeting at the White House by simply counting the limos pulling into the South Portico. Gradually, presidents developed a tendency to gather smaller ad hoc groups around them in crisis. John Kennedy brought together a fourteen-member executive committee to give him options for responding to the Soviet missiles in Cuba.[89] Lyndon Johnson used a similar Tuesday lunch group for advice on Vietnam.[90]

Morton Halperin and Daniel Hoffman noted that Nixon narrowed his circle of advisors as he prepared his historic China policy initiatives and the plans for extensive bombing in Cambodia. Only the president, Chief of Staff H. R. Haldeman, national security advisor Kissinger, and one member of Kissinger's staff were privy to these policies before the president went public with them.[91] Since that time, presidents have followed these leads keeping the crisis circle as tight as possible.

When the White House decides that it is time to inform some members of the bureaucracies, the creativity of the president's men is put to the test as they try to devise new classification schemes to see that information doesn't spread farther than they want it to. Finding new labels to perch atop documents to limit their distribution is not always an easy proposition as the Nixon administration found out as it racked its brains for a new classification system before *The New York Times* began serializing the *Pentagon Papers*. On one of the Watergate tapes, the president did the following thinking aloud to H. R. Haldeman, John Erlichman, and Egil Krogh:[92]

> maybe another approach to it would be to set up . . . a new classification system. . . . Don't use *top secret* for me ever again. I never want to see *top secret* in the God damn office . . . shall we call it uh, John, what would be a good name? President's secure? . . . Eyes only, is a silly thing too. It doesn't mean anything anymore.

Fortunately for presidents, if they decide to share information with one bureaucracy and not with others, they can use that agency's own internal secrecy codes. The codes were created so that one bureaucracy could shield information from competitors for the president's ear in other bureaus. This limited distribution system (LIMDIS) was approved under a national security memorandum (1972) that provided that[93]

> the originating department or other appropriate authority may impose . . . special requirements with respect to access, distribution, and protection of classified information and material, including those which presently relate to communications, intelligence, intelligence sources and methods and cryptography.

The White House can develop its own security systems to keep some departments in the dark as to its plans. It was widely reported that a naval officer assigned to National Security Assistant Kissinger's staff during the Nixon years was used by his naval commander to spy on what Kissinger was planning.

When bureaucracies develop their own internal systems of classification, they normally make the titles classified. Persons seeking information must know the classifications that exist before they can ask for information. Rarely is the security surrounding these classifications breached, but David Wise recounts an interesting example of the competition between the CIA and the FBI to learn about each other's classification codes. In March 1965, *The New York Times* ran an article about Johnson's national security assistant McGeorge Bundy, which included a picture of Bundy holding a notebook labeled "Top Secret Dinar." The picture had been in The New York Times files for some time and was pulled out for that particular article. At 9 A.M. the following morning a CIA agent rushed into the *Times* seeking the negative that he feared could be blown up to reveal the text of the document that could explain its nature. He was relieved to learn that he had arrived before "another agency" (evidently the FBI) could. Eventually the CIA retired that particular classification. Wise suggests that the cost of retiring them is prohibitive since every document so stamped had to be retrieved, typed again, and then reclassified. Interestingly enough, the executive order then applicable forbade security classifications other than "top secret," "secret," or "confidential." It is no wonder that the Senate was flustered to find that the other systems existed in violation of White House directives before 1972.[94]

DANGERS OF THE SECURITY MAZE. If the president is to act as skipper of his own foreign affairs ship, he must make himself accessible enough to listen to views that differ from the consensus of those closest to him. The more classifications systems there are, the greater the capacity of bureaucrats and White House aides with clearances to manipulate the president by seeking to control the flow of information and analysis to and from the White House. In effect, the president can become the victim of the monster he has created or is perpetuating. Since presidents hear little but praise from their staffers, they may become accustomed to "team players" and attempt to pressure dissenters back into line.

With the inauguration of Democratic president Jimmy Carter, congressional attempts to legislate some solutions to the secrecy problem ground to a halt. The Freedom of Information Act, hailed as monumental reform legislation when it was passed in 1967, has had little effect on the security system because Congress included exemptions from automatic declassification of "national security" documents. No provision was made to provide for Congress or the courts to decide what constituted "national security" so that is left up to the president. In the concluding section of this chapter, we shall discuss some possible reforms in this area.

## NATIONAL EMERGENCIES AND THE WAR POWERS

While reforms in the classification system to limit the president have stalled, Congress has been more willing to question the extent of the president's emergency and war powers. Nevertheless, when a crisis is perceived as emerging, Congress has normally been generous in providing presidents with sufficient leeway to handle it in the manner they judge best. Richard Pious estimated that there were approximately 470 statutes providing powers to the president to act "in case of emergency" by issuing executive orders. In passing legislation of this type, Congress acknowledges the leadership role of the executive.

EMERGENCY POWERS. Emergency powers have permitted a president to control the economy, regulate imports and exports, impose rationing, intervene in labor disputes, freeze wages and prices, suspend civil liberties, impose censorship, and otherwise control the information the free press can publish.[95] Most of these pieces of emergency legislation enabled the Congress to terminate these authorities by concurrent majorities. Under this type of legislation, for example, Woodrow Wilson approved the arming of merchant ships prior to formal U.S. entry into the war based on previously unrevoked emergency powers. Likewise, John Kennedy used a state of emergency that hadn't been rescinded by Congress since its passage during the Korean conflict to freeze Cuban assets in U.S. banks.

Theodore Sorensen commented on a chilling example of Congress's tendency to lavish emergency powers on the president virtually without investigation during 1974. The House Armed Services Committee, after thirty minutes of hearings, voted to extend a civil defense statute under which a Nixon executive order authorized any president who *anticipated* an attack on the United States to impose total controls on free expression, free enterprise, and free labor and free education.[96] It is hard to imagine that a committee of Congress could be so lacking in political awareness as to be oblivious to the potential for mischief that this type of authorization represents.

In recent years, Congress has become more vigilant in crisis situations as a result of the efforts of the Senate Special Committee on National Emergencies and delegated powers (the Church committee). In 1976, the National Emergencies Act provided for the rescinding of most emergency statutes and created a new method for handling them in the future. Legislators were sensitive to the need for extensive White House latitude in crisis, but they had learned that authorities once granted could be assumed forever. Today, presidents may declare a state of emergency to run for a year. On ninety days' notice to Congress, they can renew emergency powers and Congress must vote every six months to permit the state of emergency and the special powers to continue.

WAR POWERS. Commonly in emergency situations involving military action, presidents tend to view any congressional role as superfluous or at best cosmetic. Presidents have considered military action as their responsibility and so have felt no great pressure to consult with Congress when action has seemed appropriate. If past history is a valid indicator, Congress has rarely shown an eagerness to tie the president's hands when he wishes to respond to any threats he perceives to U.S. national security. A House foreign affairs (now International Relations) committee study researched by the Library of Congress identified 165 cases of uses of U.S. armed forces abroad from 1798 to 1970.[97] During that same period there had been only five declared wars, four of which merely recognized that a state of war already existed. More recently, however, in response to the Southeast Asia policies of "war by increments," Congress began to seek limits on the powers of presidents to entangle the nation in seemingly endless conflicts. Few legislative-executive conflicts pose more difficulties than the constitutional ambiguities evident in the placement of the war powers. Merlo Pusey, in *The Way We Go to War*,[98] tries to point out the basic practical questions involved in who shall assume leadership:

The basic question is not the good intentions of the President . . . we may assume that [he] will be guided by what he deems to be the best interest of the country. But Presidents, even more than other men, are likely to be caught in a rushing stream of circumstances and, even if they could always be trusted to make wise decisions, *our system rests on the assumption that many minds are more trustworthy than one on questions of war and peace.*

In empowering the president to make war while leaving the "declaration to Congress," the framers were giving the president the power to "hold an enemy at bay while Congress could make the decision as to whether further hostilities would be in the national interest."[99]

Early in our history, presidents adopted the concept of "defensive war" to justify use of troops without a congressional declaration. President Jefferson, a strict constructionist, sent the American marines and navy to the "shores of Tripoli" in an attempt to clear the Mediterranean sea lanes of the pirates who had been playing havoc with American shipping. Jefferson ordered the navy to board the Tripolitan ships and disarm them and then return them to their home ports. No invasion of Tripoli was authorized because Congress had not declared war. While subsequent chief executives usually nodded to the duty of Congress to declare war, American history is a veritable collage of examples of presidents' sending troops into battle without a declaration of war. Declared wars to date include War of 1812, Mexican-American War of 1845, Spanish-American War of 1898, World War I, and World War II. Evidently, the distinction between making and declaring war has been blurred sufficiently that it is no longer a major consideration in White House decision making.

W. Taylor Reveley, III, takes the view that the issue of war powers is best framed in terms of limits on the president's authority to pursue a foreign policy that might lead to armed conflict.[100] This view would make consultation with Congress necessary if limits were to be realistic. Unfortunately, what Congress considers "consultation" and the views of the Nixon-Ford administration did not jibe when it came to the application of the War Powers Act (1973). This legislation, which Nixon vetoed but Congress overrode, provided that the president must "consult" when possible with congressional leaders in any situation in which hostilities including the use of armed forces appeared imminent. In addition, the president, should he order military operations, must report to Congress within forty-eight hours about the circumstances necessitating his actions and the estimated amount of time involved in the operations. If, within sixty days, the Congress has not specifically authorized the president to continue to use force, then he must order the troops to disengage from the conflict. The president may get a thirty-day extension with the approval of Congress or may be given thirty days in which to get the troops home. At any time during this sixty- or ninety-day period, Congress may order the president to remove all U.S. forces from conflict. Opponents of the War Powers Act argued that it would strip the president of the military leadership he required to deal with national security crises.

TESTS OF WAR POWERS ACT. The first tests of the results of the War Powers Act involved the evacuations of Americans from Saigon and Phnom Penh. The Ford administration followed vintage SOP (standard operating procedures) in orchestrating those two operations. Ford informed selected congressional leaders after he had already made the decisions to order the marine operations.[101] Not long after this, in 1975, the Cambodian government seized an American freighter, the *Mayaguez,* in international waters near an island off the coast of Cambodia. Although the Democratic leadership complained that the president sent in the troops even before attempting to consult with Congress, most members, in the flush of patriotic fervor and euphoria of the freeing of the thirty member civilian crew, cheered the success of the operation. Freeing the crew also buoyed the sagging morale of a nation dispirited from its ignominious exit from Vietnam. In each of these cases, Ford's interpretation of "consultation" might have put him in compliance with the letter of the War Powers Act, but he was clearly not acting within the "spirit" of the law. State Department Legal Advisor Monroe Leigh admitted to congressional investigators that, by the time the president made his reports, the last American armed forces were already out.[102] Presidential Counselor Roderick Hills indicated that[103]

> The President believed that informing Congress of his actions satisfied the requirements under the War Powers resolution that he consult with Congress before beginning military operations of this type.

Speaker Carl Albert, Representative Thomas P. O'Neill, and Senators James Eastland, Clifford Case, and Majority Leader Mike Mansfield groused that they were *informed,* not consulted, at the time of the *Mayaguez* incident.[104]

Raoul Berger, prolific and probing analyst of the Constitution, saw future problems with the application of the War Powers Act in light of the precedents set in 1975, "The Senate Foreign Relations Committee," he suggested, "set its seal on the President's exercise of his constitutional powers in sinking the Cambodian patrol boats. Suppose the patrol boats the U.S. sunk . . . had been those of the Soviet Union. Is it alone for the President to make the fateful judgment that may plunge us into war?"[105] Congress bowed low to presidential leadership in crisis by permitting the White House to adhere to the letter of the War Powers Act without living up to its spirit.

While the Carter administration had its share of problems with Congress on everything from arms sales to arms control, it never crossed swords with the Democratic leaders on Capitol Hill over the use of troops. Carter did complain about congressional restrictions on his ability to assist U.S. friends in Africa in light of Russian and Cuban adventurism all over the Dark Continent, but he declared himself satisfied with the War Powers Act.

Clearly, the War Powers Act has not proven to be a precedent-setting act of congressional self-assertiveness capable of curbing presidential monopoly over the use of the tools of war. The mere passage of legislation, after all, does little to change ingrained patterns of behavior. Some critics of the act have envisioned the war powers legislation, which was watered down from the original Senate version created by Senator Thomas Eagleton,[106] as a statutory justification to presidents to use powers that the Founding Fathers were careful not to bestow. It does nothing to forbid any initial commitment of American forces, so it hardly ties the president's hands in crisis. Once the American colors have been flown, though, and lives of Americans are jeopardized, it will always be difficult for Congress to withdraw funds or forces from such engagements.

White House consultation with Congress in crisis seems unlikely. Presidents seem to prefer congressional involvement in the form of massive endorsements of actions that the White House has already planned or executed. Presidents will consult only when political considerations seem to warrant. Defining the term consultation will continue to cause difficulties because the term has different meanings depending on which end of Pennsylvania Avenue is doing the defining. Alexander Bickel has pointed out that "there is no way you can define the term other than . . . an assumption that, in the future, the Presidents will act in good faith."[107] Leadership and good faith may be one thing; but good judgment is quite another.

Probably the most potent weapon in the Capitol Hill arsenal for defending its role in foreign policy from power-oriented presidents is the control that the Constitution gives Congress over the purse strings. It can support the president with dollars for a Marshall Plan or it can restrict him by providing that no money be spent for certain purposes such as the invasion of Cambodia during the Vietnam conflict.[108] There are well over seventy such constraints and numerous legislative vetoes now a part of legislation on foreign affairs, and the number increases yearly. Provisions of this type are usually a part of such legislations as (1) arms export control legislation, (2) foreign assistance acts, (3) foreign aid appropriations, and so forth. They can be used to prohibit funds for a particular type of military operation, sale of weapons to a certain type of nation, and assistance to specified nations and even to limit operations of a particular federal agency around the world. As of 1974, the Foreign Assistance Act provided that no funds under any act can be spent for CIA operations other than intelligence gathering. On the surface, at least, that seemed to tie the president's hands in approving covert operations. But, to the contrary, Congress was unwilling to go so far as to assume a role in clearing covert operations so the act provided that these restrictions applied "unless the President finds each such operation important to the U.S. national security and reports his findings to the appropriate congressional committees in a timely fashion."[109] It is left purposely nebulous as to what "timely" means.

## MODELS OF REFORM FOR EXECUTIVE LEGISLATIVE INTERACTION IN FOREIGN AFFAIRS

Despite Representative Les Aspin's lament that "Congress is too unalterably political for reform,"[110] others have done quite a bit of brainstorming about reinvigorating the checks-and-balances system in foreign affairs. Table 6.2 summarizes the areas in which suggestions have been made: (1) internal legislative branch reforms, (2) adaptations of existing inter branch relations, and (3) plans that call for changes in the Constitution. Space constraints forbid a thorough evaluation of each of these, but they provide food for thought.[111]

### COMMITTEE JURISDICTIONS AND INTERNAL REFORMS

Overlap and duplication of effort are a way of life in foreign affairs organization on Capitol Hill. In the House, seventeen of the twenty-two standing committees have jurisdiction of some sort in foreign policy. Only one committee in the Senate has

## TABLE 6.2
## REFORMING PRESIDENTIAL-CONGRESSIONAL
## RELATIONS IN FOREIGN AFFAIRS

*Internal legislative refinements (encompassing various plans for restructuring Congress from within)*
1. Streamlining the committee structures and jurisdictions
2. Upgrading the role of House International Relations and Senate Foreign Relations Committees
3. Creating a joint committee on intelligence or national security
4. Establishing joint hearing of foreign policy committees from both houses
5. Enhancing roles for the party leadership in foreign affairs
6. Improving congressional sources of information and analysis

*Adaptive approaches*
1. Bringing the Senate in at earlier stages of the treaty or executive agreements processes
2. Creating an informal joint executive-legislative council to meet regularly on foreign affairs matters
3. Developing question-answer sessions with the cabinet members' going regularly before Congress
4. Placing members of Congress on the National Security Council
5. Establishing congressionally created and staffed liaison offices between national security community and relevant foreign relations committees on the Hill

*Constitutionally innovative models*
1. Establishing a parliamentary system
2. Providing for no-confidence votes in Congress to yield new elections
3. Requiring senatorial consent for all foreign policy-related presidential staffers
4. Requiring more status for the House in treaties because they are closest to the voters
5. According new congressionally mandated standards for classification of national security documents limiting authority to classify documents; some establishment of automatic declassification systems subject to periodic review
6. Establishing congressional statutes that more clearly define the scope and substance of executive rights to claim privilege and national security to withhold information from Congress

Source: Adapted from Frank Kessler, "Presidential-Congressional Battles: Toward a Truce on the Foreign Policy Front," *Presidential Studies Quarterly*, Spring, 1978, pp. 119-124.

no foreign policy role, and that is the Senate Rules and Administration Committee.[112] A number of analysts have suggested that congressional access to sensitive information would improve if both houses agreed to set up one committee on intelligence or national security. In recent years, well over one hundred joint committee plans of this sort have been paraded before a less than enthusiastic Congress. Recent supporters of the Joint Committee on Intelligence[113] include Republicans Howard Baker and Lowell Weicker in the U.S. Senate.[114] Both have suggested that a committee of this sort could make effective oversight of the "company" CIA possible. Other joint committee devotees have extolled the blemish-free record of the Joint Atomic Energy Committee,[115] which has proved much more leak proof than some of today's nuclear reactors. The last five presidents have lent their vocal support to one of these committees and former CIA Director William Colby chimed in before congressional investigators that "a joint committee could better retain secrecy."[116] A former "high State Department source" (as Secretary of State Kissinger reveled in calling himself in background briefings) complained constantly that he was forced to spend entirely too much of his time briefing too many committees.[117] He also sniped that he might just as well have been giving briefings to *The New York Times* or the *Washington Post,* because his information ended up there anyway. The Rockefeller commission report on intelligence, the Murphy commission report on the organization of government for the conduct of foreign policy, and such respected legal scholars as John Norton Moore have also sung the praises of joint committees as facilitating cooperation between the White House and Capitol Hill.[118] Each sees value in consensus decision making in foreign policy, but none prefers "war by committees" as the cure for the imperial presidency.

With all this high-powered support, one might reasonably wonder why these proposals have not moved beyond the drawing boards. The reasons why joint committees are an anathema on the Hill give real insight into the second-class role that Congress plays in the foreign policy process. The answer in this case seems to be that others, notably those from Capitol Hill, have serious reservations about them. Former Senate Majority Leader Mike Mansfield, a foreign affairs moderate by any standards, suggested numerous arguments against a joint committee championed by the Murphy Commission, but they basically boiled down to the following[119]

1. The committee would decrease the authority of standing committees.
2. The executive could easily abuse it.
3. No more national security information would necessarily be promised by the White House if a joint committee were instituted.
4. It would be a barrier to sensitive information reaching standing committees whereas, under the Murphy plan, the joint committee could not initiate legislation on its own.

The makeup of a joint committee could also present difficulties. If the party leadership and the chairpersons and ranking minority members of the appropriately related committees from both houses were members, the committee would be ridiculously cumbersome.[120] Time and scheduling factors would be monstrous even if subcommittees did most of the joint committee work. Scheduling problems now force representatives and senators to try to bilocate as it is without such a committee. No matter how theoretically attractive these committees might seem, in the final analysis, their proponents seem fated, like latter day colleagues of Sisyphus, to push these boulders up Capitol Hill only to watch them roll inexorably to the bottom again. If, after Vietnam and Watergate, the Murphy commission survey of Congress showed minimal support for a national security for each house, is it logical to suppose that Congress, which grudgingly approved standing committees on intelligence for each house, would eagerly press for a joint one?[121]

## CONGRESSIONAL
## INFORMATION AND ANALYSIS

The role of Congress will depend on its ability to accumulate and analyze sufficient information to answer such seemingly simple questions as (1) What went on? (2) What is going on now? and (3) What is being planned for broad future policies? "Too often," as Joseph Califano so neatly phrased it, "Congress must depend on instinct rather than on evidence."[122] Without adequate sources of information and methods of analysis, congressional "watchdogs" seem doomed to spend more time dogging than watching.

Although Congress has been eager to blame the White House for its lack of information, legislators on the Hill bear at least some of the responsibility for their information handicaps. The stock solution has been to add more staff. In recent years committee staffs have ballooned and Congress has created service institutions like the Congressional Budget Office and the Office of Technology to aid in research. Comptroller General Elmer Stats who heads the General Accounting Office suggests that Congress was not even taking advantage of the information it already receives. Stats put it this way[123]

> I don't share the view that just more people will answer Congress's problems of exercising oversight to find out how programs are working. . . . We have trouble getting people on the Hill to read GAO reports despite summaries and précis of our findings. You would think they would want to ask their staff what is available.

Members of Congress seem to prefer blissful ignorance to the responsibilities of being privy to foreign policy information, especially if it is sensitive. Many members might prefer being left in the dark to being held accountable for supporting poor executive decisions. A. Ernest Fitzgerald, the Pentagon specialist who uncovered the huge cost overruns of the air force's C-5A, accuses Congress of copping out on the C-5A with the lame excuse that it lacked the resources necessary to challenge the Pentagon on "national security issues."[124]

> Cancellation of the program was never the issue on the C-5A. They just wanted to stay ignorant. If they had gotten the facts, there was just no way they could have justified continuing the program. . . . They claim they couldn't understand the issue. The issue was *lying, cheating, and stealing.*

Unfortunately, internal reforms proposals such as restructuring committee jurisdictions, creating new joint committees, enhancing the role of party leaders as receptacles of secret information, and beefing up congressional techniques of information retrieval and analysis depend on the determination of Congress to have a role in international affairs. The adaptive models could be attempted without too much danger of permanent damage to our system of government. None of these would be constitutionally locked in so that they could be scrapped if unworkable. Still, these suggestions of more interaction between the White House and the Hill hinge on the president's willingness to share his preserve with the poachers from the other end of Pennsylvania Avenue. The constitutional innovations, while initially attractive, still would require more tampering with the "system" than either Congress or the public would likely approve. If Watergate proved anything, it showed that the responses to "imperial presidents" could include impeachment. Louis W. Koenig, cognizant of the broader sweep of American history, cautions against such constitutional panaceas as introduction of a "no-confidence" vote. He fears, and rightfully so, that tampering with the present checks and balances could be a "recipe for the Presidency's destruction." No confidence, and most of the constitutional innovative proposals, would be an overreaction to the Watergate abuses.[125] Most of the recent calls for dismantling the powers of the presidency are based on the erroneous assumption that the Richard Nixons are, and always will be, the White

House rule. Ultimately, would a "no-confidence vote" ensure congressional will to deal with presidential abuses more than the powers of the purse and the impeachment option have?

Since it is nationally recognized that White House staffs are no longer merely advising the presidents but are often making and implementing policy virtually on their own, Congress must be careful to consider the possibility of making some of those more sensitive appointees subject to Senate approval. At this point, however, the chances of Congress's being willing to divest the president of his right to staff confidentiality and the right to choose his own team make reforms along this line unlikely. Arthur Schlesinger, Jr., has suggested that Congress make a concerted effort to enact new systems for documents classification to make the president and his advisors more forthcoming with Congress; but Congress doesn't seem eager to do so because, unlike Schlesinger, they see too much to be lost in the way of legitimate presidential leadership in protecting national security information via claims of executive privilege.

A POSSIBLE FRAMEWORK FOR COOPERATION. The day-to-day *conduct* of foreign policy should logically be the president's job. His capacity for reacting quickly cannot be matched by a cumbersome institution like Congress. The *making* of foreign policy is another matter, however. An informed Congress, in closer contact with the voters can assist the White House as the president tries to convince the electorate that his initiatives warrant their support. To educate the electorate, legislators must be willing to "take the heat or stay out of the kitchen." Numerous senators, in voting for the twin Panama Canal treaties in 1978, were toying with political suicide in doing so. They had to convince their constituents of the wisdom of their decisions.

Congress will only be able to assume a useful role in checking potential presidential excesses and developing consensus behind national policies if it makes a concerted effort to accumulate usable information. Congress must then (1) take advantage of already available executive information sources, (2) improve its analysis capabilities to ensure the accuracy of the information it receives, and (3) put the president on notice, by legislation if necessary, that Congress is interested in and capable of handling national security information. Presidents, for their part, could consider the value of the adaptive approaches, especially those involving as early a system of consultation with the Senate as possible.

## CRYSTAL BALL GAZING INTO THE 1980s: PARTNERSHIP OR CONFRONTATION?

The reassertive Congress of the 1970s has developed the habit of leap-frogging from nation to nation in placing restrictions on presidential options in Angola, Cambodia, Chile, and so forth. This tendency to multiply the number of legislative vetoes on foreign aid, foreign trade, and military aid legislation has discouraged presidents from cooperating with Congress. Neither the president nor the Congress seems willing to take the bold leadership necessary to chart a broad-range foreign policy for a scaled-down American role in the world of the 1980s. Our difficulties in "winning" in Vietnam and our increasing dependence on foreign sources of energy and raw materials have been bitter pills for Americans to swallow. It becomes difficult for either the White House or the legislators on the Hill to convince the public that the "good ole days" of a U.S.-dominant post-World War II world have long since disappeared.

Congress cannot and should not be expected to guide the day-to-day operations of U.S. foreign policy, but it would be in the interests of the nation for a president to bring them into the long-range policy process as often as possible. The alternative might be congressional attempts to legislate an expanded role for themselves and White House attempts to return to Nixon-Johnson practices of deception and disrespect for democratic process.

## NOTES

[1] Arthur Schlesinger, Jr., "Congress and the Making of American Foreign Policy," *The Presidency Reappraised*, ed. Thomas Cronin and Rexford Tugwell, 2nd ed. (New York: Praeger, 1977), p. 216.

[2] *Christian Science Monitor*, November 14, 1979. Later the Supreme Court let stand a federal appeals court decision favoring the president's right to abrogate treaties without Senate consent.

[3] Robert D. Novak, "Washington's Two Governments," in *The Effective President*, eds. John C. Hoy and Melvin Bernstein (Pacific Palisades, Calif.: Palisades Press, 1976), p. 95.

[4] David J. Vogler, *The Politics of Congress* (Boston: Allyn & Bacon, 1974), p. 3. See also Malcolm Jewell and Samuel Patterson, *The Legislative Process in the U.S.*, 3rd ed. (New York: Random House, 1977), pp. 5-18.

[5] For more on this, see John S. Saloma, *Congress and the New Politics* (Boston: Little, Brown 1969), p. 185.

[6] Congress in 1970 had a mere ten computers, most of which were used for payrolls, inventory, and personnel work as reported in U.S. Congress, House, Select Committee on Committees, Staff Report, *Congress and Technical Information*, 93rd Cong., 2d sess., May 1974, p. 32. Joseph Califano estimated that, at the midpoint of the 1970s, the White House had available for presidential uses about 4,000 on-line computers in Joseph A. Califano, Jr., *A Presidential Nation* (New York: W. W. Norton, 1975), p. 57.

[7] Robert Sherrill, *Why They Call It Politics* (New York: Harcourt Brace, 1979), p. 108.

[8] Leroy N. Rieselbach, *Congressional Reform in the Seventies* (Morristown, N.J.: General Learning Press, 1977), pp. 8-9.

[9] U.S. Congress, Senate, Committee on the Judiciary, Subcommittee on Separation of Powers, Hearings, *Executive Privilege*, 92nd Cong., 1st sess., 1971, p. 345.

[10] Good discussion of these problems in John T. Eliff, "Congress and the Intelligence Community," in *Congress Reconsidered*, eds. Lawrence C. Dodd and Bruce I. Oppenheimer (New York: Praeger, 1977), p. 201.

[11] See the testimony of Harold Seidemann of the University of Connecticut in U.S. Congress, House, Select Committee on Committees, Panel Discussion, *Committee Organization in the House*, vol. 2 of part 2 of 3, 93rd Cong., 1st sess., 1973, p. 389.

[12] Califano, *op. cit.*, p. 55.

[13] Panel Discussion, *Committee Organization in the House*, p. 390.

[14] Leslie Gelb and Anthony Lake, "Congress: Politics and Bad Policy," *Foreign Policy*, 20 (Fall 1975), 123.

[15] Rowland Egger and Joseph P. Harris, *The President and Congress* (New York: McGraw-Hill, 1963), p. 2. See also Arthur Schlesinger, Jr., *The Imperial Presidency* (New York: Houghton Mifflin, 1974), chaps. 1, 2, pp. 13-46.

[16] Erwin C. Hargrove, *The Power of the Modern Presidency* (New York: Knopf, 1974), p. 168.

[17] Thomas Cronin, *The State of the Presidency* (Boston: Little, Brown, 1975), p. 13.

[18] *Ibid.*, p. 13.

[19] See Robert Wendzel, *International Relations: A Policy Making Focus* (New York: John Wiley, 1977), pp. 39-44.

[20] As an example of leaks see the discussion of Daniel Schorr of CBS leaking information to the *Village Voice* on classified House committee materials on intelligence gathering. See David Ignatius, "Dan Schorr: The Secret Sharer," *Washington Monthly*, (April 1976), 6-21. See also *The New York Times*, July 23, 1976.

[21] On the problem of secrecy and interbranch relations, see Peter W. Hebeling and Amitai Etzioni, "Executive Deception: Capitol Hill's Growing Problem," *Trial*, (January 1976), 6.

[22] *National Journal*, September 7, 1974, p. 1344. Ironically, *N.J.* found that there were at least 225 instances in which executive branch agencies (1964-1974) refused to provide information to Congress. Ninety percent of them came under Richard M. Nixon.

[23] Schlesinger, *Imperial Presidency*, p. 179.

[24] Tom Wicker, *J.F.K. and L.B.J.: The Influence of Personality on Politics* (Baltimore, Md.: Penguin Books, 1972), pp. 224-225 as cited in James A. Nathan and James K. Oliver, *United States Foreign Policy and World Order* (Boston: Little, Brown, 1976), p. 394.

[25] On the *Pentagon Papers*, see Neil Sheehan, Hedrick Smith, et al., *The Pentagon Papers, New York Times* (New York: Bantam Books, 1971), p. 240. See also U.S. Congress, Senate, Committee on Foreign Relations, Hearings, *The Gulf of Tonkin, the 1964 Incidents*, 90th Cong., 2d sess., 1968.

[26] David Wise, *The Politics of Lying* (New York: Random House, 1973), p. 65.

[27] See as a good summary in Nathan and Oliver, *op. cit.*, pp. 361-363. Also see Anthony Austin, *The President's War* (Philadelphia: J. B. Lippincott, 1971), pp. 292-293.

[28] See John Galloway, *The Gulf of Tonkin Resolution* (East Rutherford, N.J.: Fairleigh Dickinson University Press.

[29] For Under Secretary Katzenbach's statements, see U.S. Congress, Senate, Committee on Foreign Relations, Hearings, *U.S. Commitments to Foreign Powers*, 90th Cong., 1st sess., 1971, p. 23.

[30] Richard Pious, *The American Presidency* (New York: Basic Books, 1979), p. 338.

[31] Schlesinger, *The Imperial Presidency*, p. 180.

[32] Wise, *op. cit.*, p. 49.

[33] *Congressional Quarterly Weekly Reports*, hereafter cited as CQWR. August 11, 1973, p. 2205. See also *CQWR*, August 2, 1975, p. 1717.

[34] On executive agreements see U.S. Congress, Senate, Committee on the Judiciary, Senate Report # 93-1286 to accompany S. 3830, *Executive Agreements*, 93rd Cong., 2d sess., November 1974, p. 4.

See also U.S. Congress, Senate, Committee on Foreign Relations, Senate Report # 92-591, *Transmittal of Executive Agreements*, 92nd Cong., 2d sess., January 1972.

See also U.S. Congress, Senate, Committee on the Judiciary, Subcommittee on Separation of Powers, Hearings, *Congressional Oversight of Executive Agreements*, 92nd Cong., 2d sess., p. 348.

A good synopsis of the problem is in Charles J. Stevens, "The Use and Constitutionality of Executive Agreements: Recent Congressional Initiatives, *Orbis* (Winter 1977), 905-931.

[35] Nathan and Oliver, *op. cit.*, p. 487.

[36] See section on the constitutionality of executive agreements in Louis Henkin, *Foreign Affairs and the Constitution* (New York: W. W. Norton, 1972), pp. 173-189.

[37] *Ibid.*, p. 173 for congressional-executive type and p. 176 for sole type.

[38] Marian Irish and Elke Frank, *U.S. Foreign Policy* (New York: Harcourt Brace, 1975), p. 456. See also John Spanier and Eric Uslaner, *How American Foreign Policy Is Made* (New York: Praeger, 1978), p. 39.

[39] On the Bricker amendment, see Stephen Garrett, "Foreign Policy and the American Constitution: The Bricker Amendment in Contemporary Perspective," *International Studies Quarterly*, (June 1972), 187-220.

[40] For a discussion of the 1967 and 1969 resolutions, see Louis Fisher, *President and Congress* (New York: Free Press, 1972), pp. 225-227.

[41] Early in 1972, hearings were held on whether some of these base arrangements should have been submitted as treaties. See U.S. Congress, Senate, Committee on the Judiciary, Subcommittee on Separation of Powers, Hearings, *Congressional Oversight of Executive Agreements*, p. 348. See also comments on this from Senator Stuart Symington who was critical of nuclear weapons deployments in *The New York Times*, July 30, 1972.

[42] On the Nixon-Thieu letters see U.S. Senate, Committee on the Judiciary, Hearings, *Congressional Oversight of Executive Agreements 1975*, 94th Cong., 1st sess., 1975, pp. 315-326.

[43] On the Jackson-Vanik amendment, see Irish and Frank, *op. cit.,* p. 303.

[44] Charles J. Stevens, *op. cit.,* contains the senator's comments at pp. 916-919.

See also *CQWR*, August 2, 1975, p. 1713. Congress was following long-standing traditions of respecting the need for presidential prerogatives in crisis in the Lockean sense that was generally accepted by the Founding Fathers. On this, see Edward S. Corwin, *Constitutional Dictatorship* (Princeton, N.J.: Princeton U.P., 1948). See also J. Malcolm Smith and Cornelius Cotter, *Powers of Presidents During Crisis* (Washington, D.C.: Public Affairs Press, 1960). See also Louis W. Koenig, *The Presidency and Crisis* (New York: Kings Crown, 1944). Further instruction in the subject can be gleaned from U.S. Congress, Senate Special Committee on National Emergencies and Delegated Emergency Powers, Report, 93rd Cong., 2d sess., June 1974. See also Frank Church, "Ending Emergency Government," *Akron Law Review,* (Winter 1975), 108. See also: John Norton Moore, "Contemporary Issues in an Ongoing Debate: The Role of Congress and the President in Foreign Affairs," *International Lawyer,* (October 1973), 738-744.

[45] Louis Fisher, *Constitution Between Friends* (New York: St. Martin's Press, 1978), pp. 208-213.

[46] Henkin, *op. cit.,* p. 371.

[47] Irish and Frank, *op. cit.,* p. 366.

[48] *Ibid.,* p. 366.

[49] Spanier and Uslaner, *op. cit.,* p. 38.

[50] See Maureen Berman and Joseph Johnson, *Unofficial Diplomats* (New York: Columbia U.P., 1977).

[51] For the provisions of the Logan Act, see Fisher, *Constitution Among Friends,* p. 157.

[52] Woodrow Wilson, *Congressional Government* (1885), pp. 233-234 as cited in Fisher, *Constitution Between Friends,* p. 194.

[53] Woodrow Wilson, *Constitutional Government in the United States* (New York: Columbia U.P., 1908), pp. 77-78.

[54] Irish and Frank, *op. cit.,* p. 274.

[55] For a discussion of the role of Congress at the Punta del Este Conference, see DeLesseps S. Morrison, *The Latin American Mission* (New York: Simon & Schuster, 1965).

[56] Irish and Frank, *op. cit.,* p. 366.

[57] Pious, *op. cit.,* p. 338.

[58] William J. Lanouette, "The Panama Canal Treaties–Playing in Peoria and in the Senate," *National Journal,* October 8, 1977, pp. 1556-1562.

[59] Arthur S. Miller, *Presidential Power* (St. Paul, Minn.: West Publishing, 1977), p. 157.

[60] See footnote 2.

[61] The Roosevelt examples come from Henkin, *op. cit.,* p. 168.

[62] On times when a president may need consensus, see Erwin C. Hargrove, *The Power of the Modern Presidency* (New York: Knopf, 1974), p. 168.

[63] William Mullen, *Presidential Power and Politics* (New York: St. Martin's Press, 1976), p. 89.

[64] Schlesinger, *Imperial Presidency,* p. 157.

[65] *Ibid.,* p. 159.

[66] For Senator Fulbright's request for this information, see Adam Breckenridge, *The Executive Privilege* (Lincoln, Neb.: Univ. of Nebraska Press, 1974), pp. 7-9.

See also negative views of executive privilege in Raoul Berger, "Executive Privilege vs. Congressional Inquiry," *U.C.L.A. Law Review,* 1044-1363. See also Berger, *Executive Privilege: A Constitutional Myth* (Cambridge, Mass.: Harvard U.P., 1974).

[67] Merlo Pusey, *The Way We Go to War* (Boston: Houghton Mifflin, 1969), p. 180.

[68] Harvey C. Mansfield, ed., *Congress vs. the President,* Proceedings of the Academy of Political Science (Montpelier, Vt.: Capital City Press, 1975), pp. 136-137.

[69] *U.S. v. Nixon,* 94 S.C., 1974, p. 3090. Chief Justice Burger supported the right of presidents to use executive privilege when the claim was advanced on the basis of "the need to protect military, diplomatic and other sensitive national security secrets."

[70] Fisher, *Constitution Among Friends,* p. 186.

See also Fisher, *Presidential Spending Power* (Princeton, N.J.: Princeton U.P., 1975), p. 207. See also Fisher, "Dark Corners of the Budget," *The Nation,* January 19, 1974, p. 75.

[71] Fisher, *Spending Power,* pp. 238-247.

[72] Nathan and Oliver, *op. cit.,* p. 496.

[73] Victor Marchetti and John D. Marks, *The CIA and the Cult of Intelligence* (New York: Dell Books, 1975), pp. 58-64, 325-327.

See also U.S. Congress, Senate, *Congressional Record,* 93rd Cong., 1st sess., April 10, 1973, p. 11504, which contains Senator William Proxmire's views on the matter.

[74] Philip Agee, *Inside the Company: CIA Diary* (New York: Bantam Books, 1975).

[75] 88 Stats. 1804, Sec. 32, 1974 as cited in Pious, *op. cit.,* p. 290.

[76] On earlier problems with CIA reorganization, see William Colby, "Reorganizing the CIA: Who and How," *Foreign Policy,* (Summer 1976), 55.

[77] Nathan and Oliver, *op. cit.,* p. 496.

[78] For an estimated intelligence breakdown, see Marchetti and Marx, *op. cit.,* pp. 325-327, and for techniques for hiding CIA money in other budgets, see Timothy Ingram, "Billions in the Basement," *Washington Monthly,* (January 1972), 40.

[79] *Ibid.,* p. 43.

[80] Fisher, *President and Congress,* p. 300, and *Spending Power,* p. 121.

[81] Fisher, *Spending Power,* p. 107. Nixon signed the Cambodian rider only because he couldn't get the rest of the money he needed without it. He then did everything he could to lessen the effect of the rider.

[82] Bill Moyers, *Washington Monthly,* February 1969, as cited in Thomas Cronin, *The State of the Presidency* (Boston: Little, Brown, 1975), p. 153.

[83] Mullen, *op. cit.,* p. 81.

[84] Morton Halperin and Daniel N. Hoffman, *Top Secret: National Security and the Right to Know* (Washington, D.C.: New Republic Books, 1977), p. 14.

[85] For Ellsberg's philosophy in releasing the documents, see Daniel Ellsberg, *Papers on the War* (New York: Simon & Schuster, 1972).

[86] Wise, *op. cit.,* pp. 59-60.

[87] See Thomas M. Franck and Edward Weisband, eds., *Secrecy and Foreign Policy* (New York: Oxford U.P., 1974), p. 100.

[88] Halperin and Hoffman, *op. cit.,* p. 27.

[89] Graham Allison, *The Essence of a Decision* (Boston: Little, Brown, 1971). See also Elie Abel, *The Missile Crisis* (New York: Bantam Books, 1966).

[90] Henry Graff, *The Tuesday Cabinet* (Englewood Cliffs, N.J.: Prentice-Hall, 1970).

[91] Halperin and Hoffman, *op. cit.,* p. 28.

[92] *Ibid.,* p. 28.

[93] Pious, *op. cit.,* p. 349.

[94] Wise, *op. cit.,* pp. 100-105, 147-148.

[95] Pious, *op. cit.,* p. 216.

[96] Theodore Sorensen, *Watchmen in the Night* (Cambridge, Mass.: M.I.T. Press, 1975), p. 115.

[97] U.S. Congress, House, Committee on Foreign Affairs, Report, *Background Information on the Use of Armed Forces in Foreign Countries*, 91st Cong., 1st sess., 1970.

[98] Merlo Pusey, *op. cit.*, p. 5. See also Alexander George, "The Case for Multiple Advocacy in the Making of Foreign Policy," *American Political Science Review*, (September 1972), 751-791.

[99] *Ibid.*, p. 47. See also Charles A. Lafgren, "War Making Under the Constitution: The Original Understanding," *Yale Law Journal*, (March 1972), esp. pp. 676-677. Also see W. Taylor Reveley, III, "Constitutional Allocation of the War Powers Between the President and Congress," *Virginia Journal of International Law*, 15 (Fall 1974), 73-147. See also L. C. Ratner, "The Coordinated War Making Power: Legislative, Executive and Judicial Roles," *Southern California Law Review*, 44 (December 1971), 461-489.

[100] W. Taylor Reveley, III, "Presidential War Making: Constitutional Prerogatives or Usurpation," in *Congress and President: Allies and Adversaries*, ed. Ronald C. Moe (Pacific Palisades, Calif.: Goodyear, 1971), p. 226. See Also Gerald L. Jenkins, "The War Powers Resolution: Statutory Limits on the Commander in Chief," *Harvard Journal of Legislation*, (February 1974), 181-204. See also Jacob K. Javits, "Congressional Presence in Foreign Relations," *Foreign Relations*, (January 1970), 320. In support of the War Powers Act, see Javits, *Who Makes War: The President vs. Congress* (New York: Morrow, 1973).

[101] U.S. Congress, House, Committee on International Relations, Hearings on Public Law 93-148, *War Powers Act: Test of Compliance*, 94th Cong., 1st Sess., May/June 1975, at pp. 9, 30, 41.

[102] On *Mayaguez*, see Roy Rowan, *The Four Days of Mayaguez* (New York: W. W. Norton, 1975), pp. 179-180.

[103] *The New York Times*, May 15, 1975.

[104] *Congressional Quarterly Guide: Current American Government*, Washington, D.C., Congressional Quarterly, Inc., Spring 1975, p. 310. Section 4a of Public Law 93-148 (War Powers Act) calls for reports in any case in which U.S. armed forces are introduced:

1. into hostilities or into situations where imminent hostilities are clearly indicated by circumstances
2. into the territory, air space, or waters of a foreign nation while equipped for combat
3. in numbers that substantially enlarge the U.S. armed forces already located in a foreign nation

See also *The New York Times*, May 15, 1975.

[105] *The New York Times*, May 23, 1975.

[106] Thomas F. Eagleton, *War and Presidential Power: Chronicles of Congressional Surrender* (New York: Liveright, 1974), p. 208.

[107] *War Powers Compliance Hearings*, p. 38. See also for Nixon's view on the legislation, Francis D. Wormuth, "The Nixon Theory of the War Powers," *California Law Review*, (May 1972), 30.

[108] Section 2415 Foreign Assistance Act, 1971.

[109] Willian Lanouette, "Carter and Congress Clash on Foreign Policy," *National Journal*, July 15, 1978, pp. 1116-1123.

[110] Les Aspin, "Why Doesn't Congress Do Something," *Foreign Policy*, (Winter 1974-1975), 73.

[111] These models were introduced by this author in "Presidential-Congressional Battles: Towards a Truce on the Foreign Policy Front," *Presidential Studies Quarterly*, (Fall 1978), 119-124.

[112] *Congressional Directory*, 95th Cong., 1st sess. (Washington, D.C.: G.P.O., 1977) used to compile this.

[113] Hubert Humphrey's Joint Committee Proposals in U.S. Congress, Senate, *Congressional Record*, April 1973, pp. 11886-11888.

[114] *The New York Times*, September 20, 1974.

[115] Harold P. Green, "The Joint Committee on Atomic Energy: A Model for Legislative Reform?" in *Congress and President: Allies and Adversaries*, pp. 166-178.

[116] *CQWR*, January 31, 1976, p. 204. Colby lowered his sights, though, in Colby, *op. cit.*, p. 55.

[117] Topic was discussed by this writer in a meeting with Secretary of State Kissinger at the Tea Room of the Muehlbach Hotel in Kansas City, Missouri, on May 13, 1975. Ironically, this was also the day that the *Mayaguez* incident became public so Kissinger was forced to cut his visit short to return for an NSC meeting that evening.

[118] See *Report to the President* by the Commission on CIA Activities Within the U.S. (Washington, D.C.: G.P.O., June 1975). For a summary of the report, see *The New York Times,* June 11, 1975.

Tiny staffs for congressional CIA watchdogs were the role with one and a half full-time staffers for the House subcommittee and one and a half for the Senate as cited on p. 76 of above report.

Robert D. Murphy Commission on the Organization of Government for the Conduct of Foreign Policy, *Report to the President* (Washington, D.C.: G.P.O., 1975), 5, 208-209. See also John Norton Moore, "Contemporary Issues," p. 736.

[119] See full Mansfield comments in *Murphy Commission Report,* p. 231. In an interview with Ambassador Robert D. Murphy, chair of the Commission and later head of President Ford's Foreign Intelligence Board, at Corning Glass International Headquarters, New York City, July 7, 1976, the ambassador indicated that, initially, congressional members of the commission had been most cooperative. He pointed out that Senator Mansfield had been generous in providing his office for meetings. Things soured when Anne Armstrong was replaced by Vice President Rockefeller. Mansfield took this as a White House effort to make Murphy and Rockefeller commission reports alike.

[120] Murphy Commission Report, Appendices, vol. 5, p. 188. See also Randall Ripley, "Congressional Party Leadership and the impact of Congress on Foreign Policy," in Appendices, vol. 5, p. 48. A somewhat less optimistic view of the potential role of party leadership can be found in John W. Kingdon, *Congress and Voting Decisions* (New York: Harper & Row, 1973), p. 31. Instructive in this vein also would be Aage R. Clausen, *How Congress Decides* (New York: St. Martin's Press, 1973). See also Randall B. Ripley, *Power in the Senate* (New York: St. Martin's Press, 1969) and also Mark J. Green, James Fallows, and David Zwick, *Who Runs Congress* (New York: Bantam Books, 1972).

[121] Murphy Commission, Appendices, vol. 5, p. 127.

[122] Califano, *op. cit.,* p. 61. Noteworthy in presidential congressional relations in foreign policy is Francis O. Wilcox, *Congress, the Executive, and Foreign Policy* (New York: Council on Foreign Relations, 1971). Also highly instructive in this area is I. M. Destler, *Presidents, Bureaucrats and Foreign Policy* (Princeton, N.J.: Princeton U.P., 1972).

An excellent chronicle of congressional reassertiveness can be found in Harvey G. Zeidenstein, "The Reassertion of Congressional Power: New Curbs on the President," *Political Science Quarterly,* (Fall 1978), 393-409.

[123] Dom Bonafede, Daniel Rapoport, and Joel Havermann, "The President versus Congress: The Score Since Watergate," *National Journal,* May 29, 1976, p. 739.

[124] *Ibid.,* p. 740.

[125] Louis W. Koenig, "A Recipe for the Presidency's Destruction," *George Washington University Law Review,* (January 1975), 376.

# The Courts:
# Complications for
# Presidential Leadership

The relationship between the president and the Supreme Court can be a strange one indeed. Presidents are elected politicians, but they are also the living symbol of the nation with all the positive sentiments that can entail. On the other hand, the nine justices are not burdened with the label "politician" since theoretically they are appointed not for their vote-getting ability but for their expertise as jurists. Since they serve for life, they give the impression of being above the dirty images that politics can conjure up in the minds of the public.

The Founding Fathers realized that politics was inevitable so they introduced checks and balances into the Constitution to make sure that no branch of the federal government could dominate the others. Still, the courts claimed the right of *judicial review* in *Marbury* v. *Madison* in 1803, which several presidents have seen as synonymous with judicial *supremacy*. Recent Supreme Courts, especially the Warren court of the 1950s and 1960s, have used judicial review as a tool of social change. Their decisions have complicated presidential leadership in the area of social policy by taking stands on issues that presidents considered too politically hot to handle. In doing so, they have forced presidents to support the court's position, half-heartedly enforce it, disregard it, or openly criticize it and try to change its position. Also, when a president tries to interpret his authority under the Constitution or statute law, he runs the risk of getting a public lesson in constitutional law from the high court.

Presidents have, as a group, been most generous with themselves when it comes to interpreting their powers. Both the president and the courts are reading the same Constitution and laws, but their interpretations on the limits of presidential powers have often been radically different. It has been said that the Bible, Karl Marx, and Thomas Jefferson could be quoted to defend almost any imaginable proposition. Given the nebulous language of the Constitution, that document could well be added to the list. Still, should the presidents themselves be the ultimate word on the limits of their own powers? Who is responsible for deciding what is meant by such imprecise language in the Constitution as "the executive power shall be vested in the President of the United States of America?" (Article II) What are these executive powers? What are their limits? Does the president have inherent powers as commander-in-chief to violate civil liberties in wartime due to his responsibilities to assure the survival of the nation? Need he enforce court decisions he does not like? May the court even order him to do anything?

The Founding Fathers, in their collective wisdom, left these and other similar questions unanswered. However, since the early days of the Republic under our present Constitution, the Supreme Court has assumed the role of final arbiter when disputes have arisen over the meaning of sections of the Constitution. From that time forward, "the law" has become, in Justice Oliver Wendell Holmes famous phrasing, "whatever the Courts say it is." A justice of more recent vintage, Felix Frankfurter, went even further to claim that "The Supreme Court is the Constitution."

Rhetoric from the lofty perch of the high court bench is one thing; cold political reality is quite another. Constitutional scholar Clifton Rossiter brushed aside the power of the court in its dealings with the White House commenting that "the President may act as if the Supreme Court doesn't even exist."[1] A more contemporary textbook author entitled a brief five-page chapter on the Supreme Court and the president "Judicial Power: A Very Minor Complication."[2] Undoubtedly, Richard Nixon would consider that an overstatement since the court publicly ordered him to turn over the tapes that provided such damning evidence of his involvement in the Watergate cover-up. Still, on the whole, the court has been uncomfortable with frontal assaults on presidential powers. One study of eight hundred cases (1790-1956) before the Supreme Court over the powers of the president found that less than 5 percent of those decisions ultimately went against the man in the White House.[3] Since the justices have shown either support or deference to the president, scholars on the presidency have tended to devote precious little time to examining these interactions.

Why spend the time studying how the two communicate if the court habitually bows subserviently in the direction of the president when his leadership is questioned? The court is important to presidential leadership for several reasons. First, its decisions can reshape the political processes of the nation by calling for redistricting of legislatures to favor urban rather than rural areas. In deciding on the constitutionality of legislation providing matching funds for presidential races, it can decide who will be able to run for president. It can make decisions that provide new constitutional rights for citizens that the president must either enforce or try to reverse. Finally, the court, in alliance with the White House, is capable of reshaping the social order of the nation with landmark decisions in areas such as legal rights, education, emergency powers, and many others.

A complex chain of social processes can be triggered by a Supreme Court decision as Table 7.1 illustrates with respect to the desegregation decision of the Supreme Court in *Brown* v. *Board of Education* (1954).[4] Public values can gradually be changed as a result.

Had the 1954 decision not been made, subsequent events might not have occurred or would have certainly been delayed. Even though a number of years elapsed between the decision and the social impact, the court decision was a catalyst to bringing it about.

Presidents and the court have often clashed over social policies too. Their differences have been aired in public creating further controversy. When the court, for example, favors busing as a method for improving education for minorities, and the public prefers to drag its heels, the court's position places the president on the

## TABLE 7.1
## THE CHAIN REACTION FROM COURT DECISION,
### *BROWN* v. *BOARD OF EDUCATION* (1954)

| THE DECISION | POLITICAL DEBATE | LEGISLATION | EXECUTIVE ACTION |
|---|---|---|---|
| Desegregate schools | Civil rights becomes a campaign issue (1955 on) | Civil Rights Act (1965), no federal funds to segregated schools | HEW guidelines follow presidential order to implement 1965 law |

*IMPACT ON SOCIETY*
School integration in Deep South by 1970

Source: Adapted from James P. Levine, "Methodological Considerations in Studying Supreme Court Efficacy" in Walter Murphy and C. Herman Pritchett eds., *Courts, Judges, and Politics*, 3rd ed. (New York: Random House, 1979), p. 415.

horns of a nasty dilemma. He may choose the "high road" and support the court, oblivious to the political backlash that is sure to develop, or he can cover his own political hide and wage a holding action that could earn him enough votes for four more years in the White House.

In this chapter, we shall examine the interactions between the justices and the president to illustrate how clashes develop and worsen. Within this framework, we shall also consider the tools that presidents have at their disposal to try to shape the thinking of the court. Finally we shall look at some of the areas in which the court has either contracted or expanded the boundaries of presidential leadership.

## JUDICIAL REVIEW:
## TWISTIFICATIONS AND PRETZEL JOBS?

Supreme Court justices have clashed with presidents, members of Congress and even their own colleagues for using judicial review to twist the law to disguise their own social philosophies in constitutional verbiage. In a recent "inside the Supreme Court" account entitled *The Brethren,* a number of justices and their clerks bemoaned the creativity of their colleagues in interpreting the Constitution. Conservative Justice William Rehnquist was especially contemptuous of the opinions of his liberal brother (a term the justices use for one another) William Brennan. After reading one case with what he considered standard Brennan form and substance, Rehnquist quipped, "Brennan has done another pretzel job."[5] His remarks echoed the laments of many a president. Jefferson, for example, called Chief Justice Marshall's creative tendencies "twistifications of the law."[6]

It is only human to expect a Supreme Court justice to view cases from his own personal set of values and prejudices and to read the law to fit them. The Founding Fathers are not available, in any event, to provide irrefutable evidence about what they meant by certain sections of the Constitution. Even if they were, it is doubtful that twentieth-century politics would always jibe with eighteenth-century legal principles. Modern political realities suggest that, when Supreme Court interpretations of presidential powers vary from the views at the White House, battles will inevitably ensue.

Even though the Constitution remained silent on the matter of judicial review, since *Marbury* v. *Madison* (1803) the court has had a base from which to launch attacks on presidential leadership. In the majority opinion of that case, Chief Justice John Marshall wrote, "It is emphatically the province and duty of the judicial department to say what the law is." He further contended that "those who apply the law to particular cases must, of necessity, expound and interpret." When conflicts arise over these interpretations, "the court must decide."[7] This theoretical high ground that Marshall staked out for the court has proven to be less lofty in practice when the president and the court have locked horns. Whenever the court seeks to substitute the view of a majority of justices for stated desires on the Hill or at the White House, their political branch "co-equals" may lay back to ambush them.

## COURT'S POWER BASE

When conflicts arise between the Supreme Court and the two other branches, one might be tempted to think that the court should be able to hold its own. After all, justices, once approved in the Senate, serve for life and their salaries cannot be lowered during their years in service. Logically, then, the court should be in a position to make demands without fear of retribution from the other two branches. However, Congress holds the purse strings and the court must depend on the legislators to provide the money for the justices to meet their expenses. Court decisions are not self-enforcing either. The justices have no army or bureaucracy at their disposal to make sure that their decisions are enforced. That is left up to the good graces of the president. In turn, presidents will be as respectful of court decisions as public opinion will permit. Ultimately, it is the weight of voter sentiments normally behind the court that binds other units of government.

## COURT TRAPPINGS

If the court is to succeed in retaining public support, it must take advantage of the mystical sort of aura of "wise men" that has tended to surround it in the minds of the voters. The very trappings of its chambers and the elaborate procedures in public hearings enhance that image. Nine black-robed justices file through long velvet curtains to take their places behind a massive carved wood bench as the audience stands and the marshall intones, "Oyez, Oyez, all persons having business before the honorable Supreme Court are admonished to draw near and give their attention."[8] Lawyers speaking before the court are resplendent in formal attire, and the time for oral arguments is scrupulously limited. Each of these special effects adds to the court's bigger-than-life image and, since the justices are not elected but rather serve for life, they are viewed as being above the dirty business of politics.

Decisions that don't jibe with voter sentiments run the risk of alienating the court's base of support. When this occurs, a president can drag his heels because there are limits to what the court alone can accomplish. According to Justice Robert Jackson,[9]

> [the court] has no function except to decide cases and controversies and its very jurisdiction . . . was left to the control of Congress. It has no force to

execute its own commands. . . . The Justices derive their offices from the favor of the other two branches . . . [and are] subject to an undefined, unlimited and unreviewable Congressional power of impeachment.

## CONFLICTS WITH INDIVIDUAL PRESIDENTS

When the president and the court do not see eye to eye, the public is put in the position of having to choose sides. Differing political philosophies provide most of the explanation for the run-ins, but personality conflicts between the president and the chief justice can be involved too.

### THOMAS JEFFERSON

Early in our history, the Federalist Supreme Court and a succession of Democratic-Republican presidents were constantly bickering. The Federalists were oriented toward a strong national government and were sympathetic to merchant and banking interests whereas the Democratic-Republicans (Democrats) were the party of states' rights and the small freeholder. President Thomas Jefferson also despised the Federalists because of the Alien and Sedition acts that Federalist judges almost gleefully applied to jail a number of fellow Democrats. He also resented John Adams and the Federalists in Congress for tampering with the court system by creating a number of new courts and making all the appointments before he (Jefferson) could be sworn in as president in 1801. The fact that President Adams appointed his Secretary of State John Marshall as chief justice before leaving office further complicated matters. Marshall, his biographers report, detested Jefferson and the feeling was mutual. Biographer Albert Beveridge notes that Marshall was unwilling to throw his support to Jefferson over Aaron Burr when the mixed-up presidential election of 1800 had to be thrown into the House. Marshall at that time considered Jefferson "totally unfit for the Chief Magistracy."[10]

Later, the celebrated case of *Marbury* v. *Madison* made its circuitous way to the Supreme Court, creating even more friction. When Secretary of State Madison, no doubt with Jefferson's endorsement, refused to give Marbury the credentials that Adams had issued for him to serve as a federal judge, he took the question to the Supreme Court seeking a *mandamus* ordering Madison to give him the credentials. Since the Supreme Court session was drawing to a close in December 1801, Marshall extended the case into the next session. In the meantime, at the president's instigation, Congress passed legislation delaying the next court term for two years while Democrats could seek excuses for removing and replacing Federalist judges on both the lower federal branches and the Supreme Court.

For starters, the Democrats in Congress swooped down on an unsuspecting New Hampshire federal district judge, John Pickering, whom they impeached and convicted in February 1803. The grounds were not criminal behavior but rather proveable insanity. The stage had been set for forays against members of the Supreme Court since Congress had set a precedent for "noncriminality-based" impeachments. Samuel Chase was to have been the first in a line of Federalists on the Supreme Court to be removed. The charges against Chase were ostensibly based on his mistreatment of some defendants as their judge in cases under the Sedition Act (1798). Congressional compassion for its wronged Democratic compatriots might have been a factor, but an even greater one was the hope of setting the pattern for impeaching justices because they were out of step with the views of Congress and the voting public. Eventually, Chase survived conviction in the Senate but the Supreme Court had received a congressional calling card with a White House seal that it was not soon to forget.

The *Marbury* decision, announced only three weeks after Pickering was removed in 1803, was a masterpiece of judicial evasiveness. Although the court tried to leave the impression that it was "above politics," its decision showed that it was hardly oblivious to political pressures. The Federalist court had been widely expected to find for Marbury. Instead, it chose to be discreet in its decision and avoided confrontation by claiming that it lacked the authority to issue a *mandamus* to Madison. While it did claim the right of judicial review it did so without directly affronting Jefferson. The threat of impeachment as a common method of cleaning house on the Supreme Court faded after Chase survived in the Senate in 1805. Also, the view that impeachment might be justified because of policy differences between the court and either the president or the Congress was laid to rest permanently.

## ANDREW JACKSON

A legendary war of words between Andrew Jackson and the Supreme Court demonstrated anew that, although the confrontations between the branches during the Jefferson administration had abated, the truce was a shaky one. Jackson hated everything the Federalists stood for and viewed the Supreme Court as an agent of the Eastern Establishment elitists bent on subjugating the small holder. He reveled in taking jabs at the court. In response to a Supreme Court decision in 1832 on the rights of some missionaries and Cherokee Indians allegedly being violated by a Georgia statute,[11] Jackson reportedly commented that "Marshall has made this ruling, now let him enforce it." At no point had the court asked the president to become involved in enforcing its order, so Jackson's politically motivated comments were a free shot at a vulnerable Supreme Court. As a philosophical states' rights advocate, Jackson wanted no part of the Supreme Court decision to void a state law.

His rhetoric became action in a later tete-à-tete with the court and the Congress over the rechartering of the Second Bank of the United States. In *McCulloch* v. *Maryland* (1818)[12] Marshall's court upheld a congressional decision to create a bank as a constitutionally implied power. Jackson, on the other hand, considered the bank a financial advantage to Eastern bankers such as noted financier Nicholas Biddle.[13] The whole system infuriated him, possibly because it was these types who had refused him a loan in his earlier days as a gentleman farmer in Tennessee.[14] When the Whigs in Congress voted to recharter the bank, he vetoed the bank legislation as "unconstitutional." In his veto message he leveled a vicious broadside at the McCulloch principle and questioned the impact that judicial review should have.[15]

> The opinion of the judges has no more authority over Congress than the opinion of Congress has over the judges, and on that point, the President

is independent of both. The authority to the Supreme Court must not, therefore, be permitted to control Congress or the Executive when acting in their legislative capacities, but to have only such influence as the force of their reasoning deserves.

Despite the fact that Jackson lashed out contemptuously at the "elitist" philosophy[16] of the Marshall court, he never once said that a president would be justified in totally disregarding an order by the Supreme Court or a high federal judge to enforce one of its decisions.

## ABRAHAM LINCOLN

During the crisis of the Civil War, Abraham Lincoln displayed none of Jackson's inhibitions about judicial decisions. In fact, in his inaugural address he served notice that he was not awed by the power or authority of the Supreme Court. As a Republican (the abolitionist party), he could not overlook the damage the Supreme Court had done in the Dred Scott case in which Justice Taney held slaves to be "property" not "persons" or "citizens" under the provisions of the Fifth Amendment. Although Lincoln was willing to recognize that many constitutional questions would have to be handled by the court and that the decisions would bind the parties in the cases, he wasn't convinced that judicial review was a very democratic way of doing things.[17]

> the candid citizen must confess that if the policy of the government on vital questions affecting the whole people is to be irrevocably fixed by decision of the Supreme Court, the instant they are made in ordinary litigation between parties in personal actions, the people will have ceased to be their own rulers, having to that extent, practically resigned their government into the hands of that eminent tribunal.

Lincoln proved to be a man of his word, willing to stand his ground in the face of Supreme Court decisions he personally judged dangerous to the Republic. The first confrontation revolved around his decisions in 1861 and 1862 to authorize his generals to suspend *habeus corpus* (right of an accused person to go before a judge to be told why he is being held) for persons accused of engaging in disloyal acts such as interfering with the draft and enlistments. Imagine if Jimmy Carter had tried such a thing during 1980 demonstrations against draft registration by eighteen-, nineteen-, and twenty-year-old males. Since the Constitution was unclear as to the president's authority to suspend *habeus corpus* in emergencies, the court was called upon to hear the issue in the case of *Ex Parte Merryman*.[18] Merryman, a Southern sympathizer living in Maryland, was jailed in a crackdown by General Cadwalader along with a number of notable supporters of the idea of secession. From the stockade at Fort McHenry in Baltimore, Merryman petitioned Chief Justice Roger Taney for a *habeus corpus* hearing. The petitioner was not even permitted to make an appearance, and Cadwalader stayed away too, contending that he was merely following a directive of the commander-in-chief. In his opinion on the case, Taney found the detention illegal because "only Congress was authorized to suspend *habeus corpus*." Although Lincoln made no immediate formal response to Taney's assertions, in a later message to Congress he labeled the decision ridiculous when emergency situations were involved:

it cannot be believed that the framers of the instrument intended that in every case the danger should run its course until Congress could be called together, the very assembling of which might be prevented by rebellion.[19]

His Attorney General Albert Bates questioned the whole idea of judicial review in uncompromising language. He could find no justification for the Supreme Court to order a president to do anything if they were from separate but equal branches under the Constitution. To be precise Bates said, "No court or judge can take cognizance of the political acts of the President or undertake to revise and reverse his political decisions."[20] The key words in Bates's comments would seem to be "political acts." Although Lincoln defended his actions as a response to a crisis of survival for the Union, the attorney general's comments could be used as justification for opponents of judicial review of presidential decisions in normal times as well. By its decisions during times of crisis, the court had shown some sympathy for Lincoln's view that extraordinary measures might be justifiable in crisis.[21]

## FRANKLIN DELANO ROOSEVELT

In no less a battle for the survival of the nation, Franklin Roosevelt found himself butting heads with the Harding-Coolidge-Hoover Supreme Court, first over the constitutionality of many of the New Deal programs and later over wartime powers the administration used without prior congressional approval. (In the years between Lincoln and Franklin Roosevelt, scuffles involving the president and the Supreme Court were infrequent and less intense than they had been during the Civil War.) Roosevelt quickly became frustrated with the court's penchant for voiding national, state, and local laws that they opposed more for philosophical than for legal reasons. Between 1934 and 1936, for example, invalidations of federal, state, and local laws was taking place in unprecedented numbers. During that two-year period, the court voided an amazing one-fifth of the total number of federal laws overturned in the history of the Republic to that date.[22] Among major actions related to the New Deal were decisions that told the Congress that it could not delegate authority to the president to set up business codes and price regulations under the National Recovery Act. The NRA eagle (a public relations symbol) had its wings clipped in *Schechter Poultry* v. *U.S.* (1935).[23] One year later the Agricultural Adjustment Act went by the wayside and with it FDR's plans to regulate agricultural production. In *U.S.* v. *Butler* (1936),[24] the court told the president that the AAA legislation was an unconstitutional use of the taxing power to, in the court's words, "effectuate an end which is not legitimate [and] not within the scope of the Constitution." Predictably, FDR resented these judicial intrusions upon what he considered legitimate policy-making concerns for both Congress and the president. Not only did the decisions themselves anger the president, but the tenor of the opinions written by the justices incurred his wrath and tested his patience. In the majority opinion in *U.S.* v. *Butler,* for example, Justice Roberts dismissed the AAA as "at best a scheme for purchasing with federal funds, submission to federal regulations of a subject reserved to the states." In one sentence, Roberts not only questioned the constitutionality of the AAA but impugned the motives of both the president and Congress in creating it.

Franklin Roosevelt was hardly one to accept affronts and rebuffs indefinitely, so the disgruntled president fired the first salvo in his war against the courts in a broadcast address to the nation in the first days of his second administration. Instead of attacking the court for complicating his task of leading the nation out of its economic woes, Roosevelt chose to take the constitutional high road and object to the court's incessant tampering with the laws passed by Congress. In his address, he complained that:[25]

> since the rise of the modern movement for social and economic progress through legislation, the Court has more and more often and more and more boldly asserted a power to veto laws passed by the Congress and state legislatures in complete disregard of original limitations. In the last four years, the sound rule of giving statutes the benefit of all reasonable doubt has been cast aside. The Court has been acting not as a judicial body, but a policy making body.

More recent presidents have had less reason to talk with such despair. Since the late 1930s, the courts have more nearly coincided in their views with the concerns of Democratic Congresses and presidents. Each has assumed that government must do more than deal with the rights of the poor, minorities, and the press. Justices have also been less solicitous of property (read business and banking) concerns. Some backsliding from this generalization has been evident in the years of the Warren Burger court. Also, during this period the court has tended to stay at arms length from the White House and has rarely attacked a president for doing something until after the fact, when he is less likely to feel the ill effects.

Each of the situations we have examined points up some of the reasons why presidents and Supreme Courts cross swords. Jefferson's personal hatred for Marshall seems to have been an exceptional case possibly because, in more modern times, Supreme Court appointees are rarely major political figures even though exceptions like William Howard Taft left the White House to later take a seat on the Supreme Court and John Quincy Adams returned to the House of Representatives. Each of the presidents referred to here voiced his resentment toward "judicial policy making" in which the court does not bow to the policy primacy of elected federal officials like the president and members of Congress. These presidents have tended to view judicial review as a thinly disguised tool of the court to create a system of judicial supremacy. Still, only Lincoln openly disregarded a court order in the *Merryman* case (and that was merely from Taney and not the whole court). Even crusty Andrew Jackson admitted, in regard to the Cherokee Indians case (*Worcester v Georgia,* 1832), that he would have obeyed a court order had one been issued. Each of these skirmishes also related to conflicting philosophies about the role of government either in federal-state relations or over the implied powers that Congress or the president can fashion for themselves by careful reading of the Constitution.

## RESTRAINING THE COURTS: AN ASSESSMENT

Since the courts possess the potential for frustrating a president's policy initiatives, one should suspect that presidents will seek ways to keep the court in line. Among the methods employed by the various occupants of the Oval Office are (1) use of the power to appoint justices to reshape the views of the court, (2) use of statutes to limit the court, and (3) use of the solicitor general to inform the court of the president's thinking.

## APPOINTMENTS

Harry Truman's observation about Supreme Court appointments, though uncharacteristically lacking in his usual salty phrasing, demonstrates the frustrations of presidents when they try to fill the court with friends or at least philosophical clones. "Packing the Supreme Court," he lamented, "just doesn't work.... Whenever you put a man cn the Court, he ceases to be your friend."[26] A person's perspectives can change in new surroundings. Political issues may look radically different from the lofty perch behind the Supreme Court bench. Other justices on the court may help to reshape the views of their new colleagues. An appointee's past may not always be a valid indicator of how he will act as a justice either. During the Senate confirmation hearings on the nomination of Hugo Black, his prior association with the Klu Klux Klan cast a pall over the proceedings. By the time Black reached his twilight years on the court, however, he was among the strongest advocates of civil rights for minorities. President Eisenhower also noticed that an appointee's past does not dictate the way he will vote on the high court. He sorely regretted his choice of former California Governor Earl Warren to serve as chief justice. Far from being the conservative Eisenhower had envisioned, Warren became the epitome of activism on the Supreme Court. To be sure that Warren's views reflected the "great ideals and common sense" for which Eisenhower had publicly applauded him, the president dispatched Attorney General Herbert Brownell to interview Warren when the vacancy occurred. In his memoirs Eisenhower referred to the Warren appointment as the greatest mistake of his presidency.[27]

FACTORS IN SELECTION. Although a potential justice's legal and political philosophies are prime considerations in the selection process, other factors carry weight as well. Friendship with the nominee is often involved in the decision to submit his name to the Senate. In most cases, the president knows the person he nominates. This could be due to the fact that presidents have so few Supreme Court nominations to make. One study found that up to the mid-1970s, presidents knew their choices personally in about three fifths of the cases.[28] Harry Truman chose his Commerce Secretary Fred Vinson; John Kennedy chose old family friend Byron "Whizzer" White and his labor secretary, Arthur Goldberg; Lyndon Johnson tapped his solicitor general, Thurgood Marshall, and named old friend Abe Fortas, only to have the latter resign under a cloud of alleged improprieties. Obviously, lawyers with, it is hoped, judicial experience, will fill the president's list of possibles. In drawing up these lists presidents typically are assisted by the attorney general and senators of his party who will have to sell that nomination on the Hill.[29] Even the sitting justices of the president's party or of the same philosophical persuasion are not shy when it comes to giving the president advice, especially when a new *chief* justice is to be appointed. The chief is especially important to the brethren because of his role in conferences and his right to assign written opinions for the majority when he is in the majority on a case. As Harry Truman prepared to appoint a new chief, two other justices put him on notice that they would resign from the high court if one of their colleagues, Justice Jackson, was nominated.

## TABLE 7.2
## THE MAJOR PARTICIPANTS IN THE
## FEDERAL JUDICIAL SELECTION PROCESS

| INITIATORS | SCREENERS | AFFIRMERS |
|---|---|---|
| President | Senators—to 1840 | Senate Judiciary Committee |
| Attorney general and staff, including deputy atty. general | Senate Judiciary Committee after 1840 | U.S. Senate |
| U.S. senators (president's party)—1840 | Department of Justice | |
| Local party leaders | FBI—1917 | |
| Judges | American Bar Association—1946 | |
| Candidates for position | Pressure groups Media | |

Source: Howard Ball, *Courts, Politics, and the Federal Judicial System* (Englewood Cliffs, N.J.: Prentice-Hall, 1980), p. 178.

In recent years the input from outside government on Supreme Court appointments has been growing. The American Bar Association passes judgment on the abilities of the appointees, and the president receives plenty of unsolicited advice from interest groups that may threaten to attack the nomination in the Senate if the choice displeases them. Presidents quickly learn to steer clear of appointees who might produce political fallout harmful to future election efforts. Richard Nixon took this insight one step farther by trying to tailor his appointments to the Supreme Court to his "Southern strategy" for election 1972. His attempts to secure Senate consent for his nominations of F. Clement Haynesworth (South Carolina) and later G. Harold Carswell (Florida) ran into stiff interest group opposition on the Hill. Those two nominations represent an ideal example of the capacity of interest groups to play havoc with the best-laid White House plans.

HAYNESWORTH, CARSWELL, AND PRESIDENT NIXON'S NOMINEE EXAMPLES. When Lyndon Johnson's crony Abe Fortas was pressured to step down from the high court under threats of impeachment, Richard Nixon prepared to appoint a replacement. His first two choices to fill the vacancy evoked fierce criticism rather than quick consent in the Senate. The administration gained the dubious distinction of being the first since Grover Cleveland's to have two consecutive nominees rejected. In fact, Nixon was the first president since 1930 to have had a nominee for the Supreme Court cast aside by the Senate.[30]

Nixon's decisions to tap Haynesworth and Carswell were in keeping with his promise to appoint strict constructionists. Attorney General John Mitchell provided a list of 170 names including mostly federal judges, some state justices, some prominent private attorneys, and others in government service. In keeping with Mitchell's baby (i.e., the Southern strategy for reelecting the president), the attorney general suggested a fifty-seven-year-old Harvard Law graduate and chief judge of the Fourth Circuit Court of Appeals from South Carolina named Clement Haynesworth.[31] Also in keeping with the southern tilt, Nixon had promised to appoint people who "are for civil rights, but who recognize that the first civil right of every American is to be free from domestic violence." Haynesworth certainly fit that description, although his commitment to minority civil rights was suspect.

Civil rights interest groups and their friends in the labor movement informed Democratic senators that they were prepared to launch a vigorous assault on the Haynesworth nomination because as a federal judge he had dragged his heels over school desegregation in Prince Edward County, Virginia. He had also voted against the majority on the Fourth Circuit Bench when it ruled that hospitals receiving federal funds could not maintain segregated facilities. On August 12, 1969 Haynesworth complained to *The New York Times* that those cases had been decided in 1958 at a time "when none of us was thinking or writing as we are today."[32] Nixon was outraged at the labor-minority coalition that formed against the nomination in the Senate. The president's wrath did not stay the axe the Senate wielded on the nomination as they rejected Haynesworth.

Although he was forced to give up on Haynesworth, Nixon did not permit that to lessen his resolve for a "Southern strategy." At the suggestion of Attorney General Mitchell, the administration selected a member of the Fifth Circuit Court of Appeals from Florida, Judge G. Harold Carswell. Five months prior to being nominated to the Supreme Court Carswell had won Senate confirmation for the seat on the Fifth Circuit without so much as a senatorial whimper. But, in January 1970, when Nixon submitted Carswell's name for confirmation to the Supreme Court, all hell broke loose. It quickly became evident that the administration hadn't done its homework in screening the nominee. The first skeleton to emerge from Carswell's closet was the issue of his role as incorporator of a "whites only" golf club. Senate liberals also accused him of being hostile to black plaintiffs and attorneys in civil rights cases. Overresponding to the criticisms that had surfaced about Haynesworth, Nixon made the tactical error of trying to make the confirmation of Carswell into a question of whether the Senate should continually tamper with the "President's right to appoint." Nixon complained bitterly that "I, as President of the United States should be accorded the same right of choice . . . freely accorded to my predecessors."[33] Senate reaction to such moaning further lessened the chances that Carswell would ever sit on the Supreme Court. Complicating matters even more, the legal fraternity considered Carswell so lackluster that many lawyers felt he didn't belong on the court and they made their views explicit to both the president and the Senate. One group of two hundred former law clerks to Supreme Court justices and deans of such respected law schools as Chicago, Harvard, Michigan, Notre Dame, and Yale wrote to both the White House and the Senate to complain about the choice.[34] With the legal community, organized labor, civil rights groups, liberal Democrats, and even some supporters of the original Haynesworth nomination massed in opposition, the Carswell selection was doomed. Nixon's eventual success in placing two other conservatives on the court was due in no small part to the cagey way in which he went about submitting the names to the public before formally presenting them to the Senate.

NIXON'S END RUN. Before submitting the names of Lewis Powell (law professor and Virginia Bar Association president) and William Rehnquist (former Mitchell aide at Justice), Nixon floated several trial balloons about possible nominees. The American Bar Association screening committee that had been generous in foregoing serious objections against Haynesworth and Carswell became highly critical of the next two nominees, Herschel Friday and Mildred Lilly. Friday, an Arkansas bond lawyer, had no bench experience, and Judge Lilly, from the federal circuit in California, had a horrendous record for having cases overturned upon appeal for judge-made errors. The ABA vote on Friday was six "not qualifieds" and six "not opposeds." Hardly a ringing endorsement. The vote on Judge Lilly was even more negative as the committee unanimously opposed her appointment.[35] After showing less than qualified candidates to critical Senate liberals, much in the way a trapper might wave raw meat in front of a pack of wolves he wanted to snare, Nixon went on national television to tell the public of the nomination of Lewis Powell and William Rehnquist even before he let the information reach the Senate. If Haynesworth, Carswell, Lilly, and Friday were unqualified, no one could question the impeccable credentials of Powell and Rehnquist. The president got his conservatives and at least one "Southerner" after all.

Even though rejection of presidential nominees to the court is rare, the Nixon experience with Haynesworth and Carswell illustrates several potential leadership complications for presidents as they appoint to the Supreme Court. His credibility as a competent leader suffers when his aides and the attorney general adopt inadequate procedures for screening candidates. Dirty linen should be discovered and the candidate disposed of before the Senate gets into the selection process.

## USING STATUTES

While presidents have hoped that judicious appointments to the high court would encourage a certain political philosophy, they have also sought congressional aid in reshaping the court to White House views. John Adams, with the support of the congressional Federalists was the first president to use statutory methods against the court. During the closing days of his administration, Congress enacted the Circuit Court Act, which reduced the number of Supreme Court justices to five with the next vacancy. The purpose of the legislation was to make sure that incoming President Thomas Jefferson couldn't change the philosophy of the court via appointments. That piece of legislation created bitterness between Jefferson and the court and led to the attempts to impeach Federalists on the Supreme Court beginning with Samuel Chase. The Senate refused to convict Chase even though the House had impeached him. Evidently, the charges were too political for its taste. Later, the president considered trying to impeach the chief justice for his role in proceedings against Aaron Burr for treason.[36] That idea got side-tracked because growing international tensions diverted the nation's attention.[37] From that period on, impeachment was discarded as a mechanism for changing the court. It was to be well over a century before the next serious attempt to tamper with the makeup of the court with the assistance of Congress would be made by a president.

COURT-PACKING PLAN: HOW A SWITCH IN TIME SAVED NINE.  Although Franklin Roosevelt swore at the time of his second inauguration to preserve, protect, and defend the Constitution, he made no such commitment to accept Supreme Court interpretations of that document. In the traditional address from the Capitol steps, he reminded the court that it had been bordering on tyranny as it dismembered the New Deal. In a thinly veiled reference to "judicial obstructionism," the president said[38]

> The essential democracy of our nation and the safety of our people depend not upon the absence of power, but upon lodging it with those whom the people can *change* or *continue* at stated intervals through an honest and free election system.

Roosevelt, never the shy type when his leadership was challenged, decided to act forcefully. The slim 5-4 conservative majorities were carving up the New Deal. His court-packing plan was merely one of a number of options that he had been toying with for a couple of years. At one point, he had considered going the constitutional amendment route, but he felt that that would take too long. He also realized that, even if he were fortunate enough to rush it through Congress on the strength of his popularity demonstrated in the election of 1936, conservative, rural-dominated state legislatures would obstruct ratification. Roosevelt had brainstormed with his aides over quite a list of possible amendments including proposals to (1) enlarge congressional authority in certain economic and social areas, (2) empower Congress to reenact laws voided by the court, (3) require a 6-3 or 7-2 vote to void an act of Congress, and (4) set age limits on justices or give them fixed terms instead of lifetime positions.[39] Any of those deviations from the custom and the Constitution would have been a radical departure. The court, for example, had been set at nine justices for almost seventy years (since 1869).

Eventually, he decided on the court-packing plan and, to that end, sent a message to Capitol Hill in February 1937. The court, he argued, was strapped with a hopeless backlog of cases and that burden was causing major complications for all the federal courts. The plan called for aid to aged and infirm justices through retirement benefits, but these baubles were dangled in hopes of swaying disbelievers in Congress to his side. At the heart of the proposals, though, was the provision permitting the president to appoint an additional justice for every seventy-year-old judge who did not resign within sixty days. This applied to all federal courts including the Supreme Court. The innovation would have expanded the high court from its traditional nine members to fifteen. Even the politically naïve could recognize that FDR was interested in majorities to undo the damage done to the New Deal. Comments about "court efficiency" and retirement benefits were little more than an elaborate smoke screen.

While the president had said publicly that "the people are with me," public opinion polls in 1935 found that voters were not enthusiastic at the idea of tampering with the court. Likewise, the Democratic Party platform in 1936 remained very low keyed on the subject of court reform.[40] Once the president unveiled his "secret" plan, newspaper and public response was both swift and almost universally negative. Roosevelt deluded himself into thinking that he could be successful if he just took his case to the people. He wrote some friends, "The source of criticism is concentrated, and I feel that, as we get the story to the general public, the whole matter will be given wide support." In March he devoted one of his celebrated radio fireside chats to this issue. In this intimate setting, he admitted to his fellow Americans that efficiency was merely one issue involved in his proposal. He complained that the Supreme Court, by its decisions, was bringing government to a standstill. In his usual artful style, he likened the American form of government to a three-horse team. Only two, the president and Congress, were pulling together; the third was not. He warned, "as a nation . . . we must take action to save the Constitution from the Court and the Court from itself."[41] A more ringing indictment is hardly imaginable.

Under political siege, in March and April, the court began a strategic retreat from its criticisms of the New Deal. At the same time, the coalition in Congress that FDR had built to push the packing plan began to disintegrate. When Associate Justice Owen Roberts and Chief Justice Charles Evans Hughes shifted support to the administration side in a Washington State minimum wage case[42] and a later case on the Wagner Labor Relations Act (1935), the court balance tipped to the left by a vote of 5-4. From that juncture, much of the urgency for the court-packing scheme disappeared.

Eventually, Roosevelt lost the court-packing battle, but he won the war to protect the New Deal. Still, he proved incapable of translating his popularity into congressional votes for tampering with the traditional makeup of the court. Nevertheless the incident put the Supreme Court on the hot seat and left its successors further evidence that issuing decisions that fly in the face of strongly held views in the White House and on Capitol Hill is risky business indeed. It would be difficult to prove that Roberts's vote in the Washington State case was influenced by fears of "court reform," but his switch and that of his colleague Charles Evans Hughes was indeed the "switch in time that saved nine."

As we noted earlier, any action that a president wants to take against the court requires some help from Congress to be effective. If the president wants to reshape the court by appointments, the Senate must approve. Should he wish to have a justice impeached and convicted, he must depend on his stalwarts on the Hill to get the job done, since he has no role in the impeachment process. Determining the size and jurisdiction of the federal courts is a duty of Congress that a president might want exercised to limit the reach of the Supreme Court. Also, reshaping the jurisdiction of the Supreme Court is an impressive weapon in congressional arsenals. In 1802, for example, Congress simply abolished an entire tier of lower federal courts.

**APPROPRIATIONS.** Should legislators wish to, they may also use the power of the purse to short-circuit unpopular court decisions. In 1975, for example, a law was proposed to undercut the school desegregation principles of *Brown* v. *Board of Education*. It included a legislative veto prohibiting the Ford administration from withholding funds from school districts that refused to participate in HEW plans for ending separate black and white schools.[43] Purse strings can also be used in other ways. Although legislators may not lower a justice's salary while he is on the bench, there are no restrictions on freezing salaries. In the original court-packing legislation in 1937, retirement benefits were waved in front of older justices to make their "golden years" off the bench seem more attractive.

**COUNTERACTIVE LEGISLATION.** Congress may also invoke its lawmaking authority to counter the interpretations of the Supreme Court. Any decision on a federal statute is subject to being reversed if Congress revises the wording with a new law.[44] In one case, legislators decided to change the appellate jurisdiction of the Supreme Court and the court agreed they had a right to do so in *Ex Parte McCardle* (1867).[45] The case involved a Mississippi newspaper editor who was arrested and taken before a military court for publishing articles in violation of the Reconstruction acts. McCardle appealed his conviction to the Supreme Court. As oral arguments progressed, Congress repealed the very provisions of the 1867 act that had made it possible for McCardle to make the appeal. President Andrew Johnson vetoed the repeal bill only to have the Radical Republicans on Capitol Hill override. Congress had feared that the court might declare all or parts of the Reconstruction acts unconstitutional. They were determined to punish the South, and the Reconstruction legislation was to be the weapon to do it. Finally, the repeal bill became law over the president's objections, and so the case was simply emoved from the court's docket. In this case, as in the situations surrounding Jefferson's impeachment attempts and FDR's court-packing scheme, the president and Congress disagreed. Johnson had hoped that the court would strike down Reconstruction while Congress had a mind of its own. The justices had no chance to side with the president in the *McCardle* case, as Congress foreclosed on that possibility with the repeal bill. Still, a president with strong support on the Hill can be in a position to encourage the courts to make decisions he can live with. Acting without Congress, presidential attempts to lead the courts in one direction or another seem destined to failure.

## GIVING ADVICE TO THE COURT: THE SOLICITOR GENERAL AND AMICUS BRIEFS

Since frontal assaults on the Supreme Court by the elected political branches have been marginally effective and then only for a short period of time, the president may try to reason with the court before it makes its decisions rather than to battle with the justices after the dye has already been cast. For this purpose, he uses the solicitor general to convey White House wishes in *amicus curiae* briefs (third-party summaries of a case) and by taking cases before the high court. The solicitor general is the third-ranking official in the Justice Department, and, since the position was created in 1870, the president appoints him with Senate consent.

Presidents tend to exercise great care in deciding whom to select since the solicitor serves as the spokesperson in sensitive dealings with the high court. In the president's name, the solicitor general determines which cases lost by executive branch agencies merit appeal to the Supreme Court. He also defends the federal government in cases it has won but are later appealed. Since the solicitor general funnels all federal agency cases and *amicus* briefs into the Supreme Court, the justices have come to expect him to separate the wheat from the chaff. They trust that he will discard cases from federal agencies that are without real merit to help save the court's time. Normally, the court holds the solicitor general in high esteem, and so it is logical that his name can be well up the list of potential Supreme Court nominees. Supreme Court Justice Thurgood Marshall[46] came to the court via that route in the late 1960s and Nixon's Solicitor General Robert Bork evidently had designs on a court seat until he got involved in the firing of special prosecutor Archibald Cox and thus tainted himself in Watergate.

When the solicitor general decides that a case has merit, the Supreme Court almost invariably agrees. In fact, the U.S. government is involved in well over half the cases that come before the court, either as a participant in the case or as an advisor to the court through an *amicus* brief.[47] The court grants special status to the federal and state governments by permitting them to file *amicus* briefs without consent of either party in a case. These *amicus* briefs submitted through the solicitor general help the president to communicate with the courts and help the justices to estimate what the president will be willing to enforce.

Within the last thirty years or so, when the United States was not in a position to bring suit over an issue, it used *amicus* briefs to get the executive involved in almost every major case pending before the courts. Solicitors general normally intervene in cases involving constitutional Amendments One through Eight and citizen rights under the Fifth and Fourteenth Amendments. Stephen Puro discovered a rapid acceleration of executive use of *amicus* briefs between 1953 and 1966. That period coincided roughly with the most productive years of the liberal Earl Warren court. Puro attributes the rapid increase to White House decisions to become more active in such issues as school desegregation, voting rights, the rights of the accused (criminal cases), and the redrawing of legislative districts.[48] In the late 1960s and early 1970s, presidents found the *amicus* avenue a convenient route for intervening in cases involving such volatile concerns as state and federal aid to private and parochial schools, women's rights, capital punishment, discrimination in education and hiring, and freedom for the press.

Solicitors general have compiled an enviable batting average in appearances before the court. The U.S. government view prevailed in almost three-fourths of the cases it entered in the years Puro studied.[49] However, we must keep in mind the fact that, in the later years especially, the presidents were very receptive to the court's activist philosophies in these areas.

The courts are sensitive enough not to issue decisions that place them at odds with their elected federal colleagues. Habitually, the justices try to sound out the White House for its views on cases even if the solicitor has not participated in them. They simply request that the solicitor provide them a brief on particular cases. Since the president and solicitors are in frequent contact, discussions with the solicitor are akin to visits with the president on an issue. The solicitor is in regular communication with the court using the proper legal language; thus he can be easier to communicate with on legal issues than the president himself, who may not always be a lawyer.

## ACTIVIST COURTS, SOCIAL POLICY, AND PRESIDENTIAL LEADERSHIP

When courts make decisions that reshape social and economic patterns and define presidential powers and imply duties for him, they can complicate his life. From the period prior to the Civil War to the late 1930s, the Supreme Court was the bastion of property rights and the defender of the sanctity of contracts against sociologically motivated state attempts to regulate wages, hours, and working conditions. Toward the end of that period, the voices of Justices Louis Brandeis, Benjamin Cardozo, and Harlan Fiske Stone were being raised to champion "sociological jurisprudence."[50] They believed that the individual needed protection by the court and lawmakers from both the real and potential abuses of corporate capitalism. After the majority shifted on the New Deal in 1937, the court became the ally and not the adversary of presidential leadership in using government to regulate economic power blocs and redistribute the wealth.[51]

## COURT AID IN
## PRESIDENT'S SOCIAL EXPERIMENTS

Working in tandem, the courts and a president constitute a potent one-two punch. During the Kennedy and Johnson years, for example, the question of desegregation was not as acute as during the Eisenhower and Nixon administrations because the Supreme Court and the White House saw eye to eye on the matter. The philosophy underlying the Warren court, like the views of Brandeis, Cardozo, and Stone, provided more than enough latitude for imaginative planners of social policy (especially in the Great Society years of the Johnson administration) to "inject the federal executive deeply into the mainstream of everyday American life."[52] The civil rights bills of the 1960s imposed affirmative action requirements for hiring of minorities and women, ordered nondiscrimination in the sale and rental of housing, and mandated open public accommodations in hotels, restaurants, and conveyances. Under Johnson's leadership and court acquiescence, HEW distributed birth control information and materials to the poor and others for their use. Likewise, the court, once the defender of the rights of business, cooperated with the president and Congress on pollution controls, safety regulations for autos and in the workplace (OSHA), wilderness conservation, and numerous other innovative restrictions on business prerogatives.

## COURT CREATES POLICY
## HEADACHES FOR PRESIDENTS

While court decisions may expand a president's leadership role in social and economic policy areas, their actions may also give him responsibilities in areas he would prefer to sidestep. This has been especially true when the court has chartered new courses in social policy as it did when it called for desegregation of schools, expanded the legal rights of the accused, and ruled abortion for "health" reasons a constitutional right of a woman in all nine months of pregnancy. Each of these issues and other controversial findings in the areas of educational and job placement on the basis of race (*Baake* v. *U.S.C.* and the *DeFunis* case)[53] have become political footballs that savvy presidents would prefer to ignore. In many of these areas, no matter what position they take on the court's decisions, they are bound to lose some votes in November.

DESEGREGATION AND BUSING. The Supreme Court's desegregation decision, and the busing controversy that grew out of it, have created political and legal problems for recent presidents. Dwight Eisenhower was president when the court wrestled with the *Brown* v. *Board of Education* case. Eisenhower had tried to convince Chief Justice Earl Warren over dinner at the White House that he and his colleagues should not find against the Topeka schools. Southerners, he felt, were not "bad people." Rather, they were merely concerned to see that their "sweet little girls are not required to sit in school alongside some big overgrown Negroes."[54] When Warren disregarded his advice, Eisenhower was painted into the corner of having to decide whether to enforce a decision he didn't agree with or risk being viewed as disinterested in the violence that developed at Little Rock, Arkansas over integrating the high school, or as a racist for opposing desegregation, or as oblivious to Supreme Court decisions.

223

Similar difficulties plagued later presidents and Congresses when federal judges began issuing court orders calling for desegregation through forced busing. How actively should the White House pursue enforcement? Should HEW compliance orders to school districts and Justice Department investigations be used? Richard Nixon was especially sensitive to these complications in September 1970 as the first major court-ordered and federally assisted desegregation of schools was implemented in the South.

In March 1970, while he announced his administration's acceptance of the sixteen-year-old principle of desegregation, he sought to have his cake and eat it too. "The Court was right on Brown," Nixon said, "but wrong on Green." He believed in the principle of integration, but he felt that forced desegregation, especially through busing, was the wrong remedy for the problem. Still, he realized that the federal courts would try to bring about integration as quickly as possible, and he wanted the judges not to worry about the White House's views on segregation. To that end he commented "Deliberate racial segregation of pupils by official action is unlawful, wherever it exists."[55] The president proposed to spend $1.5 billion on disadvantaged schools, but he knew that middle-of-the-road position would make few friends for him.[56]

> I am aware that there are many sincere Americans who believe deeply in instant solutions and who will say that my approach does not go far enough fast enough. They feel that the only way to bring about justice is to integrate all schools now, everywhere, no matter what the cost in disruption of education.

Nixon chose not to directly attack the federal courts for calling for busing, and one of his aides, Pat Buchanan, was convinced that the president had missed "a golden opportunity" because he had not taken the leadership against the judges ordering desegregation. His attempts to use specially sculpted presidential messages to reassure the courts in hopes of heading off accelerated efforts at integration through busing failed miserably. With the election of 1972 looming on the horizon, Nixon certainly didn't want to be viewed in the South as the first president to support federal funds for busing or, as he put it,[57]

> I am aware . . . that there are many equally sincere citizens—North and South, black and white—who believe that racial separation is right, and wish the clock of progress would stop or be turned back to 1953. They will be disappointed . . .

From the late 1960s to the present, desegregation and busing as a tool have been recurrent issues in each presidential election.

RIGHTS OF THE ACCUSED. Activists on the Warren court created another issue that became a heated subject in presidential politics, especially in 1968 and 1972 by reshaping the rights of the accused. In a series of cases the court expanded the protections of individuals from evidence obtained in searches (*Mapp* v. *Ohio* and *Terry* v. *Ohio*).[58] The justices also assured citizens the right to lawyers at all stages in the legal process whether the accused could afford them or not (*Escobedo* and *Miranda*).[59] Presidents had to decide whether the Justice Department should help to pay for those attorneys. Other federal judges were ordering more humane treatment of prisoners via better correctional facilities to house them. Should federal tax funds be used to match state funds for these purposes? Would leadership in this area by the White House backfire on the president? After all, couldn't the advocates of "law and order" accuse him of coddling criminals?

ABORTION. Although desegregation and law and order evoked political response across a broad spectrum of the electorate, neither was couched in the raw emotion and passionately held positions that the Supreme Court elicited in its *Doe* and *Roe* cases on abortion (*Doe* v. *Bolton* and *Roe* v. *Wade*).[60] If abortion is killing to "pro life" forces, can one expect them to compromise and permit federal assistance in the performance of the procedure if the numbers are cut from an average of well over 1 million a year to say 500,000? Since those decisions, presidents have been placed in the politically unenviable position of having to decide (1) whether abortion, in and of itself, is right or wrong, (2) whether any circumstances should justify it, (3) whether the administration, through the Department of Health and Human Services (formerly HEW) should actively pursue abortion as a social policy for population control among welfare recipients whose children may become a further financial burden on society, or (4) whether the administration should support a call for a constitutional amendment outlawing abortion except when the life of the mother is endangered. Once again, the president is in a no-win situation. In election 1980, for example, Ronald Reagan followed his Republican Party's support for the constitutional amendment while Jimmy Carter opposed his party's position for federal funding for abortion on demand. One position would seem to be similar to the other, but Carter, who said he believed that abortion is wrong and shouldn't be funded, did not support the constitutional amendment to ban most abortions. This somewhat ambiguous position won him little support from "pro lifers" and their legions of regular voters.

In each of these areas, the president is forced into a no-win situation. He must choose up sides on controversial issues and, in the process, he is likely to alienate some segments of his normal constituency. These cases provide further evidence that, in many areas of social policy, it is the court that takes the lead and the president who is often reluctantly goaded into action.

## EMERGENCIES, NATIONAL SECURITY, AND CIVIL LIBERTIES

While the court may or may not follow the president's views on strictly domestic matters, in times of national emergencies, the court has tended to put checks and balances on the shelf and deferred to presidential leadership.[61] Evidently the justices agree with President Kennedy who once said, "domestic politics can only defeat us; but foreign policy can kill us."[62] Traditionally the president declares when emergencies exist, not the court. When he issues a declaration he may claim a broad range of powers over individuals, property, and communication. Theoretically, the Constitution takes a back seat to the survival of the nation, but it has been generally accepted that the president should continue to use emergency powers only with the consent of Congress. Crisis response and limits on presidential authority envisioned under the Constitution present some of the most perplexing dilemmas for a modern democracy like ours. In several cases in our history, the courts have been called in to answer the question "Does national survival justify any means the president wishes to adopt toward that end?" Presidents Lincoln, Roosevelt, and Truman each received a tongue-lashing from the high court for their disregard of civil liberties. The first two were castigated for withholding civil liberties from individuals who were being "detained illegally," and Truman was criticized for seizing property without congressional authorization during the Korean conflict. In a letter to his friend A. G. Hodges, Lincoln admitted some of his actions during the Civil War didn't jibe with the Constitution, but he felt they were justified nonetheless.[63] Other presidents have invariably tried to defend their actions in emergencies by citing chapter and verse in the Constitution or harkening back to some present or long-past emergency legislation.

Persons born since the Great Depression of the 1930s have lived the better portion of their lives under some form of presidentially declared emergency. When the U.S. banking system teetered on the brink of chaos, Franklin Roosevelt responded with a national emergency declaration. As World War II was erupting in Europe in 1939, Roosevelt declared a "limited national emergency," and later, as matters deteriorated further, he called an "unlimited" one in 1941. Harry Truman followed in Roosevelt's footsteps by adopting emergency measures in 1950 to assist him in dealing with the Korean conflict. Neither Presidents Johnson nor Nixon dealt with Vietnam on this basis, but Nixon did declare two emegencies: one to deal with a postal strike so he could use troops to move the mails and another to cope with serious deficiencies with our balance of payments.[64] Historically, and modern times have been no exception, national emergencies are called in time of military conflicts and economic downturns, although wartime use of emergency powers is the most common and easily defensible.

## THE DUAL STANDARD
## IN WAR OR PEACE

The Supreme Court has adopted a dual standard for dealing with presidential actions that violate civil liberties in wartime. During the military action, the president is placed on a pedestal, but, when the shooting stops in the trenches, sniping begins from the Supreme Court. Lincoln's experiences with Southern sympathizers, Franklin Roosevelt's handling of Japanese-Americans, and Truman's decision to seize the Youngstown steelworks are excellent examples of how this dual standard has applied.

LINCOLN AND THE COPPERHEADS. Political and legal complications frustrated Lincoln as he attempted to come to grips with Civil War. All along, he had contended that the South had no legal right to secede. A number of Southern sympathizers in the North and in border states adamantly and vocally opposed his policies. To muffle that dissent before it swelled into a crescendo of support for secession or collaboration with the South, the president decided to place the border states under martial law. He set up military commissions to replace existing civil courts. Since these areas were not, for the most part, war zones at that time and since civil courts were capable of operating, the president was treading on shaky constitutional ground. In the *Merryman* case, Justice Taney chastized the president and reminded him that the power to suspend *habeus corpus* was a congressional power that should, in any event, be exercised with due caution. Lincoln did not formally refute the court's arguments, preferring instead to go back to Congress for further justifications for his decisions. Radical Republican legislators affixed their stamp of approval on the president's suspension of *habeus corpus* after acrimonious debate by enacting the Habeus Corpus Act of 1863.[65]

With the support of Congress, military arrests of the Copperheads (as the sympathizers to the South, outside the Confederacy, were called) continued unabated. When a case similar to *Merryman* (*Ex Parte Vallandigham*, 1864)[66] was appealed to the high court from one of the military commissions, the court had to decide how to handle it. Clement Vallandigham, a Southern sympathizer from Ohio, publicly sided with the Confederacy, calling the war a battle waged not to preserve the Union but to crush liberties. By doing so he was arrested under martial law. The justices, in the time-honored tradition of ducking an issue, ruled that the court had "no jurisdiction." Technically, military commissions were not under the Supreme Court in the Constitution or by statute. Had the court wanted to decide otherwise for a broader jurisdiction, nothing in the Constitution or law would have forbidden it from doing so.

Like a hurricane that has touched land and has returned to sea to build up more steam, the issue of the Copperheads did not dissipate with the *Vallandigham* case. Another, along the same lines, reached the Supreme Court in 1866. Lambdin Milligan (*Milligan* v. *U.S.*),[67] an Indiana resident, had been sentenced to death for involvement in an organization aimed at the overthrow of the U.S. government, resisting the draft, conspiring to seize weapons from a munitions depot, and other treasonous acts. Andrew Johnson, hoping to use his presidential powers to lessen some of the passions aroused by the war and reintegrate Southerners and Southern sympathizers into the nation, commuted Milligan's sentence to life in prison in 1865. By the time the case reached the court, the war was over and Lincoln was no longer in the White House. The situation had changed and, as the majority decision noted, "Interests prevailed which are happily terminated. Now that the public safety is assured, this question as well as others can be discussed and decided without passion." For this reason, the court reversed its wartime opinions. In *Milligan*, the majority held that Lincoln presented flimsy justification for placing Indiana, which was never a battleground, under military commissions when civil courts were operating without incident (note that the same thing could have been said in both *Merryman* and *Vallandigham*). The court in *Milligan* said, "The Constitution . . . [applies] equally in war and peace and covers . . . all classes of men . . . under all circumstances."

If that principle was to be credible as a limit on presidential leadership in crisis, it should have applied in future crises, but the court returned to protecting presidential prerogatives in wartime in the next two cases in which the issues of military tribunals and the rights of civilians in wartime came before it. One case dealt with a team of German saboteurs (*Ex Parte Quirin*, 1942) and several others addressed the president's authority to limit the movements of Americans of Japanese ancestry during World War II (*Hirabayashi* v. *U.S.*, 1943, and *Korematsu* v. *U.S.*, 1944).

ROOSEVELT, GERMAN SABOTEURS, AND JAPANESE-AMERICANS. The *Quirin* case involved eight saboteurs (seven Germans and one American) who were transported aboard a German submarine and disembarked in the ocean near New York and Florida to infiltrate and destroy U.S. munitions industries. With weapons in hand, and having disposed of their German uniforms, they found the FBI waiting for them before they could begin their operations. President Roosevelt created a special military commission to handle the case. The administration argued that the saboteurs had violated international laws of war by not wearing fixed emblems to demonstrate that they were military personnel and not merely civilians. The court refused the defendants' requests that their convictions by the military commission be overturned. The justices argued that the president was merely following standard practice, since 1806, that spies and saboteurs be handled by military courts. More important for presidential leadership in future conflicts, the high court refused to distinguish between the powers of Congress to create courts and the powers of the president to create military tribunals. The defendants' cries that their Fifth and Sixth Amendment rights were being violated also fell on deaf ears since the justices found no justification for applying those rights to noncitizens, especially foreign agents.[68]

If the German agents could claim no protection from presidential decisions, would the same principle apply to nonbelligerent American citizens? Could a president in wartime place Americans' civil liberties in limbo with national security as his justification? The questions arose after an executive order in February 1942 that called for resettlement of all persons of Japanese ancestry living on the West Coast of the United States. The order noted the potential of sabotage by these people due to their ties to Japan. Since the Pearl Harbor attack two months before the order, Roosevelt had been under severe pressure from persons on the West Coast to uproot the Japanese from the area and move them farther inland. Eventually, over 112,000 persons (70,000 American citizens) were moved into ten "relocation" camps in Arkansas, Arizona, California, Colorado, Idaho, Utah, and Wyoming. One year later, the Supreme Court reviewed Roosevelt's order taking note of congressional approval given it in March 1942. The court did its best to skirt the issue of relocation in a 1943 case *Hirabayshi* v. *U.S.*.[69] *Hirabayshi* had been convicted for violating a curfew at one of the "relocation" centers. The justices merely upheld the conviction for curfew violation without addressing the constitutionality of the camps. It was wartime and Hirabayshi would only serve a short term, so why, the court seemed to be saying, should we press the issue of the settlements themselves?

The justices could not evade the issue indefinitely, however, as the case of *Korematsu* v. *U.S.*[70] reached the court in 1944. Once again, the president was given a green light to use his commander-in-chief powers in the national security interest even though civil liberties were being compromised in the process. The majority approved of relocation during wartime to mitigate fears of invasion on the West Coast. Korematsu's crime was that he had refused to leave his California home for one of the relocation camps. In a scathing rebuttal dissent, Justice Roberts complained that the decision of the majority amounted to punishing a citizen for not submitting to imprisonment in a concentration camp without any proof that he belonged there for being disloyal. Justice Jackson was likewise uncomfortable with the precedents being set in the case. He claimed that the *Korematsu* principle would lie about like "a loaded weapon ready for the hand of any authority that can bring forth a claim of urgent need."[71]

When the war was over the majority moved toward the dissenters in a case dealing with martial law in Hawaii that had been imposed after the bombing of Pearl Harbor (*Duncan* v. *Kahanamoku*, 1946).[72] In that case, the court reversed the conviction of a civilian tried by a military tribunal for assaulting two marines on sentry duty at a Hawaiian naval yard. Justice Hugo Black, who had written the *Korematsu* decision accepting the relocation camps, now held that the governor of Hawaii and the president had no justification for permitting continued use of military tribunals to try civilians more than two years after the attack on Pearl Harbor. He contended that civil courts were operating and that the military threat had subsided. The decision bore striking similarities to the *Milligan* case discussed earlier. Both of them criticized the suspension of civil liberties, but the court had no qualms about the president's and Congress's acting in that manner in real or potential theaters of hostilities in wartime. It is important to note that *Duncan* was an after-the-fact reminder rather than any attempt on the part of the court to say that under no circumstances could presidents do what Roosevelt had done in wartime.[73]

## EMERGENCIES, PRESIDENTIAL POWERS, AND PRIVATE PROPERTY

In each of the preceding cases, the court recognized the right of a president to protect the nation from individuals whose activities during wartime might have endangered the survival of the nation. A much more complicated question arises when presidents try to justify seizing private property for national security reasons. Six months prior to the direct U.S. involvement in World War II, Franklin Roosevelt used his declaration of unlimited national emergency from early in 1941 to seize North American Aviation. A strike had paralyzed the company, and it was unable to meet its weapons supply obligations to the government. The president reasoned that the national defense would be endangered without those weapons. During the war itself, Roosevelt also seized shipyards, a railroad, and other aircraft plants that he felt could operate more efficiently under government direction. In his judgment, as leader of the free world, he had no choice but to assure the success of the war effort even at the expense of tampering, temporarily, with the free enterprise system.[74]

Were such tamperings legal? The Supreme Court stepped in to answer the question in a later case involving President Truman's decision to take over Youngstown Sheet and Tube Company. The president ordered Secretary of Commerce Sawyer to run it for the government and directed the steelworkers who had been on strike to return to their jobs immediately. While the Defense Production Act of 1950 had authorized the president to seize businesses if they failed to grant priority to defense contract orders, only the 1947 Taft-Hartley Act gave him any authority to call workers back to their jobs. Workers could have returned to work for the eighty-day cooling-off period provided under Taft-Hartley while owners, workers, and federal mediators worked out a better arrangement. Truman decided that the danger to the Korean war effort justified his decision to disregard Taft-Hartley (which he preferred not to use, probably because he had opposed the "slave labor law's" passage). He seized the mills solely under his responsibilities as commander-in-chief.[75]

In *Youngstown Sheet and Tube* v. *Sawyer*,[76] the court continued to point out to the president, as it had in the Civil War and World War II cases we just examined, that it recognized a need for presidential leadership in crisis but that, when his acts border on the unconstitutional, he has a much better chance of seeing them ap-

## TABLE 7.3
## SELECTED FEDERAL COURT CASES ON LIMITS OF PRESIDENTIAL LEADERSHIP

| BROAD TOPIC AREA | ISSUE | LEGAL QUESTION | CASE | RESULTS/IMPACT |
|---|---|---|---|---|
| Foreign affairs | Nationalizing state militias | Can president call up militias when no invasion has taken place? | *Martin v. Mott*, 12 Wheaton 19 (1827) | Presidents should be able to mass forces to deter enemy arrival. |
| | Lincoln's blockade of the South | Can president blockade without congressional declaration of war? | The *Prize* cases, 2 Black, 17 L. Ed. 459 (1863) | President can respond to acts of war by others without awaiting formal congressional declaration of war. |
| | Embargo on sale of weapons imposed by president | Can Congress by joint resolution delegate embargo authority to the president? | *Curtiss Wright Export v. U.S.*, 299 U.S. 304 (1936) | Congress can delegate in this manner but president has rights in this area as sole negotiator for the United States. |
| Administrative | Firing a federal postmaster | Can Congress restrict president's removal of political appointees? | *Myers v. U.S.*, 272 U.S. 52 (1926) | Power of removal is part of the president's power to appoint, not the Senate's consent power. Congress cannot deny presidents, even by legislation, the right to fire in these cases. |
| | Dismissing a member of the Federal Trade Commission | Are independent regulatory commission members removed like other executive branch appointees? | *Rathbun* (Humphrey's executor) *v. U.S.*, 295 U.S. 602 (1935) | These commissions are part legislative and part judicial so presidents may remove members only for cause . . . dereliction of duty or illegal activities on the job. |
| | NRA codes | Can Congress delegate authority to the president to regulate commerce? | *Schechter Poultry v. U.S.*, 295 U.S. 495 (1935) | National Recovery Act voided as an unconstitutional delegation of the commerce power. Roosevelt considers reshaping the court. |
| | Murder of an assailant by guard assigned by executive order | Can the president use executive orders to protect the lives of federal judges? | In re *Naegel*, 135 U.S. 1, 10 S. Ct. 658 (1890) | President may take any measures necessary to protect a federal judge . . . threatened with personal attack. |

| | Topic | Question | Case | Ruling |
|---|---|---|---|---|
| Administrative (cont'd.) | Enforcing reconstruction acts | Can a president be restrained by court order from executing his duties under a law of Congress? | *Mississippi v. Johnson*, 4 Wallace 475 (1867) | Court has no jurisdiction to enjoin the president in performance of his duties. Mississippi cannot get a court order to stop enforcement of Reconstruction. |
| | Domestic wiretaps | Can a president use wiretaps on domestic groups without prior judicial warrants? | *U.S. v. U.S. District Court*, 407 U.S. 297 (1972) | National security claims do not justify wiretaps on domestic organizations on presidential authority alone ... prior judicial warrants are required to protect against Bill of Rights violations. |
| | Executive privilege and Watergate tapes | Does a president have absolute right to confidentiality in his communications? | *U.S. v. Nixon*, 418 U.S. 683 (1974) | Executive privilege may not be used to withhold evidence in a criminal trial. |
| | | Is a president immune from injunction in light of *Mississippi v. Johnson*? | *U.S. v. Nixon*, 418 U.S. 683 (1974) | In this case the president is not immune from judicial process. |
| Presidential-Congressional jurisdictions | Bill signing | When can a president sign a bill? | *La Abra Silver v. U.S.*, 175 U.S. 423 (1899) | President not restricted to deciding on a bill to times when Congress is in session. Could sign bill but within ten days of receipt. |
| | Pocket veto | Can a president pocket a bill during recesses? | *Kennedy v. Sampson*, 511 F. 2d 430 (D.C. Cir. 1974) | Brief recess is not adjournment. Bill on family practice medicine becomes law without president's signature. |
| | Senator's standing to sue | Can a senator sue the president? | *Kennedy v. Sampson*, 511 F. 2d 430 (D.C. Cir. 1974) | Senator Kennedy could challenge president's actions. |
| | Impoundments | Can a president impound appropriated funds? | *Train v. City of N.Y.*, 95 U.S. 839 (1975) | Congress did not approve limitless withholding of spending funds under the Clean Water Act. Domestic impoundments rendered suspect. |

Sources: Theodore Sorensen, *Watchmen in the Night* (Cambridge, Mass.: M.I.T. Press, 1976), pp. 122-132. Paul C. Bartholomew, *Summaries of Leading Cases of the Constitution* (Totowa, N.J.: Littlefield, Adams & Co., 1974), pp. 91, 179, 189, 192, 199, 212, 219, 262, 267, 360. Arthur S. Miller, *Presidential Power* (St. Paul, Minnesota: West Publishing, 1977), pp. 39, 100, 115, 118, 176, 177, 178, 117, 197, 208, 109, 115, 273. Louis Fisher, *The Constitution Between Friends* (New York: St. Martin's Press, 1978), pp. 18-19, 22, 80-81, 97-98, 112, 114-115, 159-161, 218.

proved if Congress goes along with him. Writing for a 6-3 majority, Justice Hugo Black criticized the president's actions and the entire concept of "inherent powers" under which Truman had been acting. If a president ever had the authority to issue an order as Truman had, Black felt that it must arise from the Constitution or a law of Congress, not from some vague "inherent powers" concept. Four of the other justices in the majority seemed more willing to imagine circumstances that would justify a president's use of emergency powers.[77]

As often happens with Supreme Court decisions, the most carefully reasoned exposition of the issues came in one of the concurring opinions penned by Justice Robert Jackson. Like Black he suggested that legality of presidential actions in these cases would be bolstered by support from Congress. He warned, however, that "When a President acts in a manner which conflicts with the 'expressed or implied will of Congress' [as Truman had by not using Taft-Hartley in the strike emergency] he invites careful court scrutiny of his decision. In doing so, he is claiming superior authority to Congress . . . and the issue becomes a question of Constitutional checks and balances."[78]

## IMPLICATIONS FOR PRESIDENTIAL
## LEADERSHIP IN CRISIS

Jackson's concurring opinion raises some interesting questions about presidential leadership in crisis. Should a president conclude, as Buchanan had prior to the Civil War, that if Congress gives no expressed or implied authority and if the Constitution is devoid of specific authorization, a president may not act? Could it be that the *Youngstown* case was not a case of checks and balances at all but, rather, a demonstration of the court's willingness to assert itself at the expense of a politically vulnerable president presiding over an unpopular "police action" in Korea? After all, Truman was under increasing fire in 1952 about Korea, and he had the lowest popularity rating of any president from the beginning of polling until Nixon at the time of Watergate and Jimmy Carter in 1980. In dealing with Lincoln's transgressions from constitutional form, the court waited until he was in his grave and the war was over to question his judgment in the *Milligan* case. Roosevelt was not issued his tongue lashing by the court in the *Duncan* case either until after the hostilities were history.

Each of these presidents seized the moment in crises and avoided the temptation to glance over his shoulder to see how Congress and the courts might respond. Voters have come to expect that kind of dynamic and forceful leadership from the person they elect to preside over the nation from the Oval Office. Still, there remains the gnawing fact that abuses of power can creep in under the guise of leadership in national emergencies.

## LIMITS ON PRESIDENTIAL
## LEADERSHIP: A BROADER SPECTRUM

Although we have emphasized the potential impact of Supreme Court pronouncements on domestic policy innovations like the New Deal and have examined the emergency powers of the president, as the court views them, the justices have hardly limited themselves to those areas in defining the limits on presidential leadership. As Table 7.3 shows, the courts have instructed the president on a broad spectrum of constitutional issues.

Table 7.3 also shows the court lost little sleep over giving the president unsolicited advice on such issues as whom he may fire, how he may cooperate or conflict with Congress, the kind of executive orders he may issue, what powers he may exercise in foreign affairs, and so forth. In each of these situations the president, often reluctantly, has felt obligated to act according to the court's directives. Still, in the majority of the cases, the court's findings were supportive rather than destructive of presidential leadership.

## CONCLUSIONS

The courts, by the decisions they make, help to shape the environment in which the president can exercise leadership. Decisions, for example, that called for redrawing of legislative districts (*Baker* v. *Carr, Reynolds* v. *Sims,* and *Westberry* v. *Sanders*)[79] give raw voting power on the Hill and in the state legislatures to urban areas. Political pressures were thus magnified to force the president to act to deal with urban problems. Court decisions in social areas required that the administrations determine whether to ignore, actively support, or openly oppose the positions the justices have taken. In this respect, it is the courts that lead the president.

Tampering with the court through impeachment threats, careful selection of appointments, court packing by legislation, and similar efforts have rarely worked for presidents. Modern-day presidents have been less tempted to resort to such methods because the courts and presidents have been more philosophically attuned to one another since FDR tried to pack the court in 1937. On the whole, the recent courts have proven to be a friend rather than an enemy of presidential leadership.

## NOTES

[1] Clinton Rossiter, *The American Presidency* (New York: Harvest Books, 1960), p. 56.

[2] Phillipa Strumm, *Presidential Power and American Democracy,* 2nd ed. (Pacific Palisades, Calif.: Goodyear, 1980), pp. 89-94.

[3] Glendon Schubert, *The President and the Courts* (Minneapolis: Univ. of Minnesota Press, 1957), Appendix A as cited in Theodore Sorensen, *Watchmen in the Night* (Cambridge, Mass.: M.I.T. Press, 1975), p. 121.

[4] *Brown* v. *Board of Education of Topeka, Kansas,* 347 U.S. 483 (1954).

[5] Bob Woodward and Scott Armstrong, *The Brethren: Inside the Supreme Court* (New York: Simon & Schuster, 1979), p. 411.

[6] Emmett John Hughes, *The Living Presidency* (New York: Coward, McCann & Geoghegan, Inc., 1973), p. 171.

[7] *Marbury* v. *Madison,* 1 Branch 137 (1803) at 177.

[8] Henry J. Abraham, *The Judiciary: The Supreme Court in the Governmental Process,* 3rd ed. (Boston: Allyn & Bacon, 1973), p. 30.

[9] Joseph A. Califano, *A Presidential Nation* (New York: W. W. Norton, 1975), p. 169.

[10] Albert Beveridge, *The Life of John Marshall* (Boston: Houghton Mifflin, 1919), vol. 2, p. 537; vol. 4, pp. 579-580, as cited in Robert Scigliano, *The Supreme Court and the Presidency* (New York: Free Press, 1971), p. 25.

[11] *Worcester* v. *Georgia,* discussed in Scigliano, *op. cit.,* p. 38.

[12] *McCulloch* v. *Maryland,* 4 Wheat. 316 (1819).

[13] Arthur Schlesinger, Jr., *The Age of Jackson* (Boston: Little, Brown, 1953), pp. 90-91.

[14] Rexford Tugwell, *How They Became President* (New York: Simon & Schuster, 1964), p. 97.

[15] Cited in James Parton, *The Presidency of Andrew Jackson* (edited with notes by Robert Remini) (New York: Harper & Row, 1967), pp. 290-291.

[16] More thorough coverage is in Robert Remini, *Andrew Jackson and the Bank* (New York: W. W. Norton, 1967).

[17] Excerpted in Robert Hirschfield, ed., *The Powers of the Presidency,* 2nd ed. (Chicago: Aldine, 1973), p. 72, which is an excellent documents and essay source on the presidency.

[18] *Ex Parte Merryman,* 17 Fed. Cas. 144 (1861).

[19] Scigliano, *op. cit.,* p. 41.

[20] *Ibid.,* p. 43.

[21] See Chapter 1 of this text.

[22] Scigliano, *op. cit.,* p. 47.

[23] *Schechter Poultry* v. *U.S.,* 295 U.S. 495 (1935).

[24] *U.S.* v. *Butler,* 297 U.S. 1 (1936).

[25] Califano, *op. cit.,* p. 164.

[26] Henry J. Abraham, *Justices and Presidents* (New York: Oxford U.P., 1974), p. 63.

[27] Excerpts from *The White House Years: Mandates for Change* © 1963 by Dwight D. Eisenhower. Reprinted by permission of Doubleday & Compnay, Inc.

[28] Scigliano, *op. cit.,* p. 94.

[29] For excellent handling of selection process, see Howard Ball, *Courts and Politics* (Englewood Cliffs, N.J.: Prentice-Hall, 1980), pp. 177-190, and David Rodhe and Harold Spaeth, *Supreme Court Decision Making* (San Francisco: Freeman, 1975). See also David Danelski, *A Supreme Court Justice Is Appointed* (New York: Random House, 1964).

[30] Dan Rather and Gary Paul Gates, *The Palace Guard* (New York: Harper & Row, 1974), p. 201.

[31] *Ibid.,* pp. 246, 328.

[32] Rowland Evans and Robert Novak, *Nixon in the White House* (New York: Vintage Books, 1972), p. 161.

[33] *Ibid.,* p. 166.

[34] *Ibid.,* p. 167.

[35] Abraham, *Justices and Presidents,* p. 29.

[36] See Saul K. Padover, *Jefferson* (New York: Harcourt Brace, 1942), pp. 322-331.

[37] Scigliano, *op. cit.,* p. 31.

[38] James MacGregor Burns, *Franklin Roosevelt: The Lion and the Fox* (New York: Harcourt Brace Jovanovich, Inc., 1956), p. 292.

[39] *Ibid.,* p. 292.

[40] Walter Murphy, *Congress and the Court* (Chicago: Univ. of Chicago Press, 1965), p. 61.

[41] Robert H. Jackson, *The Struggle for Judicial Supremacy* (New York: Knopf, 1941), pp. 342-345, as cited in Sickels, *op. cit.,* p. 248.

[42] *West Coast Hotel* v. *Parrish,* 300 U.S. 379 (1937).

[43] Walter Murphy and C. Herman Pritchett, *Courts, Judges, and Politics,* 3rd ed., (New York: Random House, 1979), p. 357.

[44] *Ibid.,* p. 358.

[45] *Ex Parte McCardle,* 7 Wall 506 (1869).

[46] For Johnson's pride in appointing Marshall and other blacks, see Lyndon Johnson, *The Vantage Point* (New York: Holt, Rinehart and Winston), p. 179.

[47] Scigliano, *op. cit.,* p. 176.

[48] Steven Puro, "Presidential Relationships with the Solicitors General of the United States: Political Science Research at Presidential Libraries," prepared for delivery at the 1978

Meeting of the Missouri and Kansas Political Science Associations, October 27-28, 1978, Kansas City, Missouri. Unpublished mimeo, p. 3.

[49] *Ibid.*, p. 4.

[50] Abraham, *Justices and Presidents*, p. 196.

[51] Califano, *op. cit.*, p. 173.

[52] *Ibid.*, p. 180.

[53] *Regents of the University of California* v. *Baake*, 98 S. Ct. 2733 (1978). See also: Allan P. Sindler, *Baake, DeFundis and Minority Admissions* (New York: Longmans, 1978).

[54] Murphy and Pritchett, *op. cit.*, p. 357.

[55] On Nixon and busing, see William Safire, *Before the Fall* (Garden City, N.Y.: Doubleday, 1975), p. 241.

[56] *Ibid.*,

[57] *Ibid.*,

[58] *Mapp* v. *Ohio*, 367 U.S. 643 (1961), and *Terry* v. *Ohio*, 387 U.S. 929 (1967).

[59] *Escobedo* v. *Illinois*, 378 U.S. 478 (1964), and *Miranda* v. *Arizona*, 384 U.S. 436 (1966).

[60] *Doe* v. *Bolton*, 410 U.S. 179 (1973), and *Roe* v. *Wade*, 410 U.S. 113 (1973); *Planned Parenthood of Missouri* v. *Danforth*, 428 U.S. 52 (1976).

[61] For the best discussion of emergency powers, see J. Malcolm Smith and Cornelius Cotter, *Powers of the President During Crises* (Washington, D.C.: Public Affairs Press, 1960). See also Chapter 5 of this text.

[62] Aaron Wildavsky, "The Two Presidencies," *Transaction*, (December 1966), as reprinted in *Perspectives on the Presidency*, ed. Aaron Wildavsky (Boston: Little, Brown, 1975), p. 450.

[63] See Chapter 1.

[64] Robert DiClerico, *The American President* (Englewood Cliffs, N.J.: Prentice-Hall, 1979), p. 308.

[65] Louis Koenig, *The Chief Executive* (New York: Harcourt Brace, 1975), p.

[66] *Ex Parte Vallandigham*, 1 Wall 243 (1864).

[67] *Ex Parte Milligan*, 71 U.S. 2 (1866).

[68] *Ex Parte Quirin*, 317 U.S. 1 (1942). An excellent discussion of this case is in Koenig, *op. cit.*, p. 250. Also see Arthur S. Miller, *Presidential Power* (St. Paul, Minn.: West Publishing, 1977), p. 175.

[69] *Hirabayashi* v. *U.S.*, 320 U.S. 81 (1943).

[70] *Korematsu* v. *U.S.*, 323 U.S. 214 (1944).

[71] Sickels, *op. cit.*, p. 260.

[72] *Duncan* v. *Kahanamoku*, 327 U.S. 304 (1946).

[73] Miller, *op. cit.*, p. 176.

[74] Koenig, *op. cit.*, p. 252.

[75] Smith and Cotter, *op. cit.*, p. 134.

[76] *Youngstown Sheet and Tube Co.* v. *Sawyer*, 343 U.S. 579 (1952).

[77] *Ibid.*, pp. 587-589.

[78] *Ibid.*, p. 589.

[79] *Baker* v. *Carr*, 369 U.S. 186 (1962); *Reynolds* v. *Sims*, 377 U.S. 533 (1964); *Wesberry* v. *Sanders*, 376 U.S. 1 (1964).

# Budgets, Bureaucrats, and Brandishing the Jawbone: Economic Leadership

Election 1980 proved again that American voters expect economic leadership from the White House. No doubt high inflation and interest rates coupled with the drawn-out hostage crisis in Iran helped to make Jimmy Carter a lame duck. Even traditional Democrats (especially Catholics and Labor) jumped ship in large numbers. Gone are the days when presidents can adopt the hands-off philosophy of a Harding or a Coolidge. Former Budget Director Frederick Malek estimates that by the year 2000 two of every three dollars spent in the U.S. economy will be traceable to national or local governments.[1] The level of government spending has become a major factor in the nation's economic health.

Whether voters realize it or not, they desire economic miracles from their president. He is doing a good job if he can produce full employment, stable prices, a rising standard of living, and a wide range of social services while maintaining a stout defense and lightening the tax load. In response to a Gallup survey done for public broadcasting on public attitudes toward the presidency, the people sampled said that the most important thing that a president should be able to do is to provide leadership (24%) and to solve economic problems (17%). These were two of the top three expectations they listed.[2] Evidently they believed that the president should have both the skill and the authority to cut budgets when necessary, deflate bloated bureaucracies at will, and convince Congress to go along with controls over the skyrocketing prices that were undermining their living standards and dreams for the future.

It may be that voter desires for presidential leadership in dealing with inflation and recession are little more than wishful thinking. Increasing voter apathy demonstrated by low voter turnout even in the presidential races[3] seems to suggest that many Americans are not at all convinced that government can handle the nation's economic woes. When the people in the Gallup sample cited were asked to list the most important problem facing the nation in the 1980s, inflation, high cost of living, and taxes topped the list (58%) with energy, fuel shortages, and gasoline costs next (18%) followed by unemployment, jobs, and recession (10%).[4] When asked how confident they were that Congress, the president, or any president could deal with the problem, the "any president" category provided some interesting insights into public attitudes toward the presidency as an effective institution. Profound skepticism seemed to be the prevalent mood as only 15% were very confident about the capacity of the presidency to handle these problems while 33% were "not confident." Between the two extremes, 44% claimed to be "fairly confident."[5] An editor of a small California newspaper probably expressed these frustrations as well as anyone:[6]

> The cost of living goes up, therefore workers want to get more money because they can't cope. So the cost of labor goes up . . . so the cost of living goes up. There's no way to stop it and everybody's trying to figure out how to stay in the same place. But, I don't know if any President can turn it around. It has its own perpetual motion machine.

Doubting Thomas types such as the one third who expressed no confidence in the presidency as an economic problem-solving institution have a reasonable foundation for reaching those conclusions. Even White House staffers are not convinced about the ability of the institutional presidency to solve national problems. Richard Cheney, President Ford's chief of staff, admitted that[7]

> I came away from my eight years of government in Washington considerably more conservative than when I came here. . . . I'm less optimistic about the ability of government to do many things for people. Policy tends to be made by advocates and it is increasingly difficult to manage government. . . . I think the best solution is for government to do nothing. Maybe you have to measure success in terms of what didn't happen.

Presidents have difficulty being economic problem solvers because, like most politicians, they have tended to be notoriously deficient in their understanding of economics. Ronald Reagan was the first of the post-1932 presidents to be a college educated economist. Given the breadth of the president's other duties, there is little chance that he could operate efficiently in these areas without an economic braintrust, most of which we examined in Chapter 4 including OMB, CEA, the Treasury Department, and the Federal Reserve.

A former chairman of the CEA, Walter Heller, has called the period since 1960 the "Age of the Economist." Economic leadership in any administration arises from within the ranks of the president's economic advisors. Resident economists have become not only the source of information for presidents on fiscal and monetary matters, but their teachers as well. Lyndon Johnson learned a great respect for economists that he came to late in his political career. In comments about a new CEA nominee, Johnson pointed out that James Dusenberg ". . . is one of the nation's leading economists. When I was growing up that didn't seem to mean very much; but since I grew up, we have learned the error of our ways."[8]

Economic advisors offer the president economic prescriptions calling for varying dosages of both monetary and fiscal elixirs. In Chapter 4 we discussed how monetary policy (money supply and interest rates) impacts the health of the national economy. Harry Truman once said that the power of the presidency involved the power to persuade and Richard Neustadt[9] noted that persuasion rather than coercion was the way in which a president must get things done. Shaping fiscal policy requires skills in cajoling and measured threatening. As Table 8.1 demonstrates Ronald Reagan, like most new presidents, soon learned that proposing budget cuts and getting them enacted are two entirely different matters. Reagan was the first president since Dwight Eisenhower to consider across-the-board cuts in federal expenditures deep enough to retard the real growth of the federal bureaucracy. Though some entitle-

**TABLE 8.1**

**THE REAGAN DIET: PROPOSED BUDGET CUTS 1981**

| PROGRAM | PROPOSED CHANGES | POLITICAL PROSPECTS |
|---|---|---|
| Medicaid | A cap on Federal aid to state Medicaid programs. *Savings: $100 million in 1981, $11.3 billion more by 1985.* | Will encounter fierce opposition. The White House will bill it as "temporary," pending fundamental reforms. |
| Disability insurance under the social-security system | Weed out unqualified recipients. Impose a "megacap" on benefits. Tighten eligibility standards. *Savings: $600 million in 1982, cumulative total of $5.4 billion by 1985.* | Opponents will mount an emotional appeal against cutting aid to the vulnerable, but even Democratic leaders give the reforms a good chance of passing. |
| Social-security student benefits | Phase out college payments for children of retired, disabled and dead workers. *Savings: $100 million in 1981, $700 million in 1982, almost $4.5 billion between 1983 and 1985.* | Past attempts to make these changes have failed, but Congressional recognition that the entire social-security system is in jeopardy may make them more palatable. |
| Social-security minimum benefits | Eliminate the $122-a-month benefit. *Savings: $200 million in 1981; $1 billion a year, 1982 through 1985* | Good chance of passing. Fewer than one-half of recipients would lose a single dollar under this plan. |
| Unemployment insurance, extended benefits | Give up the national trigger for extra benefits once the number receiving insurance reaches 4.5 percent of the work force, and use a state-by-state trigger. *Savings: $570 million in 1981 and $4.7 billion over the next four years.* | Organized labor will resist, but the Senate passed such a measure last year, and Democrats say it has a chance. |
| Trade adjustment assistance for workers displaced by foreign competition | Provide aid only after regular unemployment insurance runs out and limit the insurance package to a maximum of 78 weeks. *Savings: $2.6 billion over the next five years.* | Labor opposition will be ferocious. The measure might pass only if accompanied by protectionist bills designed to reduce imports. |
| Food stamps | Reduce food-stamp benefits by 35 cents, instead of 30 cents, for every dollar earned. Cancel planned amendment to liberalize benefits. *Savings: $2.6 billion in 1982; $3.4 billion in 1983 and 1984; $3.5 billion in 1985.* | Chances for the whole package are not good. Some changes will pass—but probably not enough to save much more than $1 billion a year. |
| Aid to Families with Dependent Children | Count income of stepparents in means tests and require tests every month. *Savings: $3.1 billion by 1985.* | Support in the Senate will be strong. Welfare lobbyists will resist, but Democrats give the reforms a chance. |

238

| Program | Action and Savings | Commentary |
|---|---|---|
| Comprehensive Employment and Training Act (CETA) | Eliminate all subsidies by the end of 1981. *Savings: $1 billion in 1981, $17 billion over the following four years.* | States and cities will squawk, but sentiment against CETA is growing, and major cuts in the program are likely. |
| Arts and Humanities | Cut subsidies in half. Limit endowments to $100 million a year starting in 1984. *Savings: $309 million by 1985.* | An elite constituency will raise a fuss, and Reagan may not get all he wants. |
| Child nutrition | Reduce various subsidies and stop aid for many private schools. *Savings: $1 billion in 1982, $4.2 billion more by 1985.* | "Difficult but not impossible," says Stockman. The probability is for some cuts, but fewer than Reagan wants. |
| Rural Electrification Administration | Eliminate access to low-interest loans through the Federal Financing Bank. *Savings (mostly in off-budget expenditures): $699 million in 1981, $13.3 billion more through 1985.* | Utilities and their customers will balk at higher costs. "This is a bread-and-butter issue for both Republicans and Democrats," says one congressman. Very tough. |
| Farmers Home Administration | A 25 percent across-the-board reduction in new lending. *Savings: $900 million by 1985.* | The agency is a favorite conduit of Congressional favors. Some cuts may be approved, but not all. |
| Tennessee Valley Authority | Reduce TVA access to Federal Financing Bank's low-interest loans. *Savings: $762 million in 1982 and $3.2 billion more by 1985.* | TVA is not very popular in Washington these days, and given its limited constituency, the Administration may get what it wants. |
| National Aeronautics and Space Administration | Defer or cancel various NASA projects. *Savings: $70 million in 1981, $1.9 billion by 1985.* | Strongest reaction will come from the scientific community, but prospects for some cuts are good. |
| Waste-treatment grants | Limit funding to big-city plants where benefits are greatest. *Savings: almost $6 billion between 1981 and 1985.* | Some cuts should go through. But Congress expects a tough fight over grants already promised. |
| Synthetic fuels | Kill five pilot projects being built with direct government funding. *Savings: $368 million in 1981 and about $1 billion a year, 1982 to 1985.* | Synfuels were billed as a way to reduce dependence on OPEC, so Reagan's men expect "negative public reaction." But Democrats concede there is room for cuts. |
| Urban Development Action Grants | Rescind $500 million in 1981 and abandon future funding. *Savings: $1.5 billion between 1982 and 1985.* | A likely winner. But some legislators warn that there could be a price—an increase in block grants to cities and states. |
| U.S. Postal Service | Eliminate all public-service subsidies by 1984. *Savings: $3.1 billion by 1985.* | The powerful postal union and champions of mail deliveries six days a week may hold savings to a minimum. |
| Export-Import Bank | Reduce new loans by 25 percent below the levels planned for the next five years. *Savings: $150 million in 1981 and nearly $3.9 billion more by 1985.* | Big Ex-Im Bank customers such as Boeing will howl, and even the Administration's argument that the bank provides subsidies to fat cats may not win the day. |

Source: *Newsweek*, February 16, 1981, p. 23.

239

ments (programs providing direct payments) were initially granted "sacred cow" status (Social Security, military pensions, etc.) the budget axe fell on programs that were the darlings of the rich (arts and humanities) and the necessities of the needy (food stamps, CETA job programs, and child nutrition). The insightful might notice that the OMB operative sent by the Reagan administration to sell these proposals to the Senate Appropriations Committee was a young man named O. Bowmann Cutter.

Presidents usually confront a withering array of opponents aligned against their spending priorities and their plans on ways to distribute the tax burden. Departmental personnel, friends on congressional committees, and interest group lobbyists who agree with them present a formidable set of competitors seeking their say in "who gets what."

## PUBLIC UNDERSTANDING
## OF THE ECONOMY

In confrontations with the legislative "whales" on Capitol Hill, the business, labor, and civil rights elements, and the departments that they serve, the president may find public support for his initiatives as a useful lever. Unfortunately for the president, the average citizen often has difficulty fathoming the intricacies of the American economic system and the government's motivating role in it. Ronald Reagan, in his first televised address to the nation as President in February 1981, gave an Economics 101 lecture with visual aids which included a dollar bill and the thirty-six cents in change that he said it was worth. Federal budget figures in the billions and trillions must border on science fiction to the median-income American family—those whose incomes are pegged at $16,000 to $25,000 plus a year.

To demonstrate the concept of $1 billion, politicians and journalists have often resorted to drawing analogies. For example, they might say that 1 billion hours ago dinosaurs roamed the earth, that 1 billion minutes ago, Jesus Christ had not yet been born, and that a billion dollar bills, if taped end to end, could produce a paper belt that would ring the earth twice near the equator and could be looped twice more across the polar ice caps.

As Gallup Poll statistics demonstrate, the soaring inflation and scarce resources evidenced in recent decades have increased public fears about the economy sufficiently that it is now politically expedient for candidates to preach the gospel of fiscal restraint. Unfortunately for the president, one person's "fat" may be another's "necessities." So, while a farmer might criticize "big government," that same farmer would hardly support massive cuts in the Agriculture Department and its price supports program. Likewise, the executives who sing the praises of our "free enterprise" system would change their tune radically if there were talk at the White House of lowering tariffs. This double standard of thinking[10] among so much of the electorate makes changes in the fiscal and bureaucratic status quo risky for the president to support. Whatever policies he advocates in taxation and spending, he is forced to decide whose ox will be gored. For every friend he makes, he creates an enemy determined to make sure that he won't be elected for four more years.

As we examine the fiscal levers that the president may manipulate to adjust the operation of the economy to his liking, we shall also demonstrate that his latitude in exercising economic leadership is limited by (1) the nature of our economic system, (2) the complexity and automatic expansion of the federal budget, (3) the games bureaucrats play to protect their turfs, and (4) the capacity of powerful interest groups to sabotage his plans on the Hill and to balk at any attempt to regulate the growth of prices and wages.

## THE ECONOMY
## IN A NUTSHELL

Independence Day orators and shirt-sleeved campaigners of most every political stripe wax eloquent about the virtues of our nation's "free enterprise" system. While the means of production and distribution of most of the nation's goods and services are in private hands (capitalism), it is debatable that we have ever had a truly "free market" system (supply and demand set the price of goods and services). In reality, when a president tries to influence the direction of the economy, he finds a "mixed economy" with monopoly practices and government price and licensing regulations affecting the supply and prices of products. He learns that he can aid businesses through his taxing and tariff policies and through price supports. Likewise, he can try to keep consumers happy by issuing (in cooperation with Congress) ceiling prices that limit the cost of such essentials as natural gas and gasoline.[11] The price the consumer will pay for a product and the harvest the producer can reap are often traceable to government regulations. Deregulation can be a boon to producers but as Ronald Reagan learned in 1981, when he freed the gasoline industry from controls, consumers are less than pleased with increases substantially greater than they had been led to expect.

### MANIPULATING
### THE ECONOMY

From the days of the New Deal and the Depression, government manipulation of the economy has become the accepted orthodoxy for most presidents.[12] John Maynard Keynes provided the intellectual imprimatur for this approach claiming that business expansion and contraction were only two of several ways in which inflation and unemployment rates could be adjusted. Government, through tax and spending policies, he argued, smooths out the inflationary peaks and recessionary valleys in the normal business cycle. Following Keynesian theory, if the nation's economy is in a period of high inflation, government should increase taxes so that the public will have fewer dollars to spend. If consumers have less to spend, demand, which had been pulling up prices, will subside and so will inflation. Keynesian economics would also call for a slowdown in government spending through budget cuts to further dampen inflation.

On the other hand, the prescription for dealing with unemployment, economic slowdown (recession), or even a full-blown depression would be for the White House to increase federal spending so that more money could be pumped through the economy, thus increasing the buying power of businesses and individuals. Classical economic theory suggests that businesses with more money to spend would expand to meet new consumer demand and hire workers to operate their enlarged and retooled facilities.

Keynesian economists were sent back to their calculators and charts in the later 1970s when high inflation (18%) and high unemployment (8%) were occurring simultaneously. The contention that high inflation would encourage high employment rates as the Phillips curve[13] theory argues gave way to a new term—stagflation —which describes the simultaneous presence of high inflation and high unemployment. Presidents and their economists then had to decide if it were possible to reverse double-digit inflation without also producing levels of unemployment above 4-5%, which economists have tended to consider "full" employment.[14]

## MEASURES OF
## ECONOMIC HEALTH

Even during the unnerving economic upheavals of the 1970s, which were due, to a degree, to the energy shortages, the government indicators used to measure economic health were not altered. Even the president's perceptions of how to manipulate them has not undergone radical change, though some of the past "givens" had to be cast aside.

Of these indicators, the inflation rate seems capable of creating most political havoc for the president.[15] Increases in the cost of living index are symptomatic of underlying inflationary pressures in the economy that hit the average voter squarely in the pocketbook. This rule is not iron-clad as Kristen Monroe and Dona Metcalf Laughlin noted. For example, they found that certain groups, such as married men, felt that the unemployment rate was the single, most important, influence on presidential popularity. They also found that the state of the economy was more important to the popularity of a president than was any government program designed to help redistribute the wealth[16] which he might have led through Congress.

## ECONOMICS OF THE 1980s:
## LEARNING TO COPE

When presidents try to use fiscal policy to deal with social and economic problems in the coming decades, they will find their spending options substantially more restricted than those of their pre-Vietnam predecessors.

During the 1980 campaign, Jimmy Carter tried to lay the lion's share of the blame for the nation's economic doldrums at the doorstep of foreign oil producers. The avarice of the OPEC cartel, according to Carter, was to blame for the double-digit inflation. Actually, he was merely spotlighting a reality that faces the American economy in the coming decades. We have begun to suffer chronic shortages in other raw materials too: for example, in 1980 the United States was importing at least one-half of its twenty major mineral needs; foreign nations were supplying 97% of the chromium used in U.S. oil refineries and petroleum plants; and over 90% of the nation's cobalt for jet engines and a wide range of heavy machinery came from overseas.[17] In addition, the 1980 price tag for OPEC oil was well over

## TABLE 8.2
## KEY ECONOMIC INDICATORS

| INDICATOR | DEFINITION | SOME POLITICAL IMPACTS |
| --- | --- | --- |
| Inflation rate | Rate of general rise in prices over a stated period of time. | When too high, it can create angry consumers who might seek cuts in federal spending and can undermine the political bases leading to the new members of Congress and a new president. |
| Cost of living index* | Cost of 400 items of daily living including food, housing, clothing, transportation, medical care, etc., compared with costs of those items in a previous base year. | May stimulate inflation expectations, worker demands for higher wages, or calls for controls. |
| Gross national product | The current value of all goods and services produced in the economy during that year. | Indicates whether the economy is growing or stagnant. |
| GNP deflator | Adjustment used to take inflation into account to judge "real" growth of the value of goods and services. | May be used to convince voters that a downturn has bottomed out. |
| Unemployment rate | The ratio of the number of persons classified as unemployed to the number of people in the civilian labor force. | President may be blamed for their plight by persons who lose their jobs. |

*Formerly Consumer Price Index.

$100 billion.[18] When so much capital is going overseas, the dollars available for social programs are bound to become increasingly more scarce.

Further complicating the president's quest for increased revenues for new initiatives will be the slow growth of the American economy due to low productivity brought on by the aging machinery in our factories, increasing labor costs, and competition from other industrialized nations. When major American corporations like Chrysler come to the federal government to bail them out, the president can hardly expect national revenues to grow until such corporations can modernize to compete with foreigners and become solvent taxpayers again.

Another factor sure to complicate the president's economic leadership in the 1980s will be the inflationary psychology that has infected the American economy. Inflation has so etched itself into the minds of the consumers that they are habitually purchasing large-ticket items (cars, appliances, etc.) at the current price by borrowing in order to buy them before the price goes up. Citizens are not saving and cooling inflation by taking dollars out of circulation; they are bidding up the cost of living index by using credit to spend beyond their means. Even when government tries to come to grips with inflation, it can help create more of it.

Because excessive use of credit had been fueling inflation, Federal Reserve

Chairman Paul Volker decided in 1980 that the Federal Reserve would impose monetary and credit controls to slow the inflationary pressures each was creating. Instead, the higher interest rates meant higher prime lending rates and higher mortgage costs to new home purchasers, each of which further ballooned the cost of living index.[19] Inflationary expectations became so pronounced that a number of presidential candidates spoke out in support of a system of indexing the income tax tables to the rate of inflation. Under the scheme, if a person increases his or her income by the same percentage as the inflation rate, the additional income would not be swallowed by moving up on the tax tables. In tandem with indexing, Republican candidates such as Ronald Reagan and Robert Dole proposed limiting the growth of the tax revenues by "cuts" of $10 billion per year over a three-year period.[20]

These same candidates were calling for a strong national defense and cuts in federal spending to slow inflation and balance the budget. Who could produce on promises like those? How much of the budget can the president actually control? In Chapter 4 we demonstrated his limits in assuming leadership roles in monetary policy matters. What are his capabilities in fiscal matters given the limitations of the 1980s? Can he divert funds from congressionally mandated social programs into creating a stronger defense? Can he readjust the tax system as he chooses without guerilla warfare erupting against him on Capitol Hill? David Stockman, Reagan's OMB Director, proposed deep cuts of $15 billion in the 1981 budget. At the same time the administration was committed to increasing defense spending by $20 billion. Knowing he had a battle on his hands, President Reagan took the initiative and went to Capitol Hill and met with leaders of Congress on their own turf. Of the twentieth-century presidents, only Woodrow Wilson, who had a special room set aside on the Hill for meeting with members of Congress, had done something similar.

## PRESIDENT'S ROLE IN FISCAL POLICY

If the president has any real influence over the American economy, it is in the area of fiscal (spending and revenues) policy rather than monetary concerns. How the president handles his fiscal responsibilities reflects his personal choices among competing groups in society and reveals, as Gerald Ford put it, "his philosophy of how the public and private spheres should be related." In acting as fiscal leader, the president may decide how the spending pie will be sliced, what the tax burdens will be and who will bear them, how the government should be organized to be most effective and save dollars, and what, if any, controls will be necessary to stem inflation or bring the nation out of recessions.

### BUDGETER IN CHIEF: PRESIDENT SETS FISCAL PRIORITIES

President Lyndon Johnson once called the federal budget a dry, unfathomable maze of figures and statistics thicker than a Sears, Roebuck catalog and as dull as a telephone book. Although presidential involvement in the intricacies of the budget process has varied from administration to administration, Lance LeLoup found that Presidents Eisenhower and Nixon soon tired of the tedious budget process after their first year in office, whereas Truman and Ford maintained their enthusiasm throughout. The first years in office evidently produce a flush of optimism in the president and campaign promises encourage the administration to seek out the dregs in the federal budget and say "no" to them. Even activists like John Kennedy and Lyndon Johnson reveled in their budget-cutter role early in their White House years. Speaking about his first budget Lyndon Johnson described his role in preparing it saying that[21]

> I worked as hard on that budget as I have ever worked on anything. . . . Day after day, I went over that budget with the Cabinet officers, my economic advisors, and the Budget Director. I studied most every line, nearly every page, until I was dreaming about the budget at night.

Presidents who immerse themselves in the budget process often do so because they see it as a method for doing a number of things that can be beneficial both to the national economy as a whole and to their political fortunes four years hence when they seek reelection. According to Dennis Ippolito, presidential involvement in the budget process helps him to retain a degree of administrative control and management over the departments by affecting the resources they can get. The president can also get the departments to better plan what they want to do and he can use OMB to test an agency's performance in meeting his policy goals as it spends federal dollars.[22]

In addition to these management advantages his involvement in the budget may permit him to monitor and stabilize the economy. By keeping tabs on inflation in this manner, he is able to plan ahead to lessen its effects.

Politically, budgeting can be a boon to the person in the Oval Office since his decisions can help to gain him support from various interest groups or regions as he provides grants to cities, tax cuts to businesses, job programs and welfare assistance for the poor and unemployed, health care to the elderly, and so on. Involvement in the nitty-gritty of budget ledgers also enables the president to emphasize one area of the budget such as defense and, as a result, to rearrange national priorities (to a degree) with at least part of the budget.

### RECENT BUDGET TRENDS

Although the choices a particular president may prefer in setting budget priorities may vary according to his philosophy or demands of the times such as international crises or depressions, there have been certain continuities of expenditures in the last several decades. Table 8.3 shows the growth in federal spending in five major categories.

As the table illustrates, payments to individuals grew a whopping $235.1 billion or increased 75% between 1971 and 1981. Most of these programs are payments to individual citizens through legislated entitlement money. Entitlements exist because Congress created them and established eligibility for benefits in the law; most benefits under the programs increase automatically with the cost of living. As Table 8.4 shows, some of these are among the most popular programs in the federal budget, and tampering with them would be risky for a president.

## TABLE 8.3
### SPENDING TRENDS IN THE BUDGET, 1961-1985*

| | 1961 | | 1971 | | 1981 | | 1985 |
| --- | --- | --- | --- | --- | --- | --- | --- |
| | AMOUNT (BILLIONS) | AVERAGE ANNUAL GROWTH | AMOUNT (BILLIONS) | AVERAGE ANNUAL GROWTH | AMOUNT (BILLIONS) | AVERAGE ANNUAL GROWTH | (BILLIONS) |
| Defense | $46.6 | 5.0% | $ 75.8 | 7.6% | $157.5 | 12.0% | $248.0 |
| Payments for individuals | 27.3 | 11.1 | 78.7 | 14.8 | 313.8 | 11.3 | 481.7 |
| Other grant programs | 4.2 | 15.1 | 17.1 | 12.3 | 54.4 | 5.2 | 66.7 |
| Net interest | 6.7 | 8.2 | 14.8 | 14.0 | 55.1 | 1.9 | 59.4 |
| All other | 12.9 | 6.8 | 25.0 | 7.8 | 53.0 | 14.2 | 90.2 |
| Total | $97.8 | 8.0 | $211.4 | 11.6 | $633.8 | 10.5 | $945.9 |

SOURCE: Office of Management and Budget; cited in National Journal 8/16/80.

*The table shows spending trends in five major budget categories from fiscal 1961 through 1985. Dollar figures (in billions) for 1981 and 1985 are Office of Management and Budget estimates. The "payments for individuals" category includes direct payments, such as Social Security, and grants to state and local governments for such programs as medicaid.

**TABLE 8.4**
**MAJOR ENTITLEMENTS, FISCAL 1981 (IN BILLIONS)**

| BUDGETED TO | PROGRAM | EST. COSTS |
|---|---|---|
| Defense | Military retirement pay system | $ 13.7 |
| Agriculture | Farm price supports | 1.6 |
| Education | Student loan insurance | 1.4 |
| Health and Human Services | Social service grants | 3.1 |
| | Medicaid | 15.7 |
| | Medicare | 39.0 |
| | Black lung disability | 2.0 |
| | Social Security | 137.3 |
| | Railroad retirement | 5.2 |
| | Civil service retirement | 17.1 |
| | Federal unemployment benefits | 1.3 |
| | Federal unemployment trust fund | 16.3 |
| | Supplemental security income | 7.0 |
| | Aid to families with dependent children | 7.5 |
| | Earned income credit | 1.6 |
| | Child nutrition | 3.6 |
| Veterans Administration | Compensation | 8.4 |
| | Pensions | 3.5 |
| | G.I. bill | 2.0 |
| State and local governments | General revenue sharing | 6.9 |
| Other entitlements | | 5.3 |
| Total | | $299.5 |

Adapted from Senate Budget Committee figures cited in the *National Journal* 8/16/80, p. 1346.

In 1970, entitlements represented about $66 billion or 33% of the federal budget; Table 8.4 demonstrates that they represented closer to 43% in 1981.[23]

The largest chunk going to individuals in the fiscal 1981 budget was beyond the president's control as has generally been the case in recent years. To exercise leadership in these areas, the president would have to take the political gamble of trying to change eligibility requirements for recipients or direct assistance or encourage Congress to cut either the benefits themselves or the automatic increases mandated for these programs. Probably the largest share of the entitlements programs is targeted to the elderly and these programs consume about 25% of the entire federal budget.[24] What president would speak out against Medicare and the rest of the Social Security system? Candidates Barry Goldwater in 1964[25] and Ronald Reagan in 1980 found that even inferences that Social Security[26] should be revamped threatened the success of their campaigns for president. Another area over which the president has little or no discretion is payment of interest on the national debt. He has little choice but to try to keep the nation's credit rating in proper order by diverting budget funds to debt service.

Problems with the "combat readiness" of the armed services that invariably arise during election years in the speeches of the incumbent's opponents also helped to

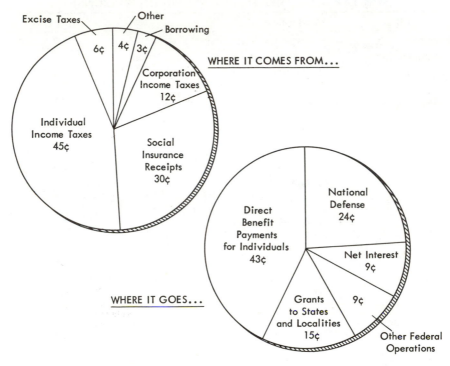

CHART 8.1    THE BUDGET DOLLAR, FISCAL 1981

WHERE IT COMES FROM...

Excise Taxes
Other
Borrowing
6¢   4¢   3¢
Corporation
Income Taxes
12¢
Individual
Income Taxes
45¢
Social
Insurance
Receipts
30¢

WHERE IT GOES...

Direct
Benefit
Payments
for Individuals
43¢

National
Defense
24¢

Net Interest
9¢

Grants
to States
and Localities
15¢

9¢

Other Federal
Operations

Source: President's Budget Message to Congress for Fiscal Year 1981, (Washington, D.C.:
G.P.O.) 1980.

account for "real increases" in recent defense budgets. When American hostages were taken in Iran in 1979 and the Soviet Union invaded Afghanistan in 1980, it became clear to the Carter administration that some sort of rapid deployment force would be needed to respond to threats such as these short of having to resort to a nuclear response. Jimmy Carter in his fiscal 1981 budget message called for 5 percent real growth in defense spending due, in his words, to[27]

> The long decline in real spending for defense. . . . I cannot ignore the major increases in Soviet military spending that have taken place in the last 20 years. I cannot ignore our commitment to our NATO allies. . . . I cannot ignore the implications of terrorism in Iran or the Soviet aggression in Afghanistan.

In defense budgeting, while it may be true that the president makes the decisions on how much should be spent and on what weapons systems are needed, U.S. allies and enemies also play major roles in shaping defense spending for him. Presidents are also limited in their control over budgeting by the fact that, in their first years in office, they must live with a budget that was formulated by their predecessors before they left office. Decisions by earlier presidents not to spend can force incoming presidents to make up for the later shortfalls in weapons or troop readiness.

248

When John Kennedy came into office, he called for massive increases in the space program to counter the Soviet *Sputnik* successes, and his Defense Secretary Robert McNamara instituted a new emphasis on conventional forces to offset the emphasis on the air force and nuclear weapons in the "more bang for the buck" days[28] when Dwight Eisenhower and Secretary of State Dulles considered massive retaliation the best defense for the nation.

Even in defense areas, the president has trouble doing much more than setting the tone for the budget. Richard Pious has estimated that at times as much as 10% of the strategic weapons funding will be rearranged by congressional committees.[29] Cooperation among the subgovernment of defense contractors, congressional committees, and procurement personnel at the Pentagon combine to push spending totals far beyond the figures set down in the president's budget proposals.[30]

## PLACES TO MAKE CUTS

If the voters are in a budget-cutting mood, and so much of the budget seems beyond the president's control, we might wonder if any areas are vulnerable to the budget axe. As the president looks at the budget pie, he may decide to consider cuts in personnel either through attrition or questioning the need for particular programs. In one of his first acts as President in 1981, Ronald Reagan instituted a federal hiring freeze. A president does so at his risk since approximately one American worker in twenty is on the federal payroll as soldier, bureaucrat, or elected politician. Which of them will lose his or her job? If the president is tempted to cut defense spending by dismantling bases or shutting down production of a particular weapons system, which states will lose the defense-produced jobs?

DEFENSE. Congress often considers defense spending more in the line of pump priming than national security. Because of this thinking, defense dollars often go to support programs that have proved less than meritorious. Senator William Proxmire and Representative Les Aspin have been outspoken about this kind of waste. Proxmire was especially critical of the C-5A transport plane that air force officials (1975) tried to defend even though the costs ended up being over twice the estimates. It had chronic difficulties with the landing gear, and vibrations caused the motors to fall off and the wings to crack.[31] Although the air force admitted that having the wings fall off at 8,000 hours was a problem, Congress found no difficulty in plucking dollars from the treasury to fund this air-craft because of the jobs involved in continuing to build it. The reasoning is simple. Secretary of Treasury John Connally in defending a 1971 loan to Lockheed argued that defense was not the only consideration in federal interest in defense contractors but that Lockheed needed the money, in his judgment, to provide employment for 31,000 in 1971 at a time when the nation desperately needed that type of employment.

STATE AND LOCAL PROGRAMS. Should the president's eye wander to the columns representing federal grants to states and local governments, he should recognize the political fallout he may suffer if he cuts funds for courthouses, recreation projects, and the like. It has become the new orthodoxy of the 1980s among both liberals and conservatives to use the budget process as a search and destroy mechanism that can ferret out entrenched programs that have long since outlived their usefulness. One classic example of a program that dodged OMB budget axes during both the Ford and Carter administrations was the Aid to Education for Impacted

Areas Program. Under it, additional dollars are targeted to school districts whose enrollments swell due to the placement of a federal installation such as a military base in the district. In 1977, President Carter sought to streamline the program since it was lavishing federal funds on some of the richest school districts in the nation. The House Budget Committee, however, voted 13-9 to restore the cuts Carter demanded. Members realized that in voting for the cuts they were simultaneously calling for either higher property taxes in their districts or lower-quality school programs. How could they vote to phase the Impacted Area programs out?[32]

For presidents dreaming of a second term, the cutting of local grants can be like slashing their own throats. If anything, in election years, the political temptation is almost irresistible to promise even more than he will be able to deliver. Edward Tufte in his study on presidential manipulation of the economy found that incumbents prefer increases in payments to individuals and local areas because they improve a president's chances by enhancing the voter's feeling of well-being at the appropriate time. The most politically effective spending in an election year involves direct transfer payments such as veterans benefits increases or Social Security bonanzas. They work better than something like a tax cut because direct payments get to the individual quickly whereas tax cuts would only trickle down to the voter over a longer period of time. Voters and local areas need a quick fix if they are to respond accordingly on election day.[33]

CREATIVE GRANTSMANSHIP SPENDING. With a budget of well over $600 billion there must be waste that the president can dispose of forcefully. Wisconsin Senator William Proxmire went so far as to provide a list of what he considered creative waste of the federal tax dollar on boondoggle project grants. These "Golden Fleece Awards" pointed out some of the more dubious grants with the hope of using public opinion to force the president and the appropriate department to take a long hard look at some of the more esoteric projects. Included were $69,111 to study the long-term storage of acorns in Poland, $21,000 to investigate the mating calls and glandular secretions of the Central American toad, and $19,300 for a study to explain why children fall off their tricycles.[34] While these particular programs, together, represent little more than ink blots on a federal budget of over $600 billion, they are indicative of some of the potentially questionable uses of the federal tax dollar.[35] But even these targets of public ridicule tend to be defended by bureaucracies that jealously guard their prerogatives to dispense "research" monies.

## BUDGETS AND ECONOMIC
## PLANNING AND MANIPULATION

As they view their budgets, presidents are less likely to worry about creeping waste than they are to consider the effect of the amount of spending on the health of the economy as a whole. In drawing up spending levels and determining tax policies, presidents also design their budgets to promote growth in the economy, stabilize it, or slow it down. Certain premises underlie their decisions to have balanced, deficit, or surplus budgets. By definition, *balanced budgets* exist when the government spends only what it takes in. In *deficit spending budgets,* the government borrows to spend more than it takes in so that the economy can be heated up from recessionary doldrums. In *surplus budgets,* the government takes in more than it spends in hopes of taking money out of circulation to lessen inflationary pressures.[36] Whichever type of budget a president selects, his goals are to maintain full employment, slow inflation and keep prices relatively stable, promote steady economic growth to maintain the "good life" or improve on it, and ensure a basic yet affordable level of community services.

In his budget message to Congress Jimmy Carter noted that[37]

> I have assumed that there will be some decline in the GNP during the course of 1980 followed by renewed moderate growth in 1981. As a result, budget receipts will be reduced and certain expenditures (welfare costs, unemployment benefits and so on) will increase automatically. . . . We must monitor the economic outlook carefully. If the economy begins to deteriorate significantly, I will consider tax reductions and temporary spending programs for job creation targeted towards particular sectors of economic stress.

The president's comments illustrate the fluid nature of the economy and the need to shift gears from fighting inflation to battling unemployment in the hardest-hit sectors of the economy such as construction trades, automobiles, and steels. Carter had called the battle against inflation and high energy costs the Moral Equivalent Of War (MEOW), but his MEOW speech soon was forgotten as unemployment skyrocketed.

Gerald Ford also learned how quickly the status of the economy could deteriorate. Not long after he replaced Richard Nixon, Ford launched a campaign to Whip Inflation Now (WIN). He even had buttons printed with the WIN logo to hype his ad campaign. Within a month, much to his chagrin, Ford's economic advisors concluded that recession was an even greater danger to the health of the economy than was inflation. Presidents try to use the little maneuvering room they have in making budget choices with only marginal success. Management and budgeting specialists like Allen Schick have suggested that, since so much of the budget is in uncontrollables and since the ebbs and flows of the economy are constantly forcing changes in economic assumptions, the president should spend as little time on the budget process as possible.[38] Contrary to Schick's tried-and-true advice, Ronald Reagan made budget cutting his first priority as president.

## THE FEDERAL BUDGET PROCESS

Preparing to spend over half a trillion dollars takes time. The preparation stage of the federal budget process consumes about thirty months. (See Table 8.5.) It involves input from the president's economic advisors (OMB, CEA, etc.), agency and department budget officers and program managers, budget examiners, congressional committees, interest groups, and the president.

As the issues facing the nation have become more complicated, costly, and international in scope, responsibility for preparing a unified budget gradually moved toward the White House. No one seriously questioned presidential direction of the economy through the budget during the early post-Depression years of the 1930s; and presidential leadership during World War II and into the mid-1960s found broad national support behind Roosevelt, Truman, and later Kennedy and

**TABLE 8.5**

**MAJOR STAGES IN THE BUDGET PROCESS**

| I. FORMULATION | II. CONGRESSIONAL BUDGET | III. EXECUTION |
|---|---|---|
| President, department, OMB | Budget committees, appropriations committees, and floor voters | All recipients of federal funds including supplementals, budget revisions, impoundments, and other changes |
| Begins 19 months prior to fiscal year | Begins 11 months prior to fiscal year | During the fiscal year |

Source: *The Federal Budget Process, Student Manual.* Management Sciences Training Center, Office of Personnel Management, May 1979. Courtesy of J. Edward Murphy.

# CHART 8.2 HOW THE FEDERAL BUDGET IS PUT TOGETHER, STEP-BY-STEP

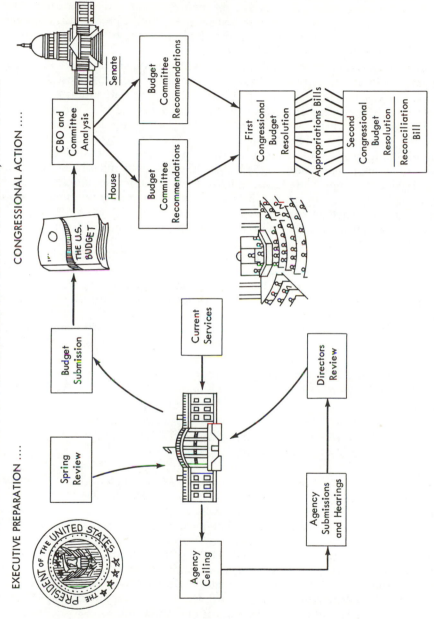

EXECUTIVE PREPARATION . . . .

CONGRESSIONAL ACTION . . . . .

Spring Review

Budget Submission

THE U.S. BUDGET

Current Services

Agency Ceiling

Agency Submissions and Hearings

Directors Review

CBO and Committee Analysis

House — Budget Committee Recommendations

Senate — Budget Committee Recommendations

First Congressional Budget Resolution

Appropriations Bills

Second Congressional Budget Resolution / Reconciliation Bill

Source: *The Federal Budget Process, Student Manual.* Management Sciences Training Center, Office of Personnel Management, May 1979. Courtesy of J. Edward Murphy.

Johnson. It was not until the era of Vietnam that Congress began to notice that it had delegated spending leadership to the president who abused it through budgetary sleights-of-hand and impoundments to fight the wrong war at the wrong time. Out of this sense of discontent, a separate congressional budget process was born and support staff were added (the Congressional Budget Office) to serve as a counterpoint to the president's budget analysts. See Chart 8.2.

Gerald Ford was the first president to deal with a new congressional budget that competed with the priorities he had set at the White House. Almost gleefully, Democrats expanded funding for most programs from the Ford estimates and proposals. As a former member of Congress, Ford knew that his old Democratic colleagues would find the budget too tight for their tastes. Still, he was determined to sell his views to the public in hopes of end-running the congressional budget by appealing to the spark of fiscal constraint latent in the souls of the American voters. In one of his press conferences on the budget, he enlisted the full cabinet, top OMB officials, and his senior White House aides to back up his presentation to the press corps. The supporting cast standing behind him was there mainly for moral support since he demonstrated an impressive personal grasp of the details of the budget.[39] Extravaganzas notwithstanding, he was still unable to get Congress to move in the direction of his "austerity" budget.[40]

In 1977, the first year that the Democrats controlled both the White House and Congress since the congressional budget reforms, the congressional and executive budgets looked much the same. The congressional spending ceiling was only $1.2 billion short of Carter's recommendations. Different revenue estimates accounted for most of the $3.6 billion between the two budgets' deficits. Congress sided with Carter on the need for federal jobs that Ford had opposed. With only a single exception, Carter recommended more spending than Ford had, and congressional budget figures were closer to Carter's figures in every instance than they had been to Ford's estimates.[41] In subsequent budget years, Carter's bubble burst as Congress balked at his energy proposals and gutted his proposed "windfall" profits tax on oil company profits.[42]

## THE EXECUTIVE BUDGET: PREPARATION, SUBMISSION, REVISIONS

Although the executive budget is not submitted to Congress until the January before the new fiscal year, which begins October 1, budget planning begins at least nineteen months before that.[43] The president's "wish book" is given to Congress in a tentative form in his State of the Union address, and specifics are spelled out more clearly in a subsequent budget message in February. Actually, there are three phases in the executive budget process: (1) the policy development stage (roughly February or March through June prior to the State of the Union address); (2) the compiling and submitting of agency estimates to OMB (roughly September through June); and (3) OMB review and presidential decision stage (approximately October through early January just before the State of the Union address.) See Chart 8.3.

As Chart 8.3 illustrates in detail, the *policy development* stage is taken up with drafting assumptions about the health of the economy, and the direction in which it is going (determined largely by CEA and OMB), and the making of preliminary decisions about whether tax and spending policies should be combined to produce a balanced budget, deficits, or surpluses. In this part of the process, the agencies inform OMB as to how much they think they will need to operate current programs at current levels, what future plans they have and their projected costs, and how economies might be realized. Next, OMB tries to reconcile these figures with expected revenues (taxes, etc.) and provides this information to the president.

Phase 2, or *compiling and submitting of estimates,* finds OMB advising the agencies on their formal budget statements by holding hearings with departmental budget officers and officers responsible for the operation of programs. After the departments have drawn up their formal requests, other interested parties (lobbyists from interest groups or state and local government or even White House aides) can make their case before OMB.[44]

Finally, in late September or October, the OMB director examines the agency budgets, once again checks the economic forecasts, and then makes budget recommendations to the president. He decides spending levels and priorities subject only to problems in the economic forecasts, and OMB relays this information to the departments. Each revises its formal budget to coincide with the president's wishes. On receipt of the changes from the departments, OMB puts the finishing touches on the State of the Union address, constructs the budget messages, and arranges for the printing of the executive budget for the coming fiscal year.

## CONGRESSIONAL RESPONSE
## AND ITS BUDGET

Even though Congress does not radically alter the spending totals of the president's budget in most cases as the Carter administration learned when it dealt with congressional Democrats, there are certain areas in which Congress tries to serve its local constituents by expanding federal outlays. Domestic programs involving poverty, community development, housing, education, and so on are likely to be ballooned from the president's proposals. The supersecret departments like the FBI and the CIA can expect to have their proposed budgets and other money hidden in various cubbyholes in other departmental budgets remain pretty much intact.[45] When Congress decides to revise White House figures, the likelihood of successful presidential action to restore his figures completely is slim. Instead, the president tries to go behind the scenes to seek some cuts in the excess or restore some muscle that has been trimmed. Jimmy Carter learned in 1978 that threats to kill appropriations bills with unacceptable programs (eighteen water projects) are not very productive. Prior to the Nixon administration, in fact, the veto on appropriations legislation was rare indeed. Richard Pious found that between 1789 and 1966 only forty were issued, and, of them, ten were overridden (including eight public works programs like those Carter wanted cut).[46]

Since June 1974, Congress sought to improve its part in the budget process by using the new CBO and developing a budget calendar of its own to parallel the president's. The congressional budget process that developed from the 1974 law has three stages: (1) developing budget targets, (2) acting on the individual bills that collectively make up the budget, and (3) reconciliating the bills to the ceilings proposed in the second concurrent budget resolution.

After the president's mid-January State of the Union address, Congress begins to work in earnest on the president's budget. In November, prior to that address, the

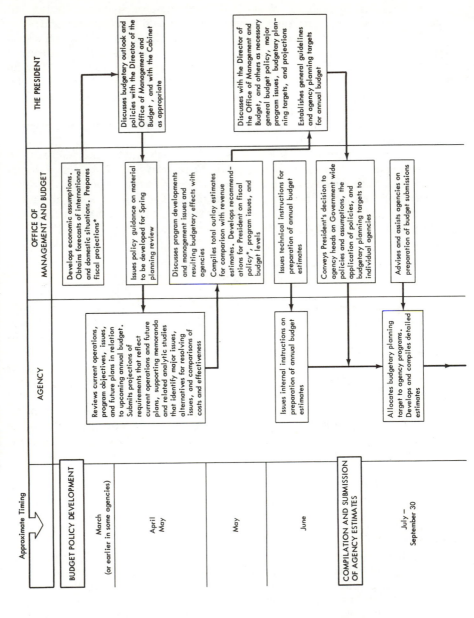

CHART 8.3 FORMULATION OF PRESIDENT'S BUDGET

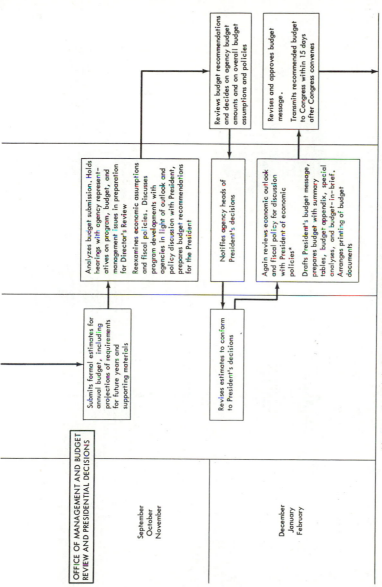

**OFFICE OF MANAGEMENT AND BUDGET REVIEW AND PRESIDENTIAL DECISIONS**

September
October
November

Submits formal estimates for annual budget, including projections of requirements for future years and supporting materials

Analyzes budget submission. Holds hearings with agency representatives on program, budget, and management issues in preparation for Director's Review

Reexamines economic assumptions and fiscal policies. Discusses program developments with agencies in light of outlook and policy discussion with President, prepares budget recommendations for the President

Reviews budget recommendations and decides on agency budget amounts and on overall budget assumptions and policies

December
January
February

Revises estimates to conform to President's decisions

Notifies agency heads of President's decisions

Again reviews economic outlook and fiscal policy for discussion with President of economic policies*

Drafts President's budget message, prepares budget with summary tables, budget appendix, special analyses, and budget-in-brief. Arranges printing of budget documents

Reviews and approves budget message.

Transmits recommended budget to Congress within 15 days after Congress convenes

*In cooperation with the Treasury Department and Council of Economic Advisors

Source: *The Federal Budget Process, Student Manual.* Management Sciences Training Center, Office of Personnel Management, May 1979. Courtesy of J. Edward Murphy.

# CHART 8.4 CONGRESSIONAL BUDGET PROCESS

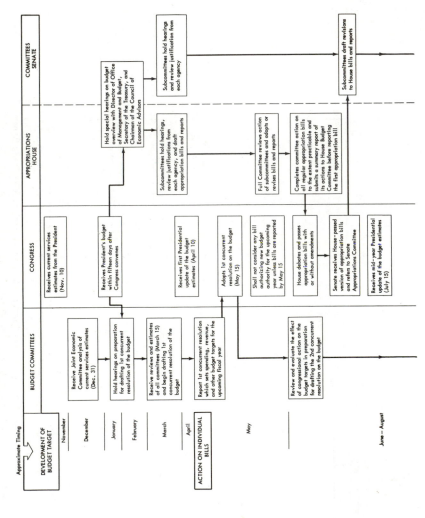

| Approximate Timing | DEVELOPMENT OF BUDGET TARGET | BUDGET COMMITTEES | CONGRESS | APPROPRIATIONS HOUSE | COMMITTEES SENATE |
|---|---|---|---|---|---|
| November | | | Receives current services estimates from the President (Nov. 10) | | |
| December | | Receive Joint Economic Committee analysis of current services estimates (Dec. 31) | | | |
| January | | Hold hearings on preparation for drafting 1st concurrent resolution of the budget | Receives President's budget within fifteen days after Congress convenes | Hold special hearings on budget overview with Director of Office of Management and Budget, Secretary of the Treasury, and Chairman of the Council of Economic Advisors | |
| February | | | | | |
| March | | Receive reviews and estimates of all committees (March 15) and begin drafting 1st concurrent resolution of the budget | Receives first Presidential update of the budget estimates (April 10) | Subcommittees hold hearings, review justifications from each agency, and draft appropriation bills and reports | Subcommittees hold hearings and review justification from each agency |
| April | | Report 1st concurrent resolution which sets spending, revenue, and other budget targets for the upcoming fiscal year | | | |
| ACTION ON INDIVIDUAL BILLS | | | Adopts 1st concurrent resolution on the budget (May 15) | | |
| May | | Review and evaluate the effect of congressional action on the budget targets in preparation for drafting the 2nd concurrent resolution on the budget | Shall not consider any bill authorizing new budget authority for the upcoming year unless bills are reported by May 15 | Full Committee reviews action of subcommittees and adopts or revises bills and reports | |
| | | | House debates and passes appropriations bills with or without amendments | Completes committee action on all regular appropriation bills to the extent practicable and submits a summary report of its actions to House Budget Committee before reporting the first appropriation bill | |
| | | | Senate receives House-passed version of appropriation bills and refers to Senate Appropriations Committee | | |
| June — August | | | Receives mid-year Presidential update of the budget estimates (July 15) | | Subcommittees draft revisions to House bills and reports |

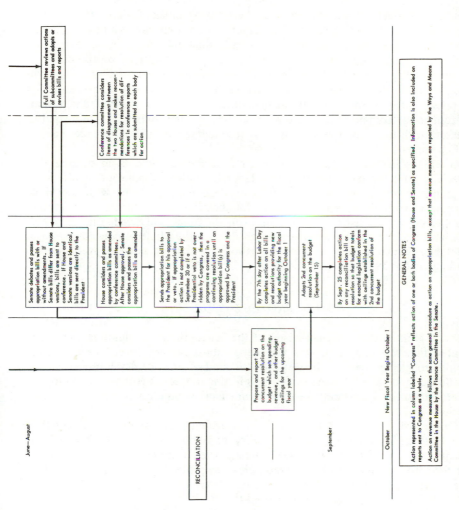

June—August

Full Committee reviews actions of subcommittees and adopts or revises bills and reports

Senate debates and passes appropriation bills with or without amendments. If Senate bills differ from House versions, bills are sent to conference. If House and Senate versions are identical, bills are sent directly to the President

Conference committee considers items of disagreement between the two Houses and makes recommendations for resolution of differences in conference reports which are submitted to each body for action

House considers and passes appropriation bills as amended by conference committees. After House approval, Senate considers and passes the appropriation bills as amended

Sends appropriation bills to the President for his approval or veto. If appropriation action is not completed by September 30 or if a Presidential veto is not overridden by Congress, then the programs are covered in a continuing resolution until an appropriation bill(s) is approved by Congress and the President

By the 7th day after Labor Day completes action on all bills and resolutions providing new budget authority for the fiscal year beginning October 1

Adopts 2nd concurrent resolution on the budget (September 15)

By Sept. 25 completes action on any reconciliation bill or resolution so that budget totals for enacted legislation conform with ceilings established in the 2nd concurrent resolution of the budget

RECONCILIATION

September

Prepare and report 2nd concurrent resolution on the budget which sets spending, revenue, and other budget ceilings for the upcoming fiscal year

October          New Fiscal Year Begins October 1

GENERAL NOTES

Action represented in column labeled "Congress" reflects action of one or both bodies of Congress (House and Senate) as specified. Information is also included on reports sent to Congress as a whole.

Action on revenue measures follows the same general procedure as action on appropriation bills, except that revenue measures are reported by the Ways and Means Committee in the House by the Finance Committee in the Senate.

Source: *The Federal Budget Process, Student Manual.* Management Sciences Training Center, Office of Personnel Management, May 1979. Courtesy of J. Edward Murphy.

259

president has given the budget committees in each house a peek at what he is planning by giving them his estimates on maintaining current expenditures for existing programs.

As Congress begins action on the individual bills in phase 2, both the budget committees and appropriations take testimony from the agencies and pressure groups affected by the particular spending bill. By May 15, Congress, at the suggestion of the budget committees, has created a tentative budget for both Houses. This first concurrent resolution sets budget targets on both revenues and expenditures. Next, each house works separately on the individual bills. Again, at the suggestion of the two budget committees, a "second concurrent resolution" on the budget is adopted by September 15. This one establishes ceilings for the total budget authorities and a floor for revenues. It also either restates the targets in the first resolution or revises them to fit more current economic realities. To this end, the various appropriations committees are informed as to how their bills might be revised to conform with the second resolution. Bills reconciling any such differences are due by September 25.

Given the involved nature of the process, it should come as no surprise that especially controversial legislation like federal funding of abortion could make keeping to such a tight schedule difficult. HSS appropriations with the Hyde amendment (forbidding federal spending for abortions unless the life of the mother was endangered) caused such battles between the House and Senate that these bills invariably ended up in conference and thus delayed the whole congressional budget timetable. Similar difficulties arose in labor and defense budgets over abortion funding in both 1979 and 1980.[47]

## BUREAUCRATIC GAMESMANSHIP: HOW TO PROTECT YOUR TURF

Edmund Muskie, the first chairperson of the Senate Budget Committee, once commented that the budget process was designed to prevent special interest from running roughshod over the budget. "If this kind of practice develops, we can kiss the budget good-bye." He was evidently referring to interest groups outside government; but to fiscal conservatives there is an enemy within too, namely, the bureaucracies.

Career civil servants are not noted for providing seminars on how to cut their own budgets. They do not lack the ability to find economies, but they lack the incentive to cut off their own noses. Bureaucracies, according to one former assistant secretary, are given to bureaucratic ploys to protect themselves. They seek to direct the department without interference from their nominal "politically appointed" bosses. Hugh Heclo has lamented that[48]

> The bureaucrats I worked for were competent and hard working but damned if they couldn't find reasons why a particular thing couldn't be done—quote the law, previous secretaries' decisions, Civil Service and General Services Administration regulations, executive orders of the past. . . . Later I found out that they knew there were ways to do things but they weren't volunteering the information.

Budget-cutting presidents and OMB examiners quickly learn that bureaucracies, cabinet secretaries, and their interest group friends on Capitol Hill will battle tooth and nail to beat back any encroachment on their budgetary kingdoms.[49] Although the public is largely unaware of these donnybrooks, it is more likely to be the president and OMB who do much of the bending. As we noted in Chapter 4, even OMB examiners can be compromised by the department they are supposed to be auditing and eventually may be working for. It has been estimated that in any particular year OMB must recruit between sixty and eighty new examiners. That is a remarkable figure in such a small organization by federal standards in that OMB has about 510 employees. Half the recruits are needed to fill gaps created by examiners transferring to other agencies in the government.[50]

When budget examiners from OMB come across programs in the departments that could be cut back or eliminated, they can expect to get some firsthand lessons in practical politics. Budget officers and program directors at an agency will roll their wagons in a circle and call in reinforcements from Capitol Hill. To congressional committees, savings is only one consideration; political impact can carry almost as much or even more weight.

During committee hearings about budget cuts in an HEW (now HSS) program, for example, the Senate subcommittee chairman reportedly said to the HSS secretary, "Mr. Secretary, I have one question. How much does my state get under this program?" The secretary replied, "$185,000." With a sense of almost righteous indignation, the senator shot back, "How can you expect me to vote against a program that puts $185,000 into my state?"[51] Often, agency budget officers can bring problems of this type to the attention of nonpolitically minded OMB examiners before they complicate matters in congressional hearings. Pork barrel can be sacred food to major figures in Congress, so OMB eventually learns a certain sensitivity toward tampering with line items, lest key congressional figures show their displeasure by deserting the president on crucial issues that might reach the House or Senate floor at a later date. As President Carter was trying to salvage his twin Panama Canal treaties, he realized that saving his plans for the "big ditch" required resurrecting plans for some smaller water projects that he had threatened to veto as unnecessary pork barrel. One political wag quipped, "I hope the Panamanians get as much out of those treaties as some Senators."[52]

When OMB examiners are seeking budget information about an agency, they cannot expect budget officers in the agencies to rattle the skeletons in their own departmental closets. Why should departmental personnel suggest places for OMB to slash programs? These same budget specialists who try to convince OMB that their agency budgets are lean are often simultaneously telling program officers to spend, spend, spend in order to justify higher spending levels next year. In the event that an agency budget officer gets wind of an OMB examiner's plans to call for cuts, the officer can always call on the departmental secretary, whom the president appointed, and on interest group heavyweights to end run the examiner to his OMB bosses and call off the proposed cuts.

## SOME POPULAR
## BUREAUCRATIC PLOYS

When intimidation by the secretary is not in the cards, bureaucracies may resort to other types of maneuvers. Leonard Reed, in a *Washington Monthly*, artfully cataloged a number of the more popular ploys. One, which he called the "king's ploy opening," involved overstating departmental needs to OMB anticipating that they will demand cuts in the department budget anyway. Successful federal, state, and local executives have known for a long time that, if one position is needed, ask for and defend with your life the proposition that three are indispensable. Because of the small OMB staff and the limited amount of time an examiner has with a particular department's budget (six or seven weeks), this ploy often proves fruitful in getting what the department originally wanted.[53]

The flip side of that technique is what Reed labels the "shortfall game." This maneuver finds the agency underestimating the cost of a popular program such as food stamps as a part of the agriculture budget. Since OMB and the president have set ceilings for departmental spending for the fiscal year, departments often understate one item of the budget request to free up dollars within the ceiling to cover programs that may not be nearly as popular on the Hill. Later on, when the number of persons actually needing food stamps exceeds the purposely low projections, the department simply goes back to Congress for a supplemental appropriation (spending authorization beyond the original appropriation) since the poor need the food.[54]

Another politically effective game is to title departmental programs so that they sound like they came straight from the president's last budget speech. If the president has stated conservation as a priority, bills should be relabeled to sound like conservation. The title "conservation" then becomes an "umbrella" to place programs under to protect them. Leonard Reed suggests that this "umbrella game" permits an agency to go to OMB asking for additional funding for old programs that have merely been repackaged to sound as if the president had required the spending to live up to one of his campaign promises. The programs gain more credibility and enlarged budgets because they sound like presidential initiatives to deal with national problems such as "environmental" concerns that might include anything from recreational lakes to more costly programs like nationwide water pollution projects.[55]

Astute budget officers in agencies and departments can also protect department dollars by manipulating priorities within their budgets in a variation of the shortfall game. In providing justification for existing programs and suggesting cuts, the department may leave the impression that certain programs popular with the public and Congress are expendable whereas less popular ones are defended as absolutely untouchable. We might label this technique the "perverting priorities ploy." It has been in vogue especially since the Carter administration initiated its zero-based budgeting (ZBB) system in 1977. The goal of Carter's ZBB was, like that of Nixon's MBO (management by objectives)[56] and Lyndon Johnson's PPB (planning, programming, and budgeting),[57] to slow the incremental growth (the percentage increase in budget items over the previous year without questioning the base costs or need for the program) of the budget.[58] The system was designed to force departments to justify their programs from the ground up and to assign them priorities.

If, for example, an agency had 200 programs, it would rank 160 of them in a "must" category and the rest might end up on an expendable list. Theoretically, Congress could then decide to delete some of the expendables. The bureaucracies, instead of automatically putting major programs on the "must" list that Congress and OMB were generous in protecting for them, would place politically popular programs and those useful to individual congressional leaders on the "expendables" list.[59] They thus suggest unpopular cuts knowing full well that the president and

OMB would be under political pressure from the Hill to restore them even if it meant raising planned budget ceilings.

Creative departmentalists made ZBB something less than a smashing success. Carter's miracle tonic had little impact on the size or character of the fiscal 1979 budget. One analyst noted that the first ZBB budget was a carbon copy of its more conventional, incremental predecessor.[60] Allen Schick was even more cutting in his criticism of ZBB:[61]

> The first president to promise a zero-base budget has delivered the most incremental financial statement since Wildavsky canonized that form of budget making years ago. . . . The FY 1979 budget hardly terminates anything of significance, continues most spending at inflation-adjusted levels and offers few program initiatives.

Despite the Nixon, Ford, and Carter efforts, the bureaucracies proved up to the task of derailing most presidential attempts to use the budget process and OMB examiners to streamline bureaucracies and change their profligate spending habits. When any president attempts to trim spending in any department, he finds senators, representatives, interest group friends, and bureaucrats themselves collaborating to shield popular programs from the budget axes.[62]

## REORGANIZATIONS AS
## A WAY OF SAVING DOLLARS

Since presidents find that efforts at saving through budgeting can be sidestepped by bureaucratic gameplayers, the temptation is great to try to solve this obstructionism by simply reorganizing the bureaucracy itself. As we noted in Chapter 5, the mere fact that the president is the nominal chief executive does not assure him of control over the sprawling federal bureaucracies.

FINE-TUNING THE CAREER SERVICES.    Of the recent modern presidents, Richard Nixon and Jimmy Carter demonstrated great personal conviction that wholesale revisions in the way in which the federal bureaucracies (departments and civil service) operate should be a White House priority. To Nixon, the federal bureaucracies had become a largely Democrat-dominated maze of career civil servants bent on embarrassing Republican presidents. On one of the Watergate tapes, Nixon reportedly complained about the lack of discipline in the bureaucracies. "We never fire . . . reprimand . . . or demote anybody. We always promote the sons-of-bitches that kick us in the ass."[63] Deputy OMB Director Frederick Malek was assigned the unenviable task of developing a method for cleaning house. His brainchild called for each department to set up a special assistant to the secretary who would write a job description for civil service openings in the department. Job descriptions would be tailored to fit particular persons the administration wanted in the open position.[64]

A variation on this scenario tried by several administrations was to have high-ranking positions in a bureaucracy transferred from career to noncareer classifications.[65] To cut costs, some of the switched positions might even be left unfilled. Jimmy Carter tried to slow down some of the politicizing of the civil service and reward efficient managers at upper levels by abolishing the old civil service system and replacing it with two new bodies: the Office of Personnel Management, responsible for administering civil service exams, salaries, and benefits, and a Merit Protection Board, with three members appointed by the president with Senate consent. The Merit Protection Board was even assigned a special counsel to prosecute political abuses and violations of the merit system. The plan also called for a separate senior executive service (SES) made up of 8,000 or 9,000 high-level managers moved from civil service by trading their job security with civil service for increased opportunity for bigger money, accelerated promotions, and enhanced chances of interdepartmental transfers. The new system also made salary increases for 72,500 midlevel civil service personnel contingent on meritorious performance rather than on longevity and automatic raises.[66] But politically appointed department heads were still left in a good position to punish "nonmeritorious" persons who strayed from the White House political views by reassigning them to new duties or even to another area of the country.[67] Some critics of the Carter reorganization have said that the system will eventually replace dedicated and talented professionals with political hacks who lack experience in public policy and managing large organizations.

Nixon OMB experts Frederick Malek and Roy Ash and the architects of the Carter reorganizations were often specialists in business management and, as a result, often overlooked the political roadblocks that litter the landscape when the president boldly seeks to reorganize the bureaucratic maze. The explanation for the obstacles is simply that members of Congress and lobbyists who enjoy access within the existing structures are bound to dig their collective heels in to delay and eventually kill reorganization. Likewise, federal employees whose jobs hang in the balance are not likely to take reorganization proposals sitting down.[68]

## WHEN FISCAL EFFORTS FAIL: MANIPULATING THE PRIVATE SECTOR

When budget juggling and reorganization fail to stem chronic inflation or to move the country out of a recession quickly, there are several other economic leadership tacks a president might take in dealing with business and labor. If more jobs are needed, a president might preach the old-time religion of either large tax cuts to business to encourage hiring or tax credits for corporations that hire the chronically unemployed, the poorly prepared, or the teenaged minorities. Taking more drastic actions, a president might try to control inflation by adopting any or a combination of the following techniques:[69]

1. Require prenotification by business to government before raising prices. The hope is that government can then *persuade* business to roll back the hikes.
2. Set salary targets for bargaining negotiations between business and labor.
3. Use public opinion and the media to discredit corporations that raise their prices in violation of presidential requests that they hold the line to stem inflation. This practice is usually known as *jawboning*.
4. Encourage Congress to authorize and the president to impose mandatory wage and price controls either on some or all wages and prices.

In recent years, talk of the last two techniques has been prevalent, but the success of these attempts at jawboning and controls is checkered at best.

When business refuses to act "responsibly," that is, when it raises prices after the president has privately begged them not to, the president may draw on his own prestige to lecture the "profiteers" whom he judges are acting in violation of the "national interest." The practice of publicly castigating industries rather than punishing them by law came to be called, with possible allusion to Samson smiting the Philistines, "jawboning." Business executives were tried and convicted by the president in the court of public opinion via calculated use of radio and television. The media became the weapon to wield against the "greedy."

One of the more celebrated and successful cases of jawboning took place during the Kennedy administration in 1962. William Blough, chairman of U.S. Steel, had decided that "we in the steel industry" must raise prices. Kennedy was incensed because the administration had prevailed upon the steelworkers' union to curb its demands for wage and fringe benefit increases and agree to a two-year pact with the industry. In a televised press conference, the popular young president lashed out at "a tiny handful of steel executives whose pursuit of power and profit exceeds their sense of public responsibility." [70] Not long after that attack on the patriotism of the steel magnates, the Justice Department and the Federal Trade Commission were prevailed upon to investigate monopoly pricing practices in the steel industry.

Kennedy personally attempted to pressure Blough in a face-to-face meeting in the Oval Office. The president was widely quoted after the confrontation as having said, "My father always told me that all businessmen were sons-of-bitches." [71] For all his venom, salty language, and public indignation about the "selfishness of big steel," the president might not have succeeded in his attempt to get a rollback of the increases had other steel company executives not voluntarily kept theirs down. Blough, fearful of losing a share of the market, capitulated to the judgment of his colleagues and ordered the increases rescinded.

Administration difficulties with U.S. Steel and the president's dependence upon the support of others in the industry to keep prices down were probably due to the fact that, beyond the investigations of the Justice Department and the FTC, Kennedy's approach amounted to "speak loudly and carry a twig." The seasoned political veteran who succeeded him in the White House (Lyndon Johnson) demonstrated that presidential leadership in dealing with business can often be more effective if the president "speaks softly but totes a tree trunk." When Johnson encountered price hikes by Alcoa, an aluminum company, he worked quietly behind the scenes to punish the industrial giant without publicly castigating it. He directed Defense Secretary McNamara to release for sale 200,000 tons of aluminum sitting in national security stockpiles. For the public record, administration officials denied that the directions given to McNamara had anything to do with Alcoa's price increases. Disclaimers fooled neither the press nor the aluminum industry. Ultimately, in an act of "industrial statesmanship," [72] as Secretary McNamara gushed, Alcoa and the other aluminum corporations rescinded the increases.

Johnson's actions in the aluminum case showed that government stockpiles could be used as a bludgeon over the head of an industry that doesn't want to have to deal with Uncle Sam as a competing supplier. In a similar vein, a president could also threaten to withhold government contracts from uncooperative companies.

Various presidents threatened to do this to assure support for some of their civil rights directives. Johnson also got what he wanted from Alcoa without inflicting a black eye on the industry. Its support, after all, could have proven useful in the future.

When Jimmy Carter began criticizing "unconscionable" price increases in the oil industry, he found the rhetoric produced little constructive aid in selling his windfall profits tax on oil companies. He acted with the belief that, since the 1973 Arab oil embargo and serious shortages, there would be substantial political capital in championing the "little man" against big oil. He had no luck convincing oil state Senator Russell Long who chaired the Senate Finance Committee that was responsible for such tax legislation. Throughout the election 1980 campaign, Carter tried to paint his opponent, who had suggested "unleashing oil companies to find more oil," as a man who would depend on the industry with its record of price gouging to chart the course of the nation's energy future. Carter's attempts at jawboning were a failure mainly because the seven majors were not even listening.

### JAWBONES PLUS TEETH: ECONOMIC CONTROLS

Many would argue that the most drastic economic measures a president could adopt in peacetime would be to impose mandatory wage and price controls. Although they have been used in wartime, it is an almost unwritten rule that they will be a last resort in other than national emergencies. In 1970, congressional Democrats gave Richard Nixon the authority to impose mandatory wage and price controls, fully expecting that he would never use them. They evidently expected to be able to criticize the president during the 1972 campaign for not using the tools they had placed at his disposal. Much to their surprise and chagrin, Nixon imposed peacetime controls in August 1971, becoming the first president to do so in American history.[73] In September he complained to the press, "You cannot have jawboning that is effective without teeth."[74]

Nixon's safari into the jungle of wage and price controls began as an unassuming expedition with showcase controls on the construction trades industry, which has traditionally been susceptible to inflationary pressures. The theory behind the limited controls was that total controls might be too unwieldy and costly to implement. The institution of partial controls was based on the belief that certain sectors including construction, steels, autos, and health care (both hospitals and doctors fees) could be effectively controlled and could aid in dampening the underlying inflationary pressures on the entire economy.

As is often the case with economic policy, its political value can be judged according to whose ox is gored. Both business and labor opposed the Nixon controls, but labor took the brunt of the policy. In phase 1 of the controls, there was a ninety-day freeze on wages. Phase 2 included systems for monitoring prices and rents by creation of a pay board and a price commission. Wage increases were held down to a 5.5% maximum while dividends, interest, and corporate profits were left uncontrolled. In phases 3 and 4 the pay and price mechanisms were replaced by a Cost of Living Council. The council proved incapable of keeping prices down when the administration moved toward removing formal controls. In April 1974, legislative authorization for the controls ran out and it was not renewed. In sum, Nixon's foray into wage and price controls, possibly because of the way in which they were constructed and the way in which they were removed, did little more than delay the impact of inflation so that it hit after the 1972 election.

Neither Gerald Ford nor Jimmy Carter followed Nixon's lead, preferring less drastic, but less immediately effective, methods such as "voluntary" wage and price guidelines and jawboning. Even though Nixon is often criticized for Watergate and Vietnam, it is evident that he was much more willing to exert presidential leadership in dealing with the economy, as through controls and attacks on the Federal Reserve, than were either of his next two successors. Only the possibility that these moves were politically motivated tarnishes his courage and "leadership" in adopting them.

Conventional wisdom among many economists says that controls do not work. Barry Bosworth, director of Carter's Council on Wage and Price Stability, and John Kenneth Galbraith, internationally respected economist, did not share these views. In an attack on the opponents of controls, Galbraith noted that every other major industrial nation has some permanent machinery for wage and price restraints. He saw these mechanisms as the lone alternative to inflation and massive unemployment. In Senator Edward Kennedy's abortive attempt to wrest the Democratic nomination from Carter in 1980, wage and price controls were at the heart of the Kennedy economic package. Galbraith concluded that[75]

> The American economy, whatever wishful analysis there may be to the contrary, is not stable at or near full employment. Wages will always shove up prices and prices will always tend to pull up wages . . .

To Galbraith, only government action, which would require presidential leadership, can effectively stave off bouts of high inflation or high unemployment. We must notice, however, that tradition discourages a president from resorting to controls in peacetime. Likewise, his leadership in imposing controls is curtailed by the fact that he may impose them only after he has convinced Congress to legislate him the authority to do so.

## CONCLUSIONS

The decade of the 1980s will be one in which cutting both budgets and taxes are likely to become accepted orthodoxy. A president nevertheless will find it difficult to exert leadership in these areas because budgets must be approved by Congress, tax policy is a constitutionally mandated legislative preserve, and the Federal Reserve acts independently of the White House. Presidents tempted to travel the road of wage and price controls must also recognize that substantial sectors of the American economy are opposed to having such controls. In effect, public expectations for presidential leadership in economic areas often overlook the severe restrictions that the president finds when he tries to manage the economy as he sees fit.

## NOTES

[1] Frederick Malek, *Washington's Hidden Tragedy: The Failure to Make Government Work* (New York: Free Press, 1978), p. 169.

[2] WHYY-TV, Inc., *Attitudes Towards the Presidency*, a national opinion survey commissioned by WHYY-TV, Inc., Philadelphia, conducted by the Gallup Poll organization, January 1980,

mimeo. p. 6 and p. 20, hereafter cited as *WHYY Study*. See also Thomas E. Cronin, "Looking for Leadership," *Public Opinion*, (February-March 1980), 14-20.

[3] On voter turnout in 1976, see Gerald Pomper, *The Election of 1976: Reports and Interpretations* (New York: David McKay, 1977), p. 72. In the 1980 race, the figures dropped from the 54% of 1976 down to 52.5%.

[4] *WHYY Study*, p. 18.

[5] *Ibid.*, p. 18.

[6] Haynes Johnson, *In the Absence of Power* (New York: Viking Press, 1980), p. 123.

[7] *Ibid.*, p. 33.

[8] Walter Heller, *New Dimensions of Political Economy* (Cambridge, Mass.: Harvard U.P., 1966), p. 3.

[9] This theme carries throughout, see Richard E. Neustadt, *Presidential Power: The Politics of Leadership FDR to Carter* (New York: John Wiley, 1980).

[10] Daniel Bell, "The Revolution of Rising Entitlements," *Fortune Magazine*, as reprinted in Bruce Steinbrickner, ed., *Annual Editions, American Government 1979/80* (Guilford, Conn.: Dushkin Publishers, 1979).

[11] On wage and price controls, see Paul Samuelson, *Economics*, 10th ed. (New York: McGraw-Hill, 1976), pp. 392-400.

[12] Edward R. Tufte, *Political Control of the Economy* (Princeton, N.J.: Princeton U.P., 1978), p. 17.

[13] Richard B. McKenzie and Gordon Tullock, *Modern Political Economy* (New York: McGraw-Hill, 1978), pp. 536-537.

[14] For the relationship between "full employment" and the health of the economy as a whole, see *Ibid.*, p. 580.

[15] *WHYY Study*, p. 18.

[16] See Kristen R. Monroe and Dona Metcalf Laughlin, "Economic Influences on Presidential Popularity Among Key Political and Socioeconomic Groups, 1965-1980," paper prepared for delivery at the Annual Meeting of the American Political Science Association, Washington Hilton Hotel, Washington, D.C., August 28, 1980.

[17] *Christian Science Monitor*, October 2, 1980.

[18] *Kansas City Times*, March 1, 1980, p. A-95.

[19] Tom Wicker, "Don't Look to the White House for Solutions to Economic Crises," *Kansas City Times*, March 1, 1980, p. A-15.

[20] Proposals such as these were usually referred to as the Kemp-Roth cuts named after the Republican congressman and senator who spearheaded the drive in Congress. For the Republican platform version, see *The New York Times*, February 14, 1980.

[21] Lance T. LeLoup, "Fiscal Chief: Presidents and the Budgets," in *The Presidency: Studies in Policy Making*, eds. Stephen A. Shull and Lance T. LeLoup (Brunswick, Ohio: Kings Court, 1979), p. 211, hereafter cited as LeLoup, "Fiscal Chief."

[22] Dennis Ippolito, *The Budget and National Politics* (San Francisco: W. H. Freeman, 1978), p. 40.

[23] Robert Sherrill, *Why They Call It Politics* (New York: Harcourt Brace, 1979), p. 306.

[24] *Ibid.*, p. 306.

[25] Theodore White, *The Making of the President, 1964* (New York: Atheneum, 1965), pp. 302-303.

[26] *Washington Post*, October 30, 1980.

[27] Jimmy Carter, *Budget Message of the President, Fiscal 1981* (Washington, D.C.: Government Printing Office, 1980), p. M-5.

[28] The "more bang for the buck" philosophy was deeply grounded in Eisenhower's belief in budget cutting as well as in his acceptance of massive retaliation as a principle of national defense. On this see Charles W. Kegley and Eugene Wittkopf, *American Foreign Policy* (New York: St. Martin's Press, 1979), p. 58.

[29] Richard Pious, *The American Presidency* (New York: Basic Books, 1979), p. 276.

[30] On the cooperation among interest groups, executive agencies, and congressional committees, see Norman Orenstein and Shirley Elder, *Interest Groups, Lobbying and Policy Making* (Washington, D.C.: Congressional Quarterly Press, 1978), pp. 53-66.

See also Gordon M. Adams, "Disarming the Military Sub-Government," *Harvard Journal of Legislation,* (April 1977), 459-503.

[31] Sherrill, *op. cit.,* p. 93.

[32] Malek, *op. cit.,* p. 175.

[33] Tufte, *op. cit.,* p. 5.

[34] Malek, *op. cit.,* p. 167.

[35] *Ibid.,* p. 175.

[36] Lance LeLoup, *Budgetary Politics: Dollars, Deficits, Decisions* (Brunswick, Ohio: Kings Court, 1977), p. 28, hereafter cited as LeLoup, *Budgetary Politics.*

[37] Carter, *Budget Message,* pp. M3 and M4.

[38] Allen Schick, "The Budget Bureau That Was: Thoughts on the Rise, Decline and Future of a Presidential Agency," in *Perspectives on the Presidency,* ed. Aaron Wildavsky (Boston: Little, Brown, 1975), p. 342.

[39] William Mullen, *Presidential Power and Politics* (New York: St. Martin's Press, 1976), pp. 61-62.

[40] "Budget: Congress Shall . . . Pay the Debts," *National Journal,* May 29, 1976, p. 743.

[41] Joel Havermann, "Congress Sets Ceiling on Federal Deficit," *National Journal,* September 24, 1977, p. 1478.

[42] For Carter's problems with Congress, see Dom Bonafede, "The Tough Job of Normalizing Relations with Capitol Hill," *National Journal,* January 13, 1979, pp. 54-57.

[43] One of the most thorough yet understandable attempts to explain the budget process can be found in Office of Personnel Management, *The Federal Budget Process, Student Manual* TOS 23AP 5-79 (Management Sciences: Training Center). For insights into the politics of budgeting, see Aaron Wildavsky, *The Politics of the Budgetary Process* (Boston: Little, Brown, 1974).

[44] Pious, *op. cit.,* p. 268.

[45] *Ibid.,* pp. 276-277. See also Mullen, *op. cit.,* p. 62.

[46] *Ibid.,* p. 277.

[47] On the role of Congress, see James P. Pfiffner, *The President, The Budget and Congress: Impoundment and the 1974 Budget Act* (Boulder, Colo.: Westview Press, 1979), pp. 131-146. On the budget committees, see George C. Edwards, II, *Presidential Influence in Congress* (San Francisco: W. H. Freeman, 1980), p. 44.

[48] Hugh Heclo, *Government of Strangers* (Washington, D.C.: Brookings Institution, 1977), p. 174.

[49] LeLoup, "Fiscal Chief," p. 198.

[50] Leonard Reed, "The Budget Game and How to Win It," *Washington Monthly,* (January 1979), 25.

[51] Elizabeth Drew, "Engagement with the Special Interest State," *New Yorker,* February 27, 1978, p. 66.

[52] Randall Ripley, "Carter and Congress," in Shull and LeLoup, *The Presidency,* p. 80.

[53] Reed, *op. cit.,* p. 28.

[54] *Ibid.,* pp. 29-30.

[55] *Ibid.,* pp. 30-31.

[56] On the management by objectives system, see Thomas D. Lynch, *Public Budgeting in America* (Englewood Cliffs, N.J.: Prentice-Hall, 1979), pp. 32-33.

[57] On planning, programming, and budgeting, see *Ibid.,* pp. 29-32.

[58] On the goals of zero-based budgeting, see Allen Schick, "Zero-Base Budgeting and Sunset," *The Bureaucrat,* (Spring 1977), 12-33.

[59] Most useful to this author in analysis of this material were source materials prepared by Allen Schick as a part of a National Science Foundation Short Course on the Politics of

Government Budgeting, Fall 1976. Included were CRS guides such as Louis Fisher, *Budget Concepts and Terminology: The Appropriations Phase* (Washington, D.C.: Congressional Research Service, HJ 205 U.S. November 21, 1974).

[60] John R. Dempsey, "Carter's Reorganization: A Mid-Term Appraisal," *Public Administration Review,* (January-February 1979), 76.

[61] Allen Schick, "The Road from ZBB," *Public Administration Review,* (March-April 1978), 177.

[62] William C. Lammars, *Presidential Politics: Patterns and Prospects* (New York: Harper & Row, 1976), p. 157.

[63] As cited in Stephen Wayne, *The Legislative Presidency* (New York: Harper & Row, 1978), p. 157.

[64] On this subject, see Robert Sickels, *The Presidency: An Introduction* (Englewood Cliffs, N.J.: Prentice-Hall, 1980), p. 322.

[65] See Thomas P. Murphy, Donald E. Neuchterlein, and Ronald J. Stupak, *Inside the Bureaucracy: The View from the Assistant Secretary's Desk* (Boulder, Colo.: Westview Press, 1978).

[66] Gregory D. Foster, "The 1978 Civil Service Reform Act: Post-Mortem or Re-Birth," *Public Administration Review,* (January-February 1979), 81.

[67] Robert DiClerico, *The American President* (Englewood Cliffs, N.J.: Prentice-Hall, 1979), pp. 143-144.

[68] Lammars, *op. cit.,* p. 152.

[69] Pious, *op. cit.,* p. 428.

[70] Louis Koenig, *The Chief Executive* (New York: Harcourt Brace, 1975), p. 273.

[71] William Safire, *The New Language of Politics* (New York: Random House, 1972), p. 317.

[72] Koenig, *op. cit.,* p. 274.

[73] Pious, *op. cit.,* pp. 328-329.

[74] Safire, *op. cit.,* p. 317.

[75] Galbraith as cited in Sherrill, *op. cit.,* p. 322.

# The Imperial Press
# and the Imperial Presidency

In the post-Vietnam and Watergate years, it has become fashionable to decry the abuses of presidential power evident in the Johnson and Nixon administrations. It was the vigilance of the American free press that brought these abuses to light and helped to "throw the rascals out." However, as we extol the virtues of the journalistic profession, we must recognize that its members can be as arrogant as any president has ever been.

Walter Cronkite, once named the most respected American in a Quayle poll (1973), habitually closed his nightly news broadcast by assuring his audience, "and that's the way it is." With similar cockiness, the masthead of *The New York Times* proclaims that within its pages the reader will find "all the news that's fit to print." David S. Broder, respected political analyst of the *Washington Post,* suggests that slogans like that are "at best gimmickry and at worst a complete fraud."[1]

All the news that is fit to print would require a ten-ton daily newspaper, and the nightly news would require hours rather than its present thirty-minute format. Because of the flood of information available in this age of electronic media, journalists have become increasingly selective in singling out some items as newsworthy and discarding the majority of the others. Selectivity implies some critieria. Picking and choosing mirrors the prejudices of the reporter, copywriter, editor, publisher, and ultimately the owner of the newspaper or television station. Although a creed of the journalistic profession would seem to be the need for objectivity in reporting, there is no such thing as neutral journalism. In fact, it was the ability of the press to have an opinion and express it that the First Amendment to the Constitution was written to protect. One of the greatest dangers to a free press is the government that it invariably criticizes.

Like the press, government can hardly be appluaded for its objectivity in reporting national and international events. *New York Times* political analyst Tom Wicker, in an article about the power of the press, noted that the government had been systematically lying to reporters about the war in Vietnam. The military was reporting on body counts in the field to give the impression that the war was turning to the South Vietnamese side in 1967. Wicker recounts meetings with Daniel Ellsberg who eventually leaked the *Pentagon Papers* on the war. Ellsberg told Wicker and his colleague, Neil Sheehan, "You guys have been conned. . . . You should have seen the figures they wanted to tell you." According to Ellsberg, the first figures that General Westmoreland and Ambassador Ellsworth Bunker wanted cabled to the Pentagon were so wild that no one in Washington would have believed them even for a moment. Pentagon officials realized that, if the figures were to have any credibility at all, they would have to be revised downward. Cables flew back and forth between Saigon and the Defense Department as the men in the field negotiated with analysts in the bureaucracy to settle on figures that they could "foist off" on the American people.[2] The ability of the press to separate fact from fantasy had been proved wanting, and since 1968 presidents and members of the press corps have continually been locking horns over what news is really "fit to print."

In this chapter we shall examine this adversary relationship between the executive branch (the president in particular) and the media. Each seems to have an exalted self-image. Such self-righteousness often gets in the way of effective working relationships between them. Presidents in search of consensus and votes often cross swords with journalists who seek the perfect headlines and copy to sell their wares. While the president has the upper hand in most of these encounters, both the White House and the press corps have some formidable tools at their disposal for manipulating each other and for shaping reality to their personal perceptions.

Competition between the president and the press can be a healthy thing for a democracy such as ours as it helps to increase the flow of information between the government and the voting public. Constant bickering and backbiting, typical of the post-Vietnam and Watergate periods can be counterproductive, however. It can encourage an unhealthy public cynicism and erode voter confidence in both the White House and the journalists who cover it. When a disenchanted electorate cries "a plague on both your houses," democracy suffers. Turnout at the polling places can shrink and the public is unlikely to yell "foul" when courts, in search of "law and order," begin tampering with the legitimate rights of the press.

Arrogance can be self-defeating. Richard Nixon and Lyndon Johnson helped to create the imperial presidency and their belief that the king could do no wrong was their undoing. There is a lesson in that for journalists as well. At a news conference just after his elevation, the "Smiling Pope" (John Paul I) reminded the assembled reporters that they were part of a noble profession and were to act as the faithful stewards of the people. He even suggested that, if St. Paul were alive today, he would be a director of Reuters Press Service. In recounting the incident, William Cheshire suggested that, in the crush of information for journalists to choose from these days, St. Paul might well have been overlooked. "Speaking as one member of an infallible vocation to another," Cheshire quipped, "I could have told his Holiness: In the United States of America St. Paul would have been lucky indeed to get his epistles published in the *Washington Post.*"[3] Because of the high esteem journalists have traditionally enjoyed in democracies, the temptation is great for them to choose the news to sway public opinion. When reporters' opinions differ from those popular in the Oval Office, the battle is joined.

## A STRAINED RELATIONSHIP

Whether a particular president gets along well with the Washington press corps or not, he soon learns that he needs them almost as much as they need him. Doris Graeber suggests that the media perform four basic functions for a president. First, they supply executives with information about current events and political settings for their policies. Next, the media can give the president insights into the concerns of the American public. Third, they serve as channels to convey his views to the public and his own government. Finally, they provide the president a stage on which he can act presidential[4] and showcase his concern for the nation.

Modern presidents have tended to surround themselves in a cocoon spun by their staffers; but they can't hide indefinitely from industrious reporters. The sixty- or seventy-member White House press corps exists solely to keep track of the president's every move. Wherever he goes, a press car or plane filled with the "pack" is in hot pursuit of a story. The twelve hundred or so members of the Washington press corps[5] compete with one another to ferret out the first inklings of a story on the Hill, at the Supreme Court, in the agencies, or at the White House. Scrutiny like that is bound to generate mounds of copy.

## DIGESTING THE NEWS

A president can ill afford to overlook what the press is saying about the way he is doing his job. Recent presidents have either done extensive personal newspaper reading and TV news watching or have depended on digests of daily commentary compiled by staffers. President John Kennedy must have been a *magna cum laude* graduate of the Evelyn Wood reading school. He combed numerous newspapers, magazines, and journals to keep informed. Each day he skimmed three papers from New York, two from Washington, two from Boston, and two from Chicago, and he chose among daily papers from four other major cities. Whenever he found a most insightful article, he discussed it with members of his staff.

Lyndon Johnson's priorities for information were a bit different. While he did thumb through *The New York Times* and *The Wall Street Journal*, he was addicted to the wire-service tickers to the point of having a receiving machine installed in the Oval Office. He worried about the coverage of his administration on television so he had a three-screened TV console set up in his office to watch the three network newscasts simultaneously. His successor, Richard Nixon, once commented, "I could go up the wall watching TV commentators. I don't. I get my news from the summary the staff prepares every day."[6] Evidently, the only television in which Nixon indulged was watching "Kojak" (a New York City-based detective story) and cheering the Washington Redskins football games. Johnson's elaborate ticker-tape and TV paraphenalia was dismantled completely.[7]

Gerald Ford continued the digests with a new wrinkle. His staff added morning TV news reports along with newspaper and magazine articles and editorials. Even snippets of books relevant to White House concerns found their way into the digest. Unlike the Nixon operation, Ford's staffers were directed to include critical comments in the digests as well as plaudits. In this way the president could be kept informed when one of his aides, cabinet secretaries, or he, himself, was the target of media wrath. Outsider Jimmy Carter didn't change things much on this score. He received a ten to fifteen-page summary of thirty to forty newspapers and the reports from morning and evening TV news. From the beginning, these digests pulled no punches. Criticism got through to the president's desk. Later, however, Press Secretary Jody Powell directed the digest staff to point out "factual errors"[8] in what they read and reported on. Invariably there comes a time in political reporting about the White House that a journalist's "facts" are an office holder's "factual errors."

Presidents find it easy to believe that the issues confronting them are too complicated for either the press or the public to comprehend adequately. Rather than attempting to inform or educate, they find it simpler to partially inform, cover up, and even misinform (a political euphemism for lying). Walter Lippmann, a giant of American journalism for over a quarter of a century, recognizing this tendency reminded presidents that they should "never cease explaining to the people directly and publicly . . . through chosen leaders what the government is doing and why."[9]

Still, at the height of the Watergate cover-up, President Nixon felt justified in sweeping the whole mess under the carpet because the disclosures were causing him political troubles. Nixon repeatedly told those who were investigating him that they risked great harm to the Republic. In their brief in the Watergate tapes case, Nixon's attorneys warned the Supreme Court that letting the lower court decision stand (he must surrender the tapes) would mean that the presidency might survive, but in a form much weaker than the office contemplated by the framers and occupied by presidents from George Washington through today. To attack him, in other words, was to weaken the presidency and endanger the stability of the nation. Must educating the electorate take a back seat to protecting the president's own political hide?

Journalists, on the other hand, revel in sniffing out juicy stories about the president and his staff. This "go for the jugular" tendency in the press encourages presidents to conclude that they are the "helpless victims" of "irresponsible" journalism. Presidents Johnson and Nixon were particularly susceptible to these bouts of self-pity. With his usual insight and artistic command of the language, Richard Nixon admitted that newspapers, "if they are against the candidate [can] give him the shaft."[10] This siege mentality was hardly peculiar to Johnson and Nixon, however. Even Napoleon Bonaparte once admitted that he feared the *Cologne Gazette* more than ten thousand bayonets. Thomas Jefferson, the architect of the First Amendment protections for the press, developed misgivings about reporters after he became president. In a letter to a friend, he groused, "even the least informed . . . learned that nothing in a newspaper is to be believed . . . a few prosecutions of prominent offenders would have a wholesome effect."[11]

## JOURNALISTS AND THEIR MEDIA

When it comes to "us against them" from the White House point of view, the press becomes the "quintessential" them.[12] Neither socioeconomic nor academic elites can be more troublesome for a president than the press corps. When a president earns their wrath, they can act as the ultimate obstructionists because they define and sharpen national issues for the voting public. Does a crisis exist in our dealings with the Soviets? Is the economy improving or is a recession in the cards? Who is the front-runner in the race for the White House?[13] Most of us get our answers to questions such as these from newspapers, magazines, through press reports, and television.

Although press reports may not jibe with White House assessments, the journalist, according to Ron Nessen (press secretary to Gerald Ford), "always has the last word and always has more words than politicians."[14] Presidents may become livid when they see what a particular editor has committed to paper, but often they can do little about it. Nixon press aide Pat Buchanan, a former editorial writer himself, put it this way, "You can yell and holler about the newspapers all you want, but you can't say that they have to change, that's their prerogative, to print what they want."[15]

The things that journalists want to print and those that the White House wants printed are often different due to the fact that each views the public as an audience from radically different perspectives. A political leader is essentially an advocate using the media channels to convince voters. Journalists view communication with the public in another vein. To them, facts have a life of their own. No matter how grim the reality or how damaging to a president's political fortunes, reporters often feel honor bound to "tell all" to the people.

Every recent administration has assumed office voicing its commitment to openness and candor. As the silver-tongued oratory began to tarnish, the reality soon became secrecy, evasiveness, and paranoia about the press. No doubt this can be traced to the fact that the reporter defines news to include not merely positions on issues but personality conflicts, controversies within an administration, scandals, and the seamier side of White House life. Reporters commonly sketch government with all its blemishes and failures.[16] Whenever they try to peek under White House cloaks of secrecy and executive privilege, they encourage retaliation. Not to be outdone, writers can take their swings too.

Few administrations survive without noticeable bruises inflicted by a disgruntled press corps. On the whole, however, the White House has been highly successful in trading news about itself that it chooses to disclose for access to media channels to the American electorate. The net effect of the interaction between these two imperial powers has been a remarkable increase in the president's leadership role in American life.[17] A president's effectiveness today increasingly rests on his ability to use the electronic media (especially television) to convince skeptics that he is steering an appropriate course for the nation.

So far, we have used the terms press, media, and journalists interchangeably. In the process, we may have left the impression that the profession speaks with a single voice. Although politicians smarting under a barrage of criticism might be tempted to accept such generalizations, they are as simplistic as they are inaccurate.

## PRINT MEDIA

Journalists divide their profession into "print" and "broadcast" media. Print media include newspapers, magazines, and wire services; broadcast refers to radio and the goldmine of the profession, television. There were about seventeen hundred daily newspapers in the United States in 1980. The numbers of independents[18] have dropped somewhat in recent years due to strikes, increased production costs (paper, typesetting equipment) and the tendency of chains to buy them out. Large, national-circulation newspapers like *The New York Times* can be an ally or a headache for the White House. A syndicated journalist who peddles his or her wares nationally can be a *persona non grata* to the president and his staff. Watergate figure G. Gordon Liddy, noted for his bizarre sense of loyalty to the Nixon administration, recently indicated that columnist Jack Anderson was considered a danger to national security by the Nixon White House and that he was marked for assassination. Even wire-service reporters for the Associated Press (AP), United Press International (UPI), and Reuters are capable of flushing out stories that the White House would prefer remain hidden.

Although journalists hate to admit it, each of them is a prisoner of deadlines. This places them at a severe disadvantage vis-à-vis the White House. They are constantly in need of something fresh and insightful to submit to their editors each day. An efficient press secretary can use this pressure to the president's advantage. He may cast pearls before them or withhold newsworthy items and bore them with banalities. Reporters for daily newspapers are especially subject to this type of manipulation.

In addition to newspapers and wire-service reports, magazines of news and opinion are also a potent political force with which administrations must contend. Popular magazines in this category (*Time, Newsweek* and *U.S. News*) and more specialized ones (*Atlantic* and *Harper's* and even *Playboy* interviews) help to mold public perceptions of national issues and political personalities. Among political elites in business and government, two dozen or so journals are widely read and respected according to a recent survey.[19] Some of these are political, for example, *The National Review, New Republic, Foreign Affairs,* and *Commonweal;* others, like the *New Yorker, Daedalus,* and *Commentary,* are more broadly based and literary but no less respected. The articles and commentary in these sources can be the seedbed of public dissent as they often were in the Vietnam era. They also may serve as places for academics and unnamed government bureaucrats to subject their innovative ideas to careful scrutiny. In this way, they provide a democracy the chance to test new ideas without having to pay the price of implementing them prematurely and finding them unworkable.

## BROADCAST MEDIA: TELEVISION

The newest member of the journalistic fraternity and the one with the largest audience by far has been network television. The three major networks have amassed huge audiences for their nightly newscasts in recent years. One circulation report several years ago estimated the CBS audience at 17.3 million, NBC at 16.2 million, and ABC at 12.0 million.[20] Those figures stood in marked contrast to the kingpins of the print media. *The New York Times* circulation at that time was 843,000, and *Time,* the weekly news magazine, had 4,325,000 subscribers. The networks supplement their nightly news programming with interview shows that probe public issues. In this category one could include CBS's "Face the Nation" and NBC's "Meet the Press" along with ABC's "Issues and Answers" and news magazines such as "Sixty Minutes," "20/20," and "Nightline." Television journalists also pepper the president with questions in televised press conferences; but, to the chagrin of the president and his aides, other commentators provide not just summaries but "instant analyses" of any White House-sponsored addresses to the nation. Once again, the journalists get the last word. To discourage "instant analysis" the Nixon administration in 1970 discontinued the time-honored practice of supplying texts of speeches before they were delivered to the public. A commentator can do little more than summarize when there is no prepublication text to follow.

# PRESS BIASES AND ROLES

Since television and the print media have such a potentially powerful impact on public perception of policy and political figures,[21] it would be only human for commentators, editors, and reporters to manipulate the news to uphold certain viewpoints they champion. Are the national press and television journalists merely fronts for some sort of Eastern Establishment liberal conspiracy, as former Vice President Spiro Agnew often complained?[22] In a monumental study of all TV network news broadcasts from July 10 to election day 1972, Richard Hoffsetter found two types of biases: (1) political bias—a tendency to favor one candidate or the other—and (2) structural bias—preference for a particular type of item thought more attuned to TV broadcasting. He found that structural biases far outweighed the amount of political bias.[23] Four years later, Thomas Patterson and Robert McClure discovered that the trappings of the race including the cheering crowds, the drama of must-win primaries, and so on presented excellent prime-time TV fare. They found that in 1976 topics of this sort took up 60 percent of the news coverage while a mere 28 percent was devoted to substantive topics.[24]

Despite these findings politicians and some journalists are still convinced that the press takes an ideological slant. Daniel Patrick Moynihan tends to agree with Agnew that there is a *liberal* bias in the press.[25] Conservative author and columnist Kevin Phillips identifies television as a part of an interlocking directorate that controls political analysis. NBC, for example, is a subsidiary of the RCA conglomerate, whereas CBS ranked at 102 on the *Fortune* 500 list of major corporations in 1977.[26] Conversely, Democratic presidential candidate Adlai Stevenson (1952) complained about a "one-party press" that was too *conservative* for his taste. In assessing press biases Stevenson said, "the overwhelming majority of the press is just against Democrats. . . . I speak of the great majority not the enlightened 10%." It was that "enlightened" 10 percent that provoked rage in Agnew and Nixon. Most of them were the large-circulation major city newspapers with a national reputation. Newspapers that could be classified as small town and conservative constituted the "overwhelming majority" that Stevenson was moaning about.

## CRUSADERS AND OPINION MAKERS

The Founding Fathers envisioned the press as a bulwark against governmental oppression. They reasoned, according to Arthur Schlesinger, Jr., that "the best antidote to despotism was the guarantee of freedom of speech and the press; and the best safeguard for democracy was the wide diffusion of information."[27] No other group outside the sphere of government was provided special protections under the Constitution. This fact has, no doubt, been a source of encouragement to each member of the Washington press corps at one time or another.

Almost as a credo of the profession, journalists tend to view themselves as crusaders in the public interest. Reporters are seekers of truth and guardians of the oppressed and the downtrodden. They are not about to permit a candidate or a president to hoodwink the electorate. Reporters convince themselves that the candidate is duping the poor voter and it is up to them to see that the poor little sap isn't conned by *this slicker*.[28] As well-intentioned as a writer might be, there is a certain antidemocratic arrogance in his or her thinking whether it is recognized or not.

As "seekers of truth" and "whistleblowers," journalists have status in the community they serve. Certain key Washington watchers tend to set the tone for appraising the performance of a president.[29] What David Broder, Joseph Kraft, Tom Wicker, James Reston, and Hugh Sidey (among others) say and think affects the way in which federal bureaucrats, members of Congress, interest group activists, and even foreign governments will view a particular president. If a president's leadership qualities are suspect to these analysts, it is likely that misgivings about him will also crop up on Capitol Hill, in the departments and agencies, and even overseas.

Anyone touring the State Department offices or cafeterias would be struck by the number of copies of *The New York Times* and the *Washington Post* that litter desks, and lunchcounters at Foggy Bottom.[30] No doubt this department is typical of official Washington in this respect. As a result of these implied votes of confidence, key correspondents of major newspapers and press services tend to view themselves as quasi-elected officials because of their popularity. Several of them, for example, suggested that Senator Thomas Eagleton's previous medical record, including treatment for depression, disqualified him for being chosen as George McGovern's running mate on the 1972 Democratic presidential ticket. Within a few days of one another, the *Washington Post,* the *Baltimore Sun,* and *The New York Times* called for Eagleton's resignation.[31] McGovern, in light of such high-powered criticism, had little choice but to jettison his selection for vice president or suffer editorial sniping for his "lack of judgment." During the early stages of the 1980 primary race for the White House, analysts questioned Senator Edward Kennedy's moral and emotional preparedness to serve as president because of the bizarre events surrounding what has come to be known as the Chappaquidick incident. Former Texas Governor John Connally was saddled with a "wheeler-dealer" label that he could not shake, and Ronald Reagan was discounted as being "too old" and "too conservative" to run for president and win in 1980. Comments of this sort showed up not just in editorials but in regular news copy. Thomas Cronin suggests that Gerald Ford's reputation as "a clumsy bumbler, a Bozo the Clown klutz" seemed to suggest mental ineptitude as well. Later such characterizations became a factor in his defeat.[32]

## INFORMATION CHANNELS
## FOR GOVERNMENT

Official Washington, which so diligently examines *The New York Times* and the *Washington Post,* often finds little time to read the president's latest policy statements or addresses to the nation. Synopses of his comments in the newspaper have become a valuable aid to a president to get his ideas filtered down through the various agencies and departments. Former presidential assistant Joseph Califano who had also served a stint at the Pentagon contends that only a handful of government officials and members of Congress read most presidential messages to Congress. "Except for a few hard-working members who study particular legislation in detail,"

Califano commented, "Representatives and Senators rely on the *Washington Post* and *New York Times* reporting and . . . perhaps read whatever verbatim excerpts those newspapers print."[33]

Since so many people in Washington and elsewhere lean on their copy for information and insights into White House operations, members of the Washington press corps in search of a story are often subject to manipulation by the president's press secretary. In fact, Russell Baker of *The New York Times* compared the modern White House, including the press corps, with the courts of the Stuart monarchs of England. He imagined correspondents as just so many courtiers in the ante chambers who were fed information designed to "make the monarch look good."[34] Unfortunately, some reporters seem quite at home in this stultifying atmosphere. In fact, they relish identifying themselves as a part of the White House press corps rather than mentioning the paper or wire service that provides them their daily meal tickets. Too many of them are willing to pay minimal attention to the fact that they can't always verify much of the information gratuitously spooned out by the press secretary. How can they verify stories when their access to the president and his advisors seems to be shrinking daily?

Limited access to the president is a reality that journalists of the 1940s did not have to contend with. During the Franklin Roosevelt years, reporters gathered weekly to bounce questions off of the president for as long as they wished. Roosevelt sat behind his desk in the Oval Office only a few feet in front of them. His spontaneous responses were disarmingly candid and spiced with his natural sense of humor.[35] What reporters couldn't glean from these sessions they sought by cornering visitors as they left the Oval Office to grill them about their meeting with the president. As the White House press staff has expanded, however, the press corps has been nudged farther and farther away from the doors of the Oval Office. Intimate sessions gave way to more structured press conferences. Once regular contacts with the president himself shrank to mere briefings from the press secretary, in-depth interviewing and investigation became increasingly difficult.

### SUPERSLEUTHING

Romantics would portray career journalists as supersleuths unearthing scandals and producing sensational headlines for each morning's newspaper. But the reality is quite different. Investigative journalism, like any detective work, can be tedious and time consuming and may lead the reporter up a number of blind alleys. Weeks might be spent in sniffing out a White House scandal. Ultimately, those labors may yield only unverifiable allegations.[36]

Journalists need not frequent bars, back corridors at the White House, or involve themselves in cloak and dagger research to dig out a story. Much can be learned from careful reading of daily briefings, off-the-record background sessions, press conferences, public speeches, and so forth. Members of the press corps normally have no access to internal White House communications and cables and dispatches from the State Department, CIA, or other intelligence agencies. Still, the determined reporter can, from gleaning documents and even reports in other media (newspapers, television, or magazines, for example), piece together a story that may be radically at odds with the official White House version of certain events. Most of us think that Woodward and Bernstein's success in exposing the Watergate cover-up could be traced to clandestine meetings with the mysterious "Deep Throat" who must have provided most of the puzzle pieces. On the contrary, the coordinator of the *Post's* special Watergate staff says that the breaking of the cover-up involved beating the pavement, innovative questioning based on deductions, and careful piecing together of already available scraps of information. Leaks from the White House, he explained, did not account for the breaks in the investigation of the Watergate saga.[37]

Some have suggested that investigative journalism about the White House is something akin to Kremlinology.[38] In Soviet politics, the appearance or absence from an important meeting or public affair such as the May Day military parade in Red Square could signal a change in a leader's status in the party. In the spring of 1980, for example, reporters didn't need a leak from the White House to know that Cyrus Vance was on his way out as secretary of state. When Vance shouldered the blame for a U.S. vote in the U.N. Security Council condemning Israeli settlements on the West Bank of the Jordan river, it was clear that he was becoming vulnerable. Not long after the ill-fated U.N. vote, which had the American Jewish community up in arms, presidential National Security Assistant Zbigniew Brzezinski, not Vance, was sent to examine the remnants of Afghan rebel groups that were hoping to drive the invading Russians out of their country. Vance's precarious position deteriorated to a point beyond redemption when he became the only close presidential advisor who opposed what turned out to be an abortive raid into Iran to free American hostages held there for almost two hundred days. Even a cub reporter could have surmised that Vance's days as secretary of state were numbered.

In-depth investigative journalism can be a calculated risk for both the editors and reporters involved. Editors may invest a fortune to get either something unverifiable or of little headline value. Reporters may invest hours in digging up a story that cannot be printed. Either can be subjected to harassment by federal agencies at the request of the White House as it seeks to punish those who have "persecuted" the president.

Sometimes, lauded investigative journalism amounts to nothing more than tripping over information dropped at the reporter's feet by a disgruntled White House staffer or department employee. Neil Sheehan was cheered for the "investigative reporting" that resulted in the publication of the *Pentagon Papers*. Columnist Robert Walters contends that David Ellsberg simply got unhappy and dumped them in the lap of *The New York Times*. In fact, he says that this is the way newspapers get most of their best stories. Walters told fellow reporter Robert Sherrill that the public was getting the wrong impression. "We shouldn't foist off on the public the idea that our reporters are out getting stuff that *nobody* wants them to have. Somebody, somewhere, wants you to have it before you'll get it."[39]

## PRESIDENTS VIEW THE PRESS

As press distrust of the White House reached its peak during the Johnson and Nixon administrations, presidential respect for journalists sunk to new lows. Certain writers who sought to curry favor with the president and the press secretary increased White House disrespect for the profession. Lyndon Johnson was both flattered and amazed at the depths to which some press people could sink to stay in his good graces. The ultimate example of this type was *Washington Star* White House correspondent Garnett "Jack" Horner. Once, when Horner was a part of the press pool riding with the president on Air Force One, LBJ invited the reporters to the front for a chat. Horner served up one cream puff question after another to the president. Later, in a Texas-sized whisper Johnson confided to an aide and half the airplane, "Boy, that Jack Horner is really a big ass kisser isn't he?"[40] Nixon White House aide Charles Colson also found the press corps easy to manipulate. "They are very much afraid of us," he commented, and "are anxious to prove that they are good guys." The harder he pressed them, the more cordial and apologetic they seemed to become.[41] Unfortunately for the administration, Nixon's hostility toward the press and his tendencies to mislead them helped to transform them from patsies and supporters of the status quo into a hostile and suspicious lot. Their normal tendency to seek out the controversial evolved in the Johnson and Nixon years into a habit of going for the White House jugular.

Nixon and Johnson were hardly the first presidents to question the professionalism of the press corps. Theodore Sorensen, close aide to John Kennedy, had also publicly bemoaned the erosion of professionalism in the journalistic community. Too many reporters and editors, he felt, were more interested in what was "salable" than in their responsibility for educating the public. They preferred examining a candidate's private life rather than his thoughts.[42] Sensational stories outsell the complexity of issue-oriented reporting. This type of reporting also tends to overlook the limits of the political process and bureaucratic realities that limit a president's leadership.

## AS TRAFFICKERS IN THE TRIVIAL

In 1976, candidate Jimmy Carter's campaign planners recognized these nonissue patterns in press reporting and demonstrated a genius for generating human interest stories about the former Georgia governor, his family, and his origins. Evidently, these stories were carefully parceled out to reporters over the long campaign trail. The Carter people sensed that news people look for personality profile stories because their editors demand them. Andrew Glass, White House correspondent for the Cox newspaper chain, noted that it "is easier to get into several newspapers with a strong story about Amy (Carter's daughter) than with one about an important policy decision. If they use both, the Amy story is likely to get on page one, while the one dealing with policy is likely to be buried on page twenty-nine."[43]

Campaigns are structured with press coverage in mind partly due to the high cost of campaign advertising. If a candidate can't afford to buy time, he must make himself news to get the time free on the nightly broadcasts. Rallies are scheduled so that there is ample time for reporters to cover them.[44] Speeches are often hyped up to create headlines for newspapers. Candidates and their aides learn how to get the most out of short telecast segments and become adept at staging media events. During the 1980 primary campaign, for example, Senator Edward Kennedy took a walking tour of the South Bronx area of New York City shortly before the New York State presidential preference primary. He attracted media coverage to help him make the point that Carter's promise to rebuild the area after his election in 1976 had not visibly improved the "bombed out" look of that dying minority neighborhood. Lessons learned on the campaign trail, as we shall demonstrate later in the chapter, are not discarded when the candidate becomes president.

Some candidates and presidents are harder to market than others. Joe McGinnis illustrates Richard Nixon's problem in the 1968 race with a statement by the producer of Nixon's staged question-answer sessions:[45]

> Let's face it, a lot of people think Nixon is dull . . . he's a bore, a pain in the ass. They look at him as the kind of kid who always carried a book bag, who was forty-two years old the day he was born. They figure that other kids got footballs for Christmas, Nixon got a briefcase and he loved it.

His public relations people were astute enough to recognize that he was a disaster on television and a caricaturist's delight. "He looks like somebody hung him in the closet overnight and he jumps out in the morning with his suit all hunched up and starts running around saying, 'I want to be President'."[46]

Since reams of triviality get front-page coverage, the public may well remember a president for the image projected of him rather than for the substance of the policies he espouses or his ability to get them enacted. To a degree, the image a president projects is a function of his popularity with the press. "Cults of personality" can be built up around popular presidents, and "credibility gaps" can dog unpopular ones. Early friendly press coverage can go sour too. Gerald Ford became news, for example, for his habit of cooking his own breakfast. Later in the administration his tendency to veto social programs helped to change press reporting about the president. Nationwide audiences were entertained with film of the president tripping down stairs, skiing on the seat of his pants on the Aspen, Colorado slopes, hitting golf balls into crowds of spectators, and bumping his head on helicopter doors.

## PHASES IN PRESIDENTIAL-PRESS RELATIONS

Journalists normally permit a president a grace period of several months before leveling broadsides at his goals and examining conflicts within his administration. This "honeymoon period," as Robert Locander points out, rarely lasts as much as a year.[47]

Two other political scientists noticed certain broad time patterns in White House press relations during typical recent administrations. Kumar and Grossman divided them into three phases: the *alliance phase,* the *competition phase,* and, finally, the *detachment phase.*[48]

### TABLE 9.1
### HONEYMOONS: TERMINATION AND REASONS WHY

| PRESIDENT | MONTH | REASON |
|-----------|-------|--------|
| Kennedy | 4 | Press management charges over Bay of Pigs |
| Johnson | 13 | Credibility questions about Vietnam |
| Nixon | 11 | Agnew media assaults |
| Ford | 2 | Nixon pardon |
| Carter | 9 | Bert Lance affair |

Source: Robert Locander, "Carter & The Press: The First Two Years," *Presidential Studies Quarterly,* (Spring 1979), p. 103.

In the *alliance phase,* which is roughly the same as Locander's "honeymoon," the needs of reporters for news and the president for publicity lead to a sort of neutral or even friendly accommodation. During this phase, the two seem to have a common definition of what is newsworthy, and reporters permit themselves to be used to convey presidential messages, free of excessive analysis. Personal stories about the president are flattering. Since the president has not had time to produce on his campaign promises in the early months and is busy trying to get his administration organized, if he avoids juicy scandals, foreign affairs fiascos, and open affronts to the press corps, he has a good chance of developing a working relationship with journalists.

The wraps come off in the *competitive phase.* The honeymoon is clearly over when reporters begin searching for and finding conflicts within an administration. Scuttlebutt and rumor about staffers and cabinet members begin to surface regularly. Journalists try to determine which cabinet people and personal aides are closest to the president. In recent years, the game has often revolved around finding the key advisor in foreign policy. Was it Secretary of State William Rogers or National Security Assistant Henry Kissinger to whom Nixon turned for foreign affairs counsel? During the Carter years the question became one of Zbigniew Brzezinski versus Cyrus Vance and later Edmund Muskie. Did the fact that Richard V. Allen, Ronald Reagan's National Security Assistant, had a basement office at the White House mean that Secretary of State Alexander Haig had more policy clout? Since the press airs the administration's dirty linen in public during this phase, the presidents soon become disenchanted with media people. To discourage damaging leaks from within, administrations resort to manipulating information, limiting regular access, and carefully structuring contacts. The president remains "visible" but less subject to hostile questions about problems within the administration.

Finally, the competitive stage gives way to the *detachment phase.* The president stays away from press contacts almost totally, leaving them to the press secretary and other administrative aides. This coincides with the reelection effort for sitting presidents. To be seen as "presidential" without having to argue politics, they adopt a "rocking chair" or "rose garden" strategy. Surrogates go out to campaign for the president. Richard Nixon used figures within his administration and Jimmy Carter leaned heavily on his wife, his son Chip, his "momma," and Vice President Mondale. While a president's meetings with foreign dignitaries are nightly news media events, his opponents might be candidly pictured with the disheveled look of a campaigner at his fifth stop in four hours. Even as the press corps in the capitol is being kept at arms length in the detachment phase, regional editors and news directors and interest groups find the White House red carpet being rolled out for them.[49] They are invited to the Oval Office to air their gripes and views as the president listens attentively across his desk. What perfect copy for local daily papers and TV news. He becomes ideal news on his own terms!

## PRESIDENTIAL INTERACTION
## WITH THE PRESS

Although we have noted some common patterns in press-White House relations, some presidents have worked more effectively with journalists than have others. Every president from FDR to the present has attempted to use the press to his

## TABLE 9.2
## MODERN PRESIDENTIAL ATTITUDES TOWARD THE PRESS

| CATEGORIES | ATTITUDES TOWARD THE PRESS | INTERACTION | PRESIDENT |
|---|---|---|---|
| Indifferent-aloof | No fear, no great respect | Regularized rigid | Eisenhower |
| Respectful-manipulative | Great respect, some fear | As personal as possible | F. Roosevelt Kennedy Truman I* |
| Suspicious-vindictive | Intense fear, antipathy | Rigid and less and less regular contact | Johnson Nixon Truman II |
| Respectful-deferential | Respect, discomfort | Neither personal nor completely rigid | Ford Carter+ |

*Truman became more suspicious of the press after the 1944 election
+Carter became increasingly critical of the press and more aloof after 1978

advantage. Presidents can be grouped into four categories based on their attitudes toward the press and their ways of interacting with journalists, as shown in Table 9.2.

## INDIFFERENT-ALOOFS

Dwight Eisenhower was clearly an indifferent-aloof type of president in his dealings with journalists. He was not naïve enough to think that the press could not hurt him; but he felt that, if he was careful with what he said, journalists would have little ammunition to use against him. He entered the White House with a tremendous reservoir of public support. Eighty percent of the nation's daily newspapers lined up behind his candidacy in 1952. Even Washington correspondents were reluctant to criticize him for fear that their readers would not like it. When he was asked about the possible pitfalls in dealing with the press, he responded, "I don't know how any reporter can hurt a President."[50]

His reputation as a wartime hero had much to do with his self-confidence. He was not arrogant enough to think that he need not be careful in his dealings with the Washington press corps. The administration hired a Hollywood writer to liven up his speeches. Press conferences were filmed with the most flattering parts to be aired and the rest ending up on the cutting room floor. It became administration policy not to permit the president to answer questions in unstructured meetings with the press. He fended off most every effort of frustrated press reporters as they tried to get him to leak a bit of gossip or say something quotable for the evening front page. Eisenhower was proud of the fact that he was "able to avoid causing the nation a serious setback through anything I said in . . . over eight years of intensive questioning."[51]

These presidents understood the legitimate adversary relationship and were willing to make themselves accessible to journalists. Their willingness to take the press seriously helped them to get friendly coverage when they needed it. As we noted earlier, Franklin Roosevelt held intimate and regular press conferences. His conferences were more like seminars with plenty of off-the-record banter and insights into the president's thinking on a broad range of issues. Only later in his administration did Roosevelt feel free to vent his frustrations with many in the press whom he saw as "the advance men for the economic royalists," his term for bankers and business people intent on ruining the social programs of the New Deal.[52] Nevertheless, until the day he died, he did little to limit press access.

Harry Truman kept the conferences up on a weekly basis, but they gradually became more formal as he moved them from the Oval Office to the old State Department treaty room. The new president didn't have the smooth relationship with the press that FDR had enjoyed in his early White House years. The former vice president still seemed to enjoy jousting with reporters, but he remained skeptical of editors and publishers. In his memoirs, Truman said[53]

> I have always made a sharp distinction between the working reporter and the editor or publisher. I always got along well with reporters. They try to do an honest job of reporting the facts. But many of their bosses . . . have their own special interests and the news is often slanted to serve those interests which, unfortunately, are not always for the benefit of the public as a whole.

When polished, youthful, intelligent, witty John Kennedy brought his own experience as a journalist into the White House, it seemed that the marriage between this president and the press had been ordained by heaven. He maintained close contacts with his "favorite" journalists and leaked blockbuster information to such respected journalists as Joseph and Stewart Alsop and Marquis Childs.[54] Stewart Alsop reportedly was a close family friend who even helped on writing and reviewing Kennedy speeches.

The Kennedy White House made a science out of manipulating the press. Reporters who gave the president favorable coverage were rewarded with visits to the White House quarters for personal information on crisis decisions. They were permitted access to government documents that their competitors could not use. Stewart Alsop and Charles Bartlett coauthored an article on the Cuban missile crisis with information from National Security Council proceedings. Key network reporters who played the game according to White House rules were permitted televised interviews with Kennedy. The president tried to woo larger segments of the press corps by using the "background briefings." Material given in these briefings could be used as "background" to articles, but none of the material could be attributed to the president. Luncheons and dinners for regional reporters in the White House proved effective in spreading goodwill beyond the Washington press corps.[55]

Among recent presidents, Kennedy was the most effective in trading the glamor of the White House and his own charisma for support in print and broadcast news reports and editorials. He was our first TV president:[56]

Kennedy gave the networks their first real opportunity to televise the President in his office, at work, and during press conferences. In return, Kennedy tacitly accepted the unstated privilege of using the networks to build a more plebiscitary Presidency than any since Franklin D. Roosevelt.

Bringing the White House under the revealing eye of network cameras proved useful to Kennedy, but he was the ultimate in "media" type presidents. He set a standard that few of his successors have been able to meet. For many of his successors, public familiarity through television bred not greater admiration but increasing contempt.

### SUSPICIOUS-VINDICTIVES

Madison Avenue's finest public relations persons would have been incapable of making Lyndon Johnson shine by comparison to his martyred predecessor. Among recent presidents, only Richard Nixon had a tougher time trying to make his peace with the press. Since both Nixon and Johnson considered the press to be biased against them, they tried to make writers the scapegoats for U.S. failures in Vietnam. Both were also convinced that the press was determined to "get them." Johnson despaired of pleasing the media because, as he put it, "I'm from the wrong side of the tracks." He once confided to *Life's* Hugh Sidey, "I don't believe I'll ever get credit for anything I do in foreign affairs, no matter how successful it is because I didn't go to Harvard."[57] Joe McGinnis agreed that a good portion of LBJ press relations problems arose from the fact that he followed Kennedy with whom the press had such a love affair. He described Johnson as "heavy and gross" and, as a result, Johnson "was forgiven nothing. . . . Johnson was syrupy. He stuck to the lens. There was no place for him in our [the press] culture."[58] Johnson, in turn, became so jaundiced with the press that his early attempts to be another Kennedy with them degenerated into outright hostility. In mock humor about journalists he once commented, "Cast your bread upon the waters and the sharks will get it."[59]

As we noted earlier, Johnson's orchestration of a Gulf of Tonkin resolution on Vietnam helped the administration to gain a reputation for lack of candor. The term "credibility gap" was coined during the Johnson years because he habitually attempted to deceive journalists and the public.[60] If he felt misunderstood by reporters, much of the problem was of his own doing. His arrogance was legendary, and he spared little of it in his dealings with the press. While Johnson seemed almost paranoid about the way in which the press treated him, it is only fair to also note that even paranoids have some real enemies.

With the advent of the Nixon administration, relations between the White House and the press went from bad to worse. Nixon's stormy political career as a crusading anticommunist representative, candidate for the Senate, presidential hopeful in 1960, and brooding loser in the race for California governor in 1962 left him with several strikes against him as he planned his race for the Oval Office. Early in his political career he tried "getting angry" with the press. In the White House, "getting even" proved sweeter still. He used the powers of the office against his enemies. The result was the sorry sight of a president trying to rewrite the First Amendment under the guise of national security to silence his most outspoken opponents. Nixon was convinced that "the press is the enemy." One aide suggested that the president's instincts were to do battle with what he was certain was ideological and personal bias against him.[61]

Doing battle effectively requires a strategy. In the fall of 1969, White House aide Jeb Stuart Magruder mapped out several scenarios for bringing the press into line.[62] He suggested, first, that the administration monitor with the assistance of the FCC all network news-related programs. Second, he noted in his memo that the Anti-Trust Division of the Justice Department might check media businesses for violations of federal law. "The possible threat of anti-trust violations," he enthused, "would be effective in changing their views."[63] Finally, he felt that the Internal Revenue Service could examine the finances of the newspapers, networks, and their executives and owners as a none-too-subtle reminder that criticism of the White House had its risks.

In another attempt to muzzle the media by discrediting it, Clay Whitehead, director of the new White House Office of Telecommunications, publicly complained about the "liberal plugola" that was being served up on network television. Instead of a fruitless frontal assault on the network moguls, Whitehead suggested that the administration try to foment mutiny among the local stations. He threatened to fight license renewal for those that did not attempt to balance the network news they beamed into local living rooms. He hoped that the chorus of complaints that was sure to arise among the flagships along the line would set the network admirals to thinking.[64]

To assure less sniping from the press, the Nixon administration resorted to extensive wiretapping not only of journalists who broke "national security"-related stories but of suspected loose-lipped White House and State Department aides. At this writing, the Supreme Court has yet to decide whether Nixon and others responsible for these taps (like Secretary of State Kissinger) can be held financially accountable for damages.

Director of Communications Herb Klein was responsible for still another effort to mute press criticism. He was tapped to generate letter-writing campaigns to newspapers and magazines and members of Congress. These were to demonstrate the depth of public support for the administration or a particular decision or action undertaken at the president's direction. This operation bore public relations fruit on a number of occasions, but one of the best examples of its success involved the spring 1970 decision to order an incursion into North Vietnamese sanctuaries in the Parrots Beak area of Cambodia.[65] That decision was bound to be unpopular because it widened the scope of an already divisive war. The day after Nixon made his address to the nation explaining the operation, the White House released pictures of a massive stack of telegrams in support of the president's initiative. No doubt many of those telegrams came from the three thousand or more Republican Party county committee chairpersons whom Klein had contacted seeking immediate statements of support. To put the best face on the incursion into Cambodia, Nixon used the event to show his own capacity to act in the best interest of the nation setting aside partisan and personal gain. He valiantly proclaimed to the public,[66]

> [some] are saying that the moves against these sanctuaries will make me a one-term President. . . . I would rather be a one-term President and do what I believe is right than be a two-term President at the cost of seeing America become a second-rate power.

Even his landslide victory in 1972 did not mellow his stance toward the press. Nixon was especially incensed with the *Washington Post* for its handling of the break-in at Democratic headquarters at the Watergate complex that greased the skids for his eventual resignation. In October 1973, he complained that the *Post* was "using innuendo, third-person hearsay, unsubstantiated sources and huge scare headlines . . . to give the appearance of direct connection between the White House and the Watergate break-in . . . a charge which the *Post* knows and half a dozen investigations have found to be false."[67]

The extensive efforts of suspicious-vindictive presidents such as Johnson and Nixon to manipulate the press illustrate some fundamental problems for presidential leadership in a democracy. Since, by definition, the people in a democracy decide, how much information available to the White House should be transmitted to the voters through the media? Most Americans would agree that some things must be kept secret lest they be used against the country by our enemies. The Supreme Court once suggested that reports on the movement of troops in a time of war as a hypothetical example of freedom of the press having limits.[68] During sensitive negotiations aimed at the release of U.S. hostages being held in Iran, President Carter called in TV anchorpersons and newspaper editors to ask their restraint in reporting on the efforts until the talks had been completed. There is always a danger that too much deference on the part of the press can be destructive to the national interest. The Bay of Pigs fiasco and numerous snafued operations in Vietnam demonstrate that secrecy may hide both woefully inadequate military plans and flawed intelligence estimates until it is too late for the Congress or the people to respond effectively. Vindictive presidents like Nixon can hide behind the mantle of national security to justify using the federal agencies to "get" their enemies both foreign and domestic.

## RESPECTFUL-DEFERENTIALS

Presidents who have no real national track record often try to develop a good reputation and working relationship with the national press early in their administrations. Both Presidents Ford and Carter came into the White House as unknowns. Ford had always been well liked by his colleagues on the Hill, whereas Carter's campaign theme of making the nation as "good and decent as its people" provided him with a similar positive image. Neither of them indulged in news management to any great extent, and neither made a habit of withholding information from reporters out of spite. Their openness did have its disadvantages, however. What incentive has a reporter to curry favor with the White House if he can get the information he wants without having to sell his soul?

To demonstrate his desire to get along well with the press, President Ford chose Jerald ter Horst from the *Detroit Free Press* as his first press secretary. Before long, ter Horst resigned because he had been left in the dark on Ford's decision to pardon Richard Nixon. To replace him, Ford settled on former NBC-TV analyst Ron Nessen. In another attempt at showing openness, Ford made an "unprecedented" appearance before a House judiciary subcommittee to "discuss" the pardon that he had already granted to Mr. Nixon.[69] Despite these efforts to divert press criticism and dispel their doubts about a "bargain," Ford's problems with the press began to multiply because his credibility had been brought into question. His decisions to use the veto to shanghai so many domestic initiatives from Capitol Hill only made matters worse.

Outsider Jimmy Carter got along well with the press during the traditional period of shadow boxing we have called the alliance phase. Jody Powell, Carter's press secretary, was not a professional journalist, but his candor, sense of humor, and down-to-earth demeanor earned him good standing with the press corps.

Neither Carter nor Ford had the personal charisma to command media deference that had been so useful to Franklin Roosevelt and John Kennedy. Their press spokespersons thus had to bear a share of the burden of improving the administration's standing with the Washington press. Without the flair of a Kennedy or a Roosevelt, these "easy-going" types of presidents are not the prime-time TV fare that the networks are looking for. They must often use their positions as president to get air time. When Gerald Ford wanted air time three weeks before the 1974 congressional elections, the networks were reluctant to accommodate him. He sought coverage of his address on the economy planned as a part of a visit to a Future Farmers of America convention being held in Kansas City, Missouri. Once the networks got wind of the content of the speech in which he encouraged the public to plant vegetable gardens, shop wisely, and observe the posted speed limits, they dismissed the speech as unworthy of prime-time coverage.[70] The president didn't permit the matter to end at that point. Instead, he made a formal request, and the networks relented even though the World Series had to be held up fifteen minutes to accommodate the speech.[71] Likewise, in December 1979, when Jimmy Carter tried to purchase TV time to announce his candidacy for a second term, the three networks each refused, ostensibly because they judged it too early to be starting a campaign. Only after the fact did a federal court side with the president, but, by then, it was too late. Carter's difficulties with coverage were not of his own making; however, the Ford "victory garden and save gas" speech led to network policy changes on requests for White House events coverage. Individual requests were subjected to greater scrutiny. As a result of these policy changes, two of Carter's nine addresses did not receive live coverage by all three networks. On February 1, 1978 ABC and NBC carried his speech on the Panama Canal in prime time while CBS broadcast it in the slot reserved for the late movie. One month later only CBS provided live coverage of the president's civil service reform speech.[72]

Although Carter was not given to battles with the press, he was not averse to setting limits on what he would discuss with them. In July 1978, for example, he told the Washington press corps during a news conference that he would accept no questions about the resignation of Dr. Peter Bourne, an old friend who had been serving as White House counselor on drug abuse control. Ironically, Bourne had signed a prescription for Quaaludes (an often-abused tranquilizer) for a fictitiously named White House aide. In doing so, he violated federal law. Seemingly, questions on the matter should have been fair game in a press conference, but Carter drew the line on them arguing that, while investigation of the incident was still in progress, answering questions on the matter would be improper.[73] Although critics complained that he was abusing the press conference format, he chose to make a plausible defense for his silence rather than hiding under a blanket of national security or executive privilege. Unlike Nixon, Carter, in his first two years made himself most accessible. Although his predecessor gave two more addresses to the nation in his first two years than Carter did, Carter held a press conference once every two and a half weeks whereas Nixon called a conference only once every two months.

By being more accessible and visible, the respectful-deferential presidents helped to keep national issues in the public eye because the president was constantly being asked about them. The only danger of regular presidential television might be that familiarity breeds contempt. In other words, the public might get tired of seeing a president day after day and thus pay no attention to his information and message.

# PRESIDENTIAL CHANNELS
# OF COMMUNICATION

Few presidents have gone so far as to wear out their welcome in the living rooms of the American electorate. Presidents continue to be prime copy for news people. For this reason, members of the press corps can be compromised into providing "good" copy in return for "inside" information. Press secretaries, staffers, and presidents themselves have become expert at using regular briefings, press conferences, media happenings, and selective leaks to whet the appetites of reporters drooling for some juicy tidbits.

## THE REGULAR
## PRESS BRIEFING

Most of the daily news about the White House that the press corps reports is supplied in regular briefings. However, press secretaries can bore correspondents with trivia and propaganda if they think it necessary. The more troublesome a particular day's briefing is likely to be, the more artful a dodger the press secretary becomes. Sometimes he will resort to the "squeeze play." To do this he simply delays starting the press conference long enough so that the press won't have time enough to summarize events, to get to a telephone, and to get the information to the wire services before noon. According to Jim McManus, a White House correspondent for the Westinghouse group now with CBS, "briefings must end by 11:45 A.M. if the information is to reach evening newspaper pages of one-edition daily papers; otherwise there isn't time enough to get the type set." Evidently, Nixon's press secretary was a master of the squeeze play. If he suspected sticky Watergate-related questions, he adopted a number of diversionary tactics to go along with the stall. He would move away from a controversial subject to one that was sure to get the press corps to frantic jotting. An especially effective diversionary tactic was shifting from the difficult question to a travel schedule for the administration's "superstar" Dr. Henry Kissinger. His comings and goings were invariably front-page news from Syracuse to St. Joe to Santa Barbara.[74]

An adept press secretary could further disarm correspondents by setting ground rules for questions during certain special briefings. Timothy Crouse explained that Ron Ziegler (Nixon's press secretary) might bring in someone like John Erlichman and then inform the assembled writers that questions are to be kept to only a limited area. One disgruntled White House press old-timer groused, "If any governor tried that, he'd be laughed out of office . . . but a lot of these guys are caught up in respect for the White House so they follow the stupid ground rules." Ziegler evidently reveled in toying with journalists. In response to a question about "dirty-trickster" Donald Segretti who had worked for the Committee to Re-elect the President, Ziegler shadow boxed quite a while before finally saying that Segretti had never been a White House employee. When the press secretary was asked why he just didn't say that in the first place, he double-talked that he had been "making a case" and that he "wasn't going to dignify the question with a comment." In fact, he was mocking the White House press and proved it by commenting, "you can't have the news funneled to you." [75] No doubt Richard Nixon would have enjoyed Ziegler's one-upmanship, but it did little to enhance the administration's standing with the press.

## PRESS CONFERENCES

While daily briefings are a fairly recent practice, the first press conferences can be traced as far back as Theodore Roosevelt's administration. A decade later, Woodrow Wilson transformed this Washington inquisition into a regular custom. Franklin Roosevelt and John Kennedy were peerless practitioners of the art. Live press conferences, a Kennedy innovation, proved to be his public relations forte. His youthful vigor, charisma, remarkable memory for details, and ability to fend off menacing questions with a raised eyebrow and crisp witticism helped him to amass plenty of political capital from these close encounters with the fourth estate. Kennedy appeared totally at ease in press conferences, probably because he spent hours preparing for them. Press Secretary Pierre Salinger and his staff mingled with the Washington media persons hoping to get wind of potential questions. On the morning of the conference Salinger cleared the president's schedule so that he and his staff could "prep" Kennedy on possible questions and feed and then quiz him on the data appropriate to suspected issues that might arise in the session. [76]

After the Kennedy years, the press conference began to fade in importance. [77] During the Johnson administration questions became progressively more pointed and almost accusatory. The president retaliated by refusing to call on "uncooperative" reporters. These mavericks who had the audacity to craft their questions to cut off every escape route for Johnson were seated on the fringes of the conference room and the president treated them as if they did not even exist. Since Johnson was determined not to be snared in any of these traps, he gradually found it in his best interest to use the press conference only very infrequently. He kept himself in the public eye with televised speeches, bill signings, and other more structured formats.

During the Nixon years, the press conference almost disappeared. Throughout his political career, there had been no love lost for the press corps on his part. For obvious reasons, his aversion for the press conference format became more acute as the Watergate cover-up began to unravel. His successors, Presidents Ford and Carter, found the atmosphere of the press conference much more congenial than Nixon had. Both called them regularly in an effort to live up to their early promises of openness and candor. Nevertheless, Carter found the Washington press corps obsession with personalities around the president exasperating. He quickly tired of questions about Bert Lance's finances, Andrew Young's sometimes undiplomatic remarks, brother Billy's antics, and his son Chip's marital difficulties. Although he did not cut back on using the press conference as a format, he hoped to get more issue-oriented questions by moving some of the press conferences out of Washington periodically.

Presidents who know how to use the press conference well possess a valuable communications tool. Opening statements can set the tone for the entire conference. Answers can be as long or as short as a president wants. If he'd rather skirt a thorny question, he can hit and run, not permitting a follow-up question. Friendly questions might be planted and can be answered with drawn-out replies.[78] Since conferences rarely last beyond thirty minutes, presidential responses must often be quick fire. If he fields questions smoothly and answers them thoroughly, he may impress voters with his grasp of a broad range of national and international issues.

### MEDIA HAPPENINGS

Some presidents simply do not project well in the question-answer format of press conferences. For these there are a number of other avenues of TV access in which they may have more direct contact with the voter without the intervention of commentators and reporters. One of these alternatives to which Richard Nixon resorted extensively was the formal address from the Oval Office during prime-time TV hours. Richard Reeves calculated that during Nixon's first one and a half years in office, he logged more television time than Johnson, Kennedy, and Eisenhower combined in a comparable period in their administrations.[79] As we noted earlier, these addresses from the Oval Office or to groups around the country do not get the coverage they once did before the Nixon-Ford years (see Table 9.3). Often, the content of an address or report can be sufficiently bland as to discourage commercial networks from airing it. Nixon found addresses from the Oval Office as the only "safe" way of communicating with the public about Watergate. In addresses from the Oval Office, he tried to convince the public that he was not a "crook" by piling a stack of typed transcripts of the Watergate tapes on his desk as he spoke with the U.S. flag to one side and a picture of Abraham Lincoln in the backdrop.

Presidents tailored these special events to their needs and to their personalities. Franklin Roosevelt's strikingly effective radio fireside chats and Jimmy Carter's

### TABLE 9.3
#### FREQUENCY OF PRESIDENTIAL PRESS CONFERENCES

| PRESIDENT | NUMBER OF CONFERENCES | NUMBER OF YEARS SURVEYED |
|---|---|---|
| FDR | 988 | 12 |
| Truman | 322 | 8 |
| JFK | 64 | 3 |
| LBJ | 126 | 5 |
| Nixon | 37 | 5½ |
| Ford | 35 | 2 |
| Carter | 41 | 2* |

Source: William Mullen, *Presidential Power and Politics* (New York: St. Martin's Press, 1976), p. 133, and Robert Locander, "Carter and the Press: The First Two Years," *Presidential Studies Quarterly*, (Spring 1979), p. 106.

*First two: 1977 and 1978.

cardigan-sweatered attempt to copy the format were both aimed at creating a personal and reassuring touch in contacts between the president and the public. Presidential public relations specialist Barry Jagoda helped Jimmy Carter add some interesting wrinkles to his media contacts. In the spring of 1977, Carter presided over town hall meetings in Clinton, Massachusetts and Yazoo City, Mississippi. Prior to those meetings he participated in a radio open-line program permitting the public to call in questions. Only 42 callers got through out of an estimated 9.5 million who tried to participate in the "Jimmy and Walter show" (Walter being CBS anchorperson Walter Cronkite). Throughout his quest for the White House, Carter had stressed that he was not "a lawyer, a liar, or a Washington insider." These innovative contacts with the voters were aimed at demonstrating his determination to retain his contacts with the public.[80]

## LEAKS, TRIAL BALLOONS, AND OTHER INTRIGUES

In politics, the grapevine often carries messages more efficiently than do telephone wires, satellites, or telegraph lines. Presidents find that selective leaking of information to the press can be useful when it is planned but devastating if a staffer tells all without authorization.

Since reporters live to break big stories, a president can purposely let out the word about a decision such as an appointment for a federal position to test public, press, and Senate response to a certain candidate. If too many thumbs are pointed down at the suggestion, he can then disavow any knowledge of how the "rumor" got started. As we noted in Chapter 7 on the president and the courts, Richard Nixon used this technique in testing out possible Supreme Court nominees before nominating William Rehnquist and Louis Powell. He could gauge the popularity of a potential policy initiative by floating it as a trial balloon. Should the idea receive rave reviews, the president could then claim it for his own. Conversely, he could deny any knowledge of the "harebrained idea" when press, congressional, and public reactions were something less than enthusiastic. Usually trial balloons are floated by "a White House official" or a "high White House source" who provides the information to a small number of reporters in "for background only briefings" commonly called backgrounders. Nixon's National Security Assistant Henry Kissinger was prone to using backgrounders. In December 1971 Dr. Kissinger was briefing five reporters who represented another eighty-eight newspeople. He asked the reporters to identify him merely as a White House official. The *Washington Post* refused to participate in the charade, arguing that[81]

> almost one hundred newspaper reporters knew who was speaking; the Russians knew, and also the Indians, and before the night was out anybody in town with the slightest interest in the question would know, so why not the readers of the *Post*? . . . Is this a game a newspaper ought to be playing? The *Post* answered no, and its managing editor vowed publicly "to get this newspaper once and for all out of the business of distributing the party line of any official of any government without identifying that official and that government."

Authorized leaks and trial balloons serve a useful purpose for an administration, but unauthorized leaks can be damaging to its credibility because the secrecy of its communications is compromised. Foreign governments will shy away from sensitive negotiations for fear that every detail of a compromise position may be splashed on the front pages of *The New York Times* or the *Washington Post*. Leaks damage an administration in other ways such as (1) showing disagreements within the administration on a policy and thus encouraging the policy's opponents, (2) foreclosing on the element of surprise when it is necessary for the effectiveness of a policy like a wage-price freeze, and (3) painting an administration into a corner on a subject it would prefer to delay acting on.

Few leaks of information were more devastating to the reputation of an administration than Daniel Ellsberg's decision to provide *The New York Times* with documents on the planning of the war in Vietnam (*Pentagon Papers*). Richard Nixon, president at the time when the documents surfaced, decided to go to court to stop publication. His decision was hardly based on a fondness for Lyndon Johnson or John Kennedy. Nixon didn't want leaking to become a habit rewarded by public adulation. He once told some of his staffers,[82]

> You're not impressing them [the press], you know, when you leak a story. They're using you and they only have contempt for leakers. They'll flatter you and invite you to all the parties in Georgetown, but they know who is weak and who is not.

While most presidents had to struggle with unauthorized leaks, few went to greater pains to plug them. In response to Ellsberg's leaking of the *Pentagon Papers,* a special unit called the Plumbers (for obvious reasons) broke into the office of Ellsberg's psychiatrist seeking to use the confidential files to discredit him. Breaking and entering was justified under "national security" because Ellsberg worked for the Pentagon and had compromised classified documents. Suspected leakers within the White House, like William Safire and Kissinger aide Dr. Morton Halperin, among others, had their phones bugged to determine whether they were supplying information to the press. In the Ford years known leakers such as Daniel Schorr of CBS news who transmitted the Pike papers on CIA covert activities to the *Village Voice* in 1976 became the target of IRS investigations of their tax returns. Schorr eventually left CBS. The totalitarian drift in the Nixon-Ford approach to dealing with leaks points up a basic problem with the public's need to know and national security. Traditionally, the public has been willing to permit a president substantial latitude in determining how national security shall be defined and how it shall be protected. In one of the classic dilemmas of modern democracy and presidential leadership, Nixon argued that the end justified the means. Horrible ethics, no doubt, but to many, acceptable politics.

## CRAFTING NEWS STORIES

An effective press staff can boost a president's stock with the voters and divert attention away from potentially damaging copy by timing White House activities to compete for space with other news. The Johnson White House, for example, synchronized a series of happenings to coincide with a major anti-Vietnam policy speech by Senator Robert Kennedy. The very day of the Kennedy speech Johnson suddenly called an unscheduled press conference, announced breakthroughs on arms control negotiations with the Soviets, and delivered a major civil rights address at Howard University. As William Small, later to become president of NBC news, noted in his 1972 book, there was little space left for Kennedy.[83]

When a president's political fortunes are at a low ebb, nothing gives him a more potent political shot in the arm than a well-orchestrated trip to a major world capital overseas.[84] Few have been planned more elaborately than Richard Nixon's preelection 1972 expeditions to the Soviet Union and China. The journey to Peking was a media event of historic importance since Nixon, who probably viewed himself as a latter-day Marco Polo, was the first American president to set foot on the Chinese mainland since Mao drove Chiang and the Nationalists to Taiwan in 1949. President Nixon and his "Madison Avenue" staff pulled out all the stops to capitalize on the occasion. No detail was overlooked that would improve press coverage. Even the president's return to Andrews Air Force Base was planned for prime time by arranging for a nine-hour layover in Anchorage, Alaska. Aides gave the transparent explanation that Nixon wanted a chance to recover from jet lag. In summing up the trip, one White House staffer gushed, "The China trip was Bob Haldeman's masterpiece, his Sistine Chapel."[85]

Most presidents are at their public relations best when dealing with foreign heads of state. Jimmy Carter's 1978 summit at Camp David with Egyptian President Sadat and Israeli Prime Minister Begin raised the president's political stock in the polls. On these occasions, the White House can use the press to put the president's best foot forward, and a healthy, albeit short, jump in public support will be forthcoming.

## PRESS RESPONSES: TECHNIQUES FOR DEALING WITH THE WHITE HOUSE

Although a president usually has the upper hand in his dealings with the press, since he has something of a monopoly of information, the press does have its ways of dealing with difficult presidents. In the years since Vietnam and Watergate especially, presidents have normally been tight lipped with the press. As a result, members of the press corps have tried to get information other than what the press secretary spoons out to them. There are a number of ways an enterprising reporter can extract information from the White House whether the president likes it or not. First, a reporter can take advantage of past contacts with people now on the president's staff, or the reporter can cultivate new friendships just by becoming familiar with aides by meeting them on a regular basis around the White House or in the social environment of Washington. If one of these officials wants a reporter to circulate a particular story or ventilate a particular issue, he often must promise that reporter some tasty tidbit in return. Insights into administration squabbles are often conveyed in this manner, and they can lead to even larger stories with careful investigative reporting. We noted earlier that a reporter can also keep the White House on its toes by carefully combing already circulating documents and stories to pinpoint inconsistencies between the stated White House position and on-the-record statements that might contradict it. Journalists may also use public opinion to pry information out of a reluctant White House staffer. During press conferences a reporter could ask why certain information was not available to the press. The television audience would undoubtedly wonder what the president was trying to hide. Newspaper editorials could be used to question White House secrecy, and congressional investigating committees might be approached to examine the issue including subpoena of the controversial documents. In many respects, this is the way the press helped to get Congress into the Watergate investigation.[86]

## ISSUES REPORTING
## AND IMAGE MANAGEMENT

The images that the media convey about an issue can buttress or destroy a president's policy on that subject. Coverage of Vietnam presents a classic example of this phenomenon. Public support for the conflict in Southeast Asia, which had been relatively strong early in the Johnson administration, faded badly as the nightly news reports began to project the brutalities of the war into American homes via television.

WHAT TO REPORT. Reports of women and children being massacred by U.S. soldiers at My Lai Four and accounts of vicious tactics being used by our South Vietnamese allies exploded the myth that Americans and their allies were above such behavior. After Walter Cronkite publicly announced that in his judgment the war could not be won, journalist David Halberstam contends that Lyndon Johnson decided to abandon the effort. While the Constitution had not imagined it, Halberstam said that "It was the first time in American history that a war had been declared over by an anchorman."[87]

Television's massive audience makes it the perfect vehicle for interest groups to use in getting their opposition to a White House policy out to the public if the networks will go along. Anti-Vietnam groups, for example, without spending a dime, used demonstrations at colleges, in churches, on the mall of the Washington monument, and even on Wall Street to raise national consciousness and eventually reverse Johnson's war policies in Southeast Asia. Special prime-time documentaries and popular news magazines of the air like "60 Minutes" (CBS), "20/20" (ABC) and "Nightline" have such broad appeal because they act as muckrakers in the best sense of the word. Well-constructed documentaries can goad an administration into acting on a problem unearthed by the network staff. Network documentaries on chemical waste dumps brought the matter to the attention of both the public and President Carter. One dump (from the Hooker Chemical Company) in the Love Canal area of upper New York State was given extensive coverage due to high incidences of cancer, leukemia, and birth defects among children born in the area. Environmental Protection Agency (EPA) investigators were detailed to the area to research the possible health hazards. For a short time, members of a neighborhood association held two people from EPA hostage demanding some prompt presidential action to aid the alleged victims of Hooker's negligence. Not long after the hostages were released, the president announced that the region would be declared a disaster area so that federal funds could be used to help in the temporary relocation of persons still living near the dump site.[88] Without television investigation and reporting of their plight, the White House could easily have overlooked the matter and let the bureaucracy follow painfully slow standard operating procedures.

HEADLINES. If recent history is any indicator, the image a president projects may be more important for his political future than any positions he takes on issues. Unfortunately for him, he is not the master of his own destiny in this regard. It is the writers or commentators and not the White House staffers who are the ultimate architects of a president's public image. The language journalists use to describe a particular president may be sprinkled with loaded words calculated to leave a generally favorable or negative impression. In a 1965 study of *Time* magazine's coverage of Presidents Truman, Eisenhower, and Kennedy, John C. Merrill searched in vain for neutral reporting. His data indicated that *Time* was heavily biased toward Republicans.[89] Using the same method of research Fedler, Meeske, and Hall looked into coverage of Presidents Johnson, Nixon (pre- and post-Watergate), Ford, and Carter. Both studies noted *Time's* ability to leave the impressions it wanted while feigning neutrality. Fedler (and the others) described bias as "any expression or variance from neutrality." *Time* habitually used headlines and subheadings to hammer home its point. This technique of labeling can be highly effective since so many people who say they have read a newspaper have merely skimmed the headlines. One article entitled "Carter's Dog Day Afternoons," with a subheading "As the President Confronts Some Tough Problems Criticism Grows," makes *Time's* view of Mr. Carter quite evident.

LABELING BY ASSOCIATION. Labeling by association was another effective technique employed by *Time* to shape a president's public image. *Time* suggested after the Watergate story broke that Richard Nixon had lost his credibility not for anything he had done but because his claim of innocence sounded hollow since his top aides were caught in a web of lies. Likewise Jimmy Carter's reputation was besmirched not because his own finances were questionable but because his friend Bert Lance was involved in making loans while he was president of the First National Bank of Calhoun, Georgia that were on the fringes of accepted banking ethics and practices.

ADJECTIVE AND ADVERB BIAS. Carter was also the target of what Fedler (and the others) called adjective and adverb bias. *Time* used a number of negatives in discussions of Carter administration policies. His approach on human rights was "grapeshot." His "missionary" foreign policy was considered "unsuitable." *Time* also used adjectives to stereotype the personality of the man in the White House. Lyndon Johnson was "demanding and difficult." Prior to Watergate, Richard Nixon was "strong, skillful and cool at his job." Later, he became "haggard, weary, grim and nervous." A carefully chosen photograph properly captioned and well placed in the newspaper can help to either improve or erode a president's popularity. A biting cartoon can have a similar effect. Such labeling and stereotyping enables journalists not only to gain the voter's attention with creative language, but they also permit the media to use that ingenuity to mold the views of their audiences.[90]

## FUTURE RELATIONS:
## THE PRESIDENT AND PRESS

The legacy of lies that surrounded Vietnam and Watergate is often blamed for the intense adversary relationship that has existed between the White House and the press corps since. In a public broadcast interview with Martin Agronsky, Jimmy Carter's press secretary, Jody Powell, was hardly optimistic as he commented, "I think the honeymoons with the president are over. . . . The basic relationship . . . has changed over the past decade. It will never be what it was."[91] While things have changed over the last few decades, many of the patterns of presidential press interaction have remained much the same.

Today, as always, the president is news, and he realizes the power in that reality. He will continue to use the media, especially television, to remind the electorate that he alone is the representative of all of the people. Even the shock of Watergate did not totally sever the ties between the public and their president. Because he is news, a president can try to monopolize the air waves; but his exalted media position creates serious difficulties for democracy. We expect our presidents to be superstars like the other media personalities on television. There is no place on prime time for a president who lacks the self-confidence necessary to promise solutions rather than solace in the midst of our nation's economic woes. Since the decade of the 1960s it has become increasingly evident that a president's charisma rather than the content of his policies sells him to the press and the voters. Nevertheless, like any superstar, presidents are expected to be miracle workers. The danger always exists that a president might begin to believe his own propaganda that he can in fact work miracles. The temptation to manipulate the press to leave the impression that all is well is almost irresistible. Vigilant journalists should be able to "blow the whistle" on failures and abuses of power at the White House. Further, they can goad Congress or the courts into action by raising the consciousness of the public. Efforts by the *Washington Post* to get to the bottom of the Watergate scandal serve as a perfect case in point.

More than the lies involved in Vietnam and Watergate, however, the relationship between presidents and the press has been altered radically through the increase of specialized media persons on the White House staff. Franklin Roosevelt borrowed speechwriters from the agencies, had no public relations personnel, and was without the guidance of "in-house" pollsters to chart his relations with both the press and the public. Today, no reasonably intelligent president could survive without his press relations staff, public relations people, gag writer, news digest operation, and so forth. The more specialized the White House media operations, the easier it becomes for the president to learn how to deal effectively if not cordially with the press. While the staff enhances the president's leadership potential immensely, it tends to serve as a buffer that isolates him from reporters and the public as a whole.

Recent experiences seem to indicate that presidents who divorce themselves from frequent press contact are more likely to become vindictive with journalists who criticize them. Although future presidents will still have the FBI and IRS at their disposal to cower their adversaries, it is unlikely that intelligent presidents will regularly resort to the kind of "hardball" tactics that became notorious during the Nixon years. Proposed charters for the CIA and FBI could serve the purpose of foreclosing those options too. "Hardball" tactics when they become public knowledge can boomerang on the president who resorts to them.

Sparring between the White House and the press corps, however, is a healthy thing for a democracy. When this sparring deteriorates into a test of wills and a fight for preeminence in the public mind, then legitimate presidential leadership can be endangered and public respect for journalists can wane. Post-Watergate press hostility has developed a sort of criticism-for-the-sake-of-criticism style of reporting. What an unpopular president does wrong is news while what he may do right is filler for the back pages. These comments are not meant to suggest that the president should be able to tuck the press in his hip pocket. No more perfect recipe for despotism could be devised. The American press corps is one of the most professional and independent in the world today, and it has a duty to rake muck where there is muck to rake. Still, emphasis on destructive rather than constructive criticism may gradually erode public confidence not just in politicians like the president but in the political process itself. If chiseling away at presidential power without regard to the legitimate need for him to exercise it continues unabated, public respect for his unique position under the constitution could be badly shaken. At present, no other set of existing political institutions seems capable of filling that leadership role as effectively.

# NOTES

[1] David S. Broder, "The Presidency and the Press," in *The Future of the American Presidency*, ed. Charles W. Dunn (Morristown, N.J.: General Learning Press, 1975), p. 258.

[2] Tom Wicker, "The Power of the Press? It's a Long Way from Absolute," in *Annual Editions American Government, 1980-81*, ed. Bruce Stinebrickner, Sluice Dock (Guilford, Conn.: Dushkin, 1980), pp. 220-221.

[3] William P. Cheshire, "The Imperial Press," *National Review*, August 17, 1979, in *Annual Editions American Government*, p. 219.

[4] Doris Graeber, *Mass Media and American Politics* (Washington, D.C.: Congressional Quarterly Press, 1980), pp. 195-196.

[5] Philippa Strum, *Presidential Power and American Democracy*, 2nd ed. (Santa Monica, Calif.: Goodyear, 1979), p. 119.

[6] Arthur Schlesinger, Jr., *The Imperial Presidency* (Boston: Houghton Mifflin, 1973), p. 214.

[7] *Ibid.*, p. 214.

[8] Strum, *op. cit.*, p. 121.

[9] Broder, *op. cit.*, p. 257.

[10] Theodore Sorensen, *The Watchmen in the Night* (Cambridge, Mass.: M.I.T. Press, 1976), pp. 64-65.

[11] Peter Ferbath and Carey Winfrey, *The Adversaries: The President and the Press* (Brunswick, Ohio: King's Court, 1974), p. 5.

[12] William Safire, *Before the Fall* (Garden City, N.Y.: Doubleday, 1975), p. 341.

[13] For a more thorough discussion of the front-runner phenomenon, see Chapter 4.

[14] Terry F. Buss and C. Richard Hofsetter, "The President and the News Media," in *The Presidency: Studies in Policy Making*, eds. Stevel Shull and Lance LeLoup (Brunswick, Ohio: King's Court, 1979), p. 20.

[15] As cited in Robert J. Sickels, *The Presidency: An Introduction* (Englewood Cliffs, N.J.: Prentice-Hall, 1980), p. 33.

[16] William Mullen, *Presidential Power and Politics* (New York: St. Martin's Press, 1976), p. 139.

[17] This is the thesis of Michael Baruch Grossman and Francis E. Rourke, "The Media and the Presidency: An Exchange Analysis," *Political Science Quarterly*, (Fall 1976), 455-470.

[18] Philip Geylin and Douglass Cater, *American Media: Adequate or Not?* (Washington, D.C.: American Enterprises Institute, 1970), p. 5.

[19] Charles Kadushkin, "Who Are the Elite Intellectuals?" *Public Interest*, (Fall 1972), 109-114.

[20] *Ayer's Directory of Publications* (Philadelphia: Ayer Press, 1980), as cited in Milton Cummings and David Wise, *Democracy Under Pressure*, 4th ed. (New York: Harcourt Brace, 1981), p. 199.

[21] Stephen Wayne, *The Road to the White House* (New York: St. Martin's Press, 1980), p. 121.

[22] Safire, *op. cit.*, p. 186.

[23] Richard Hofsetter, *Bias in the News* (Columbus: Ohio State U.P., 1976), p. 202.

[24] Thomas E. Patterson and Robert McClure, *The Unseeing Eye: The Myth of Television Power in National Elections* (New York: Putnam, 1976), p. 31.

[25] For more on Moynihan's views in this regard, see Daniel P. Moynihan, *Coping: On the Practice of Government* (New York: Random House, 1971).

[26] Kevin Phillips, "Beating the Media Trusts," *Harper's,* July 1977, pp. 23-24.

[27] Schlesinger, *op. cit.,* p. 233. See also Robert M. Kaus, "The Constitution, the Press and the Rest of the United States," *Washington Monthly,* (November 1978), p. 55.

[28] David S. Broder, "Political Reporters in Presidential Politics," as excerpted in James I. Lengle and Byron I. Shafer, *Presidential Politics: Readings on Nominations and Elections* (New York: St. Martin's Press, 1980), p. 497.

[29] Richard Neustadt makes this point in his *Presidential Power: The Politics of Leadership from FDR to Carter* (New York: John Wiley, 1980), p. 47.

[30] This comment is based on author's experiences in 1974 and 1975 participating in week-long and day-long conferences of professors related to foreign policy at the U.S. Department of State, Washington, D.C., March 1975 and June 1975.

[31] Theodore White, *The Making of the President, 1972* (New York: Atheneum, 1972), p. 270.

[32] Thomas Cronin, *The State of the Presidency,* 2nd ed. (Boston: Little, Brown, 1980), p. 108.

[33] Joseph Califano, *A Presidential Nation* (New York: W. W. Norton, 1975), p. 116.

[34] Timothy Crouse, *Boys on the Bus* (New York: Random House, 1973), p. 207.

[35] *Ibid.,* p. 210.

[36] Marian Irish and Elke Frank, *U.S. Foreign Policy, Context, Conduct, Content* (New York: Harcourt Brace, 1975), pp. 16-19.

[37] Grossman and Rourke, *op. cit.,* p. 467.

[38] *Ibid.,* p. 463.

[39] Robert Sherrill, *Why They Call It Politics,* 3rd ed. (New York: Harcourt Brace, 1980), p. 282.

[40] Crouse, *op. cit.,* p. 233.

[41] For Colson's comments, see U.S. Congress, Senate, Select Committee on Presidential Campaign Activities, Report, 93rd Cong., 2nd sess., June 1974, pp. 281-283.

[42] Kandy Stroud, *How Jimmy Won* (New York: William Morrow, 1977), p. 202.

[43] Michael Baruch Grossman and Martha Joynt Kumar, "The White House and the News Media: The Phases of their Relationship," *Political Science Quarterly,* (Spring 1979), 41.

[44] Stephen Wayne, *The Road to the White House* (New York: St. Martin's Press, 1980), p. 213.

[45] Joe McGinnis, *The Selling of the President, 1968* (New York: Simon & Schuster, 1969), p. 103.

[46] *Ibid.,* p. 103.

[47] Robert Locander, "Carter and the Press: The First Two Years," *Presidential Studies Quarterly,* (Spring 1979), 106.

[48] Grossman and Kumar, *op. cit.,* pp. 40-51.

[49] Locander, *op. cit.,* p. 116.

[50] Patrick Anderson, *The President's Men* (Garden City, N.Y.: Doubleday, 1969), p. 217.

[51] Dwight D. Eisenhower, *Mandates for Change,* 1953-56 (New York: Doubleday & Company, Inc., 1963), p. 151.

[52] James McGregor Burns, *Presidential Government: Crucible for Leadership* (Boston: Houghton Mifflin, 1965), p. 199.

[53] Harry S. Truman, *Years of Trial and Hope, 1946-1952* (New York: Doubleday & Company, Inc., 1956), p. 41.

[54] Strumm, *op. cit.,* p. 127.

[55] Louis Koenig, *The Chief Executive,* 3rd ed. (New York: Harcourt Brace, 1975), p. 108.

[56] Cronin, *op. cit.,* pp. 96-97.

[57] Theodore White, *Making of a President, 1968* (New York: Atheneum, 1968), p. 125.

58 McGinnis, *op. cit.,* p. 30.

59 White, *Making of a President, 1968,* p. 125.

60 William Small, *Political Power and the Press* (New York: W. W. Norton, 1972), p. 119.

61 Safire, *op. cit.,* p. 342.

62 Magruder memo cited in Mullen, *op. cit.,* pp. 136-137.

63 Sickels, *op. cit.,* p. 32.

64 Mullen, *op. cit.,* p. 135.

65 *Ibid.,* p. 136.

66 *The New York Times,* May 1, 1971, as cited in Cronin, *op. cit.,* p. 111.

67 Sickels, *op. cit.,* p. 33.

68 *Ibid.,* p. 35.

69 Mullen, *op. cit.,* p. 138; on the hearing, see Sorensen, *op. cit.,* p. 64.

70 Mullen, *op. cit.,* p. 139.

71 *Ibid.*

72 Locander, *op. cit.,* p. 113.

73 Cronin, *op. cit.,* p. 98.

74 On the squeeze play, see Crouse, *op. cit.,* p. 212.

75 *Ibid.,* p. 213.

76 See Pierre Salinger, *With Kennedy* (Garden City, N.Y.: Doubleday, 1966),

77 William Lammars, *Presidential Politics* (New York: Harper & Row, 1976), p. 189.

78 *Ibid.,* pp. 189-190.

79 Richard Reeves, "The Prime Time President," *New York Times* magazine, May 15, 1977, p. 18.

80 Locander, *op. cit.,* p. 115.

81 Sherrill, *op. cit.,* p. 286.

82 Safire, *op. cit.,* p. 295.

83 Small, *op. cit.,* p. 114.

84 See Chapter 1 of this study on "summitry."

85 Dan Rather and Gary P. Gates, *The Palace Guard* (New York: Harper & Row, 1975), p. 287.

86 These three examples are in Grossman and O'Rourke, *op. cit.,* p. 463.

87 David Halberstam, *The Powers That Be* (New York: Knopf, 1979), p. 6.

88 *Christian Science Monitor,* May 15, 1980.

89 John C. Merrill, "How *Time* Stereotyped Three U.S. Presidents," *Journalism Quarterly,* (August 1965), 563-570.

90 These techniques are examined in Fred Fedler, Mike Meeske, and Joe Hall, "*Time* Magazine Revisited: Presidential Stereotypes Persist," *Journalism Quarterly,* (Summer 1979), 353-359.

91 Grossman and Kumar, *op. cit.,* p. 37.

PART

# 4

# CHOOSING
# AND
# DISPOSING
# OF PRESIDENTS

# The Keys to the Kingdom: How to Get the Top White House Job

Gone are the days when the delegates at a nominating convention could point to a George Washington as the "obvious choice" for president. The field of contenders has widened considerably since then. In 1976, for example, on the Democratic side alone, at least fifteen candidates were vying for their party's nomination, either actively or through groups serving as stalking horses for them. Even the incumbent president, who is normally a shoo-in for his party's nomination, found himself less than the "obvious choice" of faithful Republicans, who evidently viewed the nomination as a toss-up between President Ford and former Governor Ronald Reagan. Among the party hopefuls who suited up for the 1976 presidential "marathon" were persons representing almost every shade of political philosophy and interest. By 1980 the cast of characters had expanded in the Republican camp, among them Ronald Reagan; a younger version of Reagan, Representative Philip Crane; an unreconstructed conservative, John Anderson; former secretary of the treasury and erstwhile Democrat John Connally; and former CIA director and "liberal" Republican from Connecticut via Texas, George Bush. Also in the field was a Senate Watergate Committee member Howard Baker from Tennessee, and rumors were rife throughout the primary season 1980 that former President Gerald Ford was soon to throw his hat into the ring. That "Who's Who" of the Republican Party represented a broad spectrum of political philosophies and regional affiliations.

The lists of candidate during the 1970s and in 1980 demonstrated that the factions which George Washington had warned against in his Farewell Address to the nation were a political way of life. His contemporary, James Madison, on the other hand saw both the inevitability and the value in conflict and compromise among groups in the government process. He saw the "spirit of party and faction"[1] as necessary and ordinary in the day-to-day operation of government.

In short, it is becoming increasingly unlikely that any one person can be expected to be the "obvious choice" for president. This is due to several factors: the very existence of political parties, increasing competition for the position, and differing views on the role of government espoused throughout the nation. This chapter will look at the selection process as it affects the dreams of contenders and public desires in the race for the Oval Office. Among the questions to be addressed are (1) How do "mass" political considerations affect the selection process? (2) What types

305

of persons are usually considered presidential "timber"? (3) How are modern presidential campaigns organized? (4) What parts do the primaries and national conventions play in the selection process? (5) Have finances of modern presidential politics made the White House the residence of the rich? (6) Is the Electoral College an anachronism in a mass democracy like ours? Finally, What dilemmas for modern democracy does our selection process present?

## THE MASS PRESIDENCY: PRESIDENT OF "ALL" THE PEOPLE

The presidency of the 1980s is light-years away from the elitist-oriented chief executive that Alexander Hamilton envisioned. The *Electoral College* that he proposed to insulate his "elected king" from the whims of the undisciplined masses still remains, but it hardly serves the function he intended. He wanted the selection to be made by[2]

> a small number of persons selected by their fellow citizens from the general mass, [and that the electors] . . . will be most likely to possess the information and discernment requisite to such complicated investigations.

One could easily view the presidency today as a "mass" or people's institution. It did not seem to bother either the voters or the electors in 1976 that a peanut farmer, former state legislator, and one-term Southern governor would be seeking the coveted chair in the Oval Office. Likewise, an unknown Illinois congressman, John Anderson, vaulted into the 1980 race and eventually charted an independent candidacy.

When Jimmy Carter was elected in 1976, it was in part because of his success in constantly reminding voters that he was not a part of the Washington establishment.[3] His was a people's campaign with a "peanut brigade" of volunteers stumping door to door for the candidate who carried his own suitcase, stayed in voters' homes rather than in motels, and, unassumingly, yet confidently, introduced himself as Jimmy. How ironic in post-Watergate years that the very qualities, such as experience and contacts in government, which had previously been considered valuable assets, now became liabilities. Carter had indeed struck a responsive chord with the public, even though the media political analysts showed little early recognition of his possibilities.[4] The Carter battle plan, with its emphasis on personal contacts with the voters and ties within the party, clearly confounded the experts who expected Humphrey to emerge as the victor from a "brokered" (horse trading of delegates) national convention. So much for conventional wisdom.

To the former Georgia governor's credit in 1976, he noticed, as did Republican George Bush in 1980, that capturing delegates' votes at the convention was akin to closing the barn door after the donkeys got out. He planned, as a result, for a long-range campaign. He formally announced his interest in the nomination on December 12, 1974, one month prior to the end of his term as governor. Three days later on NBC's "Meet the Press," he made it clear that he was aiming at getting the delegate support he needed *before* the New York convention.[5]

> The concept of a brokered convention is obnoxious to me . . . I don't believe that is the proper approach to take. I am going into the primaries and into

the states that select delegates by conventions with the full intention of winning a majority of these delegates before the convention. [6]

Carter and others like him who seek the presidency recognize all too quickly that the road to the White House is not the road to be trod by the weak. Among the things that can be surmised about any candidate who survives the rigors of the race is that he has at least the physical endurance, self-discipline, and vote-getting know-how to reach his goal. While each of these qualities is to be admired in candidates seeking the highest office, there is no iron-clad indication that they bear any direct relationship to the competence required to provide leadership in the impossible job of being president.

## THE PRESIDENTIAL BREED

What manner of man does our "mass presidency" of the late twentieth century demand? Can the requisite energy, discipline, and administrative and leadership ability be found in any mortal? Could this same superman understand the role of the common person in a democracy such as ours? Was Andrew Jackson right in supposing that any citizen should be able to be president? Surely, "Old Hickory" didn't expect the inexperienced to be capable of administering a budget of well over half a trillion dollars and a national government of 2.8 million employees, armed services of 2.2 million, and a population of over 215 million persons. [7]

AVAILABILITY.  There is a rather curious term used in American politics to describe the personal, social, and political characteristics that the parties seek in their presidential nominees. If an individual measures up, he is considered "available." [8]

Every red-blooded American views himself or herself as presidential material. The bare constitutional requirements do little to discourage those grandiose dreams. To be eligible for the office, via election or otherwise, a person must be at least thirty-five years of age, a natural-born citizen of the United States, and a fourteen-year resident of the United States. [9] This last requirement disqualified people like Henry Kissinger (German-born) and S. I. Hayakawa (Canadian-born). Even though the Constitution does little to narrow the field of contenders for the parties, certain backgrounds have been considered necessary, though not formally stated, for potential nominees. The composite candidate would possess some or all of the following basic prerequisites: *He* would be a white male from a large-population state, a Protestant, of forty to fifty-odd years of age, and a decisive leadership type with some record of success in government or similar credentials.

LARGE-POPULATION STATE.  Not all those valued characteristics of the typical nominee have survived intact to the present, but state size is still a consideration. The nomination of a person from a large-population state seems likely to remain important, if not vital, as long as the Electoral College weighted system of voting continues. A candidate from a large-population state should be expected to carry his own state and states like it. Victories in the ten largest electoral vote states today would leave a candidate a mere eleven votes short of a majority in the Electoral College. [10] From 1896-1976, only five of the persons originally nominated by a party convention came from the smaller (seven electoral votes or less) states. None of the five—Landon of Kansas, Davis of West Virginia, Bryan of Nebraska, Goldwater of Arizona, or McGovern of South Dakota—emerged victorious in the November elections.[11] The nomination by the Democrats in 1976 was not much of a deviation from that pattern since Jimmy Carter's Georgia would have close to the large group with twelve electoral votes.

AGE AND RELIGIOUS FACTORS. The importance of age and religion seems to be fading for future elections. As the population itself ages and as longevity becomes a possibility for more persons because of medical technology, hopefuls will likely be required to prove merely that they are in sufficiently robust health to survive the rigors of the election grind. In election 1980, for example, Ronald Reagan's age did not inhibit the Republicans from making him their standard-bearer.

The religious affiliation of potential candidates has become less important, too, at least as far as Catholic aspirants are concerned. After the Democrats' disastrous nomination of Al Smith, the Catholic governor of New York, in 1928, the party shied away from Catholic nominees until 1960 when John Kennedy surprised Hubert Humphrey in the West Virginia presidential preference primary. West Virginia,[12] in fact, is one of the most highly Protestant states in the nation. Kennedy's victory in November, slim though the margin may have been, seemed to lay to rest the "Catholic issue." Since Catholic voters represent a major segment of the Democratic coalition and a growing percentage of the population, they are likely to be seen as possibilities for either the top or number two spots on the party ticket. Religious ticket balancing will continue to be a major consideration of Democratic candidates especially since the Republicans have been making efforts to disengage the various ethnic Catholics from the Democratic coalition. George McGovern in 1972 was no doubt looking at Senator Tom Eagleton and later Mayor Kevin White of Boston and finally Kennedy-once-removed Sargent Shriver as Catholics who could help his chances for the urban ethnic Catholic vote.

OTHER SOCIAL FACTORS. Race, sex, and marital status factors have been undergoing changes in recent years. The American voter of today would be more amenable to blacks in high office than in the years prior to 1960.[13] Obviously finding a black candidate for president would still be a difficult chore partly because there are no black governors and there has been only one black senator (Edward Brooke of Massachusetts as of 1978) since Reconstruction. Shirley Chisholm, a black congresswoman from New York, make a brief and abortive run for the Democratic nomination in 1972 but had only a limited constituency of blacks and activist and left-leaning youths.[14] In 1976 another woman, Ellen McCormack, had her name placed in nomination more as a symbolic gesture than anything else. This homemaker's nomination would not have been possible but for the existence of matching funds for presidential candidates, convention rules that broadened the potential for lesser known candidates, and the fact that she represented a growing and increasingly activist segment of the population opposed to the 1973 Supreme Court decision legalizing abortion.[15] Even prior to the 1970s, marital status and considerations about divorce began to recede in importance for potential nominees. The fact that Adlai Stevenson had been divorced did not deter the Democrats from nominating the Illinois governor in 1952 and 1956. Ronald Reagan was elected in 1980 although he had been divorced from Jane Wyman, the mother of his first children and had remarried Nancy Davis, who became the First Lady.

LEADERSHIP AND DECISIVENESS AS FACTORS. American voters have clearly favored candidates promising strong leadership, especially in times of crisis. Some hopefuls who might possess the necessary administrative background or leadership potential prove to have neither the temperament nor the stomach for the race entailed in winning the office. Senator Walter Mondale pulled out of the 1976 race commenting in November 1974 that he "didn't relish the prospect of sleeping at so many Holiday Inns." As he so aptly phrased it, "I don't think anyone should be President who is not willing to go through fire."[16]

Weakness or indecisiveness is often gauged by the voters in terms of the way in which candidates react to stressful situations, whether the crises are of their own making or are the result of uncontrollable pressures. One could view the experiences of Senator Edmund Muskie during the 1972 campaign as a case in point. As Hubert Humphrey's running mate in the photofinish against Nixon in 1968, he was recognized widely as the party spokesperson and the odds-on favorite for the 1972 nomination. Even as "front-runner" he was required to undergo the U.S. ordeal by fire known as the New Hampshire primary. As the nation's first, it sets the tone for the rest of the preconvention campaigning. After an unusually furious week of campaigning in other states soon to have their own primaries, Muskie returned to New Hampshire for the homestretch there. During the last weeks of February, William Loeb's newspaper, the *Manchester Union Leader,* nationally recognized as a tabloid, began to level broadsides at Muskie's sometimes flamboyant wife Jane. The paper also painted Muskie as disrespectful of French Canadians in the area because he laughed at an attempt to slur them as "New Hampshire blacks." A combination of fatigue and anger at the time left Muskie making a public speech with tears in his eyes at the way even his wife was being vilified. The incident was recorded for the nation to see on the CBS-TV Saturday news. Muskie came across as weak and out of control. The senator from Maine later commented about the incident that "It changed people's minds about me. . . . They were looking for a strong, steady man and here I was weak."[17]

Muskie's opponent for the nomination and the eventual choice of the Democrats in 1972, George McGovern, was given to making statements and decisions that created doubts in the public mind about his judgment, decisiveness, and strength of character under pressure. Examples of indecision on McGovern's part were numerous, but his guaranteed income program and his "waffling" on the nomination of Senator Thomas Eagleton were indicative of his problem. During the campaign, his $1,000-per-year proposed grant to each American as a part of a tax reform package backfired. When it turned out that the idea would cost the federal treasury $30 billion, he had to back off. The much-reported Eagleton affair showed McGovern to be both deficient in his research before the selection of the Missouri senator and ill advised in his premature statement of 1,000 percent support for his vice-presidential choice. As Eagleton's previous medical history surfaced and as unsubstantiated stories about "drunken driving tickets" appeared in Jack Anderson's column, the senator became a liability to the ticket, and he was encouraged to resign. In each of these cases, premature decisions showed poor planning. The fact that the candidate would not admit his errors did not enhance his image as one strong enough to admit mistakes. The careful candidate avoids mistakes and flaps, but the smart one should be able to get out of them too. In April 1976, candidate Jimmy Carter, in answer to a New York *Daily News* reporter's question about the chances of survival of the black central cities surrounded by white neighbors came up with his "ethnic purity" *faux pas*. Carter said "I see nothing wrong with ethnic purity being maintained. I would not force a racial integration of a neighborhood by government action."[18] There is always a danger that candidates who shoot from the hip might hit their own feet. Carter acknowledged that he was "careless in the words" that he used much in contrast to Muskie's complaints about press coverage. The former Georgia governor recounted his record of sympathy for minorities and support that they had given him. Admitting an error immediately showed great self-confidence, and the storm blew over as quickly as it had arisen. Carter campaign strategists in 1980 hoped for a gaffe by Ronald Reagan when they agreed to a pre-election debate.

Strong, decisive, self-confident types clearly provide the leadership demanded from the modern American president, but will these types value democratic institutions enough to respect them in pressure situations? Our selection process can do very little, at present, to weed out the nondemocratic types. It may be that the best we can hope for is that emphasis on democracy in the workings of all our social institutions might sift out some of the destructive types before they seek the Oval Office.[19] Greater emphasis on democracy in the selection of leadership for Congress by doing away with the rigid seniority system and limiting the power of committee chairpersons might prepare nominees emerging from Congress for taking a more democratic view of the political process.

PRIOR EXPERIENCE. Our present haphazard process for selecting the president cannot even ensure the election of a person capable of handling the office. As one noted political analyst so aptly put it,[20]

> In our system, there is nothing to prevent a man who is absolutely incapable of being President from becoming president. He runs in the primaries, if he has money, if he has charisma, he can win the nomination and move into the Presidency as an absolutely untried character. . . . There is no way that you can assure that . . . you are always going to get men of competence and integrity.

Given the broad spectrum of responsibilities assigned to the president and the domestic, foreign, political, and administrative competencies required to do the job well, it should be obvious that there is no perfect training ground for the White House. Nevertheless, certain backgrounds have historically been recognized as valuable during the primaries and at the nominating conventions. Of the first forty occupants of the Oval Office, twenty-seven had prior experience in one or both houses of Congress. Of the thirteen exceptions, seven were governors (Cleveland, the two Roosevelts, Wilson, Coolidge, Carter, and Reagan), two others had administrative experience (Arthur and Hoover), and one (William Howard Taft) brought judicial know-how with him to the White House.[21]

GOVERNORS AND SENATORS. A quick look at Democratic and Republican hopefuls from 1976 shows governors or former governors and senators as the most numerous aspiring nominees. In 1972 ten Democratic senators, almost one fifth of the party members in the upper chamber, were either announced or considered possible nominees. Early front-runner Edmund Muskie, former vice president Hubert Humphrey, undeclared Ted Kennedy, and eventual nominee George Mc-

Govern were senatorial names prominent in the 1972 Democratic presidential sweepstakes. The Federal Election Campaign Act of 1974,[22] with its provision of matching funds, broadened the Democratic Party field even further. Still, among the most "serious" challengers, there were more senators than governors or representatives.[23]

While simple logic would show that governors, as elected executives, should be better prepared for the administrative duties of the Oval Office, senators are better prepared politically because of their national exposure in the print and broadcast media. Senator Harry S. Truman became a possible vice-presidential nominee with Franklin Roosevelt in 1944 because of his notoriety as chair of a Senate committee investigating waste in the war effort. Estes Kefauver of Tennessee became the choice of the Democrats for vice president in 1956 partly because of his daily battles with gangland figures during the telecast Senate rackets hearings. More recently, Senator Howard Baker of Tennessee was catapulted into the vice-presidential and later the presidential limelight through favorable exposure as a part of the Ervin committee investigating Watergate (Senate Select Committee on Presidential Campaign Finance).

Unlike governors, senators are not forced to grapple directly with the "no-win, no-hide" problems of writing and administering budgets that are able to both soothe irate taxpayers and please "poverty-stricken" state employees.[24] When the situation dictates, a senator can fade into the background behind ninety-nine other colleagues whereas the governor is usually perched like a sitting duck at the apex of state governmental machinery. The public normally hears about governors when they are from large states; other governors with national reputations are commonly the ones who have been under fire. Senators are also blessed with a six-year term whereas governors have a mere four years. Until recently, many states have had gubernatorial and presidential elections that coincided so that a governor seeking the White House has often had to weigh the options of a race with the real chance of sacrificing the statehouse chair if the quest for the White House falls short.[25]

Members of the Senate have the advantage of possessing at least some experience in foreign policy matters, whereas governors are usually deficient in this area. Since World War II, presidents have found themselves devoting an inordinate amount of time to international policies. Governors who do not possess readily recognized credentials in foreign affairs are often at a disadvantage to senators and must establish their credibility as internationalists by traveling overseas on "fact-finding" missions, as Governor Adlai Stevenson did in 1952 and as Governor George Romney did in 1968. Romney's attempts to prove his expertise in world affairs helped to spell the end of his presidential hopes. Upon his return from Vietnam in 1968, he made an offhanded statement on a Detroit TV show that the military and diplomatic corps had brainwashed him on Vietnam policy. It was picked up a few days later in the national press and led to severe criticism for his tendency to be swayed so easily. Even after the fallout from the brainwashing incident, Romney continued trying to prove his ability in foreign affairs, but, as Theodore White recounts, to little avail:

> He flew to Paris to polish his image as a foreign affairs expert, at least on European affairs, and fell into additional befoulment with the press as he claimed that reporters had misquoted him.[26]

Governor Jimmy Carter had acquired his international spurs in two ways. As governor of Georgia, he traveled extensively in Latin America to encourage international trade for Georgia. He also participated in the work of the Tri-Lateral Commission, a group of business, banking, and intellectual persons from the United States, West Germany, and Japan looking into the issues of international peace. It was with this group that Carter came into contact with the man he would choose to be his national security assistant, Zbigniew Brzezinski, then a professor at Columbia University.

While senators have tended to have an international relations head start on governors in the presidential sweepstakes, it has always been assumed that governors who lived not in Washington, but in the home state, had a leg up on senators when it came to using the party organization to get national convention votes. Until 1972, when national convention rules changed for the Democrats, state governors could control the pols who made up their state delegations and broker with other governors for additional support. The revised rules in both 1972 and to a degree in 1976 put women, minorities, and youth in many of the Democratic Party convention floor seats that had previously been occupied by party pros. These new convention delegates were not as easily unified into a bloc that state governors could control.

On balance, then, it would seem that senators have a better shot at being chosen as party standard-bearers than do sitting governors. This rule of thumb does not necessarily apply to ex-governors as the respective Carter and Reagan campaigns of 1976 and 1980 so graphically illustrated. Both had begun organizing their campaigns far in advance. Carter, for example, was being advised to run as early as 1971. In July of that year he discussed the matter with Dr. Peter Bourne, a psychiatrist who had worked with Governor Carter's wife on mental health matters for the state. Bourne asked Carter, "Have you ever thought of running for President," to which the governor replied, "No, I haven't; but if I did, here's what I'd do. I'd run for four years, the same way I did for governor." [27]

## VICE PRESIDENTS
## AND INCUMBENCY FACTORS

An increasingly likely potential nominee often overlooked in discussions of potential nominees is the vice president. In the twentieth century, vice presidents have fared well when they sought to move up from bridesmaid to the top of the ticket. Since 1956, both times the incumbent president opted against a renomination bid, his running mate was tapped to replace him (Nixon in 1960 and Humphrey in 1968). In 1972, *Time* cameoed Nixon's then blameless vice president as the "Spiro of '76." [28] The enhanced role given to the vice president under Jimmy Carter could upgrade the chances of future junior partners on presidential tickets being nominated for "chairmen of the board." A major liability for the vice president, though, is the fact that he must often be an apologist for the failures of the president he served. Hubert Humphrey learned in 1968 how impossible it was to rid himself of voter dissatisfaction with Johnson's war in Vietnam since he had been Johnson's vice president.

Sitting presidents who actively seek their party's nomination at the national convention will receive it. In fact, Chester Arthur was the last incumbent, back in 1884, to be refused, although Gerald Ford came dangerously close to sharing that dubious distinction in 1976, and Ted Kennedy made a surprising run at Jimmy Carter in 1980. One might wonder today, however, if that old prescription is iron clad any longer. After all, no president has, for various reasons, served two full terms since Dwight Eisenhower (1953-1961). Since then, there have been several challenges aimed at unseating occupants of the Oval Office. In two of those cases, the presidents decided to forego the battle for renomination due to poor showings in early primaries (Truman in 1952 and LBJ in 1968).[29] In a third case, Gerald Ford had to quell a barracks revolt from the right within the Republican Party to wrest the nomination from his surprisingly potent opponent, Ronald Reagan, in 1976. Admittedly, the Ford situation was unique since he was the first nonelected president seeking office in his own right. Unlike Truman and LBJ, he had no proven organization at the national level. His good track record in races for Congress from his home district in Grand Rapids, Michigan was hardly proof of his viability as a campaigner at the presidential election level.

While recent history would tend to point up many of the negative aspects of incumbency, a sitting president is not necessarily occupying the hot seat if he knows how to use the office. In fact, he should be able to consider his position as an asset rather than as a liability. The president, his family, his habits, his hobbies are all considered newsworthy. During the Kennedy "Camelot" years, for example, the press and the public clamored for tidbits about Jacqueline and later the two Kennedy children. Everything about a president is news.

ACTING "PRESIDENTIAL."  The occupant of the Oval Office is easily more visible than his opponents. He may assume an "above-the-battle" posture and remain "presidential" as Richard Nixon did in his race against McGovern in 1972. He may indulge in grandstanding diplomacy with trips to the Soviet Union and the People's Republic of China as President Nixon did prior to the 1972 elections. The incumbent also has a vast reservoir of public adulation to tap as he travels from media event to media event in Air Force One with the strains of "Hail to the Chief" resounding in the ears of numerous awestruck onlookers and striking a responsive chord in living rooms across the nation. Another advantage that presidents usually have over their competitors is the fact that they are proven campaign organizers, fund raisers, and vote getters throughout the country. Their organizations of previous years need merely be dusted off, refined a bit, and set into motion; they do not require organization from the ground up.

MANIPULATING THE ECONOMY.  No opponent can manipulate fiscal and monetary policies to help create a rosy economic picture for November the way in which a president can. A president can judiciously time economic benefits to interest groups or certain segments of the electorate to ensure their support on election day. Timing of Social Security increases provides a classic example of this point. Checks went out in October 1972, one month before the elections, with the following memo enclosed and personally approved by President Nixon to each of the 24.7 million Social Security recipients:[30]

> Your social security payment has been increased by 20% starting with this month's check by a new statute enacted by Congress and signed into law by President Richard Nixon on July 1, 1972.

> The President also signed into law a provision which will allow your social security benefits to increase automatically if the cost of living goes up.

This example from the Nixon administration is hardly unique. Edward Tufte, in his extraordinary work on political control of the economy, demonstrates that a pattern of timing transfer payments (funds paid directly by the federal government to individuals, groups, or public entities) exists. Looking at election year correlations with transfer payments, he has found what many had suspected but never proved.[31]

> In four of the last seven election years, governmental transfer payments have reached their yearly peaks in October and November; in the eight surrounding odd-numbered years . . . transfers reached their yearly maximum at the end of the year in December with one exception.

The political presupposition behind this obvious manipulation is that the voter would be unwilling to shoot Santa Claus in November.

There are numerous other examples of the economic advantages available to the incumbent. Candidates may decry low farm prices; presidents can increase subsidies. Candidates can complain about import quotas or duties; presidents can raise or lower them. In other words, candidates can articulate solutions to problems during the campaign, but presidents can act to solve them. These economic management tools can, however, constitute a double-edged sword. The president who has power over the economy can also be held accountable for its woes. On the whole, however, the president has a plus in his column in this area.

To sum up on prior experience as a factor in the selection process, it could be said that (1) basic characteristics of party nominees have not changed radically since the turn of the century, (2) senators have become more visible as potential nominees than have governors and other types of hopefuls, (3) an increasingly visible vice presidency could become a stepping stone to the White House even though it has been a millstone to some, and (4) an incumbent president will still be able to gain his party's nomination if he is adept at using his preeminent media position, previously proven campaign machinery, and the political and economic tools of his office to their utmost.

## THE PREPARATION STAGE: PLANNING FOR THE RACE

The road to the White House has become a veritable maze strewn with obstacles. No single national law applies to the U.S. presidential nomination process in toto. State laws in each of the fifty states affect the selection of delegates to the national conventions that nominate the party standard-bearer. As a result of the hodgepodge of regulations, hopefuls are subjecting themselves to a grueling chore of developing strategies and organizing.

The situation is complicated further by the time frame of the formal part of the process. In both 1976 and 1980, the formal pre-general-election phase dragged on through six long months. The first of the delegate selection caucuses was held in January, and the two party conventions did not meet until July and August. In 1980 political pundits even began looking at non-binding straw-polls being held before the caucuses in Florida. We shall examine the caucuses, the primaries, and the national convention in more detail later in this chapter; but it cannot be over-stressed that the mere logistics of campaigning for delegates across the nation could present mind-boggling problems. Any candidate who can piece together a winning campaign organization certainly displays at least *some* administrative talent.

The race for the White House, as Richard Nixon so characteristically described it, becomes a *battle* to be won.[32] An effective general should be able to develop strategies, delegate responsibilities, and bite the bullet when difficult decisions reach his desk. Likewise, no candidate for president can expect to win in spite of his organization. A general, after all, is only as successful as the soldiers who fight under his command will make him.

## THE DECISION:
### GO OR NO GO

As the lessons of U.S. involvement in Vietnam so graphically illustrated, no massive undertaking should be entered into piecemeal with goals, costs, and possibilities of success left unaddressed. Likewise, in political campaigns, the potential competitor must realistically assess his chances of winning the nomination and set up his strategies far in advance. He must honestly evaluate not only his capabilities and liabilities but must also judge whether he can command more recognition than other old faces and new that are in hot pursuit of the coveted nomination. He must also assess his standing with respect to other "unannounced" potential nominees.

A case in point could be the early planning of the candidate who came from virtual oblivion to capture the Democratic nomination in 1976. During September 1972, Governor Jimmy Carter and his closest political advisors—Hamilton Jordan, Gerald Rafshoon, Dr. Peter Bourne, and Landon Butler—began carefully assessing his chances for 1976. Even prior to that, Rafshoon and Jordan had tried to convince Democratic presidential nominee George McGovern that a Southern governor would make an excellent running mate in 1972. As they were returning from the frustrating meeting with McGovern's pollster Pat Caddell, Rafshoon wondered aloud to Jordan,[33]

> Why can't Jimmy run for President? He's not going to run for the Senate. And, four years from now we certainly aren't going to go around here trying to curry favor with somebody [asking] to put an ex-governor on as Vice President.

Carter later admitted to his friends that he had broached the outrageous subject of his running for president with his wife. Recognizing some of his more glaring weaknesses, he told his political associates[34]

> We [Carter and Rosalyn] tried to assess and inventory everything that existed in the way of assets or a problem including the financial requirements, the fact that I was not in office, I was from a little town, the fact that I was not in Washington, the fact that I was not well known, the fact that I had no power base and so forth. We enumerated all of those problems and tried to figure out how we could either minimize the problem or make an asset out of it.

In November 1972, Jordan drew up a fifty-page how-to-do-it memo. It evaluated potential opponents (for example, George Wallace and Ted Kennedy); it discussed public dissatisfaction with the "Washington establishment"; it mapped out ways in which Carter could get media coverage in the *Washington Post* and *The New York Times*. It also took notice of one of the most important strategic elements that Carter was to adopt for his campaign by suggesting that the bandwagon get rolling very early if its last stop were to be the White House and not somewhere along the primary trails in the backwoods of New Hampshire or the swamps of Florida. As basic strategy, the Jordan memo[35] proposed that Carter

1. Demonstrate in the first primaries your strength as a candidate. This means a strong surprise showing in New Hampshire and a victory in Florida.
2. Establish that you are not a regional candidate by winning early primaries in medium-sized states outside the South such as Rhode Island and Wisconsin.
3. Select one of the large industrial and traditionally Democratic states which has an early primary to confront all major opponents and establish yourself as a major contender. Pennsylvania and Ohio would be possibilities.
4. Demonstrate consistent strength in all primaries entered.

Notice that the last two strategies did not say "win" but merely "establish yourself" as a contender and demonstrate strength. This audacious memo could have been mistaken for the work of Jonathan Swift as it was hardly a "modest proposal." While the plan was well thought out on paper, implementing it seemed to require a work force that would have been the envy of the Pharoahs of ancient Egypt.

## ORGANIZING
## FOR THE GRIND

Once a candidate decides that he is sufficiently masochistic to bear up under the strain of the race, he and his political intimates must piece together an effective campaign machine. It must attract a pool of sufficiently experienced workers who can recognize and cultivate the candidate's natural constituencies and identify and target the undecided voters. In the period prior to the national convention, the organization will be a personal one; but, if "the next president" is to emerge victorious, it is important that the organization be sufficiently flexible to work in tandem with the established national party organization during the general election portion of the quest. One of the many factors that severely handicapped the efforts of George McGovern in 1972 was the fact that his long-haired loyalists did not mix well with the traditional labor leaders, ethnics, and big-city pols who represented the mainstream of the national organization.

Campaign organizations are, to a great degree, an extension of the personality and prejudices of the presidential candidates. Still, there are enough similarities that a rough sketch of these structures can be drawn for the typical campaign of the 1980s. See Table 10.1 and Chart 10.1.

The picture-perfect organization chart may prove totally unworkable when the human element is added to bring it to life. The success of a campaign can often hinge not only on the charisma of the candidate but also on the quality and quantity of volunteers and other personnel it attracts.

## TABLE 10.1
## ROLE OF MAJOR CAMPAIGN OPERATIVES

| POSITION | DUTIES AND ROLE |
|----------|-----------------|
| Campaign Manager | Coordinates campaign<br>Assigns duties to committees<br>Supervises operations of all staffs and committees |
| Director | Liaison with party organization<br>Liaison with interest groups including ethnic groups<br>Special fund raiser |
| Campaign Committee | Advisory body for candidate<br>Meets only when called by the manager<br>Reflects the views of the candidate's voters (labor, minorities, women's rights, activists, etc.) |
| Finance Chairman<br>(Treasurer) | Principal fund raiser<br>Contact point with professional fund raisers<br>Accountant<br>Signs checks<br>Responsible for purchases<br>Develops mailing lists for names of contributors<br>Prepares federal financial reports |
| Public Relations Director<br>(Media Affairs) | Helps develop theme for the campaign<br>Finds candidate's image strengths and exploits them<br>Some involvement in media spending priorities |
| Legal Advisor | Explains campaign-related laws to volunteers and staff<br>Monitors compliance with laws in operation of the campaign (federal and state)<br>Reviews all spending contracts<br>Reviews campaign literature for possible libel or slander<br>Goes to court or government agencies when necessary<br>Monitors fairness in media coverage of the candidate |
| Press Secretary | Develops contacts with media<br>Issues press releases<br>Creates and schedules media "happenings" for no cost coverage<br>Handles transportation for the media people to follow the campaign trail<br>Keeps track of media reporting for future uses |
| Research Director | Searches backgrounds of candidate and potential opponents<br>Compiles position papers on "issues" including developing new approaches to solving problems<br>Obtains data on habits and views of voters<br>Identifies and targets natural voter support<br>Updates briefings on "issues"<br>Plans in-house polling or assists manager in hiring polling firms |
| Volunteer Director | Recruits workers<br>Arranges transportation of volunteers<br>Assigns volunteers to committees<br>Keeps data on volunteers<br>Helps to get the voters out on election day |

TABLE 10.1 (cont'd.)

| POSITION | DUTIES AND ROLE |
| --- | --- |
| Scheduling Director | Schedules candidate visits to localities<br>Hires experienced advance people<br>Checks on advance people in the areas of:<br>    arranging press conferences<br>    housing for candidate and staff<br>    finding places to speak<br>    organizing demonstrations of support<br>    contact with local party organizers |
| Liaisons with Special Groups (State Parties, Ethnics, Various Interest Groups) | Coordinate the activities of non-campaign organization groups supporting the candidate |

Sources: Hugh A. Bone, *American Politics and the Party System* (New York: McGraw Hill, 1971), pp. 322-360. James Brown and Philip M. Seib, *The Art of Politics: Electoral Strategies and Campaign Management* (Port Washington, N.Y.: Alfred Press, 1976), pp. 55-71.

The Kennedy campaign of 1960 was often recognized for the brain power it brought to bear on the race for the White House. Theodore White colorfully portrayed the cast of characters that supported the attractive, young, Massachusetts senator. For his "idea men" Kennedy raided the halls of ivy with the assistance of Professor Archibald Cox of Harvard Law who prevailed on his friends and associates to enlist in the cause. At the center of the ideas team was Theodore Sorensen whom Kennedy called his "intellectual blood bank." To organize the campaign, Kennedy harnessed the talents of a long-time campaign cohort Lawrence F. O'Brien. O'Brien's campaign manuals have become the "bible" for political organizers since that time.[36] Scheduling and advance were the duties of a corps of battle-hardened political veterans from earlier Kennedy successes. The group, headed by Kenneth O'Donnell, came to be known somewhat affectionately as the "Irish Mafia." As a close advisor and freelance troubleshooter, John Kennedy used his brother Robert. Although the senator did not always take his brother's advice as was the case with JFK's decision to put Lyndon Johnson in the number two slot on the 1960 ticket,[37] JFK had the advantage of having a trusted aide who would provide constructive criticism when the need arose. Bill Moyers filled a similar role for Lyndon Johnson in 1964, and Robert Finch did likewise for Richard Nixon in 1968, with Hamilton Jordan doing likewise for Jimmy Carter and Edwin Meese for Ronald Reagan.

Even though John Kennedy is often viewed as the quintessence of the packageable media-type presidential candidate, few candidates recognized the necessity of effective media and public relations-educated personnel better than Richard Nixon did in 1968. Nixon surrounded himself with pinstriped public relations types. At the pinnacle of the organizational pyramid was H. R. (Bob) Haldeman, a forty-two-year-old former advertising executive with J. Walter Thompson Associates, a New York and California public relations firm. Haldeman had also earned his political spurs by suffering through the previous Nixon campaign losses in 1960 (presidential) and 1962 (California governor's race). Others in communications and public relations were hardly uninitiated newcomers. Frank Shakespear was a CBS execu-

**CHART 10.1  PRESIDENTIAL CAMPAIGN ORGANIZATION**

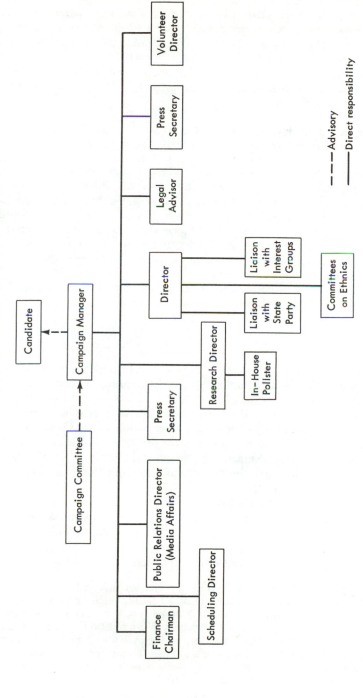

tive on leave; William Safire and Patrick Buchanan brought journalism experience to the cause; Herbert Klein, who headed up the press operations, was a public relations figure with Nixon ties dating back to 1960. Also in the press operations was former U.S.C. graduate, Disneyland tour guide, and later J. W. Thompson ad executive, Ronald Ziegler.[38] The Nixon operation points up the fact that candidates have come to depend more and more for election not on their "idea men" and the issue stands but on the images that are projected. Marshall McLuhan recognized in the 1960s that[39]

> Policies and issues . . . are too specialized. . . . The shaping of a candidate's integral image has taken the place of discussing conflicting points of view.

This tendency to divert from issues to images portends problems with effective citizen participation in our democratic processes. British philosopher Edmund Burke's concept of representation emphasized the importance of public officials' retaining the freedom to exercise their good judgment in carrying on the affairs of state.[40] However, the public should have more to go on in choosing a candidate than his personal appearance, vocal resonance, and talk show personality or acting ability. The American electorate, because it tends to be apathetic, can be swayed by posturings and images because national problems are so complex that study would be required to understand them. In the free market system of American politics, the voters get only what they demand and are willing to pay for.

## CAMPAIGN SKIPPER

No matter what types of themes or organizations the candidate selects to keep his bandwagon rolling, he must ultimately do the steering. A clear chain of command is needed so that the candidate has some idea of what deeds are being performed in his name. The excesses of the Nixon campaign were possible partly because the president delegated responsibility for his reelection to the Committee to Re-elect the President. Later, on national television, the president had to accept the responsibility for the bugging, campaign law violations, malicious "dirty tricks" aimed at Democratic hopefuls, and the entire chronicle of abuses that have come to be known as the Watergate affair.

Candidates provide leadership for their organizations through the strength of their own personalities. If a candidate cannot hold the ship on course, infighting in the organization is bound to erupt. In 1972, for example, George McGovern's team began to fall apart mainly because he was unable to rally his own troops and keep them united. As Theodore White explained the unfortunate turn of events,[41]

> At his Washington headquarters, by the second half of October, when the upturn failed to come, a condition had set in which I had never known before; it was not the condition of bleak despair, or the black-humor surliness of the Goldwater headquarters in 1964; it was a condition which passed disloyalty. Men and women whom I had known for over a year as disciples now despised their own candidate. They were not disaffected with the cause, but contemptuous of the man; betrayed not by his beliefs, which they still shared, but by the absence of that hard quality of leadership that they sought.

# THE ROLE OF THE PRIMARIES:
## ACCELERATING THE BANDWAGON

Since most of those lusting after the party's ultimate prize have not previously been occupants of the Oval Office, the parties need some evidence that one of them can handle the opposition in November. The presidential preference primaries were originally envisioned as a way of determining which of the would-be nominees could be the viable choice at the national convention.

After 1968, however, the primaries began increasing in both number and importance.[42] At that time only fifteen states and Washington, D.C. had primaries that elected some of their convention delegates. By 1972, the figures had increased to twenty-three states plus the District of Columbia, and, in 1976, thirty states held them and accounted for over 70 percent of the delegates. The 1980 figure was thirty-six and future years promise even more primaries.

While there are certain similarities among the primaries, state laws provide for a veritable tossed salad of variations. State legislatures can create them as mere "beauty contests" showing nonbinding voter preferences. They may also institute primaries to select delegates to the national conventions. In some cases these purposes can be combined. Ultimately, when the primaries are viewed nationally, there are four types: (1) pure preference, (2) delegate selection only, (3) the two combined, and (4) the two separated. State laws also vary with respect to the extent to which convention delegates are bound to a particular candidate when the national convention meets.[43] Potential candidates for the party nomination must become conversant with the peculiarities of each state's primaries since delegates are involved and electable images are often built or shattered at the various stops along the primary trail.

### PRIMARIES AND THE IMAGE
### OF INEVITABILITY

Primaries are the stuff of which momentum is made in the preconvention period of the race for the White House. Since the advent of television, primaries have become media happenings focusing national consciousness on the selection process unfolding in each of the states. Candidates no longer need to "win" primaries since a "strong showing" (usually defined generously by the candidate and more rigidly by the media reporters, especially those on TV) is enough to turn an unknown like Jimmy Carter in 1976 into a bona fide candidate or even front-runner. "The Lord gives and the Lord takes away." The press can make a front-runner and can also push him back into the pack or possibly out of the race. A case in point might be front-runner Edmund Muskie in 1972.

Muskie's experience illustrates that media coverage of the front-runner in the primaries brings along with it press expectations of their anointed hero. On January 9, 1972, David S. Broder, respected and influential political writer for the *Washington Post,* wrote from New Hampshire that[44]

> As acknowledged front-runner and resident of the neighboring state, Muskie will have to win the support of at least half of the New Hampshire Democrats in order to claim a victory.

The senator from Maine would have been pleased with being the leader whether he collected 50 percent of the vote or not. When Broder questioned Muskie on his "disappointing" showing, the candidate became testy. Broder pressed on, though, asking the senator what effect the New Hampshire primary would have on his chances in Florida and elsewhere. Muskie fired back,[45]

> You'll tell me and you'll tell the rest of the country because *you* interpret this victory. This press conference today is *my* only chance to interpret it, but you'll probably even misinterpret that.

GETTING IN EARLY. Although the primary season is getting to be longer than the professional basketball and football seasons, the early primaries can be devastating to the hopes of front-runners and also-rans. In 1976, the primaries were spread out over six months. Still, the New Hampshire primary, in a state not exactly representative of the United States, has the potential for sounding taps for the leaders and the hangers on. In 1968, President Johnson was shocked and embarrassed by the surprising horse race in New Hampshire with antiwar activist Senator Eugene McCarthy from Wisconsin. The primary results sufficiently emboldened Senator Robert Kennedy to enter the fray and encouraged LBJ to reexamine his chances for nomination.[46]

In that same year, George Romney was humiliated there by Richard Nixon and eventually limped out of the race. John Kennedy's bandwagon was given a crucial boost in 1960 by his showing in small, poor, rural West Virginia because his victory proved that Protestants could vote for a Catholic candidate.[47] Today's primary setup gives an inordinate amount of power to the electorate in small, rural, and conservative states while potentially limiting the field from which the voters in larger more liberal states may make their selections. Mercifully, for the lesser known "rest of the pack" candidates, the early primaries permit a budding campaign maximum national exposure at minimum cost. A "good showing" early may soon swell badly depleted campaign coffers.[48]

THE LONG ROAD. The length of the primary road both in months and miles aids candidates with the time free to travel it with no distractions. The Ronald Reagans (1976-1980) and Jimmy Carters (in 1976) who were not holding public office have the advantage of being able to develop grass-roots organizations at least a couple of years in advance of the primaries. Still, traveling through thirty-six or more states can be financially and physically taxing. In 1976, for example, between March 2 and May 2 primaries were held in nine states including such pivotal ones as Massachusetts, Florida, Illinois, New York, Wisconsin, Pennsylvania, and Texas. From May 4 through June 8 there were nineteen other primaries culminating in the bonanza of delegates for the digging in California.[49]

## DEVELOPING STRATEGIES

Since there are so many primaries, no candidate can expect to win them all, so it has become common for campaigners to select those that seem friendly and avoid being maneuvered into others. This time-tested strategy has become harder to follow in recent years especially for Democratic hopefuls, since such a large percentage of the delegates to the national convention are now selected in primaries. It behooves candidates in a crowded field to gather delegates where they may and as soon as possible.[50] In August 1978, for example, Representative Philip Crane, back-bench Republican from Illinois and darling of the new conservatives, confidently announced his intention to contest for the 1980 nomination in all thirty-six primaries over two and a quarter years prior to election day. Before 1976 such an announcement, if covered by the press at all, would have elicited peals of laughter to rival a Marx brothers' film festival. But, in the summer of 1978, no one was even snickering.[51]

Whenever someone enters the fray, he must always have a quick explanation for "temporary setbacks." If a candidate does not do well in a particular state, he can chalk it off to a lack of time and funds that limit getting deeply involved in every state. He might also blame crossover voters for a poor showing since few states have figured out effective ways of stopping Republicans from voting in Democratic primaries, and vice versa. Sometimes the purpose of crossing over is to nominate the weakest possible opponent for your candidate in November. The role of Republicans in the large George Wallace vote in the Wisconsin Democratic primaries in 1972 was curious to say the least. There was no real Republican contest and the Alabama governor garnered 22 percent of the vote, while neighboring Senators McGovern and Humphrey could muster only 30 percent and 21 percent, respectively, and Senator Muskie tallied a meager 10 percent.[52] Any candidate could alibi that in some states his name was placed on the ballot against his wishes as was the case with Senator Ted Kennedy and Hubert Humphrey in the 1976 primary in Nebraska. Senator Frank Church from nearby Idaho paced the field in that particular primary.[53]

The mushrooming numbers of primaries place a premium on the ability to develop numerous local campaign organizations and to transfer workers from state to state as needed and prearranged. Manning far-flung outposts requires legions of volunteers prepared to offer their total commitment. Prior to the convention, candidates with strong issue identification or personal magnetism have a decided advantage over their more middle-of-the-road competitors when searching out volunteers. Eugene McCarthy and later George McGovern capitalized on the strong antiwar sentiments and liberal leanings among younger (especially college-aged) Americans to develop their massive "kiddie corps." Barry Goldwater[54] and Ronald Reagan stirred up the adrenalin of the conservative faithful in their quest of the Oval Office. In both Goldwater's and McGovern's cases, the "true believers" engineered the nomination at the national convention, but the ideological positions to which they adhered left them too far out on the political fringes to attract moderate voters in November.

Success in the primaries cannot be translated automatically into assurances for November. For one thing, voter turnout in primaries is always substantially smaller than it is in general elections.[55] A majority of convention delegates might support a candidate who is attractive to them but unpalatable to the average voter. Goldwater and McGovern are proof of that. Neither party seems to learn from the other's mistakes. Evidently George Santayana was correct in his assertion that those who cannot remember the past are condemned to repeat it.

WHY MORE PRIMARIES? In light of the numerous difficulties with the primary system already noted, it might seem contradictory to suggest that the number and importance of primaries are sure to increase. Still, recent trends would indicate that this will be the case into the 1980s. We could suggest several plausible explanations for the proliferation of primaries. First, primaries are a Chamber of Commerce bonanza of national TV coverage and print media exposure. Second, with the candidate and his advance persons and close entourage come the "boys on the bus" (the press corps), and all of them need accommodations, food, and entertainment. Probably the only more lucrative exposure possible for a city would be to host a party's national convention. For Kansas City in 1976 it was a public relations coup to host the Republican convention to show American vacationers that there were no cows in the streets and no hitching posts. Detroit in 1980 proved it was not the burned out inner-city shell many Americans had imagined. A third reason for the increasing popularity of primaries is the fact that they provide, in this post-Watergate era, for an opening up of the presidential nomination process to the average citizen who would otherwise not be active enough in politics to take part. This last point puts the parties squarely on the horns of a perplexing dilemma. Introducing democracy into the party selection process is indeed laudable, yet as the Democrats have come to realize since 1972, doing so can encourage amateurs to take over the nominating process and win a major battle for their candidate but torpedo the nominee and the party in November.

## ADJUSTING THE PRIMARY SYSTEM

Most of the proposals for clearing a path through the thicket of presidential preference primaries that have sprung up in recent years follow one of three approaches: (1) cutting down on the number of dates during which primaries may be held, (2) setting up five regional primaries to assist the candidates in travel, and (3) developing a single national primary.[56] These proposals recognize that the candidates have little time to develop knowledge on many issue areas given the grueling pace to which they must adhere. In addition, the candidates are not in any one state long enough now to give the public time to get more than a cursory look at them. Also, under the present system, the press must spread itself tissue-thin, juggling events in several states simultaneously. As a result, in preparing for coverage of the next primary, reporters have little time for analysis of results but must depend on gut-level surmisings that are often superficial at best. In 1968, for example, Senator Eugene McCarthy's unexpectedly solid showing in the New Hampshire primary was being interpreted and recorded as proof of public disenchantment with Lyndon Johnson's policies in Vietnam. That *post hoc, ergo propter hoc* (after the event, therefore because of it) logic proved difficult to defend in retrospect since McCarthy voters in the New Hampshire primary supported[57] George Wallace over Humphrey and Nixon in the general election.

For the foreseeable future, the serious candidates for president must gather delegates wherever they are available, even if this means undergoing the migraine of entering all the primaries, as Jimmy Carter did in 1976. The strategy of avoiding some or all of the primaries and waiting in the wings to be drafted by the national convention is becoming increasingly less plausible. Possibly, a sitting president who can use the office and party machinery to get delegate support could survive by playing presidential and staying out of the primaries; but even incumbency does not completely assure nomination any longer. While it is true that Hubert Humphrey was nominated in 1968 without entering the primaries, he was able to simply let McCarthy, Kennedy, Wallace, and the others eliminate one another while he awaited the call of the party to serve. He expected the same strategy to work again in 1976, but, to his chagrin, the brokered convention he foresaw did not materialize because Jimmy Carter had done such an effective job of beating the bushes for convention delegates that there were few bargains left to be struck.

The fact that the primaries can deteriorate into popularity contests and can be won by pluralities rather than majorities brings into question their value in helping the *party* select a person who represents the broad views within the party. Worst of all, pluralities in the primaries might be translated into nomination at conventions; but, too often, majorities in November are not as likely.

## THE CAUCUS OR MINI-CONVENTION PROCESS

Until the 1960s these state and local methods for selecting national convention delegates were carefully orchestrated by party bosses.[58] Delegates selected at the congressional district level and state-wide usually voted as a bloc or unit and they were rarely inextricably tied to one candidate. In 1964, though, Barry Goldwater rallied his followers to get them involved in the congressional district and state caucuses and conventions. His grass-roots strategy won him the Republican nomination.[59]

While the specifics of these convention processes may vary a bit from state to state, Chart 10.2 shows the flow of delegates from the early precinct caucuses all the way to the national conventions.

Richard Stearns who directed McGovern's 1972 delegate hunt in nonprimary states estimated that, if 5-6 percent of registered Democrats turned out as pro-McGovern forces at the precinct caucuses, it would have been enough to have dominated them.[60] To the dismay of unprepared party regulars, the shoeless, bearded, neophyte McGovern believers upset many a previously smoothly rolling applecart at the precinct and county levels.[61]

**CHART 10.2    DEMOCRATIC MINI-CONVENTION SYSTEM 1972, 1976, AND 1980**

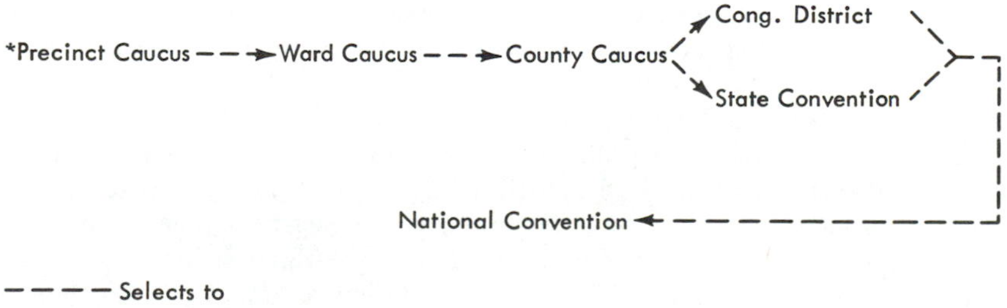

*Precinct Caucus − − →Ward Caucus − − →County Caucus< Cong. District  State Convention → National Convention ← − − − − − − − − − − −

− − − − Selects to

* Participants need only declare themselves by signature as democrat

Both Ronald Reagan and Jimmy Carter followed the Stearns outline in 1976 and 1980 on the presupposition that delegates committed by personal preference to the candidate would hold firm. Infiltration of the faithful at the precinct level, they reasoned, would ensure eventual solid blocs of delegates that could not be brokered by party regulars at the national conventions. (This proved true in dramatic fashion at the 1980 Democratic convention when Senator Kennedy was unable to woo Carter delegates to his side.) Delegates chosen through the caucus system today are likely to either owe blind allegiance to their personal hero or be under the thumb of party leaders or elected officials in their states. In either case, they could hardly be viewed as a microcosm of voter opinion since they each represent a tiny activist segment of a much larger electorate.[62]

## AMASSING CAUCUS DELEGATES

Influencing nonprimary national convention delegates requires long-range preparation. Candidates find it necessary to employ analysts and develop contacts who can assess whether state delegations and individual delegates are "firm" or "mushy." Nonprimary state delegates played an important role in the nominating conventions for both parties in 1976. Even an incumbent president, Gerald Ford, learned that delegates can't be taken for granted.

In early June, when the last of the Republican primaries had been held, eleven of the twenty-one states that chose delegates through caucuses and conventions had completed their work. Ronald Reagan had won 178 delegates in these states whereas Ford had only 114 to show for his efforts, with 64 remaining uncommitted. That left 270 more delegates to be chosen in the ten other nonprimary states. Those delegates could easily have spelled victory for one of the competitors since the early tallies at the Kansas City convention left a microscopic spread between the two.[63] The Ford forces had overconfidently deemphasized the need for attracting nonprimary delegates early in the race. Later, when they realized that the Reagan candidacy was not just a flash in the pan, the president's men depended upon state party machinery to carry the load of encouraging local delegates to vote for him at the convention. As one Ford operative put it, "We never thought we'd need the convention states so we were woefully outorganized by the Reagan forces in them. . . ."[64]

These state party pros proved to be the Edsels of the Ford campaign. Then Missouri Governor Christopher (Kit) Bond's efforts to gather delegate support for the president became a terrible personal embarrassment for both, since Mr. Ford had come to Springfield shortly before the state convention to buttress what he had been told would be a substantial count for his camp. Reagan, however, because he had done so well at the congressional district conventions, collected all but one of the nineteen delegates selected by the state convention.[65]

Fortunately for Ford, the primaries had produced one hundred uncommitted delegates for the president to proposition. Eventually, he had to resort to the advantages of incumbency to cajole the "gettable" delegates expected to show up at the national convention in Kansas City. The president invited wavering and uncommitted delegates to the White House and lent a friendly ear to their pork barrel requests. Delegate counter James Baker later admitted that each delegate who was uncommitted was handled individually:[66]

> What I tried to do was to find out whose judgment was most respected by a party delegate. Once we had determined who that was, we tried to get that person to work on the delegate. . . . Ultimately, I'd say 150 people were the ball game, and the President himself probably talked or visited with practically every one of those.

In a similar manner, Jimmy Carter tried to woo Chicago Mayor Jane Byrne with several million dollars in transit subsidies before the 1980 Democratic Convention. Even an incumbent president had to learn that in the "new politics" of the 1970s and 1980s fresh faces were entering the nomination process and were not necessarily willing to be bargained with in the traditional ways. They expected to be dealt with as individuals. The party professionals proved incapable of marshalling the troops as they had done in the simpler past. These delegates were not to be swayed by simple marching orders from on high. Future uncommitted delegates promise to be no less intransigent.

## THE NATIONAL CONVENTION: CORONATION OR CONTEST?

When most of us think of a national convention, we envision long-winded speeches, "spontaneous" hoopla, tense balloting for the presidential nominee, and mystery over his choice of running mate. In the 1980s, if present party rules continue, the convention may well become merely a small, final skirmish for the well-organized and well-funded candidate. Kennedy forces in 1980 tried to have delegates freed of any obligation to vote as their states had in selecting them. He wanted an "open" convention. The major theaters of war in the battle for the White House will become the state and local trenches where hand-to-hand combat will determine which camp will accumulate the needed primary and caucus delegates. Brokered conventions seem less and less likely, and uncommitted delegates could, as in the case of the great white whale, become an endangered species. Personally committed delegates, because they are not likely to be party pros, will stand by "their candidate" whether he has a chance or not. Nelson Polsby and Aaron Wildavsky, in their work on presidential elections, give a classic example of this type of unwavering loyalist. They related the experiences of a Shirley Chisholm delegate at the 1972 convention who was chosen from a black district in a sparsely populated state.[67]

> The delegate . . . had been selected because she had shown up at a meeting to back her candidate. Even before she left her home, she had received calls from the McGovern forces asking her to vote against the Humphrey challenge to the seating of the California delegation. . . . [Instead] the delegate approved the challenge because it meant more votes for Chisholm. She was not moved by the argument that McGovern would thereby lose his majority.

She didn't even yield under the pressure of a personal visit from Coretta King, wife of slain civil rights hero, Dr. Martin Luther King. This example illustrates not only the tenacity and faithfulness of committed delegates but also the need for the presidential candidates to keep track of the delegates who might be needed to swing a first-ballot victory. Monitoring delegate counts can be an enormous proposition too. In 1960 the Kennedy forces built an impressive floor communications system to keep on top of delegates who might stray from the fold. "State Shepherds" were assigned to make the task possible. Floor managers, Governor Abraham Ribicoff and Robert Kennedy, coordinated the convention-night operations via eight dualcommunication walkie-talkies carried around the convention floor.[68] McGovern's headhunter, twenty-seven-year-old former Rhodes scholar, Rick Stearns, had a computerized list of all of the delegates according to nineteen variable personal characteristics.[69] Ronald Reagan assembled a comparable organization under John Sears in 1976, and James Baker served as his counterpoint on the Ford convention team. Ironically, Baker took his considerable skills to the Reagan campaign replacing Sears in 1980 and later became Reagan's White House chief of staff.

## PARTY RULES AND
## THE CONVENTION APPARATUS

Unlike the virtually immutable laws of science, party rules are subject to human manipulation and rewriting. They need not be based on accepted principles about party operation. In fact, they are more likely to be the end product of infighting among party pretenders to the throne. Rules are often purposely designed to favor one candidate over another. The national parties will usually have their committees choose commissions to make recommendations on changes. It behooves candidates to do what they can to get their supporters on these commissions. Commission reports almost invariably arouse at least some protest. Who writes the rules can play the most effective game but makes the most enemies, too.

For example, one of the most commonly voiced complaints leveled at the 1978 Winograd[70] commission report for the 1980 Democratic convention and delegate selection process was that it was tailored to assure Jimmy Carter's renomination. Carter aide Mark Siegel's presence on the commission lent credibility to those charges.[71] Kennedy's attempts to have those rules changed in 1980 were aimed at freeing the lock on convention delegates that the incumbent, Jimmy Carter, had fashioned.

## PARTY RULES
## VERSUS STATE LAWS

Party rules have begun to eclipse state laws in the area of delegate selection. Movement in this direction began in 1948 when the Dixiecrats rose up against the civil rights plank in the Democratic Party platform. Non-Southern states then made an effort to introduce national rules that discouraged selection procedures based on race. In 1968, the regular Mississippi delegation was denied seats on the Democratic convention floor because its selection violated national party principles even though the procedures fully complied with Mississippi law.[72] In litigation over a similar set of problems with the California and Illinois delegations in 1972, the Supreme Court upheld the right of the national parties to set their own rules.[73]

Changes in Republican Party rules contributed to making the 1976 convention such a cliff hanger. Shifts in apportionment rules (methods of allotting delegates to each state) favored candidates attractive to the South and the Far West, and, unfortunately for President Ford, that was Reagan country. Also, the president lost potential supporters because there were fewer Eastern and Midwestern delegates.

Gerald Pomper theorized that, if the old 1952 apportionment system had been maintained, Ford would have won handily with 56.6 percent of the vote. Had the Republicans adopted a proportional representation rule (a candidate gets state delegates according to the percentage of the state primary vote he wins) rather than allowing a winner-take-all arrangement, Reagan, who carried the whole California delegation to the convention, would have surrendered fifty-nine delegates to Ford and thus have been in no position to seriously challenge the president.[74]

In the final analysis, most conflicts over party rules can be boiled down to such political questions as (1) What regions of the country and states should carry the most weight?[75] (2) Should loyal party regulars permit their power to be diluted by "candidate-oriented" zealots who might "deep six" election chances? and (3) Should conventions choose candidates on the basis of their appeal to the faithful or be expected to consider the potential electability of each candidate?

## CONVENTION ORGANIZATION

Conflicts at the convention are first aired before the major committees. Long before the opening gavel, these committees have been at work preparing for the quadrennial extravaganza. It is through their efforts that the national convention, which had been in hibernation for four years, awakens to its triple tasks of choosing nominees for president and vice-president and writing a party platform. The four major committees are, in order of importance,

1. Credentials, which makes up the official delegate list for the convention.
2. Rules, which sets convention regulations and procedures for selecting the nominee.
3. Permanent organization, which selects permanent officers for the convention.
4. Platform, which compiles the party position on issues.[76]

The successful aspiring nominee is often the one who has courted the national party apparatus, especially the national committee, to have his lieutenants placed in crucial committee positions for the convention. Well-placed friends on the Platform Committee can save the candidate the embarrassment of having later to disavow parts of his party's platform. Friends on the national committee could also assist a would-be nominee by selecting a keynote speaker attuned to his philosophy and goals. Stalwarts sprinkled liberally throughout the Credentials Committee could be invaluable since credentials issues have played a prominent role in numerous national conventions. General Eisenhower's victory over Senator Robert Taft at the 1952 Republican convention was due in part to credentials.[77] In 1972 credentials fights loomed important in the eventual Democratic convention selection of Senator George McGovern. At that convention, scrupulously even-handed Washington lawyer Patricia Roberts Harris (later to become HEW Secretary under President Carter) and her Credentials Committee were asked to evaluate an amazing eighty-two challenges, twelve of which were handled. The floor votes on credentials fights related to the California, Illinois, and South Carolina delegations sent through the party shock waves that did not subside until after the general election. Chicago Mayor Daley's Illinois delegation was judged to lack proper proportions of women, minorities, and youth to fit the party (McGovern-Fraser) guidelines. It made little difference that the delegation was constituted legally under existing Illinois law. The decision to unseat the delegation incensed party regulars, organized labor, and the Illinois party pros.[78] Like Pontius Pilate, they washed their hands of the Mc-Govern candidacy, and during the period prior to the general election they refused to lift a finger on his behalf, even though their support would have been invaluable to party success in November. The floor vote to unseat the Illinois delegation in 1972 was a show of McGovern strength, whereas the votes on California and South Carolina proved to be tests of McGovern strength prior to the balloting. While this situation was nothing new for national conventions, once candidate McGovern cleared those floor hurdles, the nomination was assured. Still, with such an angrily divided party, the nomination proved to be as much a curse as a prize.

## CONVENTIONS AND THE FUTURE

The major parties have, in recent years, made valiant efforts to streamline their conventions as one or both of them have dispensed with long nominating and seconding speeches, limited or eliminated "spontaneous" demonstrations, discouraged "favorite son" delaying tactics, and limited bloc voting by state delegations. In the backlash of public mistrust toward politicians, both parties have been attempting to "democratize" the conventions by bringing more rank and file voters into the selection process via the primaries and caucuses. The states have, at the behest of the Democratic Party, begun to bring their statutes into compliance with party guidelines governing primaries and selection of delegates to the national convention. When party rules unseated two delegations in 1972, the resulting litigation found the courts on the side of the parties, even though state laws (in California and Illinois) and party guidelines conflicted.

If the patterns of recent election years continue, the national convention will be eclipsed by other factors that have become more crucial in the selection process. A simple look at the number of first-ballot nominations by the two parties since 1956 would indicate that decisions were possibly being made elsewhere. None of the nominations by either party from 1956 through 1980 took more than one ballot.[79] The increasing number of delegates chosen via primaries has led to new casts of characters in succeeding election years. Delegate recruitment has become a critical job for candidates long before the convention itself. The McGovern (1972) and Carter (1976) campaigns show the importance of unearthing delegates from the farthest reaches of the nation and using the party rules to their utmost to win nomination. With campaign images being projected through mass media and with public opinion polls to measure voter reaction to the themes and images[80] each candidate presents, even the uncommitted delegates are in a position to make their decisions prior to the convention, should they wish. Unless the rules change, the conventions seem destined to become coronations rather than contests. Incumbent presidents seem likely to hold a slight edge if they seek their party's nomination. Still, rules changes and federal matching funds may improve the chances of political unknowns as they compete for the party's ultimate prize, the nomination.

# THE GENERAL
## ELECTION CAMPAIGN

For each nominee, staffer, and volunteer who celebrates the wisdom of the convention delegates, there is a legion of disgruntled losers. Party decorum requires that bygones be bygones, but people involved in heated primary and convention skirmishes often find it hard to actively support their erstwhile enemies in the larger battle ahead. The successful nominee must be able to hold his party's normal coalition in line behind his candidacy. If every person who is identified as a Democrat turned out to vote for the party nominee, the candidate would have little need to seek out disenchanted Republicans and independents. In 1976, for example, 48 percent of those asked by the Gallup pollsters to state their party preferences called themselves Democrats while 23 percent identified themselves as Republicans with the remainder being independents.[81] Some might suggest that these figures represent a Watergate backlash, but the Center for Political Studies of the University of Michigan and the Gallup organizers have found similar figures since 1952.[82]

The traditional Democratic coalition has generally been the gravy train of American politics since 1932. The candidate who gets aboard and convinces labor leadership, urban politicos, Catholic ethnics, blacks, and Southern Democrats to stay with him can often ride it all the way to the White House. Maintaining support of such a diverse lot can require the dexterity of an Olympic gymnast.

The Democratic fortress has not been impregnable, however, as Dwight Eisenhower, Richard Nixon, and Ronald Reagan wooed and won Democratic voters. Actually, Eisenhower's two victories should be attributed to the charisma of the man rather than to a weakening of party ties among Democrats. As proof, one need only look at the races for Congress in those years to see that Ike had only one session in which he dealt with a Republican majority and that was in 1953. The election of John Kennedy, a Catholic, over a well-recognized vice president—Nixon—was further evidence that there was enough vitality in FDR's coalition to overcome some formidable obstacles. Lyndon Johnson's cakewalk in 1964 was possible in part because all the major segments of the traditional coalition, with the single exception of the South, made their marks on the proper spot on the ballot. Hubert Humphrey's near miss in 1968 may not be interpreted realistically as a breakup of the FDR coalition either, since George Wallace siphoned off 13.6 percent of the vote, which was just enough to elect Nixon.

The Wallace phenomenon had pointed up some potential cracks in the coalition, and Nixon planned to exploit them in 1972. He theorized that the "solid" South was ripe for the plucking. The president shamelessly courted suburbanites, blue-collar workers, and Catholic ethnics. His "Silent Majority" (middle-class white America) marched to a new drummer in 1972, and some journalists like William Rusher and Kevin Phillips[83] interpreted that vote as the beginnings of a New Majority that has yet to materialize. Evidently, reports of the total demise of the Democratic coalition in 1972[84] were, as Mark Twain described the news of his own death, "greatly exaggerated."

In 1976, Jimmy Carter had modest success with the basic elements of the old Democratic coalition that had been scattered to the four winds in the aftermath of

## TABLE 10.2
## CARTER'S COLLAPSE: THE ANATOMY OF REAGAN'S VICTORY

| | PERCENT FOR REAGAN | PERCENT FOR CARTER | PERCENT FOR ANDERSON | CARTER SHIFT FROM 1976 |
|---|---|---|---|---|
| **Sex** | | | | |
| Male | 54% | 37% | 7% | −14 |
| Female | 46 | 45 | 7 | − 7 |
| **Race** | | | | |
| White | 55 | 36 | 8 | −12 |
| Black | 14 | 82 | 3 | 0 |
| Spanish-speaking | 36 | 54 | 7 | −28 |
| **Age** | | | | |
| 18-21 | 43 | 44 | 11 | − 5 |
| 22-29 | 43 | 43 | 11 | −12 |
| 30-44 | 54 | 37 | 8 | −15 |
| 45-59 | 55 | 31 | 5 | − 9 |
| 60 and over | 54 | 40 | 4 | − 8 |
| **Family income** | | | | |
| Under $10,000 | 41 | 50 | 7 | −11* |
| $10,000-$15,000 | 42 | 47 | 8 | − 9* |
| $15,000-$25,000 | 53 | 38 | 7 | −12* |
| $25,000-$50,000 | 58 | 32 | 9 | NA |
| Over $50,000 | 65 | 25 | 8 | NA |
| **Job head of house** | | | | |
| Professional/manager | 56 | 33 | 9 | −10 |
| Clerical/white collar | 48 | 42 | 8 | − 8 |
| Blue collar | 47 | 46 | 5 | −13 |
| Job hunter | 36 | 55 | 7 | −12 |
| Union member in house | 44 | 47 | 7 | −14 |
| **Religion** | | | | |
| Protestant (white) | 62 | 31 | 6 | −12 |
| Catholic | 51 | 40 | 7 | −14 |
| Jewish | 39 | 45 | 14 | −23 |

the disastrous McGovern nomination in 1972. Carter also made inroads into areas that had recently been leaning Republican, especially in the South. Organized labor posted 62 percent of its vote in the Carter column, which constituted a better showing for the Georgia governor than John Kennedy had amassed in 1960. Only Lyndon Johnson had surpassed that showing since 1952. He carried 54 percent of the South in contrast to McGovern's 28 percent in 1972. Although the Catholic vote was down from its usual, in the low 60 percent area, the vote for Carter among Catholics of 55 percent was a marked improvement from McGovern's 40 percent support figures. The normal Democratic candidate since the 1930s has carried 80 percent of the votes of nominal Democrats; Carter carried 82 percent.[85]

As we look into the 1980s, however, it is not clear whether the Democratic coalition, even if it holds together, will be able to produce the votes necessary to elect a president. The "big-city vote," for example, which has been so crucial, has, like the urban population, been shrinking steadily. As an illustration, one could

TABLE 10.2 (cont'd.)

| | PERCENT FOR REAGAN | PERCENT FOR CARTER | PERCENT FOR ANDERSON | CARTER SHIFT FROM 1976 |
|---|---|---|---|---|
| 1976 presidential vote | | | | |
| Carter | 29% | 63% | 7% | – |
| Ford | 83 | 10 | 5 | – |
| Special categories | | | | |
| "Born again" whites | 61 | 34 | 4 | NA |
| Teachers | 46 | 41 | 10 | NA |
| Kennedy supporters | 24 | 66 | 8 | NA |
| Family financial status | | | | |
| Better (17%) | 37 | 53 | 8 | NA |
| Worse (36%) | 63 | 25 | 8 | NA |
| Same (43%) | 46 | 46 | 7 | NA |
| Education | | | | |
| Non-high school grad. | 45 | 50 | 3 | NA |
| High school grad. | 51 | 43 | 4 | NA |
| Some college | 55 | 35 | 8 | NA |
| College grad. | 51 | 35 | 11 | NA |
| Size of place | | | | |
| Rural/small town | 54 | 39 | 5 | –11 |
| Small cities | 48 | 43 | 7 | NA |
| Suburbs | 55 | 35 | 8 | –11 |
| Large cities | 36 | 53 | 8 | –10 |
| Party identification | | | | |
| Republican (28%) | 84 | 11 | 4 | 0 |
| Democratic (43%) | 26 | 66 | 6 | –13 |
| Independent (23%) | 54 | 30 | 12 | –16 |
| Ideology | | | | |
| Liberal | 27 | 57 | 11 | –18 |
| Moderate | 48 | 42 | 8 | –11 |
| Conservative | 71 | 23 | 4 | – 7 |

*figures adjusted for inflation

Source: CBS News/*The New York Times,* as cited in the *National Journal,* November 8, 1980.

point to the city of Chicago and the role of its legendary political machine. Carter rolled up approximately two thirds of the vote there in 1976, but Chicago's share of the Illinois vote had plummeted from one third of the state vote in 1960 to one fourth in 1976.[86] The coalition also stands to be hurt by the fact that today more voters are calling themselves independents than in the earlier heydays of the Democratic coalition. The 1972 election proved that numerous Democrats were capable of jumping ship (two in five to be exact) at least in the presidential race. Although most of them returned to the fold in 1976, Jimmy Carter hardly won in a runaway. Ronald Reagan's 51 percent to 42 percent pasting of Jimmy Carter in 1980 saw the Democratic coalition fall into shambles. Industrial northeastern states like New York, Pennsylvania, and Ohio moved into the Democratic column. A new Republican majority materialized in the Senate as labor-union members and Catholic ethnics marked the ballots in the unfamiliar Republican column.[87] The unresolved fate of the American hostages in Iran played a part in Jimmy Carter's defeat in 1980; but the resurgence of conservative politics helped to defeat not only Mr. Carter, but a number of his liberal Democratic colleagues such as Senators Mc-Govern, Bayh, and Church. Even Carter's native South, once the solid Democratic bastion, elected Republican senators and governors. Traditional habits or party-label voting were disappearing. See Table 10.2.

Since presidential candidates will find that party labels alone are not dependable sources of large blocs of votes, they will continue to be forced to develop the machinery necessary to arouse more personal support for their campaigns. In deciding the shape and direction that their organizations will take, they must address and quickly reach solutions to such basic postconvention questions as (1) What, if any, changes will be needed in the organization? (2) What personal image should be presented through public relations and the media? (3) How will the potential opponent affect the image choices to be made? (4) Who should be targeted? and (5) How can limited resources be best allocated in light of federal spending ceilings?

## THE PARTY AND
## PERSONAL ORGANIZATION

The successful nominees might, in the euphoria of their victories, be tempted to take on the opposing party's candidate using the same organization that served them so well in vanquishing the primary and caucus also-rans. Still, prudence would dictate that they make use of the extensive party organization earned by emerging victorious from the convention. Some candidates have mistakenly felt that they could retain party support and ideological purity under the assumption that the party regulars had no real alternative in November. This benighted thinking held sway in the Goldwater camp in 1964. In his acceptance speech, he told the assembled Republican conventioneers that he would welcome others to *join* the cause. He also dismissed any suggestions that he should modify his views to gain support of regular Republicans and the public at large. As far as he was concerned,[88]

> Those who do not care for our cause, we don't expect to enter the cause in any case. And let our Republicanism, so focused and dedicated, not be made fuzzy and unthinking by stupid labels. I would remind you that extremism in defense of liberty is no vice. And . . . that moderation in the pursuit of justice is no virtue.

With the gauntlet thrown down, conciliation among factions became virtually impossible. Even meetings between Goldwater and all the Republican governors and congressional candidates hosted by President Eisenhower in August[89] did little to bridge the cavernous gap.

Other factional candidates, unlike Goldwater, might be eager to use the party organization to help down the homestretch toward November. Often, however, their preconvention campaigns have alienated them so totally from the mainstream of the party that pleas for unity fall on deaf ears. George McGovern, for example, had a truncated Democratic organization to work with because he had sacrificed his image for the general election in his effort to win the nomination. He expected to be nominated by the left and reunite with the centrists of the party, but, unfortunately for him, they were totally disenchanted. A twenty-fifth-ward Democratic leader from Chicago reflected the sentiments of the old guard:[90]

> I have been here since 1920. For all that time now I been seeing these do-gooder boobs come and go and I'm still here. They come up overnight and think they're going to take over the machine. . . . Those kooks couldn't even be elected street cleaners in Chicago.

To add to his woes, McGovern alienated the Kennedy forces with his ham-fisted handling of the appointment of a national chairperson for the party. Incredibly, he gave the nod to Ms. Jean Westwood, an unknown to most party regulars, after having promised it first to Kennedy and party stalwart Lawrence O'Brien and then to JFK's former press secretary, Pierre Salinger. In both cases, he pulled the rug out from under them with no warning.[91]

Jimmy Carter learned well from McGovern's colossal blunders. At the conclusion of his term as governor, Carter volunteered to aid the 1973 Democratic Party chair, Robert Strauss, in any way he could. He was named chair of the finance committee of the national committee in 1974, and he worked closely with Strauss in coordinating the campaign after the 1976 convention. While the ultimate decisions were being made by the candidate and his "good ole boys," Hamilton Jordan and Gerald Rafshoon, the Carter people were not standoffish. Carter's decision to open his general election bid in Warm Springs, Georgia, Franklin Roosevelt's old retreat, was aimed at demonstrating his close ties with long-standing party philosophies and traditions.

Party regulars are a supportive plus to a candidate's personal organization should he be willing to use them. Numerous calamities can befall those who leave the complicated business of organizing a fifty-state election to legions of politically unsophisticated volunteers. Party regulars provide contacts with state and local party organizations. They are familiar with those personal comments that should be made by the candidate in their particular region. They can help the candidate's speechwriters with information to tailor his "set" speech to his individual audiences.

Nelson Polsby and Aaron Wildavsky recalled Adlai Stevenson's problems with inappropriate speeches. Stevenson prided himself on writing his own. One of his speeches went over the heads of an audience of party workers in Connecticut in 1956 because the punch lines were highly literary and tailored to Yale and Princeton humor. The audience was unprepared and, worse than that, they were uninspired to rally to the cause.[92]

It is on election day, though, that cooperation with the party organization pays its largest dividends. Getting the vote out for a presidential race requires the same mechanics common in state and local races. A candidate may well be "Galluping" away with an election according to political analysts, but, unless the voters turn up in large numbers on election day, first place in the polls won't win a White House job. Party regulars and their leaders are familiar with the mechanics of precinct lists, canvass cards, and telephone banks as tools to bring the faithful to cast their ballots. Few candidates could match that expertise, even with a most highly experienced personal entourage.

Finally, the party organization could serve as a check on excesses that might be undertaken by zealots in the name of the candidate. The Committee to Re-elect President Nixon stands as an unfortunate example of what can happen when a candidate has amassed a whopping ($60-million) war chest[93] and virtually ignores the party. Party leaders might well have served as a moderating influence on CREEP in cases involving some of the more blatant violations of propriety and the law. Their incentives for blowing the whistle, early when necessary, would stem from their realization that public airing of these abuses would wreak havoc on every Republican candidate for office.

## THEMES AND IMAGES

While organization is important, image is crucial. In our media age, products are often foisted off upon gullible consumers who seem to enjoy being fooled. Psychologists, market analysts, ad-agency people, and television technicians band together to create and exploit images with which the public can readily identify. Products are hawked through association with persons and things that the public respects. Today's candidate then cannot be the "typical politician." He must represent what is good and decent about America.

Pat Caddell, former McGovern pollster and president of Cambridge Survey Research, argued, even before Carter hired him, that a candidate who puts together a *thematic* campaign rather than stressing narrowly defined "issues" would stand a good chance of capturing the imagination of the electorate in 1976.[94] McGovern's campaign exhortation, "Come home, America," was rich in this Caddell type of thinking. Jimmy Carter's low-key sermonette style, concentrating on what a "good, decent, honest, and fair nation" America is, struck a responsive chord with the electorate nationwide. Even his purported "fuzziness" on the issues did not short-circuit the advantages his themes and images had provided for him. Jules Witcover, who followed Carter across the country during the campaign, logged this assessment of his style:[95]

> It occurred to me as Carter talked that he was not especially talking down to those children, but that his standard speech itself was a subtle exercise in talking down to an audience, adult or child. . . . enveloping them with his smile and his message of goodness and love that could overcome all adversity.

Effective campaigners make every effort to integrate their overall themes in every media contact with the voters, be it spontaneous or rehearsed.[96]

In well-organized presidential campaigns, themes and images are selected with meticulous attention to such factors as (1) the coalition of voters to be tapped, (2) any tarnish that must be wiped from the candidate's shining armor or advantages to be emphasized, and (3) the value of artful mud slinging. Coalitions were discussed earlier; but, at this juncture, we should note that coordination between pollsters and public relations people is imperative. Public opinion analysts pick up fluctuations in the normal coalition; then the media people produce remedial messages. Soon, pollsters are able to evaluate the success or failure of those spots and ads.

Glossing over or correcting a candidate's image deficiencies can be a demanding if not impossible task. In 1968, for example, Richard Nixon's image-makers sought to create a "new Nixon"—less abrasive, more pleasant, more self-confident, and so forth. As Joe McGinnis illustrates so graphically in *The Selling of the President, 1968,* each of Nixon's media contacts with the public was carefully orchestrated.[97] Ironically, without the intervention of George Wallace's candidacy in 1968, it is questionable whether the "new Nixon" would have been any more successful than the "tricky Dick" of 1960.

Some candidates, especially ideological purists like Goldwater, can be the cause of splitting headaches for their media teams. How can public relations people improve voter perceptions of a man who, like Barry Goldwater, speaks out against labor unions in Detroit and questions the value and viability of the Social Security system in Florida?[98] He also made two disastrous comments about nuclear weapons, suggesting that (1) they be used for jungle defoliation (tactically) in Vietnam and (2) NATO field commanders be given freer rein over tactical use of nuclear weapons. These proposals provided the mud for Lyndon Johnson to sling in an artfully done commercial that depicted a little girl picking petals from a daisy. "Ten, nine, eight, seven, six, five, four, three, two, one . . . (pictures of a nuclear blast). These are the stakes. To make a world in which all of God's children can live . . . or to go into the dark. We must either love each other or we must die. . . . The stakes are too high for you to stay home." Goldwater insisted upon defending himself against this characterization; but it was virtually impossible for his image-makers to convince the voting public that he was much to the left of Attila the Hun.

When Ronald Reagan was cast by the Carter campaign as a candidate who, if elected, would lead the country to war and separate Jew from Christian, men from women, and blacks from whites he reacted most effectively by denying the implications and standing on his record as governor. He argued that under his administration women and minorities had been actively recruited and appointed to high positions. During the only Carter/Reagen debate in 1980 when President Carter spoke critically of Reagan's committments to civil rights, approaches to Social Security reform, and the tendency to use the big stick in foreign affairs, the challenger kept his composure by laughing and referring to his opponent's negative comments by mumbling into the mike, "there he goes again. . . . I didn't say that." Reagan effectively counteracted both the President's debate tactics and his campaign ads which attempted to portray Reagan as a man who lacked compassion for the down-trodden and who was reckless enough to take the nation to war.

Presidential campaign advertising detoured in early 1972 from slick gimmickry to *cinema verité*. Ads began to resemble news broadcasts rather than commercials for deodorant soap. The decision to change came in light of research into the factors that most affected voter views on candidates. Walter DeVries found in 1970 that TV ads ranked twenty-fourth while TV news ranked first.[99] Whether tomorrow's voters will think the same way is for the public opinion analysts to ascertain. It could be that American voters are becoming more selective as they expand their educational horizons.

Ticket splitting[100] may also be a product of these environmental changes. Two researchers into the ticket-splitting phenomenon have found that these voters glean the information they use to make voting judgments through the media.

## MEDIA COVERAGE:
## IMAGES AND ISSUES

Since increasing numbers of voters are depending on journalists for their political information, media decisions on the coverage of events become crucial to all candidates, especially those incapable of funding a media blitz. Editorial conceptions of "what is news" shape coverage patterns because of the extensive number of events from which to select and the limited time and space in which to report. Oliver Wendell Holmes once said that "the law is what the courts say it is." Walter Cronkite could well say, "the issues are what I say they are."

In an analysis of presidential campaign coverage in 1972, Doris Graber found that campaign coverage heavily emphasizes personalities of candidates much more than professional qualifications and issues.[101] She also found that foreign policy and social issues moved out of the limelight with the ebbing of passions over Vietnam and the calming of the once explosive racial tensions of the late 1960s. Nevertheless it could be argued that Carter's inability to bring about the release of the American hostages in Iran cost him the 1980 election. Candidates may attempt to be all things to all people on the issues and still be elected on the basis of their images. A major part of Jimmy Carter's success in 1976 was his ability to come across as moderately liberal to liberals and moderately conservative to conservatives.

THE GREAT DEBATES. Since the famous Kennedy-Nixon debates in 1960, incumbents and their challengers have found it necessary to weigh the pros and cons of challenging or being goaded into face-to-face televised confrontations. Monday morning quarterbacks after the 1960 encounters faulted Nixon for playing into Kennedy's hands. The young Massachusetts senator gained an aura of respectability by being placed on equal footing with the vice-president of the United States. Nixon, on the other hand, was forced to defend the lackluster record of the Eisenhower administration. Kennedy's pleasing appearance and skill as an orator were perfectly attuned to the television medium. The vice president had an image problem that he hoped to dispel by his performance in the debates. To overcome his image as a volatile, vindictive, and coldly calculating personality,[102] he tried to be polite with Kennedy, but it came across as deference. A CBS-sponsored Roper poll[103] found that nearly 2 million voters chose JFK over Nixon largely on the basis of the debates. Considering that the final vote margin between the two was well under 200,000, the debates were crucial to Kennedy's success.

The Carter-Ford encounters in 1976 were handled more as a combined press conference, with each candidate responding to press questions than in a standard debate format.[104] At the time the meetings were agreed to, Carter was riding high in the polls. Ironically, it was Ford, the incumbent president who needed to make political capital in them.[105] By October, when they took place, Carter was reeling from the backlash of a *Playboy* magazine interview in which he had used foul language and admitted to human frailties not to be expected of a "born again" Christian. He also needed to shore up his sagging popularity with the ethnics, especially Catholics, and to show that he could address issues and not always sidestep them.

Carter's campaign continued on its downhill skid even though he did reasonably well and opinion polls had given him a clear victory in the second of the series. Debates always seem to be to the advantage of the trailing candidate. Ford had strategized the debates well. He took the offensive early in the first meeting leaving "Governor" Carter seemingly flustered and deferential to the "president." Although Carter regained his composure in the second debate and scored well, Ford still maintained his presidential advantage until he surprised the audience with the revelation that Eastern Europe was not under Soviet domination. In one sentence, Ford had solved Carter's ethnics problem for him. Throughout the three debates, Ford was on top of figures and facts about pending legislation in response to questions from the press. Carter, as an outsider, did not present the image of being on top of the issues that any president would be asked to deal with. These debates proved once again that front-runners run a great risk of faltering in one-on-one confrontations with their adversaries.

The "debate" held between Jimmy Carter and Ronald Reagan during the 1980 campaign was virtually devoid of the gaffes that crept into the prior televised sparring matches. Reagan's polish as a professional performer and the fact that he didn't put his foot into his mouth brought into question the Carter decision to debate. The race which was a virtual dead-heat began tilting towards Reagan.

## THE FINANCIAL FACTOR

Creating images costs money but this represents only a portion of the cost of a race for the White House. Campaign budgets today bear little resemblance to the items listed and dollars spent in George Washington's day. In his 1757 race for the Virginia House of Burgesses, Washington listed expenditures for the "customary means of winning votes," which meant rum, wine, beer, and hard cider.[106] The ledger for a modern-day presidential campaign is more likely to include such entries as expenditures for (1) professional consulting firms; (2) computer experts to target voters and seek out volunteers; (3) direct-mail fund-raising experts and purchased lists of potential contributors; (4) public opinion analysts (pollsters); (5) public relations, media, and film-making professionals; and (6) secretarial and housekeeping needs such as rent, paper, mailing costs, travel, costs of getting the vote out, and so forth. Even discounting inflation and the large electorate to be reached, costs of today's national elections are astronomical due to the numerous functions to be performed by the organization. Polling costs depleted the Humphrey and Nixon coffers to the tune of $261,521 and $348,102, respectively, in 1968. The total cost of the 1972 campaign was estimated at $140 million, and Nixon alone amassed a personal campaign war chest in excess of $60 million. In 1968 and 1972, the largest expenditures were directed toward TV and radio advertising.[107] In 1976, however, expenditures for television dropped, as did total spending due to 1974 campaign finance legislation, which we will discuss in more detail later in this chapter. While most discussions of campaign finance relate to presidential nominees, the costs of the campaigns also include the start-up costs of all of the potential nominees who braved the primaries.

Presidential candidates spent more in 1976 on their prenomination races than they did in 1972, according to the Federal Election Commission.[108] The most profligate spender was Ronald Reagan, who spent $16.1 million. Next came Gerald Ford at $13.8 million followed by Jimmy Carter at $12.8 million. Other candidates spending more than $1 million included George Wallace ($7.6 million), Henry Jackson ($6.3 million), Morris Udall ($4.3 million), Lloyd Bentsen ($2.3 million), Jerry Brown ($2.0 million), Frank Church ($1.6 million), Fred Harris ($1.4 million) and Birch Bayh ($1.0 million).[109] While the 1974 campaign spending law set a prenomination ceiling on expenditures of $13.1 million, the figures cited for each candidate listed include expenses exempted from the limits under the law.

The *National Journal* found that primary expenditures in 1976 were considerably higher than were those in 1972:[110]

The $77.9 million in pre-nomination expenditures is considerably higher than the estimate for 1972 spending given by Citizens' Research Foundation director Herbert E. Alexander in Financing the 1972 Election (D. C. Heath, 1976). Alexander estimated Democratic expenditures at $32.7 million and Republican at approximately $21 million including $19.7 million spent by President Nixon. Since the Republican nomination was not contested seriously, Alexander said that most of Nixon's expenses probably should be considered general election expenses.

While total reported expenditures were up in 1976, the Democratic nominee, Carter, spent about the same amount of money as his predecessor, George McGovern. In Carter's day, though, the dollars he had to spend were worth much less than they had been for McGovern in 1972, so it could be said that he exercised less buying power.

AMASSING A WAR CHEST. Before 1976, the costs of campaigns were growing astronomically, forcing candidates to tap every previously known source and conjure up new ways of feeding their monstrous organizations. Some candidates had the advantage of raiding their own personal fortunes. In 1968, for example, Nelson Rockefeller gave at least $350,000 to his own campaign in addition to $300,000 he had contributed to George Romney's effort. Rockefeller's step-mother advanced $1.5 million to the New York governor's race for the White House. Likewise the Kennedy family is widely recognized as having bankrolled large portions of the preconvention campaigns of both sons, John and Robert.[111]

For those born without silver spoons in their mouths, there have always been a few "fat cats" willing to help make them competitive. David Adamany, in researching the effects of "big givers" between 1952 and 1972, determined that each election year found more money available and larger numbers of "big" contributors.

From 1952 to 1960 givers of $10,000 or more numbered about one hundred in each presidential year with gifts totaling between $1.6 and $2.3 million. In 1964, their numbers rose slightly to 130. . . . The 1968 campaign was a watershed: the number of $10,000 givers jumped to 424 and their total contributions exceeded $12.2 million. 1972 was an orgy of big money. Big givers were now defined at the $50,000 level, and the Nixon-Agnew drive wooed 124 such givers who anted up $16.8 million.[112]

Insurance executive W. Clement Stone personally contributed well over $2 million and others contributed close to that figure. Walter Annenberg ($254,000) was considered for an ambassadorial position partly due to his generosity.[113] Buying positions may provide funds for a candidate, but the practice hardly ensures capable public officials.

GROUP CONTRIBUTIONS. Interest groups patriotically open their purses and commit volunteers to friendly presidential contenders. The Committee on Political Education of the AFL-CIO has been an invaluable source of support for Democratic candidates. In addition to contributions in dollars, organized labor since 1952 has also been generous with contributions in kind (i.e., things other than money that the candidate would otherwise have to spend for). This includes volunteers to handle canvassing, voter registration, and manning phones to help get the vote out. They can be especially helpful to candidates in the primaries, as Henry Jackson expected in the 1976 Pennsylvania primary.[114] Conventional wisdom places big business contributions in the pocket of the Republican nominee, and that thinking is essentially accurate. Business giving was especially evident to the Committee for the Re-election of President Nixon in 1972. The gifts list among members of the oil and gas industry, for example, was a "Who's Who" of the field. Contributions by officers and stockholders in these companies accumulated nearly $5 million for the Nixon effort.[115] They had made it clear to Mr. Nixon during his first administration that they resented the activities of the Anti-Trust Division of the Justice Department, which was sounding dangerously like Teddy Roosevelt (trustbuster) in its investigations of monopoly practices in the industry. Attorney General Mitchell had to give a political lesson in a meeting of the anti-trust group. Journalists Rowland Evans and Robert Novak described Mitchell's unannounced visit as follows:[116]

> Speaking briefly and laconically, Mitchell urged the task force to practice extreme caution. "Don't put the President in a box," he said. No further explanation was needed. He was gently instructing the task force to forget its long months of economic computations rather than embarrass the President with his allies in big oil. After Mitchell's intervention, the task force markedly scaled down the scope of its recommendations.

For every dollar of oil money, there is potential for milk money, medical money, defense dollars, and numerous other campaign revenue sources.

In addition to interest group monies, the candidate can draw, should he wish, on funds available through his party's national committee. It should be noted, however, that the role of the party has been steadily declining with the rise of intense campaign organization by the candidate long before the earliest of the primaries. In 1972, Nixon's Committee to Re-elect the President declared its independence from the party machinery.[117]

> The Committee for the Re-election of the President had the responsibility to get the President re-elected; the Republican National Committee had the responsibility for other candidates. We very definitely do not want Nixon perceived as the Republican candidate for President, but as Richard Nixon running for re-election, or the President running for re-election.

The Carter organization went so far as to present a set of goals to the Democratic National Committee (DNC) based on using the party machinery and most of its revenues to "get out the vote" for all Democrats across the nation. The campaign finance legislation limited party spending on the ticket to $3.2 million in 1976, but no limits were placed on party-building efforts not directed toward a specific candidate. Mark Siegel, executive director of the DNC, discussed its role as Carter viewed it:[118]

> After spending $3.2 million directly on the Carter-Mondale ticket, he would like to see the DNC spend between $2 million and $2.4 million on voter registration, $1.2 million on getting the vote out, $1 million for polling, $1 million for DNC operations and $300,000 for candidate training and education.

The voter registration drive was similar to the program in which the Republican National Committee had been involved. Siegel even gave targets for voter registration numbers:[119]

We are aiming at registering one million people. There are 55 million un-registered people in the country and at least two-thirds of them, if they were registered, would vote Democratic.

FEDERAL ELECTION FINANCE LEGISLATION. The election of 1976, funded partially through federal matching funds, opened a new chapter in presidential campaign financing. Although many analysts prefer to view these finance reforms as a reaction to Watergate, the pool of funds used in 1976 was collected on the basis of legislation (the Revenue Act) passed in 1971.[120] The legislation permitted taxpayers to divert $1 of their tax payments into a presidential election campaign fund that was intended to match dollars raised by each candidate for president. During that same year Congress enacted the Federal Election Campaign Act to plug up some of the glaring loopholes that had not been sufficiently addressed under the Corrupt Practices Act of 1925. The emphasis of the new legislation was exposure of campaign finances through disclosure requirements. Political committees receiving or spending over $1,000 in a year for *any* federal candidate were required to register with the government. The information required included reports on major ($100 or more) contributors and expenditures. The act also restricted the amount a candidate for federal office could spend on media (radio, television, newspapers, magazines, billboards, etc.) to 10 cents per voting-age person in the contested area (i.e., congressional district, state, or nation as a whole).

Unlike other expenditures that might be hidden in a maze of figures on a campaign ledger, these expenditures could be easily verified through investigation of payments made to outside firms. This Federal Election Campaign Act[121] went a long way toward assuring the public's right to know who is providing the financial backing for presidential hopefuls.

The Watergate scandal and the reported "dirty tricks" and other campaign abuses of the Committee to Re-elect President Nixon aroused angry demands for more far-reaching reforms. In 1974, new campaign finance legislation was enacted and its provisions profoundly affected the race for the White House in 1976 by opening up the quest to more hopefuls and reducing the "fat cats" of past campaigns to a more slender role (see Table 10.3).

Federal matching funds lengthened the list of hopefuls in 1976. Requirements that matching funds go to those who collected $5,000 in small contributions in twenty states also forced the potential candidates to make very early "go- no-go" decisions. Joel Goldstein, in an in-depth study of the influence of money on the 1976 presidential selection process, found that federal funds helped to produce "serious" candidates, some of them two years prior to the nominating conventions (see Table 10.4).[122]

The fact that fewer dollars were spent on the race for the White House in 1976 than in 1972 can be attributed largely to the reform legislation we have just examined. Media spending limits from 1971 legislation and spending ceilings imposed in 1974 were the major contributing factors braking the momentum of big-dollar presidential politics. Also, 60 percent of the $114 million expended in 1976 was provided by federal funds, thus lessening the role of large single contributors.

Incumbency advantages were magnified by these reforms. Gerald Ford was better able to budget his limited resources since he had instant media access at no cost. Jimmy Carter, therefore, needed more money just to make himself and his views

## TABLE 10.3
## MAJOR PROVISIONS OF CAMPAIGN FINANCE LAW OF 1974

| GENERAL SUBJECT | SPECIFIC REGULATIONS |
|---|---|
| Matching funds | Candidates must raise $5,000 in each of 20 states in contributions of $250 or less. |
| | Candidates must agree to spending limits if federal funds are accepted. |
| | Federal dollars will match candidates' contributions to the ceilings. |
| Ceilings on spending | Candidate may spend only $10 million on the preconvention campaign (inflation factor for future years: $11 million in 1976, $ 17.2 million in 1980). |
| | Candidates may spend only $20 million on general election campaign (inflation factor for future years: $22 million in 1976, $35 million in 1980). |
| | Candidates may spend amounts equal to 20% of their total spending for fund raising—*not counted in ceilings.* |
| Political parties | Each major party may receive up to $2 million to pay for its national convention. |
| | Parties may spend 2 cents per voting-age person on behalf of presidential candidates. |
| Contributions | Candidates may spend no more than $50,000 on their own campaigns (Supreme Court outlawed this provision in *Buckley* v. *Valeo*). |
| | A person may contribute up to $1,000 directly to candidates in each primary and general election. No more than $25,000 total may be contributed to federal office candidates by one person in one year. |
| | Organizations are limited to contributions of $5,000 per candidate per year. |
| | Supreme Court declares that persons may spend their own funds for a candidate as long as they do not cooperate with a candidate's organization in doing so. |
| Enforcement | A six-person federal election commission was established (selection process modified by the Supreme Court). |

Sources: Adapted from: Frank Sorauf, *Party Politics in America*, 4th ed. (Boston: Little, Brown, 1980), pp. 316-320, and Herbert Alexander, "Financing Politics: Money, Elections and Political Reform" (Washington, D.C.: Congressional Quarterly Press, 1980), 30-38.

known to the public. Under the 1974 law, however, since both the president and the contender had accepted federal matching funds, spending ceilings became a factor. By the end of the campaign the Carter budget for mass media had become tight, and frills like bumper stickers and campaign buttons became as precious to collectors as the works of Van Gogh.[123] Even at the time of the convention, though, Carter buttons were being hawked by industrious entrepreneurs around Madison Square Garden for as much as $25 each.[124] Due to Gerald Ford's incumbency, his campaign organization was able to use its media money sparingly, saving up for a

## TABLE 10.4
### CANDIDATES IN 1976 AND DATE OF INITIAL CORRESPONDENCE WITH THE FEDERAL ELECTION COMMISSION

| CANDIDATES | DATE |
| --- | --- |
| Democrats | |
| Bireh Bayh | August 5, 1975 |
| Lloyd Bentsen | February 14, 1975 |
| Edmund G. Brown | March 22, 1976 |
| Jimmy Carter | November 14, 1974 |
| Frank Church | December 12, 1975 |
| Fred Harris | January 28, 1975 |
| Henry Jackson | June 17, 1974 |
| Ellen McCormack | July 8, 1975 |
| Terry Sanford | June 21, 1974 |
| Milton Shapp | June 25, 1975 |
| Sargent Shriver | July 15, 1975 |
| Morris Udall | February 10, 1975 |
| George Wallace | December 2, 1974 |
| Republicans | |
| Gerald Ford | June 20, 1975 |
| Ronald Reagan | July 24, 1975 |

Source: Federal Election Commission, *FEC Disclosure.* Series No. 7 (Washington, D.C.: G.P.O., 1976, and Joel H. Goldstein, "The Influence of Money on the Pre-Nomination Stage of the Presidential Selection Process: The Case of 1976 Election," *Presidential Studies Quarterly*, (Spring 1978), 166.

media blitz closer to election day. The spending ceilings also made planning expenditures more important than it had ever been in the preceilings past. Obviously, when a race is close, an outsider can ill afford to run out of money in the last weeks of the campaign and leave the air waves to the incumbent.

Supporters of Ronald Reagan in 1980 helped him overcome the problem of overspending the federal campaign law limits by forming private committees not linked to the Reagan organization. Five groups in particular, the North Carolina Congressional Club, the National Conservative Political Action Committee (NCPAC), the Fund for a Conservative Majority, Americans for Change, and Americans for an Effective Presidency contributed millions of dollars to the Reagan effort while scrupulously avoiding consent of the candidate or his campaign organization. These groups took advantage of the Supreme Court decision in *Buckley* v. *Voleo,* 1976. The Court argued that it was unconstitutional to limit expenditures for or against political candidates so long as individuals or groups making them did so without approval of the candidates themselves or their campaign organizations.[125]

One 1980 candidate for the Republican presidential nomination, John Connally, decided not to take federal funds in order to avoid the spending limits forced on recipients. His well-heeled friends bankrolled his South Carolina primary race to the tune of $12 million. This Texas-sized budget resulted in only one convention delegate. Even if he had been successful in South Carolina, it is doubtful that he could have kept up his fund-raising success indefinitely. His delegate was history's most expensive.

# REGIONAL STRATEGIES AND
# THE ELECTORAL COLLEGE

While strategy is important in the pre-convention organizational spending phases, the Electoral College system dictates many strategic decisions for both major candidates as they move down the homestretch from the convention to the November elections. Under the existing mechanics, which have not changed measurably throughout U.S. history, candidates gain electoral votes only if they are popular vote winners in a particular state. Since winner takes all, the voice of the minority of voters in each state has no bearing on who will sit in the White House. The system encourages hopefuls to concentrate their efforts in states that they think they can win, especially the ones with large electoral vote counts.[126] Typically, Republicans will concentrate on the agricultural Mid-West, the Yankee Northeast and the Far West. Democratic nominees depend upon the populous Urban Northeast and the old South. Prudent candidates tend to absent themselves from the opponents' turf. Still, no candidate can afford to side-step the large pivotal states like California, Illinois, Texas, Pennsylvania, Michigan, Ohio, and New York. Victories in just these states would insure 211 of the 270 votes needed for victory in the electoral college.

## CHART 10.3    ELECTORAL COLLEGE BREAKDOWN BY STATES IN 1980

In 1976 Carter sought to at least split the vote in thirteen states whose electoral votes totaled 291. Half those votes added to the South and "safe" Democratic states were considered enough to put him over the top. The basic Carter game plan worked for him as his final vote totals showed his greatest strength in the South and in the traditionally Democratic sections of the East. In fact, of the ten states Carter won with more than 55 percent of the vote, all were in the South and East (see Table 10.5).[127]

### TABLE 10.5
### ELECTION 1976: VOTE BY REGIONS

|  | EAST | SOUTH | MIDWEST | WEST | NATIONAL VOTE | NATIONAL % OF TOTAL |
|---|---|---|---|---|---|---|
| Jimmy Carter | 51.5% | 53.7% | 48.3% | 45.7% | 40,828,587 | 50.1% |
| Gerald Ford | 47.0 | 45.0 | 49.7 | 51.0 | 39,147,613 | 48.0 |

Source: Special Report, *President Carter*, Congressional Quarterly Service (Washington, D.C.: G.P.O., 1977), p. 70.

## DEMOCRACY
## AND THE ELECTORAL COLLEGE

Few of our American political institutions have come under more concentrated political fire than the Electoral College. It has been criticized as an archaic remnant of antidemocratic thinking abroad in the land at the time of the Constitutional Convention in 1787. Article II of the Constitution as amended by the Twelfth Amendment simply provides that

1. Each state shall be apportioned electors according to its total representation in the U.S. Congress (senators and representatives).
2. State legislatures set the patterns for choosing electors.
3. Electors meet in their states to cast ballots.
4. Votes are counted before both houses of Congress.
5. A majority vote constitutes election.
6. When no candidate gets a majority, the House makes the determination by majority vote, each state having only one vote.

Twice in our history, the electors yielded to the House of Representatives to make the selection because of deadlock (in 1800 and in 1824). Two other times since the Civil War, candidates won in the popular vote but lost in the Electoral College (in 1876 and in 1888). The possibility that the popular vote could be overturned in the Electoral College constitutes a glaring anachronism for a nation that prides itself on being a representative democracy. The mechanisms violate the one-person, one-vote principle because custom, and some state statutes, dictate that the candidate who wins the general election in a state, even if only by one vote, gets all its electors. This is tantamount to disenfranchising minority voters in a state even if they constitute 49 percent plus of the vote. The apportionment of electors to the states gives the large-population states more leverage in selecting the president than their smaller counterparts. Since the Constitution does not bind electors to follow the views of the majority in their home states expressed in the November election, it is possible for them to cast ballots according to their own judgment. However, this rarely happens. In 1976, for example, of 538 electors, only 1, a Republican, voted for Reagan although Gerald Ford had carried that elector's home state, Washington.

Numerous proposals have surfaced in Congress to attack the inequities of the existing system. The list could be summarized into the following categories: (1) those that would do away with individual electors, (2) those that call for dividing the electoral votes according to the proportion of the state popular vote each candidate receives, (3) those that propose selection of electors from congressional districts rather than on a statewide basis, and (4) those that aim to do away with individual electors who might deviate from the voter's choice, but retain the electoral winner-take-all vote in the states.[128] While proposals have been as numerous as pigeons in Central Park, Congress has balked at reformation of the system because of the uproar that changes would elicit from the traditionally omnipotent Northern urban states that hold the trump cards in the present Electoral College game. The last serious attempt to amend the Constitution with respect to the Electoral College was made in 1968.[129] The amendment would have abolished the college in favor of the popular vote alone. In the event that no candidate garnered 40 percent of the popular vote, the top two candidates would participate in a runoff election. The idea passed the House but was fillibustered to death in the Senate by small-state and Southern senators. Paradoxically, the Northern urban states did not oppose the change. While it is true that candidates strategize on the basis of the large-state votes in the Electoral College, it is the small, rural, and Southern states that are overrepresented in the system, since they get electoral votes for their two senators regardless of the fact that they have small populations.

## PROBLEMS WITH THE SELECTION
## PROCESS IN SUMMATION

Our present system of nomination and election of the president presents numerous difficulties both in ensuring effective leadership and in maintaining vital democratic processes. As things stand today, there is no preprimary system for weeding out incompetent hopefuls who know how to become popular through projecting a salable image. The growing popularity of the preference primary system has enhanced citizen participation in the nomination process but, their growing numbers, the fact that they are bunched together on the calendar, and the fact that crucial primaries can be taking place at opposite ends of the country on consecutive Tuesdays makes in-depth discussion of issues in any one state virtually impossible. Media coverage of the preconvention stage of the process could have great potential as a vehicle for airing issues, but time restrictions on the grueling campaign trail have encouraged reporters to emphasize personalities over issues.

Adjustments in party rules on delegate selection and convention procedures have loosened the stranglehold that party pros have had on the nominating process. The changes, however, have worked to the advantage of personalist candidates rather than recognized, electable party leaders who represent the mainstream of their party. Revolutionary campaign finance reforms, especially those since 1974, have opened the doors to the White House to contenders who in the past would have been unable to accumulate the necessary capital to make the race without selling their souls to the groups that would bankroll their campaigns. While the role of large single contributors has been noticeably curtailed, it has not been totally eliminated. Mandated spending ceilings in both the primaries and the general election seemed to minimize the likelihood of Watergate-like abuses because so little money was left for more legitimate expenditures as polling, media advertising, and getting out the vote. However, the emergence of the five large support committees for Reagan in 1980, which provided needed services to the campaign through funds collected outside of the candidate's campaign umbrella, brings into question the effectiveness of the spending limits since the Supreme Court in *Buckley* v. *Valeo* (1976) opened up this massive loophole.

In light of the other moves toward democracy in the earlier stages of the selection process, the Electoral College stands out as a relic of the past hardly befitting a modern democracy. Since it ensures no more capable administrators than more direct democracy alternatives do, there seems to be little justification for its continuation beyond regional political considerations.

## NOTES

[1] James Madison, *Federalist 10* in *The Federalist: A Commentary on the Constitution of the U.S.*, ed. Edward Meade Earle (New York: Modern Library, 1937), pp. 53-62.

[2] Alexander Hamilton, *Federalist 68* in *Ibid.*, pp. 441-442.

[3] Congressional Quarterly Service, *President Carter, Special Issue* (Washington, D.C.: G.P.O., 1977), p. 6.

[4] This was probably due to the fact that the media had not recognized that a brokered convention might not be inevitable.

[5] In 1973, Jimmy Carter appeared on the television and went virtually unrecognized, yet by the following year he was actively involved as Democratic National Committee Finance Chair and as a guest on "Meet the Press." On the matter of the recognition factor and Jimmy Carter in his race for the White House, see Gerald Pomper and colleagues, *The Election of 1976: Reports and Interpretations* (New York: David McKay, 1977), p. 10.

[6] *President Carter,* p. 3.

[7] On number of federal employees, see Jimmy Carter, "Accompanying Message to the State of the Union Address," as cited in *Congressional Quarterly Weekly Reports,* January 28, 1978, p. 209.

Population figures from the U.S. Department of Commerce, Bureau of the Census, *Current Population Reports: Population Estimates and Projections,* Series P-25, No. 647 (Washington, D.C.: G.P.O., February 1977), p. 1.

[8] Frank J. Sorauf, *Party Politics in America,* 3rd ed. (Boston: Little, Brown, 1976), p. 298. Availability is also handled well in Stephen Hess, *The Presidential Campaign: The Leadership Selection Process after Watergate* (Washington, D.C.: Brookings Institution, 1974), pp. 23-35.

[9] U.S. Constitution, Article II, Section 1.

[10] The states involved are California (45), New York (41), Pennsylvania (27), Texas and Illinois (26 each), Ohio (25), Michigan (21), Florida and New Jersey (17 each), Massachusetts (14), and Indiana (13).

[11] Some would argue that, since more candidates are likely from the Senate, the population size is less important since small-state senators are TV visible. But will they be popular in large electoral states?

[12] A good discussion of the implications of the West Virginia primary can be found in Theodore White, *The Making of the President, 1960* (New York: Mentor Books, 1961), pp. 116-126.

[13] George Gallup, *The Gallup Poll Public Opinion, 1935-71* (New York: Random House, 1972), p. 2327.

[14] Hunter S. Thompson, *Fear and Loathing on the Campaign Trail, 1972* (New York: Popular Library, 1972), p. 59.

[15] Ellen McCormack, who had no previous political experience, ran as a Pro Life Democrat and had her name placed in nomination to dramatize her opposition to the Supreme Court's *Doe* v. *Bolton* and *Roe* v. *Wade* cases that permitted abortion on demand for "health" reasons. McCormack was one of four nominated for president in 1976, joining Carter, Morris Udall, and Jerry Brown. Before the advent of federal matching funds, campaigns like hers would have been impossible.

[16] President Carter, p. 11.

[17] Theodore White, *Making of the President, 1972* (New York: Atheneum, 1973), p. 106.

[18] Jules Witcover, *Marathon: The Pursuit of the Presidency, 1972-1976* (New York: Viking Penguin, Inc., 1977), p. 321.

[19] Erwin C. Hargrove, "What Manner of Man: The Crisis of the Contemporary Presidency," in *Choosing the President*, American Assembly Series, ed. James David Barber (Englewood Cliffs, N.J.: Prentice-Hall, 1974), p. 33.

[20] James Sundquist, "What Happened to Our Checks and Balances," in *Has the President Too Much Power?*, ed. Charles Roberts (New York: Harper's Magazine Press, 1974), p. 110.

[21] Robert Peabody and Eva Lubalin, "The Making of Presidential Candidates," in *The Future of the American Presidency*, ed. Charles Dunn (Morristown, N.J.: General Learning Press, 1975), p. 28, provided the basis for this information up to the Nixon administration.

[22] This act will be discussed in more detail later on in this chapter.

[23] Good discussion of the list of hopefuls in Pomper, et al., *op. cit.*, pp. 10-17.

[24] This situation has become especially acute in light of what has come to be known as the Proposition 13 mentality. This refers to the California initiative led by Howard Jarvis, which was approved by California voters. It cut property taxes by one third, which had an unavoidable effect on the security of state and local government personnel.

[25] Congressional Quarterly Services, *Politics in America*, Special Edition (Washington, D.C.: G.P.O., 1969), pp. 148-155. Also see Robert Walters, "The Quirks of the Political Creature," *National Journal*, November 6, 1976, p. 1605.

[26] Theodore White, *The Making of the President, 1968* (New York: Atheneum, 1970), p. 74. The "brainwashing" speech and its fallout are discussed (pp. 69-73).

[27] Witcover, *op. cit.*, p. 116.

[28] "And Now Here's Spiro . . . for '76," *Time*, November 20, 1972, p. 19.

[29] Dom Bonafede, "The Veep: A Heartbeat Away or Only as Close as the Polling Place," *National Journal*, July 10, 1976, p. 968. This article discusses the efforts of the Harvard study group on the vice-presidential selection process conducted under the auspices of the Harvard University Institute of Politics.

[30] It is noteworthy that, of the forty U.S. presidents, one third or thirteen of them served as vice-presidents. During this century, six of the fourteen presidents had occupied the vice-presidency including three of the last five (Johnson, Nixon, and Ford). U.S. Department of Health, Education, and Welfare, Social Security Administration, *DHEW No. SS A 73-10322* (Washington, D.C.: G.P.O., October 1972), as reproduced in Edward R. Tufte, *Political Control of the Economy* (Princeton, N.J.: Princeton U.P., 1978), p. 32.

[31] *Ibid.*, p. 39. See also Rowland Evans and Robert Novak, "Nixonomics," in *Nixon in the White House* (New York: Random House, 1972), pp. 177-210.

[32] Erwin C. Hargrove, *Power of the Modern Presidency* (New York: Knopf, 1974), p. 46.

[33]Witcover, *op. cit.*, p. 115.

[34]*Ibid.*, p. 118.

[35]*Ibid.*, p. 123.

[36]Theodore White, *Making of the President, 1960* (New York: Mentor Books, 1967), pp. 56, 283ff., discusses the Kennedy staff before and after the nomination.

[37]Theodore White, *Making of the President, 1964* (New York: Signet, 1966), p. 310. This selection discusses the bad blood between Robert Kennedy and Lyndon Johnson.

[38]Dan Rather and Gary Paul Gates, *The Palace Guard* (New York: Warner, 1975), pp. 179-185. See also White, *Making of the President, 1968*, p. 174.

[39]Joe McGinnis, *The Selling of the President, 1968* (New York: Pocket Books, 1970), p. 21.

[40]For a discussion of Burke's philosophy, see Dante Germino, *Modern Western Political Thought: Machiavelli to Marx* (Chicago: Rand McNally, 1972), pp. 221ff.

[41]White, *The Making of the President, 1972*, p. 338.

[42]Nelson Polsby and Aaron Wildavsky, *Presidential Elections*, 4th ed. (New York: Scribner's, 1976), p. 107.

[43]For a generalized study of the primary system, see Polsby and Wildavsky, *op. cit.*, pp. 95-96. A more updated discussion of the role of the primaries can be found in Warren E. Miller and Theresa E. Levitin, *Leadership and Change: Presidential Elections from 1952 to 1976* (Cambridge, Mass.: Winthrop Press, 1976), pp. 189-240. As clear a summation of the differences among the types of primaries can be found in Sorauf, *op. cit.*, pp. 274-278.

[44]Timothy Crouse, *The Boys on the Bus* (New York: Random House, 1973), p. 47.

[45]*Ibid.*, p. 48.

[46]White, *Making of the President, 1968*, pp. 109-111.

[47]An excellent discussion of the "religion issue" can be found in Herbert Asher, *Presidential Elections and American Politics* (Homewood, Ill.: Dorsey Press, 1976), pp. 143-147. See also Philip E. Converse, "Religion and Politics: The 1960 Election," in *Elections and Political Order*, eds. Angus Campbell and associates (New York: John Wiley, 1966), pp. 112-113.

[48]*President Carter*, p. 6.

[49]For a full listing of the total vote and the Carter percentage in the Democratic primaries of 1976 including the dates of each, see Pomper et al., *op. cit.*, pp. 14-15.

[50]Pomper, et al., *op. cit.*, p. 13.

[51]*The New York Times*, August 4, 1978.

[52]White, *Making of the President, 1972*, p. 140.

[53]"The ABC's of How a President Is Chosen, *U.S. News and World Report*, February 18, as reprinted in Annual Editions *American Government 80/81*, 10th ed., (Guilford, Ct.: Dushkin, Sluice Dock, 1980), 200-201. In nine states in 1976, the secretary of state placed the names of nationally recognized presidential candidates on the ballot. They were California, Idaho, Maryland, Massachusetts, Michigan, Nebraska, Nevada, Oregon, and Tennessee. In five other states, a special nominating committee determined which presidential candidates would be listed: Florida, Georgia, Kentucky, North Carolina, and Wisconsin. Eleven states required that candidates or supporters file petitions with specified numbers of signatures to be on the ballot. In five states, the candidate's name didn't even appear on the ballot.

[54]The best discussion in detail of the Goldwater strategies can be found in John Kessel, *The Goldwater Coalition* (Indianapolis: Bobbs-Merrill, 1968). Also see Stephen Shadegg, *What Happened to Goldwater* (New York: Holt, Rinehart and Winston, 1965).

[55]Turnout in the primaries is handled well in Austin Ranney, "Turnout and Representation in Presidential Primary Elections," *American Political Science Review*, (March 1972), esp. p. 2137.

[56]Hess, *op. cit.*, pp. 33ff. The most democratic of the proposals and the best known plan for a direct national primary was introduced as a constitutional amendment by Senators Mike Mansfield and George Aiken in March 1972. It calls for a primary in early August and, if no candidate wins at least 40 percent of the vote, a run-off election twenty-eight days later. Candidates would qualify for the primary by filing petitions signed by a certain percentage of voters nationwide. The purpose of the conventions would be to write the platforms and pick the vice-presidential nominees.

Opponents of the national primary proposals include Paul T. David, Ralph M. Goldman, and Richard C. Bain, *The Politics of National Party Conventions* (Washington, D.C.: Brookings Institution, 1960), pp. 489-490.

For useful discussions of problems with the primaries as they exist, see Robert Sickels, *Presidential Transactions* (Englewood Cliffs, N.J.: Prentice-Hall, 1974), pp. 6-7. Also William R. Keech and Donald R. Matthews, *The Party Choice* (Washington, D.C.: Brookings Institution, 1976). A good discussion of primary rules on the selection of presidential candidates is in James I. Lengle and Byron Shafer, "Primary Rules, Political Power, and Social Change," *American Political Science Review,* (March 1976), 25-40. On the increasing importance of the primaries as a determining factor in who gets the nomination, see Arthur T. Hadley, *The Invisible Primary* (Englewood Cliffs, N.J.: Prentice-Hall, 1976).

[57] A discussion of the Wallace and McCarthy phenomena can be found in Phillip Converse, Warren Miller, Jerrold G. Rusk, and Arthur C. Wolfe, "Continuity and Change in American Politics," *American Political Science Review,* (December 1969), 1092-1093. On the history of the primaries, see Louise Overacker, *The Presidential Primary* (New York: Macmillan, 1926). A more recent historical discussion can be found along with extensive discussions of the implications of the primaries in the election of the president in James W. Davis, *Springboard to the White House: Presidential Primaries—How They Are Fought and Won* (New York: Crowell, 1967).

[58] Citizen participation in party politics including the primaries is discussed in John S. Saloma and Frederick M. Sontag, *Parties: The Real Opportunity for Effective Citizen Politics* (New York: Vintage Books, 1973).

[59] On Goldwater's campaign strategy and his quest for the nomination, see F. Clifton White, *Suite 3505: The Story of the Draft Goldwater Movement* (New Rochelle, N.Y.: Arlington House, 1967).

[60] Donald R. Matthews, "Presidential Nominations: Process and Outcomes," in *Choosing the President,* p. 60.

[61] Possibly this is why many states are going to primaries to keep these types from complicating state politics and state conventions. For further discussion on the role of neophytes in the selection process in 1972, see Jeanne Kirkpatrick, *The Presidential Elite* (New York: Russell Sage Foundation, 1976).

[62] In 1976, for example, only 21 million participated in major party primaries whereas 81 million voted in the general election.

[63] Witcover, *op. cit.,* p. 461. For more on this see Pomper, et al., *op. cit.,* p. 26.

[64] Witcover, *op. cit.,* p. 462.

[65] *Ibid.,* p. 463.

[66] *Ibid.,* p. 469.

[67] Polsby and Wildavsky, *op. cit.,* p. 127.

[68] White, *The Making of the President, 1960,* p. 182.

[69] White, *The Making of the President, 1972,* p. 226. Stearns decided that 1,442 votes were frozen for McGovern, that another 187 coalition votes were disturbed by conscience, and that a possible 106 more could have been reached by deals.

[70] The Winograd commission was chaired by Morley A. Winograd, Michigan State Chair who was asked to look into Presidential nomination and party structure. See Paul Clancy, "Battlelines Are Being Drawn Over How the Democrats Pick Their Candidate," *National Journal,* February 11, 1978, pp. 227-229.

[71] *Ibid.,* p. 229.

[72] *Ibid.,* p. 83. A complete analysis of the credentials fights can be found in John R. Schmidt and Wayne W. Whalis, "Credentials Contests at the 1968 and 1972 Democratic National Conventions," *Harvard Law Review,* 1438-1470, as cited in Hugh A. Bone, *American Politics and the Party System,* 4th ed. (New York: McGraw-Hill, 1974), p. 301.

[73] *O'Brien* v. *Brown,* 409 U.S. 1, 1972.

[74] Pomper et al., *op. cit.,* p. 19.

[75] The whole concept of "bonus" delegates is based on the belief that states should be rewarded with additional voting power if they have elected party candidates to office in the state

and supported the national ticket in previous elections. On bonuses, see Bone, *op. cit.*, pp. 288-289.

[76] For a thorough discussion of the roles of the four major committees, see V. O. Key, *Politics, Parties and Pressure Groups*, 5th ed. (New York: Crowell, 1969), pp. 412-422.

[77] On the Taft-Eisenhower conflicts, see *Ibid.*, pp. 417-418.

[78] The vitriolic credentials fights are discussed in White, *Making of the President, 1972*, pp. 212-221.

[79] In recent years that could be due to the fact that the primaries are more numerous and visible.

[80] *Gallup Poll Opinion Index*, no. 137, December 1976, 2-4.

[81] *Ibid.*, pp. 2-4.

[82] Polsby and Wildavsky, *op. cit.*, p. 198.

[83] Kevin Phillips, *The Emerging Republican Majority* (New Rochelle, N.Y.: Arlington House, 1969).

[84] On the Democratic coalition, see Asher, *op. cit.*, p. 49. Also, for weaknesses in it, see Richard L. Rubin, *Party Dynamics: The Democratic Coalition and the Politics of Change* (New York: Oxford U.P., 1973).

See also *Gallup Poll Opinion Index*, no. 125 (November-December 1975), 104. In addition see Pomper, *Election 1976*, pp. 61-62.

[85] *Gallup Poll Opinion Index*, no. 137 (December 1976), 2-4.

[86] Pomper et al., *op. cit.*, p. 64.

[87] "Carter's Collapse: The Anatomy of Reagan's Victory," *CBS News/The New York Times*, as cited in the *National Journal*, November 8, 1980.

[88] John Kessel, "Strategy for November," in *Choosing the President*, pp. 95, 98-100.

[89] *Ibid.*, p. 99.

[90] *Ibid.*, p. 110.

[91] White, *The Making of the President, 1972*, pp. 250-255.

[92] Polsby and Wildavsky, *op. cit.*

[93] See *Congressional Quarterly*, October 6, 1973, p. 2659.

[94] Michael Malbin, Dom Bonafede, and Robert Walters, "After 8 Long Years on the Outside, the Democrats Want to Come Inside," *National Journal*, July 24, 1976, p. 1024.

[95] Witcover, *op. cit.*, p. 247.

[96] Robert Agranoff, *The Management of Election Campaigns* (Boston: Holbrook, 1976), p. 338.

[97] McGinnis, *op. cit.*, pp. 1-18.

[98] For Goldwater on Social Security, see White, *Making of the President, 1964*, pp. 360-362.

[99] *Congressional Quarterly Weekly Reports*, May 4, 1974, pp. 1105-1108. See also L. Patrick Devlin, "Contrasts in Presidential Campaign Commercials," *Journal of Broadcasting*, (Winter 1973), 17-26.

[100] On ticket splitting, see *Gallup Poll Opinion Index*, no. 137 (December 1976), 7. See also Walter DeVries and Lance Tarrance, *The Ticket Splitter* (Grand Rapids, Mich.: Eerdmans, 1972).

[101] Doris Graber, "Effects of Incumbency on Coverage Patterns in 1972 Presidential Campaign," *Journalism Quarterly*, (Autumn 1976), 508. See also David S. Myers, "Editorials and Foreign Affairs in the 1976 Presidential Campaign," *Journalism Quarterly*, (Spring 1978), 92-99. Also useful in this area is Stephen Hess, "Foreign Policy and Presidential Campaigns," in Stanley Bach and George T. Sulzner, *Perspectives on the Presidency* (Lexington, Mass.: D. C. Heath, 1974).

[102] Nixon's reputation for wielding the political axe against his opponents by innuendo as in the cases of early foes in races for the House and Senate in California Jerry Voorhis and Helen Gahagan Douglas is well chronicled in Gary Wills, *Nixon's Agonistes: The Crisis of the Self-made Man* (New York: Signet, 1971), pp. 74-92.

[103] White, *Making of the President, 1960*, p. 332.

[104] See Sidney Kraus, ed., *The Great Debates* (Bloomington: Indiana U.P., 1962).

[105] Witcover, *op. cit.*, p. 610.

[106] George Thayer, *Who Shakes the Honey Tree* (New York: Simon & Schuster, 1973), p. 25.

[107] Advertising finances in the 1968 race are discussed in Herbert Alexander, "Political Broadcasting in 1968" *Television Quarterly,* (Spring 1970). See also *Congressional Quarterly Weekly Reports,* September 12, 1969, p. 1701. Further information can be found in Polsby and Wildavsky, *op. cit.,* p. 167, and in Sorauf, *op. cit.,* p. 319.

[108] "Washington Update," *National Journal,* October 2, 1976, p. 1399.

[109] *Ibid.,* p. 1399.

[110] *Ibid.,* p. 1399.

[111] Bone, *op. cit.,* p. 400. For more on Rocky's finances it is estimated that his family spent tens of millions on his presidential plans in David Adamany, *Campaign Finance in America* (North Scituate, Mass.: Duxbury Press, 1972), p. 151.

[112] David W. Adamany, "Financing National Politics," in Agranoff, *op. cit.,* p. 392.

[113] *Washington Post,* September 30, 1973. In fairness to Nixon, the practice of "selling" ambassadorships was a long standing tradition at the White House.

[114] Martin Schramm, *Running for President 1976: The Carter Campaign* (New York: Stein and Day, 1977), p. 119, as cited in Joel Goldstein, "The Influence of Money on the Pre-Nomination Stage of the Presidential Selection Process: The Case of the 1976 Election," *Presidential Studies Quarterly,* (Spring 1978), 179.

[115] See Adamany in Agranoff, *op. cit.,* p. 395. Executives of major oil companies later paraded into court to plead guilty to making contributions in excess of the legal limit to CREEP.

[116] Evans and Novak, *op. cit.,* p. 58.

[117] Ernest R. May and Janet Fraser, *Campaign '72: The Managers Speak* (Cambridge, Mass.: Harvard U.P., 1973), p. 223.

[118] Malbin et al., *op. cit., National Journal,* July 24, 1976, p. 1033.

[119] *Ibid.,* p. 1033.

[120] For a more thorough discussion and notes on the wording of the legislation, see Hess, *The Presidential Campaign,* p. 76.

[121] See *Congressional Quarterly Weekly Reports,* June 17, 1972, pp. 1459-1460. Also see Hess, *The Presidential Campaign,* p. 76.

[122] Joel Goldstein, *op. cit.,* p. 166. Author has done the most thorough job on the subject matter available in article form.

[123] Pomper et al., *op. cit.,* p. 71.

[124] Demand exceeded supply mainly because everyone wanted to be recognized on the floor as a "long-time" supporter of the nominee.

This author owes the chance to be in New York for the convention to a grant from the National Endowment for the Humanities providing for participation in a Seminar for College Teachers directed by Prof. Louis W. Koenig of New York University. The seminar, entitled "Presidential Power and Democratic Constraints," provided many of the insights that encouraged me to undertake this book. My debt to Professor Koenig for his inspiration and encouragement to in-depth research is gratefully acknowledged.

[125] Maxwell Glen Political Report, "Free Spenders—The 'Other' Campaign for Reagan," *National Journal,* September 13, 1980, p. 1512. On the 1980 campaign see David Broder, Lou Cannon, Haynes Johnson, Martin Schramm, Richard Harwood, and the staff of *The Washington Post, The Pursuit of the Presidency, 1980,* (New York: Berkley Books) 1980 by arrangement with *The Washington Post.* See also Gerald Pomper with colleagues, *The Election of 1980: Reports and Interpretations,* (Chatham, N.J.: Chatham House) 1981.

[126] One of the most thorough handlings of the Electoral College and alternatives to it can be found in Wallace S. Sayre and Judith Paris, *Voting for President: The Electoral College and the American Political System* (Washington, D.C.: Brookings Institution, 1970).

[127] Malbin et al., *op. cit., National Journal,* July 24, 1976, pp. 1024-1028.

[128] On the implications of reforms, see Lawrence D. Longley and Alan G. Braun, *The Politics of Electoral College Reform* (New Haven, Conn.: Yale U.P., 1972).

[129] On the vote to amend the constitution relative to the Electoral College system, see Sorauf, *op. cit.,* p. 271.

# 11

# Leadership and Accountability

For well over two decades, no president has served two full terms. Deaths and resignations are obvious factors, but voter expectations that the presidents will be miracle workers have also made reelection a difficult proposition. Presidential hopefuls have, like the public, imagined that they could do the impossible once they moved into the Oval Office. Lyndon Johnson warned his successor Richard Nixon to be realistic about the limits of the office:[1]

> Before you get to be president you think you can do anything. You think you're the most powerful leader since God. But, when you get in that tall chair, as you're gonna find out, Mr. President, you can't count on people. You'll find your hands tied and people cussin' you. The office is kinda like the little country boy found the Hoochie-Koochie show at the carnival; once he'd paid his dime and got inside the tent: "It ain't exactly as it was advertised."

With that same sense of the possible, Lyndon Johnson had recognized the futility of any attempt on his part to get his party's nomination in the face of the anti-Vietnam sentiment that crystallized in the campaign waged by Robert Kennedy in 1968. Both Gerald Ford and Jimmy Carter had to withstand determined assaults on their positions as incumbents from within their own parties in 1976 and 1980. While each won his party's nomination, neither proved capable of returning to the Oval Office. The rap against both was similar, "nice guy, poor leader."

As the quadrennial presidential elections approach, American voters scan the political landscape in search of that elusive superstar with the mental acumen of a Jefferson, the courage of a Lincoln, the charismatic flare of a Kennedy, and a sense of the common man evident in the likes of Jackson and Truman. Sensing those sentiments, Jimmy Carter presented himself in 1976 as an "outsider" not tainted by the Washington "establishment." His above-the-fray, white-knight posturing captured the fancy of the voting public.[2] They seemed to think that he might be capable of leading the bureaucracies of the federal government without being swallowed up by them.

In this type of storybook environment, it would certainly be justified for presidents to worry about the extent to which they should assume leadership. In the last three decades, presidents have been berated for either being weak or for abusing the powers of the office. As the electorate searches in vain for a modern Washington in whom to place its confidence, the job description of the office continues to grow. George Washington would find it hard to compete for the office today because the job description has ballooned from the days of the first Constitutional Convention at Philadelphia. He would be lacking in the requisite campaigning, management, and foreign affairs skills that would be required to first be elected and then to manage the massive federal bureaucracy of the 1980s.

Both custom and necessity help to explain the expanded roles of the presidency especially since the Depression days of the 1930s. With an increased role for government in the economy, presidents have often been typecast as economic saviors. Two world wars, a Cold War with the Soviets, and nuclear weapons with lightning-like striking capacity have made presidents both the guardians of the "free world" and custodians of the button that could unleash a nuclear holocaust on the entire world. With each new crisis situation, bureaucratic support machinery has grown. Since Franklin Roosevelt's terms, the White House staff has also mushroomed. Gradually, the presidency became the motive force in the American political process, far surpassing any expectations of the Founding Fathers who created the institution. They had feared abuse of power by Congress and clearly spelled out legislative duties in Article I. At the same time, they left the responsibilities of Washington and his successors a mass of very broad generalizations.

Clearly, the job had outgrown the constitutional provisions sculpted for it. As the office grew, so did the need for improved management skills. Since the advent of the electronic media, however, the process of selecting candidates and the press reporting of it have tended to emphasize personalities, straw polls, primary tally sheets, and national convention delegate counts at the expense of examining the management competence or issue positions of presidential hopefuls. In Jimmy Carter's now famous interview with *Playboy* magazine in which he admitted that he had lusted in his heart, the former Georgia governor griped that the national media had absolutely no interest in issues.[3]

Under the glare of modern cameras, a technocrat like Herbert Hoover, who was notoriously bland, makes nary a splash even though he might, like Hoover, be a highly competent administrator. FDR noted that management skills were not enough. He once said of the presidency that it was more than an engineering job and that it was preeminently a place of moral leadership.

Whenever one reads of the modern presidency, he or she is likely to stumble over the term "leadership" in every other line.[4] It has become the appropriate buzzword in American political and academic circles. Gerald Ford and Jimmy Carter demonstrated that being "honest and decent" was not enough to get things accomplished.[5] Leadership boils down to a capacity to get things done but also the ability to motivate others to help. Effective leaders demonstrate the courage and self-confidence to propose new directions for solving chronic problems and the capacity to mobilize others to more than lip service. Timid presidents who prove uninspiring to the press, the public, Congress, and the interest groups seem destined to fall victim to the modern syndrome of a "four-year, no-reelection" presidency.

# CONSENSUS IN THE
## "ME" GENERATION:
## LEADERS NEED FOLLOWERS

In noting that Gerald Ford lacked these enobling qualities, Richard Reeves titled his book on the former president, using Ford's own words, *A Ford Not a Lincoln.*[6] Creative titles notwithstanding, attempts to compare presidents prior to the mid-1960s with their predecessors on the quality of leadership should be considered suspect because leadership might well have been more possible in the past when national consensus was more easily attainable. Too many laments about the vacuum in political leadership from the White House in recent decades have overlooked the problem of followership. In Chapter 5, we noted that leading Congress can be difficult for a president since there are so many power centers on Capitol Hill as the caucus has replaced the once-powerful standing committee chairpersons who must now demean themselves to seek support for reelection to their positions. Deceptive presidents also made Congress increasingly skeptical of following presidential leadership. The 1970s saw legislators penning bills to limit presidential war powers, emergency powers, and budget and impounding authorities. Legislative vetoes have become an increasingly common way for Congress to restrict presidential options, especially in foreign affairs areas.

James McGregor Burns has suggested that leadership involves not only an ability to anticipate needs for change and the strength of character to shift policy when the need arises but also a capacity for building coalitions behind the president's programs.[7] In the modern era of single-issue politics and the "me generation," forging effective alliances among interest groups, members of Congress, and large sectors of the electorate can be difficult indeed. Madison Avenue constantly reminds the television viewer, as one commercial puts it, "you can never do enough for yourself." This preoccupation with the individual and de-emphasis on community complicates immeasurably any efforts that a president might want to make to lead the nation behind a set of goals. Successful presidents in the coming decades will be those who can convince the public that thinking in terms of "us" will, in the longer run, be in the best interest of each individual in the "me" generation.

If campaign rhetoric is to be taken as an indication, political pros still sense that many voters seek something or someone to believe in and someone to lead.[8] Candidates for the White House, on the other hand, desire the power to provide that leadership. Presidents who prove capable of sensing these needs and the deepest aspirations of the American public and are able to articulate them forcefully should be able to use the resultant public support to ride herd over the bureaucracies to motivate careerists and to meet at least some of these popular needs and aspirations. Congress, the press, the courts, and the interest groups will doubtless compete with any president who proclaims himself to be the articulator of the American dream. Checks and balances operate that way. Democratic political processes also force a president to exercise restraint in using government in what he perceives to be the national interest. Clinton Rossiter suggests that, when history examines the leadership of a president, if he is not regularly accused in his lifetime of subverting the Constitution, he has little chance of being judged truly "great" by future generations.[9] It is the Lincolns, the Jeffersons, and the Franklin Roosevelts who overlooked constitutional limitations and not the scrupulous constitutionalists like James Buchanan and William Howard Taft who top historians' lists of noteworthy presidents. Crises predispose the public to accept the judgments of their presidents.[10] Building coalitions and exercising forceful leadership are easier when the economic or physical survival of the nation is at stake. It is during the noncrisis periods that building coalitions becomes so difficult. Presidents tend to be judged by voters at these times not just on the basis of leading the nation right or left but on their ability to keep the nation out of military involvements and to sidestep serious economic downturns. In essence, there is a danger that the president will be credited for what doesn't happen while he is in the Oval Office. He will become a mere chief damage control officer.

## LEADERSHIP QUALITIES AND THE MODERN PRESIDENTS

If presidents are to help shape the future rather than be mere guardians of the status quo, a number of leadership qualities can be helpful in their forward-looking pursuits. The list of these traits would be long indeed. In a study entitled *Candidates and Their Images,* Dan Nimmo and Robert Savage had groups of college students on two campuses write brief essays on the qualities they expected or observed in the "ideal president."[11] Over two hundred distinguishable traits were suggested and Nimmo and Savage distilled them down into fifty-two sentences describing the "perfect" public official, party leader, person, and communicator. In another examination of presidential traits, Herman Finer capsulized the qualities of leadership into twelve categories ranging from conviction to conciliation and from creativity to constitutionality.[12] From the perspectives of leadership, accountability, and effectiveness, our list here will include the following "Ps": perspective, purpose, power and perseverance, patience, and personality and performing skills.

### *PERSPECTIVE*

No president can be expected to fully comprehend all the subtleties of the numerous problems that cross the threshold of the Oval Office daily. Still, competent presidents cannot hope to exercise leadership if they lack the native intelligence to assess those issues on the basis of information that their advisors can provide. Without these basic capacities, a president might relinquish leadership to expert aides because they alone possess the capacity to comprehend the complications of specific problems.

Modern administrator-politician presidents require skills in identifying problems, formulating policy solutions, adopting policies, implementing policies, and reevaluating policies to determine if continuation is prudent. Identifying difficulties needing federal action immediately can be perplexing since the president often has little expertise in many of the areas in which problems arise. Jimmy Carter, for example, was a trained nuclear physicist, but that did not necessarily prepare him for the foreign policy issues that might have called for the threat or even the use of nuclear weapons. Ronald Reagan's background as actor, union leader, governor, and radio-sage left him similarly deficient in international affairs. Often the president needs assistance to understand the nature of the situation at hand.

JUDGE OF THE CHARACTER OF THE STAFF. Since the president is so dependent upon his staff for sharpening his perspectives on issues, his success in policy making depends to some extent upon an ability to seek out and judge competent persons for the White House staff. The shameful saga we have come to know as Watergate illustrates the problems Richard Nixon brought upon himself both because of the aides he chose and the reelection demands he made of them. It has been suggested that the lack of political savvy and knowledge of the Washington scene that characterized Jimmy Carter's Georgians like Hamilton Jordan and congressional relations figure Frank Moore got the administration off on the wrong foot and were part of the reason Carter was soundly defeated in his 1980 reelection bid.

Finding quality aides may be one thing, but convincing them to take demanding jobs in the federal government, especially if they are senior executives with prior government experiences like Ronald Reagan sought in 1980, can be quite another. Former high officials in the Nixon-Ford years such as George Schultz and William Simon rejected offers by Reagan to return to government, partly because of the massive drop in salary they would have to take and partly because of tough conflicts of interest legislation.[13] Lyndon Johnson also found the search for aides a real challenge. Johnson had the reputation for being so impossible to work for that one of his aides saw him as a cross between Roman Emperor Caligula and Dagwood Bumpstead's boss, Mr. Dithers. He had great difficulty in retaining the Kennedy staffers bequeathed to him and in getting replacements when they left for greener pastures. Johnson was not above flattery to convince capable persons to sign on with the administration. In a characteristic appeal, in this case to Eric Goldman, he groveled[14]

> You know how I came to be in this room . . . I don't know how long I will be here. As long as I am the President I have one resolve. Before I leave, I am determined to do things that will make opportunities better for ordinary Americans, and peace in the world more secure. But, I badly need the help. . . . And I especially need the help of the best minds in the country.

Even with the best of staffers, the problems that saddle presidents are often so complex that presidents must remain calm in the realization that there are no simple solutions on the horizon. They are still held accountable for adopting initiatives to attack long-standing problems even though they are virtually unsolvable.

ECONOMIC REALISM. Presidents in the decade of the 1980s will be viewing economic realities that will limit the options to something less than was available to their predecessors as recently as the 1960s. They are unlikely to be able to follow Lyndon Johnson's lead in attacking domestic ills. Broad-range goals adopted and enacted through numerous pieces of legislation packaged as the "Great Society programs" can be very costly propositions. If a major problem needed solving during Johnson's tenure, cost rarely was the major obstacle. On the other hand, people such as White House special assistant Joseph Califano were expected to design a plethora of programs even though they realized that cost factors might not prove favorable. In the summer of 1965, Califano received the following directions from the president:[15]

There are three areas of urgent concern for the 1966 legislative program. The transportation system of the country is a mess. I want to do something about it.

Second, we must show the people of this nation that the cities can be re-built. I want a program to totally rebuild the ghettos of the nation.

We need an open housing bill. School desegregation and equal employment are not enough. We'll pass voting rights this year.

Johnson's pet programs, budgetbusters all, would not sit well with today's inflation-conscious voters. As the public moved moderately to the right of the political spectrum in the later 1970s and into the 1980s, the pressures for balanced budgets have increased along with demands that federal deficits be trimmed. Voters felt that government was spending too much and this was a major component in high rates of inflation (see Table 11.1).

Ironically, it was Califano, the architect of many of the Great Society programs, who became HEW secretary with marching orders from President Carter to evaluate the cost effectiveness and fiscal soundness of many of these programs with an eye toward budget cuts that the views in Table 11.1 seem to demand.

LEGISLATIVE REALIST. The modern president must be able to set legislative priorities clearly and use power judiciously to get programs enacted. Presidents will find it increasingly difficult to ram domestic programs down the throat of Congress as FDR and LBJ were able to do early in their administrations. Unless presidents have proven coattails, they are likely to experience difficulties in passing major social legislation. Thomas Cronin has even suggested that it is unrealistic to expect any president to be able to bring about major social change in the near future.[16] A massive influx of legislation lacking priorities will surely overload the fragile legislative machinery. Attempts to get "everything" will also severely test the already fractured system of party loyalty and produce few credits on legislative tally sheets. As the Carter administration was preparing for the transition to a Reagan presidency, Carter's Chief of Staff Hamilton Jordan noted that one of the greatest mistakes the administration had made was not setting clear legislative priorities. Presidents Truman and Kennedy were likewise criticized for having impatient ways of dealing with Congress.[17]

Future presidents would do well to heed the words of theologian Ignatius Loyola as they try to develop a sense of the possible and set their priorities. In asking God for a sense of perspective, Loyola prayed for "the courage to change the things that I can change, the serenity to accept the things that I cannot change, and the wisdom to know the difference." Presidents with this sense of perspective would be more likely to spend their power wisely throughout the four years of their first term lest they invest too much of it on early unwinnable situations and find themselves bankrupt later on.

## PURPOSE

Being realistic about "what will sell" is no excuse for a president to forego establishing a definite set of high-minded priorities. A sense of purpose entails a sense of direction and a belief that the nation is capable of reaching new higher plateaus. As the labels liberal and conservative can become emotionally charged in election years,

## TABLE 11.1
### MOST IMPORTANT PROBLEM:
"WHAT DO YOU THINK IS THE MOST IMPORTANT PROBLEM FACING THIS COUNTRY TODAY?"

*September 12 - 15, 1980*

| | Inflation, high cost of living | Un-employment | International problems | Dissatisfaction with government | Energy | Government spending | Moral decline | Crime |
|---|---|---|---|---|---|---|---|---|
| NATIONAL | 61% | 16% | 15% | 6% | 4% | 3% | 3% | 2% |
| **SEX** | | | | | | | | |
| Male | 59 | 18 | 16 | 7 | 4 | 2 | 2 | 1 |
| Female | 62 | 14 | 14 | 5 | 4 | 3 | 3 | 3 |
| **RACE** | | | | | | | | |
| White | 61 | 16 | 16 | 6 | 4 | 3 | 3 | 1 |
| Non-white | 57 | 19 | 11 | 5 | 2 | * | 4 | 3 |
| **EDUCATION** | | | | | | | | |
| College | 64 | 15 | 14 | 9 | 4 | 4 | 3 | 1 |
| High school | 60 | 18 | 16 | 5 | 3 | 3 | 2 | 2 |
| Grade school | 55 | 13 | 13 | 4 | 3 | 3 | 3 | 3 |
| **REGION** | | | | | | | | |
| East | 61 | 20 | 15 | 6 | 3 | 1 | 1 | 2 |
| Midwest | 64 | 19 | 15 | 4 | 3 | 2 | 3 | 1 |
| South | 60 | 10 | 15 | 6 | 4 | 4 | 4 | 2 |
| West | 56 | 18 | 15 | 9 | 5 | 4 | 2 | 1 |
| **AGE** | | | | | | | | |
| Total under 30 | 63 | 16 | 19 | 5 | 4 | 3 | 1 | 1 |
| 18 - 24 years | 64 | 14 | 22 | 6 | 2 | 3 | – | 1 |
| 25 - 29 years | 62 | 19 | 15 | 3 | 6 | 3 | 3 | 1 |
| 30 - 49 years | 61 | 18 | 13 | 7 | 3 | 3 | 4 | 1 |
| 50 & older | 58 | 15 | 13 | 6 | 4 | 3 | 3 | 3 |

| | | | | | | | | |
|---|---|---|---|---|---|---|---|---|
| **INCOME** | | | | | | | | |
| $25,000 & over | 68 | 16 | 13 | 6 | 5 | 3 | 2 | 1 |
| $20,000 - $24,999 | 64 | 14 | 18 | 5 | 2 | 4 | 2 | 2 |
| $15,000 - $19,999 | 65 | 14 | 16 | 5 | 3 | 4 | 2 | 2 |
| $10,000 - $14,999 | 58 | 16 | 16 | 7 | 3 | 3 | 3 | 2 |
| $ 5,000 - $ 9,999 | 55 | 21 | 12 | 6 | 3 | 1 | 3 | 2 |
| Under $5,000 | 50 | 14 | 16 | 6 | 4 | 2 | 7 | 1 |
| **POLITICS** | | | | | | | | |
| Republican | 66 | 11 | 14 | 7 | 4 | 4 | 2 | 2 |
| Democrat | 60 | 19 | 16 | 5 | 4 | 2 | 3 | 2 |
| Independent | 58 | 17 | 12 | 9 | 3 | 2 | 3 | 1 |
| **RELIGION** | | | | | | | | |
| Protestant | 61 | 13 | 15 | 6 | 4 | 3 | 3 | 2 |
| Catholic | 61 | 25 | 15 | 3 | 3 | 3 | 1 | 1 |
| **OCCUPATION** | | | | | | | | |
| Professional & Business | 64 | 15 | 15 | 7 | 4 | 4 | 3 | 1 |
| Clerical & sales | 60 | 15 | 15 | 5 | 8 | 2 | 3 | 1 |
| Manual workers | 60 | 18 | 15 | 6 | 3 | 2 | 3 | 2 |
| Non-labor force | 58 | 15 | 15 | 6 | 3 | 3 | 2 | 3 |
| **CITY SIZE** | | | | | | | | |
| 1,000,000 & over | 61 | 25 | 13 | 4 | 2 | 1 | 2 | 2 |
| 500,000 - 999,999 | 64 | 16 | 15 | 5 | 3 | 3 | 1 | 2 |
| 50,000 - 499,999 | 60 | 15 | 17 | 8 | 3 | 4 | 3 | 1 |
| 2,500 - 49,999 | 63 | 15 | 13 | 8 | 5 | 3 | 2 | 2 |
| Under 2,500, rural | 58 | 12 | 15 | 6 | 5 | 3 | 4 | 1 |
| **LABOR UNION** | | | | | | | | |
| Labor union families | 57 | 23 | 14 | 6 | 3 | 3 | 1 | 1 |
| Non-labor union families | 62 | 14 | 15 | 6 | 4 | 3 | 3 | 2 |

Source: Gallup Opinion Index #181, September 1980, p. 10.

*Less than one percent.

a consistent set of values can have its political liabilities. George McGovern was soundly trounced in 1972 due in large measure to the fact that he was viewed as too liberal. In 1980, Ronald Reagan was able to allay public fears fanned by his opponent Jimmy Carter that he was so conservative that he would dismantle Social Security and Medicare and would set back the social betterment of minorities and women.[18] Jimmy Carter in 1980 made a desperate attempt to label Reagan more conservative than Barry Goldwater (who was defeated by LBJ through use of the same tactics). Reagan's victory with 51 percent of the popular and over 490 electoral votes suggested that the public wasn't buying what Carter was trying to sell.

If a candidate's retreat toward the voters is not calculated judiciously, it may hurt his or her political reputation. In California, for example, Governor Jerry Brown doggedly opposed the Proposition 13 property tax rollback legislation in his state because of the detrimental effect it would have on funds available for social services for the disadvantaged. By the time his own race for governor commenced in 1978, Proposition 13 had been enacted by the voters and he threw himself into the spirit of making it work. To his critics, he simply responded that he was trying to make the best of the situation, but skeptics remained unconvinced.

Providing a sense of purpose to the public can be a valuable asset for a president if he is capable of doing so. Jimmy Carter learned that the voters will not accept directions from a president to lower their sights. Presidents who dreamed great dreams and had a sense of mission carved their niches in the history books. Jefferson is revered for his imagination in purchasing the better part of today's United States. "Trustbuster" became the proud label adorning Theodore Roosevelt's place Nicolas Biddle and the other stalking horses for the Second Bank of the United States. "Trustbuster" became the proud label adorning Theodore Roosevelt's niche in history, and Woodrow Wilson is remembered for his dream of trying to make the world "safe for democracy." Likewise FDR's efforts for the "forgotten Americans" during the Depression and Harry Truman's dogged determination to improve the status of labor and minority groups earned them the plaudits of historians who measure presidencies on both efforts and performances.

Modern presidents have even greater potential for leading the public to higher goals because they are able to be in more intimate contact with the public through the electronic media. When a sense of purpose is deeply felt, the White House can be an even more "bully" pulpit than Theodore Roosevelt had imagined.

MORAL VOICE. Pulpits are the offices of preachers, and Clinton Rossiter described the president as a "moral spokesman" for both the nation and the free world. To perform this function effectively requires the ability to talk the "language of Christian morality and American tradition."[19] The president's chief of state role not only provides him the advantage of claiming moral leadership but also the responsibility to provide it. When a president betrays this responsibility as Richard Nixon did by involving himself in the Watergate cover-up, his credibility suffers irreparable damage. The Watergate tapes illustrated that Nixon did not expect the public to believe John Dean and others who implicated him in the cover-up. Ultimately, however, his decision to resign was both an admission that he could no longer govern and that the House would impeach him if he continued in office.

There is a danger, Herman Finer reminds us, that expressions of purpose will spring not from the personal convictions of the president but from the pens of creative public relations people who can point out the philosophies that will sell much in the way that they can target a market for deodorant soap. The place of prominence in American politics and world affairs transforms a president into "chief teacher of political values" along with his other often cited "chieftan" roles.[20] British philosopher Edmund Burke would suggest that he has the duty not merely to serve as an amplifier of uninformed public opinion but also as an educator and architect who helps to define and shape issues using his own judgment and defending his decisions to an increasingly skeptical public.

At times, moral leadership may entail political risk. Although four presidents were involved for fourteen years in negotiating a Panama Canal treaty, Jimmy Carter had to try to sell it to a voting public that had been convinced that the Canal treaties represented a sellout to a "two-bit tin-horn Communist dictator" (General Torrijos). Carter was bequeathed the gargantuan job of educating the electorate to the need for the treaties, including moral imperatives such as respect for Panamanian sovereignty. He also had to neutralize the educational crusades launched by the opponents of the treaties led by Representative Phillip Crane (R., Illinois) and enhanced by the active and visible support of Ronald Reagan. Even as the treaties neared the ratification vote, public opinion lined up on the opposing side.[21] Still, Carter steered the pacts through the Senate with a slim one-vote margin. Some senators like Floyd Haskell of Colorado who supported the president in this endeavor paid dearly in the following elections.

While morality and a sense of purpose are necessary for effective presidential leadership, there are dangers that moral imperatives could lead to rigid behavior. Wilson could not compromise on the "fourteen points" and the League of Nations. Hoover cringed at even the slightest suggestion that any good could come from a federal relief program even when that seemed to be the only way in which to feed the growing unemployed sector (25 percent) of the American population. Few are more zealous than moral crusaders, but the danger exists that the public might disagree with the goals of the crusade.

## POWER AND PERSEVERANCE

When presidents realize that crusades are not in the cards, they have other tools at their disposal to encourage public cooperation. Often, appeals to patriotism and sacrifice in the national interest fall on deaf ears. Promises of governmental rewards or threats of reprisals may be in the offing. Threatening the titans of industry (jawboning as Kennedy did with the steel industry and as LBJ did with Alcoa) to get price rollbacks require leaders in the White House with a strong sense of the powers of the office.

Raging inflation may encourage White House discussions of wage and price guidelines (voluntary) or controls (mandatory), but controls are rarely invoked. Voluntary guidelines, such as those adopted by Jimmy Carter in 1978, have done little to even ease the problem of inflation. Carter found that all his 7 percent wage increase guidelines and complicated price guidelines did was to make enemies for him in the labor movement. George Meany, the crusty and outspoken patriarch of the AFL-CIO, berated Carter for being the most conservative president since Calvin Coolidge. Even under such severe buffeting, the president is expected to persevere.

Drawing the lines between perseverance and bull-headedness can be difficult. What could be seen as self-confidence in one situation could be viewed as arrogance in another. Still, presidential leaders of the 1980s and beyond must be capable of standing their ground in the face of single-minded opposition by zealous and well-organized single interest opponents attacking their proposals.

## PATIENCE OR TOLERATION

While it is true that presidents should have the strength of their convictions, it is also true that they should have patience with the differing views espoused by others. Self-confidence can aid effective leadership, but haughtiness can destroy the necessary lines of communication. The intelligent captain, when informed by a subordinate that he is steering a collision course, would hardly be expected to continue full-speed ahead. Presidents in James David Barber's negative categories had the unhappy penchant for freezing at the helm. Wilson refused to compromise on the League of Nations; Hoover was adverse to government doles; and Lyndon Johnson was determined to "win" the war in Vietnam even when voices within his inner circle were being raised about the futility of the situation.[22]

As we noted earlier, the world of the presidential advisor is too often one of a bootlicker expected to dote on the president's every word. When a president will not brook even private criticism, he will receive none at all. Staffers and advisors may be men with strong egos because they have demonstrated the drive to take on the demands of the jobs. It should be no surprise that LBJ, who treated his staff like his personal servants, had a revolving door administration with staffers coming and going. In six years, LBJ employed five press secretaries. Even worse for the self-esteem of high-level presidential employees is to be forbidden access to the president himself. Nixon's staffing system isolated him from political realities within his administration and left him defenseless in the wake of public outcry over the excesses of his reelection committee. His distaste for criticism encouraged his staffers to withhold information about unfavorable public reaction to his role in Watergate. As Woodward and Bernstein recounted in *The Final Days,* it was not until almost the day he announced his decision to resign that he realized that he could not ride out the storm.[23] A president needs alternative sources of information and must be willing to take dissent along with adulation.

## PERSONALITY AND
## PERFORMING SKILLS

Presidents who are attuned to the democratic process would find less difficulty in accepting criticism and, as a result, should be more effective leaders than those whose personalities need constant stroking. Louis Koenig, in his classic study *The Chief Executive,* suggests that certain personality types (high democratic) lend themselves to democratic practice and that others (low democratic) are more oriented toward disregard for the need for public support. Koenig insightfully theorizes that low democratic types, in attitude and behavior, are apt to be engrossed in themselves (i.e., they are ego defensive). In expressing a decided preference for the "high democratic," Koenig suggests that they will (1) revere and support civil rights, (2) support programs aimed at the public as a whole and not at merely a privileged few, (3) make themselves accessible, (4) discuss issues while campaigning, (5) value candor in dealing with staff and others, and (6) be responsive to democratic values.[24]

These typologies require that the high democratic types have the personality to sell their goals to Congress and the public. In this media age, the meek are unlikely to inherit the White House. Communications analyst Marshall McLuhan has suggested that the medium is the message. Putting it another way, it is not so much what you say as how forcefully you are able to say it that counts.[25]

Certain types of personalities are attuned to the public relations and persuasive aspects of presidential leadership. Herman Finer suggests that, among other factors, a president who aspires to effective leadership must be clever, charming, and conscientious. But cleverness, however valuable in leadership, may be manipulative and may be used to weaken the democratic process. As a case in point, one might look at Franklin Roosevelt's creativity in attempting to deal with an uncooperative Supreme Court. Since court decisions in the *Schechter* case outlawing the AAA (Agriculture Adjustment Act) and subsequent outlawing of the NRA codes under the National Recovery Act were playing havoc with his hopes for institutionalizing the New Deal, he cleverly concocted a plan to make the court cooperative by changing the composition of the court to fifteen members from its usual nine.[26] While the court-packing plan permitted him to appoint six new liberal judges who would support his views, it represented a political attack on the constitutional process.

Personal charm can be a real asset to a president in helping him to assert leadership. Magnetism (charisma) can be the product of physical characteristics or personality traits. In our media age, looking like a president becomes an increasingly important commodity. When Senator Stuart Symington of Missouri was being considered as a presidential possibility at the time of the 1960 Democratic convention, one of his most valuable assets was the impression that he had the silver-haired look of a president.[27] The eventual nominee that year, John Kennedy, had the advantage of physical attractiveness and an image of youth and vigor. One of his main campaign themes was to contrast his promise of "New Frontiers" to Nixon's likelihood of producing "more years of worn-out Republican administration." His dynamic personality lent credibility to his promise to get the nation moving again.

Charm also played a crucial role in the meteoric rise of Jimmy Carter in 1976. His calm, self-assured, optimistic manner served him well not only in the race for the White House but in delicate situations like the Middle East peace negotiations at Camp David, Maryland in 1978 in which he brought Egypt and Israel to at least a temporary meeting of the minds when few observers thought it possible. Cartoonist heaven would no doubt be populated with political figures possessing Lyndon Johnson noses and ears and Jimmy Carter smiles. Although his "picket fence" grinned from caricatures on many an editorial page, that smile, and the sense of warmth that it represented, was a major plus for him in the presidential sweepstakes. Jules Witcover provided a vignette of Carter on the campaign trail that illustrates how his personality endeared him to persons who had previously had little or no knowledge of the one-term governor from Georgia.

During the New Hampshire preprimary campaign, Carter visited St. Patrick's School and spoke to the primary students. As he launched into a slightly scaled-down version of his standard sermonette, he asked the students if they agreed with him. "What we need is for our government to be as good as our people. Wouldn't that be a great thing?" He beamed broadly at them and they returned his smile. In a later talk to the seventh- and eighth-graders, he launched into his standard fare in his typical, low and reverent tones. When he concluded with the comment,

"I love all of you," and he raised his arms high over his head, the students swarmed up to him to receive embraces from him or to tug at his leg. Jules Witcover recounts the awed reaction of one of his colleagues, "suffer little children to come unto me." Carter didn't treat children as adults; it was more like he treated children and adults alike, capturing them with his smile and his message of hope, goodness, and love.[28]

Carter later followed the tradition of his predecessor Franklin Roosevelt with his fireside chats.[29] Again he was attempting to use his low-keyed and confessorial style to forge links with the public to aid him in pushing controversial programs through a balky Congress. While his personality did not lend itself to television as Roosevelt's melodious voice lent itself to radio, Carter nevertheless hesitated to abandon a good thing that had worked so well for him in face-to-face campaigning. *Washington Post* analyst Haynes Johnson told a Political Science Association convention audience that Jimmy Carter only decided to stop using the fireside chats because they weren't working as he had hoped. Johnson noticed that Franklin Roosevelt devoted each of the "chats" to specific and simple single issues. Jimmy Carter tried to tackle more complex problems like "energy," and he was simply ineffective in arousing public fervor or understanding of the reality of the problems.

If proper media personality alone were to be sufficient for leadership, Robert Redford could make an excellent candidate for president. Some critics of the Carter-Reagan debate noted that Carter didn't have a public relations chance against a polished professional actor like Ronald Reagan. Accomplished thespians may well be able to win the White House, but, without an understanding of the complexities of the job, an ability to choose effective advisors, and an ability to accept advice, it is questionable that they will fill the shoes of a Washington, Lincoln, or Roosevelt.

## LEADERSHIP RESTRAINED

There is a danger that those who sit in the same chair as giants in history might tend to overestimate their authority. The Founding Fathers didn't overlook this possibility.

### IMPEACHMENT

For those who would betray the public trust, the Constitution provides retribution. Despite the enormous power alloted to the president, the executive may be removed through impeachment and conviction for "treason, bribery and other high crimes and misdemeanors." Undoubtedly, the procedure is more genteel than were the methods that the French chose for disposing of Louis XVI. But, when resorted to, impeachment can be just as politically deadly. It was expected that impeachment would be "extreme medicine" to handle the ills of the American body politic.[30] The process was intended to be quasi-judicial rather than strictly political even though handled by political figures. British experiences with impeachment led Thomas Jefferson to comment that "impeachment has been more an engine of passion than of justice."[31] He also disdainfully referred to the process as a "mere scarecrow." The Founding Fathers expected that, in the United States, impeachment would be used sparingly and certainly not for partisan reasons that might have encouraged votes of no confidence in parliamentary systems.[32]

DEFINING IMPEACHABLE OFFENSES. Originally, at Philadelphia, the grounds for impeachment were limited to treason and bribery. Although neither of the terms was expressly defined in Article I, treason was defined in Article III and bribery was considered self-explanatory. To broaden the basis for impeachment, George Mason suggested that the phrase "other high crimes and misdemeanors against the state" be added.[33]

The debates on grounds for impeachment at Philadelphia contrasted the views of British philosophers Edmund Burke and Lord Blackstone.[34] The Burkean approach encompassed a broader interpretation of punishable offenses. Blackstone saw impeachment as justifiable only as a prosecution for violation of already known and established law, whereas Burke included "abuse of power" and "violation of the public trust" as impeachable offenses. British precedent in these areas was, at best, ambiguous. Impeachment had been used early much in the way that "no-confidence" votes would be used later. Conviction, though, under trial decision by the House of Lords meant possible jail and heavy fines for the convicted. Even as the convention was deliberating, a celebrated case was beginning to unfold in England, and Warren Hastings, British governor-general of India, would undergo impeachment in 1788 for *betraying his public trust.*[35] The delegates at Philadelphia eventually adopted a broad Burkean interpretation of the meaning of impeachable offenses.

As the impeachment process has evolved in American constitutional practice, it had become common for defense lawyers to argue from a more narrow Blackstone perspective. Still, in American practice the concept has been handled in broad-based political terms. Hamilton expressed the common view in *Federalist 65* that impeachable offenses were[36]

> Those offenses which proceed from the misconduct of public men, or, in other words, from the abuse of or violation of some public trust. They are of a nature which may with peculiar propriety be denominated political, as they relate chiefly to injuries done immediately to society itself.

In choosing the term "propriety," Hamilton was admitting that he recognized that impeachment might be abused for petty partisan reasons. Still, the delegates at Philadelphia judged this a worthy gamble and preferable to no method of removing the president who might become a danger to the nation by remaining in office. Impeachment was intended to be an act of last resort, not a vote of no-confidence. Mere policy conflicts were not to trigger it.

In 1834, Congress tested a less devastating alternative in censuring President Andrew Jackson over the Second Bank of the United States incident. Characteristically, he did not back down from his position even in the face of censure by the Senate. Jackson threw down the gauntlet to Congress. If Congress meant what it said, Jackson taunted, the House should have impeached him and the Senate tried him. If he were in fact violating the law, the tongue lashing of censure by Congress was as inappropriate as it was ineffective. The battle over the Second Bank of the United States illustrates that the Constitution provided Congress no effective "halfway house" for impeachment.[37]

ANDREW JOHNSON CASE: IMPEACHMENT FOR POLICY REASONS. Only twice in American history have presidents been subjected to the embarrassment of an impeachment investigation before Congress. When Andrew Johnson disagreed with the Radical Republicans over Reconstruction, he laid his career on the line. The impeachment provisions under the Constitution presented almost as many questions as it answered.

Johnson was being harassed by the Radical Republicans in Congress because of his conciliatory attitudes toward reconstruction of the South. No doubt, the fact that he was a Democrat did little to endear him to the Republicans who were eager to punish the South for its transgressions.[38] Because the Constitution provides that a two-thirds vote of the Senate is necessary for conviction on impeachable offenses, Johnson escaped the ignominious stigma of removal and the nation avoided a destabilizing precedent of "political" impeachment by a mere single-vote margin.

The trial in the Senate was little more than a charade. Patrick Henry had refused to participate in the Philadelphia convention because he said that he smelled a rat. The odor of a skunk pervaded the impeachment proceedings on Capitol Hill. The facade of a case was constructed around the constitutionally flimsy Tenure of Office Act of 1867. Under that legislation, the president was forbidden to remove civil officers whom he had appointed with Senate consent unless the Senate likewise approved the dismissal. It could be said that Johnson brought the problem on himself, to a degree at least, because of his wholesale house-cleaning of the executive in 1866.[39] He seemed bent on making indigenous Republican bureaucrats an endangered species. He argued cogently that the legislation severely curtailed presidential administrative direction in a way not envisioned by the Founding Fathers.

The act became a vehicle to oust Johnson when he decided to dismiss Secretary of War Edwin Stanton. The secretary had been a holdover from the Lincoln cabinet and he had "sneaked out Cabinet secrets to the Radical Republicans."[40] Johnson was so deeply convinced that the Tenure of Office legislation was unconstitutional that he fired Stanton and tapped General Lorenzo Thomas to succeed him. Stanton, not being one to give in easily, barricaded himself in his office.[41] The House, disagreeing with the president's interpretation, impeached him for violation of the act.

In the Senate, a kangaroo court atmosphere permeated the chambers. How impartial could justice be when the chief justice, responsible under the Constitution to preside, himself had designs on the White House. Even more potentially destructive of justice was the fact that Benjamin Wade, president pro tem of the Senate, was both a voter on conviction and the next in line to the Oval Office under the operative Succession Act of 1792.[42] Johnson was given little time to mount a defense and did not have anything remotely approaching the mass of legal talent paid for at public expense that Richard Nixon would have over a hundred years later. To make things even worse for Johnson, the Senate even recessed for ten days so that votes against him could be lined up.[43]

Thirty-six votes were required to convict (two thirds) and on three of the counts Johnson survived conviction by a slim one vote (35 to 19). Radical Republican arm twisting had failed. Impeachment as a "partisan" tool for removing presidents had suffered a setback. Congress proved incapable of amending the intent of the Constitution through practice, so impeachment did not become a vote of "no confidence."[44]

Had the Radicals succeeded in their scheme, not only would they have altered the presidential-congressional system, but the trauma of conviction and the virtual halt of presidential leadership during any transition process would have been a serious blow to a nation plagued already with the difficulties of binding up its wounds after a protracted Civil War.

Several times Congress attempted to curb the president's powers or change a policy by impeaching his appointees. In the 1790s, the House of Representatives, angry at the provisions of the Jay treaty with Britain, sought to impeach the man who negotiated the "disgraceful" document. President Washington refused to be intimidated and stymied the effort by refusing to provide congressional headhunters with his instructions to Jay. During the scandal-riddled Grant administration, his secretary of war escaped conviction in 1876 by resigning two hours before the House impeached him.[45] President Truman in December 1950 saw Republican members of the House and Senate in their respective conferences setting their sights on removing his Secretary of State Dean Acheson. The joint Republican resolution seeking Acheson's ouster, while not a formal impeachment, was aimed at forcing Truman to replace the secretary. Instead of frightening the president, the resolution steeled Truman's resolve to protect his comrade under fire.[46]

From the 1950s to the early 1970s, it seemed likely that impeachment would be unnecessary except in the most extreme cases of moral turpitude in the White House. Clinton Rossiter confidently predicted in 1960 that "the next President impeached will have asked for a firing squad by committing a low personal rather than a high political crime . . . shooting a Senator, for example."

PRE-NIXON PRECEDENTS. Earlier congressional investigations of Presidents Jackson and Andrew Johnson had been less complicated than the Nixon case would be in one important respect. In the first two cases the presidents had done what they were accused of doing and did not question the fact that they had. Jackson transferred funds from the Second Bank of the United States contrary to congressional wishes and he never denied doing so. Johnson had fired Stanton in violation of the Tenure of Office Act of 1867 and, likewise, he did not deny having done so. Both argued that what they had done was not grounds for impeachment but, rather, was within presidential powers under the Constitution. In Nixon's case, however, the most inflammatory accusation against him was that his involvement in the cover-up of Watergate constituted an obstruction of justice and warranted impeachment. Nixon steadfastly refused to admit any involvement in the cover-up and guarded the evidence capable of proving or disproving his contention.

The Founding Fathers had left Congress with no process for demanding evidence short of impeachment based on refusal to provide it. If the evidence Richard Nixon held could have implicated him in a felony, were his Sixth Amendment rights to trial by a jury of his peers being violated by impeachment? Could he invoke his Fifth Amendment rights in refusing to incriminate himself? Were his transgressions such that he would be held liable to trial in criminal courts after impeachment proceedings had run their course? In each of these cases, the Constitution remained frustratingly silent.

THE CASE AGAINST RICHARD NIXON: HOW MUCH LEADERSHIP IS TOO MUCH. If the impeachment process had been discredited by the shoddy way in which the Radical Republicans had handled the case of Andrew Johnson, Congress vindicated the process in 1974. The series of scandals later lumped together as "Watergate" began to surface in the spring and summer of 1973. Soon thereafter a chorus of congressional voices began calling for Nixon's ouster. On July 31, 1973, Massachusetts Representative Robert Drinan introduced a resolution of impeachment.[47] At that time the proposal languished because the prospect of Spiro Agnew in the White House represented a frightening alternative to the status quo. When Agnew resigned on October 10, the way had been cleared for House Judiciary Committee action on the resolution later in the month. Nixon was convinced that he could "tough it out." His career, after all, had been a series of "crises."

In early February, the whole House by a 410-4 vote gave the committee a virtual blank check empowering it to investigate the situation, including subpoena powers needed to uncover necessary information. At issue before the committee in the formal hearings was a lengthy list of alleged abuses of power.[48] Committee Counsel John Doar and his staff collected thirty-eight volumes of evidence on burglary, wiretapping, use of the IRS and FBI against White House enemies, withholding evidence from an impeachment investigation, violation of campaign finance laws, establishment of a secret domestic surveillance organization (Plumbers unit), violation of income tax laws, and bombing Cambodia in violation of previously enacted law. Any one of these could have served as a basis for indictment.

Unlike Andrew Johnson, Nixon had ample time to prepare his defense, and he used every weapon in the presidential arsenal. He invoked executive privilege and expressed fears for national security as justification for withholding the Watergate tapes from House and Senate investigators and even from the courts. To calm public anger, he provided typed transcripts of the tapes. He argued through his attorney, James St. Clair that he sought merely to protect the "integrity" of the presidency. As one editorial cartoonist portrayed the situation, a shrinking Nixon hid behind the bigger-than-life presidential seal. For public consumption he argued, impeach me and you weaken the presidency.

St. Clair and Nixon also borrowed from Lord Blackstone in that they argued that impeachment would be justifiable only for serious crimes perpetrated by a public servant himself while acting in his official capacity.

Legal arguments notwithstanding, the ultimate judgment rested with political figures in the House and Senate who would determine if the evidence warranted impeachment and conviction. The president needed to build at least a senatorial coalition to survive conviction. By 1974, however, Nixon was virtually a lame duck. He had hoped to coalesce Senate support using the same Southern Democrats and Republicans from the upper Midwest and West who had cooperated in dismantling the Great Society. It is generally conceded that the strength of a president as party leader depends on the durability of his coattails. The administration had proved unwilling or at least inept at extending presidential coattails down the ticket so that Republican representatives and senators could ride along on the landslide. In 1970 when Nixon sent his vice-president out to stump for Republicans, Agnew became the kiss of death. His bombast sealed the fate of many a frustrated GOP hopeful. Because of Nixon's habit of blowing substantial leads by going out to campaign, the Committee to Re-elect sent out thirty-six surrogate Nixons while the candidate remained above the battle. If he had coattails, Nixon made little effort to extend them, and, in the one case he did in 1974, the Michigan candidate for Congress lost.

In creating a separate committee to Re-elect the President and funneling most of his campaign funds through it, Nixon also slighted the Republican National Committee. Once again he brought into question his respect for the party whose support he so desperately needed to survive impeachment and conviction.

The president's house of cards began to tumble in late July 1974. First, the Supreme Court by an 8-0 vote ordered the White House to turn over the Watergate tapes as material evidence in the trials of several of Nixon's colleagues.[49] The most damaging blow to Nixon's case was not the vaunted eighteen and a half minutes that was attributed to an "accidental" erasure by the president's apparently acrobatic secretary, Rosemary Woods; rather, it was the content of his three June 23[50] conversations with Chief of Staff H. R. Haldeman which pointed unmistakably to the president's involvement in attempts to use the CIA to shanghai an FBI investigation of the Watergate break-in.

Within a week after the taped bombshell exploded, the House Judiciary Committee, with only one Republican still opposed, followed televised debates with a list of articles of impeachment. The first article cited the president for obstructing justice by using his presidential powers to impede the investigations of Watergate. The second article accused him of abuse of powers by using the CIA, FBI, and IRS against his enemies and by acquiescing in the formation of the "Plumbers" unit which used illegal surveillance techniques in violation of the First Amendment. Finally, Article III charged the president with refusal to comply with the committee request for tapes needed to pursue the impeachment investigation.[51] Presidential stalwarts on the House committee like Congressmen Sandman, Maraziti, and Mayne had been lied to as had equally trusting Senate Minority Leader Hugh Scott. Nixon soon found friends a precious commodity in short supply.

On August 8, Senators Scott and Goldwater and House Minority Leader Rhodes informed the president at a private White House meeting that he stood little chance of avoiding impeachment in the House and conviction in the Senate. This news plus the gentle prodding of his new Chief of Staff General Alexander Haig helped Nixon to realize that his case was hopeless.[52] The drama was played out a bit over a year after it had formally begun with a terse resignation letter from the president to the secretary of state, a tearful farewell to the Nixon staff, and a bold wave from the steps of the helicopter that was to carry him on the first leg of his trip to forced retirement.

THE PUNISHMENT FOR IMPEACHMENT. Nixon had escaped impeachment, conviction, and the attendant punishment even though he suffered the loss of the White House. The punishment for conviction upon impeachable offenses was set down in Article I, Section 3 of the Constitution, which provides that

> Judgment in cases of impeachment shall not extend further than removal from office, and disqualification to hold or enjoy any office of Honor, Trust, or Profit under the United States; but, the party convicted shall, nevertheless be liable and subject to Indictment, Trial, Judgment, and Punishment according to Law.

By resigning, Nixon also retained his secret service contingent, virtually assured a transition staff and expenses, and retained the generous presidential pension for his years of service. On the other hand, he left the door open to grand jury subpoenas related to Watergate trials and the possibility that he could be indicted himself on one of the many charges that the House and Senate had uncovered, especially those related to obstruction of justice, tax evasion, and violation of campaign finance legislation.

Speculation about the possibility that Nixon could have been the first president to be placed behind bars subsided when Gerald Ford decided that, to save the nation from "prolonged and divisive debate" over Nixon's culpability, he would grant his predecessor a "full, free, and absolute pardon." It covered all crimes that Nixon had or may have committed while he was president. Numerous interesting legal questions were left unanswered in the wake of the pardon. Since that time, there has been no recognizable effort to adjust the system to deal with complications related to evidence, subpoenas, and testimony as they relate to separation of powers.

Honest people could differ over the propriety of House Judiciary Committee arguments against the president's right to bomb Cambodia to protect withdrawing U.S. forces in nearby Vietnam. Others might question the justification of "national security" wiretaps[53] being cited as a reason for impeachment. Few, however, would doubt that Nixon's complicity in the Watergate cover-up alone was sufficient grounds for impeachment. Those actions involved personal criminal activity (obstruction of justice) on the president's part. The House Judiciary Committee can testify to the fact that surmising presidential complicity and amassing evidence in the president's possession to prove it are two entirely different things. Nevertheless, the unusual events of 1974 demonstrated that public discontent, if focused enough and adamant enough, can help to strengthen the resolve of the Congress and the courts to think the unthinkable and bring antidemocratic presidents to their knees.

IMPLICATIONS FOR PRESIDENTIAL LEADERSHIP. In the later months of Nixon's struggle to fend off impeachment, his arguments that impeachment might weaken the presidency (not just the president) became more and more poignant. In a February 26, 1974 press conference, he told the assembled reporters that he would not resign from office because of lack of popularity in the polls. He reasoned that lack of support in the polls should not be permitted to undermine the stability of the presidency no matter who the occupant of the Oval Office. To make his point, he cited numerous policies that were contingent on strong, stable presidential leadership, and he expressed fears about arms limitations talks (SALT) with the Soviets and the success of the Middle East "shuttle" diplomacy being undermined by the impeachment process.[54]

Throughout his ordeal, Nixon tried to characterize the investigation as "politically" motivated for "partisan" gain. Future presidents, he contended, would be forced to temper their authority and penchant for leadership with the realization that Congress could trump up charges for political rather than legal reasons as they had done with Andrew Johnson. He seemed to judge presidential leadership, especially in foreign affairs, as beyond being held captive to political processes like impeachment because it could be initiated for less than altruistic reasons. Nixon's attempts to prove himself indispensible were harmless enough; but a subsequent president might be tempted to enmesh the United States in a conflict to divert attention from his own problems at home. The longer the process drags on, the greater the likelihood that either the president might use crises to his advantage or he might permit domestic and foreign policy problems to fade into a limbo of inattention as he fights for his political life.

The fertile minds of several analysts of the American political scene have envisioned an almost total overhauling of existing presidential-congressional relations that would touch on removal. Herman Finer, Charles Hardin, and James Sundquist have seen advantages in parliamentary systems. Sundquist, a rigorous and prolific observer from the Brookings Institution, sees a vote of "no confidence" as the ultimate panacea.[55] According to Sundquist, speaking in support of Representative Henry Reuss of Wisconsin's proposal for a "no-confidence" constitutional amendment,[56]

> If the no confidence procedure were introduced into our Constitution, a President, to keep his office, would have to do more than just keep himself free of indictable crimes. He would have to satisfy the Congress, and therefore, the people as well . . . . [he would] find it necessary to consult with Congressional leaders . . . it would be dangerous to flout them.

Some have suggested that a national recall of the president would be a more "democratic" way of handling the removal of a president that the voters have selected. Recall would force many of those who voted for a president to vote against him. No doubt the president's crime or incompetence would have to be blatantly obvious for this approach to work well. It could also be contended that this approach would ease the transition to a new administration because public apprehensions could be minimized by voter participation in removal. Unfortunately, a system of this type would be costly and difficult to administer and could create deep cleavages in the electorate. No doubt, a national recall could not be organized overnight, so there would be a protracted delay, though not as long as a year as in the Nixon case.

Imaginative proposals such as these, while initially attractive and more "democratic," still require more tampering with the constitutional system than the public or Congress itself is likely to countenance. If Watergate proved anything, it pointed out that impeachment is indeed a remedy, even if it is rarely resorted to and is undertaken with great reservation and trepidation on the part of Congress. Louis Koenig, recognizing the broader sweep of American political history, cautions against panaceas like the Reuss proposal. He envisions such tampering with the checks-and-balances system as "a recipe for the Presidency's destruction."[57] Both no-confidence approaches and recall elections could be viewed as an overreaction to Watergate abuses. Each seems to assume that the Richard Nixons will be the rule rather than the exception.

A less dramatic adjustment that might assure that the duties of the Oval Office do not go unattended could involve the vice president. If a president were impeached, he could temporarily relinquish the office to the vice-president for the duration of the Senate trial. The vice-president, as he may do now under the Twenty-Fifth Amendment, would become acting president until Senate action is completed. To ensure that the Senate would not unduly delay the process to keep the elected president from returning, a time limit could be set for a conviction decision. Upon acquittal, the president would resume his office. This method would speed up the process, limit the chances for drift in dealing with domestic and foreign policy problems, and remove the president from the chance to "show-boat" for public consumption in hopes of surviving a Senate trial unscathed.

## RESIGNATION

Given the herculean effort involved in being elected to the presidency, it would seem unlikely that any incumbent would willingly resign. Before Richard Nixon stepped down from office, only Woodrow Wilson considered resignation seriously enough to discuss it openly. Wilson's biographer, Ray Stannard Baker, recounts two different situations in which the president considered resignation. The first time, Wilson considered the possibility that he might become a lame duck president in 1916 if he lost to Charles Evans Hughes. With war imminent, Wilson tried to determine a way to make a smooth transition to a new administration. He decided to request the resignation of Secretary of State Lansing and then that of Vice-President Marshall and finally he could appoint Hughes secretary of state in time to fill the vacancy that would be created by Wilson's possible resignation.[58] Fortunately for the president, the plan didn't materialize—his pursuit of a second term was successful.

In 1919 Wilson considered resigning and then standing for reelection under the provisions of the applicable Succession Act (1886) that allowed for a special election to fill a presidential vacancy. He hoped to make the special election a sort of referendum on the Versailles Treaty and the League of Nations, which he had been unable to sell in the Senate.[59] As fate would have it, he again decided against resignation. It is frightening to imagine the presidency's being left, even for a short time, in the hands of Vice-President Thomas Marshall. In all his years as vice-president, Marshall's only contribution to history was his offhanded remark, "what this country needs is a good 5¢ cigar."[60] He had no aspirations to be vice-president and, fortunately for the nation, he wasn't thrust, even temporarily, into the presidency.

In 1974, Richard Nixon became the first president to resign. Although administrations had been under fire before for the excesses of the president's men (Grant, Harding, and Truman had these problems), in no previous case had the president himself been wallowing so deeply in the mud. Graft and corruption for personal financial gain were not unusual though inexcusable. Until the 1970s, however, never had so much evidence surfaced about illegal practices aimed at increasing an administration's political power vis-à-vis its adversaries. Nixon's decision to vacate the Oval Office was tantamount to his admission that he was indeed impeachable and that impeachment and conviction were no longer out of the question.

## FILLING LEADERSHIP VACUUMS

DEATH. Of our forty presidents to date, eight have died in office. Four died of natural causes (Harrison, Taylor, Harding, and Franklin Roosevelt); four were the victims of assassins (Lincoln, Garfield, McKinley, and Kennedy). Other presidents were targets of would-be assassins (Jackson, Theodore Roosevelt, FDR, Truman, Ford, and Reagan). It is frightening to realize that 20 percent of our American presidents have been stalked by murderers. The office itself is physically and psychologically murderous as well. The typical president between 1932 and 1976 was in his mid-fifties when he assumed the strains of the office.[61] These considerations illustrate that death in the White House is a distinct possibility and must be reckoned with.

The Founding Fathers were vague on the constitutional provisions relating to death and disability, and they left the question of succession beyond the vice president up to Congress to be broached at a later date. Because of the frequency with which death has caused presidential vacancies, the words of the Constitution on these matters have been perused again and again. Article II provides that

> In case of removal of the President from office, or of his death, resignation, or inability to discharge the powers and duties of the said office, the same shall devolve upon the Vice President, and the Congress may by law provide for the case of removal, death, resignation, or inability, both of the President and Vice President, declaring what officer shall then act as President, and such officer shall act accordingly until the disability be removed, or a President shall be elected.

As has too often been the case, the constitutional provisions raised more questions than they answered. Did the Founding Fathers mean that the vice president became president on the death of his former mentor, or was he merely "acting" president? What constitutes disability? Who is to judge whether an individual president is disabled? Once removed for disability, can a president resume his duties? How does he prove that he is no longer disabled? If someone other than the vice-president succeeds to the White House, must that person permanently vacate any other government position, such as speaker of the House, that he held? The answers to a number of these questions were to evolve through custom over a period of years and some would await the ratification of the Twenty-Fifth Amendment.

The first test of the constitutional mechanisms for filling a presidential vacancy came in the wake of the death of President William Henry Harrison. From the outset, Harrison's vice president, John Tyler, believed that he assumed not just the powers and duties of the office, but the office itself. Some would argue that this viewpoint contradicted the "intent of the framers" who in a later stage of the Philadelphia convention had worded the death and disability provisions to say that "the Vice President shall exercise those powers and duties until another President be chosen, or until the inability of the President be removed." Whether the Founding Fathers intended it or not, the Tyler precedent has been followed ever since upon the death of a president. Custom in these situations made the vice president the president in the fullest possible sense of the word.[62] On March 30, 1981 as Ronald Reagan was being wheeled into surgery at George Washington University Hospital, Secretary of State Alexander Haig began an impromptu press briefing aimed at showing the nation that "someone was indeed minding the store at the White House" while the President was temporarily incapacitated. Was Reagan's situation comparable to just being asleep? Could things continue without his relinquishing the duties of his office? If he did step down, could he come back? Presidential disability creates severe complications for smooth administration in times of crisis.

DISABILITY. The death of a president leaves no pretender to the throne waiting in the wings, but, in the case of disability, if the vice president takes over as "acting" president, the elected president may seek to return as quickly as possible. After Lincoln was shot, he lingered for such a short time that no long-standing leadership crises developed. When President Garfield was felled by an assassin's bullet, the situation was infinitely more complicated. For eighty days, the wounded president clung tenaciously to life, thus placing his vice president, Chester Arthur, in a terrible bind. Arthur, who had supported Ulysses S. Grant, not Garfield, for the Republican nomination, had been inserted on the presidential ticket to bind up wounds among disaffected Grant supporters. Some Garfield believers were convinced that Arthur was intimately involved in the plot to kill the president. It did little to help matters when Charles Giteau, Garfield's assassin, expressed his gratification that Arthur would be president. On Giteau's person at the time of his capture was a letter addressed to the White House calling Garfield's death a "political necessity."[63]

Within a month after the shooting, the cabinet began to suggest that Arthur assume the duties as president under the disability provisions of the Constitution. Arthur steadfastly declined to take the reins of power. Garfield, himself, remained secluded throughout his protracted illness and saw only his wife and doctors and virtually no other visitors. In fact, he performed only one official function, that of signing an extradition paper for the State Department after his doctor read it to him.[64] Throughout this period, Arthur shunned the limelight. By August, the president's condition had worsened so much that the cabinet began looking into the status of the vice president (powers he would have) should he assume the office of president. They tried to decide whether Arthur would stay on for the duration of the term or whether Garfield could be reinstalled. By a 4-3 vote, they determined that, once Garfield gave way to Arthur, he could not return to the Oval Office. The members of the cabinet were removed from the horns of this most perplexing dilemma when Garfield died on September 16. The problem of disability now solved by an act of God was gingerly returned to Pandora's box and the lid was hermetically sealed.

Questions about presidential disability were destined to bedevil four subsequent administrations. The first arose in April 1919 as President Woodrow Wilson, reportedly suffering from influenza, returned home from a European tour during which he had been drumming up support for the League of Nations. Rumors persisted that the "flu" was in fact a mild stroke. In early September, the president embarked on a tortuous twenty-seven-day marathon of speeches seeking domestic acceptance of the controversial League of Nations Covenant. The extended swing ended abruptly on September 25 as the president first complained of a persistent headache and battled a flareup of his chronic asthma. On the last day of the tour, in Pueblo, Colorado, he seemed on the verge of collapse. The public was to learn on the next afternoon that Wilson had suffered a "complete nervous breakdown." From October 2 to April 14 Wilson remained a virtual recluse.[65] The interim was perplexing indeed for all involved. The Versailles Treaty and the League of Nations were still unfinished business in the Senate, and the task of adjusting both the society and the economy to peacetime had scarcely begun. At the suggestion of Carl T. Grayson, Wilson's personal physician, Edith Bolling Wilson, the president's wife, labored mightily to free her husband from as many of the strains of the office as she could.[66] Those wishing to communicate with the president did so with Mrs. Wilson as an intermediary. In her memoirs, Wilson's wife reported how she filtered information coming from cabinet advisors. She wrote "tabloids" or summaries to submit to her husband. In defense of her nonconstitutional if not unconstitutional role, she wrote[67]

I myself never made a single decision regarding the disposition of public affairs. The only decision that was mine was what was important and what was not, and the *very* important decision of when to present matters to my husband.

During Mrs. Wilson's interegnum, the cabinet remained without direction. Secretary of State Lansing, who had served previously as secretary to the cabinet, took it upon himself to call cabinet meetings. At one point, the cabinet even tried to prevail on Vice President Marshall to take over during Wilson's disability, but Marshall would have no part of the idea. When word reached Wilson that Lansing was calling cabinet meetings without presidential or congressional direction, the president implied in a letter that Lansing's resignation was in order.[68] Fortunately for the nation, the machinery of government during this period may have sputtered and chugged, but it did not grind to a halt.

The illness and subsequent death of President Franklin Roosevelt illustrated how ill prepared vice presidents could be to assume the duties of the Oval Office when called upon due to death or disability. In the fourth Roosevelt administration Vice President Harry Truman was clearly an outsider. Truman once commented that "I don't think I saw Roosevelt but twice as Vice President, except at Cabinet meetings and Roosevelt never discussed anything important at his Cabinet meetings."[69] The "Man from Missouri" would later admit that he had known nothing about the Manhattan Project and the atomic bomb it was creating until Secretary of State Stimson informed him about it after he had become president. In fact, word that he was president had leaked to the press before the White House even informed him. In his memoirs he recounts his first inklings that something was brewing.[70]

I turned to Rayburn [speaker of the House, Mr. Sam] explaining that I had been summoned to the White House and would be back shortly. I did not know why I had been called . . . I imagined that he [the president] just wanted to go over some matters with me before his return to Warm Springs.

A more fatalistic and superstitious man might have worried about assuming the office on Friday the thirteenth. Upon learning of Roosevelt's death, Truman asked if there might be anything he could do for Mrs. Roosevelt. Eleanor's reply was indicative of the situation in which Truman found himself: "Is there anything we can do for you?" she asked, "for you are the one in trouble now." Truman recognized that many of his difficulties were beyond his control. "It is a mighty leap from the Vice-Presidency to the Presidency," he declared, "when one is forced to make it without warning. . . . The Vice President can't equip himself to become President merely by virtue of being second in rank."[71]

Subsequent presidents seemed to view it as their duty to keep their vice presidents at least conversant with foreign policy issues. Vice presidents tend to be better prepared to assume the presidency in recent years. President Eisenhower brought Richard Nixon more into the mainstream of policy making than his predecessors had done with their number two men. John Kennedy appointed Lyndon Johnson to chair the Space Council and the President's Commission on Equal Opportunity, sent him on a fact-finding trip to Vietnam in May 1961, and included him in the "Ex-Com" that advised the president during the Cuban missile crisis. Johnson and Nixon sent Humphrey and Agnew overseas to speak for their administrations and permitted them to chair domestic committees. Gerald Ford showed his confidence in Vice President Nelson Rockefeller by assigning him responsibility to conduct an investigation of the intelligence community. Jimmy Carter made Walter Mondale a more recognized factor in his administration than many of his predecessors were. Historian and former Kennedy aide Arthur Schlesinger, Jr., told the *National Journal* that[72]

> Undoubtedly, Carter is making a more serious effort to use [Mondale] than any President since Andrew Jackson. But I would guess that his influence varies in reverse ratio to the extent that the Carter team doesn't know the Washington terrain.

Ronald Reagan gave George Bush the same upstairs White House office that Mondale had occupied. Another respected president watcher and former White House fellow, Thomas Cronin, also emphasized Mondale's valuable ties with Congress and the party. Analyst of presidential organization and Brookings fellow Stephen Hess opined that the new vice-presidential role won't have a long-lasting effect because there are "no infra-structures; the whole thing rises or falls on two people."[73] Nevertheless, the recent tendency to include the vice president in discussion of major domestic and foreign policy issues ensures that he will not be totally unprepared should the presidency be suddenly thrust upon him.

DISABILITY: THE EISENHOWER-NIXON ARRANGEMENT. At three different times during his two terms, Eisenhower suffered illnesses that rendered him temporarily incapable of discharging his duties as president. His heart attack, stroke, and bout of ileitis (including needed surgery) did not produce the confusion and inertia in government that presidential disability commonly caused in the past. Order prevailed mainly because Eisenhower and Nixon, under the watchful eye of Attorney General Herbert Brownell, devised a personal arrangement for dealing with presidential disabilities.[74]

1. In the event of inability, the president would, if possible, inform the vice president, and the vice president would serve as acting president, exercising the powers and duties of the office until the inability had ended.
2. In the event of an inability that would prevent the president from so communicating with the vice president, the vice president, after such consultation as seemed to him appropriate under the circumstances, would decide upon the devolution of the powers and duties of the office and would serve as acting president until the inability has ended.
3. The president, in either event, would determine when the inability had ended and at that time would resume the full exercise of the powers and duties of the office.

A similar agreement was in force between President Kennedy and Vice President Johnson on that fateful November 22, 1963 in Dallas when the president was assassinated. As with the Nixon arrangement, it was a transitory agreement binding only on the signatories. No future presidents and vice presidents were bound to follow the lead in this area except for the fact that they would be spurning a recently developing custom.

DISABILITY AND THE TWENTY-FIFTH AMENDMENT. In the aftermath of Eisenhower's illnesses and the Kennedy assassination, pressure began to build for a constitutional amendment to assure that the stability of the nation would not be left to "informal" agreements. As President Kennedy lay dying in Parkland Memorial Hospital, the "football" remained nearby. (The football is the small briefcase containing the codes necessary to unleash the U.S. nuclear strike forces.) Had Kennedy lingered and a nuclear strike against the United States been reported, could Vice President Johnson have made the decision to respond in kind on the basis of their informal agreement? Could the informal Brownell arrangement between Eisenhower and Nixon have legally given Nixon as "acting president" all the powers of the office while the president was under anesthetic for his ileitis surgery? In an age requiring immediate response in crisis yet demanding adherence to democratic process, it becomes difficult to determine at what point a person not elected to the White House can serve as if he were.

The Twenty-Fifth Amendment, carefully sculpted by the Senate Judiciary Subcommittee on Constitutional Amendments, is complex indeed. The skeptical or melodramatic could view this amendment as a constitutional justification for *coup d'état*. They might imagine that, as in Fletcher Knebel's novel, *Seven Days In May,* the vice president, in collusion with the cabinet and highly placed military officers, could wrest the presidency from its elected incumbent. Careful reading of the amendment, however, shows that keeping an elected president out of office on grounds of disability is difficult to do.

Basically, the amendment provides that either the president, himself, or the "Vice President and a majority of the principal executive officials" (meaning the cabinet) or others "as Congress shall provide" (meaning medical experts) could declare the president incapable of handling his duties. Upon receipt of this declaration by the speaker of the House and the president pro tem of the Senate, the vice president becomes "acting" president. By letter to the House and Senate, the president may at any time declare the disability corrected and seek return to office, but the vice president, members of the cabinet or others may register their own disagreement within four days, saying that the president is still incapacitated. In the case of this eventuality, Congress must come into session within forty-eight hours to deal with the problem. Within twenty-one days of congressional receipt of the views of the vice president and "the others," Congress must decide whether the vice president should continue to act as president. A two-thirds vote in both houses voting separately would be required to permit the vice president to continue as "acting president." In dealing with this leadership versus democratic process question, the Twenty-Fifth Amendment places the burden of proof on the vice president to show that the elected president cannot physically or psychologically provide the leadership he was elected to provide.


## LEADERSHIP AND ACCOUNTABILITY: A MODERN DILEMMA

Can the president serve two masters? Is the American public expecting too much of him? Is it possible for him to provide the firm and decisive leadership necessary to handle complex international and domestic economic questions and still remain responsive to constitutional concerns? Since he must rely on a broad base of public support, which includes the other branches of government, his party, numerous interest groups, and so forth, the odds are great that in pleasing some he risks angering others.

As the early chapters of this book demonstrated, the Founding Fathers created a potentially powerful single executive who was independent of direct legislative and judicial control in his day-to-day activities. Ironically, however, the presidency has become the captive of its myriad responsibilities, the desires of the public, and the information network erected to serve the White House. While custom and usage, rather than changes in the Constitution, have enhanced presidential power and prestige, presidential roles as economic manager, architect of domestic progress, and guardian of national security have become millstones around his neck. Presidents are simply incapable of being all things to all people.

The perplexing dilemma of the modern presidency, then, is the gap between public expectations and the limited human and constitutional capabilities that any president has to meet those aspirations. Theodore Sorensen put it best in his study of decision making in the White House: "No President is free to go as far or as fast as his advisors, his politics, and his perspectives may direct him." The excesses of the Nixon years illustrate that the temptations are great to overstep those bounds. Constitutional checks and balances provide some disincentives to presidents willing to consider abusing their powers. Impeachment provides a last resort to discourage disrespect for constitutional process at the White House. Ultimately, it is the vigilance of the president's constituents that provides the greatest bullwark against the excesses of unfettered leadership.

The handsomely endowed presidency that stood as the darling of advocates of social change from the 1930s through the 1960s became the antidemocratic demon of the 1970s. Had the institution changed or was it just the aberrant behavior of a few incumbents that encouraged the outcries? A real danger exists today in overreaction to recent abuses of power at the White House. Was Richard Nixon correct? Did the specter of impeachment weaken the presidency? Were the sins of Nixon visited upon his successors via congressional attempts to reassert that body's roles in the areas of the budget process and foreign policy? Watergate and Vietnam alerted the public and Congress that presidential leadership had become an excuse for congressional abdication of responsibility. The American governmental system seems to be returning to the model that the Founding Fathers envisioned. Once again, the president must be capable of persuading the public and the other branches of government to follow his lead. In seeking cooperation, the leader becomes accountable.

## CONCLUSIONS

The presidency of the 1980s must be viewed as an institution in flux. Whether it can maintain its prominent position in the policy process depends upon several factors: (1) continued public respect for the office and its incumbents, (2) ability of future presidents to adjust their sites to a changing U.S. role in an increasingly interdependent world economic community, (3) the ability of the voters to recognize leadership qualities in candidates while not overlooking the ego drives of hopefuls that might lead them in directions disrespectful of democratic processes, and (4) perception by the president, other branches of government, interest groups, and the public at large that only crisis situations can generate support for massive social change because the voting middle class is proving basically conservative and willing to accept evolutionary but not revolutionary change.

## NOTES

[1] Lyndon Johnson to Richard Nixon, quoted in Bobby Baker with Larry King, *Wheeling and Dealing* (New York: W. W. Norton, 197?), p. 265, as cited in Thomas Cronin, "Presidential Power Revised and Reappraised," *Western Political Quarterly,* (December 1979), 381.

[2] Gerald Pomper, *The Election of 1976* (New York: David McKay, 1977), p. 11.

[3] Martin Schramm, *Running for President* (New York: 1977), p. 11, as cited in Nelson Polsby and Aaron Wildavsky, *Presidential Elections: Strategies of American Electoral Politics,* 5th ed. (New York: Scribner's, 1980), p. 180. See also Herbert Asher, *Presidential Elections and American Politics* (Homewood, Ill.: Dorsey Press, 1980), pp. 227-268.

[4] James McGregor Burns, *Leadership* (New York: Harper & Row, 1978). See also Richard E. Neustadt, *The Politics of Leadership from FDR to Carter* (New York: John Wiley, 1980). Also see James McGregor Burns, *Presidential Government: The Crucible of Leadership* (Boston: Houghton Mifflin, 1965). Of more recent vintage and in article form, see Thomas Cronin, "Looking for Leadership: 1980," *Public Opinion,* (February-March, 1980), 14-20.

[5] Frank Kessler, "Presidents and Congress: The Domestic Tangle," in *Dimensions of the Modern Presidency,* ed. Edward Kearney (St. Louis, Mo.: Forum Press, 1981).

[6] Richard Reeves, *A Ford Not a Lincoln* (New York: Harcourt Brace, 1975).

[7] Cronin, "Looking for Leadership: 1980," p. 14.

[8] Gallup Organization, "Attitudes Toward the Presidency," a national opinion survey commissioned by WHYY-TV, Philadelphia-Wilmington, January 1980.

[9] A number of studies have dealt with presidential greatness. Among the best are Arthur Schlesinger, Jr., "Our Presidents, A Rating by 75 Historians," *The New York Times Magazine,* July 29, 1962, pp. 12ff. See also Malcolm Persons, "The Presidential Rating Game," in *The Future of the American Presidency,* ed. Charles Dunn (Morristown, N.J.: General Learning Press, 1975), pp. 74-75. See also Clinton Rossiter, *The American Presidency* (New York: Harcourt-Brace, 1966), pp. 436-437. More on "greatness" is available in R. Gordon Hoxie, "Presidential Greatness," in *Power and the Presidency,* eds. Phillip Dolce and George Skau (New York: Scribner's, 1976), pp. 261ff.

[10] On this see John Mueller, *War, Presidents and Public Opinion* (New York: John Wiley, 1973), pp. 58-59.

[11] Dan Nimmo and Robert Savage, *Candidates and Their Images* (Pacific Palisades, Calif.: Goodyear, 1976), p. 242.

[12] Herman Finer, *The Presidency: Crisis and Regeneration* (Chicago: Univ. of Chicago Press, 1960), p. 137.

[13] On Ronald Reagan's problems seeking cabinet-level appointees, see *Washington Post,* November 20, 1980.

[14] James D. Barber, *Presidential Character: Predicting Performance in the White House* (Englewood Cliffs, N.J.: Prentice-Hall, 1972), p. 80.

[15] Joseph A. Califano, *Presidential Nation* (New York: W. W. Norton, 1975), p. 80.

[16] Thomas Cronin, *The State of the Presidency* (Boston: Little Brown, 1975), p. 239.

[17] Truman and Kennedy's tendencies toward "buckshot" sending of large amounts of unprioritized legislation to Congress is thoughtfully examined in Louis Koenig, *The Chief Executive,* 3rd ed. (New York: Harcourt Brace, 1975), pp. 171ff.

[18] On these tactics, see *Christian Science Monitor,* September 29, 1980.

[19] Clinton Rossiter, "The Presidency: Focus of Leadership," as reprinted in Stanley Bach and George T. Sulzner, *Perspectives on the Presidency* (Lexington, Mass.: D. C. Heath, 1974), p. 38.

[20] This theme ties together one of the best texts on the presidency by Louis Koenig in his *The Chief Executive*. Most introductory American government texts have adopted this organizational framework for their discussions of the presidency.

[21] For public opinion on the Canal treaty prior to Senate approval, see *Gallup Opinion Index*, no. 153 (April 1978), 15-24.

[22] Barber, *Presidential Character*, p. 58.

[23] Bob Woodward and Carl Bernstein, *The Final Days* (New York: Simon & Schuster, 1976), p. 31.

[24] Koenig, *op. cit.*, pp. 336-339.

[25] Finer, *op. cit.*, p. 137.

[26] On the court-packing plan to add one new justice for each judge over seventy years of age to a total of fifteen members, see Arthur Schlesinger, Jr., *The Age of Roosevelt: The Politics of Upheaval* (Boston: Houghton Mifflin, 1960), pp. 451-453.

[27] According to Theodore White, one of the major things that Missouri Senator Stuart Symington had going for him was that he "looked" the part, while young John Kennedy resembled a boy. See White, *Making of the President, 1960* (New York: New American Library, 1961), pp. 51, 327.

[28] Jules Witcover, *Marathon: The Pursuit of the Presidency, 1972-1976* (New York: Viking Penguin, Inc., 1977), pp. 247-248.

[29] On Carter and the fireside chats and so on, see *The New York Times*, February 3, 1977 and February 4, 1977. On his "peoples" inaugural, see *The New York Times*, December 16, 1976.

[30] Clinton Rossiter, *The American Presidency* (New York: Harcourt Brace, 1960), p. 53.

[31] *Ibid.*, p. 53.

[32] Raoul Berger, *Impeachment* (New York: Bantam Books, 1974), p. 83.

[33] George Mason's statement cited in Arthur Schlesinger, Jr., *The Imperial Presidency* (New York: Houghton Mifflin, 1974), p. 393.

[34] Berger, *Impeachment*, p. 351.

[35] *Ibid.*, pp. 51, 128, 351.

[36] *Federalist 65.*

[37] Schlesinger, *op. cit.*, pp. 390-391.

[38] *Ibid.*, p. 81.

[39] Rossiter, *1787: The Grand Convention*, p. 56.

[40] Berger, *Impeachment*, p. 271.

[41] Koenig, *op. cit.*, p. 67.

[42] Schlesinger, *op. cit.*, p. 82.

[43] Koenig, *op. cit.*, p. 52.

[44] Rossiter, *The American Presidency*, p. 52.

[45] Schlesinger, *op. cit.*, p. 83.

[46] Rossiter, *The American Presidency*, p. 53. Truman's resolve would be tested with Matthew Connelly and T. Lamar Caudle, aides who stood before federal courts, for, among other things, tax evasion.

[47] Report of the steps of the process in U.S. Congress, House, Committee on the Judiciary, *Report, The Impeachment of Richard M. Nixon* (Washington, D.C.: G.P.O., 1974).

[48] Good summary of the situation in Robert DiClerico, *The American Presidency* (Englewood Cliffs, N.J.: Prentice-Hall, 1979), p. 99.

[49] For a summation of Nixon's legal arguments to protect the tapes from other ears, see Richard Pious, *The American Presidency* (New York: Basic Books, 1979), pp. 78-79.

[50] *Ibid.*, pp. 78-79.

[51] DiClerico, *op. cit.*, p. 99.

[52] Theodore White, *Breach of Faith* (New York: Atheneum, 1975), p. 9.

[53] On the wiretaps, see U.S. Congress, Senate, Committee on Foreign Relations, *Dr. Kissinger's Role in Wiretapping*, 93rd Cong., 2d sess., 1974 (Washington, D.C.: G.P.O., 1974).

[54] *The New York Times,* February 26, 1974.

[55] Charles Hardin, *Presidential Power and Accountability* (Chicago: Univ. of Chicago Press, 1974).

[56] Insightful in vein too is Sundquist, "The Case for an Easier Method to Remove Presidents," *George Washington Law Review,* (January 1975), 472-484.

[57] Louis Koenig, "A Recipe for the Presidency's Destruction," *George Washington Law Review,* (January 1975), 376.

[58] Corwin, *op. cit.,* pp. 358-359.

[59] Koenig, *The Chief Executive,* p. 413.

[60] Corwin, *op. cit.,* p. 346.

[61] The exact figure is 54.7.

[62] Marcus Cunliffe, *History of the Presidency* (New York: Simon & Schuster, 1968), pp. 132-133. See also Warren, *op. cit.,* p. 635.

[63] Birch Bayh, *One Heartbeat Away* (Indianapolis: Bobbs-Merrill, 1968), p. 16.

[64] Koenig, *Chief Executive,* p. 77.

[65] Gene Smith, *When the Cheering Stopped* (New York: Time, 1964), p. 146.

[66] Edith Bolling Wilson, *My Memoirs* (Indianapolis: Bobbs-Merrill, 1939), p. 288.

[67] *Ibid.,* p. 289.

[68] *Ibid.,* pp. 300-301.

[69] Barber, *op. cit.,* p. 249.

[70] *Ibid.,* p. 250.

[71] *Ibid.,* p. 250.

[72] Dom Bonafede, "Vice President Mondale: Carter's Partner Without Portfolio," *National Journal,* March 11, 1978, pp. 376-384.

[73] *Ibid.,* p. 381.

[74] Bayh, *op. cit.,* p. 26.

# Appendix A

# The Terms, Party, State, and Age for Presidents of the United States

|  | YEARS IN OFFICE | PARTY | STATE | AGE |
|---|---|---|---|---|
| George Washington | 1789-1797 | Fed. | Va. | 57 |
| John Adams | 1797-1801 | Fed. | Mass. | 61 |
| Thomas Jefferson | 1801-1809 | Dem.-Rep. | Va. | 57 |
| James Madison | 1809-1817 | Dem.-Rep. | Va. | 57 |
| James Monroe | 1817-1825 | Dem.-Rep. | Va. | 58 |
| John Quincy Adams | 1825-1829 | Dem.-Rep. | Mass. | 57 |
| Andrew Jackson | 1829-1837 | Dem. | Tenn. | 61 |
| Martin Van Buren | 1837-1841 | Dem. | N.Y. | 54 |
| William Henry Harrison | 1841 | Whig | Ind. | 68 |
| John Tyler | 1841-1845 | Dem.-Whig | Va. | 51 |
| James K. Polk | 1845-1849 | Dem. | Tenn. | 49 |
| Zachary Taylor | 1849-1850 | Whig | La. | 64 |
| Millard Fillmore | 1850-1853 | Whig | N.Y. | 48 |
| Franklin Pierce | 1853-1857 | Dem. | N.H. | 50 |
| James Buchanan | 1857-1861 | Dem. | Pa. | 65 |
| Abraham Lincoln | 1861-1865 | Rep. | Ill. | 52 |
| Andrew Johnson | 1865-1869 | Union Dem. | Tenn. | 56 |
| Ulysses S. Grant | 1869-1877 | Rep. | Ohio | 46 |
| Rutherford B. Hayes | 1877-1881 | Rep. | Ohio | 54 |
| James A. Garfield | 1881 | Rep. | Ohio | 49 |
| Chester A. Arthur | 1881-1885 | Rep. | N.Y. | 50 |
| Grover Cleveland | 1885-1889 | Dem. | N.Y. | 47 |
| Benjamin Harrison | 1889-1893 | Rep. | Ind. | 55 |
| Grover Cleveland | 1893-1897 | Dem. | N.Y. | 55 |
| William McKinley | 1897-1901 | Rep. | Ohio | 54 |
| Theodore Roosevelt | 1901-1909 | Rep. | N.Y. | 42 |
| William H. Taft | 1909-1913 | Rep. | Ohio | 51 |
| Woodrow Wilson | 1913-1921 | Dem. | N.J. | 56 |
| Warren G. Harding | 1921-1923 | Rep. | Ohio | 56 |
| Calvin Coolidge | 1923-1929 | Rep. | Mass. | 55 |
| Herbert C. Hoover | 1929-1933 | Rep. | Calif. | 54 |
| Franklin D. Roosevelt | 1933-1945 | Dem. | N.Y. | 51 |
| Harry S. Truman | 1945-1953 | Dem. | Mo. | 60 |

| | | | | |
|---|---|---|---|---|
| Dwight D. Eisenhower | 1953-1961 | Rep. | N.Y. | 62 |
| John F. Kennedy | 1961-1963 | Dem. | Mass. | 43 |
| Lyndon B. Johnson | 1963-1969 | Dem. | Tex. | 55 |
| Richard M. Nixon | 1969-1974 | Rep. | Calif. | 56 |
| Gerald R. Ford, Jr. | 1974-1977 | Rep. | Mich. | 61 |
| Jimmy Carter | 1977-1981 | Dem. | Ga. | 52 |
| Ronald W. Reagan | 1981- | Rep. | Calif. | 69 |

# Appendix B

# Background of Nominees for President, 1932–1980

| NAME | AGE | STATE | PARTY | RELIGION | OCCUPATION |
|------|-----|-------|-------|----------|------------|
| Roosevelt | 51 | N.Y. | Dem. | Episcopalian | Lawyer, State Legislator, assistant secretary of navy, governor |
| Hoover | 58 | Calif. | Rep. | Quaker | President |
| Roosevelt | 55 | N.Y. | Dem. | Episcopalian | President |
| Landon | 49 | Kans. | Rep. | Methodist | Banker, oilman, governor |
| Roosevelt | 59 | N.Y. | Dem. | Episcopalian | President |
| Wilkie | 48 | Ind. | Rep. | Episcopalian | Lawyer, industrialist |
| Roosevelt | 63 | N.Y. | Dem. | Episcopalian | President |
| Dewey | 42 | N.Y. | Rep. | Episcopalian | Lawyer, governor |
| Truman | 64 | Mo. | Dem. | Baptist | President |
| Dewey | 46 | N.Y. | Rep. | Episcopalian | Lawyer, governor |
| Eisenhower | 62 | N.Y. | Rep. | Presbyterian | Professional soldier |
| Stevenson | 52 | Ill. | Dem. | Presbyterian | Lawyer, journalist, governor |
| Eisenhower | 66 | N.Y. | Rep. | Presbyterian | President |
| Stevenson | 56 | Ill. | Dem. | Presbyterian | Lawyer, journalist, governor |
| Kennedy | 43 | Mass. | Dem. | Catholic | Journalist, U.S. representative, U.S. senator |
| Nixon | 48 | Calif. | Rep. | Quaker | Lawyer, U.S. representative, U.S. senator, vice president |
| Johnson | 56 | Tex. | Dem. | Disciples of Christ | Teacher, U.S. representative, U.S. senator, vice president |
| Goldwater | 55 | Ariz. | Rep. | Episcopalian | Business executive, U.S. senator |
| Nixon | 56 | Calif. | Rep. | Quaker | Lawyer, U.S. representative, U.S. senator, vice president |

| | | | | | |
|---|---|---|---|---|---|
| Humphrey | 57 | Minn. | Dem. | Congrega-tionalist | Teacher, mayor, U.S. senator, vice president |
| Nixon | 60 | Calif. | Rep. | Quaker | President |
| McGovern | 50 | S. Dak. | Dem. | Methodist | Teacher, U.S. senator |
| Carter | 51 | Ga. | Dem. | Baptist | State legislator, governor, farmer |
| Ford | 63 | Mich. | Rep. | Episcopalian | U.S. representative, vice president |
| Carter | 55 | Ga. | Dem. | Baptist | President |
| Reagan | 69 | Calif. | Rep. | Disciples of Christ | California governor, professional actor |

# Appendix C

# The Presidency...
# According to the Constitution

## ARTICLE I

SECTION 3. (6) The Senate shall have the sole power to try all impeachments. When sitting for that purpose, they shall be on oath or affirmation. When the President of the United States is tried, the Chief Justice shall preside; and no person shall be convicted without the concurrence of two-thirds of the members present.

(7) Judgment in cases of impeachment shall not extend further than to removal from office, and disqualification to hold and enjoy any office of honor, trust, or profit under the United States; but the party convicted shall, nevertheless, be liable and subject to indictment, trial, judgment, and punishment, according to law.

SECTION 7. (2) Every bill which shall have passed the House of Representatives and the Senate shall, before it becomes a law, be presented to the President of the United States; if he approve he shall sign it, but if not he shall return it, with his objections, to that house in which it shall have originated, who shall enter the objections at large on their journal and proceed to reconsider it. If after such reconsideration, two-thirds of that house shall agree to pass the bill, it shall be sent, together with the objections, to the other house, by which it shall likewise be reconsidered, and if approved by two-thirds of that house it shall become a law. But in all cases the votes of both houses shall be determined by yeas and nays, and the names of the persons voting for and against the bill shall be entered on the journal of each house respectively. If any bill shall not be returned by the President within ten days (Sundays excepted) after it shall have been presented to him, the same shall be a law, in like manner as if he had signed it unless the Congress by their adjournment prevent its return, in which case it shall not be a law.

(3) Every order, resolution, or vote to which the concurrence of the Senate and House of Representatives may be necessary (except on a question of adjournment) shall be presented to the President of the United States; and before the same shall take effect, shall be approved by him, or being disapproved by him, shall be repassed by two-thirds of the Senate and House of Representatives, according to the rules and limitations prescribed in the case of a bill.

# ARTICLE II

SECTION I.  (1) The executive power shall be vested in a President of the United States of America. He shall hold his office during the term of four years, and, together with the Vice President, chosen for the same term, be elected as follows:

(2) Each state shall appoint, in such manner as the legislature thereof may direct, a number of electors, equal to the whole number of Senators and Representatives to which the State may be entitled in the Congress; but no Senator or Representative, or person holding an office of trust or profit under the United States, shall be appointed an elector.

(3) The electors shall meet in their respective states and vote by ballot for two persons, of whom one at least shall not be an inhabitant of the same state with themselves. And they shall make a list of all the persons voted for, and of the number of votes for each; which list they shall sign and certify, and transmit sealed to the seat of the government of the United States, directed to the President of the Senate. The President of the Senate shall, in the presence of the Senate and House of Representatives, open all the certificates, and the votes shall then be counted. The person having the greatest number of votes shall be the President, if such a number be a majority of the whole number of electors appointed; and if there be more than one who have such a majority, and have an equal number of votes, then the House of Representatives shall immediately choose by ballot one of them for President; and if no person have a majority, then from the five highest on the list the said House shall in like manner choose the President. But in choosing the President the votes shall be taken by states, the representation from each state having one vote; a quorum for this purpose shall consist of a member or members from two-thirds of the states, and a majority of all the states shall be necessary to a choice. In every case, after the choice of the President, the person having the greatest number of votes of the electors shall be the Vice President. But if there should remain two or more who have equal votes, the Senate shall choose from them by ballot the Vice President. *[This paragraph was superseded by the Twelfth Amendment]*

(4) The Congress may determine the time of choosing the electors and the day on which they shall give their votes, which day shall be the same throughout the United States.

(5) No person except a natural born citizen, or a citizen of the United States at the time of the adoption of this Constitution, shall be eligible to the office of President; neither shall any person be eligible to that office who shall not have attained to the age of thirty-five years, and been fourteen years a resident within the United States.

(6) In case of the removal of the President from office, or of his death, resignation, or inability to discharge the powers and duties of the said office, the same shall devolve on the Vice President, and the Congress may by law provide for the case of removal, death, resignation, or inability, both of the President and Vice President, declaring what officer shall then act as President, and such officer shall act accordingly until the disability be removed or a President shall be elected. *[See also the provisions of the Twenty-fifth Amendment]*

(7) The President shall, at stated times, receive for his services a compensation which shall neither be increased nor diminished during the period for which he shall have been elected, and he shall not receive within that period any other emolument from the United States or any of them.

(8) Before he enter on the execution of his office he shall take the following oath or affirmation:

I do solemnly swear (or affirm) that I will faithfully execute the office of the President of the United States, and will to the best of my ability preserve, protect, and defend the Constitution of the United States.

SECTION 2. (1) The President shall be Commander-in-Chief of the Army and Navy of the United States, and of the militia of the several states when called into the actual service of the United States; he may require the opinion, in writing, of the principal officer in each of the executive departments, upon any subject relating to the duties of their respective offices, and he shall have power to grant reprieves and pardons for offenses against the United States, except in cases of impeachment.

(2) He shall have power, by and with the advice and consent of the Senate, to make treaties, provided two-thirds of the Senators present concur; and he shall nominate, and, by and with the advice and consent of the Senate, shall appoint ambassadors, other public ministers and consuls, judges of the Supreme Court, and all other officers of the United States, whose appointments are not herein otherwise provided for, and which shall be established by law; but the Congress may by law vest the appointment of such inferior officers, as they think proper, in the President alone, in the courts of law, or in the heads of departments.

(3) The President shall have power to fill up all vacancies that may happen during the recess of the Senate, by granting commissions which shall expire at the end of their next session.

## ARTICLE IV

SECTION 4. The United States shall guarantee to every State in this Union a republican form of government, and shall protect each of them against invasion; and on application of the legislature, or of the executive (when the legislature cannot be convened) against domestic violence.

## ARTICLE VI

(2) This Constitution, and the laws of the United States which shall be made in pursuance thereof, and all treaties made, or which shall be made, under the authority of the United States, shall be the supreme law of the land; and the judges in every State shall be bound thereby, anything in the Constitution or laws of any State to the contrary notwithstanding.

## AMENDMENT XII (1804)

The electors shall meet in their respective states and vote by ballot for President and Vice President, one of whom, at least, shall not be an inhabitant of the same state with themselves; they shall name in their ballots the person voted for as President, and in distinct ballots the person voted for as Vice President, and they shall make distinct lists of all persons voted for as President and of all persons voted for as Vice President, and of the number of votes for each; which lists they shall sign and certify, and transmit sealed to the seat of the government of the United States, directed to the President of the Senate. The President of the Senate shall, in the presence of the Senate and House of Representatives, open all the certificates and the votes shall then be counted. The person having the greatest number of votes for President shall be the President, if such number be a majority of the whole number of electors appointed; and if no person have such a majority, then from the persons having the highest numbers not exceeding three on the list of those voted for as President, the House of Representatives shall choose immediately, by ballot, the President. But in choosing the President the votes shall be taken by states, the representation from each state having one vote; a quorum for this purpose shall consist of a member or members from two-thirds of the states, and a majority of all states shall be necessary to a choice. And if the House of Representatives shall not choose a President whenever the right of choice shall devolve upon them, before the fourth day of March next following, then the Vice President shall act as President, as in the case of the death or other constitutional disability of the President.

The person having the greatest number of votes as Vice President shall be the Vice President, if such number be a majority of the whole number of electors appointed; and if no person have a majority, then from the two highest numbers on the list the Senate shall choose the Vice President; a quorum for the purpose shall consist of two-thirds of the whole number of Senators, and a majority of the whole number shall be necessary to a choice. But no person constitutionally ineligible to the office of President shall be eligible to that of Vice President of the United States.

## AMENDMENT XX (1933)

SECTION 1.    The terms of the President and Vice President shall end at noon on the 20th day of January, and the terms of Senators and Representatives at noon on the 3rd day of January, of the years in which such terms would have ended if this article had not been ratified; and the terms of their successors shall then begin.

SECTION 2.    The Congress shall assemble at least once in every year, and such meeting shall begin at noon on the 3rd day of January, unless they shall by law appoint a different day.

SECTION 3.    If, at the time fixed for the beginning of the term of the President, the President elect shall have died, the Vice President elect shall become President. If a President shall not have been chosen before the time fixed for the beginning of his term, or if the President elect shall have failed to qualify, then the Vice President elect shall act as President until a President shall have qualified; and the Congress may by law provide for the case wherein neither a President elect nor a Vice President elect shall have qualified, declaring who shall then act as President, or the manner in which one who is to act shall be selected, and such persons shall act accordingly until a President or Vice President shall have qualified.

SECTION 4.    The Congress may be law provide for the case of the death of any of the persons from whom the House of Representatives may choose a President whenever the right of choice shall have devloved upon them, and for the case of the death of any of the persons from whom the Senate may choose a Vice President whenever the right of choice shall have devolved upon them.

## AMENDMENT XXII (1951)

No person shall be elected to the office of the President more than twice, and no person who has held the office of President, or acted as President, for more than two years of a term to which some other person was elected President shall be elected to the office of the President more than once. But this article shall not apply to any person holding the office of President when this article was proposed by the Congress, and shall not prevent any person who may be holding the office of President, or acting as President, during the term within which this article becomes operative from holding the office of President or acting as President during the remainder of such term.

## AMENDMENT XXIII (1961)

SECTION 1. The District constituting the seat of government of the United States shall appoint in such a manner as the Congress may direct:

A number of electors of President and Vice President equal to the whole number of Senators and Representatives in Congress to which the District would be entitled if it were a State, but in no event more than the least populous state; they shall be in addition to those appointed by the States, but they shall be considered, for the purposes of the election of President and Vice President, to be electors appointed by a State; and they shall meet in the District and perform such duties as provided by the twelfth article of amendment.

## AMENDMENT XXV (1967)

SECTION 1. In case of the removal of the President from office or of his death or resignation, the Vice President shall become President.

SECTION 2. Whenever there is a vacancy in the office of the Vice President, the President shall nominate a Vice President who shall take office upon confirmation by a majority vote of both Houses of Congress.

SECTION 3. Whenever the President transmits to the President pro tempore of the Senate and the Speaker of the House of Representatives his written declaration that he is unable to discharge the powers and duties of his office, and until he transmits to them a written declaration to the contrary, such powers and duties shall be discharged by the Vice President as Acting President.

SECTION 4. Whenever the Vice President and a majority of either the principal officers of the executive department or of such other body as Congress may by law provide, transmit to the President pro tempore of the Senate and the Speaker of the House of Representatives their written declaration that the President is unable to discharge the powers and duties of his office, the Vice President shall immediately assume the powers and duties of the office as Acting President.

Thereafter, when the President transmits to the President pro tempore of the Senate and the Speaker of the House of Representatives his written declaration that no inability exists, he shall resume the powers and duties of his office unless the Vice President and a majority of either the principal officers of the executive department or of such other body as Congress may by law provide, transmit within four days to the President pro tempore of the Senate and the Speaker of the House of Representatives their written declaration that the President is unable to discharge the powers and duties of his office. Thereupon Congress shall decide the issue, assembling within forty-eight hours for that purpose if not in session. If the Congress within twenty-one days after receipt of the latter written declaration, or, if Congress is not in session, within twenty-one days after Congress is required to assemble, determined by two-thirds vote of both Houses that the President is unable to discharge the powers and duties of his office, the Vice President shall continue to discharge the same as Acting President; otherwise, the President shall resume the powers and duties of his office.

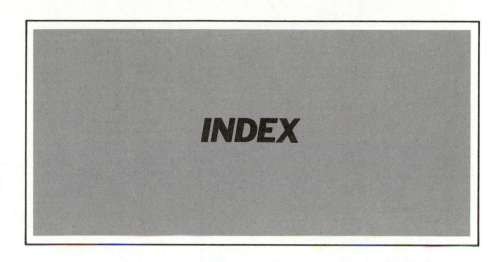

# INDEX